DECLINE
or
RENEWAL?

DECLINE
or
RENEWAL?

France Since the 1930s

by Stanley Hoffmann

The Viking Press | *New York*

Acknowledgment is made to the following for permission to quote material:

The American Political Science Association: *The Rulers: Heroic Leadership in Modern France* by Stanley Hoffmann, Copyright © 1966 by The American Political Science Association.

Daedalus: Obstinate or Obsolete: The Fate of the Nation-State and the Case of Western Europe by Stanley Hoffmann, Summer 1966 issue.

E. P. Dutton & Co., Inc.: From the book *The Sorrow and the Pity: A Film by Marcel Ophuls*. Introduction by Stanley Hoffmann. Copyright © 1972 by Outerbridge & Lazard, Inc. Published by E. P. Dutton & Co., Inc. (Outerbridge & Lazard, Inc.) and used with their permission.

Journal of International Affairs: "Perceptions, Reality and the Franco-American Conflict" by Stanley Hoffmann. Copyright by the Trustees of Columbia University in the City of New York. Permission to reprint from the *Journal of International Affairs*, Volume 21, Number 1, 1967, is gratefully acknowledged to the Editors of the *Journal*.

Revue Française de Science Politique: "Aspects du Régime de Vichy" by Stanley Hoffmann, March 1956.

John Wiley & Sons, Inc.: "Protest in Modern France" by Stanley Hoffmann, which appears in *The Revolution in World Politics* edited by Morton A. Kaplan. Copyright © 1962 by John Wiley & Sons, Inc., Publishers. Reprinted by permission.

The University of Chicago Press: "Self-Ensnared: Collaboration with Germany" by Stanley Hoffmann, September 1968 issue of *Journal of Modern History*, Copyright © 1968 by The University of Chicago Press.

To Michel Crozier and Jean-Marie Domenach

Preface

Old France, worn down by history, bruised by wars
and revolutions, going back and forth endlessly
from grandeur to decline, but restored from
century to century by the genius of renewal.

—DE GAULLE, *War Memoirs*

The essays collected in this volume have been written over a period of eighteen years. Some of them were written for this book. The others, published earlier in either English or French, have been revised, often quite drastically, to become part of a coherent volume. In all of them, I try to answer one underlying question: what has been happening in the French political community since the 1930s? How has France been affected by the winds of change? Have they blown away the cozy society that emerged from the French Revolution, the parliamentary regime which in the early years of this century seemed to have brought stability at last to French political institutions, and France's age-old great-power status? Are the spectacular transformations of France's economic and social system, her constitutional order, and her role in the world a successful response to a formidable challenge, or a brave but ultimately doomed fight against internal paralysis and external decline?

This question is examined here from four different angles. First, from the sinister viewpoint of the war years. The tragi-comedy of the Vichy regime and the drama of French collaboration with Nazi Germany showed France at her nadir. Yet only if one examines Vichy's contradictions—caught as it was between its frantic desire to protect an obsolescent society by means of reactionary institutions, and its deadly dependence on the good will of the occupying power—can one understand fully France's postwar drive for modernization and independence. Nor can one otherwise explain the continuing reluctance of the French body politic to acknowledge its temporary acquiescence of a generation ago to Pétain's reassuring delusions. The nostalgia for a simpler past and *de facto* acceptance of a minor-power status have been recurrent temptations in the postwar era. It is obviously still too painful for the French to admit that the regime which surrendered most completely to them and ended in shame and blood started with broad popular support. Rather than reminding the nation of its fall and its sins, the Gaullist or Resistance myth tended to make Vichy a scapegoat; today, anti-Gaullists of the Left and Right tend to look at de Gaulle as the scapegoat for France's failings.

A second angle is provided by the internal transformation of French society. Here, the central problem is that of change vs. continuity. How much of "old France" is still present, even in the way in which change is carried out? How and when is the shift from the largely rural economy and bourgeois society of yesterday to the industrial economy and "consumer society" of today also going to affect authority relations, and such apparently unshakable institutions as the French civil service and school system? What would be the social and political costs if the residues from the past were unyielding? The chapters which examine this problem are part of a kind of conversation I have enjoyed over the years with my friend Michel Crozier, the brilliant sociologist. Twelve years ago, the ideas which he was on the verge of developing in his *The Bureaucratic Phenomenon* influenced and reinforced those which five colleagues and I presented in a book entitled *In Search of France*. His model of French authority relations inspired an essay of mine on heroic leadership (included in this book). Our first interpretations of the "events" of May 1968, written in the summer of that tumultuous year, were also quite similar. The French title of his most recent book, *La Société bloquée,* is borrowed from my description of prewar France. No writer on postwar France, whether or not he endorses the analysis and prescriptions offered by Crozier and his remarkable team at the Centre de Sociologie des Organisations, can afford to ignore their writings. We all must come to terms with a theory that is so powerful it sometimes seems to explain everything.

A third angle is that of France's attempt to find a new role in a world apparently dominated by superpowers, and to define her relation to the rest of Europe. She has tried to contribute to the emergence of a West European will, while avoiding being absorbed in an entity whose goals might be either dictated by the United States or obscured by intra-European squabbles. Here, the central problem is that of the meaning and possibilities of independence for a middle power, in an age not merely of giant states but also of transnational forces, which reveal the limits of middle- and small-power control far more cruelly than those of superpower autonomy. That the West Europeans should have shown themselves unable to join forces and respond in unison to the contradictory pulls and pushes of the giants; that the rest of the world should be so relatively unrewarding an arena for a nation which had been used to thinking of itself in the first rank and which saw in economic growth and industrial might a way of repairing the losses of World War II and overcoming the blows of de-colonization—these have been particular vexations for the French, especially under Gaullist leadership.

The fourth angle is the vision of one man: Charles de Gaulle. There are many objective reasons why he should be the central figure of this book. In the war years, he was the head of the Resistance, the symbol of opposition to Germany and Vichy, the promise of internal renovation and external *redressement*. No other French political leader, except for Richelieu or Napoleon, has been more concerned with economic modernization and political strength aimed at power and influence on the world stage. The very style of his authority, and the priority he gave to *grandeur*, sharpened the basic French contradiction between widespread modernization and an atavistic process of change at home, and between redesigned ambitions and apparently unalterable limitations abroad. Moreover, whatever the scope of his achievements, his personality is likely to exert fascination long after historians have given a final verdict on his statecraft. In the gallery of great men who provide French history and culture with so much of its intensity, humanity, and color, there are not too many statesmen. De Gaulle was a statesman eager to serve as an example for posterity, an intellectual concerned with increasing public consciousness of the problems facing the French of his time, and a great artist of action and of language. No discussion of France in the era of Charles de Gaulle can fail to try to give a temporary balance sheet of his successes and failures, and to ask whether he will appear in the books as a man who deflected the course of history or only as a brilliant parenthesis.

De Gaulle called his last writings *Memoirs of Hope*. What hope is there for the state which he left behind? He had intended it to be strong enough to promote the transformation of society and to with-stand its traditional resistances and divisions. But is not France today perhaps too much the expression, indeed the culmination, of a tradi-tional style whose virtues, in Crozier's words, are exhausted? What hope is there for the French nation-state? De Gaulle had wanted France to contribute to the coming of a new international system in which she would be a major actor. But is there anything left of such ambitions, and does a nation that has discovered, after his disap-pearance, the limits of her possibilities still have any *projet* other than her own prosperity?

These, then, are the issues. The reader will find that my attempts to discuss them are essays, not monographs; questions about France's fate, politics, behavior or beliefs, not a history or survey of France since the 1930s. While I did not write them for scholars and specialists, they assume a certain familiarity with contemporary French affairs— and a certain tolerance for discontinuities and gaps. Unity is provided by the central question and common themes. Different angles yield different views of the same landscape; also, I am sometimes of several minds on the same issue, and do not feel like apologizing for it: complexity does not mean contradiction. For instance, I stress both the diversity of Vichy, and the way in which all of Vichy, like the French Revolution, was propelled by a single logic, by the mad momentum of an infernal machine that, once launched, stopped only when it crashed: even if this was not the intent of the men who signed the armistice of June 1940, their signing it meant choosing to be in one of the two camps in an international civil war. Later, I suggest why psychological studies of leaders tend to be flawed, and why a political perspective is preferable; yet another essay offers a psychological interpretation of General de Gaulle. Later still, I express my admiration for the sweep and skill of de Gaulle's foreign policy, for his exhortation to the French to "be themselves," and my doubts about the role of middle powers in the world today. It is not by accident that the title of this book, borrowed from de Gaulle, is in the form of a question. The chapters in this book represent an internal dialogue rather than a demonstration of a thesis; they express my conviction that the truth has many facets rather than my failure to arrive at conclusions.

The readers should not expect (or fear) that this book is an exercise in political science. Some of the chapters have certain pretensions of that kind, including an attempt at dispassionate analysis. Others, though, are different. The central essay on de Gaulle, written jointly by my wife and me, is a restrained attempt at psychohistory, inspired far more by Erikson than by Freud. The chapter on the film *The Sorrow and the Pity* and much of my approach to General de Gaulle are unashamedly subjective.

Even a historian writing long after the events he describes cannot help his subjectivity: his values, indeed his whole personality, are reflected in his choice of issues and in his conclusions. But when one has lived the dramas one analyzes, it is even harder not to take sides. I would add that there is a terrible risk of blandness, of an inappropriate bending backward, an inconclusiveness, in pretending to be neutral. (Also, the kind of history that results often makes the historical actors look like well-meaning bunglers overtaken by events.)

And there is a real possibility of being partisan anyway: awareness is a better guide than repression or denial.

In this instance, my own emotional involvement in France since the 1930s explains both what some may call my bias, and what I have referred to as my ambivalence. As for my bias, it is simple. In my early teens, I spent four long years in Vichy France. Having passionately clung to the voice of de Gaulle, speaking from London, as the voice of hope, honor, and freedom, I have never been able to shake off the memories of it, even when I disagreed with his tactics or deplored his policies. All the misunderstandings that later developed between him and former *résistants* or Free French never really eroded the bond of admiration and gratitude forged in those desperate years; the emotional outpouring that followed his death proved it. As for my ambivalence, it results from a mix of commitment to and detachment from France. I owe to French education whatever I may be today; I was blessed in my school and immediate postschool years with helpful teachers whose warmth and kindness I can never repay; my deepest friendships are in France, along with the landscapes imprinted in me. And yet I have chosen to live and teach in the United States, for reasons that have to do with those stifling rigidities of the French social, educational, and political system which the reader will find discussed here. But some people are born to be outsiders looking in, and the distance from which they thereby benefit, and even the sweet longing for belonging, are adequate compensations for partial estrangement or uprootedness.

I would like to thank my stimulating, wise, and learned friend Professor Nancy Roelker, and Professor Robert E. Herzstein, for having volunteered to translate some of my essays originally written in French; my colleague Professor Laurence Wylie, whose fresh intuitions and powers of empathy are so often devastatingly original; Professors Suzanne Berger and Peter Gourevitch, from whose arguments, writings, and examples I have gained much knowledge and pleasure in the years of our association; Pierre and Catherine Grémion, whose understanding of the intricacies of France's system of territorial administration are unsurpassed; and my undiscouraged editor, Elisabeth Sifton. This is the third book of mine on which she has worked, and I sometimes believe that one of the few incentives for the agonizing task of writing is the prospect of having her edit the end result.

In addition to Michel Crozier, I dedicate this book to Jean-Marie Domenach, the ardent director of *Esprit,* generous fighter of good causes, disciple and biographer of Mounier, revealer of Barrès, and *résistant.* He represents in my eyes what is best in a nationalism that synthesizes all French traditions, and in a culture that still questions the purposes to which growth and profit are put, or still remembers that easy optimism about peace and prosperity often lead to the *retour du tragique*.

Stanley Hoffmann
Summer 1973
Cambridge, Massachusetts

Contents

I
The Fall

1
The Vichy Circle
of French Conservatives

Few historical phenomena offer the possibilities to political science that the Vichy regime does. A considerable literature already exists dealing with the sociology of revolutions; a study of Vichy would provide a fine contribution to a sociology of counterrevolution, just as it would complement recent studies on the Right in France, and on totalitarian experiences in the twentieth century.

If one examines the host of magazines and journals of every kind published under this paradoxical regime—which censured pitilessly everything that did not suit either its own ends or those of the occupying power, while it subsidized everything useful to itself (including a certain amount of material of little direct benefit to Vichy, but which the occupier imposed)—two distinct tendencies of thought emerge. On one hand, we have a group of intellectuals hotly pursuing a kind of pseudo-Latin mirage, a vision of a static, classical society, governed by the values of order and hierarchy that characterized the great periods of Western civilization—the Pax Romana and the Middle Ages. This society would see to it that everyone stayed in his rightful place, under the enlightened guidance of far-sighted elites, to whom the Christian religion would bring spiritual support and police protection. At the opposite extreme we have intellectuals tortured by a pseudo-Nordic mirage of a dynamic, romantic society, extolling the values of heroism and struggle, blood and earth, inscrutable forces and revolutionary masses. There is nothing new about the infatuation of French intellectuals with the fashionable political myths of the day, and for the regimes that claim to incarnate them. If today it is the intellectuals of the opposite persuasion who cause the greatest stir and attract the

Translated by Professor Robert E. Herzstein and the author from "Aspects du régime de Vichy," *Revue française de science politique,* March 1956.

most attention, at the time of the Vichy government, as was only to be expected, it was the disciples of Charles Maurras or Henri Massis, admirers of Pierre Drieu la Rochelle or the latest works of Henry de Montherlant, who evinced a comparable failure to come to terms with contemporary French society and a suspicious tendency to smoke the opium of the moment. This, however, is not the point that I want to emphasize here. Certain aspects of the political process will detain us longer.

The view of the Vichy regime as a "bloc" is beginning to lose its force, and it is right that it should. For the notion of Vichy unity, like that of the unity of the French Revolution, was in large part the creation of its enemies. The solidarity between the nationalist-traditionalist Vichy of the summer of 1940 and the Fascist-collaborationist Vichy of spring 1944 is no greater than that between Montagnards and Thermidorians. No less, either, we might add: while there were undeniable antagonisms in the intentions and psychology of the actors and in their social backing, at the same time there was a chain connection, as it were, a relentless determinism. This is what led the play inexorably on to its denouement, from the moment when the first actors, who "had not wanted this to happen" and proclaimed as much before the tribunal of history, set in motion forces which they were incapable of stopping, in spite of all their protestations. In both cases, there is the same negative solidarity against a deposed regime—which means that the biographer's or the philosopher's judgment cannot be the same as the sociologist's.

I

The most surprising discovery, for someone who has a preconceived notion of Vichy as a monolithic "bloc" or as two successive and opposing systems, is that Vichy was as diverse at any given moment of its existence as it was through time. From 1940 to the end of 1943 at least, Vichy was a pluralist dictatorship.

Pluralism was manifest throughout the different ministries, subministries, general secretariats, etc. The Secretariat for Youth came out in 1941 for a "united" youth movement, as against a "single" one, and appeared resigned to the fact that the Compagnons de France, which it sponsored, would have no monopoly on rallying all the unorganized young. It also tolerated the experiment of the École de Cadres at Uriage, whose leaders were inspired by pure personalist philosophy, light-years away from the Maurrasian views of Pétain's aides. But in the Secretariat for Information, pseudoclassicists and pseudoromantics shared power and established a national École de Cadres of their own opposed to Uriage, which was deemed heretic.

The State Secretariat of Labor sought to make trade unionism the basis of social organization, even though it meant making labor union organs of something which had been repugnant to most syndicalists. Yet in Marshal Philippe Pétain's privy council, many members were determined quickly to reduce trade unionism to impotence, to eradicate it immediately. The Peasant Corporation's theorists were quite ready to assert that agriculture must become once more the foundation of French society and economy. On the other hand, the activities of the Committees of Organization for industry and commerce ultimately strengthened the powers of the big French employers.[1] * Big business predominated on these committees, largely because of the very cumbersomeness of their machinery, but the Veterans' Legion vowed to defend small and middle-size businesses and vehemently denounced the "trusts" in its propaganda. The regime waged a constant, insistent, at times embarrassing campaign to get the support of the Church, but at the same time there were Vichy officials determined to create a monopolistic trade union, to mobilize all youth across the board to step up political repression—all of which alienated the Catholic hierarchy. And over and above all of this, the ideology was vague enough to allow everyone to appeal to the "thought" or "doctrine" of Marshal Pétain.

"Pluralism" was carried even further when opposite tendencies struggled with each other within a single agency. Thus, in 1941 and 1942, a conflict arose between Joseph Darnand's activism and the inertia, encouraged by the leaders of the Veterans' Legion, of most veterans. In 1942, within the Secretariat for Youth, a moderate, pluralistic, and nonpolitical Secretary-General coexisted delicately with an Under-Secretary General who was a spokesman for impatient collaborationists in Paris and a great inventor of stillborn formulas for a state youth movement.

What was behind this seething cauldron of ideas and experiments, this morass of administrations, this unstable division of labor? The Vichy regime was the consequence of the disappearance of the parliamentary Third Republic and the accession to power of all of the forces which it had kept on the sidelines or whose assigned role in it had not been as big as they desired. It was a great revenge of minorities: we are talking basically about conservative forces who, for at least sixteen years, had been feeling that the Republic was no longer conservative enough. These forces of conservatism did not coincide with the French "middle classes"—a term that, in any case, covers a multitude of different realities. But they might be defined as including the following: an appreciable fraction of nonsalaried social groups (farm owners and operators, heads of businesses, shopkeepers and artisans, members of the

* Notes begin on page 487.

professions) and "cadres," a smaller percentage of public and trade-union officials, office workers, and independent workers. For these people, the Republican regime had been unsatisfactory. They disliked it for the rise of the left-wing parties, the pressure from the working class, the growth of communism in politics, labor, and (particularly) the intelligentsia, as well as its financial crises and government scandals. To them, the regime seemed to favor the subversion of a social order that had long been stable. The pluralism of Vichy resulted from divisions within these conservative forces and, above all, from the social ideal of its principal tendencies.

Pluralism resulted also from the presence in Vichy and Paris of a small fraction of the Left itself: the intellectuals, politicians, and labor leaders who had deserted the Republic for a number of reasons—anticommunism (especially among politicians upset by the sudden growth of the Communist party and among labor leaders displaced or demoted by Communists after the merger of Communist and non-Communist unions), pacifism, and disgust with the failure of the Popular Front. Especially in the last two years of the Third Republic, these disgruntled members of the Left met with many of their counterparts on the Right, particularly on the grounds of opposition to the coming war. But they were not going to play the crucial role in Vichy (although one of them, René Belin, became Minister of Labor, and many of them were prominent among the collaborationists); and I want here to focus on the conservatives who predominated in Vichy.

The problem of group access to state power is one of the most important in political science.[2] Briefly and sketchily, one can state that in classical representative democracies, at the national level, there are two main techniques of access. The first is the genuinely political technique—access to power through the political parties. The second is the specialized technique—access through pressure groups that defend and promote the interests of their members. Access of the second type is always indirect, since the interest groups are private associations without rule-making powers granted to them by law, and they must get in touch and deal with the central institutions of the state—parliamentary committees, ministries—whose decisions seal the fate of the claims they present on behalf of the social forces they represent. In other words, if they want to receive favors from the state, they must in some way control these institutions first. The better technique of access is the political one—access through the political parties is the only fully decisive one. From the viewpoint of the social forces who use parties as their intermediaries, even though the regime is a representative and not a direct democracy, access to power can be either direct or indirect. It is direct when the victorious party is one to which the members of the social group concerned have massively adhered and which is ruled by them: in this case, the party is the means by which the *pays réel* and the *pays légal* are made identical. Access is indirect when the party is merely a collection of *notables* ruled by its parliamentary representatives; in that case, the party is at the same time the instrument of the social group's participation to power *and* a screen between the group and power: the party is only a link between the real country and the legal country.

Under the Third Republic, the French middle classes' access to political power was always indirect. The parties they voted for were parties of *notables* who went looking for constituents (rather than the other way around). As for their interest groups, they were not very well organized in the individualistic society of the time. There was nothing wrong with this state of affairs, so long as access was not a vital necessity for the middle classes, in other words, so long as their social authority went unchallenged. Toward the end of the Third Republic that authority was shaken for the first time. At that moment the conservative forces, for whom access to political power was the only means of fending off the threat to their "real" power with legally authoritative measures, discovered that they were cut off from access —or, rather, that they had cut themselves off by their reluctance to take collective action. The unions had displayed a superior grade of specialized formal organization, permitting the working class to compensate at long last for its economic inferiority in the competition for access to political power. The better organization of the conservatives' opponents was especially in evidence in the decisive area of political technique: the mass parties (in other words, the parties of the Left) made themselves masters of power in 1936 with the complicity (the betrayal) of the Radical party, thus providing direct access to power for the forces of what the Right called "subversion." The problem, therefore, for the conservative forces, since their indirect access to power using the political technique was turning out to be disastrous, was how to substitute a direct means of access.

Apparently, there were only two ways of doing this. One was the democratic way. This would have meant accepting the representative regime but turning away from parties of *notables,* which lived only for and through the parliamentary game; these had become useless now that the game was no longer under their control. The conservatives would have had to re-establish contact and trust (now broken) between themselves and their representatives; they would have had to resign themselves to mass participation in a mass party, for which they would have to provide more than just a clientele at election time. The other way was the Fascist one, of direct access through anti-Republican action. This would have meant organizing a totalitarian instrument for seizing and keeping power and excluding other social groups and parties from it. The French conservatives for a while seemed attracted by both formulas, each equally new to them, and they hesitated between them: hence the simultaneous increase in membership of Colonel François de la Rocque's reactionary but moderate Parti Social Français (PSF) and Jacques Doriot's rabid Parti Populaire Français (PPF) in 1936–37, and some celebrated transfers from one to the other. In reality, neither formula suited most of the conservatives.

For these formulas had the same flaws: both required collective action—although repugnance to collective action explained why, in the past, the conservatives had resorted to parties of *notables* and misused the only important collective instrument they had had before 1934, the Bloc National of 1919. And both formulas required politicizing the conservatives. Now, conservatives always tended to confuse politics and disorder, and they tended to believe, as the platform of the PSF paradoxically explained, that only the elimination of politicians could lead to the reconciliation of all good Frenchmen. But, as we shall see, their schemes for social reconstruction made no room for political action.

The formula of direct democratic access had obstacles of its own. To the conservatives, scalded by the Popular Front, it seemed that only a strong state could restore France's threatened social order. But the Republic (which had failed to reform itself in 1934) was no longer capable of being such a state: to seize power within the framework of Republican institutions was to do too little and too late. Indeed, the parliamentary machine was so run down that only the conquest of the executive branch seemed at all interesting. Parliament was spending all its time abdicating, by granting to the cabinets the power of legislating through decrees. In other words, Parliament was useless, nothing but a huge obstacle. As for the formula of direct Fascist action, this required not only a conception of the state radically different from that held by most of France's conservatives, but also a willingness to stage a *coup d'état*—which neither Maurras nor Colonel de la Rocque, for instance, ever evinced, either before or after the bloody riots of February 6, 1934.

Thus, the conservative forces went on feeling alienated from the old techniques of political access without finding any substitute for them. They followed whomever seemed to serve them, and then they deserted them if their leaders appeared to go too far or not far enough for their tastes. Doriot, la Rocque, even Édouard Daladier were first the beneficiaries, later the victims of this mood. Then the Germans invaded France, the Republic fell. There was now a *tabula rasa,* and the conservatives were saved from further embarrassment.[3]

The conservatives during the Vichy regime can be divided into two main groupings. On one side, there were those who remained faithful to the idea of a representative regime and to political-party competition, and who believed that forces for social order would find their best chances for survival and success in an intelligent and modern use of the techniques of democratic access. In June 1940, these men might have accepted, at most, a kind of Roman dictatorship, aimed at preserving France's substance while waiting for peace, without major constitutional or social ambitions or ideological pretenses. This was the attitude of that old nationalist leader of the Right Louis Marin, and of the conservative champion of prewar appeasement, Pierre-Étienne Flandin, who tried to bring the regime closer to public opinion during his brief period of service in Vichy. On the other side, there were all those who tried to insure direct access to power outside of the democratic ways. The classic distinctions made by René Rémond must be accepted and supplemented here.[4] He divides France's Right into three categories: the counterrevolutionaries, the Orleanist or liberal conservatives, and the Bonapartists. The counterrevolutionaries, followers of Maurras, were still fighting the Enlightenment and the French Revolution, nostalgic for a hierarchical society, and dreaming of a decentralized monarchy. Liberal conservatives were the heirs of those nineteenth-century ideologues who accepted only the early part of the French Revolution: the triumph of the *haute bourgeoisie,* a state with balanced powers, and government by consent. But they remained fearful of democracy, universal suffrage, and unfiltered popular pressures for social reform. When the social order seemed threatened, these men were always willing to sacrifice temporarily the trappings of liberalism—public liberties, parliamentary government, unregulated economic enterprise—in order to save their deepest values: property and the limited state. The Bonapartists were the activist captors of the old Jacobin instinct for direct action and decisive government but, as Tocqueville had already remarked, the plebiscitarian rule they demanded would be "in the name of the people yet without the people," it would be "government with the enlightenment classes" and would try to satisfy "the passions of envy" and "the sentiments of equality" of the masses while satisfying the rich "by assuring them material order, the tranquil possession of their goods . . . continued well-being and opportunities of enrichment through official positions." [5] The conservatives who rejoiced about Vichy were much more numerous than the Maurrasian counterrevolutionaries and the "Bonapartist" League members of the 1920s. After February 6, 1934, an authoritarian fever had affected them all. A kind of Bonapartist push (sometimes jazzed up by Fascist gimmicks) had radicalized many men of the liberal, "Orleanist" Right without driving them all the way to genuine fascism. (A similar fever produced by comparable events in 1851 had brought

France's conservatives to Louis-Napoléon.) But men who came from the old counterrevolutionary Right or from the Bonapartist Right were sometimes pushed all the way to fascism.

Disciples of Maurras, Fascists and conservatives disgruntled with the Republic had only one thing in common: the determination to regain direct access to power outside of the classical representative regime— i.e., to end that famous divorce between the conservatives' *pays réel* and the *pays légal*. Thus, they agreed on using Maurras's old motto "politics first"—"politics" meaning that the sudden, providential seizure of power had to be exploited to institute direct access once and for all. But they disagreed about the techniques. For the Fascists, the slogan would be "politics forever." The technique of political access must be the totalitarian mass party. Society should not be independent from the state, which expressed itself through this party. The divorce between the legal country and the real country would end because the former would absorb the later. The specialized technique of access to power would, therefore, also be confiscated by the state. But other conservatives feared that in a Fascist state their access to power would once again become indirect: the party, while consisting of the masses of "conscious citizens," would probably end up being run by a minority whose composition might not at all be reassuring; and so a new screen would appear between power and the forces of law and order. Also, even if everything were for the best, the interest groups authorized by the state would once again depend on the whims of bureaucratic agencies or the state apparatus; at worst, they might even be eliminated and replaced by minor subdivisions of the party.

If it is true to say that fascism is a "revolt of the socially displaced," then the Vichyism of 1940–41 was created by all of the people who wanted to avoid this fate. But the thing they were afraid of was precisely the inherent dynamism of the state, the revolutionary potential of a single-party state, the risks involved in mobilizing the masses— inevitable factors under such a system. If the Republic in its final years had seemed to them to encourage the rise of disorder from below, the Fascist state now appeared as an infernal machine that threatened to spread disorder from above. The basic attitude of Vichy conservatism was distrust of the state. This distrust led them to oppose the methods of fascism. Their object was the dilution of "official" France in the "real" France.

So from the very first their conception of the ideal France was poles apart from that of the Fascists. It was not fundamentally different from that of the conservatives of the Orleanist tradition (from which they would not have departed but for the pressure of recent events): a society that was capable of existing by itself without need of the state, that was its own guarantor of a stable order; a "nightwatchman" state

with strictly limited prerogatives, for which governing would be ad-
ministering, and which would administer as little as possible. This was
the absolute negation of the state as the Fascists conceived it. "Politics
first," in the sense I defined it above, was supposed to permit the establishment of a society and state whose watchword would be "no politics." It was the old laissez-faire ideal of a society functioning for the
best so long as nothing came along to interfere with the golden rules
of liberalism. If only the "politicians" or "professional syndicalists" refrained from distorting those rules, the reconciliation of all Frenchmen
(the other great theme of the men of the Right) would once more become possible.

However—and it is an important exception—they were convinced
that the nation they wished to re-create could not be viable so long as
the intangible rules were those of classical liberalism. (It was on this
issue that the authoritarian conservatives parted company with those
who remained faithful to liberalism.) Nor was this all. They insisted
that it was those very rules that were responsible for the state of disorder that justified the "National Revolution." Political access through
the party system, to their minds, had corrupted society. It would have
served no useful purpose to restore a liberal France in accordance with
the principles of John Stuart Mill: the same causes would produce the
same effects, the reign of politics and individualism would once more
lead to collectivism, socialism, and statism.

In the reconstructed society, the motto was to be "priority to economic and social concerns." Specialized means of access to power were
to be privileged, in contrast to the situation under a democratic or a
Fascist regime. This choice was a clear indication of their deeply felt
repugnance for mass action as being too inchoate and demagogic. Powerless special-interest associations were to be replaced by autonomous,
hierarchical, disciplined communities, empowered to regulate the conduct of their members: an individualistic society would give way to an
"organic" society. In this way, some of the functions and prerogatives
presently usurped by the state would be restored to organized groups.
The role of the state itself would be reduced to that of a general-polic-
ing body, whose duty it was to see to it that nothing disturbed the
order established by these groups. As a consequence, we can scarcely
continue to describe the manner of access to what is left of the state as
"political"; the whole point was that the state must be depoliticized so
as to be at once strong and circumscribed in its powers. In order to
manage this, therefore, the forces of conservatism would have no need
to assume a political structure—the party system. They would have direct access, as community groups whose representatives participated in
the exercise of state power within its central institutions (the corporate
state), and also as privileged social forces that supplied cadres and doc-

trine directly to the state. State leadership would no longer be subject to the hazards of election, and the civil service would be subject to strict discipline.

Thus we arrive at a blueprint for a society of all but autonomous professional organizations, a society in which the economy is protected and the free circulation of ideas limited so as to avoid any threat to social stability. Nothing is left of liberalism but a few isolated values—property, the limitation on the prerogatives of the state, the nondependence of order on central power—to which all others are sacrificed. In this blueprint, the conservatives who had broken with Orleanist liberalism could see eye to eye with the traditionalists. Wasn't this exactly the doctrine of Maurras, with his hatred of representative government, his propaganda for decentralization and "natural communities"?

The whole of Vichy in 1940–41 can be explained in terms of this meeting of minds between two forms of opposition to the Republic. For the old, more doctrinaire opposition, the adversary had always been the democratic conception of the French Revolution, the dogma of equality (which led to universal suffrage and hence to a divorce between the real country and its official representation), the dogma of freedom of thought (which led to the triumph of *laïcisme* and secret societies); the enemy was first and foremost the democrat, the "Republican." For the more recent opposition, more anxious to defend threatened interests than ideas, the chief bones of contention were the rise of the French working class, the effects of socialization and (in many cases) industrialization, and the Popular Front. It looked as if, in their search for the "good society" (to use the original title of Walter Lippmann's famous book), a considerable number of French conservatives had concluded that since the classical liberal blueprint for society was unsatisfactory, a counterrevolutionary plan had to be adopted, so that the Fascist prescription would not carry the day. This is why the National Revolution gives us the impression of a kind of Maurrasianism of the market place. True, all that the Vichy conservatives preserved of Maurras's elaborate construction were the main outlines. The parts that seemed too utopian or too sectarian were an embarrassment to them. They favored organized professions, but not corporatism; they could hardly take seriously a folkloristic regionalism or the restoration of the monarchy. They had no intention of throwing out the entire heritage of 1789, which made the bourgeoisie the dominant class. But once these rough edges were smoothed out, they were quite prepared to go along for a good deal of the way.

This convergence also explains Vichy in another fashion, and again sets the Vichy conservatives against the Fascists. Not only did they differ as to their conception of the aims of the coming revolution, but their respective ideas of the means to be used to bring it about were diametrically opposed. For the Fascists, a revolution could only be made by immediately creating a totalitarian apparatus. For their adversaries, the notion of "politics first" meant simply a seizure of power in the naked state—providentially stripped of both parties and Parliament, but without the powers of a totalitarian state—by the naked forces of conservatism, without any solid organization, of either a political or an interest-group nature. This was certainly dictatorship, with all consultation and popular representation suppressed, but without an apparatus; a dictatorship that would legislate in the abstract, trusting that the laws would be applied without a murmur and that the new France would emerge without effort. It was an act of faith in the omnipotence of the Word and of Law. Indeed, its creators believed that their plans were designed merely to re-establish the natural order of things. Since their designs were "like the brilliant rays [*faisceaux*] of pure reason," [6] why shouldn't their necessity impress itself as self-evident upon men's minds? In that case, the state would not have to brainwash or bully its citizens: it would be enough to educate them.

It is not easy to indicate how the social components of the middle classes distributed themselves among the various political tendencies —democratic Left, Republican conservatives, Vichyite or collaborationist Left, anti-Republican conservatives, counterrevolutionaries, and Fascists. What makes an answer difficult here is, first, the political instability of the conservative forces in the 1930s, and, second, the fact that French political forces have been studied mainly in their parliamentary and ideological aspects rather than from the viewpoint of their social bases. This is particularly regrettable in the case of the French Right, given its indifference to ideas. One can only say that each one of the social components of the middle classes was represented in each political tendency, and that the Fascists found much of their clientele in the right-wing fraction of the professions (the component of the middle classes most deeply concerned with politics) and among small shopkeepers, employees, and independent workers closest to proletarization—an obviously urban clientele in the main.

II

The conservative disciples of Maurras and the "authoritarian" conservatives seized power in the summer of 1940. At once, they set about building the communitarian society and the safe state (strong, but limited in scope) that I have just described. They organized direct access to power through community institutions. If the specialized organization of conservative forces had been weak under the Republic, Vichy legislation now sped up their consolidation; embryonic organizations that had existed under the Republic were used, insofar as they were deemed won over to the new ideal, as engines for the new machine. Thus, rural syndicalism, which had even before the war campaigned for corporatism,[7] now saw its wishes fulfilled: its leaders were asked to establish Vichy's Peasant Corporation, endowed with the legal means of expansion that syndicalism had never had. The political agitator of the French peasantry in the 1930s, Henri Dorgères, who had been much more truculent in organizing part of France's rural population, was now put in charge of the Corporation's propaganda. And in order to weave its network of Committees of Industrial Organization, Vichy resorted to a large extent to pre-existing employers' associations, at the same time eliminating the men who were too well known for their activities under the previous regime, or who were too committed to classic liberal positions. Thus, the modern part of the economy came to be governed by employers' organizations, transformed into branches of the state administration. To the cadres, fairly disorganized before the war, Vichy gave the possibility of grouping themselves in an autonomous and general fashion, since the Charter of Labor pronounced its blessing to the syndicalism of the cadres and engineers and assured them of considerable representation on the social committees. The same work of organization went on in those milieux where it had been lacking, or where it had only shown up in the form of unions that had to be suppressed as dangerous—the liberal professions, where corporative, protectionist, and disciplined "orders" flourished. These groups all received considerable rule-making power. Hence, in order to open up this means of access to power, Vichy practiced "organic" pluralism: each group, when suitably organized, received control over its own domain. As a corollary, the specialized groups whose rise, during the last phase of the Third Republic, had threatened the social power of the conservatives were emasculated: white-collar unions were abolished; blue-collar unionism was deprived of its interprofessional agencies, subjected to the state as regards its statutes and the choice of its leaders, restricted to a part of its former prerogatives, "made wiser" through the new formula of the exclusive and compulsory union.

The opening of a direct-access route to the state was equally interesting. As could be expected, the political technique of democracy (or of fascism)—parties—was immediately replaced with the technique of direct access by the "forces of order" *as such,* which foreshadowed and prepared for the setting up of definitive central institutions, postponed for the time being. First came depoliticization. The political personnel of the Republic was eliminated; the civil service and all of the local institutions were purged, Freemasons were hunted down. One of the consequences, secondary but significant, of the divorce between much of the Right and its delegates to the Third Republic's "legal country" was that conservative parliamentarians could play only a very small and awkward role in Vichy. To be sure, some quite prominent ones were used in the government and civil service, but only if they had displayed antiparliamentary feelings before the war or if they were, due to their social standing, "representative gentlemen" who owed nothing to elections—if I may use a distinction made at the time by François Perroux. The bad adaptation French conservatives had made to the prewar Republic, and their tendency to antiparliamentarism in times of crisis, made it very difficult for a right-wing senator or deputy to carry out his parliamentary mandate.

Then came the second phase of the operation: once the way was cleared of politicians, the machinery of state was to be manned by the healthy, uncontaminated forces of society. Three conservative groups were thus privileged. The army and the navy were given extraordinary influence in a state that proclaimed France's military defeat—were they not, as Maurras wrote, the very archetype of the "real forces" held down for so long?—and officers of both the army and navy were installed in ministerial positions, prefectures, as directors of the Chantiers de la Jeunesse, as local heads of the Veterans' Legion in many *départements*. Civil servants with conservative ideas were promoted, sometimes to cabinet positions. And the local *notables* once rejected by universal suffrage were richly rewarded, especially at the head of *communes* and *départements*. In this way, the image of a pluralist society was complemented by that of a dictatorship of the forces of law and order.

In order to protect these two new techniques of access to power, i.e., in order to prevent the communitarian society's being subverted by social groups that were left out of the privileged organizations or reduced to dependency, and in order to eliminate opposition to the authoritarian state and to the oligarchic recruitment of its ruling personnel, the men in power saw to it that France would be put in a socially conservative strait jacket. Much of Vichy's legislation, especially toward youth, education, the family, and also Vichy's policy toward the Church, was aimed at consolidating the rule of those elites. To be sure, not all the measures had this objective. Indeed, the divorce between the real country and the legal country was much more serious, and had more aspects, than a simple dissociation between conservative forces and Republican institutions.

Thus, some of Vichy's reforms, designed to restore "realities" which the Republic had neglected, meant more than social reaction—its pro-family demographic policy, its vindication of physical fitness, its upsurge of "fraternity," and the mixing of classes within the Chantiers or the cadre schools—even though, in truth, Vichy did no more than develop tendencies that were already apparent in the last years of the Republic. Nevertheless, the elaborate demonstration of respect toward the established order—the participation of the Church in government demonstrations, moral indoctrination, the reign of virtue, apprenticeship to civic discipline in the Chantiers, the whole effort to form conformist elites (support for educational youth movements, reform of the educational system so as to bind the child to his social milieu and combat social uprooting), the return, if not to the soil, at least to nature, far from the dangerous cities (lairs of Republicans, but also of Fascists)—all of this corresponds to a concern for social safety.

Such were the aims. Such were the laws. But, practically from the start, the disciples of Maurras and their conservative allies were caught in a contradiction. French society in 1940 was so far removed from the orderly and hierarchical society of which they dreamed that mere seizure of power in a state whose institutions dated from the liberal era was simply not enough. France was infinitely more complicated than Portugal, which the conservatives liked to take as an example in 1940–41, and the shock that had disturbed French conservative forces before 1940 had been quite strong. It thus became quickly apparent that the instruments available to the men in power would be absurdly weak should these means be conservative, or dangerously revolutionary should they be efficient.

Depoliticization, the organization of communities, the "return to reality"—this presupposed Draconian measures that terrified people who wanted a strong state but only within narrow limits. They could see very well that only generalized, intensive, and permanent use of power could possibly restore the power of the forces of conservatism in society and consolidate their annexation of the state. Yet they distrusted the state, that producer of collectivism. They realized they had to mobilize the masses, but what would this do to the theory of France as a "nation of *notables*" and to the static dream of specialized, conservative communities? Inversely, if they resigned themselves to a dictatorship without strength, they again risked facing disorder and discovering that their interpretation of "politics first" was the negation of politics. Charles Péguy's famous quip about Kant, which the conservatives loved to quote in this period of reaction against Rousseau and Kant—"Kant had pure hands, but he had no hands"—could thus be applicable to them.

After the Communists had seized power in Russia in 1917, they had been faced with the same choice. They too wanted a withering away of the state and a spontaneously harmonious society; they too wanted a merely temporary dictatorship; but they were not afraid of the state or of the requirements of mass action. So they chose the totalitarian means, the all-engulfing state and the single party, and were able to stay in power at the cost of seeing their original objectives wither away instead of the state.

The men of Vichy, caught between their admiration for Mussolini's methods and their sympathy for Swiss society and the Swiss state, tried to come up with a compromise. They decided against transforming the state into an instrument of totalitarianism. They nonetheless decided to strengthen their dictatorship and to view the exercise of dictatorial power—in the context of a state whose prerogatives far exceeded those of the ideal state they had in mind—no longer as a passing expedient that would make possible a social restoration and a return to the ideal state, but instead as a permanent necessity to protect society after, as well as during, such a restoration. The ideal state was dropped. This sacrifice of one part of their program in order better to preserve the other had disastrous consequences. The pluralist society, far from being saved, was eaten away little by little by an encroaching state; yet the state, which became more and more totalitarian in its pretensions, lacked the backing of the party that might have endowed it with popular support and public terror. It became a paraplegic. Whichever way you looked at it, Vichy was the loser.

The contrast between the state's pretensions and the means placed at its disposition was apparent in all the efforts used to mobilize the masses in the service of the regime. The single-party system was considered pernicious as of the summer of 1940; in the absence of that particular instrument, Vichy tried to come up with a number of alternatives, but it was never bold enough to go all the way to the logical totalitarian conclusion. The most famous example is that of the Veterans' Legion. An exclusive movement, its task was to disseminate the doctrine of the Marshal—but its role was reduced to a purely "civic" one, without legal means for political action: it was therefore fated to be transformed into a parallel administration, and to become embittered in its own passivity. Time and again, noisily heralded instructions and directives drafted by its leaders or by the government reminded the members of their duty to serve as intermediaries between the people and the regime, to inform the public, to educate but not usurp the powers of the government and of its agents, "the only trustees of the central powers' constitutional authority." It is not surprising that despite constant warnings from Legion leaders, the veterans turned from propagandists to informers, became a gigantic pressure group, a network for the settlement of political accounts, collided with exasperated public officials, and thus deprived the regime of the benefits it could have derived from its plea for depoliticization, without bringing to it in exchange the advantages of dynamic and constructive activities.

The policy pursued with regard to youth movements presents an even more striking contrast. Vichy's determination to channel the enthusiasm of young people for the National Revolution was apparent from the start; but once again no one dared to go all the way to a state-directed movement. A choice had to be made. One possibility was for the regime to staff an exclusive, or specially favored, youth movement with "revolutionary" cadres—that is, in the absence of cadres formed by the doctrine of the new state and equipped for mass action, cadres chosen from among the Fascist youth groups. The other possibility was to choose the cadres from among the prewar nonpolitical youth movements (largely Catholic), but in that case, though they might provide strong ideological guarantees of respect for the established order and the established regime, it would be impossible to create a single, exclusive movement. If Vichy decided to settle for a specially favored movement, it was only to be expected that the cadres, considering their origin, would make sure that its activities did not have any adverse effect on other movements, and, considering their formation, would be more likely to provide young people with a civic training than to involve them in direct political action. This was in fact the choice that Vichy had to make in the case of the Compagnons movement. Vichy chose sound but nonpolitical organization over dynamic but dangerous mobilization, and consequently closed the door to the political enlistment of youth in the service of the regime. Each time it looked as if it wanted to exert pressure in that direction, Vichy ran up against the combined opposition of the old movements—and of the new one, which, for want of orthodox cadres, it had been unable to reduce to servitude.

In reality, there was an insoluble contradiction in the matter of youth mobilization as well as in the political mobilization of adults. It was hard to use *notables* whose only ideal was to repudiate politics for mass action, nor was it any easier, through mere "educational" propaganda, to rally the masses behind a doctrine that consisted in destroying their political power. When Minister of the Interior Pierre Pucheu said that Vichy had to re-establish contact with the people "by creating a popular and national force on which the state would lean" but which would be "the very opposite of a party," because the time for parties was gone and because the French needed a kind of mutual amnesty, he merely expressed the embarrassment of authoritarian conservatives in 1941. The "technique of the *coup d'état*" was no longer enough; what was needed now was a policy of permanent revolution.

By resisting (not without anguish) the temptation of the totalitarian state, Vichy seemed to give up on any rapid enforcement of the National Revolution; but by trying nevertheless to extend the powers of the state, by giving in to the temptation of *étatisme* for which it had so much abused the Republic, Vichy itself destroyed the sketch of an ideal society drawn by its exuberant legislators. As the state and the bureaucracy extended their hold, the mirage of "natural communities" and organized "necessary liberties" disappeared from the horizon. Consider, for example, the self-destruction of the National Revolution in the realm of education. According to Maurras—who was approved of by all those who insisted on the family's primary responsibility for education, on the role that corporatism had to play in this area, and on the shrinking of the state's activities—the goal was to transform education into a free, autonomous association over which the state played a general supervisory role.[8] But even Maurras the decentralizer added that in the near future, the school, having been corrupted by the Republic, had to stop being a "soviet" and become again "the school of the French state," and he congratulated himself that the French would at last enjoy "a regime in which the state once more becomes the master responsible for reading, writing, spelling, grammar, letters, arithmetic, and civics." An ardent campaign developed for the abolition of Republican textbooks and for a radical purge of the Ministry of National Education. The best-selling conservative writer Henry Bordeaux, who had noticed that Nazi textbooks did not mention Germany's defeat at the battle of the Marne, suggested that the new French textbooks should show the same discretion about France's defeat in 1940.[9]

It was the same story with local administration. The regime never tired of singing the praises of a return to a provincial structure, the resurrection of the old *pays*, the reawakening of regional traditions. But in spite of elaborate preparatory studies, the new provinces were never officially mapped, and decentralization gave way to a municipal law that abolished elections in *communes* of more than two thousand inhabitants, as well as to a law that suspended the *conseils généraux* and the *conseils d'arrondissements*. Once again, Maurras was there to applaud: the "municipal tyrant," the product of universal suffrage, was no longer to be tolerated; the mayor must be the representative of the central power, for the Revolution had annihilated the old *communes,* local assemblies, provincial estates general. These same local assemblies (in which, or so he claimed, he had placed his hopes since childhood) had become polluted. The Communist dialectic of a temporary dictatorship preparing happiness for tomorrow was thus used by the National Revolution. It had to recognize that the "national communities" were not so natural as all that.

And the same contradiction appeared in the organization of the economy. The founding fathers of the Peasant Corporation had tried to limit the hold of the state on it as much as possible. Of course, even here they had had to admit that the French peasantry had no natural leaders and that the delegates to corporative organizations would have to find those leaders themselves; but they were often careful not to impose their choices on the peasants. Yet, soon, the very builders of this difficult and gigantic enterprise expressed their alarm: the Corporation's independence was being seriously threatened by its contacts with the state. The Corporation, which was supposed to have autonomous powers, in fact had none; it became an appendix of the bureaucracy, dependent on the state for its resources, and it received from the state, toward the end of 1942, a new statute that increased government controls. As for those who had hoped that industry would receive a corporative organization, or at least a relatively autonomous government by industrialists themselves, they were disappointed early enough. To be sure, it was not the state that took over here, but the Organization Committees composed of professional businessmen; however, only select businessmen—the biggest—were adequately represented, and there was almost total symbiosis between the committees and the civil service. The Organization Committees became bureaucratic and led eventually to industry's being run by an all-powerful minority of professionals. Defenders of small and middle-size businesses who had so often denounced, under the Third Republic, the impious collusion of socialism and big capital, were now able to sound off against the "synarchic" coalition of big capital with the administration.[10] It had not been their intention that the seizure of power by the forces of order and tradition —which look with favor, as we know, upon family businesses and with disfavor upon anonymous capital—should lead to this kind of government planning.

The spread of state control ended up by destroying the privileged access to power that the Vichy conservatives had wished to open up. There was no question any more of divesting the state of some of its principal functions. From 1940 to 1942, the basic means to power remained political: the control of the state. Things were back where they started; it was "politics forever." But the point was that the people who controlled the state, the conservatives, were without the means to do so effectively. By re-emphasizing the state while weakening it, they were signing their own death warrants, cutting themselves off from the only approach to power they had left. For the traditional liberties they had wanted to restore, they had substituted what the conservative and proappeasement ex-Minister Anatole de Monzie, in a letter to Marshal Pétain, referred to as "improvised abuses," when what was clearly called for was an organized reign of terror. And in this fashion Vichy caused the scale to weigh in favor of Fascists and crypto-Fascists. These men, for their part, had never believed in the dissolution of the state and the creation of static conservative communities; they had fewer qualms about shelving the dream. They also had no qualms in pushing the policy of state control initiated by the conservatives to its logical conclusion. Through 1942 and 1943, the conservative position was eroded.

Within Vichy France, in the very heart of the institutions that Vichy had created only to condemn them to inertia, a number of "activists" began to emerge. Out of the Veterans' Legion, considered too soft and cumbersome, Darnand carved a Service d'Ordre Légionnaire (SOL) which became the Militia, a "chivalric force" entrusted with a summary but brutal program of political action and repression. Then, in order to neutralize the Fascists in Paris, Vichy thought it expedient to give important posts to men of the same political persuasion as they. They in turn naturally took advantage of their position in the highest places in the French state to build an empire for themselves, to gain a sort of Fascist bridgehead. This showed in the propaganda of men in the Information Service throughout France, and in the repeated attempts by certain groups in the Secretariat for Youth to start up a "single youth movement." In addition to this twofold infiltration of the conservative Vichy regime, there was an open struggle with the Fascist groups in Paris, who were in no way disarmed by the "competition" from the wolves admitted to the Vichy sheepfold. On the contrary, they found therein at once a band of accomplices and one more reason for hostility toward Vichy. The contest of Vichy with Marcel Déat and his supporters was brutal; that with Doriot and the PPF, which was allowed to recruit members in the Southern (i.e., Vichy) Zone and North Africa, was more subtle. The contest was all the more dangerous for Vichy, since the illusory nature of the closed society that the conservatives wanted to build, and the simultaneously ineffective and obnoxious nature of the means they employed, enabled the Fascists to denounce Vichy in the most demagogic terms. Déat stressed its chauvinism and clericalism. Doriot emphasized the plutocratic side. Alfred Fabre-Luce talked about a war between the "monarchists" of Vichy and the "Bonapartists" of Paris. The contrast is indeed striking between the tepid and moralizing propaganda of conservative Vichy and the mass meetings organized by the groups in Paris, or the parades of their followers in the Southern Zone.

Vichy could do nothing but lose at this game, and the same went for Pierre Laval's game—Laval the subtle, the oversubtle tactician. To prevent the triumph of the Fascists, he tried to divert and turn the anti-Vichy sentiments they exploited to his own advantage. One by one, he removed the conservatives from power; he got rid of the military; he made no bones about snuffing out the little legionary flame; he buried the National Council. Beyond that, he seemed determined to close off the Fascists' access to political power by "repoliticizing" France somewhat, i.e., by restoring the political cadres the conservatives had endeavored to abolish.[11]

The year 1943 saw the same conservative forces that had "made" the National Revolution break free from Vichy, and, in many cases, join up with the Resistance. This was the year of the divorce between the Church and Vichy, of the compulsory labor laws sending young Frenchmen to Germany, the year in which certain people who had been among the Marshal's closest companions in 1940 went into exile or were deported. Although Laval had tried to keep the overly "dynamic" forces that had emerged from Vichy's concepts and concessions, like the SOL, or the Information Service, under his personal control, he was outflanked by them and by the groups in Paris who were supported by the Germans. They were all there was left to take over power. By undermining the National Revolution without having any personal support, he had sawed off the branch he was sitting on. He was simply the syndic of the failure of the Vichy conservatives: both he and they played the classic part of the sorcerer's apprentice.

The final months of Vichy are by no means the least interesting. The conservative forces, driven from power by the Fascists and clinging to the few community institutions they had created, found themselves face to face with a social threat far worse than those that had so upset them in the past. The "left wing" republic of 1936 had alarmed them more than it had hurt them, and out of this fear (and in the absence of serious wounds) Vichy had been born. In 1936, certainly, the "disorder" had seemed the more menacing in that it came from the very depths of society; however, the machinery of the state—a weak state—was not a driving force but merely a supplement and even, to a certain extent, a brake. The disorders of 1944 were less profound: the subversion no longer came from below, but from above; the state itself had provoked it, not one particular class. But to the extent to which this state had become totalitarian, the damage seemed all the worse, and the ill effects less insidious but more brutal: deportations, assassinations of "law and order" types throughout the country, escalation of summary executions, looting, a diffused civil war. The sit-in strikes of 1936 seemed child's play compared with the police terror of 1944, and the Popular Front a small thing next to the National Socialist Front.

The conservatives were thrown into the arms of the Republic (which they had so vilified in 1940) by the Fascists. By now most of them realized that the golden age of conservative society was not within reach, and that they had better make their choice somewhere in between the iron age of the totalitarian state and the age of the Republic—less brilliant perhaps than the latter, but more flexible than the former. I have stressed that we must not confuse the "middle classes," even the nonsalaried middle classes, with the forces of conservatism. Present in the ranks of the Resistance and among the leaders of Free France were numerous representatives of the middle classes who were not political conservatives, as well as conservatives who had given precedence to their determination to resist the invader over their desire to build a society in conformity with their political and social ideals. This appeared to be, to followers of Marshal Pétain, a guarantee against the risks of social upheaval after the Liberation: reconciliation with the Republic was the only chance left to avoid open civil war (which would no doubt end in victory for the forces of subversion), even to restore a conservative republic. Pétain himself seemed to understand this point: the draft constitution he drew up at the end of 1943 was interpreted, by two men * who had never lost hope in the mirage of conservative society, as an "aggravated return to 1875."

III

Thus France's conservative forces came full circle. The Resistance's "revolution through law" was after all less dangerous than the "revolution from the top" of the summer of 1940. For the creation of radically new institutions or for the revival of very old, half-legendary ones (which amounts to the same thing), the mere seizure of power by teams reluctant to use political organization and political methods— such as police terror and the mobilization of opinion—was useless. But whereas the temporary use of powers of a nontotalitarian state is insufficient, the totalitarian state, which is necessary, soon becomes an end in itself, and the teams in power can no longer get rid of it. The Bonapartist solution—a "popular" state led by forces of law and order without either totalitarian apparatus or democratic freedoms, i.e., a left-wing facade, a conservative substance, a dictatorial reality—was no longer possible. But the revolutionary potential in a Fascist mobilization of the masses, the Fascist *étatisme* that turns the whole population into employees of the state, were repugnant to French conservatives. The state corrupts the revolution even and especially if it is a "national" revolution; but without a state, there is no revolution. "The worst kind of Utopian thinking is that which ignores the solidarity between good and evil, or the incompatibility between equally precious goods." [12] The distinction between society and state, which is essential to conservatives, can survive today only in a democratic regime, for it will then be preserved by a coalition of conservatives and antitotalitarian men of the Left.

The new *ralliement* of conservatives to the Republic was not shattered after 1945. In the Fourth Republic, threatened by the great social push of the Liberation and by inflation, French conservative forces tried to use the two methods of indirect access to power as well as possible. They perfected their specialized organizations in the economic realm, developing and completing the structures consolidated by Vichy. The Conseil National du Patronat Français, the Fédération

* Xavier Vallat and Dommange.

Nationale des Syndicats d'Exploitants Agricoles, and even the Confédération Générale des Petites et Moyennes Entreprises, were heirs
of Vichy's institutions. And, in the realm of politics, they groped for
parties in which they would feel at ease. For a while, de Gaulle's
Rassemblement du Peuple Français (RPF) appeared as a possible instrument of direct access to power. But in 1952, the breakup of the
RPF—which combined an appeal to the masses (especially for a "la-
bor-capital association") with an appeal to the forces of law and order
(in its critique of a Republic that seemed too weak to resist pressures
from below)—proved that the *ralliement* was solid. For it was the most
conservative elements of the RPF that seceded and dropped de Gaulle
in favor of the reassuring Antoine Pinay, having become worried by
the "demagogic" possibilities of Gaullist doctrine and the mass structure of the RPF. On the whole, French conservatives in their sedate
elitism continued to prefer the classical parties of *notables* despite all
their inconveniences. What made their indirect access to power tolerable was the division in the forces favoring change; with the labor unions divided between Communists and two main kinds of non-Communists, with the political Left torn between a Communist mass party,
a Socialist party that was not much more than a party of militants,
and a Radical party of ambivalent *notables,* French conservatives
could feel quite safe.

But it would be wrong to imagine that France's middle classes had
all become converts to the Republic. Inflation and economic growth,
and the resulting discrepancies in living standards and regional incomes, tended to create a new dividing line. Above it, the more prosperous and respectable conservatives behaved as Republican citizens
converted to civic action. Below it, categories that came close to economic death and proletarianization once again found the indirect political procedures frustrating, but they remembered the horrors of 1944
well enough to shun the adventure of totalitarian and *étatiste* parties.
If direct action without political tools was ruled out, if direct action
with an instrument like a mass party was bad, the only remaining
thing was to have a specialized professional organization (made in the
image of the ideal communitarian society), give it a political role, and
throw it into action for the conquest of power. This is what the Poujade shopkeepers' and peasants' movement tried to do in 1953–56, but
neither direct, i.e., violent, action nor parliamentary action succeeded.[13]

When the Fourth Republic fell, under blows delivered not by
French conservatives but by France's settlers in Algeria and by the
French Army, the conservatives found a haven in the Fifth Republic.
Here was a regime that was representative yet endowed with a strong
executive, in which they had no reason to fear social subversion and in

which the two indirect techniques of access to power worked well. The RPF's mass aspects had worried them, but the new Gaullist party chose not to be a party of masses or militants. French conservatives were at last able to square the circle: the party for which they voted became France's largest party at election time, dominated the Parliament (after 1962), and became increasingly a party of *notables*.

Interestingly enough, when, after the near revolution of May 1968 a tremendous conservative upsurge led to the smashing Gaullist victory in the elections of June 1968, General de Gaulle chose to give this victory a reformist meaning rather than that of a victory for law and order. Enough middle-class conservatives deserted him in the referendum of April 1969 to insure first his defeat, and then the election to the Presidency of a man who both perpetuated the Fifth Republic and gave it the solid conservative color that de Gaulle had wanted to change. That is a long and complex story, but it is difficult to understand the political attitudes and evolution of France's conservatives if one ignores the Vichy background.

2
Self-Ensnared:
Collaboration with
Nazi Germany

Almost thirty years have passed since the Liberation of France in 1944, and the flood of books about Vichy and the Resistance has not receded. However, there is no satisfactory French treatment of the most delicate of all the problems raised by the fall and divisions of France: collaboration with the German occupant. This may be due in part to the nature of the subject. Vichy can be discussed—I won't say objectively, but without reopening the wounds that the events of 1940–44 inflicted on French self-confidence and national consciousness. For there is enough apparently convincing evidence behind the thesis of Vichy—that it was a shield protecting the French body politic while London and the Resistance forged a sword—to allow the French public to face without too much shame such facts as Marshal Pétain's early popularity and Vichy's original appeal. The Fascist gangs and writers of Paris could be dismissed as a noisy but tiny, repulsive but insignificant, minority, an exception that confirms the rule of French decency despite French divisions. To deal with the subject of collaboration as such would make retrospective reassurance far more difficult. For one would have to realize that the cancer that was gnawing at France's sense of national identity had spread beyond the narrow confines of the "Paris traitors."

The historians and social scientists of France, where that sense of national identity appears to have triumphed at last over the ordeals which nearly thirty years of ghastly tests had accumulated, may feel less inhibited today about scrutinizing an ugly past. However, there is a second reason for timidity. The subject is infernally complicated. Vichy, the pluralistic dictatorship, is complex enough. Yet it is easier to distinguish the phases, clans, ideas, and issues in the maze of

First published in the *Journal of Modern History,* September 1968.

Pétain's regime than it is to do so in the story of French collaborationism. There seem to have been almost as many collaborationisms as there were proponents or practitioners of collaboration. This may help explain why, if we look for full treatments, we find only two volumes —one [1] written by a former collaborationist, who throws amazingly little light or heat on what purports to be his subject, and another written by an incisive young political scientist [2] who does a fine job of reviewing themes and factions but is limited by the nature of her assignment, which was to focus on the press.

There may be a third reason why there is no entirely satisfactory treatment of French collaboration with the Nazis—and why there may well never be one. Paradoxical as it may sound, the subject turns out, upon analysis, to be more elusive than substantial. I do not mean to suggest that there was no collaboration after all. There was a lot of it. What I want to suggest is that the subject is interesting only if one looks at it not from the viewpoint of Franco-German relations in Hitler's Europe but from that of Franco-French relations, so to speak.

In this chapter I propose an analytic distinction between two kinds of behavior. There was, on one hand, *collaboration with Germany* for reasons of state, i.e., to safeguard French interests in interstate relations between the beaten power and the victor. This was to a large extent the necessary if unintended by-product of the existence of a French state in Vichy. Even here, what is most enlightening is not the story of French negotiations with German officials, but the contrast between Vichy's theory of (limited) independence and Vichy's practice— a contrast imposed by the realities of France's situation. On the other hand, there was *collaborationism with the Nazis,* in the sense of an openly desired cooperation with, and imitation of, the German regime. We find in collaborationism not so much seduction by or fascination with the Nazis (although there was some) as a means to a variety of internal *French* ends. In very few cases did the collaborationists know much about what the Nazis were really like; even to the ideological collaborationists, fascism, or national socialism, was more a myth than a political and social reality clearly seen and analyzed. French collaborationism in World War II can best be viewed as the most extreme form of what I have called elsewhere the breakdown of the Republican synthesis—a "mix" represented by the stalemate society and the parliamentary regime.[3] The collaborationists were among the most determined rebels engaged in the destruction of that synthesis. At the same time, the practitioners of collaboration and the champions of collaborationism reflected many of the features of the polity against which they rebelled—features conflicting with those of the foreign regimes they appeared to admire and those which the Vichy doctrine was calling for.

I

I am not suggesting that all forms of collaboration were parts of the "Franco-French war." The national situation of France after the armistice was such that a modicum of collaboration with the victor was inevitable. On one hand, as Article 3 of the armistice agreement stipulated, the French administration in the three-fifths of France occupied by the Germans could not avoid having to collaborate with German military authorities; the coexistence of two bureaucracies in the same territory made it impossible for the French to practice *le silence de la mer*. On the other hand, as the war became more cataclysmic and German needs more intense, the pressure on French authorities to participate more fully in the German war effort—through the production of weapons for the German war machine, the export of food products to Germany, the sending of workers to German factories—was bound to increase. Again, a modicum of collaboration was inevitable. Since there existed a French government in France (by contrast with the situation in countries like Belgium or Norway), the Germans instead of imposing their decisions directly could always put the French authorities before the dilemma: collaboration or "Polandization." Even the most rigorously *attentiste* or anti-German of all possible Vichy regimes would have had to give in from time to time, due to France's defeat and partial occupation. Also, the Germans detained a huge mass of French war prisoners as hostages for this kind of pressure and blackmail; until November 1942 the implicit threat of total occupation was always suspended over Vichy; even after November 1942 there was always an implicit threat of eliminating the regime itself, of obliterating its last shreds of authority. In other words, a basic contradiction was going to annihilate, over time, all of Vichy's best intentions. There was a French government in France, determined to save whatever could be saved after the disaster of 1940, rather than wage battle outside. But its very existence sufficed to turn what in other occupied parts of Europe would have been a pure and simple fact of domination and effect of conquest into what might be called a *collaboration d'état* (if I may be forgiven a French play on the two meanings of the word *état*). Moreover, the regime's own stake in protecting what it had saved (the empire, the fleet, and Vichy France)—i.e., its margin between limited independence and Polandization—facilitated Germany's task and aggravated the bent toward such collaboration.

This is a most important point for three different reasons. First, Vichy was in an "objectively collaborationist" position, however much individual Vichyites or the scriptures and servants of the National Revolution may deserve to be called "subjectively" anticollaborationist. Many have said that de Gaulle's consistent condemnation of

Vichy as a regime marked *ab ovo* by the sin of the armistice was a sectarian refusal to acknowledge the services Vichy rendered to the French body politic in preventing Polandization. They failed to see the point I am trying to make, and to understand the nature of de Gaulle's concern: he worried about French self-respect, honor, and moral integrity rather than French physical integrity. For many of the conservatives who surrounded Pétain, the virtue of the armistice was that it allowed a French regime to prepare a domestic *redressement*, prerequisite either to French external recovery in case of an ultimate German victory, or to French mediation in case of a deadlock in the war, or to French revenge. But this patriotic dream had no relation to the realities of total war. In such a war, there would be no opportunity for *redressement*, no distance from the occupant's demands, and Vichy would be more like a pressed orange than like a tough nut—as Pucheu discovered when he selected, in effect, German-held hostages for the Nazis to shoot in retaliation for Resistance sabotage. The drama of Vichy was not in the murky motives but in the catastrophic consequences—and, alas, the ethical value of a policy has to be assessed in light of the outcome, not the intentions: circumstances placed *l'État français* in a situation of mandatory, involuntary collaboration. Vichy prided itself on its "return to reality," and Laval saw himself as a great realist. But Vichy's return to reality was a mixture of resignation to and obstinate self-delusion about an untenable reality, and Laval's realism led to a series of small Munichs. In order to preserve their chances, they had to give them up one by one.

Second, only a short step separated *involuntary* collaboration for reason of state from *voluntary* collaboration for reason of state. If giving in to enemy demands could be justified by the need to save one's last holdings and hostages, then anticipating at least some of those demands or adopting an "understanding" attitude toward German economic and military imperatives could be defended as a way of warding off dangerous pressures, enlarging one's domain, or improving the prisoners' or nation's lot. Many Vichyites who can hardly be accused of pro-Nazi sympathies and who were sure that their policy was one of serving strictly French interest moved to voluntary collaboration out of conviction that Germany would win the war. Involuntary collaboration was the price they had to pay for having misjudged France's situation; voluntary collaboration was a price they chose to pay because they misjudged Germany's. This was slippery ground indeed, and there was no clear yardstick to indicate where reason of state ended and folly began. In the fall of 1940, at Montoire, Pétain's acceptance of the "principle" of collaboration meant that he had put a finger into the machine. That he did not want to put the whole hand in was proved by his dismissal of Laval, guilty of having pursued a policy of voluntary collaboration with excessive zeal and dangerous concessions.

But Admiral François Darlan was to adopt a tactic closer to Laval's than to the "Montoire line" in the first months of his own brief reign. Precisely because voluntary collaboration for national-interest reasons was so slippery, especially in a situation where the enemy promised very little and conceded even less, there would always come a time when the practitioners of that dangerous art suddenly realized how risky it was and try to pull back, to withdraw into dilatory procedures and a strict interpretation of the armistice. Inevitably, the realities prevailed—i.e., the Germans exploited all the resources which the national situation of France and Vichy put into their hands, tightened the screws, and destroyed the Vichy officials who had dared to halt the squeeze.[4]

Third, both involuntary and voluntary *collaboration d'état* provided a backdrop, a cover, a pretext, or a springboard for collaborationism, that is, for what might be called desired or deliberate collaboration. Involuntary collaboration reluctantly recognized necessity; voluntary collaboration for reason of state was a foolhardy attempt to exploit necessity. Neither one implied acquiescence to Nazi ideology or enthusiasm for the "new order" that Germany was proclaiming in Europe. Collaborationism, however, did entail at least one of the two following things. It could mean deliberately serving the enemy—perhaps rationalized in traditional terms of "national interest," yet divorced in daily practice from calculations of net advantages for the nation and based in the final analysis on calculations of personal advantage. (I am thinking here of various shady characters like Fernand de Brinon and Jean Luchaire, whose careers were staked on close Franco-German relations and who saw in Germany's victory the condition and guaranty of their own importance.) Or collaborationism could mean deliberate advocacy of cooperation with a force which, even though it was foreign, was deemed to be the champion, guarantor, or model of necessary domestic transformation. To simplify, we can distinguish between *servile* collaborationism and *ideological* collaborationism (we must of course remember that these are ideal types). Now, neither type of collaborationism would have been as much at ease as they were—in a country that was basically deaf to their appeal—if there had been no *collaboration d'état*. Precisely because the latter always tended to slip from involuntary to voluntary, the collaborationists could indulge in one or both of two tricks: they could point with satisfaction to the closeness between their own policy and the Vichy-sanctioned objective of collaboration with the Third Reich—i.e., argue that Vichy's doctrine was their behavior; and they could point indignantly to Vichy's shortcomings, hesitations, and betrayals—i.e., charge Vichy with sabotaging its own doctrine. A gigantic distance separated a firmly *attentiste* Vichyite like Maurras or Pétain's friend René Gillouin, from a

Jacques Benoist-Méchin or Drieu la Rochelle. Yet the former's situation provided a platform for the latter, and their weaknesses gave license for the latter's excesses.

Men of little experience, bad judgment, and good faith, like Jean Bichelonne, moved imperceptibly from voluntary *collaboration d'état* to collaborationism. Anticommunism provided a link. It allowed servile collaborators to parade behind a cause and served to fuel the internal and external energies of ideological collaborators. Vichy gave its blessings to the ultracollaborationist Volunteers' Legion against Bolshevism. Anglophobia also provided a link.

Between voluntary *collaboration d'état,* servile collaborationism, and ideological collaborationism, the difference was often obscure. The rather demonic Laval of 1940, who scared Pétain's advisers so much that they had him overthrown, was gambling on improving France's lot by pleasing the German winner, enjoying a colossal personal revenge for the humiliations of 1936–40, and talking in doctrinaire terms about the death of democracy and the coming of the authoritarian age. The much tamer Laval of 1942, who on the whole withdrew into a besieged policy of involuntary collaboration, still thought he had to make himself accepted and respected by the Nazis by publicly stating that he wanted a German victory to save Europe from Bolshevism. Collaboration, like the French Revolution, is both a savage story of inexpiable inner splits, and *un bloc,* insofar as even its more extreme forms were propelled by or developed from its more moderate ones. How much, given Vichy's situation, *collaboration d'état.* But Darnand himself, stubborn soldier and simple mind, by the efforts of Laval to keep in the good graces of men like Déat or Luchaire for as long as possible. How much, given the state of French opinion, collaborationism needed to lean on mere collaboration is shown by the fact that in September 1943, even collaborationists who had lost patience with Laval's temporization still insisted that only he could be France's Premier. The Laval of 1943 needed a Darnand as a bloody collaborationist cover behind which he could more easily pursue the laborious rearguard action of mere involuntary *collaboration d'état.* But Darnand himself, stubborn soldier and simple mind, found in *collaboration d'état* an invitation to collaborationism.

II

Thus, the situation devised by Hitler in 1940—which deprived Germany of some of the immediate advantages to be had in occupying France totally, yet provided her with countless opportunities for exploiting French weakness—accounts in large part for the phenomena I discuss. But a coherent polity could have limited the damage from *col-*

laboration d'état. The heart of the matter is that France was not a coherent polity. What made Hitler's apparent "moderation" of June
1940 so devilish was its ability to maximize France's inner tensions. A
Carthaginian Hitler would have made collaborationism inconceivable
and, in all likelihood, would have ruled out the very conditions that
made for *collaboration d'état:* an armistice with a government that
chose to stay in Metropolitan France. Of course, the emergence in Bordeaux of a government determined to stay in France indicated that
the country's cohesion as a polity was shaky. This had always been
Hitler's conviction. By making French acceptance of the armistice
terms relatively easy, and by sending back as ambassador the young
Otto Abetz, known by many potential collaborationists as a friend
of France, Hitler did his best to exacerbate the "Franco-French
war."

I have tried in the previous chapter to describe in some detail the
forces which in the 1930s turned against the "Republican synthesis"
and later took advantage of the fall of France to impose their views.
They can be divided into three groups, although there is something
arbitrary about a division which exaggerates the distinctions between
categories and takes no account of the fluidity of ideas and men.
There were the followers of Maurras, who viewed the Third Republic
as an evil regime: it had corrupted the French polity by splintering
power and letting "alien" ideologies infect the mind of the public, and
weakened French society by dislodging its "natural elites" from power
and letting urbanization, industrialization, and proletarization proceed. Then there was a sprawling mass of conservatives who had
turned anti-Republican on grounds not of constitutional principle but
of social discontent, since the regime, in the 1930s and especially in
1936, had seemed unable to preserve "stability" and had thus, in their
eyes, lost legitimacy (which had never been better than conditional,
dependent on the performance of a specific social function). Finally,
there were the Fascists—Fascist political gangs and Fascist intellectuals—with notions of French regeneration or revitalization either
through direct, plebiscitarian action led by a totalitarian party or
through tough, heroic, virile, redeeming action repudiating Republican talk and democratic decadence. One must add to these three
groups a significant number of men who could in no way be called
rightists, men who came from parties of the Left and from labor unions
—Marcel Déat, Gaston Bergery, Georges Dumoulin, Charles Spinasse,
René Belin—who nevertheless ended up in the Vichy camp or in the
Paris political ghetto.

Two feelings served to cement these disparate forces together. One,
already mentioned, was anticommunism. The rise of the Communist
party in France had provided the Right with a convenient devil

theory of French social upheavals and had provoked the migration away from the Left of the politicians and unionists just mentioned. The other feeling was "appeasement" pacifism. This was much more complex. On the Right, it usually amounted to a determination to avoid military confrontation with Germany, at least as long as France herself remained politically and socially weak and as long as the main beneficiary of such a war would be the Soviet ally. This might be called conditional pacifism; in most cases, it yielded to a kind of resignation to war after Hitler's invasion of Bohemia or after his quarrel with Poland over Danzig. But on the Fascist right, there were individual cases of unconditional pacifism with no ideological overtones among French conservatives: Laval in this one respect remained faithful to his distant political origins and close to the leftist group. For pacifism was also unconditional among the ex-leftists I have mentioned; here, it was often due to a visceral hatred of war, but anticommunism played a large part too.

In the large mass of men found in and around Vichy early in July 1940, who were the collaborationists? One can distinguish four groups.

First, there was a group composed largely of journalists whom it would be difficult to tag as leftist or conservative. They had all been members of the sprawling and largely corrupt journalistic establishment of the Third Republic. They had, over the years, either served the cause of Franco-German reconciliation, like Luchaire and Brinon, or absorbed the varieties of pacifism prevalent in the mid and late 1930s. Many of them had come from the circles around Aristide Briand and Joseph Caillaux (even though Briand was dead by 1933 and Caillaux had veered sharply in the days of Munich from his attitude during World War I). Others had been close to the Action Française, but found it too stifling and musty and thought its basic anti-German bias old-fashioned. Laval knew these men well and used many of them as informal emissaries and intermediaries during the occupation. For this amorphous group, collaborationism was much less an ideological commitment than a splendid opportunity for jobs. These men were literally put in control of the Paris press and radio by Abetz. This was to be their day, their reward for not having come closest to pure opportunism; and yet we must remember that even servile collaborationism is not entirely mercenary, since it was practiced by men who had become disaffected from the so-called bellicist policies of the Third Republic. They were now serving new masters, but without having to suppress old beliefs.

Second, there were Fascist intellectuals: the men of *Je suis partout,* writers like Alphonse de Chateaubriant, Drieu la Rochelle, Abel Bonnard, Louis-Ferdinand Céline. The nature of their fascism has been well analyzed by others.[5] It was, indeed, a romanticism—elitist, sentimental, attractive in its nostalgia for rejuvenation and action, and repulsive in its pose of virility, its perfume of decadence, its *fin de race* character, and above all its vindictiveness. These were men to whom the petty, compressed, depressed, and querulous France of the 1930s was anathema, who "were violently opposed—emotionally, intellectually and morally—to bourgeois society and bourgeois values," [6] who saw in democracy a form of bourgeois decadence and in Marxism a hideous, collectivist degradation of the individual. They were dreaming of a society that would no longer be based on money, ruled by mediocrity, and wracked by the masses. They were driven to collaborationism by, for one thing, admiration for "Fascist man"—the new type of heroic, fraternal human being whom fascism and nazism had allegedly created. Here we find the one instance of actual sympathy for or fascination with the enemy's system—and even here one must note that in some instances it was a fascination with Italian or Spanish fascism more than with national socialism. The other factor in their collaborationism was the intensity of their hatred for the elements in France which Nazi ideology also aimed to destroy: the Jews and the Communists in particular. Collaborationism here was almost purely ideological—although it also had the advantage of giving these men an influence they had not enjoyed before.

What is remarkable is the degree to which their ideological predilection obscured in their own eyes what might be called the classic interstate aspect of the problem. After all, collaborationism *also* meant subscribing to the victory of Germany over France. In this respect, the Fascist intellectuals were not of one mind. Some prewar Fascists did not slip into collaborationism, precisely because concern for the French nation remained predominant in their minds; neither Thierry-Maulnier, who remembered his Action Française origins, nor Bertrand de Jouvenel embraced the Nazi cause. Lucien Rebatet, at the other extreme, was, as we know, literally a defeatist, rejoicing in the *décombres* of France. Bonnard, in a more convoluted way, shared this masochism. But neither Drieu la Rochelle nor Robert Brasillach had been unmitigated admirers of Germany; both had advocated French fascism as the only way of resisting German might, and they had been classically anti-German during the Phony War. From June 1940 to 1943, however, their ideological predispositions overrode their scruples as French citizens. Brasillach subordinated his to his concern for internal French regeneration and (after June 1941) for anti-Communist crusading; Drieu la Rochelle saw occupied Europe as an opportunity for realizing an old dream at last—that of a unified Europe with a virile France saved from decadence—and he rationalized away France's humiliation by arguing that every federation needs a federator, so that if it had to be Germany, at least it was a Fascist Germany. [7] It was only in 1943 that Drieu la Rochelle's and Brasillach's ideological faith slumped. Both men discovered that the problem of relations among nations had not been obliterated by ideological transnational solidarities. Drieu la Rochelle became disenchanted with the quality of German fascism; he at last discovered that not only was it not as socialistic as he had hoped, but also not as universal and European as he had believed. Brasillach began to worry about the degree of "denationalization" that collaborationism entailed. Thus, the Fascist intellectuals ended by splitting. Most of them continued to embrace the German cause, whatever the cost to France, because the France that was being battered by civil war and Nazi repression was one they hated anyhow. These were men of resentment, in whom the dream of a new man had less force than the impulse of destruction. Some of them, like the two novelists, quietly stepped back, appalled by some of the consequences of their original choice and aware that their dream had been a delusion.

Third, there were men who had aped fascism before the war, by setting up would-be single parties and ersatz totalitarian movements. Many of the leagues that so upset the Republicans in the 1930s were nothing but rallies of conservatives who thought that the best way of restoring the quiet social and political order of their dreams—one in which elites would rule, so to speak, apolitically—was to borrow a plebiscitarian leaf from their adversaries' book, a calculation that had begun with Boulangism. When Daladier restored order, most of that agitation stopped. When Vichy appeared, the conservatives flocked to it and, in the summer of 1940, killed the notion of a single party. But, in the 1930s, there had also been genuine embryos of fascism: Doriot's PPF, the conspiratorial "Cagoule" headed by Eugène Deloncle, of which Darnand had been a member, and smaller gangs like Marcel Bucard's. Between them and the conservatives grown temporarily rabid, the differences were not primarily in the realm of social doctrine, for the program of these gangs was quite fundamentally conservative and appealed to the deep instincts of stability and equilibrium in the stalemate society.[8] The differences were, rather, of politics and temperament. Whereas the conservatives wished for a depoliticized society, organized so as to take care of itself without parties, parliaments, and politicians, the Fascists believed that the "reconciled" society of their programs would need to be firmly run by a political elite whose dual task would be to wage a permanent battle against the corrupters of France (i.e., purges) and to place under their own control the various economic and social activities of the nation (i.e., ruling). Both the conservatives and the Fascists appealed to the *"sans-culotte"* heritage, to the Jacobin impulse, to the plebiscitarian tradition, but the conservatives deeply distrusted what they felt they had to use, whereas the Fascists were in their element. A movement like the Croix de Feu and a gang like the

PPF each had their share of the modern, urban *sans-culottes:* shop-keepers, restaurateurs, garage mechanics, employees, traveling salesmen, clerks, etc. But the conservatives used temporary Jacobin methods for Girondin ends, while the Fascists wanted to combine social stability with permanent political agitation.

The largest contingent of collaborationists was provided by the Fascist gangs: Doriot's PPF, Deloncle's new and adventurous Mouvement Socialiste Révolutionnaire (MSR), later Darnand's SOL and Militia. These were the activists. As in the case of the intellectuals, there was one huge negative component in their ideological collaborationism: the desire for internal revenge (not only against Jews and Communists and the Republican Left, but also against the tepid conservatives of Vichy who were trying to set the clock back and institutionalize *les valeurs du père de famille* by reserving for themselves all the positions of power in the state and by excommunicating all politics). But whereas the ideological collaborationism of Fascist intellectuals was at least partly positive—in the sense of being moved by the myth of Fascist man—that of the Fascist gangs was largely imitative. They were fascinated by the institutional innovation of fascism and nazism—the single party and the paramilitary elite group, the armed gang of modern *chevaliers* rooting out asocial weeds on behalf of a doctrine of national resurrection, under the control of a tough political leadership. The development of the SOL and Militia by Darnand, whose interest in Nazi techniques led him to become *Obersturmführer* of the Waffen SS, is particularly significant.

Once again, ideological predispositions obscured interstate considerations. In the intellectuals' case, the latter were either abolished by defeatism or swept away by illusions about a fraternal European order. In the case of the gangs, the story is more complex. There was no inherent or pre-existing sympathy for Nazi Germany, even if there was a desire to learn from its political techniques. Doriot, after the crisis that hit the PPF in the post-Munich days, had adopted the same nationalist stance which the minority of dissidents who resigned had advocated. Darnand, a former follower of the Action Française, had been anti-German most of his life. Collaborationism was merely a foreign-policy corollary of a domestic political stance. With Vichy in the hands of *les modérés,* the activists, intent on a thorough purging of France and on seizing power, decided to collaborate with those who not only fought the same enemies with the same intensity but who were also most likely to favor groups that imitated Nazi practices. "The enemies of my enemies are my friends; the models of my behavior ought to be my supporters."

The irony lies in the fact that the Germans in France were rather reluctant supporters of these Fascist gangs. They realized, correctly, that they were unpopular and isolated. Their existence contributed to France's desired weakness, but the Germans got more advantage out of blackmailing a Vichy leadership group that had popular support and respectability than they could have gotten from putting ill-experienced and widely detested gangs in power. The story of Doriot's relations with Abetz and the Germans is a rather stormy one. Doriot's services were kept at arm's length; his long periods of combat in Russia were, for him, escapes from the frustrations of inaction in France and, for the Germans, a convenient way to keep the PPF under wraps. As for Darnand, the Germans decided to give his Militia arms as well as access to northern France only when it became clear that they would, in effect, serve as an auxiliary in the fight against the Resistance. Thus, a man like Doriot, who sought in collaborationism a road to power and who entirely identified French interests with Germany's in the process, was treated with disdain; but a man like Darnand, convinced that he was serving nothing but the interest of France—an interest which he redefined in intensely and exclusively ideological fashion—was deemed more deserving by the Germans, precisely because he appeared more genuine, less servile, and hence more likely to be effective.[9]

Finally, there were the members of the prewar pacifist and anti-Communist left. Their attitude is in many ways the most interesting. Here, there was no particular enthusiasm for Fascist man, the cult of the virile hero, youth movements, and Olympic games; nor had there been any enthusiasm for totalitarian political techniques. These were former parliamentarians quite at ease in Parliament, former members of the Socialist or Radical parties and of reformist labor unions. And yet, in the summer and fall of 1940, Déat emerges as the champion of the single party and of collaborationism. What had happened?

Once more, the explanation is to be found in domestic French terms. Exactly like the conservative Vichyites and the Fascists, these men had a burning desire to settle accounts with the political class of the fallen regime—with the Socialists, Radicals, and Confédération Générale du Travail (CGT) leaders who had made so many mistakes. They had let the Communists impose their bellicism, had frightened into conservatism the peasants and middle classes which the neo-Socialists and some union leaders of the 1930s had wanted to woo, and had failed to wrest control of the French economy from the famous "two hundred families," from the trusts and munitions makers. On the other hand, they were temperamentally alienated from both the conservatives and the Fascists. Their anticommunism and their determination to take revenge on what might be called the "Popular Front establishment" did not spill over into a dogmatic aversion to parliamentarism, to Freemasons and Jews. They remained marked by their left-wing origins—they had been part of the Republican machine (in a way that a Doriot, for instance, had never been, since his career had taken him directly from the extreme left to the far right, i.e., from one ghetto to another). They had reasons to hate the bosses of that machine but not the whole personnel. To Déat and his friends, Vichy's clericalism, ruralism, antilabor corporatism, and elitism were unpalatable (and so were its big-business connections), whereas the Fascist politicians resented only Vichy's aversion for politics rather than its social conservatism. Nor did these men have the dictatorial or plebiscitarian temper of a Doriot and the conspiratorial itch of a Darnand. In the "amalgam" of beneficiaries of France's fall, during the summer of 1940, in that great moment of revenge, they were a minority among minorities; they represented the Left.

Their collaborationism and Déat's decision to "go Fascist" and build a "single party" of his own were timely reactions to their predicament. There was no room for these men in Vichy. The regime of General Maxime Weygand or Yves Bouthillier could absorb one Belin, but it could not accommodate a whole group. Déat decided to do what the conservatives had done earlier: to appeal to the plebiscitarian impulse, not, like la Rocque, so as to play the pied piper of "order and stability," but so as to fish in the pond—now *disponible*—of former left-wing voters. The time of parliamentary parties was over. The fishing had to be done with the one available and fashionable rod: the pseudototalitarian one. Collaborationism was a means to power, as it was for Doriot. But Déat and his friends had one asset Doriot did not have: Abetz's sympathies. Hitler's ambassador shrewdly realized that men who came from the Left, who had some good words to say about the Popular Front or the late Republic, and who were hostile to clericalism, Vichy militarism, "moral order," and political purges of schoolteachers and local *notables* would have more influence among the French than a Doriot or a Bucard. Thus, for Déat, collaborationism was much less a logical commitment than a tactical necessity. Isolated in the new French order, they could count only on the Germans; the Fascist gangs, at least, had either pre-existing machines of their own or some sympathies in Vichy because of the conservative orthodoxy of their social (although not their political) doctrine. Moreover—and this is the only area in which ideology played some part—other prewar factors made this group's conversion to collaborationism in a totalitarian guise seem not so startling: their anticommunism, their pacifism (which "dictated" cooperation with a power that they considered as having won the war), and a tentative prewar interpretation of Nazi Germany not as a right-wing dictatorship but as a rough, dynamic, and demagogic version of what the *néos* had once advocated: *ordre, autorité, nation,* the control of the trusts by the state, a planned economy, an alliance of peasants, workers, and the lower middle classes. And they now also saw in Nazi Germany a model and matrix for a European economic federation that would rationally exploit the continent's resources.

Thus, collaborationism in all its forms—from the purest to the most corrupt—partook of one important feeling: a sense that Germany, whatever reservations one might have had about her before June 1940, was the wave of the future, and that the correct political future could only be achieved by clinging to the policies and aping the institutions of Hitler's state. So we come back once more to a point made earlier —how blurred the distinction was between voluntary *collaboration d'état* and collaborationism. For the former also entailed a decision to support German policies. Still there were differences between the two, although in individual cases these dwindled into mere nuances. Collaborationism downplayed calculations in terms of *raison d'état* and ignored the interstate aspect of Franco-German relations (yet Darnand and Benoist-Méchin apparently convinced themselves that ardent collaboration would restore to France all she had lost). Collaborationism was advocated by men who were out of power in order to get political control of France, whereas *collaboration d'état* concerned itself with governing France (yet, once risen to power, collaborationists like Darnand pursued their policy). Collaborationism went beyond mere support of German policies to an imitation of Nazi institutions—and this is what limited its appeal.

III

If one tries to generalize about Frenchmen engaged only in *collaboration d'état* and those who were collaborationists, one social difference becomes clear. The Vichyites who were not collaborationists represented a political class which had been, so to speak, in exile or opposition during the Third Republic and which, as such, had a revenge to take, but these political "exiles" were socially very well established. They represented the top of the cream of the civil service, the armed forces, the business community, the social elites of landowners or professions or local *notables*. The drama of the French Right was precisely in the divorce between political power, which the Third Republic shifted to a political class representative of Léon Gambetta's *"nouvelles couches"* (the lower middle classes, the peasants, the *"petits"*), and economic or social power, whose possessors had remained much higher on the social ladder. Vichy was a revenge perpetrated by men who felt they were the natural governing elite of the French state—who believed they represented French continuity and stability.

On the other hand, the collaborationists were to a large extent *déclassés*—social misfits and political deviants. Not only had they not exerted political power, but they were not among the established "social authorities" either. Their ideas had segregated them from the Republican establishment—the high commands of the parties and unions—and from the conservative social establishment which was suspicious of Fascist gangs, amused by the verve but not converted to the views of Fascist intellectuals. And apart from the staid reviews and circles of conservative *académiciens,* Fascist intellectuals were only cliques of *copains;* the journalists had been living precarious lives as salaried spokesmen for business tycoons or politicians. So collaborationism was largely a bilious outlet for them. They had good reasons for embracing the German cause: without the Nazis, their chance of gaining power in France was nil; and in Germany the Nazi party and regime had made use and given a sense of mission to comparable misfits. A century earlier, Louis Blanqui had celebrated in the *déclassés* the "secret ferment," the "reserve force of the revolution"; now, they were the public ferment and reserve force of a very different sort of revolution. Some of the most prominent collaborationists, like Paul Marion or Jean Fontenoy, had gone through a variety of movements or newspapers, at ease nowhere, too cynical for intellectual daydreams, too undisciplined for the gangs, accumulating only grievances against all established orthodoxies.

Of course there were important instances of men who straddled the fence between the two milieux of collaboration. In particular, Laval, who had for a while been a prominent political leader on the French Right, too intimate with political power in the Third Republic to be quite as much of a misfit as the collaborationists, nevertheless was fundamentally a *déclassé* in Vichy's brand of orthodoxy. Vichy conservatives were suspicious of parliamentarians (even their own), and the self-made *nouveau riche* who had traveled a long and shady road from the far left to the Senate was never entirely respectable in the circles of *la bonne société.* Laval remained a devious and deviant, distrusted and lonely wolf in Vichy.

Another difference between the Vichyites and the collaborationists was a psychological one. The *collaborateurs d'état* were men of prudence, temporization, cautious managers of a society that needed, they believed, a respite from agitation above all. The collaborationists were activists, muckrakers or crusaders, men of direct action, demagogues and demonstrators. Again, this distinction throws some light on important individuals. For there were collaborationists who seemed indeed to belong intellectually or socially among conservative *notables* and yet who embraced collaborationism with savage ardor: Philippe Henriot, Catholic polemicist and conservative deputy, was driven to his death by the intensity of his passion.

Ultimately, however, it is the historical solidarity of all kinds of collaboration that I want to stress, and not for the sake of paradox. Collaborators and collaborationists agreed in their critique of the "old regime," even if they disagreed in the formulation of remedies. Moreover, by their behavior, they demonstrated that the very values and habits they wanted to destroy were all-pervasive. Collaboration and collaborationism were not just, respectively, the by-product of a national situation and an extreme reaction against a certain domestic order; they were mirror images of the features they pretended to supersede. France in the 1930s and during the war can be seen as a huge auto-da-fé—I dare not say a Götterdämmerung, for far more dregs than Gods were doomed. The fiasco of collaboration was a replica of the Republican fiasco—smaller in scope, more extreme in its manifestations.

In the first place, the foreign policy of the Republic had been marked by features that did not change during Vichy. A nation weakened by the bloodbath of World War I, from which it had emerged with the illusion of victory, had gradually realized that the *status quo* could not be defended by her efforts alone.[10] As a result, French diplomacy had slipped from the old imperatives of autonomy to increased dependence on the support and initiatives of external allies, especially Britain. In the 1930s, British placidity led to French *abandons;* British appeasement bolstered and justified French appeasement. Collaborators and collaborationists bitterly denounced the Third Republic's "abdication"—not for its diplomatic effects but because, they said, it had led France in 1939 to fight a war for His Britannic Majesty that was not in France's interest and that Winston Churchill wanted to keep inflicting on France. Yet both subordinated—unwillingly or deliberately—whatever French autonomy was left, or could have been restored, to German primacy. One after the other, Vichy accepted German demands of the most humiliating sort, and collaborationism went so far as to summon Vichy to do for Germany what had been deemed abominable when *bellicistes* had wanted to do it for the Czechs, Poles, or British—i.e., accept total military solidarity in an ideological war.

French diplomacy and strategy in the 1930s had shown remarkably little understanding of events and leaders in foreign countries, and the politicians of the Third Republic had tended to interpret them in familiar terms—projecting, so to speak, onto the external present either irrelevant French domestic experiences or obsolete international ones. An educational system that was heavily centered on things French, little interest in travel, a mixture of intellectual rigidity and fatigue were largely responsible for France's attitude. Collaborators and collaborationists displayed the same naïveté, complacency, illusions, and ignorance. Laval remained convinced that he could "handle" Hitler and manipulate the Nazis just as he had managed the French National Assembly or (he thought) Stalin. Vichy believed in the myth of France's qualitative superiority and intellectual skill offsetting Germany's brute force. The collaborationists' ideas of Germany and Italy were Rorschach tests of their own domestic orientations: each found in Nazi Germany whatever it wanted to forge in France. In particular, the Fascist intellectuals took Nazi and Fascist vaticinations about the "new man" so seriously that they never really bothered to find out; some clung to the myth until the bitter end, less because they refused to face facts than because they could not afford to face them—and the two writers who did, as we know, went quietly to their death.

The same continuity can be seen in French domestic policies. The political life of the Third Republic had been marked by excessive political fragmentation and instability; the substitution of defensive programs for positive ones and of moralistic or ideological dogmas for concrete reforms; the final triumph of decay beneath surface immobilism. Collaboration and collaborationism can be described in exactly the same way. Indeed, its fragmentation and instability reached a rare degree of absurdity. The rivalry between Déat and Doriot faithfully reproduced, in the Paris microcosm, the old split between Left and Right, and the story of the relations between the various cliques of collaborationists, and between them and Vichy, is of byzantine complexity. Personal antagonisms, attempts at *noyautage,* expulsions, reconciliations, maneuvers, and manifestoes composed a tangled web, compared with which the parliamentary politics of the Third Republic look eminently Cartesian. The height of folly was reached when the exiles who fled to Germany in August 1944 continued to plot, to bicker, and to haggle.

And the more one reads the writings of these men—both what they wrote at the time and what they have been pleading since—the more one is struck by the negativism and the hollow moralizing bent of their politics. The Popular Front had been primarily a defensive reaction against "enemies of the Republic" (as in 1899) rather than a positive alliance to deal with the roots of France's troubles. Similarly, *collaboration d'état* was primarily a defense against Polandization rather than a clear program of French *redressement;* and collaborationism was above all a mobilization against enemies common to Germany and to the collaborationists—namely, Jews, Gaullists, Communists, the so-called terrorists of 1943–44. Advocates of *collaboration d'état* appealed plaintively to the sense of discipline, moral responsibility, and civic trust of the citizens; the collaborationist program seemed evenly divided between drastic demands for exemplary purges and simple slogans about social solidarity, moral purification, class cooperation, etc.

Collaboration was presented as a straightforward moral duty: that of sharing in the construction of the fine new European order. Slogans were endlessly repeated; here—as in so many platforms of the Third Republic's parties—catchwords had a Pavlovian function and served as refuges from real political analysis.

Also, most importantly, there was again a combination of surface immobility and underlying decay. Pétain remained *la couronne* (as Drieu la Rochelle and Brasillach had called him), in full serenity and fast senility. Laval, for more than two years, played a steadfast, sacrificial, and desperate role trying to prevent a complete takeover by the collaborationists. Official doctrine remained intact: the National Revolution at home, defense of French interests abroad. (In July 1944 as in July 1940, the more extreme collaborationists could only express their displeasure at Vichy's timidity. Vichy France had not formally become Hitler's ally.) But behind this façade, what foulness! *Collaboration d'état,* in a zigzagging resistance to through-and-through collaborationism, yielded inch by inch under pressure, thus demonstrating the absurdity of Vichy's original wager. In order to ward off pressure, Darlan and Laval had repeatedly played the game of *donner des gages* to the collaborationists; the hope was to neutralize them by giving them some power, the result was to put more and more of their wine into Vichy water. Vichy's use of men like Benoist-Méchin, Bonnard, Marion, Brinon, Darnand—men deemed preferable to the gang leaders (or, in Darnand's case, a gang leader deemed acceptable because of his lack of independent political sense)—succeeded in increasing the Germans' hold, in delivering to the collaborationists essential sectors of the Vichy state, and in whetting their appetite for more. As for the collaborationists themselves, who set themselves the formidable challenge of seizing power *and* of converting more Frenchmen to their cause, not only did they fail to get full control of the pitiful *État Français,* but they became precisely what in their "franco-centrism" they had neither wanted to become nor sufficiently foreseen that they might become: subaltern agents of the Gestapo, the SS, and the Wehrmacht, butchers of their compatriots, French voices of Nazi propaganda. The revulsion against collaboration, even among those conservatives who had originally backed Vichy, ended by benefiting the very enemies whom Vichy and the collaborationists had wanted to destroy: the Republic, the democrats, and, above all, the Communists.

Affinity for Nazi Germany was rarely the dominant motif of French collaboration. Germany was an immovable force for some, a providential ally for others. Nevertheless, even when collaboration had "good" motives—the protection or promotion of French interests or the quest for a new man—it was doomed by the convergence of two factors. The objective one was Germany's defeat; collaboration in most (but not all) of its manifestations was based on the expectation of German victory. The subjective factor was the fundamental opportunism that tinged all forms of collaboration: involuntary *collaboration d'état* sought to exploit Germany's superiority (however much one hoped that it would not last) in order to wrest some advantages or preserve some assets; and voluntary *collaboration d'état* as well as collaborationism went much further in the same direction, or in the direction of using Germany's triumph for domestic political purposes—seeing a "divine surprise" not only in the Republic's fall but in the Nazis' glory. This is what most of the French could not bring themselves to accept—stunned though they were by defeat and eager to find scapegoats. They realized that collaborators and collaborationists were blind to what, by the end of 1942, had become obvious—the fact that in this game only the Germans won, at France's expense. It was Gribouille's game. In order to ward off a future, hypothetical evil (the vengeful wrath of a spurned, victorious Germany or the horrors of victorious Soviet hordes), one accepted or even increased the immediate, certain, and tangible evils of Nazi occupation and repression. Eventually, the much vaunted material benefits to France to be gained from cooperation with the victor vanished, while the moral damage spread. *Collaboration d'état* played into German hands—saving the Germans from having to rule France directly or from having to let the small cliques of collaborationists mess up things, and encouraging naïve or fanatic Frenchmen to believe that collaborationism had Pétain's sanction. And collaborationism played into German hands too —allowing the Germans to blackmail Vichy with the threat of letting the tough ones take over.

The more hostile the French became to the obvious implications of collaboration, the more collaboration took on a desperately anti-French tone. Laval, a misguided patriot, turned into a masochist of unpopularity, determined to save the French despite themselves. The collaborationists became more and more shrill in their advocacy of repression, more and more determined to punish the nation for its resistance to their delirium. Finally, collaboration, which had started as a reaction against certain forces, practices, beliefs, and habits of the fallen regime, became a reaction against France. The significance of collaboration was not quantitative but qualitative—it was the triumph of forced or enthusiastic masochism.

Thus, collaboration was the most hideous aspect of an ugly, collective wash of dirty laundry, a decomposition of a polity that marked the 1930s and the war years. Its only merit, apart from the occasional merit of individuals, was that it taught a lesson about the price of stalemate and the cost of concentrating on domestic settlements of accounts, which postwar France, despite all its troubles and turbulence, appeared not to have forgotten—at least until 1968.

3
In the Looking Glass:
Sorrow and Pity?

I

Like all works of art that probe the truth about a society, *The Sorrow and the Pity* is a mirror presented by the authors to their audiences. How clear a mirror it turns out to be, compared with novels or even with plays, not to mention memoirs or histories! Words in print, or words acted on a stage, are no substitutes for the faces, voices, gestures of "real" people. No written flashback has the power that explodes on the screen when a scene from 1940 and a scene from the present are juxtaposed, showing the same man at thirty years' distance. No narrative, no fictional reconstruction matches the newsreel or the live interview. And especially when the subject is nothing less than a nation's behavior in the darkest hour of its history, it is not surprising that the reactions should be so passionate.

The first group reflected in the mirror is today's audience. The reactions of American reviewers and spectators to a film like this tell us something about the troubled America of the early 1970s. The cruelties and frailties that this movie exposes cannot be dismissed as mere evidence of French decadence or Nazi beastliness. We know now that the "banality of evil," self-deception, the thousand ways in which people deny or repress guilt so as to preserve or restore their self-esteem, are not just tales from abroad. The question which this movie raises for Americans is not: Under similar circumstances, would we have behaved better? It is: Under different but not incomparable circumstances, have we behaved better? *The Sorrow and the Pity* could be the title of a very similar documentary on Americans and the Vietnam

First published as the introduction to *The Sorrow and the Pity: a Film by Marcel Ophuls* (New York, 1972).

45

war. We all know American counterparts of every one of the human types who appear on the screen.

But it is of course the reactions of the French audiences that are the most interesting. What do they tell us about France today? The intensity of the response to the film shows that the time has not yet come in France when an attempt to come to terms with those gruesome years can be met with equanimity. The divisions among the French, which this movie sets forth for all to see, are still too deep. Any debate over the issues that divide them becomes a psychodrama. For almost thirty years, France has been flooded with memoirs, pamphlets, accounts of trials, charges and countercharges, case studies, biographies, revelations, and press reviews concerning the years of Vichy and occupation. But there has been only one attempt to write an over-all history,[1] and it gained general acceptance only because it was bland. Maxim Litvinov once said that no arbitration of conflicts between the Soviet Union and capitalist countries was conceivable, because only an angel could be objective. Today, it is still impossible for a Frenchman to deal with the Vichy period without choosing his camp deliberately—or actually taking sides even if he does not want to.

The Sorrow and the Pity underscores once more that the dividing lines were far from straight. Each side was an unstable and unhappy forced coalition. The supporters of Pétain were highly uncomfortable about those Frenchmen who took the old man's words too seriously, or who took them too far and, like Christian de la Mazière, decided to fight in a German uniform. The Resistance was torn by rivalry between Communists and non-Communists, by old suspicions between Left and Right, by differences of emphasis between those who in occupied France fought above all the Germans and those who in Vichy France (which was not occupied until November 1942) saw the reactionary regime of Pétain as their main foe. Nor was there ever perfect harmony between the Resistance in France and de Gaulle in London and Algiers. Moreover, as the movie so penetratingly shows, many people took refuge in the humble and often painful tasks of daily survival, and did their best (if that is the right word) to stay out of the battles and away from the heat. But, to paraphrase Paul Valéry, if mankind lasts because of the masses of people for whom endurance has a higher value than action, its fate is determined by those who choose, act, and decide. And that minority—it is always a minority—was split into two irreconcilable, if heterogeneous, groups. Their internal divergences were subordinated to common goals: the liberation of France on one side; accommodation to Nazi Germany (assumed, with enthusiasm or resignation, to be victorious or unbeatable) and concomitant antidemocratic reform on the other side. Therefore, today, when one tries to write or to talk about those years, one cannot avoid making up one's

mind; such were the stakes, such was the depth of feeling, that any effort to be "fair" to each side usually annoys both, and serves History
no better than it helps reconciliation.

The Sorrow and the Pity, by Marcel Ophuls and his associates, does
have a point of view: it is on the side of the Resistance. Obliquely—
through editing, and by putting them in embarrassing positions, by
extracting damning statements from them—it exposes the German ex-
occupiers, the officials of Vichy (such as Pétain's former Youth Minister, who has forgotten his "revolutionary" fervor of 1940), and of
course Laval, whose rise to a kind of feudal lordship is unforgettably
revealed in his son-in-law's attempt to get beneficiaries of Laval's special favors to testify to his goodness. If de la Mazière is presented in a
better light, it may be because he carried his convictions, however evil,
to their logical conclusion and was able to look back with candor (not
untainted by complacency). The movie denounces Vichy's complicity
in the anti-Semitic propaganda campaigns and, above all, in the deportation of Jews. As a result, the defenders of Vichy who are still
around (including Laval's son-in-law) have vigorously criticized the
movie and trotted out again the arguments that show that Vichy actually protected France from a worse fate, defended French Jews from
extermination, and served as a sacrificial shield. But, as I have argued
elsewhere, and as Robert Paxton shows in his book *Vichy France*, Vichy's interest in collaboration far exceeded the "necessities" of shield-
ing France. In any event, the Vichyites' protests do not damage the
case so vividly made by this movie: even if Vichy saved France from,
say, the fate of occupied Poland, and even if Laval did his best to
delay the arrest of French Jews, the moral price paid was horrendous;
Vichy France made moral choices that no government should be willing to make—about which hostages should be shot (Communists),
which Jews should be delivered (foreign ones, including children the
Germans had not planned to grab). It lent France's police, judicial apparatus, penitentiary administration, not to mention its controlled
media to the Nazis, or used them (as in anti-Resistance repression) for
purposes that served the Nazi cause. Next to this, homilies about
Pétain's good intentions, harangues about Laval's good deeds, hag-
glings about comparative results all wilt. But that is precisely what
Vichy diehards do not want to face.

If Ophuls is on the side of the Resistance, why, then, has the response to the film from those who fought in it been so embarrassed?
As is well known, France's television network (ORTF, a state monopoly) never showed *The Sorrow and the Pity*, which had been made
for Swiss and West German television companies, and the head of
French television allegedly never found time to see it. Released as a
movie, it reached hundreds of thousands of Frenchmen instead of the

millions of viewers it would have had on home screens. In this respect, what the mirror reveals about present-day France is doubly fascinating. Gaullist officialdom had two contemporary reasons for resenting Ophuls' work. Ophuls and his associates had worked for the ORTF until the "events" of May 1968. At that time, they took part in the strike which crippled the network and marked a rebellion of many of its employees against government control (especially over news programs). Ophuls and his associates were among those whom the government dismissed, once the strike was over. The relative liberalization introduced, after de Gaulle's retirement, by the new Premier, Jacques Chaban-Delmas, did not go so far as to endear Ophuls to the management of the ORTF. It did not encourage the top bureaucracy of that faction-ridden and politically sensitive state enterprise (constantly criticized by vigilant conservative Gaullists for any departure from social orthodoxy and political conformity) to show a film in which an old French peasant suggests that eighty-year-old leaders should be fed to the pigs! While in the film two of de Gaulle's wartime supporters and ministers, Pierre Mendès-France and Emmanuel d'Astier de la Vigerie, speak very highly of de Gaulle, there isn't much else about him—the short newsreel clipping that shows him reading a speech on the BBC is hardly flattering. Even people less finely attuned to the nuances of anti-Gaullist *contestation* than the bosses of the ORTF could find in the film traces of the "spirit of May." Would this movie have been entirely the same if it had been made, say, in 1967?

On the other hand, and quite apart from this, the movie challenged what might be called an official French myth that had become hallowed with time and buttressed by official emphasis and general public silence: not the "myth of the Resistance" (the movie itself shows that the Resistance was a noble and formidable reality), but the myth of the French being massively enrolled in or at least standing behind the Resistance, with the exception of a handful of collaborationists and a small clique of reactionaries. This official version of history portrays France as a victorious power, temporarily defeated in an early battle yet faithful throughout to her cause and her allies, thanks to the Resistance, and fully engaged in her own liberation and in the defeat of Nazi Germany. The Vichy regime—whose existence so sharply differentiated France's case from that of the other occupied countries whose governments had moved into exile in London—is dismissed as illegal and illegitimate since its creation: a point on which de Gaulle remained intractable, despite the reservations of French courts. How this version developed is easy to understand. The dramas of the war, occupation, and Liberation eliminated practically the whole of France's political class: the Vichyites were purged; most of the political leaders of the Third Republic—whom Vichy had discarded, berated, and sometimes jailed or worse—were still held responsible for the years of internal turmoil and external appeasement in the 1930s and for France's execrable state of unpreparedness in 1939–40. The new political class that appeared after the war was of Resistance vintage— whether its members belonged to new parties, such as the Christian Democrats, Mouvement Républicain Populaire (MRP), or old ones, such as the Communists and Socialists. The biggest recruiting asset of the Communist party, after the Liberation, was its heroic role in the Resistance, which it exploited shamelessly by calling itself the party of the "75,000 shot." Jacques Duclos, the most important leader of the Communist party underground, continues to cling to this theme, as the movie shows. There was no major difference between the Fourth and the Gaullist Fifth Republics in this respect—except that a regime headed by General de Gaulle was even less willing to challenge the accepted version of history and, thanks to its self-assurance and cohesion, was even more capable of seeing to it that radio and television, not to mention constant public ceremonies, reminded the French at every opportunity of the role of the Resistance and the Free French, and of the great days of the Liberation. De Gaulle's battle for emancipation from American or "Anglo-Saxon" dominance led to an ever greater underplaying of the Allies' role in the war. Many of the leaders of the Gaullist party had been war heroes; there was an elite of a few hundred "compagnons de la Libération," distinguished by their deeds in occupied France or in de Gaulle's ranks. Not so paradoxically, the fact that in the early 1970s the Gaullist state was headed by Georges Pompidou (who had not served in the Resistance; he had taught in a Paris *lycée* during the war), and the Communist party by Georges Marchais (who had volunteered to work in Germany for the Nazi war machine rather than joining the *maquis*) made it even less likely that the official version would be abandoned by its promoters.

The weight of this version of history, the persistent, if often submerged, division between the two camps of the war years, and most probably the discomfort felt by all those who had lived through those years without committing themselves or had come to regret their commitment, who knew the inaccuracies of the official version, but feared the squalor of a truer one—all of this resulted in a general unwillingness to dismantle the myth. The only challengers were the surviving Vichyites, whose casuistry, unrepentant shrillness, denigration of their foes, and obstinate arrogance only strengthened the official version. In primary and secondary schools, little was said about the war years (partly, of course, because contemporary history is rarely taught). What was said or written in texts conformed to the official version. Caught between the regime's celebrations and the schools' scanty sketches of the myth, surrounded by elders who either preferred not to talk about those painful years, or draped themselves in the glory of their exploits, or marinated in rancor, France's younger generation grew up with a mixture of indifference, ignorance, and exasperation toward these crucial years: they knew little, except that their parents' occasional discussions sounded to them like old veterans' tales of bygone ages.

It is no surprise that the audiences in the movie houses where *The Sorrow and the Pity* is shown are largely composed of young men and women who have found in this film a way of learning without indoctrination. It is no surprise that the French government has been less than elated. While the Communists, whose role in the Resistance is stressed in the movie, have not complained, they have not greeted it with enthusiasm: after all, the film punctures the *image d'Épinal* of a nation led by the working class, rising against the oppressors under the guidance of the Communists. . . . Gaullist politicians, privately or in interviews, have denounced the movie as unpatriotic. History is chaos, so goes their argument, and any selection or interpretation is arbitrary. The official version may not be the total truth, but it has an essence of the truth in it, and it has a vital function. To be sure, there were collaborationists, traitors, torturers; a huge majority of the French, after the debacle, had applauded Pétain's determination to take France out of the war and to change the regime. To be sure, many of the people who cheered de Gaulle on the Champs-Élysées on that glorious day in August 1944 had come to salute Pétain when he visited the capital four months earlier. But the most important thing for France was to overcome her weaknesses, to play a vital role in the world, to regain her rank, and to strengthen her material and moral resources. This could only be done, not so much by explicitly denying the real shame or "sorrow," as by explicitly emphasizing the equally real heroism and *redressement*. If one wants people to win victories over their worst flaws, one must appeal to what is noble in them. If one wants to bring out the best in them, it is the best that one must celebrate. Man, said de Gaulle to André Malraux, was not made to be guilty, sin is not interesting; the only ethics are those which lead man toward the greater things he carries in himself.[2] If the official version had a self-serving function (in that it legitimized and supported the postwar political elite), it had even more of a therapeutic mission.

It is high time that a debate take place about the merits and demerits of this version of history. Its strengths cannot be dismissed out of hand. France's gravest problem throughout the 1930s and the war years was a crisis of self-esteem. De Gaulle set himself up as the nurse of France's self-respect. Whatever the failings which the movie exposes —ranging from cowardice for survival to crimes against humanity— they did not compare with those of Nazi Germany: the collaborationists and the murderers were a small minority, the Vichyites grew fewer and fewer as the war went on, popular support for Pétain kept dwindling and turned to pity, dismay, and disgust. There was, therefore, little need to stare at one's evil deeds, to face one's guilt, to purge oneself of lies and sins in order to be sure never to commit them again and to be able to look into the eyes of another. Public contrition was not a precondition of self-respect. In public affairs, moreover, ethics and politics are hard to separate. In West Germany, denazification was the precondition of the nation's march toward status and power, which Konrad Adenauer led. But in France any wallowing in shame, any prolonged and extensive purges aimed at weeding out all those who in any way had done wrong would only have served those among France's allies who wanted to relegate her to a minor role in the postwar world, and, domestically, the Communists, who were calling for drastic purges and hoped to fill the vacuum. For the last half-century, France's air had been filled with mutual recriminations, charges and countercharges about who is responsible for decadence and degradation. If other nations tended to project their troubles on their neighbors and had to be forced to look at themselves, the French had made the mistake of locking themselves in a cage and tearing themselves apart in it; it was time for them to overcome their demons and get out into the world again. Vichy, in search of a quiet niche in the victorious enemy's domain, had plunged the French into an orgy of breast-beating, which had, as usual, turned into a ritual chase after scapegoats. This was not to be repeated in 1945.

And yet there were serious flaws in this approach. Official therapeutics and widespread malaise—or justified lack of pride—concerning the national performance in 1940–44 combined to create a sort of conspiracy of silence about much of what had really happened. It made a genuine assessment of the period far more difficult than for any other troubled and divisive period of French history. The Algerian war, however recent, and even though it was tainted by tortures and massacres, can be more easily discussed than the war years, perhaps because it carried no overtones of treason. And while aimed at overcoming French weaknesses, the official approach toward 1940–44 reflects these weaknesses insofar as it deems the French too immature or too fickle to face themselves without lapsing into demoralization or chaos; there is a good deal of paternalism here. Anyway, an attitude that may have been justified in 1945 is much harder to condone in 1974. When the French population consists so largely of people who were not even born when the war ended, and to whom those distant traumas are hardly different from the turmoils they read about in their history texts, why should the taboo not be lifted? If the revelation of Vichy complicity in Nazi crimes on one hand, of widespread mediocrity and

passivity on the other, lifts a veil which the elites and the older generations are eager to keep wrapped around their nakedness, why should
the young feel ashamed or guilty? After all, the very "generation gap"
keeps them from feeling solidarity with their elders. The official answer would be, I suspect, that one of Gaullism's assumptions and
objectives is precisely to preserve French solidarity, that the duty of
each new generation is to take on—*assumer*—the sum total of French
history.

II

There was still another reason for the postwar political elites not to be
happy about *The Sorrow and the Pity*—a reason that has little to do
either with May 1968 or with the official version. Here we must turn
to the second entity mirrored in the movie: wartime France. Some critics of the film did not much mind that it shook the Gaullist tree, but
they thought it gave a distorted view of France during the war—a
myth was in danger of being replaced by a countermyth. Maybe the
very strength and resilience of the first myth had invited so devastating
a rebuttal as this one, but two excesses do not make one truth. Perhaps the French should be obliged to watch this film and face at last
the other, seamier side of the story, compare the indictment with the
legend. But was there not a danger that foreign audiences, especially
in nations that had reasons to resent postwar France, or to suspect that
the official version had been a whitewash, would only too willingly accept *The Sorrow and the Pity* as the real and whole truth?

That it is the "real" truth cannot be questioned. It is easy to use a
movie camera for lies—propaganda films sometimes do so brilliantly.
But there are no lies here. In an interview, Marcel Ophuls has stated
that his intention was to show the discrepancy between present testimonies and past reality, the distortions of memory and the soothing
role of oblivion for many souls who need to find peace. This he has
done superbly—for instance, when he asks Marius Klein, a shopkeeper, about the wartime advertisement he placed denying that he was
Jewish; or when he interviews two ancient high-school teachers who
do not seem capable of bringing their past back to life; or when
d'Astier de la Vigerie, on the eve of his death, repudiates his 1944 demand for drastic purges; or when every German in the film denies responsibility for atrocities or arrests (they were, invariably, another service's responsibility). But Ophuls does much more with the passage of
time than recording lapses, denials, and inconsistencies. He has shown
how diversely time affects different people. He records the bitter and
vivid memories of some: the two humane, quietly heroic, and so mov-
ingly matter-of-fact old peasants, the brothers Grave, who say that

their Resistance feats gave them a bad reputation; the successful busi-
nessman who used to be Colonel Gaspar in the Resistance, who now
drives a Mercedes-Benz but remains haunted by the events of those
years, upset by the false claims of "the Resistants of the last hour" and
contemptuous of those who took no risks then but lie to themselves
now. Christian de la Mazière, the former Fascist and Waffen SS, is still
smarting from Pétain's refusal to see him; as for his revolutionary
"past" (he quite perceptively remarks that for the son of a traditional
French counterrevolutionary officer to become a Fascist was a form of
contestation—just as it is today for the son of a Communist to become
a *gauchiste*), it has left him skeptical of ideologies and fearful of commitments. And there is, of course, the unforgettable character out of a
Mauriac novel or a Clouzot movie: the hairdresser, Mme. Solange, ar-
rested, tortured, and jailed after the Liberation on what she considers
to be a charge trumped up by a close friend who imitated her hand-
writing in an act of vengeance aimed both at her own husband and at
Mme. Solange. Whether *her* story is true, we will never know, but
about her own sufferings, resentments, and firm "apolitical" love for
Pétain, her hands, her voice, her face, her words allow no doubts.
Also, Ophuls shows men who have not changed at all, and regret nothing: on one hand, former Captain Tausend, still proud of German victories, cheerfully self-righteous, and convinced that Alsace is German,
or that other ex-soldier of the Third Reich who still resents his capture by the *maquis;* on the other hand, Mendès-France, as incisive,
tough-minded, devoid of illusion or cant, articulate, combative, ironic,
and proud today as when he was being hounded as a Jew and tried on
a fake charge of desertion. If M. Verdier the pharmacist (in a way the
movie's antihero) has changed at all, it is only to become rather opu-
lent, as he smugly admits; his feelings have not altered.

Truthful when he shows us what time has done to his characters,
Ophuls is also right when he tells us what went on in the war years.
The thread is provided by two figures. One is the invariably bouncy,
mindlessly optimistic Maurice Chevalier, singing his silly little patriotic ditties during the Phony War, then under Pétain, then after the
Liberation. He symbolizes both the average guy's resilience and talent
for passing through all regimes, and the breezy mediocrity and shallow
self-satisfaction that survive all ordeals. (It must be said, however, that
there was much more to Chevalier than this; the use of his songs and
dances is a perfectly fair statement of a theme, but it is unfair to the
man, however much on target as far as his audiences are concerned.)
The other figure is M. Verdier, who reveals himself as the perfect
Français moyen of those years. All events are reduced to him—at best,
to him and his family: he let the front come to him, as he put it; the
French defeat was like losing a rugby match; eating and prudence

were his mottos—out of fear of starvation he overfed his son, born in 1942; the big event of 1943 was the resumption of hunting. A monster, a scoundrel? Assuredly not. His horizon may be low, his sense of solidarity may be weak, his display of that form of individualism Tocqueville prophesied (and detested) may be annoying, but the other side of the coin is that he has a kind of soft humanity—he refused to kill a German soldier whom he could have shot, he helped two Jewish girls, his powers of sympathy were genuine enough. But indignation and rebellion are not his forte; the only reaction one could have to the deportations of Jews, he says, was tears—hidden tears, in one's cellar. . . . Ophuls reveals other characters as even more mediocre: the hotel-keeper at Royat, whose bad memories are limited to the fact that he did not get paid by the Germans who took over his hotel and to the night when German soldiers tried to bring girls up to their rooms; the bicycle champion who saw no Germans in a city which was not merely occupied but the scene of violent disturbances. If the movie so often seems a prosecutor's brief, it is not because of the interviewers' questions—the screenplay makes this clearer than the film itself—it is because of the answers they get.

What is, ultimately, frightening about *The Sorrow and the Pity,* is that it reveals to some of its viewers and reminds the others what the climate of quasi-civil war and Nazi occupation was like. It is Verdier who, characteristically, talks about sorrow and pity: soft feelings again. What seeps from the screen is fear, hatred, and contempt. D'Astier, in 1969, explains his bloodthirstiness of 1944 by the fact that throughout the war years he had lived in fear. It is fear that the two high-school professors remember, amidst the ruins of their memories, as the main reason why repression and arrests went unchallenged by their colleagues. It is fear which Dennis Rake, the British agent, sees as the reason for the bourgeois' caution and cowardice. It is hatred, Mendès-France reports, the kind of hatred that breeds and feeds civil wars, which inspired the followers of Pétain and Laval in their campaign against the parliamentarians who sailed on the *Massilia* in order to keep fighting, and in their attacks on Léon Blum, the Socialist leader of the Popular Front (whom they blamed, absurdly, for France's fall, because the Popular Front had frightened them). It is hatred which the monarchist *résistant* Colonel du Jonchay (an almost cartoonlike figure) still feels toward Communists and toward Mendès-France. It is hatred which bloated Vichy's anti-Semitism and the fascism of young men like de la Mazière, raised on a diet of antiliberalism, anticommunism, and disgust for foreigners and Jews. It is hatred which led to the Vichy Militia's abominations. It is hatred, as well as envy and pettiness disguised as patriotism, which turned poison-pen letters into an industry. It is hatred and a passion for hasty vengeance which swelled the inevitable wave of summary executions in the weeks preceding and following the Liberation. As for contempt, the movie is steeped in it: the contempt which we, as spectators, cannot help feeling toward some of the characters on the screen; the contempt which the former German occupiers obviously still have for the French who served them—on the black market or in bed—or who came asking for services, such as the right to hold horse races; the sardonic contempt, barely curbed by pity and empathy, which old General Sir Edward Spears, Churchill's adviser and de Gaulle's friend-turned-foe, suggests for a nation that let Britain down and turned to military saviors even in defeat; the contempt of de la Mazière for the glittering nights of occupied Paris—and for the drab soldiers of France compared to the healthy torsos of the Nazis; the contempt of Mendés-France (and his lawyer) for the men who tried and jailed him. Whoever has not lived through such a period will absorb its poisons while watching *The Sorrow and the Pity*.

There is another truth that emerges in the film, one I have mentioned before: a truth about what united each camp in occupied France. The men of Vichy were those for whom order was the highest good. War was chaos and a permanent threat of subversion; only an authoritarian and reactionary regime could restore and consolidate "society," undermined by democracy and labor unions and "excessive" freedoms and "foreign" miasmas. In the other camp were all those for whom freedom came first, whether it was the lay, Republican, humanitarian ideal of freedom the brothers Grave absorbed in their Socialist milieu and in the Third Republic's public school, or the somewhat less liberal, more narrowly patriotic instinct of freedom from foreign invaders which seems to have animated Colonel Gaspar. And the secondary truth—the diversity of each camp—is also brought home. Lamirand, the amiable, gullible engineer who tried in vain to convert French youth to the cult of Pétain, and de la Mazière hardly seem to belong to the same world. D'Astier, an eccentric aristocrat who describes himself as the black sheep of his family and who, after years of Communist fellow traveling, died a left-wing Gaullist, proclaims autobiographically that only "ill-adjusted" people were ripe for the risks of the Resistance; but those admirable brothers Grave, so much in harmony with their hills and their land and their farm, were obviously well-adjusted men who decided that what they had was worth fighting and dying for.

Finally, the film's portrait is true, if painful, of those people who—under a barrage of propaganda and later a deluge of bombs, fearful of famine and reprisals, caught between armies and police forces, uncertain of the future, afraid of the disastrous effects of any commitment—found whatever security was still available by locking the doors of their homes and hearts, clinging to their daily tasks, trying to remain unnoticed, and praying for survival. Self-preservation is not the noblest of aims, but it is the most elementary. In the torn country of 1944, with all communications cut, battles raging, rumors on the rampage, executions and ambushes everywhere, each man, each family, each village or town tended to become a little sovereign island again. That this did not prevent an extraordinary revival of community and an explosion of national enthusiasm became clear at the Liberation—about which the film shows us very little, and whose excesses only are mentioned.

If nothing here is false, it is still not the whole truth. Foreigners should beware of judging wartime France on the basis of this movie alone. *The Sorrow and the Pity* lasts four and a half hours: it is much too short a time for a fair sketch of France in those years. I wish Ophuls could have made a movie twice or three times as long, or a series. Whole chunks of history are missing. The complex, slow way in which public opinion woke up from its escapist dream of archaic reaction and sheltered neutrality, realized that its love affair with Pétain was based on delusions, and gradually recoiled from the harsh realities of oppression and collaboration—this is not well shown. There were turning points: Laval's return to power in April 1942; the Allied invasion of North Africa and Pétain's failure to leave Vichy in November 1942; the landings in Italy, etc., which are not indicated. The spectator remains under the impression that the parties, *salons,* theaters, and collaborationist movie stars of occupied Paris were representative of French slackness or corruption throughout the period; this is not at all the case. The Resistance itself was not, of course, the subject matter of the movie, but, even so, it could have been less arbitrarily presented. The movie focuses on Clermont-Ferrand, the capital of Auvergne; but it does not report the Resistance activities of the faculty and students from the University of Strasbourg, in exile in Clermont-Ferrand— which led to massive Nazi repression—nor the Resistance activities at the big Michelin rubber factory, in which management as well as workers took part (one person mentions the arrest of Mme. Michelin). While the statement, so often made since 1945 and echoed here by Dennis Rake, that the "people" and especially workers joined the Resistance but the bourgeoisie did not, has some truth in it, it is much more true of the industrial and commercial bourgeoisie (with important exceptions, as in Clermont-Ferrand) than of the bourgeoisie of the professions. One would not know this from the film. It shows us very little of a group whose effect was enormous, in days when the printed and the spoken word had such a resonance: the intelligentsia. One rather crazy pro-Nazi novelist, Chateaubriant, is shown; why not, on the other side, Malraux or Vercors? More seriously, the diversity and complexity of the French Resistance movements is only barely suggested. Why Duclos, who had little to do with Clermont-Ferrand, appears on the screen is not clear. It was, of course, important to evoke the Communists' skills and sacrifices, but it would have been equally fair to stress the role of Christian Democrats and priests in the Resistance (the former head of the MRP, Georges Bidault, is interviewed, but talks of other things). Too much emphasis is put on Colonel du Jonchay, who manages to make the Resistance look pretty silly; and while there are moving scenes with ex-Colonel Gaspar, some spectators may have felt sorry that the true hero of the movie (along with Mendès-France), the marvelous old farmer Grave, who knows who was responsible for his deportation but refuses to avenge himself, was a member of the *British* Intelligence Service, not of the *French* Resistance. This is a small point, perhaps, for foreign audiences today, but it is a sore one for many Frenchmen, especially since Vichy and the Nazis kept denouncing the rebels as a rabble manipulated by London and Moscow.

These omissions bother me less, however, than the inevitable subtle distortion due to the process of selection. The whole truth is not here, not only because of what was left out, but because of what was emphasized. Of course the Resistance was not a mass movement—less than 250,000 "membership cards" were given out by the Veterans' Administration after the war. But would it have been impossible to show how hard it was to reach even that many people in a largely *petit-bourgeois* country, where most citizens *do* have something to lose—beyond their lives and freedoms—if they abandon their daily routine and throw themselves into the adventure of clandestinity? Of course, Vichy's anti-Semitic legislation, however autonomous, and Laval's ghastly decisions about the Jews, bitterly recalled by Claude Lévy, one of his young victims who survived to write eloquently about that sinister episode, represent hideous complicity with Nazism at its worst. But to say, as Lévy does, that *France* was the only European *country* that collaborated is to equate the Vichy regime and its police with France, and it neglects all the Quislings and Oustachis elsewhere. Moreover, it leaves out all those in France who helped Jews, foreign or French, to escape and survive. To be sure, Rake and Evans, the British pilot downed over France, pay tribute to the people who hid them. But—such is the power of the camera—what they *say* is less deeply convincing than what is *shown,* and so much of what is shown is grisly or shameful. The Resistance, small as it may have been, would not have even had a chance of getting started and organized, of surviving the efficient hounding of the Nazis and their well-equipped French accomplices, if it had not had—especially in 1943–44—the active and passive support of millions of Frenchmen who provided the *maquisards* with false identity papers, food, clothing, shelter, and information. Some people —such as de la Mazière—preserved their "innocence" and closed their eyes and ears when victims were rounded up and sent to camps and jails. But there were many more who knew, and did their best to save or help those victims. All of this may have been unspectacular, but it was important, in itself and for the record. One does not see much of it in *The Sorrow and the Pity*. It is as if the right tune were being sung, but in the wrong key. For Americans—who have never experienced sudden, total defeat and the almost overnight disappearance of their accustomed political elites; who have never lived under foreign occupation; who do not know what Nazi pressure meant; who have never had an apparently legal government, headed by a national hero and claiming total obedience, sinking deeper and deeper into a morass of impotence, absurdity, and crime; who have never had to worry first and last about food and physical survival—the wise and gentle warning of Anthony Eden must be heeded: do not judge too harshly. Especially one must keep in mind that not everything has been recorded here, and that the movie is both a revelation and a weapon in the painful domestic battle which the French are waging with their past.

III

The Sorrow and the Pity not only mirrors the French of today and those of the war years. Like all works of art, it reflects its author. I had never met Marcel Ophuls, but his film helps me to know him. He came to France, as a child, when his German parents fled Nazi Germany. Max Ophüls, his father, the famous film director of *Liebelei, la Ronde, Lola Montès,* became a French citizen, like many refugees from Central Europe, and served in the French Army when the war began. His son, like so many children of aliens, must have been caught in that French melting pot that is almost as effective as, and less publicized than, the American one: her school system, her universalistic culture, the seductiveness of her intelligence and logic. Then came the catastrophe, and Vichy, the statute that discriminated against Jews in various professions—especially the movies—and its vendetta against naturalized refugees. The Ophüls family left for the United States in 1941. They did not return to France until 1950. Max Ophüls, unrecognized in Hollywood, once again found fame in France. Marcel also became a film director in France.

Their history, I think, explains a great deal about *The Sorrow and the Pity*. France is Marcel Ophuls' country: how well he knows her ways, her landscapes, the tones of conversation, the language of glances and gestures peculiar to her folk, the rhetoric of official propaganda, the atmosphere of her provincial towns! But, obviously, his country deeply hurt him, as a child, in 1940. *The Sorrow and the Pity* is partly an exploration of the wound, partly the cry of a grieving convert—a child in flight from Nazi persecution who had found new roots in France. As once-uprooted people do, he had probably adopted France ever so passionately while she adopted him legally. He no doubt came to love the wisdom and poetry of French classics, the turmoil and intensity of French history, the ease and harmony of French daily life, the witty humaneness of the French *peuple*. Growing older, Ophuls must have found himself drawn back to these traumatic months of collapse, eerie revolution, sudden reversal of all values, sudden fear; he may have felt a need to come to grips with his own experience, and an annoyance with France's unwillingness to face the past, with official boastings, with the one-sidedness of the standard—the victors'— history. Both his resentment of the Germans, who uprooted him a second time, and his grievances against the French who shattered his love affair fill the screen. The subtle distortions I have mentioned are not accidental: they tell a story—his own. How do I know this? By listening to the cool, sometimes insinuating, often cutting voice that interviews so many of the characters; and by listening to myself, whose personal history has many points in common with his own, except that I came to France some years earlier and not as a refugee, when I was a few months old, and that I remained in France throughout the war as a Frenchified Austrian—French by education and feeling, Austrian by passport only, a partly Jewish alien in a xenophobic anti-Semitic police state.

Hence my sympathy and my dissent. The first half of the movie— "The Collapse"—is almost unassailable. Ophuls was there, lived through this, and gives us the best account of it since the first half-hour of René Clément's *Forbidden Games*. This was the feeling of cowardly relief and collective concussion, the stunned flight from the war, the terrible blow (incomprehensible then, and, for many, even now) delivered by the British when they attacked the French fleet at Mers-el-Kebir, the search for peace and quiet and discipline—and scapegoats—under that grand old oak Marshal Pétain, the clarion calls for atonement, the arrogant wails of self-flagellation, and the daily miseries of partial occupation and food shortages.

But Ophuls was not there later on: hence the weaknesses of the second half of his film, "The Choice." He was not there when the "armies of the shadows" gathered in the woods, when Resistance networks defied the Gestapo and the Vichy Militia and dropped coded messages in city mailboxes, when the morale of an exhausted and restless nation was upheld on the exhortations of a handful of spokesmen at the BBC and by the eloquence of writers whose real names were disguised at the bottom of ill-printed columns in clandestine newspapers and confidential pamphlets. These were days of hope and fervor, when even those who were not heroic began to live vicariously with the heroes in an atmosphere of passionate anticipation that makes anything in the postwar world seem drab or drained by comparison. The grand Gaullist metaphor of a nation that overcomes its initial weakness, daunts its demons, climbs the slope again, and makes the final victory partly its own, surely flatters the French too much, down-playing as it does the doubts and divagations of the earlier period, and the opportunism and savagery that marred the Resistance. But it is not, basically, false. Who did not live in a French town or village during the weeks before and after the Liberation does not know the bliss of being alive at the end of an unspeakable ordeal, the bliss of being happy with and proud of the people with whom one has survived. Much of what went on earlier could be forgiven—the little capitulations, the small acts of selfishness and meanness, if not the cruelties and calls for murder—because of the price paid, and because of the slowly opening eyes, the *revanche* that was also a redemption, later on. If Maurice Chevalier tells one part of the story (a part I remember well, from the miserable radio of 1939 or 1941), surely Jean Moulin, the martyred leader of the Resistance, and de Gaulle's inflexible genius tell the other.

Both parts are true; but since we all judge—maybe we should not, but we cannot help it—my own verdict is not so severe as Marcel Ophuls'. On the scales of history, the great things are weightier than the mean ones. In Ophuls' movie, Verdier and the two almost senile schoolteachers contribute a nagging, almost deafening counterpoint to the Graves, to Gaspar, and to Mendès-France. In my memory, the schoolteacher—now seventy-five, and still vibrant—who taught me French history, gave me hope in the worst days, dried my tears when my best friend was deported along with his mother, and gave false papers to my mother and me so that we could flee a Gestapo-infested city in which the complicity of friends and neighbors was no longer a guarantee of safety—this man wipes out all the bad moments, and the humiliations, and the terrors. He and his gentle wife were not Resistance heroes, but if there is an average Frenchman, it was this man who was representative of his nation; for that, France and the French will always deserve our tribute, and have my love.

II
Authority and Society

4

The Rulers: Heroic Leadership in Modern France

I. On the Study of Political Leadership

The study of political leadership has been the orphan of contemporary political science. Empirical studies of political life have focused on the behavior of groups rather than on the statecraft of leaders; efforts at theory have produced a glut of typologies and models of political systems, often written at a level of abstraction that freezes out the role and effect of political leaders. Only political philosophy has continued to be concerned with the phenomenon of statecraft—under such headings as authority and legitimacy—but all too frequently without sufficient regard for empirical data. It is in the analysis of totalitarian systems and in the realm of what has been called political pathology that political scientists have paid most attention to the scars left by leaders on their countries and on the world. But statecraft is of the essence of all politics. At a time when so many regimes are nothing but a leader writ large, general and abstract frameworks and models run the risk of collapsing like sand castles whenever the leader falls. Whatever the virtues of systems theory, it is no substitute for the empirical analysis of political leadership. Indeed, when so many systems approaches seem to be based on a metaphoric assimilation of the political universe to a physical, cybernetic, or economic model, the study of statecraft may become the last refuge of political analysis.

There seem to be two different perspectives for the investigation of leadership. One is psychological: its focus is on the personality of the leader, whose behavior, beliefs, techniques, and works are studied as

First published in Lewis J. Edinger, ed., *Political Leadership in Industrialized Societies* (New York, 1967).

expressions of his personality and as clues to his character. The other is political: its focus is on statecraft, the way in which the leader conceives and carries out his role as statesman, his relations with and effect on his followers or opponents. In practice, of course, the distinction often gets blurred. The study of statecraft cannot ignore the personal idiosyncrasies of the leader, especially when—if I may use a metaphor suggested by Robert Tucker—the leader is not merely an actor (however great) in a play but the playwright as well, while the psychological study must scrutinize political behavior, since the deeds are the clues to the psyche. But each student of political leadership must choose between the two approaches lest he lose focus completely, for there is inevitably some tension in trying to use both at once. They pull the analyst in different directions: one asks him to elucidate what is always a mystery—the coils and springs of character; the other asks him to illuminate a performance. Although in each case he examines how leadership roles are selected, defined, and played, the emphasis in one is on how personality traits shape and are shaped by these roles, and in the other on how those roles shape and are shaped by the polity.

My own viewpoint here is the second of these. To begin with, it is a matter of training. Successful use of the psychological perspective requires a solid and subtle training in psychology and psychoanalysis. Nothing is more irritating than people playing amateur psychoanalyst. Good psychologists are aware of the gaps between personality, social psychology, and political behavior, but political scientists insufficiently grounded in psychology and psychoanalysis may leap imprudently over these gaps, producing oversimplified political analysis and crude personality studies. Then too, even the most competent handling of the psychological perspective has serious drawbacks, given the current state of psychoanalytic and psychological theory. To a large extent, a political leader will be seen as a man driven by needs, tensions, and forces (of which he is only dimly aware) toward beliefs and behavior patterns that will help him meet those needs, cope with those tensions, and appease those forces. Until psychological theory provides us with more satisfying tools, and unless political scientists learn to avoid shortcuts, this approach risks sending us on a seductive rather than productive detour. It has the fascination of an adventure story—a search for the missing clue or missing link, a search in which everything revealed is treated as a sign of something concealed, and things expressed are deemed the revelation of things repressed. All too often (as in a certain contemporary approach to political philosophy) the fascination of the search itself induces the searchers to find in everything overt a covert meaning, which makes the open record read like an exercise in deception.[1] This is both risky and limited: risky, since we are reduced to hypotheses, endlessly intriguing yet tantalizingly endless; limited, because it tends to neglect the conscious part of statecraft. Leaders, especially great leaders, discover and exploit the personality traits and the psychological techniques required for successful statecraft, even if at the outset of their careers they are innocent of the techniques and exhibit only latent or minimal aspects of the needed traits. What is needed depends, of course, largely on the political circumstances—another reason for adopting a more directly political perspective, which, I repeat, involves a consideration of character whenever necessary.

A comparative study of political leadership requires hypotheses about the most important variables, for these allow for the development of typologies, a first step toward theory. (In few areas would a proliferation of theories unsupported by empirical evidence, characteristic of much political science, be so ludicrous). In the psychological perspective, we would expect the development of personality models.[2] If the focus is on statecraft, we would have to find a middle ground between two extremes: case studies so descriptive that analysis and comparison are hopeless; and general propositions so "universally valid" as to be meaningless. We need this middle ground because the study of statecraft is the study of interaction between distinctive personalities and distinctive milieux.

For comparative purposes the following three variables are of special importance; they are analytically distinct, although in practice they interact continuously.

1. *The style of authority in the society in which the leader operates.* Political scientists, at last following the indicators offered by great sociologists of the past, are beginning to pay attention to this, and it is at the heart of recent studies of political systems and civic cultures. The resilience of patterns of authority, even in societies whose social and political structures are in flux, points to the importance of the ways in which decisions are made, individuals and groups cooperate, and conflicts are handled—and to the importance of the society's views about these matters. Since the political scientists' study of authority patterns and of beliefs about authority is not far advanced, it is not surprising that the first efforts here have suffered from "globalism"—from trying for an overview which neglects significant variations of beliefs and behavior within a given society. In the study of political leadership, the *style* of political authority is of special interest: i.e., the relations (and notions about relations) of authority in the political sphere. By "political sphere" I mean both the political system in the narrow sense (the pattern of power, interests, and policies) and the community at large in its dealings with the political system. Any empirical study of statecraft must investigate the relations between a political leader and the

style of political authority in his society: does he express it,[3] or is he trying to change it, and, if so, from what to what? A typology of styles of political authority is a prerequisite to a typology of political leadership.

2. *The nature of the political system.* By this I mean: the institutional setup, which defines the various leadership roles, sets limits (flexible or not) within which the leader can operate, shapes the orientations and techniques of his statecraft, provides him with (or deprives him of) various kinds of legal and political power; and the nature of the system's political legitimacy, i.e., the "political formula," which includes the way in which political leaders are selected and how power is distributed among them, as well as the scope and depth of consent to the political formula, which depends on how the citizens evaluate and appreciate these processes of selection and distribution. Political legitimacy is a notion that ties together the institutional setup with the elements of what some writers call the political culture—the style of authority, the political opinions, and the social values prevalent in the community at large. A given style of authority, a given consensus among social groups about the structure of society rule out and are compatible with a number of different political systems; a political system, in order to be legitimate, not only must be congruent with the style of authority and be based on a consensus about the social order, but must express a consensus about the polity as well. A distinction that comes to mind immediately is that between political leaders who operate within legitimate political systems and political leaders who do not, who come to power when the previous political system has broken down or who destroy it once in power.[4] Within each category there are other obvious distinctions: in the first group depending on the political system; in the second group depending on the institutional setup and political formula the leader imposes or shapes after the breakdown.

3. *The nature and scope of the tasks performed by the leaders.* Here, several important factors intersect: the purposes of the leader, set partly by his own beliefs, dogmas, and hierarchy of values, and partly by the nation's circumstances as he perceives (or misperceives) them; the economic system, social structure, and the various groups' values, which constitute the givens (yet certainly not the unchangeable givens) of statecraft; the external situation, if we look at the leader's foreign policy. Various typologies can be built here. The way in which the leaders define their tasks can provide one spectrum—from pragmatic to dogmatic; the means they use in carrying them out suggests another—from moderate to violent. If the question concerns the scope of the tasks undertaken, one may want to place leaders along a spectrum from "single issue" to "total system" (domestic and interna-

tional). If one is concerned with social change, one can classify political leaders as reactionary, conservative, reformist, or revolutionary; if one is interested in the relation of the nation to the world at large, a different set of categories can be developed, etc.

I am well aware of the rudimentary character of these remarks, yet they may have at least one (negative) virtue. They suggest that the most fruitful way of studying political leadership may not be to distinguish between leadership in industrialized societies and leadership in "developing" countries. The style of authority in a given society has a way of being partly independent of the social and economic structure: patterns forged during a preindustrial phase live on, indeed shape the pattern of industrialization. The relative autonomy of politics owes a great deal to the autonomy of authority relations, and to the fact that institutional arrangements and the legitimacy (or lack thereof) of a political system are the products of political forces and beliefs related to, but only partly dependent on, the economic and social systems. We all know that industrialized societies at comparable levels of development display a bewildering variety of political regimes. The same is true of the underdeveloped countries. Industrialization certainly affects the tasks of statesmen, but there are entire ranges of issues whose connection with the modern economy is tenuous or indirect; the ways the economy is managed or the ways the social groups share its burdens and benefits are as varied as the political regimes. For underdeveloped countries it is absurd to assume either that "modernization" is the overriding, necessary concern of all political leaders or that the techniques of "political development" are so clear-cut and predetermined that they force statecraft into a necessarily small number of distinct molds. The political implications of the construct "industrial society," or of the process "modernization," are very few if we think of the necessary consequences, and infinitely varied if we think of the possible concomitants.

This chapter presents only a few suggestions for the study of political leadership in one country—France. I am no foe of comparative undertakings, and I realize that comparison becomes hopeless when the scholar is faced with empirical studies that celebrate the uniqueness of an experience. But it is of little value to bring together phenomena that have artificially been made comparable by conversion into a common language that conceals essential differences. Perhaps the most fruitful approach consists in accumulating empirical data upon which one can base an analysis of the essential features of political leadership at a given time and place. This would, of course, focus on what appears "distinctive" (a word not synonymous with unique). But if one asks questions of general interest for any study of political leadership, if one examines variables that are significant for most investigations of statecraft, subsequent comparisons will be made possible and meaningful. Often what appeared distinctive at an early stage of the scholarly process will be seen as characteristic of a much broader category of phenomena. It is therefore quite possible that the hypotheses presented here about political leadership in France are no more peculiar to France than, say, the behavior of parliamentarians analyzed by Nathan Leites is "peculiarly French." [5] But this will have to be determined at a later, more inclusive stage of analysis—and that more general stage cannot be validly reached by any shortcut.

My use of the word "heroic" is a probably vain attempt to avoid the heady, if largely sterile, discussions provoked by the word "charismatic." "Heroism" is a relative notion: a man who is a hero to my neighbor may be a calamity to me. Maybe it would have been preferable to speak about crisis leadership in France—the point being that whereas there are frequent crises which produce leaders whose behavior will be discussed here, not all of these act heroically. However, in some French emergencies the crisis leader makes no pretense of being unusual. What concerns us here are crisis leaders who either see themselves or are seen by the public as different from the norm— whether their ultimate accomplishments vindicate this view or not. Specifically, I will concentrate on three figures and assume for brevity's sake that their exploits as well as the context in which they operated are familiar: Marshal Philippe Pétain, Pierre Mendès-France, and Charles de Gaulle. I will, in the next section, present a very general framework for an analysis of their statecraft. The nature, functions, and limits of French crisis leaders can best be understood by reference to the style of authority prevalent in French society in general, and in the French polity in particular, as well as by reference to the political system whose crisis brings them forth. In the following two sections I will put some flesh on these bones; first I will describe with more detail the style of "heroic" leaders, how they conceive of, establish, and maintain their authority; then I will discuss the substance of their statecraft, the kinds of tasks undertaken by them, and their performance in carrying out those tasks.

II. Heroic Leadership in France: a Framework

The general framework for our investigation is provided by recent studies of the French style of authority. Here the pioneer is Michel Crozier, whose extraordinarily rich and provocative work offers a sweeping interpretation of authority relations in France's bureaucracy, industrial organization, education, and political system, in both their structural aspects (how are such relations arranged) and cultural aspects (what are the values served by those arrangements).[6] Major contributions have also been made by two other sociologists, Jesse R. Pitts and Laurence Wylie. Elsewhere I have tried to use their findings for the purpose of political analysis.[7] Philip Williams has also applied them in his masterpiece on the Fourth Republic.[8] Our common debt to Tocqueville need hardly be stressed.

Crozier's model is that of a system of authority relations in which each stratum, as he calls it, is isolated from other strata and governed by impersonal rules decreed by a superior authority entitled to set such rules but severely limited in scope and means. Within each stratum there is a fierce insistence on equality that the impersonality of the rules guarantees. The joint activities of the members of the stratum are primarily negative, i.e., aimed at preventing two kinds of encroachments: from outside, to protect the stratum against excessive or arbitrary acts of external authorities; and from inside, to deny any members the possibility of taking over the leadership of the group. Such a structure of authority relations results in a society both centralized and hierarchical: centralized, since decisions are referred to high echelons; hierarchical, since every stratum is concerned with and dedicated to the preservation of its own peculiar rank and status. Yet centralization goes along with strict limitations on the superior's rule-making power, constantly held in check by the ruled, and within each rank there is a fierce resistance to privilege and inequality. This structure also results for the individual in a kind of double bookkeeping: he complies with the rules (explicit and assumed) of the social units he lives and works in, as long as they are not arbitrary; yet his private beliefs remain unaffected by, and often are quite contrary to, his public behavior.

The values served by such an arrangement are many. One is what Crozier has called *"l'horreur du face-à-face"*: a dislike of the form of freedom known as participation (also a dislike of the *face-à-face* of totalitarianism, which abolishes all freedom and turns all life into public life); a desire to avoid direct, interpersonal conflict, which might result in permanent entanglement or personal dependence; a preference for *in*dependence, for as broad as possible a sphere of uninvaded private thought and action.* Defense of the private sphere provides the main,

---

* The hypothesis of *l'horreur du face-à-face* has recently come under attack by William Schonfeld, who prefers a functional explanation for the behavior of French primary and high-school students, and by John Ambler, who finds that answers to a questionnaire about authority relations do not confirm the hypothesis.

In Schonfeld's case, it is hard to understand why school children—who find, roughly after primary school, that the earlier oscillation from *le chahut* to what Schonfeld calls the teacher's Caesaristic legitimacy is no longer functional—should adopt what he calls (cryptically) "learned coverage" behavior, i.e., what Crozier describes—unless one posits Crozier's hypothesis. (To be sure, one can argue that the students have to conform to an institutional system that leaves them little

almost the only excuse for occasional joint action; perpetuation of it is assured by the paucity of communications among categories, as well as by the combined effects of decision-making from above and restraints on the decision-makers' sphere of action. Another value served is what one might call a preference for homeorhetic change. The word "homeostasis" implies a return to the *status quo ante* after each crisis is over; it does not apply to the French example, which is not that of a stagnant society. The word "homeorhesis" implies the acceptance of change *and* a return to equilibrium after change. It therefore better fits the French polity, where there is a pervasive dislike for change that disturbs the existing hierarchy of ranks and statuses and the existing leveling within each stratum, a willingness instead to tolerate either the *status quo* or, if it is untenable and provokes excessive strains, change that affects the whole society yet preserves the delicate harmony of hierarchy with equalitarianism. What is resisted is change at the end of which certain groups find themselves in a situation more disadvantageous than the one they held before or than the one they had been led to expect as the outcome of the change. Homeorhesis means, to be precise, a refusal to retrogress or a resentment at failing to progress during a process of change that improves the lot of others; it is the rejection of absolute or relative *déclassement*. It is based on the fear of insecurity.[9]

The matrix for this extraordinary set of arrangements and values is France's school system. Its historical origins are preindustrial, a blend of feudal remnants and rebellion against feudalism. They have worked as a corset within which French industrialization has been forced and contorted. Modern France, from the Revolution to World War II, perfectly blended the style summarized above and a socioeconomic system which slowed down industrialization and preserved a peculiar "bal-

---

choice, but then one has to explain the origins and formidable resilience of this system.) Gérard Vincent (in *Les Professeurs du second degré,* Paris, 1967) shows that *le chahut* does not end with primary school and continues in high school to play the role of an outlet against authoritarianism.

In Ambler's case, there are two confusions. First, the fact that Frenchmen *say* they would prefer face-to-face relations only tells us something about their opinions, and nothing about their actual behavior. One of the key features of the "Crozier model" is that a wide-ranging freedom of utopian thought is made possible by the bureaucratic system that protects independence yet makes the thought ineffective. Second, in Crozier's model, face-to-face relations do have an important role—as an "under the counter," semi-legitimate corrective to the anonymity of hierarchical bureaucratic relations. But these face-to-face relations are *hidden*, and aim at avoiding conflict—by contrast with the kind of bargaining face-to-face model that is Crozier's ideal and a democratic myth. Being a form of pressure on one's superior and, frequently a hidden exchange of favors rather than an open responsible deal, the face-to-face relations that exist confirm and perpetuate the patterns Crozier describes.

ance"; this blend produced what I have called the stalemate society. As Crozier has shown, the French style of authority produces an alternation of routine and crisis. The absence of face-to-face relations, the distance between strata, the concept of a higher authority unsharing and bound by impersonal rules—all these condemn such authority to abstraction and rigidity. In ordinary circumstances, the disadvantages are reduced by informal, "parallel," under-the-counter relations that violate the sacrosanct equality within each stratum and fill the gap that exists between above and below, but this is at best a palliative, especially since the violation is covert, the link suspect. Subordinates' resistance to their superiors and the superiors' inability to innovate result in short circuits, i.e., crises when the "rules of the game" either fail to prevent a deterioration of the subjects' status, contribute to a loss of status, or seem to impinge on their independence. Then, the normal rules of the game are suspended and changes are introduced.

Thanks to Crozier, we have a convincing model of routine authority as well as change. But the model of crisis authority is barely sketched in. Just as routine authority is an odd mix of opposites (hierarchy and equality, dependence on and distrust of superior authority), crisis authority is a blend of extremes. On one hand, it represents the collapse of the norm—both in a substantive sense, since it introduces total change into a previously immobile system, and in a procedural sense, since it corresponds to a collapse of the "delicate balance of terror" which exists in routine authority relations. It bespeaks a sudden willingness of the strata to find a way out of crisis, a relief from stress, a blank check given to a superior no longer bound by restraints and bullied by resistance. Crisis authority reasserts personal authority—one might almost say reasserts aristocratic values, as opposed to the antiaristocratic value of distrust and drive for impersonality.

On the other hand, crisis authority performs a *function* for the system, rather than a *change of* system. The way change is thereby introduced often still conforms to the basic value of France's style of authority—the avoidance of face-to-face relations and the preference for homeorhetic change—as if the authorities to whom power had been given by and for the crisis understood exactly the nature, conditions, and limits of the power delegated. The structure and values of French authority relations are so firm that a crisis leader's attempt to change its style would end in fiasco. Thus crisis leadership in France has two aspects. It has a cataclysmic side, which sets it off from crisis leadership in, say, the United States or Britain. In those two countries, a crisis is usually just a particularly strong challenge that can be handled by the normal procedures of authority; in France, those procedures are suspended and crisis leadership becomes not only a response to the challenge but a sort of revenge against the normal procedures.

And it has a functional side—which sets it off from the leadership of totalitarian countries, for there is an aspect of continuity or even complicity. During routine periods, the "parallel relations" (so largely personal) adumbrate (and help avoid) the relations that exist in a crisis:
they are the shadow of crisis authority in the impersonal light of routine authority patterns. Even when the shadow takes over, the limits
voluntarily observed by or forced upon crisis leaders are a glimmer of,
and a promise of return to, that impersonal light in temporary eclipse.
A country whose language has no equivalents for the words "statecraft" and "leadership" but contains such cold and static abstractions
as *le Pouvoir* and *l'État* will be tempted to see in grand leadership a
kind of heroic exercise in self-expression, a holiday from rules and routine, an exalting spectacle. Yet the distrust of arbitrariness which the
vocabulary suggests reminds the leader of the spectators' determination
to stop the show if it threatens to turn the audience into stage props.
Crisis leadership represents, in this sense, a return to the highly personalized authority to which the French are subjected in their early
childhood: at home and in the first grades at school, parents and
teachers are face-to-face superiors, as well as makers or transmitters of
impersonal rules that apply to them as well as to the child. Crisis leadership, in order to be effective, must be more than the temporary
triumph of the "parallel" procedures that normally exist behind the
legal façade: it must avoid arbitrariness and somehow turn the heroic
show into the impersonal rules of "total" but harmonious change, just
as the personal dependence of the early family and school years turns
into the system of depersonalized hierarchy and rule-surrounded independence later on. Thus the function crisis leadership performs is double: it is both the agent of social change *in* the system, and the preserver *of* the system against the mortal threat of destruction by
immobility or a change of system.

As Crozier has shown, these very general considerations apply to
French political life; the alternation of representative regimes and saviors ("techniques of evasion" from a citizens' "participant" culture)
represents, in the political sphere, oscillation from routine to crisis.[10]
But in order to understand heroic leadership, one has to take into
account several specific factors of national political life.*

---

* A case can be made to show that in local politics, especially in the small *communes,* what is crisis leadership on the national level is really ordinary leadership,
and vice versa—which confirms the point made above about the functionality of
crisis leadership (see Mark J. Kesselman, *The Ambiguous Consensus,* New York,
1967). One could argue that in early or small units—small communes, small enterprises, the family and the classroom for the little child—the norm in authority relations is the "personal" superior. His legitimacy depends, however, not merely on
his individual qualities ("personal authority") but also on the fairness of the rules

First, there are factors distinctive to the *style of political authority*. Some of the features Crozier analyzed in general terms are accentuated in the political sphere. The negative and brittle character of associations, the difficulty in cooperating and reaching compromises that do more than confirm respective statuses are usual features of French political parties (with the partial exception of the extreme left). Especially true of French parties and interest groups is a tendency to try to obtain what they want by blackmailing higher authority. Hence the resort to a frequently "revolutionary" vocabulary that conceals far more limited intentions yet reveals a general attitude toward change (all or nothing) and authority (defiance and dependence). The lack of communication between strata, the distance between each stratum and higher authority, are characteristic of a political regime in which the citizens elect representatives who tend to behave as a caste of sovereign *camarades*.

But French history and the divergences among Frenchmen concerning political legitimacy have also introduced three features that are *peculiar* to the political sphere. The most obvious is addiction not merely to revolutionary talk, but to violence. In other words, the degree of willingness to observe the rules of the game when the results fail to give satisfaction is low. Also, the centralizing efforts of the *ancien régime,* the work and ideology of the Revolution, and the mistakes made by the post-1815 monarchies injected into the whole political sphere a special kind of equalitarianism. Crozier is concerned only with equality within each stratum (otherwise determined to preserve its rank privileges). But authority patterns in the political sphere are distinguished by national equalitarianism, that is, an insistence by most of the population on, and the superior authority's somewhat grudging acceptance of, the dogma of equality before the law, irrespective of social privileges. Hence the existence of *le Peuple,* which does not mean the "presence" of the people as participating citizens in a democratic civic culture, but suggests an aspect of universal suffrage that is important even for elites and leaders fundamentally hostile to what Tocqueville called democracy: that it is impossible to act in the political sphere as if the various strata were completely isolated from each other and political decisions involved only certain select groups of society (this is why one finds a plebiscitarian component even

---

he makes or transmits, on his being part of a hierarchy of general, impersonal rules. In these units, the personal link affords relief from the anonymity and rigidity of the rules, and the rules protect the subject from the personal arbitrariness of his superior. In larger and later organizations, the heavy costs of personal dependence are eliminated, but the "parallel" relations—last preserve of the "aristocratic" values of prowess and seduction—remain as an escape from anonymity and inflexibility.

in the most antipopular movements). The third feature is a nostalgia for unanimity and consensus—a by-product of equalitarianism, a reaction against the curse of violence.

All those features point in the same direction: to the fragility of "routine authority." It is challenged, pressured, milked by groups that offer more stress than support, more resistance than service; exercised over citizens used to violence, distrustful of privileges for the neighbor, and yet reluctant or unable to handle their own problems; torn between expectations of over-all equalitarianism or unanimity that render the continual resort to "parallel relations" illegitimate, and demands for special protection and favors that make them indispensable. "Routine authority" is bound to be excessively abstract, unimaginative, distant, and sclerotic. In other words, the "revenge" aspect of heroic leadership is bound to be especially important. "Throughout French political history . . . there have been two 'tempers' which may be called Jacobin and Girondin: each can be found at the same time or in rapid succession in every sector of French opinion. It was the Jacobin temper which the parliamentary game left out." [11]

One must take into account the *nature of the political system* itself. Limiting ourselves to the Third and Fourth Republics, we can fill in the framework in the following fashion. Certain features reinforce the conclusions derived from our study of the style of political authority. The institutional setup of the parliamentary Republics afflicted "routine authority" with a kind of anemia that went far beyond the general weakness described in Crozier's model. The reason for this was to be found in the ideological divisiveness of French political life. Given the framework of the French style of authority, French parliamentarianism was probably the only way of insuring the peaceful coexistence of clashing ideologies. Nevertheless, the number and nature of the parties (shaped either for the mere occupation of power or for sterile opposition); a deliberative rather than representative Parliament concerned with general principles rather than reform; impotent cabinets; the need to govern *au centre* almost all the time; multiple brakes and no motor—all this made "routine authority" almost a caricature of Crozier's model.

The structure of the two Republics allows one to present what the French would call a *portrait-robot* of the kind of leader who would succeed best in a system of that sort. One could call him the nondirective leader, the perfect broker, and compare him usefully not to executive leaders in other political systems, but to successful legislative leaders in a highly decentralized assembly such as the United States Senate. What he needs is a certain indifference to policy outcomes, resignation to letting events impose decisions which can then be "sold" as inevitable (instead of risking trouble by suggesting decisions which anticipate events), a Byzantine respect for ritual, inexhaustible patience for bargaining with a wide variety of groups, scrupulous observance of the dogma of equality among members of Parliament and of the sacrosanct distance between them and the electorate (that is, no appeal to the people above the heads of the parliamentarians)—to make sure that, should he be overthrown, he would not be ostracized later. He needs, finally, the art of manipulating the "parallel relations," knowing how to use the key men who, behind the façade of impersonal equality, nevertheless have their hands on the levers of influence. Smooth unobtrusiveness, self-effacing procedural skill, flexibility, what the French call *astuce*—these are the functional requirements of "routine authority": we recognize men like Camille Chautemps, Henri Queuille, Edgar Faure (until he asserted himself and dissolved the Assembly in 1955) and even Briand or Blum.

However, the institutional setup and political formula of the Republics also presented features that gave to their routine authority a resilience that somewhat alters the routine-and-crisis pattern suggested by Crozier. Routine authority, despite its tendency toward paralysis, nevertheless functioned, and the two parliamentary Republics showed a remarkable aptitude for self-preservation. The colorful deadlock of parliaments and cabinets should make us forget neither the bureaucracy, grinding out impersonal rules at a distance from the public and also taking part in the game of parallel relations, nor the consensus on which the Republics rested. Among social groups and political forces, beneath all the ideological differences about the ideal society and the best regime, there was a broad consensus favoring a limited state, congruent with the prevailing style of authority; *in most circumstances,* a career bureaucracy together with a parliamentary system more adept at checking than at moving that bureaucracy corresponded exactly to what was desired. Legitimacy was conditional; to most social or political groups and forces the regime was acceptable as long as its activities left intact their sphere of independence while settling conflicts to their satisfaction. And this was precisely what happened most of the time. The political formula produced a political class diverse enough to appease the characteristic equalitarianism of the political sphere; the setup admirably divorced equalitarianism from social reform and thus pleased most groups and parties, at the same time condemning those that wanted change to play the homeorhetic game, i.e., to ask for all or nothing (thus usually playing into the hands of those who wanted nothing). As a result, the political system was informed with a sense of legitimacy that disappeared only in major crises where the conditions for legitimacy ceased to be met.

In certain kinds of emergencies the system was even capable of injecting into "routine authority" a certain amount of efficiency for a while. This temporary closing of the ranks was essentially defensive: the Third Republic managed to defend itself against attacks from outside authorities threatening the regime. Two kinds of techniques were used. One was attrition: attracting the enemy into the game—into Parliament—where he would spend and waste his energies and means of action; this was a gentle death, and it worked against most antiparliamentary movements. The other technique, used against both antiparliamentary movements and against foreign powers or domestic forces of subversion that operated outside the political sphere, was to get everyone to agree to back a trusted parliamentarian and burden him with the responsibility of eliminating the threat: René Waldeck-Rousseau, Georges Clemenceau, Raymond Poincaré, Gaston Doumergue, Édouard Daladier, Guy Mollet received such temporary delegations of effectiveness.

When less extraordinary threats or strains, instead of being resolved by the political system, resulted in deadlocks among the parliamentarians, hence in the fall of the government, the system resorted to the "cabinet crisis," a mechanism of considerable interest, well analyzed by Williams. It was part and parcel of "routine authority" insofar as it aimed at and usually succeeded in avoiding the switch to crisis leadership, followed ritual rules that reflected the structure of the parliamentary game, and resulted in frustrating foes and defusing threats rather than giving a new impulse to society. Yet the cabinet crisis was in a small way a kind of crisis leadership, insofar as it resulted in a (temporary) resolution of deadlock and achieved this largely through "parallel relations."

I seem to have derailed from the track of heroic leadership onto the sidetrack of routine authority. But it remains true that heroic leadership can only be understood by reference to its counterpart. The nature, resilience, and deep roots of routine authority in France explain in particular the following propositions.

Within the parliamentary regime there was occasional room for limited executive authority, as long as its temporary trustee respected the style and rituals of parliamentarism. But any attempt to act "heroically" within the confines of the regime was bound to fail: the hero would be stifled and his leadership could unfold only when the formal procedures had collapsed altogether. In the earlier period of the Third Republic, the depressing fate of Gambetta had been instructive enough. And in the twentieth century, the parliamentarians' resentment of Clemenceau's wartime style was effective as soon as peace returned. More recently, nothing has been more enlightening than what happened to de Gaulle and Mendès-France's attempts to combine a style of heroic leadership with opposition to and within the Republic:

both the RPF and the Radical party turned from vehicles for their leaders' return to power into splintering, fiercely negative organizations, leading a short, nasty, and brutish life, torn between job-seekers ready to be absorbed in the "system" and hyperbolic champions of *la politique du pire,* reduced to proving their existence through their capacity to destroy.

The tension between routine and crisis authority is greater in the political sphere than in the rest of French society. The resilience of routine political authority explains why resort to a different kind of leadership is postponed until a situation breeds something like a national sense of emergency, a conviction that there is no other alternative. This, and the peculiar weakness of normal leadership, explains why heroic leadership is met with chiliastic hopes that facilitate change. It is worth noting that the emergency of 1940, the greatest in modern French history, engendered not just one but two rival heroic leaders. This kind of charged atmosphere and these large hopes induce a violently emotional repudiation of routine authority. Yet this very repudiation condemns the heroic leader to a perpetual quest for a legitimacy of his own, and makes his singularity a prison.

Insofar as the political system merely exaggerated features of the national style of authority and represented the wishes of most social "consensus groups" and most political forces, heroic leadership, although free from the special limits imposed by the "games, poisons, and delights of the system," still had to pay heed to the inherent limitations of that style, those desires, and those wishes.

If we try to define the relations between French heroic leadership and the style of authority and the political system, we come to the notion of a vicious circle in French heroic leadership, for it perpetuates the style and preserves within the political system a tension between two extreme types of authority, which fight yet need each other.

Heroic leadership is the statecraft of an "outsider" who cleans Augeas's stables so that Augeas does not have to do what he hates above all—getting involved, alienating what he considers his right to privacy, to independence, to (vigilant) absence. Heroic leadership arrives when change can no longer be delayed. But what it provides is direction without mobilization, and the citizens who are led respond with support yet without participation. The unwritten contract of French patterns of authority is respected, the bonds and trust of democracy *à l'anglo-saxonne* and the bondage and terror of totalitarianism are avoided. Heroic leadership is indeed a *spectacle*—the leader has the double prestige of rebellion and prowess: he reasserts individual exploits after and against the impersonal, anonymous grayness of routine authority.

Yet the spectacle itself is part of the whole drama of French authority, for the leader performs in a way that perpetuates nonparticipation —he turns the show into a monologue addressed to the whole people, instead of channeling the structured participation of his supporters in either totalitarian or democratic "face-to-face" organizations, and his "personal power" confirms his adversaries in their own purely *negative* associations and in their distrust of strong leadership. As Pitts has incisively suggested, "prowess is created by the recognition of the spectator as much as by the actions of the hero." [12] Equality—that constant value—is preserved, since the hero addresses himself to all the spectators indiscriminately; independence—the ultimate value—is preserved, since prowess is a mode of "seduction," not participation: heroic leadership is a thing to be admired (passively) or imitated (individually). To be sure, it establishes a theatrical *face-à-face* between the leader and his people; yet it perpetuates *la peur du face-à-face,* if by *face-à-face* we mean the direct bargaining and involvement of democracy. De Gaulle did not try to organize a political force of his own until after his resignation in 1946 (even then he called it a Rally, not a party); and Mendès-France's battle to gain control of the Radical party began only after he had been overthrown in February 1955.

At first sight, it seems as if each heroic leader, although unable to break the pattern of distance and noninvolvement, should at least be able to violate the other chief value—the preference for homeorhetic change—since there are no brakes on him. The authority patterns of heroic leadership seem a triumph of *le bon plaisir,* manifest both in the mass (or mock) equalitarianism of the *spectacle* and in the important extralegal systems of parallel personal relations behind the scenes, where the decisions are made. Yet brakes exist, for leadership (like power) is not merely an attribute, it is a relationship. There is no effective leadership without support. And support is facilitated when the forms of impersonality and the *respect des droits acquis*—i.e., respect for the hierarchy of ranks and statuses—are observed. Here is where the bureaucracy comes in again: preserver of the basic trend behind the wild zigzags on the parliamentary fever chart, it is also the regulator and routinizer of heroic leadership. One cannot contrast a representative and an administrative tradition [13] in French political history, because the administrative reality behind the changing political façade is permanent. What varies is the way the administration operates. In "representative" periods—which are the routine—it receives some impulses and is submitted to stringent checks from a distrustful and stalemated political class. In "savior" periods, some of the checks are lifted and the impulse is invigorated (yet still tends to translate itself into general rules). Support would disappear and heroic leadership would be pitifully checkmated if the leader forgot the formidable capacity of opposition of the various "strata" to schemes that promote the "wrong" kind of change: French society dispenses its antidotes to totalitarianism along with its resistance to voluntary participation. This explains why, behind the proud façade of rule by fiat and self-inspiration, the heroic leader is often as frustrated as his despised "routine" predecessors, obliged to coax, bargain, and compromise, to rule by "equivocation, prevarication, and slow elimination of every alternative." [14] Vichy's labor policy, de Gaulle's handling of the Algerian war, the contrast between Vichy's official views of industry and the actions undertaken, the dismissal by the Fifth Republic of most of the reformist suggestions made by the Rueff-Armand Committee, the educational and regional reforms in the Fifth Republic made before the fateful spring of 1968, the miners' strike in 1963 are cases in point. Heroic leadership likes to cloak itself in de Gaulle's stentorian phrase: *le pouvoir ne recule pas.* As a witty critic put it, reality is different: *le pouvoir ne recule pas, il circule.* The vigilance of the "strata" also explains why a revolt against heroic leadership can occur. In May 1968, de Gaulle faced a revolt by groups worried about their status and protesting against the current mixture of public *immobilisme* and detrimental state interference. In April 1969, even his mild reformism appeared threatening to many.

This impression of a vicious circle is reinforced if one considers the relations between heroic leadership and the political system. The drama of French heroic leadership lies in its symbiotic relation to the political system it denounces—like the two mortal foes handcuffed to each other in the agony of Death Valley, in Erich Von Stroheim's classic *Greed.* This drama takes the form of a quest for legitimacy. Both Pétain and de Gaulle were determined to be properly christened by the Republics they intended to lay to rest—and the wretched parliamentarians were willing to sprinkle the waters on their assassins' brows. The parliamentarians endorsed charisma both because by preserving "the silken thread of legality" [15] they wanted to remind the heroic leaders of their limits and because they saw them as protection against others who would be less respectful of the French way of authority: the advocates of a single party on the Nazi mold in July 1940, or the paratroopers in May 1958. Regarding the heroic leaders, their insistence on receiving a proper delegation was, *nolens volens,* recognition of the essential legitimacy of the fallen regimes—as if the new legitimacy they wanted as a direct verdict of the nation would be incomplete without legality, i.e., without the endorsement of the previous regime. Even the de Gaulle of the Resistance years, eager though he was to make a clean break with the fallen Third Republic, ended by reviving its parties in order to gain a full measure of internal and international legitimacy.

A second, and more important, aspect of the symbiosis between the

new regime established by the heroic leader and its routine predecessor is that the former is plagued by being basically uninstitu-
tionalizable. It is hard to overcome the contradiction between regular
leadership and heroic leadership: the heroic leader comes from the
depths of history to give a solo performance of patriotic prowess—and
insures by his acts that regular leadership after him may well, in
reaction against him, not be leadership at all. Both the Vichy regime
and de Gaulle's Fifth Republic were marked by a permanent concern
about legitimacy: neither the endorsement of the prior regime nor the
plebiscites of the crowds seemed to suffice. De Gaulle's fatal referendum of April 1969 was at least as much an attempt to rekindle the
legitimacy which the events of May 1968 had doused, as an attempt to
gain approval for specific reforms. Characteristically, legislative elections, however triumphal, do not end the quest for the Grail. Both
Pétain and de Gaulle tried to find security and solace in arguments
that nonetheless underlined the fragility of the construct: one was that
the leader had a "historical" legitimacy deriving from his past deeds,
another that the services rendered by the new regime gave it legitimacy (in other words, legitimacy is once again conditional).

To the problem of legitimacy we may add that of transition: of how
to move back from heroism to routine. By 1943, Pétain, having
reached the end of the frayed rope that had tightened around his
neck, wanted to give power back to the very Parliament that had
blessed him and that he had disgraced. De Gaulle's first exercise of
power ended in his resignation, and there was a total restoration of the
"routine" political system. In his second regime, he tried to build
something that would preclude any return to the old routine, especially through the procedure of popular election for the President, and
the transition to Pompidou, in 1969, was assured with remarkable
smoothness. Yet it is still far from clear whether his system will not
some day turn out to be a façade behind which a new restoration will
triumph, or will not be dismantled by opponents victorious after long
frustration. For the Fifth Republic to depart from the traditional pattern, what is required is something like a realization of Gaston Defferre's concept of 1965 (it was largely inspired by men such as Crozier):
the President as leader of a majority party or majority coalition. But
the prerequisite is an end to splintering, and though Pompidou won
with such a formula four years after Defferre's fiasco, France is still far
from accepting this unanimously. De Gaulle's conception was simple,
fierce, and self-fulfilling: since French parties are hopelessly splintered
and condemned to behaving like "delinquent peer groups," the President must be "the nation's man." This would not really end the oscillation from parliamentary regime to "savior," but it would institutionalize the savior. The trouble was that treating the parties as

delinquents helped to keep them that way—negative associations concerned with winning power and excluding others from it—and the regime's parliamentary features offered enough chances for deadlock to justify fear of either an "escalation" into dictatorship or a return to routine impotence. If the party system deteriorates (i.e., if the Gaullist coalition explodes) or fails to reform further (i.e., if the Left fails to match the considerable transformation and regrouping on the Right), or if on the contrary a united Left, under Communist guidance, successfully challenges the constitutional system and cripples its Presidency; if finding a "nation's man" at regular intervals is impossible (the notion of criteria for charisma is somewhat elusive!), then all the provisions of the Constitution will be useless to stop the Presidency from fading back into the blurred blandness of Third and Fourth Republic premiers. De Gaulle, who in 1962 believed that the popular election of the President was a sure deterrent to such a decline, in December 1965 proclaimed almost desperately that constitutions were mere "envelopes" and that the condition of the political parties made him, de Gaulle, a continuing "national necessity." But the heroic leader cannot become immortal, and all "heroic" regimes recurrently tamper with their constitutions so as to ease a transition back to "normalcy." It had been the case with both Napoleons. The Fifth Republic had three constitutional referendums under de Gaulle, in 1958, 1962, and 1969.

The return to normalcy has now, for the first time, been less than tragic. The two Napoleons ended in national disaster, Pétain's regime in the horrors of insurrection and invasion, but de Gaulle's regime broke out of the vicious circle. Still, as the momentous year from May 1968 to April 1969 showed, the difficulty remained: heroic leadership in France is connected too closely with a cataclysmic sense of emergency and with the notion of "total" transformation to handle a process of gradual evolution easily and well. Napoléon III tried—by a gliding descent into parliamentarism—and failed. Almost by definition, a *gaullisme des tempêtes* looked better than a *gaullisme de croisière,* but when the latter sailed into the tempest of May 1968, the French people first turned to de Gaulle for shelter, then moved away from his old way of calling on and taming tempests, and from his newer, brisker *vitesse de croisière.*

III. The Style of Heroic Leadership

My preceding remarks offer a very rough indication of what heroic leadership is like in France. Here I want to sketch in more detail some of the main features of its style.

When I say that the heroic leader is, with reference to "routine authority," the outsider, I mean this in two different ways. He tends to be a man who has not played the political game, either because he has had little contact with it (an indispensable factor if the crisis that brings him to power amounts to the collapse, and not merely the stalemate, of the regime) or because he has shown impatience with its rituals and rules. He is thus in strong contrast to, say, a Roosevelt or even Churchill. Pétain and de Gaulle fitted the first category: although both had had governmental experience before June 1940, this merely heightened their sense of power and their distaste for the crippling conditions imposed by the Third Republic on its exercise. The second category includes Clemenceau, who was called to head the war government of 1917 precisely for the qualities that had made him obnoxious to his colleagues in peacetime, and Mendès-France, who had been a sharp and intransigent (if loyal) censor of the Fourth Republic until the Dien Bien Phu emergency brought him to power.

Moreover, the heroic leader has been a rebel against the prevalent order of things or the prevalent ideas. When those ideas are believed or proven to be bankrupt and the order breaks down, he has the kind of prestige that best fits in with French notions of authority—prestige that comes from defiance, from nonconformity, from not having participated in the errors of the evil way. His personality and behavior have shown that he has the necessary ingredients for heroic leadership: he has maintained his independence from superior authority, he has said no, he has been right when such authority was wrong, and he usually suffered for it, either through setbacks to his career or through temporary withdrawals from the public scene.[16]

And yet there is a difference between being "out" and being an adventurer, between defiance and nihilism, between being outside routine authority and being outside the over-all pattern of French authority. The French turn to heroic leaders when there is no "normal" alternative, but their selection of a hero is not haphazard. Clemenceau had been in the wilderness through much of his career—yet he was a former Premier and tested leader. Mendès-France had resigned with *éclat* from de Gaulle's cabinet in 1945 and mercilessly denounced the colonial and economic policies of de Gaulle's successors —yet he was in many ways a devoted servant of the parliamentary Republic and the Radical party. Pétain's military career before 1914 had suffered from his advocacy of a defensive strategy at a time when the high command was wedded to the offensive—yet he had become one of the military glories, a minister, and ambassador of the Republic. De Gaulle's career had known rough days for reasons inversely symmetrical to Pétain's—yet he too had tried to gain influence through the ordinary channels, not in plots against them. True, the temporary twostar general of 1940 literally stepped out of France's institutions and exerted a brand of heroic leadership—pure, unbound, and self-made —that is unique in French history; but his success in rallying the Free French and the Resistance around himself was due not just to his character and his statecraft. The rebel hero was not *n'importe qui;* he had served (however briefly) in the cabinet and had had a distinguished (if difficult) career. He was admirable, but he was also respectable. One might suggest that there is a rapprochement between this willingness to endorse and applaud rebellion when the rebel seems not only vindicated but in other ways "notable," and the tolerance of adolescent rebellion because one knows it is a prelude to adult conformity.

With respect to heroic leaders' beliefs, we find some interesting features that contrast with those of the "routine leaders." To begin with, there are areas of unshakable dogmatism: a conviction of possessing certain truths, the triumph of which is the condition of France's salvation and the purpose of one's leadership. Indeed, it is worth scrutinizing the words of leaders like Pétain, Mendès-France, and de Gaulle for their references to perdition and salvation, for expressions of their therapeutic approach—France being a beloved patient badly treated by puny quacks but at last to be cured by a doctor who knows exactly what is wrong and what is to be done. To be sure, each leader had his own dogmas, and each one was capable (or had to show himself capable) of flexibility in action. Yet Pétain's austere doctrine of authoritarian regeneration through suffering and the restoration of rural values, de Gaulle's doctrine of a strong state engaged in a permanent struggle for greatness on the world scene, Mendès-France's doctrine on the primacy of economics—all contrast with the skepticism of many parliamentary premiers and the willingness of many other leaders with principles and ideals to set them aside when they came to power.

Partly because of their previous experience of having been right and unrecognized, the heroic leaders' image of themselves is a peculiar blend of self-orientation and identification with a cause. Self-orientation is hardly limited to heroic leaders—French politicians' capacity to project their personality onto the center of the stage and to discuss issues in terms of the issues' effect on their own psyches is remarkable. But there is a difference between the narcissism of Édouard Herriot or Léon Blum and the vanity displayed by heroic leaders. The vanity of Pétain, de Gaulle, or Mendès-France was not narcissistic but active and self-transcending; each one saw himself as the carrier of a message greater than himself. Mendès-France, the least vain of the three, had serene confidence in his own ability; Pétain "gave his person to France in order to alleviate her misery"; de Gaulle turned himself into a "somewhat fabulous character" whom he discussed in the third person, who was clearly the agent of destiny and whose moves had to be carefully thought through precisely because they shaped France's fate.

This self-perception accompanies a coldly or caustically harsh perception of the nonheroes: in all three cases, there is an undeniable sense of superiority. Mendès-France once confided to the deputies that France had been unlucky in some of her leaders before him. Pétain's treatment of his opponents, his indifference to the personal fate of his followers, his obvious lack of sympathy for individual members of the elites he was trying to shore up collectively were not just symptoms of that "shipwreck," old age. And de Gaulle's way of using his own followers as instruments or treating them as part of the "heavy dough" he had to knead—a "king in exile" attitude detected by one of his superiors at an early age [17]—the haughtiness that froze the ardor of so many *résistants* when they met him for the first time needs no elaboration. We have here a clue to their personalities, too: nongregarious men who exhibit in different degrees that melancholy so well described by de Gaulle, the most self-analytic and gifted of them; a propensity to solitude in the midst of action, as well as proud and bitter solace once duty has been performed. After all, it is perhaps fitting that heroic leadership should be exercised by men who are loners by personality as well as origin.

The political behavior of heroic leaders seems to display a permanent contradiction.* There is, on one hand, the aspect of revenge I have often mentioned—the repudiation of and reprisals for the routine pattern and its servants. On the other hand, there is a nostalgia for unanimity and reconciliation. This nostalgia is in a way related to the revenge, since the routine pattern is blamed for being divisive and for not having represented the "latent" general will, but it is partly contradicted by the exclusion of the "old regime" from unanimity. The drive for consensus, however vague, mystical or personal, is indispensable for marshaling support, since the heroic leaders shun the structured support provided by the ordinary means (parties and established interest groups) and would be at sea if faced merely with the hostility of discarded *notables*. The drive for punishment is also necessary; it gives the leader's most enthusiastic supporters a sense of accomplishment (as well as jobs), and it provides him with an argument whenever support wanes: "Do you want a return to the old mess?" Thus heroic leadership always seems to have two faces: a sectarian one and a Rousseauistic one, with the leader in a position comparable to Rousseau's legislator. In Vichy, the sectarian face was particularly evi-

---

* My observations here apply primarily to Pétain and de Gaulle. They are less true, or more unevenly true, of Mendès-France, largely because he operated within the constraints of the Fourth Republic; but to the extent that they do apply to him, they show how far he went in trying to distinguish himself from the pattern of routine authority.

dent, yet Vichy too had its myth of latent unanimity: it supposedly was reasserting "natural" community structures that had been hidden but never erased by the defunct Republican superstructures. De Gaulle's regime offered the clearest image of the two faces—constant flaying of the "parties of the past" and celebration of the "will of the nation," which they had not heeded. Mendès-France was not in a position to "punish" the political forces that had fought him, yet there was an element of vindictiveness in his relations with the MRP and with right-wing Radicals, and in order to get the indispensable support of the leaders of parties and interest groups, he too resorted to the myth of unanimity, thus putting (unsuccessfully) popular pressure on a restive Assembly.

Heroic leaders also tend to behave in a way that constitutes a pointed reversal of routine authority, even when punishment or revenge is ruled out. Whereas the life of the ordinary Premier is absorbed by a kind of pure game of politics—a perpetual process, engaged in by professional players—the heroic leader tries to make the public (presumably fed up with such politics) believe that he is not playing politics: the others are politicians, he is a statesman. (Vichy's official designation was *l'État français,* and de Gaulle's first decision upon his arrival in liberated Paris was to "put the State back in its center, which was of course the Ministry of War," before meeting the Resistance leaders in the Hôtel-de-Ville.[18]) Ordinary politics means a method rather than a set of goals, a procedure for making (or avoiding) decisions rather than the decisions themselves; the leader who aims at goals and lives for decisions denies that his policies are politics. To a social scientist, politics means difficult choices among values and difficult confrontations of ideas; the heroic leader, even when he proclaims that to govern is to choose, tends to propose to the public that *his* policies are a suprapolitical course of action dictated not by necessity, but by the higher good of the country. De Gaulle's "in the interest of France," Vichy's "eternal truths," even Mendès-France's *dossier* —facts and statistics leading to necessary conclusions—constitute three very different approaches to "depoliticization": in reverse order, an economist's version, a mystical (yet basically right-wing) one, and an astutely political one. Politics also means bargaining and the public banter of horse trading. The heroic leader tried to maintain a façade of rigorous hostility to such debasing procedures, although a great deal of private trading goes on behind the scenes. Pétain liked to announce "his" decision in trenchant terms and terse decrees when the incessant clashes of personal cliques and clans had temporarily halted. De Gaulle's disdain for negotiation, his preference for unilateral offers (and vetoes) to which others must adjust and which preserved the appearance of sovereignty, marked his handling of the Algerian war, indeed of all foreign policy; his transfiguration of bargaining into "arbitration," and even his paradoxical attempt to institute "participation" in *his* way, marked his handling of domestic affairs. Mendès-France, true enough, had to bargain more than he originally wanted to, and more still as his time in office ran out, but it cramped his style and proved the incompatibility between the "system" and his leadership. Routine authority is legitimate because of what it *is*, the heroic leader is legitimate because of what he *does*.

As one punster has put it, the style of such leadership is Caesarean. For ordinary premiers, politics is a French garden of rules and regulations where they move with caution; but the heroic leader, even when he observes the unwritten rules of French authority, refuses to be bound by the "ordinary" rules of the political system. Even Mendès-France, a normal Premier, tried to tell the National Assembly that he had his own conception of the executive, one that was quite incompatible with the rules of a game that made premiers the mice of parliamentary cats. Pétain violated outrageously the terms of the delegation he had received from Parliament. De Gaulle went even further, since he continually reinterpreted his own Constitution—always in the same direction and often in contradiction to the letter and procedures of the text—to reinforce the President's position.

Ordinary politics all too often mean the demise of responsibility: responsibility is dismembered and buried by the too numerous occupants of power, is repudiated by temporary leaders with a variety of reasons for wanting to appear as merely the executors of collective compromises or as the foster parents of "other people's children." The heroic leader seizes responsibility as a sword, instead of hiding behind the shield of committee procedures; he puts the spotlight on his acts and claims personal authorship even for measures actually instituted below him. Sometimes, these claims are pathetic and even repulsive, as with many of Pétain's punitive "decisions," actually initiated by his entourage or forced upon him by the Germans. Sometimes there is an aspect of deliberate and (again) spectacular provocation, as when de Gaulle personally took responsibility for vetoing Britain's entry into EEC instead of letting Macmillan's application get lost in the procedural side streets at Brussels, when he turned against Israel in 1967, when he called for a free Québec, and when he defied the rebellious French on May 30, 1968. The heroic leader tends to thirst for responsibility, just as the routine leader longs for absolution: Pétain's proud statement to his judges and de Gaulle's claim to all the social and economic reforms of the Liberation are cases in point. Ordinary men doubt and change their minds. The heroic leader acts as if he never hesitated and, when he writes—as de Gaulle did so abundantly—erases all trace of the roads he once thought of taking but did not, or took but abandoned.

Ordinary politics take place in a fishbowl, and the ratio of words to deeds is extraordinarily high. Heroic leaders certainly do not shun words, but the flow of explanations and justifications is thinner, and above all they depend to a high degree on secrecy and surprise. Secrecy and surprise are necessary ingredients of the spectacle, components of prowess, ways of renewing the alertness and applause of a people whose support is needed but whose participation is unwelcome.[19] Moreover, the obstacles found *below* the political surface, where the relevant "strata" resist change, oblige the heroic leader to resort to concealment and cunning, for he has to preserve the myth according to which past inefficiency was due only to the rules of the political game (the myth of heroic omnipotence), and he must be able to conclude deals and make retreats behind the scenes which, if public, would make the Emperor look naked—i.e., he must disguise the reality of his limitations. Mendès-France's steeplechase suspense in dealing with Indochina, Tunisia, and the European Defense Community (EDC) was both functional in the short run and dysfunctional (rather early) *à la longue,* in that it infuriated the parliamentarians, who were made to look silly. Because they had to fight heavy odds in constraining situations where candor could have been fatal, Pétain and de Gaulle resorted to ambiguity, cunning, and deviousness, often deceiving every group in turn. But when similar constraints confronted routine leaders, they usually could not even resort to that black magic: cunning may well be a resource of the weak, but the parliamentary premiers were *too* weak, and when they tried it they often could not control events. (One thinks of the sequels to Faure's devious dealings over Morocco in the summer of 1955—leading far more rapidly to independence than he had wished—or of Mollet's Suez operation in 1956.) Routine authority is characterized best either by blustering statements in sad contrast to the outcomes ("No German guns pointed at Strasbourg," "French Algeria forever," etc.) or by plaintive confessions of impotence ("We are condemned to live together," "My subordinates did not obey my orders"). Heroic leadership—and this speaks volumes for the tragic circumstances in which the French turn to it and for the limits within which the hero must operate—is characterized best by Mendès-France's month-long self-ultimatum for a Geneva settlement, and by de Gaulle's dazzling first words to the Algerian crowd: *"Je vous ai compris."*

A third aspect of the heroic leader's conduct concerns his behavior toward the citizenry as a whole, his quest for effusive unanimity, not revenge. Here we find one, but only one, feature common to our three statesmen. It is what might be called their constant call to collective prowess. Heroic leadership offers the spectacle of the hero defying the Gods, and it mobilizes the spectators' enthusiasm by presenting the performance as a national undertaking. So, to rally support, the hero makes a conscious attempt to promote the audience's identification with the character on the stage, thus wrapping his legitimacy in their complicity. This identification *ipso facto* evades the problem of organizing and channeling support: simply, each citizen is asked to feel like a hero.

In Mendès-France's case, the quip reported by Alexander Werth is eloquent enough: his heroic rush after deadlines, his swift successive confrontations with France's enemies and allies, his slayings of the domestic dragons of alcohol and "Malthusianism," *c'était du cinéma.*[20] But it would perhaps be more accurate to switch metaphors: it was like an Olympic race, for in Mendès-France's own attitude and in the behavior of his supporters there was something of the ardor, good humor, and grim earnestness of competitive sports (alas, it turned out to be a 500-yard race, not a marathon). In the antiquarians' dreamhouse of Vichy, built on the Maurrasian notion that the people had had altogether too much to say in recent French history, Pétain nevertheless made vigilant efforts to rally enthusiasm—by tear-jerking displays of the self-sacrificing old man's stigmata and by beating drums for the National Revolution. Here, the appropriate metaphor (derived from an oddly cheerful song of Maurice Chevalier) is that of workers who rebuild a fallen house under the guidance of the wise old master-builder. In the Fifth Republic, although the population was kept in a state of mental and emotional alert by de Gaulle's incomparable sense of personal drama—well-spaced and well-prepared public announcements, trips sublime or familiar, recurrent crises—there was always an effort to present his actions as the reaching toward and the unfolding of a "great undertaking," a *grande affaire,* a "national ambition." Here, the simile most congruent with the General's own idea of himself (or at least—given the man's complexity—his public version of his self-image) would be that of a modern Moses guiding his flock toward a (very misty) Promised Land.

The public conduct of the three men was quite different in other respects. Mendès-France's style was a fascinating, heterogeneous mix between the seemingly unavoidable style of French authority (expressed in his perception of self and others) and his own personal ideal, much closer to the model of democratic face-to-face discussions in a "participant political culture." There was tension between character and convictions: on one hand, the man himself maintained, especially toward his aides, the kind of distance that enhances mystery and a sense of fruitful solitude; his rigor and uncompromising austerity in matters of basic importance to him (such as the fight against the alcohol lobby) projected the image of a confident loner unburdened by friendships and foibles. Yet his very emphasis on *le dossier,* the simplicity of his fireside chats, his plain, flat way of stating the unadorned truth as he saw it, his preference for clear contractual relations between Parliament and Premier—as if the Fourth Republic could be turned into the British political system—suggested a very different political style, which his intelligence and democratic convictions admired, although his temper and training were not wholly fitted for it. The qualities of his temper and training contributed to his popular appeal, but also to his parliamentary downfall. Whether the citizenry was moved more by his attempt to treat them as rational human beings, entitled to a faithful accounting of public affairs by their trustee, than by his personality and prowess—and whether they were at all aware of a tension between Mendès-France's heroic activism and his aspirations to be merely effective—is impossible to know.

In the cases of Pétain and de Gaulle, no such tension existed. Mendès-France, for whom the problem of legitimacy was simplified by his being a regular Premier, could be satisfied with (and indeed democratically believed in) the self-evident eloquence of deeds. But Pétain and de Gaulle needed and wanted more. Conditional legitimacy based on achievements past and present is fragile—hence the effort to give it deeper roots by digging, so to speak, into the national psyche. Their style of heroic leadership represents a return to the mold of the *ancien régime,* adapted to modern circumstances: a baroque version of a classic style. Here, too, we find a sense of distance between the leader and the led. The two military men, like the Radical politician, were singularly unbending and ungregarious characters. But whereas Mendès-France struggled somewhat against this, Pétain and de Gaulle cultivated it: Pétain by developing (and letting his sycophants develop) a drooling cult of the idol who was "assuming" France's woes as a sacrificial priest; de Gaulle by rigorously following the precepts so exaltingly laid down in *The Edge of the Sword.* In both cases, there was a repudiation of familiarity, a cult of separateness from the herd, which somehow recalls the distance between the subjects and the King. Mendès-France wanted his popularity to be based merely on respect for things well done, although his precarious position required him to whip up respect by means of drama; Pétain wanted from the French the dependent love and anxious trust of children; and de Gaulle, cynical or contemptuous of love, preferred consent based less on reason than on awe. Mendès-France tried to mitigate the sense of personal separateness and the budding personality cult that grew around him by stressing his team. Pétain and de Gaulle tried to compensate the personal distance that removed them from the crowd with dips into the crowd and receiving delegations from the crowd, thus paying homage to the requirement of equalitarianism. But, as in the *bande,* "where," as Pitts has described it, "all members are equal in their common subordination to the leader," [21] this merely confirmed the purely personal, uninstitutionalized nature of leadership and the abyss between Him and Them: it was paternalism on a grand scale. In a homogenized community with rapid communications, these methods of personal command and contact accentuated the contrast between impersonal administration (including the anonymity of the ministers, *commis* who served the Leader) and personal responsibility, between impersonal immobility and personal action. They re-created the situation that existed when *le bon peuple* cursed the King's aides, saved its love for the King, and lamented *Si le roi savait!*

The natural milieu of French heroic leadership has always been monarchic: the two Napoleons established empires. Pétain transferred and transformed his 1917 technique of command by personal presence and appeal into a pseudomonarchy—with the cramped ceremonial of Vichy's Hôtel du Parc and the pomp of provincial tours, masses in cathedrals, dedications of symbolic trees, pictures of the Leader in every home, schoolchildren's letters to "le Maréchal" and food packages from him. De Gaulle (who inclined toward Louis XIV rather than Saint Louis) had his rites of press conferences, parades, receptions, and motorcades. They all cultivated mystery and cunning, in the best imitation of *le secret du roi.*

This half-instinctive, half-deliberate re-creation of an old tradition shows once again the two aspects of heroic leadership: repudiating one set of rules on behalf of personality, and framing personal power in a reassuring alternate set. Heroic leadership is original insofar as it accepts, develops, and exploits the plebiscitary implications latent in the *ancien régime* (a regime that once engaged in battle against the political power of the feudal elites, just as the heroic leaders battle the political power of "routine authorities"). It was the neglect and dessication of those plebiscitary possibilities that were largely responsible for the *ancien régime's* decline and overthrow. The *ancien régime* had become anti-equalitarian and too impersonal, just as routine Republican authority became too anonymous for crises; the enthusiasm for personal rule, which produced the leadership of Robespierre and Napoleon, today breeds personality cults around every potential heroic leader, however unrewarding (Pinay), chilling (de Gaulle), unworthy (Pétain), or reluctant (Mendès-France). Certainly, the French heroic leaders' approach to *la population* [22] differs from the resolutely anti-plebiscitarian "heroic leadership" of Spain or Portugal. It differs even more from totalitarian concepts of people or *Volk* (which require not just cheering spectators but structured, self-sacrificing slaves) and from the Republican notion of *le peuple* (unfortunately more a myth than an organized force). The heroic leader is neither the *peuple's* son (or rather the bourgeois' son) nor gang leader or big brother. He is a personalized king—without camaraderie or concentration camps.

A clue to the endurance of the classical style is provided by the two leaders' rhetoric. (In studying this rhetoric, one could also do a fine analysis of its contrasts with the less self-conscious flow of Republican eloquence and with the delirium tremens and ideological gobbledygook of totalitarianism.) Pétain (who rarely wrote the first drafts of his speeches) prescribed for himself a codelike simplicity and directness of style that seemed to dismiss all the impurities and excrescences grafted on the French language in the nineteenth and twentieth centuries; stark formulas worthy of medals and frontispieces were his form of eloquence—and, in a highly word-conscious nation, not the least of his appeals. De Gaulle's range was greater; where Pétain liked his sentences short and striking, de Gaulle indulged in long and complex phrases, as if to display his incredible memory—indeed, as his age increased, so did the length of his phrases.[23] Yet he too, so much addicted in other respects to Chateaubriand's precept of "leading the French through dreams," had a style closer to Corneille or Retz than Chateaubriand or Hugo: his fondness for archaic words and sentences that often seem translated from Latin gave an early seventeenth-century flavor to speeches that were (therefore) almost impossible to translate well. The fact that both men were educated by the Jesuits, steeped in classics, and worked on literary projects partly explains this, but only partly: de Gaulle's speeches as a statesman differed in style from his prewar writings; the older he became, the heavier the classic patina.

Imitative resurrection always finds a response in times of emergency: the strait-jacket state described by Richelieu is a natural refuge from and remedy for intolerable centrifugal forces. But it does not suffice to bring solace to the people or support to the leader, even with the full flowering of plebiscitary seeds. The *ancien régime,* before the "age of the democratic revolution," could afford to be nonideological, and its kings could be just statesmen (or weaklings surrounded by statesmen). As Charles X discovered, there are limits to mere restoration. What modern heroic leadership needs is not only the techniques of undifferentiated unanimity, which are within the realm of means, but also a grandiose sense of purpose. The heroic leader, to use Max Weber's distinction, must be both statesman and prophet; his dogmas serve him well, and if his dogmas are too sketchy or too dry, he must somehow wrap them in a prophetic vision. The classicism of the statesman must be united with a prophetic romanticism. The literary style, to be most effective, should convey all the allusions and associations of France's golden classic age; the modern heroic leader must rule by the romantic resonance of his language as well as by the weight of deeds. Even Mendès-France, least romantic of men, communicated a vision of economic progress, social change, efficiency, and fraternal "concert" that, in the cesspool climate of 1954, attracted those perpetual seekers after romantic causes, the young and the intellectuals. Even Pétain, flayer of ideology and foe of romantic disorder, tried to be a quaint sort of prophet: the prophet of a return to *"une francité archaïque,"* [24] the awakener of a romanticism of youth camps, physical fitness, folkloric revival, imperial duty, and agrarian utopia. And what was wartime Gaullism if not a prophecy of resurrection, a romanticism of patriotic exploits, an adventure against a formidable foe in order to save French honor, an epic of an unknown leader "too poor to bend," spiting the Allies in order to save France's future? If the second coming of Gaullism saw the prevalence of statecraft over prophecy, of stately prose over epic poetry, the prestige of the *Rex* of the 1960s still rested fundamentally on the myth and mystique of the *Dux* of 1940. And de Gaulle's foreign policy served a vision sufficiently sweeping and remote to be termed a prophecy.

IV. The Substance of Heroic Leadership

My analysis of the style of heroic leadership was aimed at elucidating the relation of heroic leadership to the style of authority and to the political system. I should like now to add the third variable—the nature and scope of tasks undertaken—and to evaluate the leaders' performances. For convenience's sake, I have divided these remarks into two categories: foreign and domestic policy. The importance of external policy for Pétain, Mendès-France, and de Gaulle justifies this division. After all, the heroic leaders were brought to power because of three international crises: catastrophe in 1940, defeat in 1954, deadlock in 1958.

Pétain, Mendès-France, and de Gaulle were nationalists, if not in the sense of men for whom the nation is the highest value and the top priority (this was hardly true of Mendès-France), at least in the sense of men for whom the circumstances of the times required that priority be put on national self-assertion. But there were other, deeper reasons for the nationalism. Heroic leadership means prowess; on the world stage, prowess and national self-assertion are twins. Moreover, for Pétain and de Gaulle, the quest for a legitimacy beyond personal deeds led, as we know, to a ritual that was inevitably nationalistic, insofar as it sought to remind the nation of its identity, to make its past relevant, and to reassure it of its permanence. Indeed, whether they originally intended to give precedence to foreign affairs or not, heroic leaders tend to find that a world stage of sovereign states provides opportunities for prowess and national mobilization which the domestic scene often denies.

In this respect, all three stand out in sharp contrast to the foreign policy of the Republics, which—at least since the turn of the century —tended to put so much importance on France's alliances that it often interpreted France's national interests in terms of her main allies' reactions. It has been pointed out most incisively [25] that de Gaulle's grating wartime insistence on national independence was a reaction against the Third Republic's excessive dependence on British support, which led to national paralysis during the Rhineland crisis and during the Spanish Civil War. Pétain's hostility to Britain may have had a similar origin. In both cases, one can go back to World War I: Pétain was, in contrast with Foch, most reluctant toward France's allies, and de Gaulle was a prisoner of war during the period that saw France become increasingly dependent on outside aid. But France's allies were not the only target. Even Pétain intended to protect Vichy France by means of a nationalist insulation that would allow her to emulate post-1806 Prussia—to rebuild her forces and play a major role after having preserved her empire and her fleet, either as a referee in a deadlocked war, or as a nonsubservient associate of a victorious but respectful Germany. As for Mendès-France, his acts in Geneva and Brussels seemed to defy the United States and to reverse commitments that many Frenchmen thought were damaging to French autonomy: hopeless rearguard actions overseas, and a scheme of European integration that benefited an economically stronger Germany. For Mendès-France in 1954 as for Pétain in 1940, domestic reform was a precondition for external success and a safeguard against external *effacement*.

Here the resemblance ends. A separate verdict on Mendès-France's external policy performance makes little sense. In some essential areas he acted as a "liquidator," [26] getting the best possible terms out of impossible situations (Indochina, German rearmament); he did not have time to see his initiatives (in North Africa, in relations with Britain) bear fruit, in "seven months and seventeen days." The conceptions were sound enough; execution, alas, was a matter of domestic politics, not diplomacy.

As for Pétain, his was a double tragedy: he was incapable of playing consistently the role he assigned himself, and it was impossible to fulfill the task; it was a bad performance of a "dysfunctional role." [27] Even within the limits of the armistice of June 1940, Pétain thought that there was some room left for external prowess. But the idea of playing Prussia to Hitler's Napoleon was a classic case of a misapplied analogy: Hitler was not Napoleon. He was determined to use the rump Vichy state as hostage, instead of letting it become a bulwark of strength. Moreover, Vichy's brand of cleverness all too often led to lamentable detours from the ideal path: instead of an uncompromising stand on the terms of the armistice, there were pseudo-Machiavellian attempts to reach the goal of French resurgence by anticipating German desires and offering "collaboration" to a victor who had not expected so much servility, however devious its intent. Tragically, each belated effort by Pétain to check the trend only increased Germany's leverage, made his position ever more "dysfunctional," and led to bigger surrenders. From the conservative viewpoint of saving French physical substance, something can be said for Pétain (although not decisively). From the perspective of his own ambition, it is a terrifying case of misheroics careening into antiheroics. The conception was wrong, the execution worse; on both counts, Pétain's statecraft was a wretched failure. National self-assertion had led to ignominy: having endangered the national identity he had wanted to preserve, Pétain payed the price of losing whatever legitimacy he had had.

De Gaulle's foreign-policy performance is a much more ambiguous subject, to be treated in detail in later chapters. But, from the viewpoint of heroic leadership, I should like to make two observations here. One concerns the nature and scope of the tasks de Gaulle set for himself. In his first period of power, he was after nothing less than an independent France returning to great-power status, present in the postwar settlements, and satisfying her security needs vis-à-vis Germany. It was a fascinating mixture of a hopeless attempt at restoration and a valiant attempt to mitigate the bad effects of the irreversible rise of extra-European superpowers. There is little doubt that the successes exceeded the failures: the purposes de Gaulle set to himself—excessive, arrogant, or downright absurd though they seemed to many of his "counterplayers"—were to a considerable extent reached; some of the failures—in particular in colonial matters and in France's German policy—reflected a tendency in de Gaulle, otherwise so keenly aware of changes in world affairs, to minimize the significance of some important new developments (such as the weakening of empires by the war, and the "devaluation" of the Franco-German conflict by the incipient cold war and by nuclear weapons). It was as if, in developing the immediate requirements of his dogma, *grandeur,* the very precariousness of France's situation led him to believe that a return to the requirements of the past was a prerequisite to meeting the needs of the future. The "second" de Gaulle's analysis of world trends strikes me as far more profound and provocative: his withdrawal from public life in 1953–58 had fascinating effects, and led both to policy renovations and personal growth. He seemed in that time fully to have absorbed the lessons of decolonization and the meaning of nuclear weapons for power, peace, and politics. His nationalism was still militant, but by universalizing it he gave a Jacobin, or left-wing, color to what had earlier seemed more like a set of right-wing, Poincaré or Bainville-like reflexes or legacies. His new aims were nothing less than to establish a new international system. *Grandeur,* of course, was still the goal; but his Fifth Republic policy objectives tried to adapt and reconvert *grandeur* to the changed and limited prospects of the new system. These objectives were not reached, and the events of 1968—France's financial troubles after the crisis of May plus the Soviet occupation of Czechoslovakia—made the vision seem out of reach. Yet the final fiasco was more a setback than a total disaster—the whole vision was so boldly long term that it would be rash to call it unrealistic—and even if the new system remained elusive, de Gaulle had succeeded in drastically changing the balance of French burdens and assets in world affairs, by comparison with the Third Republic after 1918 and with the Fourth Republic.

In both instances, there were remarkable aspects to the Gaullist performance itself. One often had the sense of a contradiction between conception and execution (apparently an old problem with de Gaulle [28]); the brutality of the performance detracted from the achievement of the purpose. (Consider, for example, the discrepancy between his behavior toward FDR and his purpose of returning France to great-power status, which required U.S. support; or between his vision of a "European Europe" and his unilateral acts that contributed to prevent the emergence of any united Europe at all.) Yet these contradictions can be explained. On the level of the issues, one can argue that whereas the performance was dysfunctional in the short run, it had at least a "Caesarean" chance of being functional in the long term—through the effects of the shock produced by plunging a surgical knife in at the right point. Behavior more immediately functional would really have been dysfunctional: meekness toward the United States would have resulted not in support but in dependence; European integration would have meant either a paralyzed or an "American" Europe. On a deeper level, vision and performance were inseparable. Fulfillment of the vision is always distant, seldom perfect, never complete, but the satisfaction of the hero and the pride of the spectators must be achieved in the performance itself. When success is never full or safe, example matters more than triumph. A brilliant, even if not immediately successful, act is its own reward; the achievement is the move, not its outcome. Apparent realization of the ideal in a way that seems to downgrade the performer would not be worth the trouble. We are in a universe of prowess. Whether such "illusionism" is "incongruent" with the present international system is a weighty matter and cannot be answered in any clear-cut way. But my own reading of the system suggests a great deal of congruence, and at any rate the performance was extraordinarily "congruent" with the French style of authority. Whereas de Gaulle, President of France, represented the authoritarian pole of the French style, de Gaulle, champion of French independence (as opposed to full participation or integration

in international alliances and agencies), represented exactly the opposite pole: celebrating the art of "drinking from one's own glass while
toasting all around," practicing the French technique of resisting and
obstructing would-be higher authority, accepting association (but
mainly of a purely contractual sort) to increase the nation's strength to
resist greater powers, defying devaluation of the franc. Domestically,
he tended to be *le pouvoir contre les citoyens;* in foreign affairs, he
was *le citoyen contre les pouvoirs.* The domestic monarch was an external *gavroche.*[29]

When we turn to domestic affairs, we find interesting lessons about
the interplay of the socioeconomic and political systems. All three
leaders were concerned with transforming France's socioeconomic system and two of them with overhauling its political system, but their
appeals and performances were extraordinarily different.

The simplest case is that of Mendès-France. He came to power
with a clear idea that economic reform was the key to all of France's
difficulties; in his speeches he talked as much like a professor as a political leader. But the irony of his turbulent sojourn in power was that
he was never able to do more than begin. He was never master of his
time. He had been chosen to cope with Indochina: this he did, and he
was duly praised for it by the National Assembly. But his determination to be more than an emergency "effective leader" within the confines of "the system" was his undoing. He did not have a stable majority behind his over-all program: he had to try to realize it piecemeal,
exploiting different *ad hoc* alignments and his capital of support while
it lasted. In order to reach what he deemed essential, he first had to
try to get more urgent issues out of the way. Thus he spent most of his
time on foreign and colonial issues because they were more pressing,
even though they were ultimately dependent, in his opinion, on the
economic *redressement* he was never allowed to launch. He had to hop
from issue to issue, instead of turning at once to his top priority—
economic reform—thus giving an impression of breathless discontinu-
ity. This was bad enough, in that it allowed his foes to wonder "where
he was going," but worse, his handling of EDC and North Africa cost
him the votes he needed for his economic projects; with each vote of
confidence forced on him by the swelling ranks of his opponents, his
majority, hence his effectiveness, declined. To be sure, he was often
clumsy in handling the deputies; [30] yet no amount of clever cajoling
would have been of much help, for Mendès-France not only wanted to
accomplish certain substantive things (not so different from what his
rival, minister, and successor Edgar Faure wanted), but he also
thought that the accomplishment would lose much of its worth and
substance if it had to be won through the laborious, devious, and
often humiliating devices of the system. Within the system, jobs could

be done in a certain way, but the performance was bound to look frayed and smell strange; yet within the system, heroic performance was impossible. To play according to the rules (as Faure did), issues would have to be delayed, distorted, or redefined until the cabinet majority reached a consensus, usually at the expense of effectiveness. This is precisely what Mendès-France wanted to avoid; in *his* game, fluctuating majorities shaping issue after issue were the only tolerable alternative to the impossible ideal world in which problems could be taken up in order of intellectual importance. He thus exhausted his credit; but he got some issues settled. After him, Faure also settled some issues; yet the way he did it made both the settlements and him look tarnished, and for all his skills he did not last much longer than Mendès-France.

Once out of power, Mendès-France's attempt to retain his charisma, his effective reputation as a leader for times of trouble, collapsed. One reason, as I have said before, was that there was no room in the political system for the kind of renovated Radical party he belatedly tried to build. It was impossible to turn that prize exhibit of "delinquent peer group" behavior, that machine for the occupation of power, into a stern and programmatic opposition.

An intense hostility arose against a man whose ideas seemed to violate the French notion of social change. In conformity with the idea that change is acceptable only when total, Mendès-France had presented his views in a most provocative and global fashion: "We are in 1788," he had said, and only a totally new approach to economic management would save France. And yet if one looks at his more specific suggestions, one sees that this apostle of budgetary reallocations, tax reform, productive use of resources, and colonial liberalism aimed not so much at moving France from one rather depressed plateau to a more exalted one, where the hierarchy of status and the vested interests would stay intact, but at demolishing some of the privileges and overhauling the hierarchy. Given these plans, his stress on total change hurt rather than helped; it sounded more like "uneven" total change than like that harmonious, massive shift of the whole which leaves relations among the parts intact. Anti-Semitism in France develops only against Jewish leaders who threaten "equilibrium"—Blum or Mendès-France, but not René Mayer. Among marginal producers—farmers or businessmen—and inefficient shopkeepers, and among wealthy *colons, mendèsisme* became a *bête noire*. Mendès-France's concept of his task clashed with the values of French society.

This would not have been fatal if his electoral base had been solid. A large mass of voters were either, in their dissatisfaction with the regime, floating from party to party, or else supporting conservative candidates without being so committed to the parliamentary regime that they preferred them to the right kind of an antiparliamentary "heroic leader," if one should emerge. Mendès-France could not count on too many of those votes, for most of this electorate was made of the social groups that felt threatened by him, and was ideologically hostile to or skeptical of the orthodox left-wing ideology he represented. He was a man of the Left, and much of the floating vote or the only "conditionally Republican" vote was a vote of the Right. In the elections of January 1956, most of these voters went to Pierre Poujade or stayed with the conservatives. The groups to whom Mendès-France appealed were largely committed to the established parties, and thereby lost to him: the MRP was his enemy, Mollet's Socialists were false friends, and his own Radical candidates were, in most cases, traditional Radicals rather than faithful *mendèsistes*.

To sum up: what Mendès-France wanted to accomplish in French society simply could not be done by a man of the Left within the French parliamentary system. When he re-emerged briefly, in May 1968, the absence of a power base prevented him from becoming the heroic beneficiary of de Gaulle's sudden fall from charisma: he was too much a statesman to be at ease, in the streets, with the *groupuscules,* and in the political arena he was crushed between Communist hostility and de Gaulle's masterful rallying of his supporters.

Marshal Pétain's domestic tasks were of two kinds: the establishment of a new political system and the creation of a new economic and social order. He failed on both counts, and not only because of the external circumstances or because of the difficulty any heroic leader meets when he tries to institutionalize his personal power. There was a deeper reason: in both realms, Pétain violated some of the most important canons of the French style of authority. In the beginning, he enjoyed extraordinary advantages. He could count on the support of all the forces of the Right that had become disenchanted with the Third Republic in the 1930s and who, after many disappointments with pseudoheroic figures, had been more or less impatiently waiting for their Godot. The collapse of left-wing parties—the suicide of the Republicans—left many of their supporters, already disenchanted with the Popular Front's fiasco, with no other resort than the old Marshal. And in some respects Pétain was the man of the hour. At the level of ideas and values, what he proposed seemed to represent exactly the preferences of most of French society, the lowest point of the trend to *repli* and stagnation characteristic of the 1930s. His views about the right kind of social order—"only the soil does not lie"— were the quintessence of the stalemate society: he was going to provide a magic that would prevent France's dissolution by the evil forces of industry (labor and big capital), urbanization, or experimentation; he was going to embalm it, by organizing it at last for the sake of its own protection and by purging it of all the political and social forces of drastic change. His masochism of regenerative suffering was simply the exaggeration of a theme often heard in the 1930s: that only through a period of insulation and self-concentration could France avoid the disintegration of its cherished "equilibrium." At the level of emotions and symbols, Pétain's appearance and speeches suggested the incarnation of a certain essence of France that had been submerged during the turmoils of the past century and a half: he was the Ancestor to whom one turned to escape from an unbearable present and a distasteful recent past, and whose appeals—of pathos and for solidarity—spread some warmth over schemes that were basically narrow, petty, and cold.

The dream of restoring and strengthening the stalemate society did indeed prove foolish. To be sure, Pétain's attempt to build a corporate society with rule-making powers in the hands of each functional body, his political system purged of politicians, fitted Crozier's model in that it intensified the distance between strata, provided each stratum with a higher authority to save its members from *le face-à-face,* and endowed each authority with impersonal rule-making attributes. But there were major violations of the unwritten rules.

First, French authority patterns show a permanent resistance to arbitrariness. But, especially in setting up Vichy's political system, Pétain gave revenge—purges, arrests, mushrooming political courts—*de facto* priority over the quest for unanimity, and gave reprisals priority over the demand for impartiality. Quick disenchantment, then hostility gripped his early supporters. This was disastrous. All heroic leaders need support, but few needed it more than the amateurs—admirals, generals, businessmen, local *notables* long discarded by universal suffrage—who had put themselves into positions from which the old political class was being expelled.

Another of Vichy's violations was that in the new political system as in the new social order, French equalitarianism was being trampled underfoot. Pétain's paternally indiscriminate forays into the crowds did not compensate for a government that seemed almost exclusively reserved for members of the authoritarian elites: the *boursier* was out, only the men with *réserves* were in, except for a few *arrivistes* like the ex-labor leader Belin. In Vichy's social institutions elitism was the rule (this was particularly so in the industrial Organization Committees and in the Labor Charter).

Lastly, and most serious, in the economic and social sphere Vichy violated the desire for "balanced," if total, change. Pétain and his advisers did not know how to distinguish between stopping the clock—as so many elements in France wanted—and turning it back. It soon became obvious that the regime's ideologues wanted, under the name of *retour au réel,* a flight back to a sort of Balzacian France; they emphasized a kind of decentralization that made sense if local issues or professional problems could be treated apart from national ones. The rehabilitation of the peasantry, rural *notables,* and small entrepreneurs, the glorification of the Catholic Church, a dislike for uprooted proletarians, adventurous businessmen, and civil servants (except those at the top): all these pointed to a somnambulistic belief in the reality of the unreal, next to which Mendès-France's faith in the "integral rationality of reality" appears positively sophisticated, and de Gaulle's assumption that *les réalités* are clear and simple to an unbiased mind seems self-evident.

Given those errors, Pétain's leadership could not escape from a basic dilemma. One possible policy was setting up the political and social institutions that his reactionary ruminations required; but they would be totally ineffective unless they actually worked in a direction opposite from the one he envisaged—preparing the stalemate society for the more dynamic and "concerted" experiences of the post-Liberation era.[31] Instead of embalming it, they would revive its circulation. Or the other possibility was that he might try to extend the scope and intensity of his power; but then arbitrariness would escalate, and his very ideal, a state that was authoritarian yet limited to the protection of a self-ruled society, would be shattered. A totalitarian Vichy would both increase resistance and violate its own precepts. The instruments Pétain selected, such as the Veterans' Legion and the youth movements, conformed to the pattern of emotional mobilization without political organization—and to the model of delinquent peer groups, primarily concerned with reporting misdeeds to the police or with the defense of their own interests. Too weak to be effective, they were cumbersome enough to be detrimental. Here, as in foreign policy, Pétain had set himself an impossible task, and here again the performance of a bad role was execrable. The old Ancestor, the living incarnation of the metaphoric "tree," was a senile man only intermittently lucid; the tree looked impressive, but it was dead.

De Gaulle's domestic leadership occurred in two very different periods. In the first, he set himself three main tasks: to unify the French resistance to the Nazis, to initiate measures of economic and social change designed to restore French power, and finally to establish a political system allowing for effective leadership. There were tensions between those tasks. The first he performed with intransigence (especially during the Giraud episode), cunning (using the political parties as a means of pressure against the Resistance movements), and masterful exploitation of what could have been a fatal flaw, his very outwardness. Not being connected with any organized political or social force made him a focal point instead of a nobody—a fact Roosevelt never grasped. He had to pay a price in order to succeed: he had to stay above all factions without any organized support all his own, bring the Communists into power, let the old parties re-emerge, and thus encourage the Resistance movements to create parties in turn. It was a cost that contributed heavily to his failure to carry out his third task. But he could not have even thought about the third, or performed the second, if he had not accomplished the first.

With the benefit of hindsight, we now see that de Gaulle's performance of his second task marked the beginning of the liquidation of France's stalemated socioeconomic system and associational life. The old consensus on the social order had broken down: the Resistance forces, largely composed of foes of or dissidents from the stalemate society, unanimously favored the measures de Gaulle advocated. The social groups most likely to be the victims of the reforms (essentially the *patronat*) were resigned to accept change as a substitute for the far more radical kind of purges the left and extreme left were talking about. In other words, de Gaulle (who remembered the lesson later) gave a kind of homeorhetic cast to changes which, although they stopped short of social revolution, created a permanently interventionist state: a state that guided more than it protected, that pushed France away from the structures and values of the traditional social system. The traditional style of authority was respected, insofar as the measures were taken from above, involved a minimum of *face-à-face,* were mostly impersonal, and maintained equalitarianism. (Indeed, it is because in one important respect he chose to be too noninterventionist, too traditional, that his objective there—social and economic reform for power—was not fully attained; this happened when he opted for René Pleven's laissez-faire finances over Mendès-France's austerity plan.)

The goal of institutional reform was not achieved at all, and this was precisely because de Gaulle had chosen to perform his other tasks. As "the symbol," as the champion of unanimity and the leader above factions, he could not *impose* his views: the parties he had encouraged and the movements he had tried to weld together filled the political vacuum left by Vichy. In a familiar swing of the pendulum, they reacted against both Pétain and de Gaulle by establishing a political system that was designed to be a bulwark against heroes. It turned out to be a barrage against leadership. De Gaulle, condemned to solitude, chose, in conformity with his conception of the hero, to get out before being thrown out or used up—for the hero who wastes his time hanging on where he can leave no mark is a fool.[32]

De Gaulle's second exercise of power was a very different enterprise.

The circumstances in which he came to power in 1958 were quite different: more like those of Pétain in 1940, but better. Like Pétain, de Gaulle in 1958 could count on an electorate that was disaffected with the Republic—voters who had supported the conservatives or had swung from one party to the other and were predominantly on the Right. But he also had the support of most of the parties: this made it easier and almost necessary for him to play his favorite role of unifier, instead of threatening revenge and punishment. So there was a large electorate available for a Gaullist party: he did not have to try, as in 1945–46, to rule above the vigilant heads of "politicians." Nor did he at any time share Pétain's illusion that one could manage a political system exclusively with social elites; indeed, many of those elites had been with Vichy, and his own standing with and feelings for them were never very good. Also, he was able to make his various tasks consistent with one another, and to be the master of his time. Now he could start with institutional reform; he handled the Algerian powder keg so that it lost much of its explosiveness thanks to political stability, economic expansion, and external successes, before he finally disposed of it.

De Gaulle's achievement of what he set himself as his first task—establishing at last the political system he had had in mind for so long—was both ambiguous and paradoxical. By preserving public freedoms, letting parties operate, allowing his own followers to create a Gaullist party, and manipulating the electoral system as well as the Constitution, he created until 1968 an effective political system for his purpose. There was opposition to him and his style, but no determined resistance either to the man or to the Constitution; and a Gaullist political class provided a transmission belt between the country and its leader. This class was largely comprised of a majority party (something the ideological *militants'* parties of the Left had never become), a nationwide "party of voters," comparable to America's parties (something that the center and right-wing collections of *notables* in France's parliamentary regimes had never been). On the other hand, the victory of the Gaullist forces was itself largely due to de Gaulle's constant attacks on the old parties, a fact that encouraged them in their determination to avoid a perpetuation of Gaullism after de Gaulle. The Gaullist party, invaluable in providing the Leader with a cooperative Parliament, was held at arm's length by this man hostile to all parties, and was devoid of any program other than following the leader. It thus tended to behave as the classic peer group, concerned primarily with being "in" and with keeping all others out—which raised the question of how it could survive after de Gaulle, being as it was far from homogeneous, and how the Presidency itself could survive, since de Gaulle had tried to keep it tied only to the undifferentiated "people" and divorced from the party system. As we have seen, if the Presidency stayed divorced from the party system, it risked constitutional deadlock, but if it became the plaything of parties eager to return to routine authority, it risked debasement. The Presidential Election of 1965 tarnished de Gaulle's personal halo yet gave him an institutional blessing, in a way routinizing an excessively "charismatic" rule. But the legislative elections of 1967 weakened and strained the Gaullist forces, revived the Left, and exacerbated its anti-executive itch.[33] Thus, suspense continued. The political system remained unsettled. This was in part because it had its own rules, different from those of the economic and social system, and was, despite all reforms, still perversely favorable to fragmentation; in part because the old style of political authority persisted. Indeed, it changed less than patterns of authority in the rest of society; at the political level there was less participation, less willingness to compromise and cooperate constructively, even less discipline than in the economic system. Insofar as it changed at all, it was in the direction of heavier centralization and weaker countervailing powers—more bureaucracy and more dependent, or more ineffective, local and professional *notables*.

It was the very disadvantages of this style, compounded by the flaws of heroic leadership, that turned the originally limited university troubles in Paris in early May 1968 into a national crisis. First, the *groupuscules,* then the unions, finally the opposition parties indulged in that kind of apocalyptic thought, revolutionary talk, and ideological stance which had been muted for several years by the homogenizing effects of industrialization, the soothing effects of economic growth and political stability. Since Parliament was irrelevant and the centralized administration was arrogantly isolated, the crisis developed primarily in the streets and caught the government unaware. In its early phase, de Gaulle left it up to the cabinet, in the hope that he would not have to commit his prestige. But the hesitations of his ministers made things worse: France was experiencing the disadvantages of both heroic *and* routine leadership. Once again, political authority had proved fragile. This time, the revolt was aimed at heroic, not routine authority, and one could see that heroic leadership had fewer institutional means of self-preservation than routine political authority.

But here is the paradox: the crisis which these flaws had produced ultimately turned near-disaster into success. First, heroic leadership, after faltering for almost four weeks, defeated its challengers through sheer force of personality: de Gaulle was not Louis-Philippe. Secondly, and unwillingly, de Gaulle helped to tilt the delicate and ambiguous balance of his regime from a charismatic/personal style to an institutionalized one. The election of a Gaullist majority on a platform of law and order, thanks to the efforts of Premier Pompidou, went a long way toward giving the majority coalition a modicum of autonomy—detaching it, at first almost imperceptibly, from its Founding Father, and suggesting to many Frenchmen that he was no longer indispensable, that his works could now live without him, and that chaos was no longer the alternative. Thirdly, the defeat of de Gaulle's referendum in April 1969 put a quiet and institutionally regular end to heroic leadership: it was not a mob on the streets but voters at the polls who ousted the hero. By prevailing in 1968, de Gaulle made democratic rejection of his leadership possible, instead of the cataclysmic rejection his opponents had hoped for. Moreover, his resignation had the remarkable effect of giving the Constitution, so often attacked when it seemed indistinguishable from him, a decisive seal of legitimacy. (Indeed, the rejection of his bill, with its massive and disparate constitutional revisions, can be seen as a vote for constitutional stability at last.) Finally, the election of Pompidou as de Gaulle's successor gave France its best chance for (although not assurance of) a synthesis. The President not only had a majority in Parliament but now was its actual leader. He had powers of "routine authority" never enjoyed under the previous Republics, yet neither the heroic mold nor the political concepts that had made de Gaulle's regime a solo performance. Out of his own defeat, de Gaulle snatched at least temporary victory for a political system he had both created and distorted by the very strength of his personality.

With respect to economic and social modernization for power, what is his legacy? Again we get an ambiguous answer. Before 1968, the liquidation of the stalemate society proceeded, and de Gaulle never hesitated to stress the imperatives of constant (not just cataclysmic occasional) change, the need for organized groups capable of cooperative action, and the duty of "public action to guide our economy." Nor did he refrain from doing what he had failed to do in 1945: hurt "established situations" and privileges by drastic financial measures. If he first enjoyed success in his role of modernizer,[34] it was partly because the ground had been prepared since 1945, and the wave of expansion, industrialization, and urbanization had been advancing for some years when he returned to power; all he had to do was to maintain the incentives and the pressures, so that there would be a continuing flow of benefits to help convert the skeptics to the virtues of growth and compensate the losers. But he appeared to succeed for another set of reasons too. Less rash than Mendès-France, he was careful not to destroy the homeorhetic image. When he sang the praise of change, it was because the "old equilibrium" had become untenable, and only *orderly* change could lead to a *new* equilibrium: change was but the condition of permanence. There had to be progress, but in stability; industrial growth, but in financial rigor and with balanced budgets. "In France, the revolution goes on regularly, day after day, because it is accepted by the public and inscribed in law." [35] Thus the style of authority was preserved, separated from the stalemate society that had so long been its symbiotic partner.[36]

What first served de Gaulle so well here was his indifference to problems of class. He was not wedded to the old order, and he was ready to throw his support to whatever group was most likely to serve his goal: the workers in 1945, the public and private "technocrats" in the 1960s. His very indifference allowed him to combine the notion of change-for-power with that of a harmonious hierarchy. This ambiguity in his performance corresponded to a tension in the man. His vision was one of "association," a kind of cooperative concert for growth and *grandeur,* different from the patterns and practices of authority in the stalemate society, yet respecting the old style—which is why, at the end, his economic and social policies suddenly seemed to turn into disaster.

There was the problem of the old style, where the state ruled above the citizens, associated groups were merely consulted, intellectual distance between strata was maintained, and the behavior of each stratum toward authority still conformed to Crozier's model. Many of the structures of the stalemate society and the values referring to its socioeconomic system were being abandoned; yet the values referring to authority—values which preceded the post-Revolutionary stalemate society—survived and preserved many residues from it, just as they had conserved in it residues of the feudal society.[37] Moreover, the very prudence which aimed at safeguarding the homeorhetic image induced de Gaulle to protect those structures from the past that had served as the legal and administrative framework of French society: the school system, the Napoleonic scheme of territorial organization, and business enterprises. This had dangerous results. Some of these institutions were overrun by the rush of economic and social change: the hierarchy of ranks and statuses and the delicate balance of expectations were upset in the very attempt to save them. And there were the uninformed, uninvolved citizens, disturbed by changes they felt that they had no grip on, pessimistic about their fate, and blaming the state for not protecting them enough.[38]

After Algeria, de Gaulle sensed that peace and prosperity were his citizens' aspirations, and he turned to Pompidou.[39] De Gaulle tried to resolve the contradiction between these aspirations and his own boredom with the "mediocrity" of happiness as a social goal by putting *la politique des interêts* at the service of *la politique de grandeur.* But the contradiction persisted. For him, the purposes of economic and social modernization had always been power, not welfare. By a symbolic coincidence, the growing French economy, having absorbed the effects of the devaluation of 1958, once again fell prey to inflation just as he was embarking on a bold foreign policy that required economic growth with monetary stability and considerable social austerity. His stabilization policy, followed after 1963 somewhat at the expense of growth and full employment, was largely dictated by a desire to accumulate a balance-of-payments surplus needed for foreign-policy goals (including the battle against the dollar) and by a desire to make French industry quickly competitive in the Common Market. Competitiveness required industrial and commercial concentration, which could not fail to antagonize the threatened laggards and *marginaux;* it also required restraints on domestic consumption and sharp limits on wage increases, which displeased the workers. The money spent on developing an independent technology—especially in the military realm —was missing for social services and equipment, further cut by the stabilization plan. De Gaulle's attention, turned on foreign affairs, was lacking for educational reform or "participation." The effort to turn France into a major economic power might have succeeded, would have met with less domestic opposition, had her foreign ambitions been postponed or slowed down. The explosion of 1968, whose financial and economic consequences deeply affected France's power, was not a revolt against de Gaulle's foreign policy (whose main features were far from unpopular) but a protest against the internal costs and burdens of external action.[40] The form it took was accidental and circumstantial, but the sudden flash of lightning illuminated dark areas. It also did considerable damage.

Homeorhesis, already affected by the combination of quantitative change and institutional prudence in social affairs, was more directly threatened in 1967—by the limited, rigid, and abrupt "Fouchet reform" in higher education, and Pompidou's ordinances on social security. The distance between the lowest wages and the highest incomes had widened, unemployment had risen. Expectations of a change that could redress the balance were frustrated by the slowness of social reform (despite de Gaulle's promises of participation in industry), and the prudence of Christian Fouchet's successor (despite the growing turbulence in higher education). This timidity was due to a fear of upsetting established positions, but it only contributed to the discontent, for it seemed to the more rebellious students and workers that the only measures taken had been repressive or regressive. Thus, groups afraid of losing status lashed out, and many particular grievances soon became a total challenge to the existing order. To be sure, things were very complex. The student revolt was obviously part of a world-wide phenomenon of protest against advanced industrial society by the young (especially middle-class and upper-middle-class young). Moreover, there was not only a classical revolt against authority that had become "illegitimate" by making and letting unharmonious change happen, but also some signs of a new challenge to the French style it-self on behalf of a different one, closer to the democratic, participatory ideal. But all these movements converged against Gaullist policy, and all the participants, having never experienced any other style of authority than the traditional one, failed in their attempt. It was when the public began to believe that the upsurge had gone too far and was beginning to threaten, instead of improve, the social order, that the tide turned.

The crisis of 1968 was thus overcome in accordance with the classical style. Heroic leadership, challenged but victorious, once more introduced necessary innovations, in accordance with the rules and values of French authority, so as to meet the most pressing grievances in industry and higher education. But de Gaulle's own further reaction to the crisis led to his fall. After the shock of May, the June elections showed that a majority of the French aspired to a period of peace and quiet. They wanted a gradual return to more routine-like authority, either under de Gaulle or without him. Only a small number thought that the *contestation* had stopped too soon. Others—Communist voters—persisted in refusing to consider the social order and its political authority legitimate, *and* in distrusting violent and anarchical contestation. Some Frenchmen hoped to develop ways of breaking through to a new style of authority.

De Gaulle's interpretation of his victory as a personal mandate to find a "third way" between capitalism and communism was not in tune with any of these moods. The idea of participation, not an ingredient of the traditional French style, was not magnetic enough. As a symbol, it was important mainly to individuals—such as young professionals [41]—who were fiercely anti-Gaullist anyhow, and they did not want it imposed from above via schemes they considered delusive, in fact perpetuating the old model. It was unimportant to most workers (far more concerned with material rewards) and threatening to many of de Gaulle's supporters, to whom his plans appeared to favor nonhomeorhetic change (especially when his new economic policy of austerity, following the crisis of the franc in November 1968, affected their incomes at a time of rising prices). Professors upset by the effects of Edgar Faure's university reform, local *notables* threatened by the plan for new regions, businessmen worried about participation in industries, shopkeepers upset by new taxes and higher payments for social security—all these turned away from de Gaulle.

Thus de Gaulle left France's modernization in a state of suspense. The transformation of France's rural economy, the development of industry, and the growth of cities had been accelerated; industrial concentration had been encouraged; the business community had embraced expansion as enthusiastically as it had once clung to stability;

the workers somehow got used to the double bookkeeping of distant millennial hopes and a daily effort to share in the benefits of mass consumption and leisure. But in practically every area, the style of authority, the matrix of modernization, was also the worst brake. Businessmen and union leaders continued to be mutually suspicious. Bad management often slowed down profitability and investment. Small shopkeepers, artisans, and peasants screamed for total protection and against taxation or attempts at keeping prices down, while state subsidies and credits resulted, not so paradoxically, both in perpetuating a mass of small farmers whose indebtedness only got worse, and in increasing the gap between them and the richer and bigger farmers, the main beneficiaries of the state's policies. In the management of modernization, state intervention all too often discouraged innovation and perpetuated inefficiency. Public policy for industrialization aimed at building up "national champions" in key sectors, with an eye on France's status in the world rather than on profitability. As a result, monopoly prevailed over competition, technical prowess over the sanction of the market. It was as if the French style of authority and the values that bolstered it allowed only two kinds of economic systems: either, when the desire for the social *status quo* prevails, a stalemate society, with sluggish economic growth and limited state power; or else, when security seems to require "balanced" expansion and orderly development instead of immobility, a *colbertiste* system, with a directing state whose mode of operation and criteria are bureaucratic, not economic, and corporate groups in need of state support.[42] Above all, the domination of narrow castes—within the civil service, the educational establishment, the business enterprises, the main interest groups—continued to breed rigidity, distance, and smoldering hostility between the "ins," established managers of the *status quo,* and the "outs," oscillating from sullen resentment to utopia.

When de Gaulle resigned, three views were in competition. De Gaulle's own, which had lost, amounted to the promotion of modernization in the old style—modified in the direction of greater "participation." The citizens would be involved, not in decision-making at every level (for it would have remained centralized), but in the preparation and execution of decisions. This might, as reformists charged, have led in practice not to increased cooperation, but to a generalization of what routine authority had been in the political sphere—a proliferation of opportunities for protest, parochialism, and protectionism, a multiplication of brakes rather than motors. At any rate, the demise of his "third way" left two drastically different views confronting each other. One, practiced by de Gaulle's successors, amounted to modernization in the old style—modifications not according to any grand scheme that might reawaken fear of change, but via *ad hoc,* pragmatic, piecemeal adaptations designed to put some oil into the rustier transmissions. The other was the conception of reformers like Crozier, who believed it possible to adopt a new style of authority not through traditional legislative reform, but through multiple experimentation—the precondition of effective modernization. Intellectually, the latter view may be more convincing; politically, it has had little leverage so far.[43]

V. The Impact and Future of Heroic Leadership

Heroic leadership alone can succeed in injecting massive doses of innovation into a national system that is suspicious of change and ordinarily combines tolerance for individual experimentation with social conformity. But since the conversion to change requires a mobilization of national energies, a reawakening of the general will, a call to national identity, heroic leadership serves also to maintain the system. When routine leaders can no longer preserve it or make change acceptable, heroic leadership saves the society by adapting it, perpetuates society by renewing it. Yet heroic leadership's importance should not conceal its disadvantages. The features of the national system that heroic leadership sustains may themselves deserve to be jettisoned, whether a style of authority that impedes participation and restrains economic and social progress, or a style of behavior on the world stage that prolongs the game of national units proud of cultivating their differences. Even if one accepts these features, there are flaws in heroic leadership of the French polity that one cannot help noting: the plague of impermanence, which drives heroic leaders into an endless and often reckless gamble for legitimacy; the rallying of support through magic rather than reason, the manipulation of frequently infantile needs for dependency, a civic culture in which mass hypnosis replaces organized citizenship; the tendency of a brand of leadership that represents the authoritarian pole of the national style to slide into tyranny or to glide from the search for unanimity into the imposition of conformity—even if the French body politic produces its own antidotes.

Good democrats would like to celebrate at last the demise of French heroic leadership. Yet to replace it requires the demise of the entire national style of authority. For heroic leadership preserves that style not only by periodically saving it from paralysis, but also, more perversely, through its own tendency to violate the rules of homeorhesis (not, as in the case of routine authority, out of anomie or neglect, but out of activism and excess)—at which point, more or less cataclysmically, a swing back to routine authority takes place. De Gaulle has written that when the traditional leadership of the old elites vanishes, the "man of character" becomes the only alternative to anonymity.

Whether a "man of character" can be found every seven years, and not only in emergencies, or whether the anonymous elites of routine French politics will resume their role remains to be seen. Even if a synthesis between the two kinds of authority should be achieved in the political system, this would not be the end of the story. For if the style of authority is unchanged in society (and in the civil service), occasional short circuits may occur comparable to that of 1968, which even a regime less personal than de Gaulle's and less impotent than the parliamentary Republics may find hard to handle. The mere synthesis of two kinds of political authority will not suffice to transform the style of authority outside political life; to do that, France's political leaders must deliberately and daringly experiment with institutional innovation in key sectors of society—education, business, the civil service, local government.

Let us look back at our three leaders: Mendès-France, Pétain, de Gaulle. We can finally (as usual) point to some fine paradoxes. In an age in which economic progress has become a primary concern of the French, the leader who made of it the cornerstone of his program owes most of his diminished appeal to the memory of the spectacle he once gave. The leader most apparently concerned with stabilizing what he saw as the essence of France and with safeguarding the existence of the French, is the one who most adventurously strayed from what her "essence" allowed and what her (if not their) existence required. The leader apparently most suspicious of dogmas, most "existentialistically" engaged in recurrent self-definition through action, without attachment to old forms of shibboleths or any other limits than the "realities" of the "situation," has been the one most aware of the unwritten rules even heroic leadership must respect to be successful [44]—at least up to 1968, but again in the way in which he made his exit. French heroic leadership is like French classical theater: it never ceases being dramatic, yet the drama must follow rules. Whether such leadership is closer to the august and candid characters of Corneille, or to the devious and driven characters of Racine, is up to the reader to decide.

5
The Ruled: Protest as a National Way of Life

There are few other nations where protest movements have been so frequent and so diverse in their origins, channels, and purposes, and so similar in their manifestations, as France.

Who are the protesters? There are times in French history when every social group and political organization seems to be protesting against the *status quo;* in other periods, protest originates in a clearly limited sector of society or politics. If we take a long-term view of France since the collapse of the Second Empire in 1870 and establish a chart of the principal protest movements, their universality will be striking.

If we look at society as a whole, we find such movements everywhere.

There are protest movements originating among the groups at the bottom of the social hierarchy or of the hierarchy of a particular occupation, aimed at the groups exerting the powers of command. Thus, there have been movements among the workers (the revolutionary syndicalism of the early CGT), the peasants (the Dorgères movement of the 1930s and the wave of 1961), the shopkeepers and artisans (Poujadism and a new wave since 1969), and the small businessmen (who joined right-wing leagues or parties in the 1930s; after the war Gingembre's Confédération Générale des Petites et Moyennes Entreprises was a noisy protest organization). Technicians and industrial employees, university students (largely *petits-bourgeois,* or sons of *grands bourgeois* who were not good enough to join the elite in the *grandes*

First published in Morton A. Kaplan, ed., *The Revolution in World Politics* (New York, 1962).

écoles), younger (i.e., powerless) members of several professions, and equally powerless students in the *lycées* all joined in the great protest of May 1968. *Lycée* students demonstrated again, in March 1973, to protest the suppression of military deferments.

There are protest movements originating also within ruling groups.[1] Some appear within the political class, which has to be subdivided, in turn, into its civilian branch and its military branch. We find protest movements against the domestic *status quo* or France's international position in the form of political parties such as the PSF or PPF before the war, the RPF after the war, the Parti Socialiste Unifié (PSU) and various *gauchiste* groups today, the Communist party since its creation. In 1972, students in the École Nationale d'Administration (ENA), the incubator of the bureaucratic elite, protested en masse against the competitive system that reserved access to the *grands corps* to the ENA's top graduates. There were also spectacular expressions of protest in the French Army during the Algerian war, culminating in a revolt against de Gaulle in Algeria in April 1961. Within the groups exercising economic power, protest during the period of the Popular Front amounted to a sabotage of the Front's economic and financial policies. The third element of the ruling groups, the Church hierarchy and the intellectuals ("spiritual" power), has also been a source of protest: the Church was a powerful force for protest in the early years of the Third Republic and again at the time of the separation of Church and state; as for the intellectuals, some groups among them—at times all of them—have been sharply critical of French political and social affairs.

Protest movements are sometimes organized (whether by political parties, interest groups, or conspiratorial groups like the prewar Cagoule and the Organisation de l'Armée Secrète [OAS] in Algeria and France in 1961–62), sometimes not. In the latter case, they appear either as sudden explosions (the Commune of Paris in 1871, the sit-down strikes of 1936, the abortive *Putsch* of April 1961), as hasty rallies from various points on the horizon around a leader (Boulangism), or as the expression of similar attitudes held by men acting within their professions (bankers and businessmen, writers and journalists). The "events" of May 1968 combined all these elements.

If we take a closer look at the French political system, we find that the universality of protest transcends all the distinctions made by political scientists.

Gabriel Almond has commented on the "poor boundary maintenance between the society and the political system in France"; he has emphasized in particular the lack of a clear separation between the functions of interest groups and those of political parties.[2] The interpenetration of these two types of bodies appears in a number of instances. Some Frenchmen carry their protest against the *status quo* into a party as well as into an interest group. (In the 1930s, Communists did this on the Left, many businessmen and veterans on the Right.) There have also been many protest alliances among such bodies: thus, the 1930s saw an alliance of left-wing parties and the labor-union movement against the Fascist threat, and a conglomeration of right-wing leagues, parties, veterans' groups, and taxpayers' movements against the Popular Front. And the protest movement against EDC in 1953–54 was an even stranger alliance of parties, businessmen, labor unionists, and intellectuals of Left and Right. Almond's remark has become much less applicable to the dominant, or *majoritaire,* side of French politics under the Fifth Republic (indeed, one might say that the explosion of May 1968 was partly due to too rigid a "boundary maintenance"). But he is still right about the opposition side: in 1960–61, opposition to the Algerian war was led by an essentially non-Communist left-wing coalition composed of unions, a small party (the PSU), the National Students Union, study groups (the Club Jean Moulin), and intellectuals. In May–June 1968, especially at the end of May, a shaky conglomeration of left-wing parties, labor unions, student *groupuscules,* and intellectuals tried to overthrow the long Gaullist reign.

Within the political parties, we find two structures particularly adapted to the expression of protest: the small ideological sect, usually dominated by intellectuals, which buys intellectual rigidity and purity at the cost of extremism and isolation; and the authoritarian league, which tries to enlist masses of people in quasi-military fashion behind much more ambiguous objectives.

Within the interest groups, we find that protest affects all the types of "interest articulation" distinguished by Almond. It affects institutional interest groups, such as the army or the Church; nonassociational groups, such as the occasional, usually short-lived, study groups that criticize the *status quo* and try to propose alternatives; associational interest groups, such as the peasants' organizations, the French labor movement, with its long history of resistance to any form of co-operation with business, or the Fédération Nationale Catholique, founded in 1924 in protest against new anticlerical measures, and the multiple unions of students and teachers in 1968; and anomic groups breaking into the political system from society, such as Dorgères's, Poujade's, and, recently, Gérard Nicoud's movements.

The issues that give rise to protest have been of all sorts. Some have been social issues concerning the status of given groups in French society; some have been national issues concerning the role of France in the world and the policy to be followed by the country toward other nations. French survival was, after all, the original issue around which

Resistance movements were formed; it was the issue in the battle over the EDC, and in the protest movement of extreme right elements against de Gaulle's Algerian policy. National issues were heavily at stake in the Poujade movement and in the protest of the Right against the Popular Front. There have also been constitutional issues concerning the institutions which the nation ought to adopt (these were at the root of Boulangism and of the RPF). Finally, philosophical issues were at the heart of the intellectuals' protest against Republican ideology around 1900, the intellectuals' protest against France's stagnation around 1930, and the intellectuals' protest against the "consumer society" in recent years. Intellectual protest movements, such as that of the "left-wing progressive intellectuals" so brilliantly denounced by Raymond Aron [3] or that of the intellectuals opposed to the Algerian war, usually develop around a mixture of all such issues. The nation-wide movement of May 1968 did also.

How does protest occur in France? It might appear that I am lumping under the heading of protest all kinds of expressions of discontent that have little in common. However, it seems that whatever the social milieu in which they originated, whatever the channels they used or created, and whatever the issues involved, those movements have shared a common style.

The first feature of this style is its fundamental destructiveness. Of course, any protest is first of all a refusal to accept a certain situation. In this respect Poujadists or the intellectuals who signed the "Manifesto of the 121," recognizing the right of young men to disobey the draft in the Algerian war, are not different from American Populists or British unilateralists. But the style of protest differs according to whether this original refusal is or is not followed by something. What characterizes almost all French protest movements is their refusal to cooperate with "the enemy" (i.e., the group responsible for the measure or state of affairs against which the protest is lodged) in order to produce a desired change.

At best (if this is the right word), the protest movement will advocate a revolutionary substitution of a new order of things. This was the case with the French labor movement at the turn of the century and with the French Communist Party in its early, militant years. In a milder and more confused way, it was also what the intellectual neutralists of the late 1940s and early 1950s hoped to achieve, since they very often associated a foreign policy of nonalignment with drastic social reforms in France (*L'Observateur* and *Esprit* argued this kind of line in that period). In an equally confused but more violent way, this seemed to be the case with the terrorist organizations and army conspiracies that opposed de Gaulle's Algerian policy. And in May 1968, there were many, often conflicting calls for a new order, ranging from the Communists' belated appeal for a new popular government to varieties of student utopianism displayed in the "liberated" halls of the Sorbonne.

At worst, and more frequently, the protest movement will simply try to sabotage public policy and practice a negative *politique du pire,* with the hope that this will lead to the collapse of the group or regime against which the movement fights. France's small authoritarian leagues, Maurras's Action Française in the 1930s (when any hope of ever setting up Maurras's mythical monarchy was quite dead), and Doriot's PPF, behaved in this fashion. So, twenty years later, did those anti-EDC leaders who were opposed to any form of German rearmament despite the obvious determination of France's allies to achieve it in some way. It was, of course, even more true of Poujade's attitude, but it was also the line of the more impassioned leaders of the RPF. Relations between business and labor in the late 1930s were marked by the same intransigence: labor, with its long tradition of class distrust, refused any concession that would permit a less disastrously rigid enforcement of the forty-hour week; and business, protesting against the legislation imposed by the state, did its best to sabotage its application. The behavior of some elements of the French Army after de Gaulle announced his policy of self-determination for Algeria showed a similar inclination to oppose and block official policy in the absence of any realistic alternative. And in 1968 the determination of various *gauchiste* student organizations to exacerbate tensions in the university, to sabotage reform and thus to "unveil" the repressiveness of even liberal institutions, brought first chaos, and later protracted turmoil in and around Paris. French protest is the rejection of reform; its purpose is not so much to redress a wrong as to punish the wrongdoer.

Another feature of French protest is what I would call "totalism," and it applies to the ideological dimension adopted by practically any protest movement. Any French protest movement expresses its hostility in terms that go far beyond the immediate occasion of the protest and that challenge or involve the very foundations of the social order, the political order, or both. In the 1930s, conservative criticism of the Third Republic for its inefficiency and corruption tended to develop into a general questioning of democracy and industrial society; the groups that demonstrated against the regime on February 6, 1934, were influenced by Maurras's counterrevolutionary ideology just as Marxism, in a more or less diluted form, colored many of the attacks on the Algerian war and the Fifth Republic, which broadened into a general assault on French and foreign capitalism. Indeed, Marxism has become the *esperanto* of all kinds of protests on the Left—from Jean-Paul Sartre to Louis Althusser, from Daniel Cohn-Bendit to Roger Garaudy—precisely because of its sweep. Nor did the proponents of appeasement in the 1930s use mere *ad hoc* arguments. They either presented a spirited and radical defense of pacifism, or developed an over-all attack on France's foreign policy and on her allies. The nationalists of the 1950s did not only protest against France's colonial retreats and her minor role in NATO, they often spoke as if there were a universal conspiracy to humiliate France—a conspiracy in which Communist inspiration, Arab hostility, and Anglo-Saxon malevolence all played a part. (*L'Aurore,* and many RPF, Poujadist, and other right-wing speakers and writers, in particular Jacques Soustelle, took this line.) A shopkeepers' rebellion against harsher measures of tax control rapidly became a call for resistance against France's decline in the world and for the summoning of a new States General. The Dreyfus Affair, with first its left-wing protest and then the right-wing protest after the victory of the Left, is the best example of how the scope of a debate may become universal. A long if grudging practice of "reformism" has not succeeded in erasing the basic hostility of the labor movement to a *syndicalisme de gestion,* which would imply not so much the abandonment of its grievances, as the explicit recognition of the "capitalist" order of society. The Communist unions' tough bargaining for quantitative advantages for the workers proceeds behind the banner of anticapitalism and the class struggle. The non-Communist CFDT's demand for "workers' power" in the factories is presented as a springboard toward a socialist new order, not as a step toward integration; it appeals to the lingering memories of early antistate, workshop-centered syndicalism which Pierre-Joseph Proudhon or Fernand Pelloutier wanted. The skilled workers, employers, and cadres of the Confédération Française et Démocratique du Travail (CFDT) thus appear closer to the artisan elite of early French syndicalism than to British or German trade unionism: *autogestion* is certainly not "participation" in the existing order.

One of the consequences of this "total" attitude is, of course, to reinforce the intransigence that results from the negative character of the protest. Another consequence is that protest battles are waged in moral terms: the moralism so characteristic of French intellectuals pervades all French protest movements; the French argue about principles, not about interests; they appeal to notions of good and evil or to traditional values.

Defeatism is a more surprising feature of French protest. Nevertheless, there is always a strand of despair about the possibility of succeeding. It is as if the very leaders of the protest knew all along that their role consisted simply in expressing that sonorous "no" without which man remains unfinished, as if they expected that however far their protest might carry them (for instance, even into power), nothing much would really be changed at the end. The gesture thus matters more than the outcome. We find this attitude among French syndicalists, for example, whose fate it has been to fall from the dream of a "total reconstruction" of society into the reality of mere permanent protest: militancy has declined, and protest talk or action, such as the vote for the most extreme party or union on Election Day, or an occasional grand holiday from work such as that of May 1968, is all that remains of the hope of collective liberation.[4] What carried Poujade's followers across France was not so much the expectation of reversing the trend toward industrialization, as the exhilarating adventure that interrupted the drabness of everyday life.[5] The men who raised barricades in Algiers in January 1960, and some of the leaders of the April 1961 *Putsch,* such as General Maurice Challe, were staging a *baroud d'honneur* against de Gaulle rather than expecting to reverse his policy: the trials of the spring and summer of 1961 revealed that many officers rallied to Challe, although they doubted that his attempt could get very far. Defeatism colored the protest of Charles Péguy, Georges Sorel, Maurice Barrès, and, later, Drieu la Rochelle, against the mediocrity in which they saw France ensconced in this century; Sartre has confessed his own sense of failure.[6] A sociologist, eager to save from the fiasco of May 1968 whatever could be made to appear both mythical and prophetic (a typical exercise, often applied in the past to another emotionally rewarding failure, the Commune of 1871), acknowledged that the movement had been creative only in what had doomed it to failure: its spontaneity.[7]

A certain lack of conviction about one's chances of success and a grudging recognition of the *status quo*'s strength contribute to explain the brittleness of most of France's protest movements. Some of their members always get discouraged earlier than others and exchange their original revolt for submission or apathy. French protest movements usually end with the absorption of many of the rebels into the system and the disappearance of the others. This absorption is sometimes reluctant and resentful, as in the case of the workers; sometimes uneasy, as in the case of some of the early neutralists who became more or less resigned to France's joining the Atlantic Alliance; or sometimes surprisingly smooth, as in the case of Michel Debré's change of attitude toward Algeria, or in the cases of many once rebellious political or interest-group leaders who were won over by the "games, poisons and delights" of the system.[8] Whichever it is, the system wins. One may ask whether protest movements fail because their leaders do not really believe in their success, or whether the leaders lose faith because of the record of past failures. It is, of course, a combination of the two: protest movements arise and fail because of the system's very structure and style.

II

Both the universality and the style of French protest result from the nature of French society and of France's political system. The nature of French society, as it existed from the Revolution until recently, created the conditions for many of the types of protest.

Society rested on a consensus that included the *haute bourgeoisie,* the lower middle classes (both independent operators and civil servants or employees), as well as the peasants. This consensus tended to preserve largely preindustrial values and attitudes and to dilute or delay industrialization. It excluded the industrial proletariat and created a major psychological barrier between the workers and the rest of the population. In particular, the bourgeoisie (whose attitude toward industrial enterprise and economic rationality never much resembled the ideal type described by Saint-Simon) insisted on applying "bourgeois" standards of social ascent (*enrichissez-vous*) to the workers and on treating them according to the degree of loyalty they showed toward their employers—one of the many aspects of the feudal hangover among the bourgeoisie. The *social* distance—i.e., differences in income, education, way of life—between the workers and the bourgeois may have been far less than in England, but the *intellectual* distance (mutual acceptance and behavior) was greater, especially since it was increased by the contrast between the bourgeois' treatment of the workers and the bourgeois' community of values with, mystical glorification of, and legal protection for the peasants. The result was that the workers could not but adopt an attitude of protest against the established order and dream of revolution or revenge.[9] By contrast with the protests of most other groups, which usually express a reaction of individual self-assertion or of defense of the "free" individual against evil forces, workers' protests expressed a sense of community, a desire for collective ascent and redemption (in May 1968, this made any genuine student/workers alliance difficult). But the numerical inferiority of the workers also made their dream a rather hopeless one: here we find the roots of negativism, "totalism," and defeatism in working-class movements.

The consensus among the other groups, which rested on a common resistance to the machine age and on an unwritten agreement to keep the middle classes as large as possible, was of such a nature that it could be threatened by external disruption. Any severe economic depression, reducing the national income, increased tensions among groups fighting for its distribution and created particularly strong protest movements among those who were most severely hit by falling prices. Hence, the rebellion of western France's peasants and the protest of the small businessmen and shopkeepers during the 1930s, for they were not as well sheltered from the Depression as the big enterprises that benefited from various ententes or government contracts. In addition, any period of rapid industrialization that eliminated marginal independent producers and shopkeepers or made things hard for them, provoked these victims of economic progress into complaining of betrayal by the state, which failed to safeguard their way of life. This was what happened in the case of Poujadism, and again in the 1970s. Thus we may conclude that the very nature of French society creates one structural protest, the industrial workers', and latent protests whose appearance depends on what French economists call *la conjoncture*.

Other forms of protest can be explained by the nature of the French political system. The fundamental factor here was the lasting split in French political thought following the Revolution, or rather double split. To begin with, there was the opposition between those Frenchmen who remained faithful to counterrevolutionary ideas and those who accepted the principle of government based on consent. And in addition, there was a division among the latter: between the liberals, who feared that any system of government in which the "will of the people" was not carefully filtered and diluted would upset the stalemate society, to which they were attached above all; the democrats, who were also attached to it but whose social conservatism was less fearful and whose respect for traditional elites was nil; and the social reformers who rejected the formula of the stalemate society altogether.

Two consequences of this basic division are important for our subject. For one, the believers in counterrevolutionary dogmas were permanently reduced to the condition of a sniping protest group; for more than forty years, this was the fate and role of Maurras's Action Française: bitter denunciation of all the institutions and men of the regime from an intellectually well-staffed but politically limited ghetto. To the extent to which the Republic was militantly opposed to counterrevolutionary ideas and the Church was wedded to them, Catholics were also obliged to create protest movements of their own. For another, although the "ideological" formula of the Third and Fourth Republics was a leftist one (an alliance between all the "heirs of the Revolution"), its "social" basis was the stalemate society. Consequently, extreme-left political parties found themselves either in part (the Socialists, until 1936) or totally (Communists) also in the position of protest groups. Although the Section Française de l'Internationale Ouvrière (SFIO), following Jean Jaurès, accepted the political institutions of the regime as legitimate, it refused to participate in the government for over thirty years or to vote the military budget in peacetime.

Because of the split in French political thought, and also because of the instability of regimes in the nineteenth century, the electoral laws and parliamentary rules of the Third Republic, and France's economic and social complexity, France developed a multiple and heterogeneous party system. The very divisions on the French political scene and the resulting incapacity at forging stable coalitions condemned the political system to immobility at important times. Any group which felt that action was vital has tended to organize a protest movement in order to break the deadlock. *Immobilisme* was less damaging and protest less frequent, as long as the function of the state was essentially ideological, but when, in the 1930s, the world outside began to disturb France's economic and social balance and the French role in the world, the load became too heavy for the multiparty parliamentary regime. As a result of the regime's fumblings and failures, the explosive issue of what de Gaulle called *le rang* provoked reactions both against the outside world and against the weakness of the government. This was the case, for instance, when the Right protested against practically the whole universe, in addition to the regime, after the Sakhiet bombing incident which preceded the fall of the Fourth Republic; the same thing had happened on a larger scale when the Left as well as the Right had attacked Blum's dead-center compromise policy of nonintervention in the Spanish Civil War.

This is why it has seemed, at times, that all organizations were engaged in an orgy of protest, pulling a paralyzed state in different directions, lashing out at one another over it, and recriminating against it for its passivity. Resulting from the nonpragmatism, nonreformism of a fragmented political system, the protest groups seemed the only alternative to complete stagnation, but they also contributed to the system's weakness. Reform through law being blocked, the first task of a protest movement was, inevitably, to attack the political system for its paralysis. This negativism made the prospect of reform even more distant, for it threw the regime on the defensive (leagues in the 1930s; RPF and anti-EDC rallies under the Fourth Republic). It also made France's adjustment to change in the world more difficult. The division of opinion regarding France's role in international affairs, or (as in the case of colonialism) the consensus of much of the population around an increasingly untenable policy was perpetuated by indecisiveness or immobility at the top. And the spectacle of a political system paralyzed by the "game" its members played according to their individual calculations produced the opposite: protests by rabidly ideological groups that preferred the vacuum of pure principles to the villainy of unprincipled power. The alternative to gradual reform was stagnation and protest.

The peculiarities of French protest derived not only from France's social consensus and political divisions, but also from features that could be found both in the society and in the polity. Fragmentation was one such peculiarity. Until recently, the inability of the French to create effective voluntary associations continued to be as it had been when Tocqueville lamented about it. Few interests were organized; the membership of business associations and labor unions, as well as political parties, remained small; the economy was splintered into a myriad of small landowners, small businessmen, small shopkeepers; the working class was dispersed among countless enterprises; the multiparty system was extraordinarily complex. Consequently, the French body politic lacked adequate institutional channels for the expression and redress of grievances. This fragmentation explains in part the frequency and diversity of protest movements: they are both a substitute for and a demonstration of the failure to create stable, broadly based channels. And the defeatism I have mentioned also stems in part from the impossibility of mobilizing a large section of the population for common, positive goals over a long period of time.

A second, and crucial, characteristic of society and politics in France has been studied admirably by Michel Crozier: it is the style of authority which defines human relations in society and in political life.[10] The French style of authority rules out participation. Instead of solving conflicts in cooperation and through compromises, individuals and groups refer the conflicts to a higher, central authority that is held responsible for the outcome. The results of this attitude are, first, centralization; second, a brittleness in the voluntary associations to which the individual belongs—their function is essentially to protect him from possible arbitrariness higher up, to promote his "public" interests, while refraining from impinging on his independence as a private individual; third, an oscillation between two forms of behavior—semi-clandestine pressuring of higher authority for special advantages, for a more "understanding" enforcement of the rules, or for the preservation of privileges, or else vocal protest when protection from above is removed; fourth, the preservation of the individual's own capacity to protest. The range of the individual's attitudes goes from apathy to resistance, with distrust coloring the whole spectrum. The lack of participation means that decisions are made by a small number of men (the bureaucrats and legislators, in the case of the political system); centralization means that they will try to preserve their privilege of making decisions alone; permanent distrust and latent resistance lower down mean that the subjects will try to limit this privilege by surrounding the decision-makers' competence with legal restrictions and themselves with vested rights; it also means that they will protest as soon as they think that arbitrariness has occurred at the top, or even in the associations to which they belong, in the expectation of being thereby more effectively protected against higher authority. Normally, conflicts between individuals in a group or between groups will be much less resolved than stifled, "arbitrated," perhaps temporarily assuaged, and quite likely perpetuated, by resort to higher authority. When protest occurs, it often expresses the same institutional intolerance of conflict in reverse, through demands for radical and definitive settlement or through dreams of frictionless harmony.

This description fits the behavior of businessmen or unionists who prefer to leave the settlement of labor problems to the government, and who are prompt to blame the government for any bad turn in *la conjoncture*. It fits the behavior of schoolteachers' unions which both demand and resist reform from the Ministry of Education. It also fits the model of political behavior proposed by Alain: the citizen is not a militant; he wants to be left alone; he abandons decisions to elites he distrusts and leaves the task of supervising those elites to representatives whom he also distrusts.

While many protest movements have resulted from the paralysis of the political system, they can also result from the malfunctioning of any subsystem or organization. Protest can be aimed either at the failure of higher authority to make the decisions referred to it, or, on the contrary, at decisions made by higher authority which seem to invade vested rights. More generally, and vaguely, it can break out whenever higher authority fails to meet the expectations of the subjects. This explains why protest movements are destructive, for many of them are initiatives taken against the exercise of initiative by others, and why they show a streak of defeatism. They are revolts against a central authority that is expected to have the final say, rebellion within an established pattern, not revolution against it. Consequently, the central authority, in order to preserve its position, usually *grants* (*octroie*) some concessions to the protest movements on its own initiative—this was the case with the "additional protocols" to EDC, the 1961 cabinet measures in favor of the peasants, and measures repeatedly taken to appease angry shopkeepers in the supermarket era. And then at that point rebellion ebbs away; harmony is restored, without cooperation, by flexibility at the top and acquiescence at the bottom. Thus, by an intriguing paradox, protest succeeds insofar as it contains a kernel of specific grievances but fails insofar as it poses a broader challenge to the decision-makers.[11]

No "protest crisis" followed this pattern more faithfully than the "events" of May 1968. Those who revolted most vocally were not predominantly the small "independent" members of the old consensus groups (peasants, shopkeepers, small businessmen). They were either workers and business employees, university and high-school students, subordinate members of increasingly bureaucratic professions, or even Catholic priests and young members of lay Catholic associations—i.e., all those, salaried or not, who function daily in hierarchical organizations run according to the rules of French authority. While their initial targets were their immediate superiors, the political system itself became the ultimate target—not only because of its direct responsibility for public education and for the public sector of the economy, but also because of the general expectation, shared by rebels and non-protesters alike, that the state, as the linchpin of French authority, had to step in—to give in, or to strike back. When it seemed that it might actually fall, there was considerable surprise among the rebels: those who were geared to the seizure of central power doubted whether the moment was ripe, and those who were dreaming of its withering away had not really thought that acting out utopia might make it real.

The structures of France's society and polity correspond to a complex of values inherited from the preindustrial past. Old aristocratic values have deeply marked not only the bourgeoisie, in its rebellion against the nobility and clergy, but also the working class, in its struggle with the bourgeoisie. In particular, there remains the prestige of prowess (individual or, in the workers' case, collective) as against more civic virtues or against what Péguy contemptuously called the "savings-account ethics," the rules of economic rationality. Also, the *ancien régime,* in its fight against the feudal order, developed the notion of a single general interest represented by the state. It encouraged the hatred of personal dependence, characteristic of the Third Estate, into becoming a general *horreur du face-à-face.* And the feudal order and the *ancien régime* of Richelieu and Louis XIV fostered a widespread attachment to equilibrium, to the unwritten imperative of a constant hierarchy of ranks and statuses. This was reinforced by the passion for legal equality within each "stratum," by the definition of arbitrariness as formal inequality, two legacies of the revolt against the *ancien régime* and against feudalism. Inevitably, as industrial values transformed the old order of *ruraux* and *légistes,* protest would arise against the spread of the new, cold, and calculating rationality and the new hierarchies and inequalities that accompanied it. Whenever the state was believed to be contributing to this tendency, protest was bound to be couched in a mix of corporatist demands and indignant defense of the "old freedoms" or "inherent rights." Thus were the demands given the legitimacy of a "general interest," while they were escalated into "totalism."

The style of protest, these being the values, was that of militant prowess. Whether against the archaic or against the new, protest is waged in archaic ways on behalf of archaic archetypes. Now, in modern society, prowess-protest is all-too-easily destructive. But given the structures and the values of France, the defense of any special interest had to turn into an attack on the state, and to wrap itself into an ideological cloak transfiguring that interest: as if its pure and simple defense were shameful, as if the state could only be challenged by another generalizing myth.

The sources of these values, of the style of authority and of fragmentation, lie deep indeed. As Crozier, Wylie, Pitts, and Shonfeld have shown,[12] they are to be found in the school system, which "tends to produce autonomous, independent and critical individuals rather than participating and responsible citizens." [13] This school system leaves little initiative to the child. Elders teach him the world, starting with general principles.[14] The competitive system—a by-product of the French mania for legal equality—increases the pressure on him. He is taught no civics or economics, but he is encouraged to sharpen his personality by using his critical faculties in scientific, literary, and psychological subjects. The dominant cultural model is derived from classical humanism: prestige is attached to a talent, the capacity for abstract conceptualization; science is a set of deductive propositions; and "practical" experience is to be provided not by experimentation but by reflecting on history and on literature, those two wombs of wisdom. The result is an individual endowed with general principles untested by practical experience, with little or no ability to organize or participate in teamwork. He has internalized the old aristocratic values, for his own success results from his "prowess"— his skill in performing tests and matching the model of the educated man as the "cultivated consumer" of disinterested disciplines. He has learned to accept superior authority in his social or public life *and* to escape from it in his inner life. In other words, obedience has *not* been internalized, and the capacity to rebel is maintained. (This model is prolonged in higher education.) As for expressing protest, all the child disposes of are peer groups which, in Pitts's words, are mere "delinquent communities," defensive protest groups against school and family pressures, recognized by neither and consequently brittle and semiclandestine.

We can understand why so many rebellious French adolescents later become the most conformist citizens and why protest movements tend to be "total," destructive, and defeatist. Protest is often the sudden public eruption of private utopias once kept within the realm of imagination, idle thought, or harmless discourse. In protest, the normal public behavior of the individual—Alain's "obedience without love" —is suspended, and the private dreams of daring change and communion without coercion are acted out. And the vehicles of protest tend to resemble the early peer groups: the protesters' exhilaration is partly due to a delicious feeling of semi-clandestinity and often emulates the schoolboys' romp, *le chahut*. Protest, like *le chahut,* is a holiday from the rules which dominate the citizen's public, i.e., social life—both from the formal rules laid down by the organizations to which he belongs, and from the myriad internalized rules inculcated in him by his family, his milieu, and his early school years. Insofar as protest is psychodrama, wish fulfillment, and liberation (one longs for a good English equivalent of *défoulement*), it is more important to listen to emotions than to examine ideas. This explains why protest movements often break off from or collide with more sedate voluntary associations —parties, unions, interest groups—whose own origins may have been equally volcanic or clandestine, and which, when faced with such challenges, must choose between joining the romp or losing their grip.

As an example of the kind of mechanism I have described, I want to take the case of the French intellectuals, for it is among them that the tradition of protest is most ancient—it begins in the eighteenth century, long before the appearance of the modern proletariat. And among them the effects of the social and political circumstances analyzed above are most interesting to observe. What we find is the persistence of a style of action that Tocqueville admirably, if unkindly, studied in a chapter of *The Old Regime and the Revolution*. This style has marked four important "intellectual crises" in the twentieth century: around 1900, around 1930, at the time of the Liberation, and in 1968.[15]

The style's first characteristic is its ideological bent: political discontent wrapped in metaphysics. The intellectual revolt against the ideology of the Third Republic took the form of a reaction against the categorical imperative, against scientism and the "sclerosis of rationalism," and for the rehabilitation of mobility, activism, and faith under the banner of Henri Bergson. The protest of the 1930s, largely aimed at the political and social flaws of a sclerotic regime and a poorly organized and badly run capitalist economy, was often couched in the language of "personalist" philosophy, which proposed to create "a new man," no longer the social atom of liberalism but a person rooted in various living communities. Marxism provided much of the inspiration for Liberation thought, and even Existentialist philosophy tried to come to terms with it. It continued to color the proclamations of students and intellectuals in 1968. Today, various French trees in the forest of psychoanalysis extend their roots in Marxist soil.

This ideological bent is a form of what I have called totalism, and it is also the product of a conviction that there are general laws, or principles, which govern human affairs whose discovery and enforcement would make the difference between chaos and order. It is this aspect of Marxism which has contributed most to its success in France, especially in the 1930s and 1940s, when the acceleration of history, as Daniel Halévy called it, destroyed all previous certitudes and seemed to require a new compass. Even the most voluntarist French thinkers —Sorel or Sartre—have not been satisfied with celebrating spontaneity, with calling for collective acts of will to overcome mediocrity or alienation in the *practico-inerte:* they have used Marxist sociology as their background dogma. But intellectuals of the Right, such as

Maurras, also liked to believe in laws of political science capable of preventing social decay and national decadence. A corollary of this belief in general principles is the search for universality, the conviction that whatever protest is made concerns not only France, but mankind. It includes a passionate interest, or belief, in "waves of the future" or streams of history. This explains why foreign examples, considered to be representative of such trends, are studied and proposed as models, lest France remain left on the shore or swimming against the tide. The belief in a key to the universe and the passion for universality can both be traced to the nature of French education.

Another characteristic of protest among the intelligentsia is a deep moralism. "The political convictions of French writers are only moral attitudes." [16] Both the protest of 1900 and that of 1930 were revolts against mediocrity, against a civilization in which virtue and heroism seemed to have no place (in this respect, many of France's intellectual Fascists were merely disciples of Barrès, without any hope left about the possibility of saving France and with the conviction that fascism represented the new wave of the future). The 1968 protest against a "programmed" society, technocracy, bureaucracy, was one more variation on this theme. The intellectuals of the Liberation often started with a moral meditation about the difficulty of human relations in the century of "the cold," and about the universal presence of death as the Emperor of the twentieth century. What followed was a denunciation of all "miserable consolers"—imbeciles, cowards, or stinkers—and a desire to transcend nihilism.

This moralism had as a consequence a lasting and sharp polarization between Left and Right. On the Left, the old quest for justice, the protest against inequality at home (i.e., for the proletariat) and abroad (for oppressed colonial peoples) [17] has dominated the French university. Here again, Marxism has found ready ground, because it presented itself not only in its scientist aspect, but also as a continuation of the old moral fight for human liberation, quenching the thirst for a secular religion which Carl Becker found already among Enlightenment philosophers. On the Right, which has dominated the academies, much theorizing and anti-Republican writing has been the result of a burning moral fear of decadence. The latest example of this polarization was left-wing intellectual protest against the Algerian war and right-wing protest against "softness" in waging the war.

Another consequence has been a tendency to substitute prophetism, or a searching out of scapegoats (such as the United States, symbol of the "cold," of the mechanization of life, of commercialism, or of capitalist inequity), or pure attachment to abstract principles, for the quest of accommodation or political solutions. The inevitable outcome of this divorce from the world of action has been some form of defeatism:

a conscious or unconscious selection of Antigone's attitude as that of the true intellectual, a clinging to slogans and rituals,[18] or a final withdrawal from *engagement* altogether.[19] No believer in a *mystique* can fail eventually to notice the abyss between *mystique* and *politique*. On the whole, French intellectuals (Sartre included, despite his denial) have been rebels rather than revolutionaries,[20] aghast at the sacrifice of purity which revolution entails and, therefore, all too often condemned to fall from rebellious fervor to futility. One cannot help being struck by the similarities between Rousseau and Sartre: both were in revolt against the social order of their time; both grounded their political philosophy in psychology; both believed that "the individual praxis is . . . the only practical and dialectic reality"; [21] both thought that man was free only when he was either by himself or part of what Sartre called a "group" and Rousseau the "general will," i.e., communities whose members are fused by voluntary striving toward a single common goal; both thus provided a standard for judging existing orders (or, as Emmanuel Mounier would have called them, established disorders) rather than blueprints for reconstruction.

A third characteristic has been, and remains, the conviction of French intellectuals that they are the conscience of society, that they are not mere specialists, entitled to respect in their spheres of expertise but deserving of no greater attention than other citizens in their views on public affairs. Crozier has denounced a "will of separation" in French intellectual fashions, which preserves the distance between the intelligentsia and the rest of society and thus partakes of that characteristically French determination to preserve one's vested rights. And, in a searching analysis, a distinguished French intellectual has recognized that even left-wing anti-Americanism contains a heavy dose of elitist dislike for a mass democracy in which this distance is not acknowledged.[22]

These were already the features of the French intellectuals in the eighteenth century, but they no longer can be explained by the causes which Tocqueville suggested. In the eighteenth century, there was an imposed separation between the world of the intellectuals, who were kept "quite out of touch with practical politics," and the world of power, which tolerated no participation. In the political vacuum around the centers of power, writers were able to become guides of public opinion. But ever since the Revolution, intellectuals have had direct and massive access to politics and can no longer be exonerated by reference to their forced ignorance of practice. Nevertheless, the symptoms of "protest intellectualism," which appeared when there *was* this divorce between ideas and action, have survived. Tocqueville himself recognized that this was already true under the Revolution, whose excesses he explains by the fact that it was led by intellectuals whose contempt for facts, desire to reconstruct the whole universe, and literary phraseology became the hallmarks of the Revolution. Ever since, French intellectuals have merged with representatives of numerous other groups within the political class (Jaurès and Blum became heads of a workers' party), but the features are still here, and the intellectuals' leadership of public opinion has not been challenged. What explains such permanence?

The answer has to be found in the nature of French society. The French intellectual has been both hero and victim of the stalemate society; in Baudelaire's terms, he was, in it, both *la plaie et le couteau*. In this society, specialization was seen as a narrowing of the mind, not a deepening of knowledge, and *la culture générale,* whose matrix is literature, was consequently the necessary condition for access to top positions. The intellectual was heir of the defeated aristocracy, since prowess as a source of prestige and prestige as a source of power continued to dominate the values and human relations of "bourgeois" society. He was also the heir of the Church, since the Enlightenment displaced religion and put lay science in its stead, and since the intellectual was called upon to provide the spiritual guidance once associated only with the Church. The humanist intellectual, mocked yet mirror-imaged by Sartre, was a sort of king, as Crozier has said, and a sort of high priest: he was accountable to none but his own genius. Politics were seen as the supreme activity of the spirit, top civil servants and political leaders were at least part-time intellectuals, and entry into intellectual or quasi-intellectual professions was for centuries the privileged method of social ascent, favored by an aristocracy whose values put intellectual achievement far above material success. This privileged position was an honor and a risk. In times of purges, the intellectuals were hit hardest, precisely because their pretense at being the conscience of society was taken seriously.

The mode of discourse encouraged by this privileged position was the same as that which had so irritated Tocqueville: "ends are discussed in relation to moral, religious and philosophical principles, and means are analyzed in a mechanistic perspective." [23] In a society overhauled by a traumatic Revolution (which the intellectual was taught to see as the direct product of intellectual challenge) and deeply marked by Catholicism, the French intellectual was bound to be fascinated by grand schemes and global designs. He could not be an "action intellectual" in the sense of "a problem solver who uses the skills and techniques of his professional training to resolve difficulties in specific areas of organized activity." [24] Yet as a "moral intellectual," he too was concerned with action and change—action and change in line with his kind of thought, action on a grand scale (hence his fascination with revolution or counterrevolution) and change through the power of ideas, through the *fiat* of spiritual *lux*.

At the same time, however, the gradual, slow evolution of French society to one far closer to other Western industrial societies contributed to increase the "protest" content of French thought. The intellectuals of the Left resented the growing importance of money and the effects of their own dependence on the market. They denounced those nations which seemed to them most advanced on the road to such corruption—first Britain, then Germany, later the United States. They looked forward to a society in which the fundamental values would be those of intellectual as well as manual labor.* The intellectuals of the Right rejected industrial society and mechanization altogether; they looked back to a society inspired by rural and aristocratic values and

* The French tradition of protest was bound to lead intellectuals into a close and tortured relation to communism. French Marxists are often the heirs of positivism; they see in communism the achievement of a scientific society led by benevolent and knowledgeable representatives of temporal power—the organizers of work, and spiritual power—the intelligentsia. French intellectuals since the Russian Revolution have had to define themselves by reference to communism and to come to terms with it—especially since World War II. At the time of the Liberation, the fascination exerted by counterrevolutionary dogmas had disappeared; the millennial aspirations of the Resistance fastened on the demise of the bourgeoisie, which was all too easily seen as the embodiment of evil, including collaborationism, and on the rise of the working class, which had massively resisted; the Communist party could appeal both to romantics in quest of action, community, and faith, and to *scientistes* in quest of total explanations and global social engineering. The key writers all either started from a Marxist position or from a critique of Marx, or else, like Mounier, Sartre, and Merleau-Ponty, "found" Marxism as soon as they began to reflect systematically on society and change.

The relation of the intelligentsia to communism has been one of constant attraction and constant tension. There has been the mirage of reconciliation—between the intellectual's esoterism, mystery, and prestige, and his desire for communion with the people; between thought and action: a reconciliation around the myth of total revolution guided by the intelligentsia on behalf of a universal class. But there has also been the crushing discomfort of a stifling and bureaucratic party. The French Communist Party tolerated no intellectual originality among its thinkers (unless, like Aragon or Picasso, their "private" activities as artists had nothing at all to do with their "public" and thoroughly orthodox behavior), nor did it appreciate charitable attempts by sympathetic non-Communists to inject some transcendence into dialectical materialism and to put human freedom back into historical determinism. Nor could intellectuals, as rebels, tolerate the party forever, for it failed to be genuinely revolutionary, its dogmas became ossified and irrelevant to new developments, and its leadership kept treating the party's intellectuals as mere tools and ornaments. Hence the periodic protests and exits and exclusions. The intellectuals went out in search of revolutionary spontaneity (sought in the early writings of Marx or in a return to pre-Marxist socialism), or a better explanation of the modern world (sought in applying Marxian methods to developments which had come to contradict his prophecies), or a new way of restoring the autonomy, distance, and authority of the intellectuals. The latest example is Roger Garaudy, who finds the key to all three quests in the passage from "mechanical rationality" (objective, deterministic, and tyrannical) to "cybernetic rationality," which is due to the new scientific and technological revolution and which restores subjectivity, autonomy, initiative, and—last but not least—the importance of *"les forces de la culture."* See *Le Grand Tournant du socialisme* (Paris, 1969).

dominated by *notables*—including the intelligentsia.

But the protest of the intellectuals is rooted also in the nature of the political system. Politics, by essence, is the art of the possible— especially in a country as stalemated as France; and yet, all French political regimes are heavily centralized (even more so than under the *ancien régime,* where bureaucracy and centralization had been far less complete than Tocqueville thought); the "conquest" of the state is a precondition for any reform, the stake of any revolution. As a result, intellectuals were fascinated by central power, encouraged in their fondness for grand schemes, incited to transfer their hopes and their homes to Paris. But they were also vividly reminded of the discrepancies between the ideal and the possible, between ends and means: nowhere was there such an abyss between the limited achievements of an ambitious and concentrated state apparatus, and the boundless constructs of an intelligentsia that made a religion of politics.

The divisions in French thought I have spoken of not only divided intellectuals and political classes; they condemned the former to be almost constantly frustrated by the conflicts or impotence of the latter. When a political regime was established on too narrow a basis (for instance, the two monarchies of 1815–48 and the Vichy regime after the initial period of unanimity), the divorce between politics and the intellectuals would reappear in a way quite comparable to that under the *ancien régime:* intellectuals supporting the regime tended to become uncompromising doctrinaires, intellectuals in opposition attacked it with the same abstract intransigence as that shown by the *philosophes.* The result was massive protest and an intellectual civil war. When a political regime rested on a much broader basis, the situation was somewhat different. In the case of a savior or strong-man regime, such as that of Napoléon III, most intellectuals would protest against its restrictions to public freedom; even when the restrictions were minimal, as under de Gaulle, there would be scores of intellectuals who resented the regime's Caesarean style. Echoes of the *ancien régime* reawakened in them their eighteenth-century ancestors' reactions to the kings—a kind of competition for the leadership of opinion (never more ardent than when the King, in the case of de Gaulle, is also an intellectual). If on the other hand the regime was democratic but *immobiliste,* the intellectuals would soon be frustrated again. In sum, intellectual protest was encouraged by the inevitable schism between a political system that functioned only by avoiding too neat a polarization and an intelligentsia that always tended toward extreme positions. The intellectuals had to choose between being the mere justifiers of the *status quo* or being dissenters of the Left or Right—or, if they did not choose, they could become both dissenters and justifiers, like Alain. One can see how uncomfortable their position would be: dissatisfied with pluralist, representative regimes because of *immobilisme,* they were even more hostile to "strong-man" regimes because of the atmosphere of forced or fake unanimity. "Unhappy consciousness" indeed!

Being both split among themselves and often opposed to the politicians in power, the intellectuals inevitably became intransigent moralists. Ever since the early eighteenth century, the absence of an intellectual consensus explains the extraordinary prevalence of moralist thinking over utilitarian arguments, even among France's liberals (by comparison with Britain's or with American "Lockeans"). And it is not surprising that the relations between intellectuals and the public would oscillate from almost complete alienation, when the country was in a mood for a savior and the intellectuals were, on the whole, in opposition (as was the case in 1958), to relative harmony, when the polarization of the intellectuals between Left and Right corresponded to a similar deep split in public opinion (1900 and 1936). Lastly, the relations between the intellectuals and the parties are almost always bad, except in brief periods of "dawn"—at the foundation of a regime, before disillusionment sets in. After that, the intellectuals begin to snipe at the compromises and maneuvers of political strategy and, particularly, at the intellectuals who, having become party leaders, are symbols of betrayal in a world *"où l'action n'est pas la sœur du rêve."* [25]

Another important source of the intellectuals' protest has been the decline of France's role in the world since the turn of the century and particularly since the 1930s. To men who believed with almost equal fervor in the universality of France and civilization, who thought, with Durkheim, that French culture was the culture of civilized man everywhere and that France's conception of patriotism reconciled the nation with mankind, this decline could not but provoke new drives into utopias, in an attempt to regain lost universality. Hence, ever since the days of Bergson and Sorel, the faith in spontaneity, in the recapturing of mastery over history by action. (This faith inspired men as different as the young de Gaulle and the young *gauchistes* of 1968; did the old man have some secret sympathy for them?) Hence also the quest for new general systems, for the recapturing of mastery over history by finding its intellectual key. (This search for determinism led "structuralist" thinkers to eliminate history altogether.) Both attitudes reflect the same unwillingness to come to terms with history, the same pride in rejecting its currents and complexity, the same preference for concepts over facts, the same atavism of prowess—oscillating "between the delirium of individual omnipotence and the schizophrenia of total determinism." [26] The more such utopias fail to return to French intellectuals—hence, in their eyes, to France—the prestige of universal relevance, the more complaints there are against the trends of modern history or against the men in power. It has seemed as if, seeing France unflatteringly reflected in foreign eyes, French intellectuals either wanted to repudiate alien testimonies altogether, or angrily urged their compatriots to adopt the apparently more successful doctrines that swept Fascist Italy, Nazi Germany, Cuba, Red China, or Soviet Russia.[27]

Until the end of the Algerian war, France's adjustment to the world continued to raise those moral issues which had provoked French intellectuals so often before into protests against one another, against the government's policy, against the outside world: issues of justice versus the national interest, survival versus decadence. In this respect, the Algerian drama was as divisive and agonizing as the Dreyfus Affair: the alignments may have been less clear, but the battles were no less fierce. It was from among the intellectuals that the most searching debates, the most passionate denunciations, and the most daring analyses of the war came—as the names of Camus, P. H. Simon, Jules Roy, Jeanson, Domenach, Aron, Mus, or Bayet, Thierry-Maulnier, Girardet, indicate. After Algeria, de Gaulle's performance—at once so personal and so unideological—did not appease the intellectual longing for a way of re-enchanting history (to parody Weber): in the alleged boredom of 1968, this nostalgia contributed first to the explosion, and later to the intellectuals' efforts to show that what had *almost* happened in France was of world-wide importance. *Ce n'est qu'un début;* France had once more been exemplary (but it was allegedly de Gaulle who said so).

Thus the intellectuals' protest was no longer mainly due, as it had been in the eighteenth century, to lack of political participation. It came from the frustrations which a "bourgeois" society and a fragmented polity imposed on a divided intelligentsia, in a world less and less fascinated by France. The immobility of the system fostered impatience in every tendency and seemed to leave a chance for every utopia. It is not surprising, if to "play the game" of politics or to accept society as it is (with its class and group tensions) means resignation to perpetual discord or gradual decadence, that so many intellectuals decided that only through rebellion could *grandeur,* solidarity, and fraternity be found again. "I revolt, therefore we are," wrote Camus. Alas, this hope turned out to be vain in almost every case. The Resistance period became a powerful and nostalgic myth because this was the one protest movement that seemed to restore unity and harmony, not only among most of the intellectuals, but between them, the parties, and the people—within the Great Alliance of Winners. But it was, once more, a negative kind of union, and the apparent triumph of the movement in 1944 came shortly before its disintegration.

III

The future of protest as a national way of life deserves some exploration. If one looks back at France from the Revolution to the 1950s, one may ask whether the kind of protest I have described, far from being "dysfunctional" or subversive to the social order, did not, on the contrary, play a vital part in saving the individual from becoming a mere cog in society, and in saving the French body politic from the Scylla of violent conflict and the Charybdis of oppression. For the stalemate society, with all its weaknesses, has long been the broadest form of consensus conceivable in France, and the *immobiliste* political system has at least preserved the underlying society and made possible the peaceful coexistence of incompatible parties and schools of thought. Such a society, such a polity, engendered protest movements for the reasons I have given, but they absorbed them as well. Indeed, the merit of the Third Republic and even of the Fourth, before 1958, was that it tamed one protest movement after another. In a nation like France, there is more than cynicism in Ernest Renan's statement that the aim of politics should not be to solve issues but to wait until they are exhausted, and more than wit in Robert de Jouvenel's maxim that stagnation is the only form of faithfulness to one's principles. For there were only two ways of keeping the nation together: one may be called the institutionalization of political stalemate; the other was Richelieu's formula of a strait jacket to contain a divided and fickle nation.

Since protest movements are the product of a certain kind of society and polity, it would seem that the transformation of the latter would bring about changes in the former. French society has indeed been undergoing a revolution, and its political system has been shaken up too. Yet the connections between economic and social change and political reform on one hand, and civic behavior on the other are anything but direct.

The decisive event in the gradual liquidation of the stalemate society since 1945 is that France has become industrialized. The stalemate society required the following structures or institutions: a limited state, whose role was to preserve equilibrium among the various groups (a protector, not a manager); a hierarchical society with a large peasant reservoir, careful social distances between the various strata which form the consensus groups, and the maintenance of as many independent operators as possible; and a clear-cut separation between the workers and the other elements of the population. All those elements are disappearing.

The government actually plays a leading role in the French economy, a fact which has been more or less grudgingly accepted by all groups in French society. The shopkeepers' revolts, the less noisy sniping by small business groups, and some protests by peasant organizations have seemed at times to challenge this aspect of state activities, because public policies tended toward the elimination of marginal producers in all these areas. But, on the whole, the attitudes in these sectors of the economy have evolved in recent years from a heroic and vain refusal to change, to a much greater willingness to adapt, and, indeed, to an expectation that the state would dutifully direct and subsidize their adaptation. Planning—its institutions and its "myth"—has helped importantly to foster a modicum of cooperation.

As a consequence of state planning and the conversion of French business to the ethos of modernization (productivity and expansion), the geographic and functional fragmentation of the French economy and society is being reduced. Advanced capitalism and the beginning of "postindustrial" society (i.e., the practical importance of theoretical knowledge, the growth of the service sector, the decline of unskilled work) have arrived simultaneously. The village is now less self-contained; [28] the family is less tight and—as in other industrial societies—an adolescent "culture" has appeared; some differences between the ranks and statuses have crumbled; a more uniform way of life emerges. As a result, the peasant basis of society has shrunk, and the new growing middle classes are predominantly salaried. The two traditional *antichambres* of the bourgeoisie—the line of wealth and the line of prestige—have become more diversified and more alike; in the *haute bourgeoisie,* property is less obsessively important. The new society seems less cramped than the old one; economic rationality has progressed at the expense of the social rationality of the bourgeoisie, reluctant to accept the challenge of social mobility and economic growth. Growth and development, rather than stability, are recognized as the preconditions of security; mass consumption, once frowned upon by the bourgeoisie, has become the motor of expansion. Interest groups are more effectively organized than before, particularly in rural France and in the business community. In those milieux change has been promoted by the cooperation of interest groups with the state.

The working class is now at least partially integrated into the nation: in part because the opposition in values and ways of life is less complete, in part because the greater specialization of industrial labor has, at the same time, fragmented the proletariat as a class and integrated a major portion of it into the firms. The worker finds himself less segregated from the rest of society, less unwilling at times to cooperate with men who in turn behave toward him as if a common interest in prosperity existed rather than an abyss. The ideal image of the proletariat may lose, but its material lot benefits from the change. As a sociologist has put it, it is the end of the trilogy "family enterprise, shopkeeper, revolutionary syndicalism." [29]

There are major changes in the political sphere also. The counterrevolutionary extreme right is practically dead. The fatal blow that the Vichy fiasco dealt to the plausibility of its doctrines, the liquidation of the stalemate society, and the extension of the state's role have relegated Maurrasian dogmas to the scholars' museum and the politicians' cemetery.

As for the other main schools of traditional French thought, the divisions among them have been blurred by the growth of Christian Democracy, by the changes in society and in the role of the state, later still by de Gaulle's success in borrowing from most ideologies so as to push them all aside, and, finally, by the general irrelevance of the old ideological categories to an analysis of (or action on) contemporary society.[30] Many of the old issues that gave rise to protest movements of the Left and Right are on the road to extinction. The issue of *laïcité* still produces an occasional corporative protest among public schoolteachers; but it is no longer a national issue. The Socialists have ceased to behave like a party of protest, and the Communists, who still do, are highly embarrassed in attempting to give a "correct" analysis of the changes in French society, and increasingly careful to keep protest from erupting into violence. The new revolutionary *gauchistes* of the far left are a noisy and often brutal lot, but neither a new school of thought nor a political force. On the Right, the Gaullists have put an end to fragmentation and created a modern, pragmatic, and dominant coalition far closer to Toryism than to any previous French conservative force.

A gradual adjustment to the outside world has brought about a surprising amount of consensus and silence where tumult and turmoil reigned just a few years ago. Even the enemy camps of European supranationalists and anti-Europeans appear to have if not exterminated at least exhausted each other, to the advantage of practical and gradual "Europeans."

Finally, signs of change appeared in the intelligentsia in the late 1950s and early 1960s. Polarization among intellectuals seemed to have decreased. The attraction of communism and Marxist orthodoxy lessened, and many left-wing intellectuals discovered that "Marxism had become the myth of the left-wing intellectuals" and was an excuse for ignoring "the entire sociological and historical reality in which they live." [31] The disillusioned and self-critical ex-Communist intellectual became a familiar actor on the French literary scene. At the other pole, many intellectuals of the Right lapsed into pure futility, and the Algerian war only briefly injected militancy into some of them. One symptom of this lowering of tension was a decline of anti-Americanism—that form of protest against the modern Western world which had so long been shared by both extremes. Another symptom was the sudden attraction of Mendès-France, a champion of pragmatic politics for so many intellectuals.

The evolution of French society threatens the pre-eminence of the intellectuals and their role as guides of public opinion. In a society where the number of specialized tasks has multiplied, where individuals belong to a broad range of organizations and communities, the appeal of the "specialist of general culture" and of his style of intransigent abstract argument diminishes. Politics is no longer considered the supreme activity of the mind. The new forms of mass culture include audiovisual and quantitative techniques, which tend to reduce the importance of literary modes of expression.[32] And the social sciences, which in France have largely developed outside the traditional university, have brought about a certain amount of experimentalism. A modern type of "action-oriented" intellectual—new in France although familiar in postwar America—has appeared.

The question has been raised whether postindustrial society would not, in France as elsewhere, usher in a world in which private concerns would divert the citizen from traditional political activity, and in which public decisions would be taken by the "technostructure" alone. Since protest was so largely ideological in France, would not "the end of ideology" mean the inherent end of protest? There are, however, obvious reasons for doubting that we are anywhere near such a fundamental mutation in French public life. Some of the most essential causes of French protest are still with us, and we were all rudely called back to reality in 1968.

The features I have described above as common to French society and to the polity have not disappeared. The style of authority not only persists, but has in some ways hardened, as will be shown in greater detail in the next chapter. "Postindustrial" society anywhere is a society of large, hierarchical, bureaucratic organizations. In France, this type of social order, like capitalism earlier, has accommodated itself to and been molded by the old structures of authority. The idiosyncratic system described by Crozier has expanded as more and more people now work in large organizations. The peculiar relationship between distant superiors and "publicly" obedient but "privately" independent subordinates has been generalized to many more occupations, and affects a greater part of more people's lives. To be sure, it has always characterized relations in the state bureaucracy, and between *administrés* and *administrateurs*. But the extension of the bureaucracy since the war has also made *those* relations more numerous and intense, now that the civil service's task, in Paris and in the provinces, has switched from accommodating of interests around the *status quo,* to the promotion and management of change. Thus, opportunities for protest along traditional lines have increased quantitatively, and there are what might be called "qualitative" new reasons as well. For the old style of authority is singularly ill-adapted to an industrial society where communication and information are essential, social distances are narrowed, the sphere of actual independence shrinks as each citizen becomes involved in a growing number of social activities, organizational units are large and must cooperate with each other, and rapid changes condemn techniques, factories, and services to early obsolescence.

The originality of the crisis in 1968 was precisely the presence in it of "pure" protests—protests that resulted neither from ideological drives nor from material grievances, but from the intolerable weight of the structures of authority. Many of the students who rebelled in the *lycées* and many of the cadres who joined the workers' strikes in factories, many of the professionals who challenged their elders, proved that a certain form of civic behavior—once visible primarily in relations with the state, or labor-management relations—had been universalized.

Protest is also a natural outcome of a clash between the economic process of constant change, and a continuing value preference for homeorhesis. For all of the conversion to expansion and development, residues of the old aristocratic disdain for economic rationality remain. French businessmen, French engineers, and French bureaucrats who control or orient industry are not really dominated by the concern for profit: their preservation of established forms and lines of authority, and their admiration for technical prowess (however uneconomical), sharply limit economic rationality; when (in an economy increasingly open to foreign competition) the sanction is failure, cadres, employees, and workers have new grounds for protest. Outside industry, all those who are forced to abandon their former professions or fall behind in the economic race find reasons to demand protection in their "humanistic" hostility to the laws of the market and to the tyranny of money, and in their equally profound attachment to "equilibrium." The same values inspired the students who flooded the university in recent years to oppose any policy that would gear studies to jobs and thereby make the curriculum more "technocratic." Simultaneously, the bureaucrats' conviction that they are the only guardians of the general interest, and are thus entitled to impose their own solution to the huge range of economic and social issues under their jurisdiction, could not but incite interest groups or local *notables* to couch their demands for attention or protection in ever more sweeping terms—defense of freedom, preservation of a humane way of life or a cultural tradition, etc.

As a result, despite the "nationalization" of the political system, brittleness and fragmentation have persisted in the realm of voluntary associations. Their membership remains small, and in almost every sector—workers, cadres, peasants, shopkeepers, students—theirs is a story of intense rivalry, splits, attempted common fronts, and mutual excommunications. Their division is an incentive to competitive outbidding; their weakness frequently causes them to lose touch with their base, which provokes outbursts there.

Conditions for protest continue to be provided by the evolution of French society; in every instance, the protest results from the interplay of substantive grievances with the French style of authority.

In the first place, the relation between workers and the rest of the population (particularly employers) remains a source of major tension. Old reflexes and attitudes have not been driven out. The workers' sense of injustice and resentment persists. In an increasingly urban nation, adequate public housing and transportation have not been provided. Access to higher education is still minimal. Major decisions affecting the workers have remained in the hands of the state which, in the 1960s, in its drive to make the economy competitive, tried to limit wage increases, especially at the bottom of the hierarchy and in public enterprises. The greater strength of the unions at the central level—where the state is—than at the factory level has kept even collective bargaining wrapped in symbolic ideology, and is often irrelevant to specific plant conditions. Within the factories, the *patronat*'s hostility to syndicalism continues to feed syndicalist *contestation* and to weaken the unions, so that the workers remain poorly organized and divided. These factors all contributed to the explosion of May 1968: unorganized workers often initiated the strikes and unions later escalated their demands. Thus, all the old tensions are still present, and new ones stem from the coexistence of traditional and more recent values.[33]

The process of modernization also provokes protest from groups that either are being eliminated or benefit from economic progress less rapidly than others. These are protests which any period of fast development produces anywhere, but, as events since 1968 have shown, they are particularly spectacular whenever the political system fails to meet the grievances adequately. Some of those protests were classical ones, in the sense of being typical of France's stalemate society as industrialization proceeded. But industralization's more hectic pace has also made these protests more frantic (as in the case of the small shopkeepers). Others are "new." Some are due to the effect of "postindustrial" society on France's pre-existing social order, as in the case of cadres displaced or demoted by the introduction of computers into their firms, or the case of the imbalance between university curriculum choices and job outlets for students. Others are less tied to the peculiarities of France's society—the complex and almost universal *contestation* of the postindustrial order by students is an example. There is another novelty as well: in parts of France that have felt left at the starting gate (Brittany, for example), the discontented have sometimes joined forces across the old social and ideological barriers and given protest an *autonomiste* regional content.[34]

France's new political system has made its own contribution to protest. Paradoxically enough, the advent of a "majority coalition," the appearance of a "voters' party," far from establishing a better transmission belt between the electorate and the executive, have in some ways aggravated the divorce and made communications weaker. To be sure, under de Gaulle this was partly due to the peculiar relations between the Gaullist coalition and Parliament on one hand, and the executive on the other: the deputies were there to vote, but the government and the top bureaucracy (largely symbiotic) were not really there to listen. Indeed, when the Gaullist majority in Parliament shrank to a handful of votes in 1967, the Premier simply decided to proceed through ordinances. But there were other reasons as well. Many discontented Frenchmen either did not vote (i.e., students under twenty-one) or voted for opposition parties whose capacity to influence the regime was nil (a phenomenon due not to Gaullist arbitrariness but to the normal functioning of majority rule). This was bound to create frustration; it made the discontented turn to other channels for the expression of their grievances (hence the resurgence of what had, earlier in the days of Gaullism, been called *les forces vives*—i.e., interest groups) and increase their militancy when the opposition, after the elections of March 1967, seemed at last close to electoral victory. On the other hand, the Gaullist party itself—whose electorate was a pretty faithful reflection of France's social and professional make-up, and which should therefore have been attuned to the desires and demands of the public —has suffered from the defects of its virtues: under de Gaulle this "voters' party" was not a party of *notables,* by contrast with previous French socially conservative political groups. Its local roots were weak: it was a national party, not only in the sense of recruiting its voters from all over France and of not being a conglomeration of little local lords, but also in the sense of not having a very intimate connection with its constituencies (many of its more brilliant younger deputies are ex-civil servants). In the more fragmented society and polity of the Third Republic, the voters sent local *notables* to Paris to keep the central civil service (whose functions were limited) under control, whereas in the *départements* the representatives of the state were engaged in a complex relation of mutual dependence with the local *notables*—a network of "parallel relations" which resulted from, yet offset, centralization. In the Fifth Republic, now that most of the important decisions are made in Paris, the voters prefer to be represented by men who are "in the know" in Paris, and who, being closer to the inner sanctum, are supposed to be better watchdogs and "pressurers" than local *notables*. The old system has become irrelevant. Yet the new one is plagued by the vices of centralization. Many Frenchmen have the impression of being subjected (through and despite their votes) to an authoritarian bureau-technocracy that takes no or little account of their grievances and that experiments in the dark. And indeed, in several important areas—education, social security, medicine, territorial administration, employment, planning—the trend has been toward ever greater administrative centralization and the atrophy of consultative bodies.[35] The citizen, despite effective majority rule, feels himself becoming more and more a mere subject.

Protest is also encouraged by the Fifth Republic's apparent combination of the high-handedness of savior regimes (yet in freedom, i.e., explosively) and the proclivity of representative regimes to *immobilisme* (yet with clogged transmission and greater centralization, i.e., also explosively). Paradoxically, one reason for its growing bureaucratic authoritarianism was the conviction that reform could come only from the highest echelon. But the conditions in which the bureaucracy had to operate—with inadequate information (relevant information often being "kept" by the lower strata or by outsiders who are not party to the decisions) and fierce resistance from below and outside (due to resentment at being left out)—smothered reform or shrank its scope. Centralization emphasized rather than eliminated impotence. Of course, there have been considerable economic changes, but their institutional and social consequences have not really been measured. The old structures that were more or less adequate in France's stalemate society—the university, the organization of authority in industry, the highly centralized *services publics* (which now comprise a major part of France's banks, industry, communications, and social-security system), the Napoleonic scheme of territorial organization, with its antiquated taxes—are bursting under and deforming the new expansion. At the same time, the effort to correct the inequities of rapid growth —to redistribute income so as to reduce discontent—without drastically changing these structures was very timid (i.e., efforts at decentralization and public housing). Or it succeeded only in burdening the budget with enormous subsidies that made little dent on inequality, delayed economic modernization instead of making it bearable, postponed the hardships of growth, and forced the state into sudden cutbacks (like the social-security reform in 1967). Protest movements have traditionally emerged either in reaction to authoritarian efforts at changing French society or in reaction against the impotence of a regime that reflected social conflicts too faithfully. The great protest of 1968, and smaller subsequent ones, erupted in reaction to a regime that exhibited a mix of authoritarianism and impotence: when there was direction, it was too haughty; when there was adjustment, it was too skimpy.

Given such conditions in society and in the political system, one should not have expected French intellectuals to lose their fondness for protest. To be sure, for a few years during the 1960s, it did look as if the old desire for total questioning and total answers had moved out of the political arena, into the esoteric constructs of "structuralism," and as if the domain of society and politics had been left (at last) to modern, modest social scientists. We did not pay sufficient attention to the effects of a dual irrelevance—the irrelevance of these new ideological systems to the world men were living in, the world of history and meanings; and the irrelevance of the new empirical research, with its (perhaps overcompensatory) indulgence in data-gathering, to the world of philosophical speculation about society's goals and man's nature. With the old ideological systems fading, but leaving a deep nostalgia behind them, the result was a kind of drought, a drying up of the emotions and the imagination. To many, this looked like a belated adaptation to the "mainstream" of the modern postindustrial age.[36] Actually, it concealed—even from the intellectuals—a continuing adherence to earlier attitudes. What was missing was a cause, in both meanings of the word. May 1968 provided it. The result was instructive, and not a little frightening.

The tendency to look for grand explanations, to treat society as if it were a field for instant, complete experimentation, the urge to turn out concepts like sausage slices, to ratiocinate and prophesy and excommunicate, to look for models and to universalize—in other words, millennialism—reasserted itself. Many French intellectuals had not resigned themselves to the demise of their pre-eminence *qua* intellectuals, and to being replaced by experts in industrial society (*vide* the resistance of so many of them to changes in education that would have sealed the fate of *la culture générale*).[37] Several of the "structuralist" thinkers now returned with a vengeance to history in the making, and applied to modern society and social sciences the methods for "unveiling" laws and functions hidden from human awareness that they had previously tried on literature, language, modes of production, or primitive societies—one more attempt at "scientific" debunking and at concealing grand ideology. Several of the "new" social scientists, eager for action, behaved not as pragmatic "action" intellectuals (in the sense of organization-minded reformers) but as ideological activists in the grand revolutionary tradition. By comparison with earlier intellectual *crises*, this one was distinguished by the prevalence of ideological attitudes over ideological substance. French intellectuals still preferred their "irresponsible royalty," to use Crozier's words, to more humble and accountable adviserdom; but again the kings had no clothes. In past intellectual *crises*, the intellectual kings had gods—earlier intellectuals who served as their inspiration, such as Proudhon or Péguy in the 1930s. This time there were no gods. The ideological drought in the politico-social realm left the kings in a state of joyous mental anarchy and confusion—to each his own theory, usually a blend of historical reminiscences and blow-ups of some aspects of the present, rolled together under a Marxist label into a preview of the future. But it also left them in a state of dependence on a single common notion—the catchall "alienation," a perfect symbol for a general resistance to the modern world, money machines, organizations, production, consumption, anonymity, organization, bureaucracy, calculations—and in a common bond with Rousseau. It was as if the death of the old ideological systems, far from releasing French intellectuals into the age of empirical action, only liberated them from the mental discipline and mental (not social) responsibility those systems had imposed, and made them even more indifferent to facts and to social consequences. It was like a re-enactment of a great past in the form of a delirium—like a long-playing record played at the speed of 78. Optimists may see in the explosion the last—if bastardized—performance of a once great act. Pessimists may argue that as long as the factors in French life enumerated above persist (the structures of authority and the values that support them, the tensions in society and in the polity), and as long as their essential substratum survives (the system of education), the atavistic reactions of French intellectuals will reappear whenever the opportunity arises, albeit in volatile and chaotic fashion. (The intellectuals' divagations on the subject of Israel and the Arabs since May 1967 seem to vindicate the pessimists.)

Daniel Bell has correctly written that "in the next few decades, the political arena will become more decisive, if anything," both because of the growing importance of national planning (vs. the market) and because of the reassertion of "communal society" (a reaction against the preponderance of great hierarchical organizations). In these respects, France as presently constituted would see a recrudescence of protests. For the national political arena will remain a contest between a centralized bureaucracy, sure of its monopolistic legitimacy, and groups excluded from the process of decision-making. (The evolution of French planning from an experimental field for *concertation* into an increasingly bureaucratic exercise of limited effect even on national decisions is a bad omen.) Even a greater role for Parliament (still in doubt) and the establishment of deeper local roots for Gaullist deputies (in process) would not redress the balance, given both the limited effect legislatures can have on the basic economic and financial decisions of modern states, and the weight of the French bureaucracy. As for French "communal society," it remains devoid of adequate institutions and resources; local groups depend on the agents of the state for support, or must escalate their demands, for in a centralized economy and political system where the old nationwide ideological fissures have disappeared, protest easily takes the form of "communal" resistance, denouncing "colonization" by Paris, its agents, and its rich.

The changes of the postwar period have helped to show where the root of the problem lies. If protests are the safety valve for conflicts and a substitute for a harmonious polity, it is not primarily because of the institutional flaws of the political system, nor because of the absence (or breakdown) of consensus on substance (domestic and foreign policies) and procedure (how to resolve disputes). It is because of the complex of values and institutions that dictate how the French deal with each other and face their conflicts. The flaws of the Fifth Republic's political system result not from constitutional vices, but mainly from the effect of the system of authority relations on the legislature and the executive. The social tensions—in a society that is almost as different from the stalemate society as it was different from the society under the *ancien régime*—are also heightened by the political system. The nonparticipatory style of authority not only escalates conflicts physically, but also perpetuates their traditional ideological aspects long after the social bases of the ideologies have disappeared: hence, for instance, among today's workers, the split that persists between those who hope their dream of change will somehow come true through conquest of the state, and those who distrust all parties and dream of a syndicalist order resulting somehow from the disappearance of the state.

Even utopian protest is functional in such a system. But the system is no longer functional for the society. It makes for a vicious circle in which the blind infuriate the blind: the decision-makers, at the top of their organizations, often do not have the information on which they should base their decisions, and they behave like charging bulls (or sleeping bulls). The subjects react equally blindly—with a mixture of vengefulness and delirium. As long as the economy was fragmented and the polity rent by deep ideological fissures, the national style of authority was an integrative force in France. It provided coherence without oppression. (Conversely, the great ideological blocs mediated, so to speak, between the centrifugal tendencies of society and of critical or rebellious subjects, and the state's permanent bureaucracy.) Now that there is a national economy, largely controlled by the state, now that the ideological blocs have been eroded, the weight of the centralized and hierarchical decision-making system of the French government in particular, of French organizations in general, becomes unbearable. It now has less need to respect differences, to take local customs and intellectual traditions into account: in the new homogeneous vacuum, all problems are treated as technical, susceptible of one solution only. And the behavior of the subjects in the system becomes disastrous. The heavier the weight of the system, the more they demand, not a new system, but what the logic of the old one has led them to demand—i.e., more rules for legal and financial protection, so as to defend their rights, consecrate their advantages, and limit their obligations; and more independence from the monster, in the form of fewer hours of work, earlier retirement, more leisure.[38]

It is not hard to list what could produce a change—a reform of the system of education (the institutions, the substance, the pedagogy), decentralization of territorial and economic administration, a reform of management techniques, etc. *How* these changes are to be introduced and made effective is another matter. For the old system, dysfunctional perhaps, is assuredly self-perpetuating. It survives crises of protest (as in 1968) by piecemeal adjustments that appease the protesters for a while and thereby also give many of them a stake in the system—i.e., it extends the sphere of protection and creates new sources of what might be called captive power (not substantive power, but the power to bargain with those above and to be consulted by them). And the "victims" of the system neither know how to change it nor appear ready to exchange the costs it inflicts for the heavy costs of "participation"—which would force them to take full responsibility for the handling of conflicts, to calculate and bear the consequences of their joint decisions, to give away the security and reassurance of "private" autonomy and public regulation for the uncertainties of constant communication, negotiation, and competition. They seem to be settled in a kind of cozy double bookkeeping. As citizens, they delegate to the political system, specifically to the leaders and members of the majority coalition, the task of insuring, on top, that change is well managed from the top. As members of different classes or interest groups, they go on protesting whenever their specific demands and expectations are frustrated.

Indeed, the style of French protest makes "participation" practically impossible. Protest as it is practiced in France attempts to protect partial independence and push full responsibility for decisions upward; it prefers the intransigence of all-or-nothing and leaves to "them" the onus of half-measures (reserving the possibility of future protest to get the other half when convenient); it pits the individual against authority; it makes "peer groups" semi-legitimate, ignored by many, distrusted by their members, resisted by higher authority, and thus condemned to oscillate from ineffectiveness to paroxysm. Between command and dissent—*le commandement* and *la contestation*—participation is ruled out: it would mean mixing the different orders of "theirs" and "ours," whereas the logic of the French system is to keep them apart.

As long as the present authority system lasts, protest will persist. The increasing social disadvantages of the system may turn protest more and more into crisis. But for the individual shaped by this system who has internalized the values on which obedience is built, can protest or even crisis really be called dysfunctional? As long as better ways of change are blocked, crisis remains the best alarm bell, even as it contributes to blocking better ways to change. Never was this vicious circle better demonstrated than in 1968.

6
Confrontation in May 1968

The most interesting aspect of France's great crisis of May–June 1968 was neither its suddenness, nor its scope, nor its spectacular ending. It was its ambiguity. What was at stake was nothing less than a nation's capacity to change not its skin (France has done that often) but its soul.

Lightning revealed, in a flash, how strong the aspirations were for change—in the citizens' attitudes toward authority, in the relation of each individual Frenchman to larger groups within France, in the traditional French conception of freedom. But the crisis also showed the resilience, even among the rebels, of the old beliefs and patterns of behavior. Lightning also revealed how widespread the aspiration was toward not only a different system of authority, but a different kind of social order altogether, how widespread was the discontent with Gaullist France's mix of features from the old stalemate society, modern capitalism, and the "postindustrial" world. But the crisis demonstrated the prevalence, among the rebels, of confusions and divisions of such magnitude as to rule out any consensus around an alternative vision of society. Since the rebels could not overcome the features they were rising against, either in themselves or in the nation, could change be worked out by the very forces they were denouncing? Was their fiasco a paradoxical prelude to the mutations they wanted, or proof of their impossibility?

The crisis of 1968 was largely due to the effect of prior widespread transformations in French life: in the educational system, deluged by masses of new students, in the economy, hit by the imperatives of growth and competition, in the regime, insufficiently responsive to pressures from below. New tensions triggered a demand for total reno-

An embryonic version of this essay appeared in the *New Republic*, August 31, 1968.

vation, but they also triggered old reflexes, reflexes which will limit the scope and meaning of any reform as long as they themselves have not changed.

In these respects, even though the government was not overthrown, the events of May–June 1968 deserve to be taken as seriously as the "successful" Revolutions of 1830 and 1848, which they resemble, or as the "National Revolution" of Vichy, of which they were, in some ways, an antithesis. The flood of books or articles that have been written about *les événements* [1] reflects their importance. (In part, it simply shows an aspect of their ambiguity: they were among other things a spectacle, and the actors, for all their attacks on the consumer society, rarely wanted to impose austerity on their potential royalties.) What makes assessment difficult is not only our proximity to these events, but also the fact that "the movement" ebbed before its various currents had had time to sort themselves out—it is therefore not surprising to find each writer using the events for confirmation of his favorite thesis.

I

The stake of the contest, and the key to its fate, was the French style of authority and of change, a style that has been described in preceding chapters. Only the main points need to be summarized here.

In a nation riddled by conflicts, the citizens have traditionally preferred to entrust the solution of conflicts to higher authority. This has been true in every group from the family to the state. But authoritarianism has always been tempered by individualism, by the citizen's determination to be protected from arbitrariness through a network of bureaucratic rules limiting the scope and intensity of authority. France is thus marked by a series of polar opposites: rigid, often stifling regulations, but also the preservation of the individual's capacity to protest, the perpetuation of his escape from involvement and responsibility; tight hierarchies controlled by a handful of important people, but also the fulfillment of the small peoples' dream of legal equality; centralization, but also fragmentation into small groups and castes; official, hierarchical relations, but also informal "parallel" relations that often find the formal superiors depending on their subordinates. Liberty is freedom *from,* not freedom *to;* it is defined as resistance and nondependence; compromise is a pejorative word. The values served by this style are, first, what Michel Crozier has called the horror of face-to-face relations; second, the desire of every group to preserve its status in society so that the over-all equilibrium (a key notion) and each group's security will, despite all changes, remain essentially intact.

In a system like this, the pattern of change is unique: the *way* of change is cataclysmic, not gradual; the *scope* of change is usually limited, especially as it preserves and perpetuates the fundamental style of authority. Except in times of turmoil, higher authority is rarely dynamic. Since most education and a huge fraction of the economy are public services, since elected local authorities have little power and no resources, any large-scale demand for change almost inevitably is aimed sooner or later at the state. Moreover, the nonparticipating citizens, when dissatisfied, behave not like reformers, but like rebels, given to wild utopianism, intransigence, and self-righteousness. In other words, in the absence of "participatory" channels of moderate change, the demand for change is radical. But rebels are not revolutionaries either: they are too negative, too much in love with protest and criticism, too concerned with preserving the basic values. So, traditionally, the rebellion disappears when central authority, aware of the rebels' clumsiness and ineptitude to build something together, grants concessions at the right moment. Thus the most indispensable changes are made possible, harmony is restored, and the pattern is reaffirmed.

The first ambiguity of the May 1968 crisis concerns its relation to this pattern. In some ways, the crisis re-enacted the French style of authority; in others, it revolted against it.

When one looks at the immediate circumstances of the eruption, one sees most clearly how familiar a drama it was, how much it was part of an age-old pattern. A fear of change in the over-all equilibrium of groups, professions, and statuses inspired the onslaught. In the case of the students' revolt, the trigger was the higher authority's sudden failure to assert itself in the expected bureaucratic way—i.e., as higher authority, but without arbitrariness. The occasion was like a school *chahut*—rambunctiousness breaking out against a teacher who had shown himself too weak or too tough. The government had responded to this *chahut* during the winter and spring of 1968 with an extravagant display of passivity at the University of Paris campus at Nanterre, followed belatedly by brutality when trouble threatened to beleaguer the Sorbonne.

A deeper cause, itself the trigger for the *gauchistes,* was the substance of recent decisions (or failures to decide) that had violated the sacrosanct principle of equilibrium. There had been a huge increase in the number of university students (almost sixfold from 1945 to 1968). The French university system is one in which access to higher education is open to all graduates of secondary schools, but it was predominantly a bourgeois preserve until about 1950. Beginning in the early 1950s, young men and women who would not have gone beyond high school in earlier decades invaded the university; most of them came from the more prosperous middle and lower-middle classes. But there were not enough opportunities available to them, either in the university, which was unprepared for the flood, or in society—especially since many of the students, guided by the traditional French scheme of values, were flocking into the humanities and social sciences, where the outlets were smallest. Traditionally, a degree had meant a career, and in this sense all French higher education could indeed have been called vocational. The new students expected to have the same opportunities as their predecessors: anything less would have been either a *déclassement,* for the bourgeois, or a drastic frustration of the will to keep up with "a process of change that improves the lot of others," for the *petits-bourgeois.* Suddenly, this promise of security seemed dubious.[2] Tens of thousands of students who had gone through the grueling maze of French exams rightly feared that they would find no jobs appropriate to their knowledge, labors, and degrees. Their revolt in 1968 was largely based on their determination to preserve their status and to vindicate their expectations [3]—on their own terms: without any *numerus clausus* restricting access to the university, without any forcible shift toward technical education, with adequate jobs for all, and with due legal and administrative protection for their rights and ranks.

The Fouchet educational reform of 1967 had not corrected any of the problems. Its measures, applied immediately not only to incoming students but to students who had already begun their university studies, were intended to raise the standards of scientific studies. But the reform was designed in order to achieve compulsory early specialization. These measures could not reduce the imbalance between curriculum choices and job outlets, since they did not touch the sacrosanct principle that the students had free access to any subject they wished to study, but they went straight against the students' values, were bound to increase the number of drop-outs, and toughened studies just as, for reasons that will be analyzed below, they seemed to become less rewarding.

By 1968 it was also well known that Fouchet's successor, Alain Peyrefitte, was under strong pressure from de Gaulle to restrict the access of students to the university in the future—a step that appeared to them as monumentally regressive, for it would have taken away their age-old right to higher educaton without any "selection," beyond the secondary schools' terminal *baccalauréat.* Thus, recent massive social changes, recent measures, and expected but resented measures, had produced a colossal set of disturbances in the balance of expectations.

As for the industrial crisis of May 1968, it too had an occasion and a cause. Workers quite spontaneously seized the moment when Premier Pompidou gave in to the students to press their own pent-up demands. In a centralized system, evidence of state weakness in one area invites *chahut* elsewhere. But the real reason for those demands was another new imbalance that had been created over the years of Gaullist rule. Here too, rising expectations in a more and more prosperous country had led to hopes and demands about better material conditions of work that had not been fulfilled. De Gaulle had had to water down and virtually abandon his old plan for some kind of association between capital and labor in the factories, thanks to the opposition of labor unions (afraid of being "integrated into the system"), businessmen (fearful about a loss of authority), and his own cabinet. Planning and the concern for a more productive economy had resulted in strengthening the bureaucracy (responsible for the public sector) and in consolidating business and its associations, whereas the workers' rate of material advance slowed down (especially in nationalized enterprises, where wages, determined by the state, were directly manipulated against inflation) and the unions remained divided and weak. The mild recession of 1967 led to unemployment among younger workers and to cuts in social services. It was not surprising that the first to revolt were often the worst hit or the most threatened: recently hired workers, afraid of being the first victims of further layoffs, young unskilled workers at the bottom of an ever-more extended scale of wages. And many of the cadres who sided with the workers had also been hit by the government's tax and social-security policies, or by measures of industrial reorganization which reduced their powers in the plants, making them, as one observer put it, more. like wage-earners than overseers.[4] Once again, a movement for change sprang from a desire for protection, from a fear of social retrogression.

Two other features of the system of French authority help to explain the May 1968 explosion. One was the condition of the voluntary associations that could have channeled grievances. The National Students Union, active during the Algerian war, had disintegrated, partly because of internal splits, partly under official pressure. As Raymond Aron put it, the students were a "lonely crowd." As for the labor unions, a number of factors hampered their effectiveness. They were stronger at the national level than in factories [5] at a time when industrial concentration was increasing the size and importance of many plants, and collective agreements negotiated at the regional or branch level were often irrelevant to conditions in the factories. The unions had lost touch with the workers—to the remarkable extent of being apparently unaware of their potential militancy and the depth of their discontent. Between nonunionized workers—the great majority—and unionized ones, between the latter and their delegates in the plants, between these and the unions' militants, there were discontinuities. Moreover, the biggest union, the CGT, was in effect subordinated to the priorities of the Communist party, busy building an electoral alliance with the non-Communist left, and satisfied with the results achieved at the polls in 1967.[6] The CGT was also focusing on Paris, not on the base. Consequently, the workers' revolt often started among those who were not union members, and had an aspect of protest against the unions' timidity and distance from the workers.[7]

The other typical feature was the government's own inadequate preparation for the crisis. Since "intermediate bodies" were either non-existent or disconnected from their bases, and since whatever information they might have had would have been retained by them as a source of power, the government's complacency was unshaken, although de Gaulle himself does not appear to have entirely shared it.[8] The authors of the Fouchet reform had thought it would be welcomed by the students!

So when, in May 1968, students and workers rebelled, it was a typically boisterous release from the impersonality and restrictiveness of French authority, an explosion of verbal and symbolic aggressiveness, a *défoulement*. It was not surprising to find writers, annoyed by what they considered a dangerous escape from reality, going back to Tocqueville's *Recollections* or Flaubert's *Sentimental Education*. These picturesque accounts of 1848 fed their irritation *and* reassured them. Once again, France was in the midst of an emotional orgy of face-to-face relations, a holiday from the boredom of everyday life, a sudden, joyous, noisy release from silence and isolation, a delirium of stream-of-consciousness discussions, debates, dialogues. It was no longer the state that was sovereign, it was the word. In a society of highly formal, contractual human relations, there was a surge of spontaneity. Neighbors who had lived side by side in mutual avoidance for years now talked to each other. In a society of separate individuals, suspicious groups, and poor communications (symbolized by the antiquated telephone system), there was a rush toward community. Students wanted to join hands with the workers and open the university to everyone. Even the beneficiaries of the hierarchy—the established professors, the *agrégés* of the university, *lycée* professors—took the lead in calling for the end of their own privileges. It was not the first time that those who had long blocked reform by an obstinate attachment to their privileges tried to get ahead of a revolution once it had begun: the first to do so had been the nobles who, on the night of August 4, 1789, abolished their special rights.

Yet this was not just one more explosive protest against specific measures or omissions for which higher authority was held responsible. Higher authority's very right to exist, not the use it had made of this right, was being attacked. Students challenged their professors, denounced the centralized controls of the Ministry of Education over the school and university systems, demanded autonomy for every academic unit, and co-management or even self-management within each. High-

school students attacked the authoritarianism of the student-teacher relation and asked for the right to participate in changing the
curriculum and examinations. In most of the professions, from architecture to medicine, the younger members challenged their less dynamic but all-powerful elders and proclaimed self-rule. The personnel
of the state-run radio and television struck on behalf of objectivity and
exerted their own right of self-expression. Young magistrates rebelled
against executive control of the judiciary. The young elite of the civil
service, training at the ENA, denounced its elitism. In some factories,
workers challenged the authority of the *patrons* and occupied the
plants as a prelude to the exercise of "worker power," and many cadres
struck for the first time, asking for a democratization of the companies.
It was not only the substance of these demands which showed that
there was something new. The rebels' behavior also went beyond the
traditional *chahut,* or holiday from rules: especially among the students there was something that had not been seen since 1789—a will
to reveal the Emperor in all his nakedness, to remove from authority
those trappings of prestige and awe on which, as Pascal had said, its
rule depended; a rage to debunk and ridicule and reduce the holders
of power to nothing; the French word is *désacraliser.* This is what
gave the posters and graffiti their wit and bite, this is where politics
and surrealism merged.

The reason for this rebellion against the very principle of authority,
and above all the reason why the explosion took place when it did
and spread as fast as it did, has to be found in the transformations of
postwar France, especially under Gaullism. In short, the system of authority that had presided over a feudal monarchy and over the stalemate society established after the monarchy's fall, once the backbone
of a deeply diverse and divided nation, had become a strait jacket.
Modern industrial and urban society needs larger and mentally less
cramped elites than the old, more static bourgeois-rural order. In industry, in education, in the professions, the rigid, authoritarian elites
were often inefficient; their decisions were ill-informed, restrictive, and
badly carried out by sullen subjects. France's centralized bureaucratic
state, while substituting for an anemic capitalism, keeps it so, largely
because of its remoteness, fragmentation into rival services, and dependence on the business elites, particularly through the networks of
graduates from the *grandes écoles.* (As Raymond Aron once suggested,
France is less capitalist and more socialistic than other advanced Western nations.) Balanced growth also required a revival of France's provinces, so long deprived of real autonomy, and a reform of the *communes,* most of which are minuscule, and whose powers are thoroughly
inadequate to urbanization. Above all, France needed a different
school system, less geared to abstract thought and essentially critical

faculties of the mind, less rigidly harsh in its early distribution of children on a very small number of different tracks that determine their whole future, more open to economics and world affairs, more diversified and experimental, based on cooperation among students as well as between them and their teachers.

The old French system could function as long as the balance between individual autonomy and social interaction, between individual creativity and group initiatives, was weighted in the direction of the former, for it fostered individual independence and self-expression within firmly established social grooves. It could only break down once the balance was weighted in the opposite direction, as it is in a modern economy. The choice for modernization had been made collectively after the tragic experiences of the 1930s and World War II, when the only alternatives seemed to be death or modernization.[9] But the consequences of that choice for France's traditional system of authority had not been suspected. (It may be that had they been, the huge effort would not have been undertaken: the principle of the hiding hand had worked well.[10]) The old system was geared to a society whose main institutions had either a small number of subjects or a limited number of functions. It was no longer adequate to cope or to operate with a huge quantitative increase in subjects or functions.

The "quantitative" transformation of France brought the nation into the age of largely urban "postindustrial" societies, with their vast hierarchical organizations. The tensions between the old and the new grew particularly sharp at three points. First, there was the problem of competence of the elites. Modern organizations must be run along meritocratic and technocratic lines. France's were still being run by elites largely composed of *héritiers* (drawn from the small sector of the population where wealth and prestige rest), and their merit and expertise were of a traditional sort—financial rather than economic, legal rather than experimental, abstract rather than problem-solving, verbal rather than group-oriented. The kind of expertise and certified merit fostered by France's educational system had already saddened Saint-Simon and made France's adjustment to the industrial order incomplete.

Second, there was the problem of change. It was not true that higher authority—in the civil service or business—resisted change: expansion, growth, and development had become, as de Gaulle wanted, a "great enterprise." But the combination of small castes and barricaded, equalitarian subjects made smooth and concerted change difficult, for it condemned higher authority to blind (hence resisted) initiatives, or to endless, essentially conservative adjustments—activities that became increasingly futile with the quantitative revolution. The bias toward the *status quo*, which had made the old system strong and resilient, now prevented the enactment of drastic reforms needed to adjust the institutions to new circumstances. It also worsened the potential crisis, by allowing for only one kind of easy decision: more of the same—more schools, more universities, more mergers into big companies—i.e., precisely the type of measure that exacerbated the contradictions between the old and the new.

Third, there was the problem of authoritarianism. Modern organizations are necessarily hierarchical, but they can be run efficiently only if the style of human relations within them allows for free communications, cooperation, and bargaining, and if there is a modicum of competition between comparable organizations. French organizations tended to become increasingly authoritarian as the quantitative changes were taking place. Depending on the degree of concentration of higher authority, and the extent of the rights and defensive associations available to the lower strata for protection and protest, the old model could appear in a more or a less authoritarian version. Recent evolution pushed toward an ever more authoritarian one. There was the simple impact of numbers. In a small organization, the old style of decision-making was saved from the excesses of authoritarianism by the fact that information available on top could be reasonably adequate, and the distant relation of the top to the lower strata could be warmed by paternalism. But when the number of subjects or functions multiplied while the ruling caste remained small and insulated, anonymity destroyed paternalism, arbitrariness due to misinformation replaced authority, and the "parallel relations" that had made some personalized humanity and a certain degree of adjustment possible were atrophied. In other words, for the dose of authoritarianism to remain the same, either the elites would have to expand and break down some of the barriers between them, or the subordinates' rights would have to be extended and their associations strengthened.

However, political factors worked precisely in the opposite direction, as far as the subjects were concerned. Within the state bureaucracy, the trend was to greater centralization—a trend of great importance, since bureaucratic decisions directly affected a huge public sector, indirectly affected the entire economy (for instance, through taxation subsidies and the control of credit), decisively affected the development of cities (through financial decisions and regulatory powers) and vitally affected the university (wholly deprived of financial autonomy, yet growing at a spectacular and unexpected pace). Whereas in earlier days the existence of a *more* authoritarian pattern of decision-making in institutions such as factories and the civil service was counterbalanced by a far *less* authoritarian pattern in the political subsystem, under the Fifth Republic the political system was twisted in the opposite direction. What had been, in Alain's intentions and day, a *counter*weight had become an *additional* weight.

It was this combination, at a time of rapid social and economic change—of inefficiency, blocked institutional reform, and rising authoritarianism—that proved unbearable. In an age that requires hierarchy yet seethes with demands for equality, the interplay of these three conditions gave France the wrong kind of hierarchy and the wrong kind of egalitarianism. The top elites were inadequate in number, in training, and in their conception of their role, which compounded the functional authority necessary for presidents and managers of modern organization, and the atavistic authoritarian *commandement* of Frenchmen in positions of power. As for their subordinates, they preferred independence to cooperation and protection to competition. Basic values thus ruled out an easy mutation: between superiors who expect loyalty, and subordinates addicted to total protest, there was no chance for that style of participation which mixes integration and detachment on all sides, nor for the smooth deferential style that functions in Japan. The postindustrial age requires that economic and political decisions be made centrally, and this means that there must be a high degree of transparency and cooperation among the main social institutions (business enterprises, public services, financial and commercial markets, academic institutions, agriculture, etc.), as well as high sensitivity to local and specialized needs and aspirations. France found herself with a series of disconnected organizations, all top-heavy.

The French university was the organization most affected by the tensions between quantitative growth and institutional inertia. The French university of the nineteenth and early twentieth centuries had been strictly tailored to the education of an elite. The cultural model was, in its abstraction and formalism, appropriate and relevant only to a small number of young and aspiring bourgeois. The structures themselves were made for a small number—with the familiar mix of centralization and fragmentation (between separate *facultés*), avoidance of competition, heavy legal protection of personnel, the distance between professors and students, isolation from the outside world, absence of an administration (the bureaucracy was above, in the Ministry of Education), and dominance of a small caste recruited by competitive examination. Values and structures came together in shaping the university's function: it had what might be called a mission of secondary selection. The principle of free access to a university education actually meant that there was a primary selection before and outside the university. Since the *lycées* were, on the whole, bourgeois, so was the university; social class and family status in effect served as the first, preacademic principles of exclusion and orientation.[11] Within this social group, the university made a second selection or, rather, an order of rank: it determined through exams the hierarchy of the future holders of teaching positions and positions of authority and prestige, although not the handful of top nonpolitical positions. The exams were both equalitarian (i.e., organized so as to avoid arbitrariness) and hierarchical (i.e., designed to act as sieves). Except in medicine, the education was essentially "general"; i.e., there was little professional training, except for perpetuating the system of education. Research took place outside the university, for the latter was organized around the *agrégation,* a teaching degree. The university was on the whole a pale and much enlarged copy of the *grandes écoles,* where the elites of civil servants, engineers, and professors were "formed." The result of those two elitist systems was to modify somewhat, but not fundamentally, the "predestination" of young bourgeois to top positions: by instituting a ranking among them, and by allowing a small number of nonbourgeois—the *boursiers*—to rejoin the *héritiers.* The exams' emphasis on equalitarianism and their hierarchical, selective function made them particularly important within the universities (as well as for entry into, and within, the *grandes écoles*). But (except for the *boursiers*) one's life did not depend on them: only one's rank or prestige or ego.

The social transformation of postwar France resulted in a sudden increase in the number of boys and girls from the middle and lower bourgeoisie who went all the way to the *baccalauréat* and from there into the universities. The government's response, especially after 1959, was an enormous building program and an increase in the number of teachers—but all within the same structures. The university, as constituted, ruled out any agreement by its various component parts on a reform of the curriculum, the pedagogy, or the institutional shells in which each group had become lodged and the statutes that traditionally defined their rights and obligations. It also guaranteed that any attempt at reform by fiat would meet with resistance. Nowhere else was the problem of change raised so sharply and so insolubly. Typically, when Fouchet, the Minister of Education, created a commission to study reforms, every suggestion met with opposition from below. The ministry, legally all-powerful, was paralyzed by its subjects' hostility; they, in turn, blamed the mess on the ministry, which totally controlled the universities' finances, curriculum, and academic manpower. Here, the subtle relations of superiors and inferiors led not merely to a stalemate but to a kind of mutual annihilation of power.

As of 1968, there had been some educational reform,[12] but it had failed to remodel the university, free it from bureaucratic strangulation, give it the freedom and resources to experiment, integrate teaching and research, create departments, make teamwork prevail over formal lecture courses, curb professorial absolutism. Yet it was just extensive enough to increase the friction between the often fussy innovations and the old structure, and to antagonize students submitted to perpetual experimentation without fundamental change. Peyrefitte, Fouchet's successor as Minister of Education, an intellectually lucid but politically prudent man, postponed further innovation. He hoped perhaps that only out of the *pourrissement* of the university could come self-reform, now that reform from above had clearly failed. He got more than he bargained for! [13]

Meanwhile, the Sorbonne in Paris and the new campus at Nanterre bore the brunt of the quantitative revolution, as the inadequacy of the old system became as glaring as its rigidity. The increased number of students radically changed the university's functions and subverted its earlier social role. The regime had been well aware of the increased enrollment, but acted as if the functions were the same. Most students now saw their access to the university in terms that only the *boursiers* from *le peuple* and the *petite bourgeoisie* had seen it in the past: as a guarantee of social promotion. The university's selective function now seemed primary—more important than social class outside and than other purposes within. Social rank still depended on profession, but profession no longer depended on family status. And yet this function could not be performed in a way that would meet expectations.

At a time when the university had to confer what it used merely to confirm—rank—it was not equipped to do so. To begin with, there were not enough "high positions" available for the new quantities of students emerging from the university. The free-access system, lack of career guidance within the schools, and the nature of the students' choices in curricula insured a disconnection between their preferences and society's needs. Most students went into fields where there were no jobs. The university's old isolation from the world had not mattered —the university was an enclave of learning for the socially well fitted —but now it meant the production of misfits. Moreover, any attempt to prevent the selective function from being submerged meant either that access to the universities would be barred to "ill-qualified" students—violating the old dogma of free access for all *bacheliers,* making the system elitist *de jure;* or that there would be increased and controlled specialization—but this ran against the cultural preferences of the students; or increased severity at exams. This last was what happened. Exams, once merely a way of reshuffling and marginally broadening the ranks of the predestined elite, now became an obsession for all students, a problem of life and death; they dominated the rhythm and curriculum within the university, and they determined the entire future of the examinees: it was a question of either-or, no longer of more-or-less. Failure or dropping out meant *déclassement* for the young bourgeois, or failure in social promotion for the young *petits-bourgeois.* As one observer put it, free access led to blind fate.

Another problem was that the university's way of "adapting" to mass education had left it unbureaucratic where it should have become more so, and hyperbureaucratic where it should not. Centralization in the Ministry of Education and the professors' exasperation with administrative tasks had meant that the universities lacked a decent administrative structure; this only underlined their lack of autonomy while increasing over-all inefficiency. The ministry had no adequate information on the number of students registered at any given place or on the size of each faculty or discipline, hence no way of planning intelligently. The need for more teachers, while protecting the monopoly of *agrégés* or *docteurs,* had led to a proliferation of *maîtres-assistants,* a new category. The *maîtres-assistants* had heavy teaching responsibilities but, since they did not have the requisite top degrees, they had lower salaries and (above all) a limited horizon. So there was a new stratum, a new element of distance between the prestigious chair-holders and the students, and a huge ferment of discontent.

Now that this massive influx into higher education had reduced its elitism, the continuing contrast between the principle of equal opportunity and social reality became even more conspicuous—a paradox well known to Tocqueville. Sons of peasants and workers continued to be at a disadvantage; the son of a farm worker had a fifty-three times smaller chance of getting to a university than the son of a lawyer. One third of the students came from a category representing less than 3 per cent of the active population (*professions* and *cadres supérieurs*).[14] The logic and frustrations of the quantitative revolution fostered a student protest against the privilege these students felt they had.

Finally, the separation between the universities and research and the resistance to "professionalization" meant that the training given those masses of young men and women, who perforce would have to occupy positions as cadres, employees, and technicians, remained mediocre and vague (while the vital importance of research would continue to be undervalued by most educated Frenchmen). There was not a huge contrast between the specialized high-quality (if not always adequate) training of the "highbrows" at the complacent *grandes écoles,* and the universities, disconnected from social needs but open to every utopia. The result was a "revolt of the middle-brows" [15]—the young students who had acceded to the university of their dreams but found it a nightmare, the teachers in purgatory without the most prestigious parchments. There was both anomie and alienation. The revolt was carefully kindled by the *gauchistes,* and began at Nanterre, where various attempts at improvement had only intensified awareness of the tensions.

In many other parts of French society, the revolt was also instigated by those who found themselves *just below* a well-defended, narrow, and isolated top. The very sharp limits which the French system of authority imposes on the capacity of the middle levels to influence the direction of an organization are much harder to accept as the number of people at those levels increases. Also, the privileges enjoyed in these strata (such as that of providing information about the lower ranks to the top) were being emptied of meaning by technical progress (computerization) and by the expansion in numbers. In industry, private or public, in many of the "tertiary" services, expansion only meant a reinforcement of centralization, rather than a redistribution of functions. The government had favored industrial mergers in order to make French companies as large as the large firms in other Common Market countries, but without making major changes in management; this had increased rigidity and heaviness, stifling internal competition as external competition grew. The partial revolt of cadres in several nationalized industries, state laboratories, and ministries corresponded to this situation; in the expanding professions—medicine, pharmacy, architecture—so did the revolt of the younger members against the handful of *grands patrons*.[16]

As for the rebellion of many *lycéens,* it reflected what was going on in the universities, insofar as the cultural model of the *lycée* was not relevant to a considerably enlarged population of students. Institutionally, to be sure, the construction of new *lycées* and colleges and the recruitment of new teachers could largely cope with the quantitative increase; but there was the problem of the *baccalauréat.* To maintain high standards at all costs would have produced for many students the same trauma that exams did later on; to lower standards only emphasized the irrelevance of the model and increased pressure on the university. Moreover, the traditional system of human relations in the *lycées* and the pedagogy that reflected it became harder to maintain, due to the relaxation of family relations [17] and because of the effect of the mass media: the boys and girls were far less ignorant of the world around them, hence more restive and less dependent on the school for information. In the *lycée,* the peer groups may still have been brittle and unprotective, but the pupil was now part of an adolescent culture that gave him support and an entirely new assertiveness.

Thus, there were strong reasons for believing that the new aspect of the 1968 revolt outweighed the traditional one: that this was an uprising of *dépendants* against institutionalized dependence, a demand for participation in a new style of authority. One could not fail to be struck by the absence from the feast of those who had, in the past, been most adept at protest according to the classic rules: the *indépendants* of French society victimized by economic change, the shopkeepers, artisans, peasants who had been so noisy in previous years. Could their silence be explained by the fact that the rebels were predominantly *de gauche,* and they were not? This would have been erroneous: many *indépendants,* especially in southern and central France, supported leftist or extreme-left parties. On the other hand, in several of the factories and services on strike, unorganized workers and members of the CFDT were going beyond professional or quantitative demands, and asking for *autogestion* or democratization of the firm or agency.

And yet there were reasons for doubt. Was the old system really being superseded? The demand presented by all the labor unions, for recognition of the *sections syndicales* in the factories, was ambiguous: to strengthen the unions could either help create a new style or simply confirm the old, with its safety valve of *contestation,* and make it more effective at the plant level. Rather than *autogestion,* workers often asked for *contrôle ouvrier* (which meant veto power) and showed continuing resistance to "participation" as long as the economy was capitalist. The behavior of the *cadres contestataires* of the public sector was mild enough to suggest that they would be satisfied with a reform of management that increased their share in decisions, rather than *autogestion:* it seemed to be more an elitist plea for rationalization than a call for democracy.[18] We know now that most of the workers' demands were classical ones concerning grievances of old standing.[19]

Many of the principal victims of the impact of quantitative expansion in old structures were silent. Not all the *dépendants* wanted to throw off the yoke. Many public services, whose theoretical autonomy had been annihilated by mushrooming state controls and by new layers of central civil servants, were unaffected by the turmoil of May 1968. Nor did most of the local *notables* rebel, even though their formal powers had been eroded by the decline of rural France, by financial stringency, and by the huge extension of the national bureaucracy into economic life. For the old system, economically and humanly so costly, did have its defenses. The public services enjoyed various legal and financial guarantees in exchange for their loss of autonomy; the insistence on security and protection at lower levels preserved the government from a genuine revolt against the system. The *notables* had, in lieu of autonomous power, the power to pressure or blackmail the state, and they owed their authority to the success of these operations: the responsibility for omissions and arbitrary moves remained the state's, yet the credit for advances and advantages went to them. In other words, they had a stake in the old system.

As for the silence of the *indépendants,* it could be explained by the flood of subsidies that had come their way from the Gaullist regime (especially when Edgar Faure was Minister of Agriculture). These funds often went to those who needed them least, but it gave these men a stake in the system (while increasing the economic irrationality of the policy). The result was to provoke revolts by the underprivileged, sooner [20] or later, but at least—given these milieux' lack of experience with any other system, *and* genuine dependence on state help—they were traditional protests. Paradoxically, the apparent *indépendants*—self-employed or locally elected—found themselves so deeply tied to the system that they did not have the option of trying to destroy it, which many of the *dépendants,* actually regimented in hierarchical or bureaucratic organizations, thought they had.

II

Some of the rebels of May 1968 still believe that they could have won, that the time for "revolution" was ripe. To be sure, the ambiguity of their movement—was it traditional protest or revolt against the traditional pattern?—would not by itself be sufficient to doom it: how many "revolutionaries" know, at first, exactly where they are heading? But they still might have been defeated by a combination of Communist tactics and Gaullist strategy. The truth is that, quite apart from these political forces, the revolutionary movement itself carried within it the seeds of its own destruction, and it grew in such a way as finally to appear as one more display of traditional protest.

Most striking was the rebels' inability really to step outside the style of authority they were attacking. Even if they were indignantly determined to change it, they *knew* no other ways of doing so than the ritual ones—the sudden shift from individualistic defense of at least partial independence and privacy to total, communal involvement, the mushrooming of "delinquent communities," the desire for *la parole totale et sans contradiction*—a mirror image of challenged authority. Centralization was out, but fragmentation was not: the reforms proposed by the students would have made every school or university a sovereign unit undisturbed by outside forces or nationwide concerns or competition. There was a mystical hope that self-management would abolish conflict magically; but, on the other hand, there was a significant shift from a reasonable and positive demand for "participation" to a romantic, negative, and absurd assertion of a right to permanent challenge (*contestation*). Groups and men unprepared for responsibility prided themselves on behaving irresponsibly. One young teacher said approvingly, "The revolutionaries are men without a program"; an inscription on the walls of the Paris Law School said, "Let us push together but let us not think together." Instead of motion, movement became an end in itself, and motions became their own reward. The nonstop assemblies and committees all too often exhibited a relentless need to hammer out legalistic plans in excruciating detail. And the participants in them fell for the grand utopian sloganeering that is typical of French protest. It also revealed a deep nostalgia for the days when France was a world pathfinder, and a desire to take the torch of revolution away from the Cubans or Chinese: "Let us change man, let us build a new civilization, let us replace the fallacious tyranny of production and consumption with true socialism," etc. These meetings often ended in discord, with each fragment insisting on the exclusive correctness of its own analysis. Or they were exploited by less naïve if equally utopian factions of ideologues—the *groupuscules* of Trotskyites, pro-Chinese or pro-Cuban Communists, etc., whose skillful nihilism merged with and manipulated the spontaneous, inexperienced rebellion of unorganized students and young workers. The whole thing had a progressive thrust but little positive content, a good direction but no road map. Auguste Comte's old warning—one can destroy only what one can replace—was pathetically answered by another statement on a wall: "I have something to say, but I don't know what." Once again, the weaknesses of France's *corps intermédiaires* gave volatility to the scene. New, self-appointed groups—study groups, reform groups, revolutionary groups—appeared like mushrooms after rain and filled the air with noisy proclamations and plans. Leaving aside the more complex case of the Communists, even the "established" organizations that joined the movement, such as the CFDT, did so out of weakness—in fear of being left behind, in the hope of gaining strength, and in the confusion of competing *tendances* and divergent local circumstances.

The intellectual substance of the movement was to a very large extent a product of this ritual. The mood was more important than the ideas, which were neither original nor profound: Marxism with more wings than body, echoes of Henry Lefebvre (better known than Herbert Marcuse), and tons of historical memories in college-outline form.[21] Once more there was a leap into utopianism—mass production of moral principles without means; there was an equally familiar tendency to put grievances into extreme language and to escalate demands to the point where it was no longer clear whether the protester had a specific change in mind or was out to overhaul society. Once again denunciations were more abundant than coherent blueprints: it was easier to see what was being opposed than what was being proposed. There was nothing new in the hyperbolic attacks on "industrial society." That had been a constant target for the intelligentsia, which despises mercantile values and applied sciences, and for the working class, half-attracted by material comfort, but half-repelled by the injustice of business authoritarianism and government deafness. Students anxious about the job market escalated their concern into an attack on the market economy. Workers whose private consumption had been reduced attacked the capitalists' consumer society.

Confusion about the kind of society and social institutions that ought to replace those under attack was total. (It has continued to complicate the lives of subsequent commentators who have found that the complexities and contradictions of the movement keep defeating their most convincing interpretations.) More lethal were the movement's divisions over political power—about what to do with it in the future, and how to deal with it now in order to win. It is here that the impact of the traditional style proved deepest. Many of the changes which the rebels talked about were of a kind that normally can begin to be carried out after a change of regime, i.e., after a successful revolution. Indeed, most of what the *contestataires* were challenging was a direct result of government legislation or policies (the educational system, working conditions in the public services), the result of government encouragement (industrial modernization and its effect on personnel), or a factor that could not be fundamentally reformed without legislation enshrining a new status, according to tradition. Therefore there had to be a *préalable:* toppling the Gaullist regime or at least the shaky Gaullist majority in Parliament. But when it came to political tactics and strategy, the rebels babbled yet were speechless.

One reason for this incoherence was the disconnection between the French political system and French society. In the previous chapter, I mentioned why and how the Gaullist regime and its majority either failed to hear the rumblings of discontent or failed to act decisively when they heard them. With docile parliaments and surface tranquillity in the country since 1962, the civil service had become disdainful of criticism, and oppressively self-confident. But a similar disconnection characterized relations between the rebels and opposition parties of the center and Left. The opposition's relative success on the second ballot of the elections in March 1967 may have encouraged rebel militancy, but it did not prevent the opposition from being just as surprised as the Gaullists when the explosion of May 1968 came. The parliamentary debate of May 22 that ended with the failure to censure Pompidou revealed how *déphasé* the language of politics and the concerns of the politicians were, by contrast with the language and concerns of the *contestataires.* Even though the "parties of yesteryear" had been doing a bit better at the polls, the social forces discontented with the government and social order no longer placed their hopes in them. The parties had spent years on lofty, complicated, and contradictory negotiations to regain control of a Parliament that the general public deemed devalued.

We must look for a deeper reason as to why the rebels failed—until after May 27—to restore the connection between politics and society. On one hand, we have to keep in mind the effect of ten years of Gaullism: it had created a kind of double disbelief, both about the political system being responsive to massive pressure for social change, *and* about its being vulnerable. It was not until after the general strike of May 13 and the sudden wave of strikes thereafter that the second disbelief was suspended. On the other hand, when the regime seemed to be threatened, the revolutionary movement was embarrassed by inner divisions and doubts.

To simplify, one could distinguish moderates and extremists in the movement—leaving the Communists for the moment aside. One group —many of the workers and cadres of the CFDT, some from the Confédération Générale du Travail–Force Ouvrière (CGT–FO), members of various professions—wanted to replace Gaullism with a more "democratic" regime that would be drastically reformist socially and left-wing politically. *Autogestion,* or power exerted in the plant or service, would be combined with the old dream of a Socialist democracy, with "socialized" means of production and central planning. But these men lacked the means to achieve their goals: they had little trust in the political parties of the center and moderate left, which they knew to be fragmented and parochial; they remembered the *immobilisme* of the Fourth Republic, and knew the decisive importance of Guy Mollet, its Socialist symbol, in the main political force of the non-Communist opposition, the Fédération de la Gauche Démocrate et Socialiste (FGDS). They turned ultimately to Mendès-France, a man without a real base. Thus, the less utopian rebels had no real political handle, and had not made sufficient efforts to create one prior to the explosion. (In the case of the CFDT, its insistence on syndicalist autonomy from the parties contributed to the distance.) As a result, while the social reformists were politically impotent, the opposition parties (politically impotent since 1958) had no social underpinning: they had voters on Election Day, but neither militants nor mass membership.

The other group in revolt against the state—nonunionized workers, some elements of the CFDT, and most of the students' *groupuscules*— proclaimed their adherence to different versions of the anarchist utopia, as expressed in pre-Marxist socialism or in revolutionary syndicalism. The longing for a thoroughly decentralized nation with power in the hands of "those who work, where they work" was as old as French socialism: the dream of Fourier, Proudhon, Sorel had never died in the labor movement, despite the Paris Commune's debacle in 1871. It now expressed itself in some workers' demands for *autogestion* and in students' and young teachers' attacks on elections and parties. This was the "spontaneity" surge. And it ran into the same problem that had already made French syndicalist organizations abandon the old dream in favor of reformism or *political* (not syndicalist) revolution: their humanely appealing blueprint for the morning after *le grand soir* was not a blueprint for winning; what were they to do if the state refused to collapse? What if the Beast, defied, defiled, and deflated, nevertheless failed to fade away? The *gauchistes* were not united on the vital issue of means—a confusion that was concealed by the adherence of some of them to a Leninist vocabulary. Some, tactically more lucid, saw the need for revolutionary instruments now, to forge the ideal society later. But these *groupuscules* were too divided and minuscule to matter. Others were pure *spontanéistes:* unwilling to become organization men in order to fight organization, knowing that the seizure of political power corrupts and insures tyranny rather than anarchy. They had no recourse other than hoping that the Beast would die of shock or shame. To provoke its demise, the rebels had at least to act in unison. Yet there were difficulties. The student groups wanted common action with the workers, but an alliance of "spontaneous," nonorganized workers and student *groupuscules* was hardly sufficient—and the more responsibly organized workers, even when they sympathized with the rebellion in the university (as in the case of the CFDT) kept their distance from the young bourgeois and the wilder forms of utopianism they spouted.

In the last analysis, the rebels had good fists, stout lungs, but no adequate political weapons. The disarray of the more moderate ones, the rashness of the more utopian, the splintering of the movement into countless factions, all this put the movement's fate into the hands of a reluctant and devious ally and a battered but resourceful foe. What the rebels really needed was the support of the one true, massive and coherent opposition force: the French Communist Party. But the party turned against them—and twice provided the Gaullist regime, on the verge of collapse, with the help it desperately needed.

In mid-May, the Communists prevented a liaison between the students and young strikers and decided to generalize the strike, so as to regain control of it. Their tactic fitted Nero's in Racine's *Britannicus:* "*J'embrasse mon rival, mais c'est pour l'étouffer.*" They insured that the drama would re-enact the ritual of protest rather than introduce a new set of authority relations. And they submerged not only the pure utopians but also the reformists. They oriented the strike exclusively toward material issues (wage increases, social security) which had accumulated over the years, instead of "self-management," and toward negotiations with Pompidou. But this was not "pragmatic" bargaining. The purpose throughout was to promote a new Popular Front which they would dominate; the party tactic was to begin by raising explicitly only the concrete issues, so as to push aside its rivals and reassure its opponents. When it began to fear that the non-Communist left was ready to move for power without it, the party decided to bring the central bargaining to a quick settlement, to keep the pressure on the government by keeping local strikes going,[22] and—still in order to gain control—to give at last an explicit political content to the strike. It now called openly for a "popular government," or popular front. This meant that it had clearly opted for legal, political action within the constitutional framework. It had thrown its weight to the side of the reformists—but crushing them in the process. This explicit politicization, following two weeks of political concealment, also meant that the party expected the regime to collapse, with a new government and new elections after de Gaulle's fall. This proved to be a fatal mistake. For although de Gaulle's first speech on May 24 had been a flop—which probably encouraged the party to count him out—the Communists' challenge gave him the opportunity to denounce as the real troublemakers, not the students and workers with whom so many sympathized, but the "totalitarian party," which so many disliked and which had imprudently, if legally, laid its claim to power.

After the crisis, and after the Gaullist victory at the polls on June 23 and 30, the Communist party's secretary-general explained that the situation had not been truly revolutionary, that the party had behaved correctly in refusing to fall into a trap laid by adventurers and *agents provocateurs,* that there would otherwise have been bloodshed and far greater losses of voters. Perhaps. Yet this way of looking at things (with eyes fixed on free elections) contributed decisively to taking the "revolution" out of the situation. Why did the party refuse to take any risk, other than that of defusing the bomb built by the students and the young workers, for the greatest (if unintended) benefit of a shaken regime which it had long denounced? We do not know whether Moscow had a large influence in the French Communist Party's bizarre strategy. (Was the unprecedented, albeit temporary, failure of the party to support Moscow in the Czech crisis evidence of autonomy or of resentment against its servitude?) But there are indigenous French reasons for its strategy which throw light on the situation.

Given its Marxist origins, its Leninist model, and its Jacobin conception of seizing power where it is—at the center—the French Communist Party had always disdained and distrusted the anarchist or federalist strains in French socialism: "worker power" in the factory would have weakened the hold of the Communist-led union, the CGT, on the workers. It would have transferred control not merely from the *patrons* but also from the CGT's representatives to either a majority of the workers (and in many industries, while the CGT was the biggest union, most of the workers were not members of *any* union) or to other more dynamic minorities, including the CFDT. The Communist party had been shaped by the French style of authority. The *groupuscules* of students who started the revolution were hostile to it, precisely because its rigid centralization, bureaucracy, and orthodoxy seemed like twins of the Gaullist regime's. Those features of the party, and the fact that it had been pretty much on the political defensive for over twenty years, made it inordinately and clumsily hostile to initiatives taken by groups that were claiming to be to its left, or under no political control at all. Instead of joining them so as to dominate them, the Communists' defensive reflex was to oppose them.[23] And yet one might ask whether it would not have been in the party's interest, in the new circumstances of May, to jettison its smooth reformism and to take control of the movement by reverting to a revolutionary line. The party was unwilling to do so. This was in part because, however tactical its reformism, and however dictatorial its behavior might be if some miracle brought it to power, it had in fact ceased being a truly revolutionary party in the sense of being "geared to the violent seizure of power." And it was in part because its leaders believed that even if de Gaulle fell, there were insuperable obstacles to revolution, both domestic and external (the army and the United States). And it was in part because of a larger "historical" factor, which I should like to examine now in more detail.

The French Communist Party's action reflected the dilemmas (and the fate) faced by all antiregime opposition movements in France— whether of the extreme left or the far right. They proclaim revolutionary goals, but, on one hand, the situation is almost never ripe for a violent seizure of power in a country that remains wedded to stability, with a still sizable peasant population that often roars but never rises, and with middle classes that are fiercely attached to their possessions and rights. On the other hand, if they try to attain their goals through parliamentary maneuvers and electoral politics, they are gradually and grudgingly absorbed into the system. This is what Jules Guesde warned Jaurès against at the turn of the century. It happened to the Socialists even before 1914; it happened to de Gaulle's RPF in the early 1950s; it was happening to the Communist party in the late 1960s, since it had decided ten years earlier that its best chance of getting out of the ghetto to which de Gaulle had consigned it was to make an alliance with the non-Communist left, now transformed into a federation headed by François Mitterrand and led by Guy Mollet. This policy brought some parliamentary gains in 1962, many more in 1967. When the crisis of 1968 came, the party instinctively denounced and tried to stop a movement that conflicted with its tactics, and to reaffirm its course in the hope that the voters would be grateful to the Communists for having helped improve the workers' material lot and for having saved France from civil war and illegality. This calculation misfired.

The Gaullists, having been as surprised as the political opposition (Communists included), but of course far more grievously, first looked as if they would not recover from the shock. Two of de Gaulle's most cherished beliefs had been blasted away. He had created a powerful

Presidency, capable of ruling France even if the Parliament were divided or even splintered; now he explained that the timidity of the executive in recent months had been due to the absence of a strong majority in the National Assembly. (A half-truth concerning the past, but one that testified to lingering doubts about the Constitution's effectiveness in the post-de Gaulle future.) He had often celebrated the "stability, security, solidity" of his constitutional system; now he discovered that France's troubles had not all been due to weak parliamentary systems and were not all curable by a "strong state." A strong state breeds problems of its own, constitutional reform does not by itself solve the most profound of France's difficulties, which lie in the heart of French society. And a third belief had been damaged. De Gaulle had proclaimed that his regime had only one leader: the President. But during the 1968 crisis, serious strains developed between him and the cabinet. Where political scientists or legal writers had feared a political split between the President (elected by the people) and the cabinet (dependent on parliamentary support), what emerged was a tactical and organizational split, which was just as dangerous. A President inclined toward forcible reactions had been confronted with a cabinet and Premier favorable to bargaining and fearful of violence. The division of labor between daily management by the Premier and general guidance by the President proved unworkable. While Pompidou was in Afghanistan during the first week of the crisis, de Gaulle and the cabinet somehow held each other at a standoff. When Pompidou came back, de Gaulle in effect gave him temporary *carte blanche* —as a result, his own speech of May 24, unconnected with Pompidou's tactics, managed to fall flat and to make things worse.[24]

When de Gaulle had returned to France from his trip to Rumania on May 18, his life's work seemed in ruins. The man who had wanted to unify the French people had apparently half the nation in revolt against him. The celebrator of the strong state presided over a paralyzed administration. The hero who had twice saved the French from disasters now faced a crisis aimed at him. His first reaction, on May 24, was ritualistic and totally inadequate. He announced a referendum—a personal vote of confidence in his own capacity to reform France, a plea to the citizens to delegate to *him* the power to organize *their* participation—this at a moment when the revolt, which was still spreading, seemed to be demonstrating that such confidence was gone and was challenging the whole notion of leaving public affairs to the sovereign wisdom of the highest authority. France is a nation that says "no" more easily than "yes" in times of anger and in the absence of a savior, and had he stuck to his proposal all the opposition forces could have combined to oust him (as they were to do when he reverted to it eleven months later).

At this point, two miracles happened. First, de Gaulle, despite his age, his well-known obstinacy, his obvious distress, and his exhaustion, realized immediately that he had blundered and, pragmatic as ever, looked for a new course. Second, the new position of the Communists gave him just what he needed. Instead of being a target, instead of pleading with his subjects for their trust, he could again become the nation's savior, leading the citizens in a fight against subversion and chaos. Up to May 29, he had been on the defensive. Now he seized the offensive (as he had in 1940 and 1958) and made the obliging Communists the focus for all those who by now were annoyed or felt threatened by growing anarchy. It was a sensational coup, in style and in substance. The de Gaulle of May 24 had confirmed his rebellious listeners' feeling that supreme authority was stumbling in the dark. *Le chahut* was given a new lease on life. The workers' rejection of the agreements of May 27 and the new political boldness of the Communist party were direct results of this fiasco. The de Gaulle of May 30, imperious and thundering, *was* authority—he was the stern schoolmaster who whistled an end to fun and games. Thus, the Paris demonstrators for law and order were given a boost, received both an injection of vigor and unforeseen reinforcements, while the *contestataires*—in factories, *cafés,* and classrooms—bitterly noted that the game was over. By shelving the referendum and dissolving the Assembly, de Gaulle disarmed the Communists, who had themselves proposed the electoral arena as a battlefield, and obliged the French to choose, not between yes and no, but between Gaullist candidates representing order *and* reform, and various squabbling kinds of anti-Gaullists who seemed to stand either for chaos or for totalitarianism or for nothing at all. As long as the battle was in the streets (or factories), France faced the prospect of anarchy or civil war between the rebels and the police (or the army). Once the battle was moved to the polls, the revolt—which was now both anti-Gaullist and anti-Communist, indeed against all existing political forces—was doomed. Things were moving back from fragmentation to centralization. The Gaullists were right in saying that in the electoral arena the only real forces were the Communist party and the Gaullist party.

The Constitution, practices, and style of the Fifth Republic are those of the more authoritarian pole of French political relations. The revolt was partly a rebellion against this authoritarianism, a longing for a more relaxed and routinelike authority of the sort which French parliamentary republics represented. And yet, paradoxically, a parliamentary system would have collapsed under the shock—the cabinet would probably have fallen and chaos ensued, as in May 1958. The Fifth Republic was the institutionalization of crisis government, with a powerful Presidency and a whole arsenal of executive controls over Parliament. And even though the crisis of 1968 proved that such a political system cannot avoid major crises, may even provoke or worsen them, it also proved that the regime can overcome them—at least as long as the strong Presidency is served by a strong President, and the cabinet headed by an able Premier.[25]

Thus de Gaulle won—a respite at least. The old tradition of regimes destroyed by barricades, of legality broken in the streets, had been defeated. With the crisis over, de Gaulle was clearly determined not to change anything in the central institutions (except the Senate). And his purge of the personnel of ORTF showed his determination to keep his grip. He replaced his Premier, Pompidou—a move which like everything he did had a great variety of reasons, but probably a major reason was his retrospective conviction that Pompidou, chosen for his prudence and practicality, had pushed prudence to the point of impracticality in his handling of those issues which were not de Gaulle's favorites. Certainly another reason was his continually reasserted conviction that there should be only one head of the executive. The Premier is not supposed to be an independent leader who comes from the majority in Parliament and follows his own line; he is but a personal representative of the President and chosen to rule that majority.[26] Since events and personal abilities had made Pompidou behave more like the former type of Premier than the latter, constitutional orthodoxy demanded that he be replaced (and be put in reserve, so to speak, perhaps so as to be, after de Gaulle, what he had tended to become under him: the second President). De Gaulle's choice of Maurice Couve de Murville to succeed Pompidou reaffirmed his decision to take personal command of domestic reform (Couve de Murville is primarily a model executor), but it also revealed his persistent taste for obfuscation: in 1944, he chose the leader of the domestic resistance, Bidault, as his Foreign Minister; in 1959, he made Michel Debré the champion of French Algeria, preside over the giving up of Algeria; Pompidou, a man primarily concerned with domestic affairs, was Premier during the period in which priority was given to foreign policy; and now, when precedence was at last given to internal reform, de Gaulle selected a man who had been in diplomacy for twenty-five years and who had the reputation of being quite conservative in financial matters.

With his renewed power and with his new (or not so new) team, what was the General up to—and up against?

III

The failure of earlier comparable movements in French history—in June 1848, the Paris Commune, the Popular Front—led to strong "law and order" reactions on the part of the public and on the part of the governments. Cavaignac and Louis-Napoléon, Thiers, Daladier of 1939, and Pétain of 1940 saw to it that *les honnêtes gens* were reassured. But de Gaulle was in a very different mood. He had always put foreign affairs ahead of everything else, and his regime's eagerness for quantitative change reflected his approach to the "internal mutation" he had so often talked about: its aim was to increase France's might. Perhaps he had thought that quantitative changes would force a real mutation which the state could then shape without having had to initiate it; perhaps his own consecration of France's style of authority had reduced the range within which he could conceive of cultural and institutional transformations. But he realized now that France did require such changes. Also, he wanted—as usual—to reconcile the French, rather than preside over the revenge of one part of the country against the other. Furthermore, he had, over the years, expressed concern precisely over the issues that now loomed most important, even though the solutions he had advocated left his associates and subordinates cool: educational reform through "selection," reform of worker-management relations, and decentralization, which he had called for on March 24, just before the explosion. Finally, he believed that the shock of May would have made even the most stalwart Frenchman aware of the need for change, as long as it was orderly— something his presence would insure.

Having thus understood and having tried to capture and channel the demands from below, de Gaulle took over the protesters' key word, *participation.* But on what kind of a social order was it possible to get the French to agree? On behalf of what kind of a society could one appeal for their participation? That was the substantive issue, but there was also a problem of method. If the idea was to arrive at a more "participatory" style, i.e., to change the old model of authority relations, what would be the best way for the government to transform patterns of behavior, values, and institutions that had endured for centuries?

This was the real drama, behind and beyond the psychodrama of May. The traditional French system of authority rules out what might be called a constructive and positive agreement on a new kind of social order, for it emphasizes the negative and the utopian. (This does not mean that the French are incapable of reaching *any* consensus. There appears to be at present a consensus for a certain kind of political system—but one that might be ineffective or might disintegrate if the Left prevails at the polls, i.e., if other issues get priority; and there has been for a long time a broad consensus against accelerated social change, on the basis of largely preindustrial values.) Efforts to change the system of authority and thereby to make a constructive consensus emerge more painlessly have foundered on the absence of a prior, positive consensus on substance, which this system has perpetuated, and on the resilience of the old style, which the absence of consensus has in turn strengthened. So long as this vicious circle remains unbroken, the old values and structures of authority linger on, and the hope for a "new society" is a delusion.

Let us begin with the problem of substance. Among the rebels of May, the only agreements were negative. This was most clear in the university. To be sure, there is nothing especially French about the problem of the big, modern university—how to keep it a citadel of critical analysis and free thought, while having it function as an instrument of social selection and training. Nor is the problem of student revolt especially French. Quite apart from local political and social circumstances, there are psychological reasons that account for the sons and daughters of the affluent, in country after country, rejecting a modern society they think is "repressive" and a university they see as its microcosm and legitimizer,[27] even if the reason why this took the form of a brief typhoon remains mysterious. But French peculiarities made this problem, and others, more difficult to solve. It would be impossible to reform the university by copying the American system of diversity and competition among units because this would be resisted by professors and students alike, given their lyrical hostility to being "integrated into industrial society," to depending on the job market or on academic degrees with declining value. Yet meeting the students' demand for no limitation on the access of secondary-school graduates to the university (a demand accepted by Edgar Faure, the new Minister of Education) and all universities having the same market value would only aggravate the imbalance between the number of students and the opportunities available for them. What gave, and still potentially gives, special seriousness to the French university crisis was precisely the combination of a transnational student revolt against a certain kind of society, and a French revolt which was simultaneously 1) a revolt inspired *by* the traditional aristocratic, antieconomic values of French society and 2) a revolt *against* the traditional pattern of authority in the French university system, which had become unbearable when extended to mass education, i.e., in the circumstances of modern, "postindustrial" society.

This is also why a positive and constructive agreement among students and teachers on a new kind of university is at present impossible. Not only is there a division among the teachers between "conservatives," fiercely attached to the old order and eager to restore it (in particular by ending the principle of open admissions), and varieties of reformists and revolutionaries. There is also the students' ambivalence. They reject the "consumer society," the rationality of which clashes with the cultural values that are residues of France's aristocratic past (individual prowess, the prestige of disinterested intellectual pursuits, a cultural model strikingly reflected—even in revolt—in the students' frequently esoteric graffiti on the walls of the Sorbonne), and which threatens to turn the ivory tower and the temple of discourse into an assembly line providing technicians for the economy. Yet they resent the traditional values and the essentially elitist cultural model; they know them to be of small relevance to a society in which experimentation and research are far more valuable than the two pillars of French culture, humanities and pure mathematics, and sense that these will not provide most new students with the rewards these had given to earlier students.[28] As Michel Crozier has pointed out, this ambivalence had resulted in an invasion of new students into the social sciences—less irrelevant than the old disciplines, yet sufficiently non-technical and critical of the new society. But the effect of this shift has been to make the crisis of finding jobs worse, without in the least providing a constructive model for the new university. The old one was attacked by those whom Alain Touraine calls the technocrats and by the students. The "technocrats"—in reality, the "action intellectuals," researchers mainly outside the university, managers of the French economy, civil servants concerned with adapting higher education to an advanced industrial society—found it hopelessly out of date. The students found it out of date too, but also willing to modernize in the wrong direction! True, lack of agreement about the purpose of a modern university is universal, and it is normally too painful to academics to be frankly discussed; but the general problem once more takes on particularly acute aspects in France because of the extra ideological and historical dimensions.

The same obstacles to positive agreement on a new order could be seen in the case of the workers and cadres. Among the workers, traditional hostility to capitalism was expressed in variations on the old theme of workers' power—the hope for a society ruled by workers in their workshops, or a society in which democratic planning and socialization of the means of production eliminated profit as the motor of the economy and destroyed the power of the *patronat*. But even here it is hard to get a clear picture of the new order. There was very little experimentation with workers' management in May; the Yugoslav model did not help, since the French admirers of it happened to be those who did not want a single party to provide cohesion and direction or "socialist" planning in the hands of state-hired managers. We are still in the French tradition of institutional blueprints based on moral principles. Moreover, this critique of a capitalist economy was made from a pre- rather than post-industrial perspective. The desire for *autogestion*, for community rather than central decisions, is everywhere a reaction against hierarchical and centralizing excesses in modern bureaucracies. But once more, in France, the general trend was shaped in an atavistic mold—by memories of Babeuf and early socialists whose values were essentially rural and *artisanal*. Critique of the present, in France, is more nostalgic than futuristic. Another critique —that of the Communists—dismissed nostalgia contemptuously, but their blueprint (more or less retouched depending on tactical necessities) was a Soviet one—cohesion being provided by a centralizing party, one of whose arms was the labor union. Between those two views, there was merely negative agreement against the present order.

Whether they belonged to the first or the second group, French workers shared an ambivalence comparable to the students'. They criticized the bases of capitalism, especially French capitalism. But they also criticized the failure of French capitalism to bring about what other capitalisms had provided (a point already made by Sorel, casting a half-shocked, half-admiring glance at the United States): better human relations and working conditions in the company, a higher living standard, greater (if not always spontaneous or early!) willingness to deal directly with strong unions instead of trying to divide and rule and of referring essential decisions to the state. Many French workers support the CGT not out of enthusiasm for the Communist blueprint, but because of the CGT's hard-headed concentration on so-called quantitative demands: in this way, while their opposition *de principe* to capitalism is maintained, the daily fight aims at making capitalism extend its blessings to the workers.[29] Once more, out of these splits and out of this ambivalence comes no positive consensus.

In the case of the cadres, ambivalence was also present. Were they revolting merely because the style of authority of French enterprises deprived them of any real responsibility and any sphere of decision, i.e., because they wanted a progressive change in this style that would satisfy them and make the organization more effective? Or were they revolting because modernization and the computer revolution were depriving them of the "captive power" they had traditionally enjoyed in the system, as a stratum between the employees or workers and the managers, indispensable to each as a "cushion" against the other [30] —i.e., was it a protest against change, on behalf of the old system? Demands for *autogestion* concealed this ambivalence, and gave a drastic, revolutionary anticapitalist flavor to what was essentially a protest against *déclassement*. But, again, the flavor of the protest and its ambiguity made it hard to see what kind of an image of the ideal enterprise the cadres could agree on.

The new postwar society having developed in the matrix of France's old system of authority, it was inevitable, of course, that the critique of the obsolescent system should be amplified into a critique of modern society, for many of the critics could not see that some of the "ills" of modern society which they denounced were due to the old French bottle into which it had been poured. Conversely, since the critique of modern society was often based on the old elitist and nonindustrial values, it was also inevitable that it would often be more old-fashioned than innovative. Touraine defines France as "an archaic society that had given itself a modern economy." [31] May 1968 provided a torrent of onslaughts against both society and economy, but it offered no consensus on a society with a modern economy, and with values and structures of authority which would allow the economy to overcome the cramping imposed by the old system and enable the French to cooperate constructively. It was most significant that Jean-Jacques Servan-Schreiber, who had recently made himself the champion of economic modernization and the prophet of the "consumer society," interpreted the crisis, when it came, as a vindication of his warnings, even though the rebels made the consumer society a target. For this resourceful journalist, it was a way of establishing negative solidarity with the rebels; they and he could commune in condemning the old structures (*they* because the new society was being introduced through them, and *he* because they slowed it down). But later, carrying further his attack on the "bourgeois" and aristocratic residues in French society on behalf of the new order,[32] he felt he had to justify his plea for modernization on the basis of France's old values—defense of human differences, man's duty to master economic forces, etc. Even modern *saint-simonisme* has to be sold in a way that pleases both young *gauchistes* and old *radicaux,* by flattering their stock of common values.

Thus, *les événements de mai* combined: a typical revolt (i.e., one in which concrete demands were turned into a general challenge) against the specific flaws of French capitalism, politically divided between Communists and varieties of socialists (the latter differing among themselves about the importance of the state in the new order); a revolt against "postindustrial society," technocracy, and economic rationality, divided into those who favored the advantages once provided by the old structures of authority (as in the case of many cadres) and more utopian dreamers (as in the case of university students); a "modern" demand for a new society, less authoritarian, fragmented and caste-ridden, more innovative, hence more capable of eliminating France's vast pockets of poverty and inequality. Add to this cacophony the ambivalence of groups that were not involved in May but demonstrated noisily a little later, such as most of the peasants and the shopkeepers. They were far from clear as to whether they protested in the name of the old stalemate society, and in undying opposition to the new society of supermarkets and business-minded farmers, or whether they protested because they neither received their share of advantages from the new order nor had the means to adapt and reconvert to it.

Nor was it clear, in the latter case, whether they believed they could receive such means and advantages through classical pressure, without drastic social changes, or whether they saw hope only in some kind of socialist transmutation, aş some young and poor farmers do. Add to all this the contradictions that affected also those Frenchmen—the silent minority—who rebelled neither in May nor later, and faithfully supported de Gaulle. Out of this comes the present state of France's consensus. If the earlier one had been negative, around an "equilibrium" acceptable not so much because of its virtues but because alternatives were unwelcome, the new condition can only be called a consensus by default. There is no alternative acceptable to anything like a majority, nor are there the factors that made the stalemate society so strong: a widely accepted set of values and structures, preference for a limited state. It is a consensus by default, not only because of the discord about alternatives, but also because of the obvious resilience of the existing social order.

The divisions and confusions on substance left de Gaulle and his government with a major problem. They could not and did not want to wait until a consensus emerged, especially as the very system of authority ruled it out; moreover, they themselves had clearly opted for making France a modern, postindustrial society—so they chose to reform the structures of authority that had distorted modernization and prevented a consensus. Yet this was, in a way, a *fuite en avant:* could one effectively change these structures and make the French join in establishing new ones, as long as they disagreed on what these institutions were for? And if their discord and their habits threatened to destroy the new structures, how far could the state allow reform to go?

This was the vise in which de Gaulle was caught when he turned to the issue of the *method* of change. *Participation* meant trying to rally the French in favor of new structures, while leaving aside the insoluble problem of "what for," in the (not absurd) belief that only out of these structures, and around the much improved society they would lead to, could any genuine agreement develop. But the evidence that there was no agreement now and fear that in jumping from the old to the new trapeze the French acrobat would crash, did not fail to affect the reformists' zeal.

For the old General, so often charged with Bonapartism, it must have been tempting to become a kind of anti-Napoleon: a man who would leave France more prosperous, at peace, and free from the yoke of Napoleon's steely centralization. Laws and decrees could establish new structures, give greater freedom to cities and regions, high schools and universities, create a framework for association within factories: progressive reformers had been suggesting this for years. But vicious circles cannot be broken by legal magic and procedural innovations.

The old system now prevented orderly change, democratic participation, and compromise; it existed precisely because of France's lack of taste for and experience with these ways of thinking and behaving. Could a greater range of freedom to act together stop Frenchmen from practicing the freedom either to command or to resist? In a first phase, inevitably, the old mentality would be very much present; the new bottles would be filled by the old wine, whose acid might corrode them. In the absence of any substantive consensus, the French were left with the habits and reactions which the traditional style of authority had inculcated in them. It was perhaps true that in the long run only the experience of "participation"—of responsibilities, competition, cooperation, compromise, face-to-face bargaining—could lead to *déblocage* and a new consensus (if not substantive, at least procedural). But it was vain to imagine this would work in the short run. The French would inevitably bring their old habits into the new channels.

Democratic participation requires not only a new legal framework, but certain kinds of organizations and a certain kind of spirit. It needs strong associations—able to speak for their members, representative of their constituencies, and capable of taking initiatives. At present, neither French labor unions nor the student bodies nor many of the professional organizations meet this requirement. Because they have so often opposed the government intransigently, the regime had, in the past, often done its best to weaken them (as it did with the National Students Union, after Algeria). Which side would now initiate the reversal of attitudes? Or would each wait for the other to reverse itself first? Democratic participation also needs a spirit of cooperation, a willingness to solve conflicts by bargaining, a readiness to deal with concrete issues rather than global designs and insoluble preconditions, a drastic shift away from the old habit of leaving decisions to superiors (who can then be blamed), a break with the old tendency of groups to look after only their own interests, and of central authority to dismiss them as illegitimate nuisances. As the crisis had shown, when each side calls for participation, it still means the miraculous and beneficial elimination of the other. When it asks for a dialogue, it often means the capitulation of all other views. The only true revolution would be one that would put an end to such attitudes, that reversed the patterns set forth in the days of Richelieu.

The Gaullist state, confirmed by the voters in June 1968, tried to hasten this revolution by setting a good example in consulting, listening, and bargaining with interested parties before drawing up a new legal network of procedures and institutions. And yet what would happen if this dialogue led to discord, and if the new institutions degenerated into chaos, or had to be given up because of the risk, or had to be established imperatively over the noise of the quarreling factions?

Once more, the old method of change would have triumphed, the old mode of adjustment-without-mutation would be operative. The odds for a real revolution were not very high—given the embittered mood of many students, the distrust of the labor unions, the resistance of the business community, the strife among teachers and in the professions, the sullenness of the non-Communist left, the bruised hostility of the Communists, the vindictiveness and power-greed of many Gaullists in the National Assembly, and the problematic chances of a mutation of de Gaulle's own personality. Yet the shock of 1968 had been deep enough to make the odds higher than at any time since the sad fiasco of the Liberation. The politicians knew this was their opportunity to make the political system relevant to an increasingly indifferent or hostile society. But the rapid evolution of French politics in the last year of de Gaulle's presidency showed in detail that there was no easy way out of the dilemma. New institutions were devised, but in most vital areas they barely concealed the old faulty structures.

First, the General (or rather his new Minister of Education, Edgar Faure) dealt with the crisis in higher education. The *loi d'orientation* of November 12, 1968, was, on the surface, very daring. It took as a basis the negative consensus against restricting admissions to the university, against competing universities, against universities too closely connected with nonacademic activities. It accepted the notions of autonomy and co-management, and set up a system of parliamentary agencies to rule the universities. It left the shape of the new "pluridisciplinary" universities to the decision of the temporary "units" into which the old ones had exploded. There was something paradoxical in seeing de Gaulle apply to the academic world the *régime d'assemblée* he had eliminated from the political system in 1958. But the university was where the explosion had been most violent, and he may have thought it wise to disconnect the university from the state administration as much as possible and let the students and teachers play with the toys they had asked for—which would keep them too busy to infect the rest of society with their viruses. Although it is a bit too early to pronounce the attempt a complete failure, it is already clear that it is not a success.

One reason was that the state was not willing after all to disconnect itself completely from the university. The National Assembly imposed various restrictions on a reluctant Faure that turned his flexible bill into a detailed regulatory code. The powers reserved by the state were important: resources are still provided by it, the state continues to set common rules on "studies leading to national degrees." Paradoxically, autonomy must thus combine with uniformity, which the strict regulation of those degrees insures; autonomy may lead to some diversity, but only in the familiar mold. Moreover, the strict limits on financial autonomy seem designed to prevent the academic managers from learning responsible self-reliance.

De Gaulle's determination to leave for the future the questions of ultimate shape and purpose meant that some essential points were untouched, and that consequently there was a strong bent toward the *status quo ante*. Thus, the university's separation from research continues and condemns "pluridisciplinary" teaching to sterility; the split between the universities and the *grandes écoles* persists; the discrepancy between student preferences and job opportunities has increased; the relative devaluation of exams may have lowered tensions, but it also perverts the selective function still more, and may in effect tend to restore the privilege which social origin once had had in providing better positions to the well-born; university autonomy without competition gives a new lease on life to parochialism and fragmentation. Most important, the absence of any reform in secondary education (except for a hotly contested downgrading of Latin) has left the traditional cultural model intact. It pushes pupils much too early into "literary" curricula; it preserves an authoritarian style of relations which fosters passivity or resentment, and contrasts with more liberal faculty relations; it keeps teachers divided into separate castes and career patterns; it perpetuates the low prestige of technical training. Yet the reform of secondary education is the key to university reform.[33] Without it, in Faure's words, there will still be, among other flaws, the division between a "general education" that is not truly general or up-to-date, and a professional training with no culture.

De Gaulle's reforms were such that the institutions of "participation" instantly became battlefields. The rivalries between *groupuscules,* factions, unions, etc., made for a maximum of heat and a minimum of light. After several years, old habits reasserted themselves: since the powers actually given to the institutions of co-management were meager at best, they are now paralyzed or deserted, and this in turn has made the ministry the dominant authority once more. The only really autonomous power the dean has is that of calling in the police or not at a time of disturbance, i.e., a power with no rewards and heavy penalties. The voluntary federation of schools and faculties into universities has been determined by political affiliations and fake marriages that in fact preserve the corporative separatism of each unit. Co-management and autonomy, under the present circumstances, thus lead to agreements only on a "corporative" basis; to conserve the *status quo,* defend established positions, mutually protect vested interests— these seem to be the only common ground. The reform has merely shifted the delicate balance between higher authority and resisting strata slightly in favor of the latter: a shift within the old pattern.[34] Could this meager result have been avoided if the state had been more daring? Clearly, something had to be done right away—one could not wait for the eventual effects of reform in secondary education. If the state had tried to impose a new conception of the university, it would have violated the principle of participation; if it had given up all powers of determination, the chances are that discord and parochialism would have grown in proportion to the stakes. Yet nothing has really been solved. Having lacked the daring to cut old ties and Gordian knots, the state has—to amend an adage—*avancé pour mieux sauter.*

The second area de Gaulle selected for reform was France's territorial administration. The bill prepared by Minister Jean-Marcel Jeanneney was far more complex and cautious than Faure's—a contrast that reflected a difference in personalities, in the pressures from below, and undoubtedly also in de Gaulle's assessment of the respective advantages to the state of major disconnection versus continuing control in the two realms. Jeanneney's bill made an attempt at decentralization, in that it gave powers of discussion and (some) regulation to new regional assemblies, and at catching not only delegates of territorial units but representatives of interest groups in the new net, i.e., it was a step toward "integration." But, on the other hand, it expressed the old Jacobin suspicion that such steps can lead to disintegration, given the tendency of political and interest groups to use new institutions as arenas to air their grievances and as stakes for control. The bill therefore carefully preserved the state's grip over the regions' financial resources, maintained each *préfet's* predominance and executive power, rejected the principle of election by direct suffrage, and gave seats in the regional councils to the regions' national deputies (a move that served the Gaullists). There was also a desire not to antagonize the local *notables,* tied to the national government in the old territorial system, which the regional reform of 1964 had actually consolidated. Therefore, the elections to regional councils were entrusted to the *notables.* Once more, at best, this would have been a shift *within* the traditional pattern, establishing at a regional level some measure of parliamentarism (although less than existed under the Third and Fourth Republics at the national level).

If the new university institutions resembled those of the Fourth Republic, the new regional ones resembled those of the Fifth. As such, the bill was fiercely criticized by reformists like Crozier, who wanted a clear break and asked for regions with popularly elected assemblies, executive power, experts, and resources of their own, and merely *ex post* supervision by the state. But the bill was opposed by other groups as well. The parties of the Left criticized it for not going far enough —less out of genuine concern for a new structure of authority than because of anti-Gaullism, indignation at the "corporatist" invasion of territorial assemblies by representatives of interests, and opposition to the accompanying transformation of the Senate (a thorn in de Gaulle's side) into a consultative emanation of the territorial assemblies and the main interest groups. The unions denounced the bill as an attempt at forcible integration. Most interestingly, the old local *notables* opposed the bill. As they saw it, it forced them to share their power with the interest groups' delegates; it diminished the importance of the districts in which their own influence had traditionally been exercised (the *commune* or *département*) without giving them any increased power in exchange at the new, higher level; and it weakened "their" central parliamentary body, the Senate.[35] They campaigned actively against the bill.

It may well be that a victory for de Gaulle at the referendum called in the spring of 1969 would have merely multiplied veto groups and veto powers, i.e., enhanced the atavistic French capacity for protest, and created new possibilities for "the most bigoted conservatisms and the most narrow corporatisms." [36] But fear of giving the "participants" extensive powers or popular legitimacy, which could be used not merely to complicate the prefects' life, but to introduce regional Fourth Republics into the Fifth made de Gaulle prefer to limit the bill's scope.[37] It was to be a safety valve for discontent, to be sure, but there was to be no disruption of the state. Again, *in the long run,* a more daring bill, like the one suggested by the reformers, *might* have led the French to behave regionally as they were now behaving in national politics—concentrating instead of fragmenting their votes. But in the short run, there was the risk that the opposition parties, well rooted locally, would prevail at the regional level and use this as a lever against the central government. De Gaulle probably saw this cautious reform as a mere first step in his battle against the local *notables*: first, catch them; later, supersede them (his reform of the French Presidency had also been gradual: in 1958, the President was the *notables'* man, in 1962 he was made the people's man). But there was to be no first step. The bill, and with it the General, fell between stools: too limited to please the *modernes,* too innovative to placate the *anciens,* and perhaps irrelevant to the most pressing problems of territorial administration: those of the growing cities, at one end, and of the small communes, at the other.

De Gaulle had no time to go beyond the law of December 1968 giving unions the right to establish *sections syndicales* at the plant level, and he did not reach what would have been the most difficult issue of all: workers' participation. The opposition of business and labor unions alike would not, probably, have been enough to stop this (after all, most French workers were not union members). But nowhere would the results have been so obviously inadequate: measures aimed at participation would have had to be imposed on the organizations on whom the chances of success ultimately depended, and the structures of participation would have been merely new channels of protest (as the shop stewards and *comités d'entreprises* had so often become) or destructive battlefields for opposing utopias and contending principles.

It is hard to judge fairly an interrupted effort, but it is possible to see in de Gaulle's design a shrewd shift within the traditional system of authority rather than a break with it. I noted earlier that for a variety of reasons the old model had become increasingly authoritarian. De Gaulle tried to reverse this trend in important areas, not by changing the nature of higher authority within them but by creating new institutions in which the subordinates or subjects could express themselves, enjoy certain rights (i.e., have a protected sphere of limited autonomy), and pressure their superiors. In this way, given the General's obvious determination to maintain the national political subsystem at the authoritarian end of the French spectrum, a certain amount of balance would have been restored: it would now have been up to the other subsystems—education, regions, business—to serve as counterweights. This was an attempt to consolidate the old system by extending to new beneficiaries (professors and students, interest groups, workers, cadres, regional representatives) the double appeal of what I have called captive power: granting them a legally guaranteed zone of action (a zone *within* the system and dependent on it, since its statute is defined and its performance supervised by the state), and giving them the opportunity most characteristic of France's older territorial arrangements—the chance to establish *notabilité* and to deepen their hold over their constituents thanks to the new influence they could bring to bear on higher authority.

If this system had been fully put through, it would not have addressed itself to two important points of tension: the competence of the elites and the problem of change. Also, by opening new (if meager) areas for their control, creating new channels for their protest, and making more room for their utopian reactions against the limits imposed from above, it would have perpetuated the brittleness of the various competing associations trying to get delegates elected. This might have made further and better institutional change even more difficult—and put an even heavier final weight on the linchpin, the state. Yet in the past, the distribution of captive power, the setting up of parliamentary or pseudoparliamentary structures, often stilled opposition, at least for a while. This time, it failed to seduce opponents and actually displeased Gaullist partisans.

The reason can be found in an analysis of the relation between France's more libertarian version of "routine authority" and the state of the underlying consensus. The libertarian version of "routine authority" corresponds, in French political history, to a society where consensus was essentially negative: against either reaction or revolution socially; against either one-man rule or the tyranny of what Blum had called unorganized masses politically. In other words, the parliamentary model was most appropriate to management of the *status quo* in a nation with deep ideological and social fissures. This also made it inappropriate to institutions—universities, regions, enterprises—whose main problem was to get out of the *status quo,* notwithstanding the lack of substantive consensus on their future. Paradoxically, the determination to overcome the *status quo* had recently led the French to repudiate the parliamentary model in the national political subsystem. There was a procedural agreement here—even though there was no substantive consensus on a new social order—that only a strong state could provide the necessary impetus for handling the problems left unsolved by the old model and for reforming the *status quo.* Now the introduction of this model into new areas risked re-exacerbating divisions and breeding chaos. When the desire to preserve the *status quo* had been a common denominator, the model had been acceptable. Now that the rate of change and expectations had become such that homeorhesis could only be sought dynamically, its generalization was opposed by conservative professors and *gauchiste* students, old *notables,* unions afraid of being regionally "integrated" and undermined by new schemes of workers' participation, business owners and managers fearing the effects of institutionalized *contestation* in their own organizations.

In the absence of an underlying consensus, de Gaulle had not wanted to break away from a system that had kept the nation together in the past by organizing the coexistence of discordant factions, and even allowed them to reach at least negative agreements. But the shift he opted for in three areas—away from the authoritarian pole—was particularly unsuited to do what he wanted it to do, since the more libertarian pole was adequate only in managing the *status quo.* Indeed, the whole system, in all its versions, was inadequate to the tasks of renovation and innovation.

Both the May rebels' mountain, and Mount de Gaulle, had brought forth mice. The rebels had violently illuminated the flaws of the old system of authority, yet the reaction they provoked at the polls had consolidated its defenders. De Gaulle's method suffered from the enormous discrepancy between his addiction to grandiose nationwide legislative schemes (reflecting the very tendency toward uniformity and fondness for legal designs characteristic of the old style) and their actual timidity (understandable, but made more glaring by the bills' cosmic pretensions). The new government of Premier Chaban-Delmas tried to be more experimental, in line with Crozier's suggestions for acting only at critical points in the system. Where de Gaulle tried to create new institutions, his successors accepted them as they were (including those he established in higher education), but tried to avoid the sterilizing (if classic) compromises between control and autonomy he settled for. The results have been mixed. The regional reform of 1972 is an empty framework, whose supporters are reduced to praise it for its "evolutive" nature: some day, someone might fill the frame. Pompidou's prudence had prevailed over Chaban-Delmas's promises. For the time being, the new regions depend on the smaller districts and on the national government for grants of power, and their only autonomous financial resource is, according to one deputy, just large enough to cover the meeting expenses of the regional councils! [38] The local *notables,* this time, were pleased: instead of being captives of de Gaulle's regions, they are captors of Pompidou's.

In social affairs—Chaban's only sphere of free action—the picture is different. In September 1969, the new Premier denounced the "stalemate" of France provoked by the style of authority and by the nature of the ruling castes in terms that amounted to quotes from (albeit without reference to) Crozier's and my own writings. Chaban-Delmas and his advisers tried to create opportunities for autonomy and cooperation by granting to public enterprises a much larger sphere of uncontrolled action, by recognizing the unions' desire not to be caught in the state's institutional cobweb in exchange for *"concertation,"* and by encouraging nationwide contractual agreements between labor and business unions on such matters as remedies against unemployment, the workers' right to professional training, fringe benefits, pensions, etc. These agreements resulted from, and led to, quasi-permanent bargaining, and set up a host of committees and procedures of consultation and negotiations. De Gaulle's successors thus hoped both to strengthen associations and to change patterns of behavior—the two prerequisites to participation.

Yet the basic dilemmas have not disappeared. Enthusiasm for the new kind of autonomy, which means involvement and responsibility, remains almost nil: to each his prerequisite for accepting the plunge. Once again, progress is hampered by traditional habits: each would-be partner asks for guarantees against risks (the state, in exchange for switching from regulation and control to guidelines or contracts; enterprises, in exchange for switching from various forms of state protection to genuine freedom of action). Progress also suffers from the absence of a substantive consensus. The unions remain suspicious of a partnership in a "new society" that would, if anything, be more purely capitalist than before, and stress the fact that whenever the relative strength of union and management changes, bargaining has to resume.

The "contractual" policy has the merit of implicating the partners *in fact* in the management of the economic machine and thereby consolidating a consensus by default; yet the very reason why the policy works is that it is ambiguous. One side of it may prepare a new model, but the other side belongs to the old one: the contracts essentially consist in definitions and distributions of rights and advantages; they allow each partner to interpret his contribution and achievements in the light of his own ideology; they keep his hands and his thoughts free, and they preserve the homeorhetic dream of security and balance. Optimists can point out there is more *face-à-face* than before; pessimists can show that it occurs only at very high levels, and that its main point seems to be to save the partners from having to change structures and attitudes more drastically, to save them from further *face-à-face,* and thereby to save face. The more peace and cooperation there is on top, the greater the risk of wildcat actions below—and the unions do not want their influence undermined in this way.

The prospects are still dim. But if there is no movement out of the *société bloquée* denounced by Chaban-Delmas, and if the "new social contract" sought by Edgar Faure—that great virtuoso of dazzling concepts and paper solutions—remains elusive, there may again be movements resembling that of May 1968. One example of graffiti that appeared in 1968 during the student rebellion seems to offer a prophetic description of France's last great upheaval: "We want a music that would be savage and ephemeral."

III
De Gaulle

7
The Hero as History:
De Gaulle's War Memoirs

I

Few publications are as fascinating for historians and political scientists as General de Gaulle's *War Memoirs*.[1] The *Memoirs* offer de Gaulle's own version of his role during the war and his conception of international and domestic politics. They provide us with a clue to most of de Gaulle's acts as founder and head of the Fifth Republic and with a means of assessing the continuity of his leadership. Finally, the *Memoirs,* like the *Testament* of Richelieu, from whom de Gaulle learned so much, are essentially a treatise on leadership.

A judgment applied by de Gaulle to Churchill fits the General himself just as well: he is "the great champion of a great enterprise and the great artist of a great history" (I, 58 *). Indeed, throughout *The Edge of the Sword,* a set of lectures first published in 1932, de Gaulle compares the leader's task to the artist's. "The true leader, like the great artist, is a man with an inborn propensity which can be strengthened and exploited by the exercises of his craft." [2] The portrait of the ideal leader to which this early book is largely devoted resembles the self-portrait that de Gaulle later painted in the *Memoirs*. There is the same mixture of romantic and classical elements. The reader of Chateaubriand, Vigny, Bergson, and Barrès emphasizes intuition as the indispensable complement of intelligence; he shows that solitude, frustrations, fights with "the stuffed dummies of the hierarchy," and an impulse to withdraw are the lot of the true leader. The reader of Cardinal de Retz and Corneille discusses the need for the leader to under-

First published in *World Politics*, XIII, No. 1 (October 1960).
* My references throughout this chapter, unless otherwise stated, are to the volumes of the English translation of the *War Memoirs*.

stand himself as well as realities in order to master events—"There is no success save starting from the truth" (III, 102); he stresses the responsibilities which leadership entails. The reader, and frequent quoter, of Shakespeare thrives on times "when danger threatens," for "history in its great moments tolerates in positions of authority only those men capable of directing their own course" (II, 75).

When the stuffed dummies were blown away by the tempest of June 1940, de Gaulle stepped into a position of authority without any hesitation, and set a course for himself from which he never departed. Thirteen years later, in describing his intentions and acts then, his account is never contradicted by the documents he appended to it, and it is written in language that is always striking and appropriate. (It is too bad—in the case of a man whose authority rests to such a degree on the might, magic, and mystery of words—that the sharp and concise eloquence of his style has been so neatly flattened in the English translation of the second and third volumes of his *Memoirs,* and that there should be so many small inaccuracies.) The author of *The Edge of the Sword* already possessed the two qualities he required of leaders: passion and self-confidence. Those qualities had served his prewar ambition to improve France's security by creating a mechanized *armée de métier.* In June 1940, a new cause appeared: it was too late to attend even to survival; now de Gaulle had to fight for resurrection, reconstruction, and renovation—no less. With each new turn of the war, and each further success of his action, his goals broadened. At first, his double objective was to put the French empire back into the war and to defend those of its pieces which he had snatched away from Vichy against Allied interference. Later, his purposes were to obtain for France a major role in postwar settlements and to build in exile a strong French state which, transported into liberated France, would preserve her from Communist subversion and could safeguard her future. He speaks of his own rule as a "sort of monarchy" (III, 270); had not his role during the war years been similar to that of the kings of France, in the days when they tried to unify the countless duchies and counties of feudal France under their dynasty?

It was the scope of de Gaulle's design that led to his clash with, and victory over, poor General Henri Giraud, who confounded national unity and military hierarchy and could not understand that war is politics. It was the nature of de Gaulle's design that led to his misunderstanding with Roosevelt, who mistook his emphasis on the political essence of his action for petty personal ambition.[3] And the scale of de Gaulle's design explains the perspective of the *Memoirs*—its passionate dialogue between the General and his image of France, the high pitch of his nationalism, his tendency to judge events only from the viewpoint of France's interests. The excesses or distortions that this perspective entailed were the consequences of de Gaulle's and France's plight in 1940–46; one man was trying to re-create a nation and a state wrecked by decadence, defeat, and division. Later, as the leader of a far more wealthy and assured nation, and of a state built according to his wishes, de Gaulle's nationalism became less strident and his concern for the world was at least as great as his concern for France. His goals had broadened again—not because he had changed, but because the situation was different. De Gaulle remained faithful to his own primordial precept: the leader must have "a keen eye for contingencies"; [4] "in economy, as in politics or strategy, there exists, I believe, no absolute truth. There are only the circumstances" (III, 136).

Still, while realities have to be reassessed constantly, de Gaulle did have a general conception that served as his map of world affairs and as his breviary for diplomatic action. His view was in many ways close to that of the "realist" school of international politics. For him, the nation-state was and would remain the basic unit. Ideologies, despite their pretensions to universality, were essentially temporary cloaks of national ambitions. (This was as true of Roosevelt's internationalism as of Stalin's communism, he believed. "Communism will pass. But France will not pass" [I, 269].) In such a world, one's power determined one's influence. The supreme mistake of a statesman would be to "rely on appearances"; this was the error of Mussolini, who, "having tried to grasp too much," finally "had nothing left to hold on to" (III, 197). The cardinal sins of a statesman are to underrate the role of force (especially military) and to subordinate his nation's armies to foreign political goals; this was the crime of Vichy and the temptation of Giraud. National survival and security can best be assured by traditional methods: the balancing of power, coalitions of convergent interests, cabinet diplomacy rather than parliamentary diplomatic posturing in either its national or international varieties. De Gaulle's own complicated diplomacy of 1944–45, which played the Soviet Union off against Britain and demanded guarantees at Germany's expense while looking forward to an association of Western Europe including Germany, had a Bismarckian ring. To complete the resemblance with the "realists," and with nineteenth-century diplomacy, there was in de Gaulle's view a definite hierarchy among the major and the minor powers, and a longing for a concert of the great powers, on whom peace depends.

De Gaulle's conception contained many elements which went beyond this familiar sketch. He had a sophisticated view of states' purposes: power, he knew, was more often a means than an end. He tended to distinguish a sphere of "interests defined in terms of power," such as national security and what he calls *le rang,* and a sphere of idealistic, "unselfish" purposes. In his vision of the world, nations were like peers whom the aristocrats' code of values expects to perform acts of individual prowess, but for the common good. The common good —de Gaulle's broadest unselfish goal—was *la querelle de l'homme;* in 1940–46, it was the struggle for freedom; [5] later, it was still the fight against totalitarianism, and the new battles against underdevelopment in much of the world, against "enslavement by the machine" in the more advanced part of the world, against foreign hegemonies all over the world. According to de Gaulle (who sounds in this respect very much like Georges Bernanos), the mechanization and urbanization of modern life offered tremendous opportunities to totalitarianism but must be turned to freedom's advantage. Another idealistic aim was the restoration of Europe, which de Gaulle considered the center of civilization. It was in part because the United States did not object to Russia's domination over Eastern Europe that de Gaulle criticized Roosevelt—and also because Roosevelt's anticolonialism was weakening Europe at a time when, according to de Gaulle, only a common Western policy toward Africa and Asia could prevent colonial territories from achieving their inevitable independence "against us." And it was in part because Britain preferred being America's lieutenant to becoming, with France, the guide of Europe that de Gaulle felt so bitter about England's behavior, then and later.[6] Both those policies seemed to him to constitute treason toward Europe; although his belief in the nation-state prevented him from looking forward to a "supranational" Europe, he was already working toward the "imposing confederation" he mentioned in the early days of the Fifth Republic. The nation may be the basic unit, but it is not an absolute: de Gaulle's concern for transnational ends and his emphasis on France's traditions of the Rights of Man made the difference between his nationalism and the integral nationalism of Maurras; *la raison supérieure de l'Europe* [7] was opposed to Germany's destruction. The belief that "in the long run there is no regime that can hold out against the will of nations" (III, 53) explained de Gaulle's hope for the withdrawal of Soviet control from Eastern Europe and induced him to accept the idea of self-government and even independence for colonies before most of his compatriots.

In the realm of means—power—there were also original aspects to de Gaulle's thinking. He was acutely aware of the changing nature of power; the sword was always essential, but economic strength was equally important—hence his emphasis on production, planning, public investments, and his own motive for nationalizations, which he saw primarily as an instrument of economic transformation and only subsidiarily as a social reform. Moreover, he did not believe that realism required that a nation's objectives always be measured by its present resources. Throughout World War II, he acted as if France were still a great power, in order to make her a great power again. Had de Gaulle violated his own precept and fallen into Mussolini's trap? I do not think so. His conduct was part of a remarkable hortatory policy: in order to get someone to do something, he should be treated as if he had done it already, and complimented for having done so.[8] In this instance, the key to de Gaulle's strategy was his certainty that France's fall could be remedied and that France would become powerful again —but only if her allies gave her a psychological and material push for a new "climb toward might." De Gaulle's policy was French power by installments.

Thus we come to a central Gaullist concept: French *grandeur*. It is by no means the clearest of his concepts, although it is the most discussed. *Why* he thought France ought to have "a great national ambition" (III, 101) was clear enough. It was part dogma, part reason. It was a *mystique,* a product of his philosophy of heroic leadership as applied to France—whom he treated as a person, as Michelet did—and of his instinctive feeling that Providence has created France "either for complete successes or for exemplary misfortunes" (I, 3). But it was also a *politique,* for he thought *grandeur* was a domestic necessity, a diversion from discord, and an international service, a factor of diplomatic wisdom and responsibility, a contribution to world equilibrium and European restoration. However, *what* he meant by *grandeur* is not so easy to analyze. He never defined it in specific terms, for *grandeur* was an attitude rather than a policy. More accurately, the policy implications of *grandeur* varied with the circumstances: they were not in the 1960s what they had been in 1945. Indeed, he believed, rigidity was the worst enemy of greatness: it was intellectual, economic, and political rigidity that led to France's decline in the 1930s, as he said repeatedly, and the problem for France was not restoration but renovation.[9] What remained fixed was the command itself: like natural law, *grandeur* was an imperative with varying content.

The imperative can be ascertained: *grandeur* meant the opposite of resignation to a passive role in the world. It meant a triple determination: first, it implied a will to be an actor, not an object, a player, not a stake; secondly, it entailed a decision to be as ambitious, universal, and inventive an actor as world politics in general and the national power basis in particular allowed; thirdly, it involved the subordination of domestic politics to the primacy of international affairs and to the requirements of status. *Grandeur* implied that the nation must be ready to bear the sacrifices such a policy requires, for there is no right without corresponding duties. Gaullism, which is not an ideology precisely because *grandeur* is not unalterably tied to any specific policies or forms of power,[10] means this triple determination.

The specific historical content of *grandeur* during the war years can be described by three terms: independence, status, self-respect. Independence did not mean isolation or autarky, but the avoidance of lasting dependence on any other unit. Hence de Gaulle's struggle against German oppression, British encroachments, and American "appeal of domination," as he saw it (II, 133); hence also his hostility to the integration of French military forces under foreign command, then and later. Status meant that France's defeat should not cost her any of the diplomatic or territorial positions she would have kept had she refused to sign the armistice of 1940. This is why de Gaulle insisted that he would negotiate France's departure from the Middle East only after the Liberation, and that France had to set foot in Indochina again before opening talks with the local nationalists there.

Self-respect was by far the most important and subtle of the three objectives. De Gaulle understood that France's image of herself had been shattered in 1940; that *grandeur* could be recovered only if France's self-pride were restored; and that she could not receive it as a gift from her allies but had to win it back through her own actions. Thus, "it was essential to bring back into the war not merely some Frenchmen, but France" (I, 80); he was not interested in merely providing the Allies with French soldiers. But his goal required that Frenchmen should fight on every front even if they were not wanted by the Allies, even if the battle were hopeless, as in Indochina in March 1945, even if the blood of Vichy Frenchmen had to be shed,[11] or even if this meant a prolongation of the war. His goal required that no free Frenchman should owe his authority to an Ally (this is why he feared that a victory for Giraud in the power struggle of 1942–43 would benefit only the Allies outside France, and only the Communists inside). He insisted on the Allies' recognizing him as France's leader only as long as this would bolster French morale and will to fight. And, he believed, the more liberal colonial policy he deemed necessary would depend on a rebirth of France's self-respect: only a confident France could really be generous—a precept he followed after 1958. Roosevelt's blindness to this fundamental goal, his willingness to deal with Vichyites, his assumption that France was finished and was anyhow more adequately represented by her easygoing prewar leaders than by this General who "had nothing of a usual Frenchman"—this is what so infuriated de Gaulle. As he told Harry Hopkins, in a remarkable dialogue, America's policy, whether it was right or not, could not but alienate the French.

The range of tactics de Gaulle used in order to achieve his triple objective was formidable. Dealing with the Allies, as he put it, "limited and alone though I was, and precisely because I was so, I had to climb to the heights and never then to come down" (I, 83); or, as he told Churchill, he was "too poor to be able to bow" (I, 243). So he went from *faits accomplis* to threats of resignation and to harsh and effective blackmail whenever his moral or material position was such that the Allies could not but give in. He never consented to agreements for agreement's sake, and he treated his diplomats' fondness for compromise as a professional disease. Dealing with his own people, his tactics were far more diverse. He remained thoroughly intransigent toward Vichy; he encouraged the Allies to make Vichy France's plight even worse so as to shock the French away from Pétain's dream world; he purged Vichyites according to their acts, not according to their intentions. But toward the enemies of Vichy, he showed much more flexibility and ambiguity (just as he did, during the Algerian war, with the military and the diehards, unless and until they defied him directly). He got rid of Giraud, but by stages. He welded the heterogeneous Resistance movements into a reasonably united force. He "wanted the Communists to serve," and he got their services. He paid a heavy price in allowing the political parties back into the picture, but he successfully broadened his support. He acted as a symbol of French unity, although this involved compromises and meant he had to soft-pedal his constitutional views. He chose Pleven's financial policy as against Mendès-France's in order not to "throw" a "sick and hurt" nation "into dangerous convulsions" (III, 136). Thus, when survival was not at stake and when conflicts put various interpretations of *grandeur* into opposition but did not threaten the principle itself, de Gaulle acted with restraint, preferred cunning to constraint, and strove for unity.

For unity was a precondition of *grandeur.* Just as his view of world affairs raised the question of the meaning of *grandeur,* his idea of French domestic affairs posed an equally crucial and complex question: the relation of Frenchmen's wishes to the constant imperative of *grandeur.*

We get a first approximation of an answer to this problem if we study de Gaulle's notion of legitimacy. A legitimate regime is one which, first, preserves and promotes French *grandeur* despite external and internal threats, and, second, receives the adherence of the nation for following such a policy. This is why de Gaulle before the 1930s approved of the Third Republic: not for ideological reasons, but because it had increased France's power and role in the world, won the *revanche* over Germany, and served those principles, "freedom, justice, popular sovereignty, without which there is no lasting strength, no solidity, no light" (III, 600, French edition). For the same reason, he disapproved of Giraud—who could never win "that elementary adherence of the French people without which a government is nothing but a fiction" (II, 90)—and of the Fourth Republic, which fumbled with *grandeur.*

Both elements of legitimacy were indispensable, but the concern with *grandeur* was, so to speak, the active principle. De Gaulle never envisaged a *coup d'état* against the Fourth Republic because of his scrupulous respect for legality,[12] but he never doubted that he incarnated "something primordial, permanent, and necessary" and thus was "a kind of capital of sovereignty" which could "remain latent" for a while, but would become effective again when popular support, in an emergency, would hurry back to him. Moreover, there were exceptional circumstances when a dictatorship of public safety was justifiable: a great national ambition or the fear of a people in peril.[13] Although de Gaulle was suspicious of the fatal and frenzied excesses to which the "great adventure" of dictatorship might lead and argued that no such temporary despotism should be prolonged more than is necessary, there was little doubt that in his mind the function of the second element of legitimacy—free institutions—was to provide genuine, untwisted, unplebiscitary ratification of national policy, rather than to initiate and define such policy.

Who could define it? In the ideal state, which de Gaulle described in his *Memoirs* and tried to establish in the Constitution of 1958, it was the chief of state. A national policy meant action, not deliberation, and action was the work of "one alone" (II, 179). Therefore no legislature could be entrusted with policy-making power, as it was during the parliamentary Republics: "assemblies, beneath their fine speeches, are ruled by the fear of action" (III, 46).[14] Leadership was a personal thing, and de Gaulle hated nothing more than anonymous power: the greatest failing of France's past regimes was their fundamental principle "Let no head show above the trenches of democracy" (III, 294). The chief of state alone was in charge of the national interest, which is not "a juxtaposition of particular interests" (III, 112 *).

The implications of this statement were huge: to de Gaulle, as to the revolutionary heirs of Rousseau, political parties—at least in France—were not the spokesmen for different versions of the national interest, but the champions of particular interests. His indictment of French parties was detailed and devastating. They were geared to permanent criticism, not to action; dominated by slogans, not by any sense of realities; always ready to put "everything at stake," instead of agreeing on fundamentals. None represented more than a small fraction of opinion, thus none could govern alone; consequently, an executive arm left to parties would be an auction of offices and influence but not a means of action. Finally, French parties had lost their "doctrinal passion" and were "shrinking until each . . . [became] nothing more than the representation of a category of interests" (III, 272). This was not the case in Britain, but it had been true in France under the Third Republic, which had "floated upon the nation's surface without directing its vital forces" (II, 77). Therefore, according to de Gaulle—just as to Richelieu—the representatives of French "categories" should

---

* My translation. De Gaulle writes *"particuliers,"* the translator writes "private."

not be allowed to take over the state. In particular, they should not select the chief of state or figure in the cabinet as spokesmen for their
groups; they might still overthrow cabinets, but their legislative powers would be smaller than in a presidential system. Hence de Gaulle's
almost complete silence on Resistance politics in his *Memoirs,* his cool-
ness toward the National Council of the Resistance which pretended
to speak for the nation, his preference for a "great administrator" instead of a political leader at the head of the Council,[15] his determination to seek "no investiture for . . . [his] authority save that which
the voice of the people would give . . . [him] directly" (II, 340).

De Gaulle's distaste for French parties and pressure groups extended
to all the "elites," the *notables* from whose ranks the representatives
were selected. The elites of France failed at first to follow him—all
they granted him was "the melancholy homage of its remorse" (I, 22).
After the Liberation, they failed to support his battle for *grandeur,* for
France's rank, and for a strong new army. They came between de
Gaulle and the people, and eliminated him in 1945 when opinion "no
longer delegated anything but parties around . . . [him]" (III, 308).
In the ideal state, de Gaulle thought, the relationship must be reversed:
it would be the people's job to put pressure on the elites to force them
to support the chief of state.

Thus, the crucial connection in the state must be the link between
the people and the head of state, the masses and their guide, as de
Gaulle called them. This link reminds one of the relation between the
Legislator and the citizens in the *Social Contract.* The national interest,
which intermediate bodies corrupt, resembles the general will, which
is not *any* will of all, but the *higher* will of each and all. Similarly, de
Gaulle distinguished "France's higher interests" as "something quite
different [from] the immediate advantage of the French" (III, 31).
The general will is always right, but the people do not always see the
common good. The Legislator helps them discover it; once they have,
people will want it. In the same way, de Gaulle believed that if the
people were shown France's higher interest, they would freely follow
the guide who disclosed it. Rousseau stressed that the Legislator's only
function was to educate the popular will and had "nothing in common with human empire"; de Gaulle's guide was also chief of state—
part Legislator, part Roman dictator, part prince. Rousseau reminded
his readers that true Legislators are rare; de Gaulle was indeed a good
one (and knew it, and said so), but what of his successors?

II

Here, we reach two fundamental questions which de Gaulle's writings
and actions have left in many minds. Was the policy of *grandeur* a realistic one after all? Was the regime that de Gaulle wanted and later

created viable? I shall ask these questions about the Fifth Republic in forthcoming chapters, but here, I should like to try to answer them with respect to the war years and de Gaulle's brief rule after the Liberation.

De Gaulle's conception of *grandeur* in those years has come under two kinds of attacks. For some—critics outside France and, in France, critics who were in sympathy with Vichy—de Gaulle's *mystique* was an anachronistic quest, a vain nostalgia for past greatness, a fruitless drive for restoration, a pretentious attempt at denying an overwhelming, unwelcome reality: France's utter dependence on the good will of the Big Three. De Gaulle's delusions and prickly pride almost squandered any such good will. A less arrogant and more skillful diplomacy could have achieved more—or at least no less. But this criticism misses the psychological meaning of de Gaulle's appeals: when he talked to the French about their greatness, it was in order to get them to adapt to, and act in, the world *as it was,* not in order to keep them in a museum of past glories. It was flattery for reform. No leader ever coaxes his people into change by telling them that they are through; as de Gaulle himself remarked, when problems appear simpler to people, "most likely they are" (III, 13). The work of the statesman in revolutionary times resembles that of Ingmar Bergman's Magician. Of course, the prerequisite to de Gaulle's success was that renovation would suffice to make a new *grandeur* possible. But the problem after the Liberation was anyhow to develop the nation's resources after the disasters of the 1930s; there was nothing absurd either about assuming that only a determined effort of growth could alleviate both material and spiritual tensions, that an appeal to pride could be the best goad for a deeply humiliated yet undaunted nation.

Resources were the precondition for *any* policy. The real question raised by de Gaulle was whether the French would want to use them primarily for and on the world stage. Was there a national will for *grandeur*? What was the likelihood of domestic support for a policy that imposed sacrifices on French consumers in return for relative autonomy in world affairs? There was in the short run no clear-cut answer. On one hand, de Gaulle's own position on the issue was not really shared by the Resistance: hence his own disillusionment throughout 1945, as the debates in the Consultative Assembly and the parties' priorities revealed the gap to him. The fact that he could not get the judges in charge of purges to adopt his own view—that Vichy's original sin was the armistice, rather than either its collaboration or its repressiveness—was symbolic of the misunderstanding. As a result, when de Gaulle resigned, French foreign policy was bound to be in a difficult position. The party and Resistance leaders had endorsed de Gaulle's ambitions and shared his demands for France's security; the level of French nationalism was much higher than before 1939, thanks to the internal Resistance and to de Gaulle's pedagogy, both of which had led to the illusion, or conviction, that France had contributed signally to the victory over Germany. But de Gaulle's successors were unwilling to give foreign affairs the priority of attention and resources de Gaulle's conception demanded, or to apply to allies the tactics he had used against all foreign states. Drawn to the world stage, he had wanted to create and develop new French resources for it. They were more impressed by the difficulty of building up French power, less single-minded about allocating these resources, yet still hopeful of somehow playing a major role. Disappointments and a nationalism of frustration could not but result from this. French policy after the war was dominated by various (to be sure, conflicting) adepts of *grandeur*. "Little Frenchmen" found little support in any party or in the electorate. The population increased, the economic and social order showed considerable progress, at least some traditional French values, routines, and protections were discarded because they had been largely responsible for France's decline, and it would have been something of a paradox to ask the nation to give up, so to speak. Even when retreat had to be ordered—in France's German policy, or overseas—it was done only under duress, and allegedly to improve the ultimate chances of cutting a grand figure. As Raymond Aron remarked, it was public dissatisfaction with France's status at a time of considerable prosperity that killed the Fourth Republic; [16] what had weakened the French role most was not a lack of resources, but the way in which the French regime had proceeded with the problem of adaptation, with finding a medium between anachronism and resignation.

Thus, whether *grandeur* is a concept for stormy times alone, for rescuing the self-pride of a nation buffeted by "the wind of history," as de Gaulle occasionally suggested, or whether a "national ambition" can remain a permanent driving force, depends in large part on the solidity and style of the regime. This was the area in which de Gaulle's disappointments, after the Liberation, were deepest. His ideal state reflected the lessons he had drawn from the Third Republic and also those he had derived from his experiences with Resistance and party representatives, business and labor leaders, and intellectuals after 1940. But he was in no position to impose his views, despite his prestige and the support of the bulk of the population. In 1946, de Gaulle's ideal was simply not achievable. The grand alliance of de Gaulle, the non-Communist Resistance, and the Communist party was a delicate balance of mutually suspicious and deterring partners. They all agreed on the urgency of rebuilding French power, hence on a deep transformation of French society and on an expansion of the state's role. But the Communists feared Gaullist rule, and de Gaulle saw them as potentially subversive in domestic and external matters. The non-Communist Resistance was—in a way Tocqueville had already noted apropos of the revolutionaries of 1789—more interested in domestic reform than in the organization of the state. And de Gaulle's own decision to introduce the parties into the Conseil Nationale de la Résistance (CNR)—both because they, having been discredited in 1940, would be more docile to him than the Resistance movements, and because he needed them as counterweights to the Communist party—carried the seeds of his subsequent defeat. The impact on the Socialists of Communist arguments derived from the old Left ideology of 1793 and from old anti-Bonapartist reflexes, and the impact on the Christian Democrats of the revival of a Socialist-Communist alliance reawakened party parochialisms and party patriotisms. The silence of the CNR's program on the subject of constitutional reform was ominous.

There was enough of a coalition to carry out an ambitious program of economic and social change. But de Gaulle became victim of the frustrations incurred by this unanimity. To campaign directly for his views about the state would have meant an overt battle with the Communists, at a time when the restoration of production and of provincial law and order required them to cooperate together. It would have obliged the Socialist party to choose between him and them—and, given the way in which it had, as Blum put it, rediscovered its old tenets, it was unlikely that he would be the winner. With the Christian Democrats as his only support, he would appear as a new Bonaparte and a champion of the Right. Thus he found himself cut off from a public that was exhausted by memories and miseries and whipped up against his government by complaints about the food shortage, the purges, the slowness of reform, inflation, etc. By the end of 1945, his only choice was between resignation and the total erosion of his authority.

The consequences were momentous. Since there had been enough agreement between him and the non-Communists to block Communist demands for the "liquidation of the bourgeoisie"—and to keep the anti-Vichy purges moderate in number and in outcome—and since in the struggle for power among his successors the Communists lost out, French society was transformed according to traditional patterns of authority—from the top—and limited ways. But the institutions of the state that presided over and oriented the changes were soon paralyzed by a return to party politics and to the party-state. Once more, the public felt left out, the bureaucracy remained unguided, and the financial price de Gaulle had already paid to unanimity (when he decided against Mendès-France's anti-inflationary policy, which had little support among the parties) continued to rise.

The Fourth Republic seemed to demonstrate *a contrario* the

strength of de Gaulle's double contention that France needed *gran-deur* to avoid external and internal disintegration, and that a regime that bypassed political parties in favor of a bond between the people and the chief of state could alone provide it. De Gaulle never failed to make these points as leader of the RPF. The considerable ambiguities of the RPF's recruitment policies, propaganda, and program; the dilemma of being antiparliamentary in a parliamentary Republic without appearing to be antidemocratic or appealing to antidemocratic elements; the difficulty of getting to power without staging a *coup d'état* or playing the game according to its detested rules—all these factors might have made the RPF look dangerous or silly, but the juxtaposition of de Gaulle's post-1946 warnings and exhortations with President Vincent Auriol's later laments and exasperations about being head of a powerless state divided in byzantine factions restores the balance.[17] Still, even a reader of de Gaulle's *War Memoirs* who knew French history only up to the fall of the Fourth Republic would be left with misgivings.

For one thing, the precedent of 1944–46 left open the key question of national support for a policy of *grandeur*. Was that support faltering or insufficient *only* because the institutions were unsettled, the parties too strong, the Chief Executive too unfree in his movements? Would constitutional reform along Gaullist lines be a panacea? For another, could the ideal regime, by the simple virtue of stability, and because of the link between the people and the diviner of the common good, solve the problems that had caused the downfall of the parliamentary Republic?

There was the problem of parties. For de Gaulle, they were a necessary evil which could not be turned into a permanently good and useful tool—at least in France. So they had to be tolerated, for they represent respectable interests, valid ideas, and genuine divisions, but must be relegated to a minor role. In the long run, however, no modern state can be managed if the parties are treated as unavoidable nuisances or, at best, cumbersome crutches that might always go off in a perverse direction of their own. Nor was the problem of French elites tackled directly by the ideal regime. Despite the brilliant light which a great man is able to project on his people while he is in power, success ultimately depends on elites capable of translating into acts and facts the intentions and decisions of the leader, while he lasts, and of making policy, when he is gone. They will not become more concerned for unity and *grandeur* when they do not participate in public affairs. Many observers had hoped that industrialization would gradually solve these two problems, and bring about a situation in which elites and parties—in France as in other industrial societies—would agree on essentials. But would the fading of old ideological issues, economic progress, and a leveling of the standard of living induce political "pragmatism"? And would even such pragmatism have any sense of purpose?

Finally, can these two problems be solved if the role of the nation is limited to passive (though free) assent and to occasional votes (either to approve executive decisions or to select rather powerless legislators), separated by long stretches in which the citizens are merely spectators and consumers of their political system? De Gaulle's permanent plea for unity, as Philip Williams and Martin Harrison have remarked,[18] and the priority he gave to issues affecting France's world status tended to limit the ideal regime's direct effect on the nation to daily administration, exhortation, and celebration.

The collapse of France's political institutions justified the Fifth Republic. It may well have been necessary to deal first with the proximate cause of all other troubles: the disarray of the state. But how far would reform of the state go toward solving the problems of substance at home and abroad, and might it not even complicate a solution at times? Somehow, this was not de Gaulle's principal worry. He was a philosopher, a moralist, an artist, and a fine historian (see II, 351–52). He was not a political scientist or a sociologist. He saw international *grandeur* as a compensation for domestic ills, but ultimately *grandeur* requires their cure. To be sure, domestic order and external successes are a powerful incentive to cure. But are they enough?

De Gaulle recognized that no man ever fulfills all his ambitions. But our doubts about his work of the future should not dim our appreciation of the man's greatness in the war years. His appeal to the French had little in common with the ebullient worship shown earlier "providential men." "De Gaulle . . . never encouraged a personality cult or even sought to perpetuate his system." [19] He was a synthesizer of French traditions; his love for France combined *ancien régime* features and the feeling of nineteenth-century French democrats; his image of France joined jealous concern for France's uniqueness with a sense of the universality of French values. His own values included faith *and* rationality. His desire for *grandeur* married past glories to renovation. He reminded his readers of the inspiration patriotism gives to man's actions, but although a world of nation-states was bound to be a world of competing forces, he never described it merely in Hobbesian terms, and he stressed the virtues of independence and association as long as the self-respect of all partners was assured.

Indeed, his fundamental preoccupation with self-respect, his regard for man's freedom, his concern for unity, his desire to lead men to act as they should rather than forcing them to do so—features that coexisted with a deep enthusiasm for action and for using all the levers and levels of leadership—remind us that, ultimately, the great political leader is an educator. De Gaulle's *War Memoirs* display all the beauties of education through example. His acts reflected the power and the limitations of such pedagogy—the power, since, largely thanks to him, France redefined her role in the world, and it is not a mean one; the limitations, since she may still lack the opportunities, the means, and the domestic structures and attitudes that make the difference between playing a role well and stumbling through one's part. That the future of France in the world depends on France even more than on the world is a poignant truth de Gaulle always understood.

8

De Gaulle as Political Artist:
The Will to Grandeur

by Stanley and Inge Hoffmann

S'élever au-dessus de soi, afin de dominer les autres,
et, par là, les événements.

—Vers l'armée de métier

The leader Charles de Gaulle, twice the savior of France, knight-errant
for her *grandeur,* believer in the cultural values embodied in a national tradition, appears all of one piece. It is as if he had chosen to
tailor himself to his role in history from the very beginning of his
childhood, as if he had carefully selected from his heritage and his personality those elements which would allow him to play the role to
perfection. When events did not conform to the demands of his self-
imposed role, he waited for the most effective entrance. Once on the
scene, he "arranged" himself so as to meet the demands, and no one,
however critical of the play, can deny the merits and mastery of his
performance.

It is therefore tempting simply to study the origins of his characteristic style, how he shaped his role, and how he imposed it on his
nation—as if he were not really much more complex. Indeed, we do
not know much more of him than the public personage. We suspect
that there was, behind it, a *face* both greater and smaller than the public figure: greater, for the public figure drew its life from the man beneath; smaller, because the man was surely restricted by the personage
he chose to become.

First published in *Daedalus,* Summer 1968; reprinted in revised form in Dankwart
A. Rustow, ed., *Philosophers and Kings* (New York, 1970). Inge Hoffmann wishes to
thank the Edward L. Hazen Foundation for its support for her research on the utili-
zation of inner tensions in creative work.

What the man demonstrated was the triumph of will over personal and national conflict, over inner doubts and external dramas. The will to restore, preserve, promote an abstraction: France, had always been more important to him than any other commitment. That "certain idea of France," of which he spoke, had to be served by a certain kind of leader. And de Gaulle's will was also, indeed primordially, to be that leader. His career showed a remarkable blend of thought and action, a rare capacity to fulfill a vocation by giving oneself and one's mission exactly the shape of one's dreams and ambitions. In other words, de Gaulle displayed an aesthetic talent refined in the political arena.

It is not the purpose of this chapter to pass judgment on de Gaulle as a political leader. Such a judgment would require an evaluation of the intrinsic merit of those dreams and ambitions, a detailed assessment of the means he used in order to realize them, and a discussion of the lasting effects of his achievements and failures. Our concern is narrower: it is to study de Gaulle as a political artist, not by looking at his techniques, at his craft, but by concentrating on what he called his gift—i.e., his "character" and the way he shaped it to fulfill the role he carried within himself.

This essay was first written a few weeks before the revolutionary events of May–June 1968 and a year before de Gaulle's second and final resignation from political leadership; we have left our analysis essentially unaltered, based as it was on our view of de Gaulle at the height of his power, on the evidence, intuition, and thoughts we had then. (Those we have since had make him appear more complex and diverse.) Here, we examine first the development of his personality, then the definition, psychological requirements, and psychological implications of his vocation, and, finally, the charismatic link between the political artist and his public—the people to whom he must communicate his gift in order to fulfill his mission. In an epilogue, we discuss the dramatic change that affected this link in May–June 1968, and its consequences.

I. Genesis

The man beneath the public figure can best be approached through a study of his family, his early reactions to his milieu, and his heroes. We are not suggesting that these influences "determined" him, but they put him on certain tracks that he never left and provided him with a point of departure that he both accepted and left behind.[1]

Charles de Gaulle was born on November 22, 1890, the third of five children, the second of four boys. His father, Henri de Gaulle, was descended from a long line of impoverished nobles—belonging to the *noblesse d'épée* and, later, mainly to the *noblesse de robe*—who lived, at first, in the provinces (Burgundy and Flanders) and, since the seventeenth century, in Paris. The fascination with history which Charles was going to display was already evidenced in his family, on Henri's side. Henri's father had written a history of Paris, had edited one of King Saint Louis, and had traced the genealogy of the family. One of Henri's brothers, called Charles de Gaulle, was a poet and scholar who, in a book about the Celts in the nineteenth century, anticipated his nephew and namesake in celebrating the resilient independence of the Celts (as well as their spread to America), and in writing that "in a camp surprised, at night, by an enemy attack, when each one fights alone, one does not ask the rank of the one who raises the flag and takes the initiative of rallying his men." [2] Henri's mother, a prolific writer of edifying novels, showed sympathy for various revolutionary figures like Proudhon and Jules Vallès, and wrote a book glorifying Daniel O'Connell.

Henri de Gaulle was forty-two when Charles was born. He had originally intended to become a *Polytechnicien* but, according to Charles's biographers, was stopped by a reversal of his family's fortune. He was wounded near Paris in the Franco-Prussian War and, later, sometimes took his children to visit the battleground. He became a professor of philosophy, history, and literature and headmaster in two distinguished Jesuit high schools in Paris. There is no doubt that his authority over Charles was great; Henri's former students have testified to his fervent love for France, and it is he who supervised his children's extensive readings in French history and in the classics of French literature, a task he accomplished with humor and ardor.

Charles's mother, Jeanne Maillot, shared her husband's devotion to France and Catholicism; she came from a bourgeois lineage—a line of austere, small businessmen from northern France, in whose families the youngest sons often pursued military careers. One of her uncles, Charles Maillot, an officer of unusual height, was legendary in the family. Little is known about her, but she appears to have been pious and vehement in her convictions. Charles's extraordinary capacity for faith was undoubtedly nourished by hers.

Charles de Gaulle's milieu was typical, and yet somehow it was *en marge,* in two essential respects. On one hand, socially it is hard to imagine a family more French than one that believes its French ancestry goes gack to the thirteenth century. Yet de Gaulle was not born in a family typical of nineteenth-century French society. As he pointed out later, his parents' outlook, concerns, and resources were not those of the bourgeoisie, and there must always have been a contrast between the dignified appearances—an apartment in Lille, one in Paris, a summer home in Dordogne—and the financial realities. De Gaulle's detachment from the class preoccupations of France's social categories thus becomes easier to understand. On the other hand, his family was typical of the values of the French Right at the end of the nineteenth century: a deep attachment to the monarchy (which the de Gaulle family had served either as officers or as lawyers), fervent Catholicism, fierce patriotism, and fear for the decline of France were characteristic of all those families to whom Maurras pitched his appeal. In one vital respect, however, the de Gaulles did not conform. Although a *"monarchiste de regret,"* Henri de Gaulle was not, it seems, moved in any way by the passionate anti-Republican hatred, the anti-Semitism, and xenophobia so characteristic of the Right. There was no sectarianism here, and Henri de Gaulle did not believe that Dreyfus was guilty. He was a man of moderation and a realist. His son inherited these virtues.

De Gaulle's family thus transmitted to him three essential messages. First, the family was profoundly inner-directed. Not only were the values it believed in, for all their lack of originality, those of a minority of Frenchmen in an impious republic (a fact that did not prevent the de Gaulles from sticking to their beliefs with dignity and firmness) but there was also a willingness to examine issues *independently,* on their own merits, and to judge them from a viewpoint of intense moderation—intense, because of the depth of Henri's "feeling" and of Mme. de Gaulle's "passion," [3] yet moderate, because the tone of the family, the manners of the father, above all the lessons of French classicism and history all seem to have pointed to the condemnation of excess. Self-respect, later so crucial to de Gaulle, was undoubtedly a family value and achievement.

Second, the values inculcated by the parents were above all public values. This was a family where a child would quickly learn to sublimate his private dreams and drives into public ones: the love of France, Christian faith, honor, the lessons of history, respect for culture, the nation as the highest temporal good and as a cultural partnership of the living and the dead, the virtues of the soldier as the defender of the nation and the carrier of the Christian faith. The remarkable—and by no means usual—harmony of the family members' views on France and the world provided young de Gaulle with a model and, in his later attempts to "gather" the French, with an inspiration and a goal. Most striking is the way in which, in this dignified but not affluent home of a family whose beliefs ran against the dogmas of the established regime, history—France's past—and the legacy of French culture seem to have served as a consolation for the present as well as a yardstick. Charles's enthusiasm for Édmond Rostand's *l'Aiglon,* which he allegedly saw at the age of ten, fits in easily.[4] It is the sentimental story of the ailing, oppressed, innocent son (played by Sarah Bernhardt) of the great Emperor, protected and inspired by a soldier called Flambeau, who symbolizes the average Frenchman and keeps the memories of Napoleon's epic alive in captivity. It could not fail to arouse in Charles the patriotic feelings and sense of service cultivated by his family and to strengthen his military vocation, already indicated by childhood games in which he always insisted on playing the role of France.

Third, and perhaps most important, Charles's milieu must have communicated to him a deep sense of distress about the present. Toward the internal situation of France, the emotions must have ranged from discomfort to disgrace, as the nation moved from the unfinished truce of the *ralliement* years to the turmoil of the Dreyfus Affair (where all sides, as de Gaulle's father saw it, behaved lamentably), the separation of Church and state, the closing of the Jesuits' schools (including Henri's), the rise of socialism, labor unions, and strikes. Externally, the dominant feeling was one of persistent national humiliation; the father and mother had been traumatized by the fall of France in the war of 1870, and remained obsessed by the need for *la revanche* and by a fear of further French setbacks like Fachoda. (This was another reason why *l'Aiglon,* with its evocation of past exploits to exorcise the humiliations of the era after Napoléon I, of which it talks, and those of the era after Napoléon III, in which it was written, would appeal to the boy.) The de Gaulles' beloved France, the "princess or madonna" of the religious and nationalistic boy, was seen and felt to be troubled, threatened, almost tragic, rather than healthy, heroic, and expanding.[5] Her present condition could only be deplored, and as for the future, one could and should of course hope, but it was hard to imagine improvement without drama. De Gaulle's martial spirit and his desire to protect thus strengthened each other.

That he picked up all those "messages" we know from the first three paragraphs of his *Mémoires.* For all its opposition to present trends, for all its nostalgia and misgivings, his family life and holidays teamed with activities, fun, and games, of which learning became a part. In short, the family provided a rich and harmonious (*nonconflicted*) cultural legacy.

The picture of a little boy slowly emerges: a "perfect little devil" who is "neither docile nor naive" ("when Charles appears, tranquility disappears"[6]), full of mischief, practical jokes, and energy (books and papers are sent flying around his room), contrasting with his austere mother, his demanding father, and his less turbulent siblings. The double concern which never left him, for statecraft and for stagecraft, began in childhood, in his fondness for reliving in his readings and in his games various episodes (usually martial ones) of French history.

The period of joyful ebullience, the passionate abandon in adventure stories and war games, gradually receded as de Gaulle approached adolescence. Someone in the family allegedly said he must have fallen into an icebox. True or not, this remark fits with his stiff, distant bearing in secondary school, where he was reported to have begun to stand apart. Why a child's sense of uniqueness, which it shares with all other growing children, should have matured into a style of life is a puzzle that we must now try to elucidate.

Maybe part of the answer can be found in de Gaulle's relation to his family. We see a tension between his respect for it, his acceptance of its beliefs, and his intense desire to make his own mark, to be his own master—*to be himself,* and not merely one more relatively undistinguished member of an old, respectable, but uncelebrated family. Independence became his claim, not just a family value. The very lessons he learned from his father and from his Catholic teachers must have created dissonance. They taught him the honor and pride of loyalty to unpopular values.[7] They, as well as the books he devoured, celebrated service, submission to causes, discipline. But these same books also revealed that history is a tale full of sound and fury, in which whole bodies of doctrines have been blown away, in which, as he was to write later, "evangelical perfection does not lead to empire." [8] Moreover, the world around him taught him that pure loyalty to traditional dogmas and the perfect practice of Christian values were no way of saving them. His books and teachers, however, provided him with an answer to the dilemma. The young reader of Corneille and history knew that mastery of self and others brings its own rewards; [9] his whole education, at home and in school, was pervaded by the Greek ideal (so powerful in France's classical age and culture, as indeed throughout continental Europe): that of the self-sufficient, self-controlled, and sovereign personality who controls events, so to speak, from within, through force of character. Thus the resolution of this tension was sought in a way that was to become typical of his style: by *transcending* the legacy.[10]

He must have experienced, at home, both opulence and deprivation —the opulence of affection, example, and high ideals, but also a double deprivation. On one hand, this obviously remarkable boy seems to have been treated, out of fairness to his brothers and sister, with no special privileges; on the other hand, as one perceptive commentator has put it, it was a "frustrated family," [11] frustrated socially and politically by France's domestic and external political conditions. There was only one way to end those frustrations *and* to emancipate oneself from them; to serve the values of the family *and* to save them from obsolescence; to remain loyal to that culture and history so dear to his parents *and* to remove culture and history from the realm of morose meditations, genealogical explorations, and imaginary recreations; to be a son and brother *and* to make a name for oneself; to remain a respectful son *and* to confront one's aggressiveness. The solution was to become a man who could save the respected past by shaping a future worthy of it, to put himself at the service of a great cause that would give him the opportunity to be great by doing great things. The cause could have been that of the Church, but the boy seems to have been too fond of battle, too much in love with temporal glory and domination. It thus became that of France, to which he transferred his religious devotion. He would serve France in such a striking way that the past would be *renewed* rather than just enshrined, and the nation might live according to the family's ideals. This meant accepting—as a precondition for success—the political framework that his parents found so distasteful: to be a nostalgic monarchist and Catholic was not going to help.

It meant, above all, rising above the family's horizons. De Gaulle says he was tempted by "the play" of French politics, whose permanent confrontation of great characters must have appealed to his imagination and love of drama.[12] But this would have hurt his family's feelings, and the play affronted its and his own values. He could, however, resolve his dilemma harmoniously. In a military career, Charles could try to do what his father had been prevented from doing by fate. He would be at the service of France, rather than of the Republic, and repudiate all divisive ideologies as so many traps.

That desire to be France's protector without intermediaries, so characteristic of his career and so clearly marked in the very first page of the *Mémoires* (where he talks first of her, and then only of his "milieu"—his word), had been, after all, authorized, indeed encouraged, by his family and education. Thus, military service was both a family tradition and a personal solution. By serving the cause of *la revanche,* he would begin to solve for all Frenchmen the problems that could otherwise not be solved for his family alone, and he would find glory in it.

He may have found the family horizons restrictive, but there was no revolt. Rather, there was a kind of externalization: a desire to fight and remove the forces that made those horizons, whether the political class of the parliamentary Republic or the great powers that had dwarfed France. De Gaulle's acts of defiance were never mere rebelliousness, nor would he ever be a revolutionary. Throughout his life, he fought all established hierarchies—but always in order to establish what he deemed a better one, with the servants of the state and himself on top in France, and with a number of great powers including France on top in the world. Thus, serving France only, and directly, was to assert his independence from all factions, as if he had originated from her alone: de Gaulle would appear both as self-made and as the product of two thousand years of history.

There is nothing unique in the case of a young man to whom history, and making its mark on it, seem the only worthy goals in life. But what was unique was the continuity of concern and purpose. The love affair with France and history, the love of battle and *"rêve de gloire au pied d'un étendard,"* [13] the determination to be at current history's rendezvous so as to be in future history's texts—these knew no interruption. What was unique was the total identification of personal with national destiny and the strength of will to fulfill the purpose beyond childhood, through a long period of trial and waiting.

In order to understand better how he managed to act out his dreams without losing touch with reality, one has to examine more carefully what seems to have happened in his early adolescence, between the ages of fourteen and sixteen. As in every important period of his life, external events coincided with internal developments. The events are well known: France's crisis between Church and state (not only a national crisis but one that affected Henri de Gaulle's career and the atmosphere at home) and the Tangiers crisis with Germany. Simultaneously, a *sense of being* different, separate, chosen was strengthened,[14] and the *will to be* unique and self-contained arose in him. These were the years when he grew to be taller than his brothers, to tower over his schoolmates, when he must have felt (and been made to feel) awkward; when he must also have felt the need to distinguish himself from that omnipresent father, who watched so closely over all the children. This was the time when his father, worried by the proliferation of Charles's gifts, by a tendency to dispersion, a lack of discipline in him, challenged him to study harder in order to be able to enter Saint-Cyr, France's West Point. Charles's reaction announces his future style: he used the challenge as an opportunity and made of the peculiarity not only an asset, but a mark. Tallness became the physical symbol of a moral ambition—to be above the others, to be straight and erect. His imagination fed his will, and his will disciplined his imagination. *Grandeur* became his motto, for himself, others, and France: he would join the army because it was then *"une des plus grandes choses du monde."* [15] Aware of how his height and his concerns distinguished him from his schoolmates, he became even more aware of his uniqueness and enchanted with it. But if there was narcissism in him, as in every adolescent (and every leader), he transcended narcissism, for his response to the threat of identity diffusion was not totalism but mobilization—or, to use two of his favorite words, *rassemblement* of all his faculties toward the goals of success and service, which would *élever* him above himself and others.

In this transition from childhood to adolescence, nothing is more interesting than a playlet de Gaulle wrote at the age of fourteen and got published the following year: *Une Mauvaise Rencontre* is his last display of youthful exuberance, and the first use of his pen toward an adult goal. It is a frothy skit about an "amiable thief" whose method of robbing is as smooth and painless as Madison Avenue's persuasions, except that there are shiny pistols which underline the persuasion.[16] This theme of coercive persuasion, and even the episodes and refrain, are taken from an inconsequential *poème à jouer* by Gustave Nadaud —a popular chansonnier-poet.[17] But Charles transformed its style into sweepy alexandrines (with a good lacing of Rostand), situated the action in Spain (the country of Don Quixote and of Hugo's Ruy Blas), and, somewhat inconsequentially, changed Nadaud's nameless "amiable thief" into César-Charles Rollet, who declares he was born brigand as others are born kings, officers, or masons (i.e., born to their own uniqueness, which they have only to fulfill), a brigand of promise who by great dramatic misfortune lost his superb garb. Unloved and hunted, Rollet "needs" to be comforted by his victim (a ruse, indeed, but one Charles supplied and elaborated). Here are some excerpts from Charles's additions to the original (emphasis added):

> César-Charles Rollet, qu'on connaît en tout lieu,
> Voleur de *grands* chemins par la *grâce* de Dieu. . . .
> Certains naquirent rois. . . Moi je naquis brigand.
> On peut le voir d'ailleurs très bien à mon costume.
> Sur ma tête, autrefois, s'agitait une plume. . . . (*avec mélancolie*)
> . . . Pourquoi me rappeler ce *superbe panache*
> Dont *un coup de bâton cruel trancha* les jours? . . .
> *O jour fatal et sombre!* Eh! Oui, Monsieur, tout passe!

These last lines, so different from Nadaud's original, make one wonder what, if anything, happened "one fatal and sinister day" to young Charles to transform him from the carefree prankster into the stiffly cordial schoolboy. And the last sigh—"everything must pass"— suggests the style of the grown man, and his fatalism half a century later.[18]

> Oh, ce fut un *combat* terrible, *horrible, laid,*
> *Grand, géant,* furieux, effroyable. C'était
> Le *chaos* monstrueux, *sans grâce,* horrible et morne
> D'un brigand *révolté* contre un homme à bicorne.
> Ma *plume* tomba près d'un gendarme à cheval,
> Auquel j'avais ouvert le ventre!
> . . . . "C'est très mal!"
> Me direz-vous. Ma foi! Je n'en sais rien moi-même.
> Personne ne nous voit, personne ne nous aime.

He describes how his featherless hat became sad—and *"selon la nature"* gradually lost its original beautiful colors.

Il restait sur mon chef droit—les *grandes* douleurs
Sont muettes—fier, *grand, défiant* la fortune.
Il rêvait, dans le jour serein, dans la nuit brune—
Partout, c'était un corps *inerte,* laid, rêveur,
Et pensant à sa *plume.*

and later:

La vie humaine n'est qu'un tissu de misères. . . .

The play reveals universal adolescent daydreams and conflicts. It also foreshadows the mature de Gaulle's mastery. The adolescent boy who wrote this play for fun added characteristic themes of his own to Nadaud's ditty: *grandeur,* struggle, chaos, and loss; loneliness, impotence, glory, and fatalism. The idea *great* is repeated again and again. Loss is symbolized by the superb feather leaving him (that is, his hat) "un corps *inerte,* laid, rêveur"; [19] also, in elaborate jest and as a ruse to arouse pity, he refers elsewhere to his loss of three sisters and three brothers. This may be a fanciful bit of analysis, but since these are de Gaulle's own additions to and changes in the original, and since they also check with the observations reported by his biographers as well as with many later Gaullist themes, they warrant being taken seriously as reflecting the principal preoccupations of young Charles.

Both versions of this boring tale cynically relied on the ultimate persuasive power of force. But Nadaud lacked Charles's subtle blend of flattery and ruse, his lusty and ironic manipulation of gullible pity (de Gaulle's *mépris* for a certain kind of man appeared early) making overt violence unnecessary. Two other changes are significant. César-Charles, before he takes his victim's new coat, gives him his own torn and tattered one (which, he says, he had received from his father) as a way of showing gratitude for articles of clothing previously extorted from the poor traveler; turning in the old for the new was to be a mark of de Gaulle's statecraft. Also, the thief "obtains" the traveler's purse by telling him that this is the only way in which the traveler can save his (*the thief's*) soul from the urge to kill; whereas Nadaud's thief forces his victim to express his thanks for the fact that he (the thief) saved the *traveler's* life: a most arresting psychological difference; César-Charles did not care whether his victim was grateful or not, but he was eager to use his own soul for blackmail. Finally, Charles added the glorification of his hero's pride and egoism; he celebrated his force and his cunning. Compare this with what the mature de Gaulle wrote some twenty years later in his prophetic "credo": "every man of action has a strong dose of egotism, pride, hardness, and cunning." [20] But the world forgives him because he dares great deeds: "he seduces those who serve under him and even if he falls by the way he retains in their eyes *the prestige of the heights* to which he wanted to lead them." Or: "Every orator waves (*agite*) grand ideas around the poorest argument." [21] Is it stretching the reader's imagination excessively to ask him to compare these lines with the feather which *"autrefois, s'agitait"* on his hero's head?

In de Gaulle's play, the thief's seduction of the traveler is so successful that the victim exclaims spontaneously (not under duress, as in Nadaud) *"Enchanté!"* at the end. Later, in his reality play with reluctant opponents (such as General Giraud, or General Raoul Salan, or foreign leaders), the victim would often, however, dream of or try for revenge after having been had.

It would seem, then, that at least at the age of fourteen de Gaulle's fate was sealed. Obviously, the young man's concern was already for the exercise of power. The play expresses a drive for mastery in a world marked by mediocrity and violence; what is missing was, so to speak, already *given*—values and a cause, on behalf of which de Gaulle would use the brigand's cynical experience and bouncy dash.

Charles's character now changed and tightened. His sister described him as "poet and soldier." [22] From now on, his pen served, first, to form reflections upon action, so as to put action in the lofty perspective that makes it meaningful, and secondly, as a substitute for action, whenever the times were not yet or no longer ripe for it. The sense of fun, so strong in his games and in his little play, did not disappear, and never would—he went on acting in plays at Saint-Cyr—but a new austerity emerged. Fun was externalized and transcended, like rebellion, used as a weapon against others and sought in the craft and pleasure of mastery. The sense of drama, so strong in the rambunctious boy, became a desire to act in a national drama for which he must prepare himself: [23] as he would say later, his gifts must be shaped by skills.[24] De Gaulle's fascination with history continued, but history was no longer a playground for childish re-enactments; it became a judge, a springboard, a reality principle. The need to protect, once turned to the defense of smaller schoolboys mistreated by bullies,[25] was oriented toward France. Later, his sense of history and his histrionic sense endowed his protectiveness with the institutional form of a plebiscitarian republic, instead of the nostalgic monarchy regretted by his more sedate parents. But already the will-to-do or will-to-be something fed on *and* magnified that something's existence; sensing his difference, he cultivated it. The desire to play a great role leads to double domination—of oneself, as a way of dominating others; [26] the strain increases the distance from others. Steeped in history, taught to find a recourse in it against the present, de Gaulle manifested his ambition by disdaining (once more, *dominer*—i.e., both stand above and mas-

ter) the petty concerns of his contemporaries and all those human entanglements that divert or slow one down. Haughtiness, separateness,
were the condition and the cost of his success.

It was as if, in those years, Charles de Gaulle experienced a loss that
stimulated his creativity (and that was reflected or anticipated in his
play): national loss, which made him fear for *his* France, and a more
intimate loss—his growing awareness of the end of childhood, the end
of family protection and mere playacting in a harsh and troubled
world, the call of responsibility.

Combativeness remained, indeed grew, but a certain note of bitterness appeared—perhaps as a reaction to those events, perhaps as a by-
product of the price he felt he had to pay, in his human relations, for
his ambition and uniqueness. The years of preparation for action suggest the double feeling which his whole career inspired: on one hand,
a sense of an extraordinarily effective use of all his resources; on the
other, a sense of a certain repression, or compression, of ordinary humanity, as if his family and education had given him enough human
warmth to avoid any real mutilation, yet had somehow made him distrust his own spontaneity and incapable of dealing with men—except
on behalf of great abstractions. For such a man, a military career—in
which his size and stiffness would be exemplary, where his awkwardness in human relations would be concealed by the hierarchy of ranks,
and where his need to serve and to command would be fulfilled—was
an excellent choice. And the selection of infantry is equally significant,
for it meant the certainty of being in the thick of battles and in contact not with men recruited from the elites and middle classes who
had been his companions in school, but with average Frenchmen—
mainly peasants—who must have appeared to him as less corrupted,
easier to lead, and easier to keep at a distance.

In the years that preceded World War I, while de Gaulle was at
Saint-Cyr, a "nationalist revival" brought back prestige to some of the
values that de Gaulle's parents and teachers had cultivated. A militant
and passionate concern for the nation's honor and rank spread from
the Right to the Republican establishment.[27] Thus de Gaulle learned
that if one sticks to beliefs one deems true and great, whatever the
costs of temporary unpopularity, one will be proven right when circumstances at last consecrate their permanent relevance and specific
aptness.

Two personal tragedies, on the other hand, aggravated his sense of
loss, his intense need for self-respect, and his isolation. (Both also
strengthened the sense that realities, however sinister, have to be accepted, that they should not crush one's will but be faced in order to
be overcome.) First, there were two years in German captivity—a
crushing blow to the young officer's dreams of glory and also, proba-

bly, to his self-respect. It frustrated him of his share in the final victory, it separated him from his comrades, and it pushed him even more into himself. Since his repeated attempts to escape were defeated by his extreme height and visibility, there was only one thing he could do: use this forced separation in order to reflect on the meaning of the great events to which he could not contribute. Out of those reflections, readings, and lectures came his first book,[28] a study of civil-military relations in Germany in World War I. It was, first, a plea for moderation, for "the limits traced by human experience, common sense, and the law"; [29] second, a study of the crucial role of morale: collective will, confidence, and unity, and of its collapse in Germany, largely because of party divisions and because of the civilian leaders' lack of stamina when faced with the rabid demands of military leaders.

The de Gaulle who came out of a German prisoners' camp immediately went to fight in Poland, against the Russian Revolution; he reflected on the strength of the Polish sense of identity across class barriers—seeing what there was and what he wanted to see. He returned to France to marry Yvonne Vendroux, the twenty-year-old daughter of a biscuit manufacturer from northern France, and to teach military history at Saint-Cyr. As a student at the École de Guerre in 1922–24, he left the same kind of impression on his superiors that he had made on his classmates as an adolescent, only stronger: that of a bright but haughty young man. He was contemptuous of the strategic "lessons" which enshrined what the French Army had learned from the war (which he who had missed half of it, obviously felt to be foolish, too mechanical, too rigid, too petty); he was extremely sure of himself and disdainful of criticism.[30]

The second tragedy was more intimate. His third and last child, born in 1928, was a retarded daughter. De Gaulle and his wife decided to keep her with them, and for twenty years the General was, it seems, the only person capable of making the little girl laugh. His powers of affection were thus lavished on a poor creature with whom no real intimacy was possible.

It is interesting to see who among the countless writers the young man was reading during these formative years, and who among the several superiors he had, impressed and influenced him most. He picked up what he needed—i.e., what resembled him and encouraged him most to be himself. As a young man, he copied a phrase of Hugo's: "concision in style, precision in thought, decisiveness in life" (qualities far more true of him than of Hugo).[31] He read Nietzsche. The vigor with which he resisted him in his own first book shows the appeal which the call for supermen had on him (it is displayed dramatically in Le Fil de l'épée), for one is always marked by what one fights so hard. Yet it also shows differences: de Gaulle denounces in supermen not only "the taste for excessive undertakings" but also the selfishness of an elite that while "pursuing its own glory believes it pursues the general interest." [32] In de Gaulle's own life, personal glory loomed large but only as servant of the general interest (as seen, of course, by de Gaulle).

He also read Péguy. The incandescent mixture he found there—of nationalism, love for the soil and people of France, and distaste for parliamentarianism (as opposed to the mystique of the Republic), celebration of France as the soldier of Christ, repudiation of the formalistic and systematic "systems of thought" derived from Kant, and the raising of Hope, active Hope, to a cardinal virtue—corresponded to his own feelings and left a mark even on his style.[33] He read Barrès, but interestingly enough saw him only as the man who "gave back to the elite a consciousness of national eternity," [34] not as a rather xenophobic, intensely conservative and frightened bourgeois writer, turned far more to the past than to a future that spelled possible decadence. He may have appreciated Maurras's (and undoubtedly Bainville's) views on foreign affairs, but there is no sign that he accepted his rigid, doctrinaire, and antiquated "system" of integral nationalism, with its "continuous song of hate." [35] Through Barrès and Péguy, on the contrary, de Gaulle shaped a nationalism akin to Michelet's, with the same epic vision of France as a person, as a chosen nation, and the same faith in the reasonableness and goodness of France's "depths," whatever the turmoil on the surface.

Above all, he read Bergson, whose philosophy of intuition (as against analytic intelligence), *élan vital* (as against established doctrines), emphasis on time as "the vehicle of spontaneous creation," and stress on how personality transcends all "stable, ready-made categories," [36] obviously attracted him. And he could recognize, not yet his own destiny, but his own aspirations, in Bergson's question:

"By what sign do we ordinarily recognize the man of action, who leaves his mark on the events into which fate throws him? Isn't it because he embraces a more or less long succession in an instantaneous vision? The greater the share of the past that he includes in his present, the heavier the mass he pushes into the future so as to put pressure on the events in preparation: his action, like an arrow, moves forward with a strength proportional to that with which its representation was bent backward".[37]

There was another influence that was even more profound because it was more direct, exerting itself in de Gaulle's own chosen career: Pétain. As a cadet, de Gaulle served in Colonel Pétain's regiment; he fought under his orders when World War I began; he became his aide and protégé in the 1920s. There were obvious differences between the cautious peasant's son and the ardent young officer, but de Gaulle recognized in his superior what he wanted to develop in himself: "the gift and the art of leadership." [38] He must have recognized himself in that man who "dominates his task through his mind, and, through his character, leaves his mark on his task"; in that "master who . . . has disdained the fate of servants—thus showing the greatness of independence, which receives orders, seizes advice but closes itself to influences—the prestige of secrecy, preserved by deliberate coldness, vigilant irony, and even by the pride in which his loneliness is wrapped." [39] "Too proud for intrigue, too strong for mediocrity, too ambitious for careerism, [Pétain] nourished in his solitude the passion to dominate, hardened by his awareness of his own merit, by the obstacles he had met, and the contempt he had for others." [40] He must also have recognized himself in Pétain's impervious disregard for official doctrine, even at a cost to his own career: for Pétain, on the eve of the war, was holding out against the established dogma of impetuous offensive—and de Gaulle was able to observe how costly that dogma proved to be, to conclude (again) that dogmas misled instead of guiding, and to learn that Pétain's concern for firepower (artillery and machine guns) was more justified than the official emphasis on manpower in a country with a relatively small population.

This was, then, the capital of influences, experiences, and resources that de Gaulle accumulated by the mid 1920s. Sure of and eager for the great destiny he had announced since he was seventeen,[41] he now turned to his first great task: the intellectual elaboration, clarification, and anticipation of his future mission.

II. Vocation

Whoever examines General de Gaulle's career as a leader cannot fail to be struck by three aspects. First, the theme of transcendence is essential: de Gaulle was a man who stretched himself all his life, so as to meet the needs created by the circumstances, and thus to fulfill himself. This required a capacity to put himself in a state of readiness and active waiting until the events occurred—he was forty-nine when France fell in 1940, and he spent twelve and a half years out of power between 1945 and 1958. It also required a capacity to grow, so as to meet new challenges not with old formulas but with appropriate inner strength.[42]

Secondly, de Gaulle was always more concerned with being right than with achieving immediate results. He showed the French intellectual's passion for intransigence and the aristocrat's concern for prowess. Throughout his career, he preferred all-or-nothing on every issue he considered important. His uncompromising presentation of the armée de métier, his tactics as leader of the RPF, his foreign policy—

all indicate a determination to be right even at the cost of immediate effectiveness or popularity, and to let events or his own acts prove that any other course than his own was wrong or bad. Pragmatic about means, which were suggested by "circumstances," because tactical inflexibility would mean inglorious failure, he was inflexible on essentials because they were the very substance of leadership. To compromise them would be to abdicate, and failure to reach worthy goals is far more glorious than resignation.

Lastly, one cannot fail to be struck by the ideological emptiness of Gaullism. Gaullism is a stance, not a doctrine; an attitude, not a coherent set of dogmas; a style without much substance—beyond the service of France and French *grandeur,* itself never defined in content, only by context.[43]

All these features reflect de Gaulle's personality and conception of leadership. What he started with—after studying what leadership should not be in his first book—was not a doctrine but a portrait. The mission was absent—because it was *generally* taken for granted, and because it *specifically* depended on events. What he presented in this new book, *Le Fil de l'épée,* was a self-portrait in anticipation: a portrait of the leader, a "Plutarchian hero created in the imagination by the values that will create in History the destiny of this hero, and thereby resembles him." [44] The values that created him were those de Gaulle had picked up from his family, from his classical and romantic readings (especially Corneille, with his emphasis on self-mastery, and Chateaubriand and Vigny, with their glorification of the lonely hero), and from the current of ideas that marked the pre-1914 nationalist revival. (The famous inquiry of 1913 made by two young intellectuals who used the pen name Agathon [45] ascribed these last to French youth: a reaction against the Republican dogmas of positivism, optimism, scientism, continuous progress, and prevalence of great forces over individual men; here, the emphasis is on struggle, competition, and above all on the great men who tame events.) Thus de Gaulle, "the man of the day before yesterday and the day after tomorrow," indeed went back to earlier notions than those of the Kantian and Comtean republic, so as to shape the future with them.

In de Gaulle's case, the values that created the great man in his imagination were primarily psychological. Like a true Corneille hero, and exactly as in Erik Erikson's concept of identity, he blended what he knew he was and what he would like to be, so as better to become what he was. The way to tame history and to leave a mark (for this was the name of the game) was to be and to have *un caractère*—the *caractère* of the leader. Without this character, no set of ideas would help—indeed, they would harm, interposing a screen between reality and the leader (shades of Sorel, and also of his reflections on World

War I)—but the right *caractère* would by definition have the craft and strength to dominate events. The leader is the man who owes his power to no one but himself,[46] who imposes himself, who is propelled by what is in him, not by other people's doctrines. He is literally self-generated and perpetually renewed by challenges, possessor of and possessed by an unexplainable gift that is somehow compelling, because men are political animals who need order and turn to leaders in periods of trouble. When de Gaulle tried to describe the craft that must shape the gift, again it was not to techniques of action or to ideas that he turned, but to psychological traits: secrecy, mystery, distance, silence, and protectiveness—all summarized as "the contrast between inner strength and self-mastery," [47] all enhanced by *la culture générale* [48]—his father's preserve.

No conception of leadership could be more alien both to the prevalent style of French political leadership of his time and to the style of incremental decision-making of modern bureaucratic systems (including armies). Yet none could be more fitting to a young man impatient for action and creation, but reduced—in his mid-thirties—to expectation and anticipation, and endowed primarily with nothing more than his own *caractère*. He accepted neither the attrition of bureaucracy,[49] nor the prevalent ideas and styles of the regime, nor the counterideologies which offended his realism and his desire for purposeful national unity. *Le caractère,* as de Gaulle defined it, would necessarily be the man who stretched his resources to meet the challenges by "forcing his own nature," the man whose "contempt for contingencies" and concern for "elevation" would dictate an unbending, all-or-nothing attitude; the man whose very condition of success was to combine energy, responsibility, and domination with doctrinal indifference and flexibility; the man remembered "less for the usefulness of what [he] had achieved than for the sweep of [his] endeavors." [50] "His character would be his destiny." [51]

Indeed, the three principal features of de Gaulle's leadership were all entailed by his conception: leadership, that mysterious gift, is an essence, revealed in acts, in attitudes, and in its very aptitude to outgrow, repudiate, and free itself from specific policies and past courses —an essence that is preserved by constant, conscious effort and renewed by practice. [52] Yet *Le Fil de l'épée* does not provide the whole picture: it does not give the full sweep of de Gaulle's conception of leadership, nor does it constitute a single key to his subsequent career.

In *Le Fil de l'épée*, de Gaulle does not describe his cyclical notion of time, in which there are shades of Nietzsche's "eternal return" and Péguy's "epochs and periods." It is expressed clearly in the last page of the *Mémoires*,[53] where he argues that history is made of peaks and depressions; nations, as well as great men, and like nature, must ride out the storms and come back up again. At any given moment, the world provides a stage, and the great man is the actor, in both the theatrical and the political sense. The metaphor of the play, of the stage, of the drama, is present in all de Gaulle's works; the actor's duty is not to follow a script, but to write his own and to play it as well as circumstances allow. The good actor must be able to play on all the registers of history. He must wait for circumstances to be ripe and, when they are, seize them decisively, for "events, in great moments, tolerate in positions of leadership only men who know how to chart their own course." [54] He must also know "how to put himself on the side of time," [55] how to discern and work for the long range. The good actor is out not only for himself. "The leaders of men—politicians, prophets, soldiers who obtained most from others—identified themselves with high ideas." So the notion of *cause* is crucial to de Gaulle's conception of leadership. The great leader fulfills himself by becoming a militant missionary on behalf of a function, at the service of which he puts all the resources of the word and of action. Charles de Gaulle identifies with France, makes himself a personage—called General de Gaulle in the *Mémoires*—whose vocation is to be the voice of the nation. History calls him in emergencies, and he calls the French on behalf of France. He has to serve the present needs of France, to protect her legacy, and to guarantee her future. He must maintain her personality, so that she can keep playing on the world stage. He must, in his own moves, follow only what he deems the national interest, apart from all categories, ideologies, and special interests. He is a unifier, by being above and lifting others above their daily selves.

Thus he fulfills a function that "goes far beyond his person." He serves "as destiny's instrument." [56] His role is to provide "that inspiration from the summits, that hope of success, that ambition of France which sustain the nation's soul . . . something essential, permanent," [57] whatever specific or institutional role he may be performing at any moment. Malraux speaks of a *dédoublement* of de Gaulle—the man and the personage. But it is really a *détriplement:* there is *Charles,* the private man, there is the public-political *de Gaulle,* the temporal leader, who happens to be the head of the Free French, or provisional Premier, or opposition leader, or President, and there is the public-historic person, the embodiment of France's cause, *General de Gaulle,* who dominates the other two, transcending the first and controlling the second. Mediating between all three, there was the political artist. Gradually emerging from Charles, he, in turn, welded the temporal-political de Gaulle and the spiritual mission of "General de Gaulle" with carefully chosen tools, fusing inner needs and outer necessities, imagination and reality, and—in his own words —"building in the secret of his innermost self the edifice of his feelings, ideas and will" in order to fulfill what was best in himself and France.

France was the entity that provided de Gaulle with the transcendence he needed and also the limits he craved. To be "France's champion" meant depending on no one yet being oneself completed; but the need to preserve France's personality and the subordination of self to her service imposed prudence, harmony, and moderation, and protected the nation and the missionary from the excesses of men (like Napoleon or Hitler) who used their nation as instruments for personal glory or to work out their ideological or psychological obsessions. The vocation was both a license and a limit. As a license, it must become the leader's *"raison d'être,"* [58] and the missionary and guide who took his cue only from history and the national interest could, as leader and trustee of the cause, take initiatives denied to lesser people. (He could rebel against the disgrace of the armistice, but others could not rebel against him, for example.) The vocation legitimized de Gaulle's ambition and gave his remarkable ego an epic hunting license. But it also restrained him, insofar as it directed, dominated, and transcended him and imposed on him the constant need not to do anything that would, by sullying his public personage, spoil the chances and soil the honor of the nation. Thus, it guaranteed France against possible excesses of his own dream—temptations of omnipotence or vindictiveness at home, of overcommitment abroad. The great leader imposes his will and denies fatalism,[59] but he must also know how to balance ends and means, how to distinguish what is irresistible from what is reversible, so as not to be destroyed by *hubris*.[60] The key is provided by the elusive but essential notion of *grandeur*.

De Gaulle's relation to his mission was the relation of a high priest to his God, executing only His will (as he sees it), and leading his people with a hand that points to the summits and hides the petty obstacles before them. Hence the mystical quality, noted by many observers,[61] and the lofty assurance of his language. Just as the religious leader must at times protect his flock from sin, at times redeem it from sin, de Gaulle's function was to redeem his nation from the secular equivalent of sin, which he himself called the fall.[62]

It was also the relation of a monarch to his kingship. One can only admire how he combined his parents' nostalgia, his own acceptance of the Republic, and his determination to give it a completely different type of leader, recalled from the monarchic past, detached from heredity, and reshaped for the dramas of the future.

Last but not least, it was the relation of an artist to his work of art. De Gaulle himself was very conscious of this. He pointed to the aesthetic dimension of military leadership [63] and statecraft,[64] to the analogy between *"le chef et l'artiste."* [65] In his books and speeches, which described or expressed the public figure, he tried to give ordinary or chaotic experience aesthetic shape, using a style that was both deliberate, given to highly structured and patterned sentences, and oratorical, as if it were written to be read aloud, from a stage. The calm that suffused his daily work routine was that of the artist who needs deep quiet to transcend the conflicts in himself and the data provided by his experience. The central themes of his published works were unaltered from his adolescence; they were constantly restated, each new statement being superimposed on the last one; each book, each major address had *all* of himself (as leader) in it, as well as something about his mission. Like any artistic act, each of his major political moves, however tortuous the means or details, formed a whole; each gesture was indivisible (could brook no compromise or partial amendment) and bore his unmistakable mark, like a painter's signature. De Gaulle had a quality that rose far above force and ruse, beyond the skillful use of all available tactics. He shaped himself and his acts (as a sculptor his stone) with art, not artifice. But if the relation of the *leader* to his mission was that of an artist to his art, so also, first of all, was *Charles*'s relation to his public self.

How did de Gaulle apply his notion of leadership to himself, make a work of art of himself and thus "create in History" his own destiny? The answer can be described chronologically and psychologically.

It may well be that de Gaulle's captivity in 1916–18, which deprived him of the opportunity to meet his first major challenge in a way that would satisfy him, heightened his fervent desire for a future chance, and saved him from rigidity, from mechanically re-enacting later in life the ways in which one successfully meets one's first test. This accident of fate left him *disponible*—for painting in his mind and works the image of the leader, and also for moving the scene of his mission from military prowess to statecraft. For his choice of a military career was not a full or satisfying answer to his need to serve by saving. The self-portrait he paints in his two books of 1932 and 1934 goes far beyond military leadership and reaches toward statecraft.[66] Only as a national leader could he solve for all Frenchmen the foreign and domestic problems that had plagued his family and his youth. If he groped toward supreme power, he did not expect it; his first moves in London, in June 1940, showed that he was still willing to serve under more prestigious French leaders, if they would reject Vichy's armistice. But he had made himself ready for supreme power, and he stepped into the void decisively.[67] Eighteen years later, he stepped into the void again, with supreme ease and tactical skill, because he had, once more, kept himself ready for the unexpected.

One can therefore say that 1940 and 1958 were two important thresholds in his career. Before June 1940, he was a military man, whose concerns far exceeded those of his superiors and colleagues yet remained essentially within the realm of strategy. From June 1940 to the early 1950s, he became—first as leader of the Resistance, then as head of Liberated France, finally as head of the Opposition—the political trustee of his beloved France, who judged all events by the yardstick of French substance and survival. His fear of loss for her was so great that on the world stage he acted primarily as a restorer and preserver of her traditional legacy, conceiving her interests in classical terms, as if the future had indeed to be the prolongation (and rectification) of the past. Finally, with the *Mémoires* and his return to power, another de Gaulle appeared, still concerned above all with France, yet more relaxed, more willing to let go, more universal (in the sense of being more able to take other people's aspirations into account, more eager to adapt and renew than to maintain and restore), and more detached—both from *Charles* and from *de Gaulle*, his temporal political self, to whom he referred in the third person from the lofty vantage point of the *General*, the historic figure.

In each case, the crossing of a threshold was prepared for by a failure of action in the previous framework, which made him again *disponible* for action when the framework collapsed. He failed in his lobbying for a motorized army in the 1930s, and he had to live through the fiasco of the RPF in the early 1950s. And it was also prepared for by the kind of catharsis which his indirect form of action—writing—performed for him. While the man of action, even when he takes as long a view or as high a vantage point as de Gaulle does, must account for the necessities of the moment, the writer can judge them in the perspective of future history. The man of action stands in the present and aims at the future, but the writer can put himself in the future and assess the present from that vantage point. Before 1940 and before 1958, writing widened de Gaulle's horizons and sharpened his lucidity—about himself (as shown by his call for a "master" in *Vers l'armée de métier* [68] and by his analysis of "General de Gaulle" in his *Mémoires*) and about the world around him. There, he also rejudges, and usually absolves, the men he had fought or condemned during the war. He wrote, quoting Faust, that in the beginning was action, not the word.[69] In his case, the word was always *about* action, it always preceded and defined action.

Chronology thus sends us back to psychology—to de Gaulle's double determination not to let failure discourage him from his mission, and to prepare himself through the disciplined reflection of writing for the role that events might allow him to play. It is as if the artist put all his efforts into shaping *General de Gaulle*, the work of art. This meant a deliberate attempt to depersonalize himself, to remove Charles from the public eye, as Malraux put it. Yet Charles the private man existed. And the public figure, the work of art, was intensely, uniquely personal.

De Gaulle's private self was not absorbed by his public role. He married a woman whose milieu was very close to that of his mother, he had three children, led a normal family life, and was a discreet but devout Catholic. There is no doubt—as he wrote himself—that "family harmony" was precious to him.[70] Private affects and public objects lived side by side. Those who were able to get through to the man found him courteous, devoid of arrogance and awkwardness. (Indeed, the descriptions remind one of those we have of his father.[71])

Still, there is a great deal of evidence about the subordination of *Charles* to *de Gaulle: Charles* seems to have been a rather reserved and traditional figure—a country gentleman—fashioned so as to leave all the energies to de Gaulle. His private life is quiet and low key —marked "neither by quarrel nor by laughter." [72] As Malraux pointed out,[73] other great men have had colorful private personalities. (He mentions Napoleon, but one could add Pétain, who, in addition to episodic liaisons, spent much of life courting a young woman to whom he wrote very intimate letters and whom he finally married.[74]) The private de Gaulle, Malraux said, was merely the one who did not talk of public affairs. His courtesy did not abolish the distance between himself and others; it protected it—indeed, it was merely, adds Malraux, a feature of his "priesthood." As far as one can surmise, there was no real intimacy between him and others. His wife was a devoted but reserved figure; his son, like himself, has chosen to devote his life to the service of France in a dutiful career as a navy officer of high rank; de Gaulle had admirers and close acquaintances, but no very close friends. Several of his colleagues agree with Malraux that de Gaulle "accepted from himself neither impulsiveness nor abandonment." [75] The private self was always on guard against indiscreet questioners who wanted to get behind the public figure, and against those who tried to take advantage of his restricted privacy to influence the public figure.[76] There is no such thing as happiness, he once "barked out," [77] under this kind of questioning. To such a man, everything that was not public life, service, the personage, and the cause—far from being a haven, a respite, a shelter—meant exile or solitude.[78] This did not mean that his family life did not provide a haven and a shelter; it obviously did, but in this refuge he always worked on his mission. Nor did it mean that he was never tempted by solitude; but when he yielded to or chose that temptation, it was in order to pursue his interior monologue or to broach the subjects closest to his heart—France and history. The monologue fed the public figure and prepared him for the next phase of his role; human warmth and entanglements might distract him from his task.

This task—the exercise of power—was also solitary, when one chose
to perform at such an altitude. Yet in *that* kind of performance lay
"the interest of life." The dominant relation between the two selves,
between *Charles* and *General de Gaulle,* could be characterized by
that Lasswellian phrase, displacement of private affects on public objects. But the displacement, here, was deliberate and elaborate—like
artistic creation. The first of public objects was none other than himself, or rather "de Gaulle," the epic figure that had to be created to fill
the part which history and Charles had prepared for it. Private feelings had to be transmuted into public service; the requirements of the
mission ruled out the personage's being influenced either by the
whims and demands of the private person or by the pressures and insults of others.[79] Malraux and Gide noted the "internal distance" this
created,[80] the refusal to let the internal monologue appear in the
open. And this accounts, too, for that gloomy, bitter, and closed look,
in eyes which "reflected nothing from the world outside," [81] during the
months after June 1940, when de Gaulle had to act out the public
figure he had created in his mind, had to meet, fit, and make its mission. The sense one gets is of a deeply passionate and sensitive man—
indeed, during the war, he seemed so scorched and raw that he could
not always control his feelings and public face [82]—but one whose
deepest passions are public, whose moods are determined by the state
of public affairs, whose serenity is the product of effort, of conquest,
and whose real dialogue is not with specific human beings but with
abstractions that *to him* are human. Gide's Thésée said: *"Je n'aime
pas l'homme, j'aime ce qui le dévore."* De Gaulle could have said: I
don't like men, I like what elevates them.[83]

As we have said, it was as if there were three de Gaulles. There was
a private person ("Charles") with a father and mother of flesh and
blood, to whom he was deeply attached. And then there were the
higher, public objects of his affections: General de Gaulle, created by
the artist as the "national necessity" for troubled times, "alone and
erect," [84] whose mythical (or real?) parents are History (the father to
whom he was responsible and who would judge him according to his
works,[85] just as others must report to him) and France (the mother—
an old cliché which the long tradition of describing France as a person
had somehow frayed, yet which finds a new force of authenticity in de
Gaulle). The feelings that animated this man were at that level, in
that realm. His failures affected him not because they were his own
but because they were France's. The warmth he needed was not the intimacy of equals but the support and sympathy of the led. The "melancholy" that was the accepted price of domination, the willing sacrifice of ordinary human relations,[86] became intolerable and led to
"ill-explained retreats" only when the *leader's* soul was engulfed by

what Clemenceau (twice quoted by de Gaulle [87]) called its worst pain: cold—the indifference or hostility of the led. The warmth he needed was public. Since his goal was not self-expression but self-fulfillment through service, and since his mission was to lead men, he could not perform his task alone; when they abandoned him, then—rather than letting his private self take over—he remained his public person, but in waiting.

Between Charles and General de Gaulle, there was probably little conflict. The stoicism with which he faced his third child's retardation resembled his imperial way of facing the realities of power. The private and the public man showed the same intense capacity to suffer, and the same ability to dominate their sensibility. If France was de Gaulle's *raison d'être*, "The General" was Charles's.

How could that double need for glory and for distance be better served than by stretching oneself into, and merging with, a function of historic significance, yet one that requires that one keep one's distance from even oneself, to make sure that the performance will be great? What a revenge over solitude and separateness to be one's own creator; what pride; and what a way to externalize and transcend narcissism! In his historic figure, de Gaulle took the pride of an artist who has mastered his craft; it was not vanity.

The values *Charles* absorbed from his family were grafted on *General de Gaulle*'s "parents." For he resembles Vigny's Moses: *"Seigneur, vous m'avez fait puissant et solitaire. Laissez-moi m'endormir du sommeil de la terre."* What saved the missionary from inhumanity was, first, a very Christian sense of man's frailty—even a great man's frailty. Second, rather than a harsh God, he serves History, which requires of its most appreciated servants that they respect moderation, and France, beacon of light, threatened princess, the nation to be saved from its vices. In thus shaping the public figure, de Gaulle resolved the basic tension analyzed earlier. The mission is a transmission of the parents' legacy (rescued and remade by the leader); the missionary is also the vehicle for the cynical lessons that history teaches, and for the ego's will to power (but to be used for a great cause).

It does not matter if we know little directly about Charles or the artist. Even if we knew the most intimate detail of his childhood, schooling, and marriage, what we are able to say about the personal life of an artist is, usually, entirely irrelevant to the evaluation of his work of art. It helps us only to understand the man who made it, not the work itself; it may provide a key to the content, but not to the intimate relation of form and content which is the essence of every work of art. Conversely, understanding this relation tells us how the man transcended himself in his art.

Indeed, the public figure (from whom the *Mémoires* writer who says

"I" strived to be detached) in the real cycle of identifications took on the features of the artist. The more he bent himself to the public figure and to France, the more the *caractère* and France resembled the artist—but as in every work of art those features were transformed, recreated, mastered. Charles de Gaulle continued to marshal all his resources. He displayed all the qualities associated with artistic creation: the mix of detachment and commitment which allows him to watch his personage from afar yet to shape its destiny; the blend of passion and decorum, so characteristic of a man whose style often appears as its own reward yet always serves a cause; the willingness to be dominated by the object—in this case, the character and France, which "haunts" him; [88] the combination of deferral and immediacy. What some opponents considered as sheer obstinacy and what represented a neurotic flaw in the character of Charles—for instance, his old need always to be right—also reflected an artist's sense of the inner appropriateness of a particular decision, of its perfect fit in the whole vision; his "feel" that his conception "works" or must ultimately work. Often, de Gaulle's skill as a craftsman (politician) *made* his conception work, even as his skill as an artist (statesman) helped him to assess the clay ("*pâte*," as he called it), the reality he was trying to reshape. It was an instinctive, instinctual activity, involving all the gifts of the artist-leader.

It is easy to see why Malraux should have become fascinated by the General. For the public figure of de Gaulle was like the embodiment of Malraux's ideal. He was a character in a novel that Malraux never wrote but that would combine all his strivings; he was also a work of art of the kind so much admired by Malraux, which takes off from past masterpieces, expresses a transcendent faith, and conquers time. De Gaulle was the adventurer with a cause that Malraux had searched for in his early years, and the cause was not the excessively abstract ideology that communism had represented and that the Soviet Union exploited for its purposes, but the preservation of a cultural entity— the nation, whose importance Malraux had discovered in defeat, and whose personality (not superiority) de Gaulle wanted to assert. De Gaulle's aim was to leave a scar on history, to shape his destiny and thus to defy death, chance, oblivion by linking creatively the past and the future. Unlike Malraux, he had kept his Christian faith, but it was faith in another world, so to speak. As for this world, faith only made it bearable and pitiable. The sense of tragedy and nothingness derives in Malraux's case from the death of God, and in de Gaulle's, from deep familiarity with that tale full of sound and fury which History tells. For both men, the temptation of nihilism,[89] "the advice of Mephisto . . . daemon of every decadence," must be overcome through action and through art, the two aspects of creation. To de Gaulle as to Malraux, men are what they do; they reveal themselves not in introspective analysis but in creative action. If creativity is the "working out of conflict and coalition within the set of identities that compose the person," [90] then de Gaulle's leadership was highly creative, even if it was not highly innovative.

Some witnesses saw de Gaulle as all of a piece. This quality was not a given, but the result of a long process—a harnessing of his gifts, conflicts, and weaknesses into unique tools and mastery of leadership. His memory became not only a thoroughly reliable servant of his eloquence but also a source of prestige and awe. His literary talent and imagination joined in the *Mémoires,* written at a time when he seems to have thought that his chances of returning to power were slim; the volumes served not only as a catharsis but also to relive the exploits of the recent past and to make a legacy of examples for the future. His gift for acting and performance became ritualized in press conferences and ceremonial appearances; and backstage, he sometimes entertained listeners with sardonic verve. His energy found outlets in constant journeys around France and across the globe, feeding his curiosity, giving him the "soul's warmth" he needed, enabling him to carry his message to all the corners of his widening stage, and preserving his sense of realities.

We have said that the army suited some of the peculiarities of his character—his sense of distance, his shying away from familiarity and intimacy, and an incapacity to share decisions that resulted from his drive for independence. All these traits became trademarks of his political leadership. The "King in exile" [91] became a Republican monarch. The mold which the army gave to his way of organizing action, its institutionalization of distance, he elevated and perpetuated in a Constitution that made the President a kind of commander-in-chief aided by a chief of staff, the Premier. His impatience with details was institutionalized. His dislike for discussions and debates, which he thought diluted the will and confused the issues,[92] and his awkwardness in small groups, led to his replacing negotiations with "consultations" in which he was usually alone with whomever he "consulted." [93] His preference for the infantry was transmuted into his political dependence on the people, short-circuiting the "elites." [94] His preference for a certain protective isolation drove telephones out of the Presidential offices and saved almost all his weekends in France for a return to Colombey-les-Deux-Églises. When some feature, left untamed, could have harmed his vocation, he curbed his own nature. The early reluctance to let himself be interviewed, photographed, or put on display was disciplined—without violating the rule about the need for mystery and surprise. And even intransigence (his trademark) was gradually limited—reserved for symbolic or protocol issues, involving "nothing but" self-respect, or vital national interests.

In addition to this transmutation of personal traits, there was a welding of opposites, or polarities, so that, far from destroying each other or the man, they complemented each other. Some of those polarities can be seen as variations on two permanent themes picked up from his parents, and later developed in memorable speeches: passion and reason.[95]

The most obvious were the polarities of rebellion and rallying,[96] defiance and assertion. The loyal son of Henri and Jeanne de Gaulle had as a child chosen the military—i.e., service and discipline—as his calling. But this most turbulent of the de Gaulle children found obedience to mediocre superiors and misleading doctrines excruciating. The natural *démarche* of de Gaulle was to defy whatever offended his concept of leadership (such as the instruction he received in military schools, the military policy of the interwar period, or the political styles of the declining Third Republic and of the Fourth Republic), or whatever "insulted the future" he hoped for and deemed possible (such as Vichy's resignation to defeat, or the two superpowers' hegemonies after the war, or the French Communists' servility toward Moscow after 1947). This defiance could be brutal and intransigent. But de Gaulle was neither a nihilist nor (adds Malraux [97]) a Trotsky. The rebel in him wanted it known, as he once told a delegation of labor-union leaders, that "General de Gaulle has no predecessors," [98] but he wanted to have successors and to represent historic continuity. The defier, or resister, defies in order to "save and put in order." [99] The purpose of his domestic calls to action was to unify the French; of his external acts of negation, to reshape the world in safer fashion, which to him meant, characteristically, to create equilibrium. But he knew he could succeed only through battle.

Another set of polarities was the General's romanticism and classicism. (His admiration for Chateaubriand, who assured the transition between the two, is no surprise.) It was the romantic who proclaimed "me and history," [100] asserted his unprecedented character, saw the world as a turmoil in which the man of action, occasionally, discreetly, discontinuously "decides and prescribes . . . and then, after action has been launched, seizes again by spurts the system of his means which facts relentlessly put out of shape." [101] It was the classicist who insisted on measure and balance, saw the leader as a kind of grand entrepreneur, the function of whose investments and innovations was to preserve the continuity and flow of history, who ruled like a Cornelian Emperor, and knew that in this century "no man can be the people's substitute." [102] Romanticism and classicism also blended in de Gaulle's military programs and use of technological innovations. He put the radio, during the war, and television, after 1958, at the service of *le caractère*. His old hostility to the "system of armed masses," which inspired his design for a professional army and later his reconversion of the French Army to the atomic age, reflected a romantic fondness for mobility, decisiveness, lightning action, which made him admire Hoche, Foch, and Clemenceau, and a classic concern for maximum efficiency in the use of limited resources, which made him celebrate Louvois and Turenne, Carnot and Pétain.

Another set of features that were kept in balance were inflexibility and tactical brutality on one hand, tactical skill and patience on the other. The former were displayed abruptly throughout his career, for it was a psychological tendency that went back to his childhood, and it stemmed from his loyalty to transmitted values and to his self-assertion. But in this transformed prankster and critical *connaisseur* of dubious means to lofty ends, there was a deliberate use of ambiguity *("je vous ai compris!")*, a willingness to wait and ponder until the moment was ripe. Temporization, it seems, was already a trait in the student and young officer whenever his mind was not fully engaged.[103]

Another tension, also resolved, existed between his taste for flamboyance and his sense of finitude. One drove him toward heroic assertions of will, toward grand attempts at making irreversible policies, the other toward a certain fatalism, a certain skepticism about the role of great men, a strange readiness, if not to accept defeat, at least to admit partial failure as the price for being human.[104] Once again, he united the two, and each reinforced the other: the more one is aware of the limits of one's possibilities—one's own, and those of "the nation as it is in the world as it is"—the more it becomes necessary to do what can be done with *panache,* flair, and style; but these qualities are justified only as long as they serve the cause realistically.

One key word of de Gaulle's political vocabulary illuminates his acts as a leader and artist, his way of mobilizing and welding his resources, and that is "arbitration." By this he did not mean mediation in the sense of finding a common denominator among pre-existing tendencies (within him) or factions (outside); it meant deciding, after taking into account all the givens of one's own nature and the "nature of things," and with the higher interest as a goal. Once again, we find mastery without mutilation; the "arbiter" was *le caractère,* determined to take charge, respectful of the need for equilibrium, and resolving inner tensions by the tough "internal discipline and heavy yoke" [105] of subordination to a higher goal.

But arbitration does not take care of all inner tensions. There was tension between de Gaulle and the cause that was supposed to transcend and elevate his private and public selves—between the artist and the mission for which he shaped his work of art. There was, in particular, a contradiction between the private man's unconscious need to assert his personality—his egotism (side by side with his deep humility), his sense of personal adventure, a certain heady enchantment with his own destiny [106]—and the historic figure's constant and conscious desire to express France, his concern for *raison d'État.* The private personality occasionally injected into the leader's acts an element of vindictiveness or into his words a paean of self-praise. The historic figure demanded self-abnegation or in any case prudence in the use of the capital, skepticism about the ego's reach. Yet reconciliation was usually provided in a way that protected the mission and satisfied the artist—by exalting the public political figure. The personality spread over the map was a *public* personage, not the private self, and since that public personage was nothing but a tool of the state, his successes, resentments, assertions, claims, and setbacks became those of the nation. To leave him "in the desert" (as the Fourth Republic did) was to waste France,[107] to slight him was to slight France, to plan his assassination was a crime against the state, to serve him was to ennoble oneself. If *le caractère* wanted full power for himself and denied anyone else's capacity to exert power adequately, it was because a mystical link between "de Gaulle" and his mission allowed him to claim historical legitimacy. De Gaulle, quoting Roosevelt, who had taxed him with egotism,[108] asked whether FDR thought him egotistic for himself or for France; in fact, he solved the problem by equating his *public* self with the *higher* interest of France.

This solution may have reconciled the artist with the final work of art—the historic personage—but it did so by boosting the *artist's* work of art, the public-political figure. And this figure, like every work of art, tended once it got under way to take on a life of its own, with its own demands for wholeness. Since its creator was so closely tied to it by his own needs and in his person, the work tended also to take over the artist. When it did so, he had failed—he was no longer master of himself, of others, or of his creation. He needed then to use his resources not to blend, but to separate. He resorted to three familiar aids, mobilized on behalf of self-distance and perspective: a sense of humor and irony, usually well controlled in public, often devastating as a safety valve in private or "after hours"; [109] the habit of describing himself in the third person; and his discipline of detachment by moving away from the all-absorbing present in time (the recourse to history) and space (travels). These three devices were instinctively and deliberately used by him, to keep himself from fusing entirely with the *éclat* and *grandeur* of his "overdetermined" work of art, so like the overdetermination of fantasy and dreams, of all rich artistic creation. A gigantic battle was waged between the artist's attempt to fuse and project his highest aspirations onto *le caractère* who lived for France, and his own narcissistic needs to hold onto that artistic projection by completely identifying with it.

What made this battle so difficult to win was not only the resemblance of the work of art, "de Gaulle," to the artist, but also the resemblance to the artist of that higher work of Gaullist art, France. Not

only did Charles turn his psychological and even physical peculiarities
into tools of leadership, but he also projected them onto his beloved
France. This was especially striking in the case of certain basic traits of
the man: he ascribed his own highest aspirations—blends of the *is* and
the *ought,* reflecting both psychological needs and moral values [110]—
to France. A pragmatist in daily politics, de Gaulle as a political high
priest was concerned above all with making France behave according
to those values. A Machiavellian in tactics, he was a moralist in his
highest goals. (An associate described him as "Caesar reshaped by
Christianity.") De Gaulle, from adolescence on, felt the need for a
strong internal discipline to guard him against waste and dispersion,
to harness his gifts and prevent internal tensions from paralyzing him.
The solution, as we know, was to unify his talents and traits in the service of a great cause, the cause harnessing and heightening the efficiency of his personality. This is exactly what he ascribed to and prescribed for France: France was full of "ferments of dispersion," often
yielded to "chimeras," was threatened by mediocrity and disasters.[111]
The harness was to be a unifying and galvanizing "national ambition,"
a "great undertaking"—*grandeur,* the "choice of a great cause," *"viser
haut et se tenir droit."* [112] Both he and France needed a higher *"querelle";* without one, he was convinced, she would not "be herself," for
she was truly herself neither in mediocrity nor in misfortune. Similarly, he was at his best only when sustained by his mission; when he
wrote of "Old France, burdened by history, bruised by wars and revolutions, relentlessly going back and forth from grandeur to decline,
but straightened, century after century, by the genius of renovation," [113] or described France as a "great people, made for example, enterprise, combat, always the star of History," [114] or said that
he always felt that Providence "had created her for perfect success or
exemplary misfortune," [115] he was describing himself as much as her.
This assurance, given so often to the French, and in the high points of
his leadership successfully communicated to them—that France was indeed "something special," different from other nations, marked by
God for great undertakings—was not merely reminiscence of Michelet
or Péguy. Was it not a projection onto France of his own sense of spe-
cialness? His conviction that France would succumb to the sirens of decadence, mediocrity, and totalitarianism unless mobilized by a higher
cause which appealed to her traditions, his belief that France would
collapse or lapse into decline unless restored to power—often repeated
by de Gaulle to his friend Adenauer [116]—were these insights from
French history or insights into himself?

The identification went further. Just as he proclaimed throughout
his life that the hero was both his own law *and* the servant of France,
he saw France both as *the* nation par excellence, and as the servant of

what during the war he called *"la querelle de l'homme"*—the cause of freedom, equilibrium, generosity in a world threatened by mechanization.[117] Just as he used all his resources in his mission, but put them at its service, he always wanted to use all the "spiritual and political families" of France, refused to discard any so long as they could contribute to the cause, tried to convert them from their separate concerns toward the common goal. *Grandeur* meant an attitude of the will and soul rather than a specific doctrine, and *grandeur* for France meant a state of mind and resolve, a rejection of pettiness, an ambition rather than a specific program. It was an ambition, more cultural and moral than political, to preserve certain values that are like a blend of Christianity's and the Revolution's.

The precondition for *grandeur,* in both cases, was the same: independence. De Gaulle's foreign policy—his central concern—aimed persistently at giving France "free hands," at restoring her freedom of decision (the more interdependent the nations of the world, the greater the need for a margin of autonomy); in later years, he made this a universal doctrine. It was impossible not to recognize in his philosophy of international relations, in his dismissal of ideologies, in his assertion of the primacy of national interests, in his stress on the incommunicable uniqueness of each nation,[118] in his view of states on the world stage as separate national essences with accidental existences shaped by the twists of history and the turns of national consciousness,[119] a projection of his concept of leadership—ultimately of his own personal stance, his own determination to "belong to all and nobody," [120] and a blend of the *is* and the *ought.* Vichy's crime was to have renounced French independence, thus it lost its legitimacy.[121] And if he was able to restore France's independence in 1944 and after 1958, it was because he had never alienated his own.

The emphasis on independence for de Gaulle and for France was tied to another essential notion: that of integrity, meaning both wholeness and faithfulness. Independence was the condition for integrity; integrity was the substance of self-respect; and self-respect, or dignity, a central value, could be found only in *grandeur.* "Not to disappoint oneself" [122] seems to be the motto he gave himself and France. There was no self-respect in humiliation, or in mediocrity, or in *"bassesse."* [123] (There may be some in failure, if it is honorable.) For the leader, there is no loss of self-respect in a resort to deception and cunning as long as the higher cause prevails; for France, there is no loss of self-respect in revising her alliances and reversing her policies, as long as her own higher goals are served. The association of capital and labor that de Gaulle kept trying to establish, so much like the combination of opposites within himself, made more sense as a promotion of dignity than as an economic reform. De Gaulle offered France's aid to French Canadians who preserved their independence and integrity and were claiming a modern role of their own, but the French Algerians who did not know how to adapt and who spoiled the image of France were less well treated by him.

Grandeur, independence, integrity: de Gaulle's leadership tended to give France his own profile, and France's leadership aimed to make the world a collection of ideal types of Gaullist nations, each one embodying unique values and virtues, and each one kept within the limits of moderation by the balancing of power. The underlying assumption here was that just as man is truly free and responsible only when he can fully develop and master his personality, there can be no true world order unless it is a structured harmony of multiple uniquenesses. And as the leader set the example for France, France must set it for the world.

Indeed, France in international relations behaved like de Gaulle writ large. This consisted of showing the way imperiously and exhorting others to follow, refusing commitments with obscure purposes and binding procedures. De Gaulle's difficulty in negotiating, his way of never being bargained out of a concession but, instead, granting (*octroyer*) [124] concessions to which the other party could respond freely —these became French vetoes, boycotts, and unilateral moves. His personal intransigence became a French toughness; his preference for dealing with other great leaders, lonely masters, and artists became a French disrespect for powers incapable of "charting their course." His need for drama became France's stealing the show in world affairs, or trying to.

The same polarities that he combined in himself he projected onto and harnessed in France. A traditionalist but also an empiricist thirsty for action, he wanted France to preserve her personality and to innovate—for without innovation, modernization, mechanization, industrialization, there was no way to be great any more. Yet all these innovations should not turn France into a bastardized America (hence his emphasis on saving her language and culture). His own mixture of narcissism and discipline became a blend of often strident French self-assertion and recognition of the need for "modesty." And just as his awareness of personal finitude increased the desire for flamboyance, so the realistic awareness of the limits of France's present power heightened the need for self-pride: French foreign policy under him combined a colossal *repli* from overseas and abandon of excessive commitments, with a spectacular determination to exploit every sphere of influence.[125]

III. Charisma

The artist does not need a responsive public immediately. He may write or paint for the "happy few" and posterity. The political artist needs a public *now,* even if his ambition is to build for the ages: without one, his work of art remains only a conception. The political artist succeeds only if public response allows the figure of the leader, privately shaped by the artist for a public role, to become a public figure. Political leadership is a relationship between the leader and his followers; and charisma is not only a gift but a form of authority, a link between a certain type of ruler and the ruled. Where there is no gift, there is no charisma—indeed, most political leaders are uncharismatic. But when the public is not receptive to the gift, charisma fails or remains dormant. If charisma is communicated self-confidence,[126] what we must discuss now is why, when, and how de Gaulle managed to impose his gift to the French, to preserve his authority after coming to power, and at what costs for the nation and for the future of his own work.

De Gaulle always knew and said that he could not carry out his mission without public support. From 1940 to 1944, he forged it. He resigned in 1946 when he felt it slipping and lacked the institutional means to preserve it *in his style*. He tried in vain to re-create it as leader of the RPF. He found it again in 1958. What were the conditions for his success?

Whenever the circumstances were exactly what the script required, de Gaulle succeeded in establishing that cycle of identifications—of France to himself and himself to France, of the people with him, of himself and France to higher causes. And then he could enact or re-enact on the stage of history the great drama he had wanted to perform: that of bringing *alone* a decisive and famous service to his nation in distress. Whenever history brought his nation to the point where his own need (for drama, leadership, call, unity, and salvation) became France's and when France at last had no alternative but to turn to the lonely leader, then the missionary who had subordinated his private self to his public function would meet men whose public drama had become a private crisis.[127] It was the man's great luck that when he projected his formidable will and imagination into the future, events obligingly provided the great dramas that he called for à la Chateaubriand (*"levez-vous, orages désirés"*). World War I had foreshadowed them in his mind, and his relative failure then had made them even more imperative for his ambition. This was an opportunity that his political genius fully exploited; but it was also part of his genius to have anticipated, announced, and denounced those events clearly.

Here we find the first ingredient of de Gaulle's charisma: the awe-inspiring capacity of *le caractère* to predict *les circonstances*—i.e., to be right. Prescience did for him what victory over paralysis did for Franklin Roosevelt in the eyes of the American people. (It is no accident that de Gaulle's symbolic domain was public, FDR's private.) His somewhat suffocating remark of May 19, 1958: "The Algerians shout:

'Vive de Gaulle,' as the French do instinctively when they are deep in anguish or carried by hope," [128] reflects a reality.

Only when the circumstances were those of extreme and irremediable disaster, when a leader could appeal both to present fears, anxieties, and sufferings of the people and to their hopes, to Péguy's *"espérance"* and Corneille's *"beau désespoir,"* when he could appear as prophet, unifier, guide toward the "summits" of self-respect and greatness—only then did de Gaulle succeed. The counterexample is provided by the long episode of the RPF. There, adequacy was missing. The General prophesied titanic turmoil and cataclysmic conflict between East and West: it did not happen. Although his goals were as lofty as ever, he could not appear as a unifier, since his very attempt to "rally" the nation outside and above the parties divided the French—a dilemma that could have been resolved (as in the fight against Vichy) only if they had gradually deserted the parties out of a personal sense of tragedy and need for salvation, the precondition for which would have been the correctness of the prophecy (as shown later, in 1958). Moreover, because "hope had kept a tragic accent for him," he had to put the spotlight on tragedy in order to justify his call for action; thus, he appealed almost exclusively to people's fears and anxieties, and exploited them stridently, with dismal results. Those who heard him and came were often those who wanted to save not France but their possessions, and of course they deserted him when the fear of loss vanished, but not without having given to the RPF a cramped, regressive, and repressive air, in which Barrès prevailed over Péguy, conservation over innovation.

For de Gaulle to be the voice of hope and effort, the disasters had already to have happened. Before, he could denounce their coming, but if they failed to occur, his prophetic gift would be tarnished, and if he tried to contribute to their coming so as to prove himself right and to awaken the missing "great ambition," he would by *la force des choses* be led to exploit the basest side of men. Moreover, his methods—intransigence, *politique du pire* yet refusal to go all the way to dictatorship (since dictatorship, in his eyes, meant excess *unless* it was prompted by a great national ambition or by a national disaster, both precisely absent) [129]—would seem destructive and keep him and his followers from power. The RPF was explicable only in Gaullist terms: at fifty-five, de Gaulle had too much energy for internal exile, and he thought France was mortally threatened. The failure of the RPF taught him that before catastrophes his strength was in solitude.[130] Writing the *Mémoires* cleansed the sullied image of the savior: he erased the re-enactment *manqué* in action by a successful re-enactment in writing.

The reason why de Gaulle's effectiveness began only in the midst of disaster had to do with the second ingredient of his charisma. Only in the depths of crisis and despair does the fear of losing one's personality stir up millennial hopes of rescue: otherwise, complacency prevails, and the would-be guide has to make an unsavory choice between frustration and deliberate contribution to the dreaded yet necessary *secousse.* But when crisis came, and when the stakes were nothing less than a national community's survival in the world, then de Gaulle's peculiar message—that France must regain her greatness by saving her identity—struck the deepest chord. For the message is far more pedagogical than ideological (and thus is related to the messages of religious leaders or a Gandhi). To de Gaulle (as to the César-Charles of his early play), what mattered most was *that* one face the turmoil, and *how* one confronts danger, rather than *what* specific measures one should take. The strength of Gaullism lay in the adequacy of a personal cause to a national one: for de Gaulle the aim in life was not to realize a program, but to be a *caractère,* to have a firm identity; for France, a very old nation, identity did not have to be defined in substantive, programmatic terms. This was necessary perhaps for new nations still unsure of their national consciousness, but positively harmful in the case of a nation where an intense feeling of nationhood coincided with fearful divisions on policies. So, in times of acute crisis in France, the thing for a leader to do was to underemphasize the substance of action but to stress its essence—which is self-respect and style. There was no need to define a French identity; there was a need to save and proclaim it, to make the French feel proud of being French and relevant to their times. Nobody felt and understood this better than de Gaulle.

In emergencies, a threat to national identity makes the citizens willing to give up their established way of life, their cherished possessions and institutions, in order to overcome the crisis. De Gaulle's personal message—mystical attachment to an idea of France, and detachment from any specific social pattern, fixed policy, overseas possession, all of which are merely transient manifestations of the mysterious essence that alone must be preserved—could thus only be heard in extreme moments, when he could play the role of innovating protector. His constant and baffling theme—France must be herself—was the second source of his charisma; for it succeeded whenever, in peril, the French needed to assert their personality in the world and to unify and adapt in order to survive. De Gaulle's charisma thus had an element of poetry in it—the sound and the rhythms of the words were more important than their actual meanings; they shaped or reshaped the meanings. In this way, he preserved the authenticity and freshness of the nation's *élan vital,* instead of hardening it in a program.

A third factor in his charisma was his appeal to a certain style of authority, a style of crisis leadership, represented in French literature in Corneille's plays and in French history by the *ancien régime* and the Napoleonic empires. The kind of leadership de Gaulle celebrated in *Le Fil de l'épée* was a French archetype.[131] "Le style du Général"—in political action and in rhetoric—fitted a mold that was perfected and conceptualized by Richelieu. His sense of distance and restraint, his conception of action by individuals each of whom must preserve his own personality and is linked, not to others on the same level as himself, but to a superior (or, in de Gaulle's own case, a higher calling), fit the Frenchman's *horreur du face-à-face* and his fear of arbitrariness.

One understands, then, the nature of de Gaulle's appeal in a crisis. He tried to address himself to people's highest qualities—sacrifice and responsibility and duty; he called on them to find in the crisis an opportunity to *grow,* rather than to succumb to the irrational fears, hatreds, and delusions so often flattered by demagogues. (Indeed, his own lack of "the physique, taste, attitudes and features that could flatter" [132] crowds, his indifference to being loved and rejection of personality cult justify Malraux's comment: "His strength lies in authority, not in contagion." [133]) Yet there is no doubt that crisis itself brings out these fears, hatreds, and delusions, induces a kind of mass regression into helplessness, and makes the helpless eager to let a decisive leader "arbitrate" for them. One finds among de Gaulle's followers different kinds of men whose attachment to him varied in motivation and intensity. There were some who needed idols or who attached themselves to the hero because of an inner need for a father figure—de Gaulle, this time, is each one of *them* completed; there were several such men in his entourage. Others were attracted more by what was compelling in de Gaulle's mission and message than by a personal need of their own—except for one common need, often neglected by political scientists: the need to admire. Some were fascinated by the artist: they were the romantics of adventure, action, and great-men-defying-history.[134] Others were occasional followers, attracted by a temporary or partial element in de Gaulle's activity, led by their own predilections and by his ambiguity to confuse this element for the essence or to misinterpret its meaning; they were grievously disappointed when they discovered their error. The closer they had been to him, the more passionate their rejection.[135]

But the qualities necessary for a charismatic (or other) leader's coming to power are not those that he needs in order to stay in power, or to protect his work. Prescience was a precondition for the success of de Gaulle's charisma, but the reason for its durability and strength lay elsewhere. It was his capacity, not merely to predict distress, but to accomplish what seemed impossible to other men, thanks to his lucidity about long-range trends, his determination to make what he wanted irresistible or inevitable, and his faith in his and France's capacity to impose their will. His mission seemed to be to realize the unlikely, to make the disputable self-evident.

The charismatic leader, having responded to and taken care of the distress that made people turn to him, may lose his charisma or his power. His role may be over. Or, in order to stay in office and to avoid the "routinization of charisma," he may perpetually re-create conditions of distress that will allow him to play the savior. (Mao Tse-tung is an example of this type.) Or, he may decide that his best way of protecting his accomplishments is to institutionalize, but then there is a problem of preserving his own charisma from the disenchantments of routinization.

De Gaulle's career managed to embrace all these alternatives. The prospects of institutionalization seem at first sight incompatible with his claim to uniqueness, to direct communication with France and history, and with the idea of the French as somewhat weak and fickle and ungrateful children or prodigal sons of France. In 1945–46, partly by inclination, partly because of the circumstances (which made him a national symbol but put institutionalization into the parties' hands), he had to choose between trying to hang onto power at the expense of his *caractère* and charisma, and saving his charisma by "leaving things before they left me" [136]—which he did, following once again the script of *Le Fil de l'épée*.

After his return to power in 1958, he ruled successfully for ten years. Conditions of distress were provided in abundance by events that were not of his creation—especially during the Algerian war. But he seized them with characteristic glee so as to re-enact his mission and to renew his charisma—when he put on his general's uniform before the television cameras while Algiers was rioting in January 1960; when he smashed the army rebellion in April 1961; when he used the 1962 assassination attempt against him as the occasion for a blitzkrieg on his political enemies. Moreover, the style of his foreign policy after the end of the Algerian drama served to produce mini-dramas, so to speak, that rejuvenated his appeal, as if he too needed to create crises for whose solutions he would be "erect and necessary." [137] The mixture of dread and excitement with which he interpreted the Middle East crisis of 1967 as a possible gateway to world war was significant, and reminded one of the false prophecies of 1947–50.

But in the late 1960s a world drama would have been not so much a challenge as a calamity, and de Gaulle was concerned above all with protecting France's heritage and future. Also, he knew that the public mood was no more heroic than the international scene was adequate for grand ventures. The problem thus became how to institutionalize his charisma in a way compatible with his unique personality. Earlier, the challenge was to grow by stretching; now it was to grow by fitting his enormous, epic frame into a more limited framework. He tried to do this by giving France institutions that corresponded to his own personal ideal and practices of leadership and to what he thought French unity, stability, and efficiency required. The distance that he needed was assured not only by the 1958 Constitution and by his interpretation of the President's role but also by the creation of a Gaullist party with which he had no direct connection, but without which he would have been in the same situation as in 1945.

Yet de Gaulle obviously doubted that institutionalizing his mission would do the trick after his departure from the scene. Leadership remains in essence a personal attribute; and he himself also tried, while alive, to preserve his charisma from the attrition of even well-oiled institutions. His decision to run for office (facing universal suffrage for the first time in his life) at the end of 1965 was highly symbolic, for it meant that while he wanted to give to his "historic" legitimacy the seal of his institutions, he doubted that the institutions could survive him. During the brief election campaign that preceded the disastrous first ballot, he resorted to apocalyptic language of fall and salvation. Elected, he continued to try to be both the first President of the Fifth Republic and "General de Gaulle." Of the three ingredients of his charisma—prophecy, stress on "being oneself," embodiment of the style of crisis authority—neither the first nor the third quite fitted the circumstances. But the second one still had appeal, as shown by the broad approval the French gave to his provocative foreign policy, which preserved France's identity even as French society and polity lost much of their old distinctiveness.

There were other factors, too, that buttressed, completed, and inspired his continuing appeal. One was collective memory—his capacity to remind people of the mess they had been in before he came to clean it up. But the very success of his clean-up attenuated the fears of a relapse, and in a youthful nation the memories began to fade away.

The other factor was the most intensely personal: his extraordinary artistry. De Gaulle's residual charisma lay almost entirely in his own *caractère*. People still followed the great actor on the stage. A charisma that once moved the French to follow him or to cling to him, in circumstances that gave him tasks commensurate with his needs, now persisted despite the narrower range of deeds and made the French watch him as a spectacle. They remembered how in the past he had stretched his potential to whatever scale was required, and they sensed that even on the more modest scale where he now operated he performed more impressively than anybody else could. He was their alibi, and they basked in the sun of his prestige.[138] And so they watched him in those grand rites that marked the institutionalization of his charisma and the periodic occasions of its reassertion, symbolically re-enacting his mission and reassuring a return to normalcy. And they watched him rebelling for France wherever he still could—against superpower hegemonies, against the power of the dollar, against American violence in Vietnam, against English-Canadian "oppression" in Québec. Times had changed. In an international system that frustrates achievements and multiplies denials, in a nation dulled and enervated by what Raymond Aron has called the "querulous satisfaction" of industrial society, a charisma once fed by accomplishments became a charisma based on drama. Statecraft became stagecraft, and remained as a protest and palliative against the banality or "melancholy" of a duller period. "Judging the leader capable of adding to the effectiveness of familiar procedures the full weight of a unique authority (*une vertu singulière*), confidence and hope keep an obscure trust in him." [139] Indeed, the suspense about how his own drama would end nourished his charisma.

Yet the problem of what would happen to his work remained. Elements of an answer can be found if one looks at some of the costs of de Gaulle's leadership. In the first place, his very identification with France, just as it had subordinated "Charles" to "de Gaulle," and both to "General de Gaulle," left out all that was not in de Gaulle's vision of France. Things which had been compressed and repressed would inevitably reassert themselves. He had, by his style of leadership, raised in acute form the problem of participation.[140] His personality and conception of leadership, on one hand, and his aversion for French parliamentary politics, on the other, created a system that might well, once the leader was gone, provoke a swing of the pendulum in the direction he had so often denounced. His exclusion of all "intermediaries" had only increased their desire for revenge. His way of unifying the French had been to rise above their differences and to ignore the different representatives. But even if some of the alignments they championed lost relevance, they were still waiting in the wings. Surrounded by able and loyal, although not servile, civil servants, and by docile politicians (whose docility annoyed him), yet incapable of keeping near him those who resisted him and whom he respected,[141] had he not eased the way for opponents he despised? The great man had dwarfed and distorted his own institutions, which remained fragile and marginal.

De Gaulle's fascination with long-range national goals—those that could be achieved on the world stage, or whatever was required for playing on it—perhaps also his personal conviction that dignity and greatness were worthier goals than mere material happiness, made him brush aside or neglect values and concerns that were of crucial importance to many.[142] The reverse side of his quest for high drama and distant perspectives was a certain indifference, or temporization and lassitude, when confronted with problems that seemed to him less essential—or less reachable by his own craft alone.[143] As for the French, their willingness to give priority to France's greatness decreased whenever the requirements for doing so ceased being the same as their own daily necessities. Once order was restored, independence insured, the threat of crisis removed, this schism led to mutual disenchantment. In the winter of 1945–46, the Frenchman's obsession with his daily difficulties and deprivations conflicted with de Gaulle's ambitions, and in the years 1965 to 1967 this occurred again. For him, these were times when the French did not live up to the imperative of *grandeur,* but satisfied themselves with mediocrity and gave the lie to his claim that France was not herself without greatness. *He* may not be himself without *grandeur,* nor could France in *his* eyes, but France can be in *theirs,* and they do not always crave it. He needed *grandeur* always; but he could enact it for France only when circumstances and the French allowed him to. When they ceased, to use a famous autobiographical quotation, being an "elite people, sure of itself and dominating" (master of its fate), the memory of what they had to do or give up to follow him made them "scowl, howl, and growl" (*la hargne, la rogne, et la grogne*).

Goals higher than those that can be served by the present system of (more or less) cooperating nation-states had also been ruled out. A man who sees his mission as the perpetuation of France, and who sees in "being oneself" the highest duty, can give to France's higher cause a noble, humanitarian tone, and this might well include extensive coordination with others. But certainly the "ambition" of disappearing into a higher grouping would be self-abnegation or abdication, the opposite of self-assertion. Every merger of sovereignties, beyond revocable association, appeared to de Gaulle like a fading of the will to live. Within France, the lack of participation and the subordination of "lower" goals led to a reaction that showed the intermediaries and the "lesser" concerns to be just as destructive as he had always warned (even more so for having been neglected); outside France, the self-fulfilling prophecy worked differently: not through reaction against what he had stood for, but through the contagion of nationalism.

Other costs had to do not with things ruled out, but with things created by his leadership. Both his deeds and his style made enemies—for himself within France, for France in the world. The occasional isolation of France in world affairs—when his initiatives or words were not followed by others, or when his words and his refusal to see things from any perspective but his own antagonized others—was a dangerous price to pay for *grandeur.* Diplomacy does not prosper or morale feed on distant chances of ultimate success or prospects of final vindication. And the inevitable domestic hostility could not please him;

he wanted to unify the French, but he exasperated many, because of his policies, his haughty style of personal leadership, or his belief that in foreign affairs dissent was tantamount to lack of patriotism. There can be no greatness without struggles; but the animosities that his struggle provoked impeded greatness insofar as, in the temporal world, leadership has to be more than a moral posture: it must bring a payment in cash.

Also, de Gaulle's high image of France, and his identification with her, often encouraged a kind of intoxicating self-delusion in him. A policy followed by other, weaker men could (indeed, must) fail. The same policy endorsed by him had to succeed—because he could speak for France, and because he was "de Gaulle." He discovered, in dealing with the Algerian Front de Libération Nationale (FLN), that this was not the case. Nor were his pronouncements and visits always followed by the results he expected. Hopes were often dashed, energies wasted, imprudent acts performed or words said—whenever his character was not convertible into material power or backed by a commitment of it, or when he misread events, or when he failed to follow up his grand moves with detailed measures of execution.

More serious, because more lasting, were the illusions de Gaulle may have created among the French. His message bred its own misunderstandings. It was pride that he wanted to restore in the French, but it was vanity that he may have encouraged. (Their reaction to his Canadian outburst was significant: he wanted to make them proud of their overseas cousins, both for their past resilience and for their new ambition; French opinion blamed him for having given France a bad name on the world stage.) He tried to replace a chauvinism of nostalgia, envy, resentment, and displaced self-doubt with a national pride in the recovery of independence, harmony, economic progress. Yet his own assertiveness often led to silly manifestations of misplaced gloating or xenophobia. In his pedagogic attempt at moving men by making them believe that they were better than they really were, so as to *make* them better, or that they were doing more than they actually did, so as to get them to do more, he spread myths—such as the unanimity of the Resistance, or the French share in the victory of 1945, or voluntary decolonization, or atomic prowess. These myths could delay the adjustment to reality which he wanted.

Ultimately, the reason why the protection of the work remained unsure is quite simple. Some of de Gaulle's accomplishments are history, irreversibly so: the Resistance and Liberation of France, the decolonization; but others are fragile—the nuclear force, the policy against supranational integration, the Constitution of 1958—because they embody a highly personal reading of reality, or an attitude rather than a program. Should the French repudiate this attitude either by deliberately choosing another course, or by showing themselves unable to follow any, then that part of his work will be lost, partly through *their* fault, and—for the reasons just given—partly through his own. His own flaws were so intimately tied to the essence of his personality and leadership that it is hard to see how they could have been avoided; and even if the fragile part of his work disappears, there would always remain the two things which de Gaulle, political master and artist, most cared about: the trail of glory and tales of greatness in the history textbooks of the future; and the inspiration and example for action. "Since everything always begins anew, what I have done will sooner or later be a source of new fervor after I have disappeared. . . ."[144] There is something contagious in greatness.[145]

We have observed that de Gaulle's conception of the leader, missionary of a national cause, had religious overtones, and that this missionary figure was itself the creation of a political artist. Most great men— artists, political or religious leaders—seem to have some common features. As Erik Erikson sums them up, they are close to de Gaulle's: the desire to fulfill the father's frustrated hopes, a strong moral conscience, and a love for "activity on a large scale"; a long effort to build up all the resources needed for the task to come; the capacity of making one's childhood crises representative of collective problems, to make one's personality the answer to historical crisis, to fill a collective identity vacuum with one's own identity, and to erase a common humiliation through one's acts or writings; the capacity to wait for the right moment, to engage one's whole personality when it comes, and to prefer settling for nothing rather than compromising one's integrity; a self-fulfilling (and early) sense of omnipotence and omniscience, combined with enormous energy and mental concentration; narcissism absorbed in charisma and lifted into deeds; a sense of being unique and unprecedented. The central values of integrity and fidelity, honor, and self-respect developed in adolescence, a kind of telescoping of the adolescent and mature stages of psychosocial identity, were also present in de Gaulle. Intimacy seems to have been limited as usual, but there was no apparent bypassing of generativity in the case of a man who had children, often expressed his concern for French youth, and wanted to be an example for future generations. At first sight, we do not find one element that characterizes many great leaders: the search for a wider identity than the one that existed before. To him, France was the highest temporal good; yet his faith in the universalism of French culture, the expansion of his horizons after the mid 1950s, his assertion of the fundamental equality and dignity of all self-respecting nations, and, within his country, his effort to transcend traditional class or ideological divisions ought not to be ignored.

If the artist is thus confirmed as a great politico-religious leader, what about the work of art to which he has devoted his life?

For an evaluation of "the work-of-art-in-history" so much *hubris* is required—even more than that of the artist who created it: in comparison with other art, its ultimate value is dependent on its timeliness, on its permanent "fit" into history, on the lasting appreciation of its audience, as well as on its intrinsic value.

By definition, the intrinsic value of a work of art is to be found not in its timeliness, nor in its social contribution, nor in the applause it gets, but in something hidden entirely within its own structure. Whether people like it or not, find it useful, pleasing or ugly is irrelevant—not just because the audience does not matter to its *artistic* evaluation, but because whether it is good or bad is not even at issue. The issue becomes, rather: is it, or is it not a work of art? If it is, then, by definition "it works, it will last," it will leave its mark somewhere, sometime.

Just as the artist, at his best, does not care about his immediate effect on his audience, one finds in de Gaulle a certain indifference to it —partly out of faith, partly out of fatalism, partly because he looked to the long-range audience of history, but mainly because he was concerned above all with his artist's work for its own sake. This concern helps to explain the relative ideological poverty of the Gaullist pursuit of *grandeur*. It also explains de Gaulle's frequent preoccupation [146] with *ending well:* like Corneille's Augustus, he had the actor's temptation to *"quitter la vie avec éclat."* [147] In the early spring of 1968, one could therefore ask: what would the rest of the story be?

The *political* artist, the man of action, needs public support. His mission might end dramatically, being repudiated after some political crisis, for example. De Gaulle could then no longer claim—as he had after January 1946—that he still represented French legitimacy, since the institutions in which the drama would unfold had been his very own, supported massively by the French people. Even rejected as a political leader, however, the historic figure—the ultimate work of art— would continue to exist: "General de Gaulle" could, like any masterpiece, be great (and thus contagious) out of office as well as in power. But for the work of art to persist and endure, the style of the exit had to be grand, like that of January 1946, and unlike that of so many other French leaders.

In other words, the real danger lay elsewhere than in the mere withdrawal of assent. It lay in that mysterious and delicate relation of the artist to his creation. Would the artist in him, despite his lucid resolve, become incapable of new creativity? There were two threats, within himself. The artist could become the captive of the public figure, from which he would have lost his distance, and which would have turned into a rigidified and uncontrolled caricature of itself, like a huge, heavy fish left on an empty shore. Or else the artist could succumb to the self-indulgence of old age, letting all the private fears and flaws, once conquered and transcended, take over, making the public figure a hostage or victim of the private man's afflictions. In either case he would be captive to his past, which he could no longer renew nor transcend.

De Gaulle, who had so eloquently described old age as a shipwreck, who warned himself against Pétain's "majestic lassitude," who watched Adenauer's decline and Churchill's decay, was surely on guard against personal exhaustion. Against irrelevance and the tendency to re-enact his missionary role incongruously, he was protected by his acute sense of reality—and also, one hoped, by his aesthetics. He needed an aesthetic end to the script he had written and the character he had shaped. Perhaps he would put an end to the work of art—public figure and mission—in time, having become again, as in his childhood and adolescence, a human being alone with his dreams. But whatever the end of his story, de Gaulle was the incarnation of Bernanos's fragile ideal—the man who never lost that *"esprit d'enfance"* inspired by all the early aspirations and ardors; he never betrayed the vision he formed in those early years, and he put a formidable mix of vitality, determination, and sheer exhilarating sense of fun and play into the realization of his dreams.

"On a l'histoire qu'on mérite." [148] This was de Gaulle's first lesson, which he read to his students when he was a young officer. Perhaps it would also be his last lesson as an old man.

IV. Postscriptum et Postmortem

The test came in May–June 1968, and in the turbulent events that followed. What accounts for the drastic change in the relations between de Gaulle the political artist and his public during his last eleven months in power? Do these changes, and his behavior during the crisis, require us to take a different view of his work of art? Was the "style of exit" sufficiently grand to allow it to endure after the end of his political leadership?

In the crisis of May–June 1968, de Gaulle's charisma at first waned so fast that his political demise appeared inevitable to many, but *le caractère* once again turned the tables on his enemies.

The crisis itself resulted from the costs of his kind of charisma. Ten years of solitary rule by a leader who needed the people's confidence but shunned their involvement made many Frenchmen eager to take their problems into their own hands. Reforms aimed at modernizing the academic system and at moving toward de Gaulle's old ideal of workers' "participation" in industry had been delayed. The high quest for *grandeur* had given priority to the financial and military demands of French foreign policy over the demands of the French consumers. Feeling neglected, they rebelled: all that had been denied and repressed exploded in May 1968. Centralization at the top of a heavily bureaucratic system had made the state unresponsive to social discontents, and had prevented the leader and his government from realizing the scope of the dissatisfaction. It insured that even a localized breakdown (such as that of the universities in Paris) would challenge the regime and spread to other sectors. During the crisis, whether out of wounded pride or out of obstinate clinging to long-range national goals, de Gaulle kept his plans for a visit to Rumania and, despite his obvious misgivings about Premier Pompidou's bargaining inclinations, he entrusted the handling of the crisis to the government. This left him at the mercy of his ministers' skills.

The crisis also resulted from the inevitable limits of any charisma. De Gaulle had given France his own features. But a nation is not a man. The crisis of May 1968 expressed deep and ancient traits of the French body politic, which no regime had been able to change. The weakness of intermediate bodies between the electorate and the government facilitated spontaneous combustion—the fire could spread without any resistance.[149] De Gaulle's contempt for those bodies, his "institutionalization of distance," had accentuated but not created this weakness. The national tendency, described by Tocqueville as well as by de Gaulle, to resist reforms unless they grew from a revolution could be found in de Gaulle's own style of leadership; but it was also, much of the time, a genuine obstacle to his own reformist inclinations of which he was cruelly aware.[150] Also, he was a very old man presiding over a nation with a vast and growing population of youth; the generation gap was colossal, and it was difficult for him to understand a student movement so different from anything in his own long experience. And by a supreme paradox, the "great mutation" of France, which he had promoted as the precondition for modern greatness, was leading to an increasingly "mechanical" society—one dominated by economic imperatives, organized along bureaucratic lines, and deprived of the *élan* of individual prowess, poor in opportunities for romantic creation or leadership, and, to many Frenchmen, dull. This may explain why de Gaulle, unlike so many of his supporters, showed some sympathy for the wave of *contestation*. The man who had, albeit in his dutifully patriotic way, sought an escape from the boredom of bourgeois society, could understand a revolt against the tedium of technocratic society. But the hierarchical anonymity of this society also explains why the rebellion broke out.

When it did, de Gaulle's charisma was almost destroyed. This time he had not only failed to foresee a crisis; he had repeatedly and recently celebrated the stability of his ten-year-old regime. What first appeared at stake was not, as in past emergencies, saving France's identity from a threat of dissolution, but appeasing a bewildering variety of grievances, both concrete and vague. The crisis was social, not national, and the ideological flag of the *contestataires* was the class struggle. This was both anathema and unfathomable to de Gaulle; he told Malraux that it was "contrary to what is deepest in me. . . . I want to unite." [151] To many Frenchmen, de Gaulle's own theme—"France must be herself"—now meant that the time had come to do without him. Yet he reacted as he had in earlier crises that attacked his leadership (such as the settlers' revolt in Algiers in January 1960). He waited, to gain perspective, then appealed to the nation to have confidence in him, and asked to be confirmed once more as the lone savior resolving France's distress. He called for a referendum that would give him a mandate for reform. But his appeal fell flat. Delay no longer seemed a strategy but a proof of his helplessness. It seemed as if a majority of the public wanted to be saved *from* him. They had revolted because of his earlier failure to reform, not in order once more to leave "public affairs to the sovereign wisdom of the highest authority." [152] Earlier rebellions against him had been limited; his strength had been his refusal to change course. This time, he offered to change it—a confession of weakness in the present and of error in the past. He did thereby appeal to hope, as he had in 1940 and 1958; but to many, the hope of change was no longer associated with him, or was associated with his fall. He had re-enacted a drama at a time when events no longer fit the conditions in which it could "work." *Les circonstances* being wrong, *le caractère* appeared like "the specter of a ghost, or the ghost of a specter." [153]

This was on May 24. Six days later, charisma was reborn and chaos tamed. The conditions had changed. The government's policy for negotiating an end to the strikes had failed. Anxiety was beginning to replace exaltation and to displace *Schadenfreude*. His antagonists were no longer a huge, anonymous mass of workers and students—i.e., "the people"—but a familiar battery of discarded politicians and labor leaders who at first were just as stunned as he had been, but who now incautiously claimed his succession, which his own fiasco of May 24 had appeared to open. The situation was no longer *insaisissable*. De Gaulle could replay, for the third time, his familiar role. He had always warned that if his own regime were challenged, the result would be anarchy, followed by totalitarianism. By May 30, that prophecy seemed convincing again. There *was* a threat of national dissolution, and he seemed to offer the only way out: once more, the heroic stance —"me or chaos"—rallied the "silent majority." An appeal for personal trust, irrelevant on May 24, worked on May 30. In the intervening days, he had somehow been retransformed from the *Président* of a stumbling regime into a *caractère* alone. Pompidou's tactics had failed, the ministers were in spectacular disarray. Thanks to de Gaulle's grand display of stagecraft—his disappearance, his visit to the French army in Germany, his use of mobility and mystery, and his apt recourse to cunning and the threat of force—the crisis now re-created 1940 and 1958. The leader won, and the historical personage now dictated the script. General de Gaulle would once more play his savior role and be the first French statesman whose regime would not be overthrown either by defeat or by a street revolt. Again, he saved so as to unify. His appeals in June were for both order and change.

But this last, spectacular re-creation of charisma contained the seeds of his final failure. This time, the mess he saved the French from was nevertheless one that had been produced by his own regime. Moreover, on May 30, as in the days of the RPF, he had to appeal primarily to the fears of the people, to their instincts for "law and order." And—at the insistence of his Premier, and in order to wage battle on the most promising ground—he had substituted new legislative elections for the postponed referendum; even though he interpreted the Gaullists' victory as a plebiscite, it reinforced a trend he did not like, reasserting the public's desire for a less charismatic, more "representative" regime.[154]

The months that followed witnessed a growing *malentendu* between the General and his people. He could no longer maintain his newly restored charisma. For one thing, the call to greatness on the world stage had been damaged beyond immediate repair by two major blows. First, the tremendous shock reverberating from the events of May had bared the fragility of French society; and the ensuing crisis of the franc exposed the Achilles' heel of his leadership, bringing back inflation and atavistic reflexes of suspicious prudence and profitable speculation which damaged the currency. This time he was unable to transfuse his self-confidence to his compatriots. He could, in November, "save" the franc alone, as he had saved France in May, but he had to save it *from* the French and by asking new sacrifices of them. His feats were becoming defensive. The second blow, the Soviet invasion of Czechoslovakia, shattered his design: his grand ideal of a reunified Europe at the expense of the superpowers was temporarily smashed.

Another of de Gaulle's strengths—the appeal to memory—was no longer so potent. People tended to be more aggrieved by the troubles of May 1968 than by the mess of ten years before, and Pompidou, dismissed in July but not disinherited, emerged as a reassuring alternative both to de Gaulle and to chaos. And the General's third asset—being a great actor on the stage—was now a liability. The new stage was drastically different, and he looked incongruous on it. Anyway, a charisma based on drama was precisely what the French were tired of.

De Gaulle was faced with a difficult choice. He could change the style of his leadership: re-enter the disenchanted world of normalcy, let charisma wane, stake his political future on institutionalization, de-emphasize the presidential monarchy, and patiently re-create the psychological and economic conditions for a new forward march. But this would have been no more in character than resigning under fire in May. He had served as a healer before, but always by rallying the French for action. He had often temporized, but only as a momentary lull in a strategy of movement. To slow down at the age of seventy-seven, in the second half of his last mandate, was to risk letting the French settle into mediocrity and losing the opportunity offered by the great *secousse*. The man who had written that only vast undertakings could offset France's "ferments of dispersion," and who knew that this was also true of himself, could not shirk his precept and shrink his personage. To act as any ordinary President—bargaining with his own supporters, balancing pressure groups—was self-betrayal.

Concerned with maintaining his work of art, rather than with maximizing his chances for political success, he gambled for the highest stakes and proposed a new national undertaking. He would not *"voir petit dans cette grande affaire."* [155] He would once more attach his leadership to the reforms he deemed essential. He would help the French save themselves from reliance on him alone, but not by dulling his leadership. He would lead them into a new social order, one that would make mechanized civilization bearable, that would be neither communism nor laissez-faire capitalism, and that would be based on "participation," in the universities, in new regional units, in industry. France would be, so to speak, "de-Napoleonized," but in his way: by him, and by becoming exemplary once more, for the new postindustrial order. This last "national ambition" corresponded to the needs of France as he saw them, and to his own need for rekindling charisma. It was not enough to propose reform; he had to stake his political future on its adoption, to ask again for a personal vote of confidence. Having won it, he could then leave soon, having launched salutary measures one last time.

But this appeal did not work. For the first time, a double contradiction appeared between the essence of his statecraft and the demands of the new mission. There was a problem of substance. Previously, he had paid attention to domestic reform because it appeared essential for France's greatness on the world stage. This was again the case, but the priorities were now reversed. Here he was on uncharted territory. The great reforms of 1944–45 had resulted from national unanimity; this time he had to reforge unanimity through reform. Then, daring was logical and timidity would have been divisive; now, *grandeur* in design was important, so as to take advantage of *la secousse,* but caution in detail was necessary, in order not to wound the body politic further. De Gaulle had to be both leader and manager. He was a great crisis leader, but he had never been a good manager.[156] He always acted as the lone embodiment of France. On the world stage, acting *for* the French, he could be brutal and bold; on the domestic stage, acting *on* the French, he could not begin to move until there was sufficient consent (created by shock),[157] and he also had to squeeze his huge frame through the narrow openings of entrenched interests and bureaucratic forts. All these difficulties were apparent in the drafting of the complicated, cumbersome, and confused bill that he submitted to the people on April 27, 1969. He had defined *grandeur* in terms of domestic reform, but his concern for balance made the measure look anything but grand.

Moreover, there was a problem of style. There was an inherent contradiction between his imperious (or imperial) style and the very notion of participation. His attempt at reconciliation was to offer participation by fiat, just as he had granted independence to Algeria. But his insistence on keeping the last word and power of execution to *l'État* emptied university and regional autonomy of much of their substance.

There was also a contradiction between "participation" and the habits and desires of the French. A nation caught for centuries in the vise of authority relations that were fundamentally nonparticipatory, knowing no middle ground between dictates from above and resistance from below, could learn the compromises of face-to-face relations only through patient institution-building and experimentation. After the shock of May, however, "the convulsions of the serpent of chaos" [158] reduced the chances of early success. The rebels of May were not interested in his balanced schemes. They wanted apocalyptic change or permanent *contestation.* De Gaulle's supporters of June wanted peace and quiet. *La secousse* of May had been strong enough to loosen his grip on them in the beginning, yet despite his hopes, and thanks in part to his own mastery, it was not strong enough to "open their eyes."

Thus, instead of a new fusion, there was a falling out between de Gaulle and the French. He disappointed those who wanted tranquillity and those who wanted not merely greatness in conception, but also boldness in execution. The doubts the French had about de Gaulle's reform bill—which appeared unsettling to some, minuscule to others, irrelevant to many—were compounded by the style in which he acted: somehow, the substance was not familiar enough, or not enough in character; the style was all too familiar, all too much in character. It was not in this way—on this ground, and by repeating the homage of their personal loyalty—that they wanted him to teach them to reform. Many who might still have been mobilized by his appeal were reluctant to follow him; many who were only too eager to participate refused to do so at the General's command.

De Gaulle's artistry may not have been at its best in the shaping of the measure on which he staked his leadership: the political leader chose to wage his customary battle on dubious ground. He was, however, as usual, more concerned with style than with substance, more with the long run than with the issue at hand, and above all with his image in history. The reform itself, for all its mediocrity, bore his mark. He was reviving the past to make it serve the future—by restoring France's provinces as regions for modern economic development. He was rallying and defying—by inviting interest groups to participate in decision-making (instead of bringing pressure to bear on it as outsiders), and by challenging hosts of local and professional *notables*. But he had higher goals. If he won, his charisma would be reaffirmed. He could draw on it to overcome obstacles to further reform; he could bring his association with his people to a quiet end on his own terms. If he lost, he would at least save *le caractère* from attrition, as in 1946, and from the possible shipwreck of old age—he would exit on behalf of a grand cause. The coldness and detachment that observers noticed in his last appeals must have reflected his discomfort with the battleground imposed by circumstances, his sense that the outside warmth he needed—the support of his people—was waning, and his greater concern with his artist's work than with winning.

Unless there could be dramatic proof to the contrary, the time had come again to "leave things before they leave me." If de Gaulle could not end in the quiet glory of a savior in harmony with his people, or in the tragedy of assassination in the service of his country, if the choice was between a mediocre, endless last act—wasted on managing a damaged *status quo* or on introducing reforms in the way of ordinary politicians—and the "exemplary misfortune" of public repudiation, he would prefer the latter as far better for the historic personage. For it would, as in the 1930s, as in 1966, as in the days of the RPF, read as a French failure, not as his own. He would stand in history as the man who, for the last time, had "been himself" in trying to guide his people *ad augusta* (albeit *per angusta*) at a moment when they wanted to stay put.[159] The end of his political leadership would come at a time chosen by him, and in his style. It was the French who were flunking their test, for the test being lost was—in his terms—that of France's will to greatness. It was symbolic that they refused to follow him on a march "to the heights" of social cooperation along a narrow path between extreme solutions. It was also symbolic that the specific issue of his downfall concerned the attempt to loosen the hold of centralized, anonymous bureaucracy. As in 1945, he would rather appear as the only true revolutionary than sink into the marsh of *immobilisme.*

There was a risk that he would thus preserve the integrity of the leader only at the cost of a debacle of some of his main achievements. His stature in history would then have been as badly hurt as if the leader had lost his grip not merely on his people but on himself. This did not happen. He made his mark by leaving in time. His last re-enactment of his old threat—"if you desert me, you will have chaos"— failed to work its magic, precisely because there *was* a chance for orderly succession. By resigning with immense dignity, he consolidated the achievement dearest to him—the regime. He provided France with her first smooth transition from charisma to normalcy. He got in defeat what he had failed to gain in triumph, and what might have eluded him had he tried to hang on until the end of his term [160]—a consensus around the Constitution of the Fifth Republic. Winning the elections of 1968 had weakened Presidential supremacy; losing the referendum of 1969 consolidated it (perhaps only for a while, but should this supremacy perish later, it would be because his successors had wasted the inheritance he had left them). He succeeded in giving his tarnished charisma that sunset glow of final defeat, so much appreciated by the French ever since Vercingétorix, Louis XIV, and Napoleon, and in leaving behind him institutions that the people promptly entrusted to his own disciples.

The political leader was dead. True, the French killed him when *they* judged that his re-enactment of his missionary role had become "incongruous" or "irrelevant." But the artist had not become "the prisoner of the public figure." [161] He submitted the political leader to Russian roulette, not out of mechanical habit but in order to determine whether his people were still willing to accept from him the only kind of leadership that allowed him to "be himself." Playing any other role would have betrayed the work of art. *Le caractère* was badly fitted for the kind of delicate reshaping that an old society needed. He could undertake it only if it were done in his style, as part of a new *grande querelle;* and he was not at all fitted for the kind of undramatic tinkering to which most Frenchmen now aspired. De Gaulle would not let his rule outlive his charisma. Even if the circumstances were no longer so grand, the exit was in style. In his last act as a leader he preserved his self-respect by committing himself to his cause, and the self-respect of his people by submitting himself to their will. Therefore, the work of art endured.

The dialogue between the private person and the historical personage persisted. Rejected by the French, de Gaulle, once more, "rather than letting his private self take over . . . remained his public person" —not this time "in waiting" for new leadership, but in writing, shaping his image the way he wanted it remembered. Whatever regrets he must have felt about losing the opportunity to repair the damage his internal and external policies incurred in 1968, whatever misgivings he may have had about the text of the reform rejected in 1969, he immediately went about transforming the story of the political leader of recent years so as to make it exemplary and magnify the impact of General de Gaulle in years to come. Only thereby could the artist reconcile the demands of an undoubtedly bruised ego and the demands of the historical personage. This last act of self-transcendence required what had served him so well in his political career: irony, detachment, perspective. The silence he imposed on himself concerning current affairs facilitated and testified to such detachment. It also raised the prestige of the historical personage: the political leader had ruled with the aura of the spoken word, the historical figure still inspired awe by a combination of silence about the present and eloquent, abundant publications about the past aimed at the future (a combination which, incidentally, allowed General de Gaulle to preserve some influence on the political leaders of the day).

De Gaulle's final place in French history is not yet clear. In the end, his stature will be measured not simply by what he did to improve that of France or by the way he came and left, but by his greatest contribution: the creation of General de Gaulle, the embodiment of a great style of French leadership, the figure who mobilized old cultural values, ancient traits of "national character," France's language, literature, and philosophy to protect France's integrity and renew France's *grandeur.* The artist, in his own quest for *grandeur,* died making history by writing it—first, the new unfinished memoirs; last, the script of his own funeral, in his village, amidst his *compagnons* and the common people, away from the pomp of officialdom—French elites and foreign dignitaries. The ultimate measure of de Gaulle as a political artist thus lay where, as a child, his artistry had begun: in the imaginative re-creation of the past, aimed at leaving a mark on the future.

9

Last Strains and Last Will: De Gaulle's Memoirs of Hope

I

No sooner had General de Gaulle resigned, following his defeat at the referendum of April 27, 1969, than he started writing a new set of memoirs. Even before his defeat—which he seems to have anticipated —he began to prepare the documents he would need in his country home at Colombey-les-Deux-Églises. For the next year and a half, aides brought him the papers he requested. He worked almost uninterruptedly on his manuscript, even during holidays in Ireland and in Spain. His daughter typed his drafts in Colombey. He had planned to write three volumes, of course—there had been three volumes of *War Memoirs,* written during his "years in the desert," and de Gaulle, like all Gaul, was an addict of the threefold division—but only the first volume of these *Memoirs of Hope, Renewal,* was published by the time of his death on November 9, 1970. Their appearance just a month before the General's fatal heart attack was a huge public (if not critical) success. He had written two chapters of the next volume, *Endeavor,* when he died. His family decided to publish them—a decision that was sharply (but I believe wrongly) criticized by some reviewers who pointed out that de Gaulle might have made further changes in the work had he lived.

However interesting the nine completed chapters of the *Memoirs of Hope,* they are but a fragment of the edifice de Gaulle had envisaged. Nothing will ever take the place of the unwritten pages he had planned on the most agitated and in many ways the least known pe-

This essay is based on "Les Mémoires d'espoir," *Esprit,* December 1970; "Les derniers chapitres," *Esprit,* January 1972; "De Gaulle redux," *The New York Review of Books,* February 24, 1972. The sections from *Esprit* were translated by Nancy Roelker and the author.

riod of his "reign" (this seems the natural word to use, did he not himself refer to his "accession?")—i.e., from the "events" of 1968 to the referendum of 1969, which was the test of all the principles and designs of his career. He had wanted the seventh and last chapter of *Endeavor* to be the keystone of the whole construction. At first, he had thought of writing "a chapter of a 'philosophical' nature, in which I shall give my personal view on the situation of France, Europe and the world." Later, he decided he would invent a dialogue between himself and the other great figures of French history—including Joan of Arc, Louis XIV, Napoleon, and Clemenceau—comparing his own situation with theirs. The only indication we have of what this might have sounded like is in André Malraux's book *Les Chênes qu'on abat:* an account of his last meeting with de Gaulle, on a snowy day in December 1969, which includes a lunchtime conversation about Napoleon. (*Les Chênes* did as well with the French public as *Renewal,* and fared much better with the critics.[1])

Is it not fitting that the unfinished work of the President of the Republic, repudiated just as he was tackling a reform of French structures, was followed by an interrupted literary work? After the voice of the people, for de Gaulle "the voice of God," came the *real* voice of God, or Destiny, to use the two words which he so deeply believed in and so often used.

Renewal, the last book Charles de Gaulle had time to finish, presents striking similarities as well as differences with the *War Memoirs.* Referring to his quarrels with Churchill in a speech to the British Parliament in 1960, de Gaulle had said, "See how Time brings out what is important and erases what matters little." Throughout all his *Memoirs* de Gaulle tried to play the role of Time for Frenchmen of today and tomorrow, to identify himself with History right away, just as in his political action he identified himself with France. What de Gaulle tried to do for his own history, death has now done for his book. Things which might have seemed questionable, exaggerated, or falsified if read during his lifetime make a very different impression when read after the disappearance of the author, who from then on belongs to History and whose book really constitutes his last will and testament. To truly comprehend it one must bear in mind that there are in effect three Charles de Gaulles. In his *Antimemoirs,* Malraux spoke of two—the private man and the public personality. But in addition to these there was a third de Gaulle: the historical figure who dominated the other two. The second was the man of action, the third was General de Gaulle the writer. Of course it was the private de Gaulle who created the other two, patiently, over time, nourishing them on his own traits of character. Just as some qualities of the private man, which he considered ill-suited to the mission of "General de Gaulle," had been deliberately repressed or left in the shadows by the statesman (such as his great sensitivity, out of place in a chief of state who "can recognize nothing but reason"), so some imperfections of the "temporal" leader were diminished and some successes enlarged in *Renewal* by the historical personage. In both cases everything is subordinated to his mission: in power, this was "to build the wealth, the power and the greatness of France"; for posterity, it was to create an image of what France could be when Frenchmen were united behind a man who championed France and incarnated the state. It was always a matter of providing France with a recourse, during his active career "in person," and in history "by the example I will have left." This is the common thread of all de Gaulle's *Memoirs*.

Memoirs of statesmen raise questions. Why should one read them? Why do they write them? Sometimes we read them in order to get the insider's view of history, to find out how things looked at the center of decision. Sometimes we read them in order to glimpse the writer's intimate personality—to discover who the man was within the statesman. Memoirs that provide neither are usually dreadful bores, like most of Lyndon Johnson's last opus. De Gaulle's *Memoirs* give one neither, and yet they are fascinating because the General's approach to his task is so different. To be sure, he too wants to vindicate himself. There are no admissions of failure or error (by contrast with his conversation with Malraux); when things go wrong, he usually pins the blame on others; when they work out well, he carefully lists the compliments he was paid. And, to be sure, he sometimes dwells on the resistance and weakness of others (a point to which I shall return), but he does this as a warning and in order to bring out what he had to do to make the true interest of France prevail. For whereas in most other instances memoir-writing is a substitute for action, for de Gaulle it was still a form of action. Needless to say, being in power had its attractions for him, but he did not live for these. His political career had not begun until he was almost fifty. He stayed out of power for twelve and a half years—largely because he refused to make compromises that might have brought him back sooner. His two regimes ended, in effect, in voluntary resignations. Power was just a means. The goal was making one's mark—he had said so as a young officer in his thirties, in that extraordinary anticipatory self-description *The Edge of the Sword*. Throughout his life, he left a scar on history, to use Malraux's old phrase, by political action, in power or in the opposition, and by literary action. One was setting a course; the other was setting an example. One lifted to the plane of statecraft what had been Charles de Gaulle's vocation since early childhood—serving France as a soldier. The other turned into literature what had been de Gaulle's father's vocation—teaching France's history.

As a result, whereas most memoir writers tell us (usually in good faith) what they have convinced *themselves* they did, and address their contemporaries above all, de Gaulle tells us what he wants *us* to think he did, and writes for posterity. He was in a hurry to assemble the record of what he had intended: first, five big volumes of speeches, published in the spring, summer, and fall of 1970; then the *Memoirs of Hope*. He told Malraux that whatever would be tried again some day for France's *grandeur,* would be the direct continuation of what he had done—not of what his successors were doing. It was fitting that a career ruled by will should end with a record of will rather than of facts: "I want there to be a testimony: 'this is what I had wanted, this, and nothing else,'" he told Malraux. Malraux comments that de Gaulle's memoirs are "a Roman simplification of events" that ignore one crucial reality. De Gaulle the tactician usually had "several irons in the fire," from among which he would choose, at the right moment, "the only efficient weapon." When de Gaulle wrote his memoirs, he left out, as much as possible, the unused irons and discarded tactics: they were the domain of the temporal leader, whereas the memoirs' purpose was to shape the historical personage, to state his strategy, to eliminate whatever was not, as Malraux puts it, "a tragedy with two characters: the French and himself," and with France as their stake.

This means, of course, that there is no point at all in looking for details, revelations, and confidences—there are none—or pointing out major inaccuracies (usually in the form of omissions). De Gaulle's *War Memoirs,* whatever their distortions, had far greater informative value, since the French, on the whole, had not known what had gone on between de Gaulle and the Allies in London and Algiers. But the events of 1958–63 are well known and were publicly discussed by de Gaulle during his far from silent Presidency. Indeed, he quotes liberally from his speeches of the period. His own doubts and changes of direction—those of the statesman, not the private man—are passed over in silence, and if he mentions a change of opinion (on Algeria or Germany), it is to show clearly that when circumstances are radically altered, reason dictates obedience to reality. His concern is not to testify but *to provide a model.*

Hence *Renewal* offers an extraordinary presentation of the Algerian tragedy that does not show the actual course of events at all: how the General, working toward a goal (disengagement without sellout) lucidly defined but at first only vaguely conceived, was obliged to revise the conditions offered to the rebel Algerians three or four times, to abandon favorable alternatives because they were unworkable, to increase his concessions in each successive speech, and to accept in the end a settlement close to that already proposed by the FLN leader Abderrahmane Farès as early as June 1958. The two remarkable chapters on the Algerian war in no way bring back to life the uncertainties, the ups and downs, the detours, the smell of blood and the screams of anguish that marked the tragic years 1958–62. They are an impeccable account of clear goals, means deliberately chosen in order to reach them, and calculated maneuvers. To be sure, de Gaulle acknowledges having had no pre-established plan—but this is no surprise, since he spent his life distinguishing between fixed policies (like the Maginot Line), which he condemned, and objectives he aimed to reach through mobility and the creative exploitation of circumstances. He also recognizes that he had to "proceed cautiously from one stage to the next," but he carefully erases the genuine vacillations and reversals that marked his progress toward a negotiated settlement. On the contrary, he paints a picture of inexorable development leading finally to the acceptance by the FLN of essential conditions established by de Gaulle himself. Here, he is trying to teach the French a double lesson: first, that Algerian independence in the framework of the Évian agreements had indeed been the goal sought, because it was in France's national interest; second, that in deciding on this goal, France showed herself mistress of adverse circumstances. De Gaulle's lesson was that one must not fall into the trap of outmoded ideas, nor be thrown off the path to the goal; one must understand that continuing openness to inevitable change and new opportunities, and at the same time unbending determination to keep the initiative, are both indispensable. "It must be France, eternal France, who, alone, from the height of her power, in the name of her principles and in accordance with her interests . . . grants to the Algerians" the right to settle their own fate. In order to transmit that image clearly, de Gaulle carefully chooses the lighting. He makes his speech of September 16, 1959, the hinge of the whole story; he interprets his speech of November 4, 1960, so that it can no longer appear as far removed as it actually was from what issued sixteen months later from Évian. The same determination explains his silence about the positions taken by the RPF on Algeria, his silence about the speed with which the *Communauté* lost its dynamism, and his elliptical and twisted presentation of his Congo policy. Here the message is that France had always supported Patrice Lumumba! The many revisions of the Fouchet Plan for West European cooperation, which contributed to its failure, are not mentioned.

The image has to be pure. Historical truth is subordinated, and sometimes sacrificed, to the didactic ideal. This explains de Gaulle's treatment of his trips to the provinces. At first, one has the impression that he was self-intoxicated as he writes, "When I broke into the Marseillaise, it was invariably taken up by the whole audience," but if we reread it we see that he has not lost his sense of reality (as is shown by his reference to "two discordant episodes"), nor is it exaltation of himself. Once again, he is there as a catalyst and symbol: "Our country thus gave itself spectacular proof of its rediscovered unity. It was moved and heartened by it, and I was filled with joy." What de Gaulle tried to give to Frenchmen for history is a memory of these dazzling but transient rediscoveries of France by herself through him as intermediary—or should one say mediator, or medium? For these were the moments when they had been fully themselves, when they had merged with him and when they had been worthy of France. In all the volumes of the *Memoirs* his eloquence is most moving when he deals with these great spurts of communion. Those of us who have lived through these episodes, as well as the incidents and setbacks that he distorts or blurs, cannot help being annoyed or incredulous, just as the leitmotiv of compliments addressed by others to de Gaulle strikes us as immodest. But for him, writing for the ages, nothing matters but to retain whatever might lift Frenchmen above themselves, "beyond all the ordeals and the obstacles and perhaps beyond the grave," and "arouse the national effort." What matters is to evoke the great enterprises, so that memory of them will remain as a remorse and an inspiration, to remind Frenchmen what a leader can accomplish when his own intelligence and character, as well as the power and support provided by his people, endow him with the means "to give a sense of national aspiration to the whole."

And yet *Renewal* is not quite like the other volumes. The *War Memoirs,* while designed to be exemplary, are still memoirs; *Renewal* reads like a report. The *War Memoirs* make us relive a period of history; *Renewal* reconstructs one. In the *War Memoirs,* the lessons emerge in the telling; in *Renewal,* they are presented analytically. *Renewal* loses in ardor and warmth what it gains in density.

I believe the key to this is given to us at the end of Chapter 1. "By contrast with the task which had fallen to me eighteen years earlier, my mission [in 1958] would be devoid of the stirring imperatives of an heroic period." There are no more giants, no more perils to raise the stakes and lift the spirits. France has lost "her special destiny" of being "constantly in danger." There are now only ordinary men, concerned less with greatness than with "that relative degree of well-being and security which passes for happiness in this world of ours." Except for de Gaulle himself, there is nothing to offset the seductions and the centrifugal claims of vested interests. The modern economy, indispensable for the power of the state, also feeds egotism, careerism, and selfish demands. Something of the essence of de Gaulle's thought is revealed in the following excerpts: "It was in a time which on all sides was drawn toward mediocrity that I must bid for greatness," in "a materially grasping and morally confused society," in "a *Zeitgeist* in which the prevailing winds were those of laxness and mediocrity." Discreetly, because he does not want to indict the French of his own time in the eyes of their posterity, de Gaulle reveals a deep personal wound. He had been a child afire with the ideal of rendering "some outstanding service" to the madonna France, a young man growing up in the era of Péguy and Agathon's *Inquiry on French Youth,* an epic hero of June 18, 1940, and of the Resistance and Liberation; having already once renounced power when those "prevailing winds" of mediocrity began to blow, he was obliged, by a second call, to resume power while they still prevailed. In his eyes—as well as for the French in general—his second reign did not have the simple, grandiose, almost mythical appeal of the war years. Then, it was a matter of resurrection. In 1958, it was at worst a matter of saving the French from tawdry suicide, at best a matter of good management. Reading *Renewal,* remembering de Gaulle's speeches, listening to recordings of his addresses to French and foreign audiences make it obvious that he committed himself, as usual, totally to his task. But he knew that he was swimming against the tide.

This fundamental discord between the crusader with great ambitions and a period resembling that of Louis-Philippe explains many things, beginning with the fact that de Gaulle could never—"being himself"—take pleasure in fully retelling often trivial episodes. The schematic nature of the book is due, not merely to the haste to finish the *Memoirs of Hope* as quickly as possible, but also to de Gaulle's profound belief that the interest of the period lay only in the uses he could make of it and no longer in "the heroic circumstances of the time." But dry analysis gives way to lively anecdote, richer language, and vivid detail when de Gaulle deals with the summit conference of 1960 and his visits to foreign countries or those of foreign statesmen to him. Even though these state occasions "no longer [had] the same dramatic character as of old," they at least took place on the stage of the only theater whose plays always thrilled him, the world stage where war and peace are decided, where greatness and decline are acted out.

The *War Memoirs* are an epic tale in which the author tells of a French resurrection from the forces of death—the Nazi enemy and its accomplices, "sirens of decadence" who were, too often, allies accustomed to a subordinate France, sickened by the French capitulation of 1940, and ill-disposed to see France reassert herself with the haughty arrogance of a de Gaulle. Above all, it was a tale of the triumph of the French people over all sorts of foreign poisons—and over themselves. *Renewal,* on the other hand, tells a story in which the principal obstacles in the General's policy, or rather in the policy of decolonization, were the French themselves, perhaps blind but acting in good faith, and the French Army, whose motives were often noble. To give the Algerian affair the dark intensity it actually had, to paint the crises of

January 1960 and April 1961 with the range of colors they deserve, to celebrate de Gaulle's exceptional triumph over so many determined adversaries, the historic de Gaulle would have had to go far beyond his familiar theme (in *Salvation* as well as in *Renewal*) of the opposition between the French elites and the people. He would have had to show how gravely civil war threatened, remind Frenchmen that the army suffered from a disease much more serious than the disintegration of the state, symptomized in ruthless search-and-destroy operations and in torture. This de Gaulle did not wish to do. The exemplary model for history was not to be the tortuous victory of a man over a considerable portion of his people and over the secular arm of the nation, but rather the righteous (albeit slow) victory of a leader supported by a people and army that were gradually enlightened and raised up by him—a victory once again of Frenchmen over themselves. In *Renewal*, there are, to be sure, many allusions to the obstacles he faced (flabbiness in the civil service, even members of his cabinet), but only among the elite. Many pages are devoted to the difficulties, so as to explain the length of the road he took, but he stays on the surface of "the sea of ignorant fear, shocked surprise, concerted malevolence." The *Putsch* of April 1961 is called "this melancholy conspiracy"—the same phrase de Gaulle had applied to the Dreyfus Affair at the opening of *Call to Honour*. It would not have served his purpose to reveal his own disappointments, miscalculations, and retreats, for this would have tarnished the image of the leader he wanted to leave behind him, and he did not stress that, at several points, only his strength of character kept the French from the abyss of civil war, for that would have sullied the portrait of the French in which he wanted them to recognize themselves. The only thing that mattered, for the record, was the fact that decolonization was accomplished in a way that left France stronger. That he never was in any way the dupe of his own "simplifications," his conversations with Malraux or with his aide Claude Mauriac [2] amply demonstrate.

Thus the genuine triumphs of de Gaulle the statesman are blurred by the historic de Gaulle in the interests of France. The absence of great dangers in a world anxious to avoid war explains a certain grayness in the style of the book, but the dangers of Algeria were certainly comparable to those surmounted fifteen years earlier, and the grayness is also due to de Gaulle's wish to arrange and to some extent spare the image of France, to remain faithful to the mythology of French unity. His notion that this unity cannot be destroyed by inexpiable quarrels, and only ceases to exist when there is no leader or when indifference and mediocrity separate the leader from the people, is very close to Rousseau's notion of the General Will. The great theme of the *War Memoirs* was the ascent of the French people through blood, tears, and fire until the war was won: one can excuse a letdown after the victory. In *Renewal,* the theme is the too-passive and vulnerable good will of the French; exposed to the same "sirens" as in earlier days, most of them are now less inclined to follow de Gaulle to the summit.

Hence, finally, the explanation of the differences in tone between the two books. In the *War Memoirs,* the events he recounts revive de Gaulle's passion, and he shows detachment only toward the accidents, the minor ups and downs. In *Renewal,* he is almost always detached from events; what excites his passion is an irritable urge to reply to his detractors (especially to the press, which is teased and criticized at least twenty times for having always taken the petty view and harmed France by denigrating him). It is also true that "in a sphere in which all is asperity," the economy, "even on the day of an Austerlitz the sun does not emerge to light up the battlefield." There is annoyance and nostalgia in this book—a far cry from the exaltation of the *War Memoirs.* There was more hope in the earlier volumes, written by de Gaulle when he had good reason to believe that destiny would never again call him to save the nation, than in these later chapters, which borrow fine titles from the Scriptures or Péguy or Malraux only in order to mask a kind of disenchanted serenity.

One must return to de Gaulle's over-all purpose. Was it not to show the French of tomorrow that even in a time of mediocrity there had been a way to bring about renewal? That the same course which had assured salvation once had also proved itself in these very different circumstances?

Those who are interested in the General's thought—not his doctrine, a word he disliked—will find no surprises in *Renewal* but confirmation, most importantly of his idea of his own role and of legitimacy. When he received his "silent but imperative" call in 1940, he was bound by a double contract: one imposed on him by "the France of the past, the present and the future," which chose him as the incarnation of "national unity and continuity," independently of and beyond all the "sacred texts." There was also the contract which bound him to the French, without whose support he could not carry out his mission, but in virtue of which he exercised all powers so long as that support existed. The limits to this power were not spelled out in texts but stemmed partly from outside, so to speak, from the people's right to repudiate it; and partly from within, from the obligation laid on de Gaulle by the first contract—to be guided only by the national interest, which includes respect for liberal traditions and the rejection of dictatorship. Within these limits, "my office, as now constituted, was the product of my initiative and the sentiment which existed toward me in the national consciousness." Repudiated, he was still a recourse, still legitimate, even though not exercising his legitimacy. The power of those who are directing the state is only "arithmetically legal" unless they feel, as he did, that "the right and the duty to uphold the national interest [as conceived by him] is intrinsic to [their] very being."

This exalted and romantic idea of legitimacy is an all-consuming conception: de Gaulle saw himself at the same time *Rex* (like the Queen of England, "in relation to whom, by virtue of the principle of legitimacy, everything is ordered") and *Dux*. The mission of this sovereign who also governs is above all to protect France against threats from without and from within. Thus stated, the notion explains his suspicion of supranational organizations and "hegemonies," and also his prudence, even timidity, about drastic changes in domestic social institutions. He did encourage, accept, and apply the austere Rueff Plan against inflation in 1958, but only in order to "lay on the firm foundation" for renewal (and also doubtless because he regretted not having done so in 1945). But when the question of economic and social transformation based on this plan arose, his old fear of exposing the flesh of the motherland to "a terrible surgery" prevailed. In 1945 France was "too weak"; in 1958 there was no catastrophe and it was therefore enough simply to "guide progress." But this should not be mistaken for a protectionist policy. In contrast to most French conservatives but following the example the British have so often set (and which de Gaulle analyzes admirably and admiringly), he wished to renovate; hence the lowering of customs barriers, hence industrialization, and hence decolonization. His aim was to "re-establish France's power, her wealth, and her influence in tune with the spirit of modern times," even if renovation implied the disappearance of many things to which de Gaulle, "being the man [he was]," was personally attached, such as the empire and rural France, of which he spoke in moving terms, but whose preservation at all costs would have condemned France to ruin or to decline.

One can draw from *Renewal* a kind of final statement on the art of governing that fills out the suggestions of the *War Memoirs* and the *Edge of the Sword*. The leader must have an over-all design rather than a specific program, even though he may carry it out only in the right circumstances. For each important part of his task, de Gaulle describes the design and shows its continuity (even if, as in the case of Algeria, it probably lacked this clarity at the start). He does this for the ex-empire, the economy, NATO, Europe, and French institutions. The leader must assume personal responsibility for all the big decisions, and thus give a face to the state, as de Gaulle does for the *Plan* "by proclaiming it my own." Being the embodiment of France, the leader must have integrity, not only in order to resist pressures, but also in order to justify the people's confidence. He who at the age of fifteen praised the use of guile explains, with good reason, that he "had struck many a blow . . . but never at the pride of a people or at the dignity of its leaders," and he repeatedly shows himself hurt by accusations of duplicity. He takes pains to distinguish between the "candor" of his over-all strategy and the hazards of his tactics. What matters about tactics is that they should not compromise the strategy's chances of success; one must therefore remain "master of the moment," "not act in haste," and when resistance is too strong, one must proceed one step at a time, use "each crisis as a springboard for further advance," and create a current of consent "powerful enough to carry all before it." This sheds a precious light not only on the Algerian affair, but on the "events" of May 1968, when his tactics were the same as in January 1960 during the Algiers rebellion. The important thing is to avoid getting mired in details, to concentrate on the essential and the enduring.

There is one subject on which *Renewal* allows one to fill out what was only glimpsed in the General's other works, and that is the personality of the author—rather of the historic personage, the "legendary character" whose "impact resulted not from his accomplishments but from the dreams he embodied and which existed before him," as Malraux puts it. When de Gaulle appears to describe the events he shaped or took part in, he really talks—and intends to talk—about himself: what he wanted and struggled for. (The same is true of most of his portraits of others: the features he praises in his ministers, or in Nehru, or in the Queen of England, or in Churchill in *The Call to Honour,* are his own.) And when he talks about himself, he really reports on a passionate, mystical, and almost (bilaterally) tyrannical affair between himself and France. This is why the "private" de Gaulle —the de Gaulle who lived amid his family, outside that liaison—was ruthlessly left out. When de Gaulle mentions his family, it is only in connection with its own service of France.

Two points stand out sharply. One is what might be called de Gaulle's relation with time. What an extraordinary combination of impatience and patience! Patience to wait—actively—for shocks, to create great designs that will apply to matters "of such scope and range that their solution would be a lengthy undertaking," to advance step by step on ground "in which nothing is once and for all achieved." Impatience with particular situations and contingencies (this is the sphere of the Premier), with men's limited daily concerns. Nobody else fused so well or pushed so far the two somewhat contradictory trends that brought back a sense of duration to the French, after the Kantian and positivistic abstractions of the pedagogues of the Third Republic. All his life this disciple of Bergson scrutinized the future and worked to project France into the vanguard of modern times, to predict coming trends so as to take better advantage of them. And this disciple of Barrès, intimately familiar with the history of France through the teaching of his own father, wanted nothing in the national heritage to be lost. In *Renewal* he speaks of the reappearance of the Franks, of the obligation to aid French Canadians, as Frenchmen, in order to correct "the historic injustice," and even of the need to "cultivate the hardy plant" still to be found in Louisiana. He invites foreign chiefs of state to the Château of Rambouillet and complains of having to live in the Élysée, where "few great events left their mark." Rarely has concern for permanence so well served as an element for identifying a man hungry for immortality with a nation which "remains herself throughout time." Rarely has reverence for the past been so closely related to eagerness for the future. (This is based on a fundamental Gaullist intuition: the creation of the future, if it is not to be a betrayal or a mere groping, must arise from awareness of the past.) Once again, de Gaulle transposed onto the collective level a personal necessity: the maintenance of filial devotion to traditionalist forebears, on the part of someone inclined to action and innovation.

Renewal also enables us to deepen our grasp of de Gaulle's striking mixture of romanticism and classicism—especially in his writing. Classicism dominates his conception of human nature—rather simple and stark, or at least without illusions—his way of seeing interests and passions behind the ideologies that disguise or claim to elevate them. His choice of means is also classical: his conception of the state owes much to Richelieu, Rousseau, and Hegel, not to mention Corneille (very little to Maurras, despite what has been said). But from this classical foundation, which gives him solidity and realism, the romantic takes flight. What could be more romantic than his personalization of his power, which he refused to let become institutionalized, and which he conceived as a mystical union between France (which he imagined, as Michelet had, as personified and ready to carry out "God's work") and her own special knight—and this in the age of sociology and political science? What could be more romantic than the Self which the General constructed for himself? He made his life exceptional by placing it in the service of a great cause and by endowing that cause with the traits of his own character. Richelieu's personality was absorbed by his career as a statesman; Louis XIV certainly left a personal mark on the state, but as a hereditary monarch, he did not have to define a mission that transcended both the state and himself. Napoleon's ambition was his only great cause. The classicist in de Gaulle disciplined his romanticism and enabled him to achieve that great synthesis of Self with Nation which Barrès had sought and which so fascinated Malraux. Yet what could be more romantic than the double image found throughout *Renewal:* that of a nation "naturally humane and historically generous," "champion of Humanity," worthy of "the cause of mankind," changing the rules of the game when she reappears on the world scene and "arousing the attention of the Third World" whenever she "was not afraid to be herself," and that of the old man (the new Moses) whose "mission was always to guide [the nation] upwards, while all the voices below continued to call her down," chosen, once and for all, "to assume [the person] of France" and "take the responsibility for . . . her destiny"? "It meant answering yes to de Gaulle, in whom [the people] put their trust because the future of France was at stake." What "the whole world" expected of France: her destiny, the motherland can demand of Charles de Gaulle, for "what else was I there for?"

Nothing is more significant in respect of this dual image than the portraits with which *Renewal* is studded; Debré, Couve de Murville, Malraux, and Mauriac are praised especially for having had faith in France and in de Gaulle. Whoever honors de Gaulle honors France and at the same time "does much to fortify" de Gaulle in his mission. Nehru may have been "continually disappointed" in his plans "by the magnitude of the task," but once more what counts most in that great man is that "he was unshakable in his faith and unwearying in his efforts."

By giving us the philosophy behind de Gaulle's foreign and domestic policy one last time in compact form, *Renewal* permits us to locate the tensions inherent in de Gaulle's conception, as well as on fundamental problems to which it does not apply. In my opinion, the tensions were accepted, if not overcome, by him. De Gaulle wanted France to serve "the universal cause of human dignity and progress," the causes of peace, of balance, of emancipation of peoples currently subjected to the rival Russian and American hegemonies, and of a Europe united and organized from one end to the other. Given the limits of French resources, this presupposed many efforts at cooperation and association. Yet his desire to disengage France from diplomatic and military constraints that might impair her freedom to act, his long rebellion against "the eagerness to submit the acts of our government" to the authorization of allies—dating, he says, from the Russian alliance in the 1890s—or to "the approval of international institutions" dominated by "the protector"; his distrust of those who "simply confine themselves to 'pleading France's cause'" instead of saying "we want" led him to turn diplomacy into a sort of bloodless battlefield, pushing others toward cooperation by "the grand game" of threats, boycotts, vetoes, and noncooperation. His deep-rooted pessimism—or, if one prefers, his conviction that, no matter what, states follow only their own interests—seemed to justify this highly military method. But even if one believes, as I do, that his concept of Europe was much less chimerical than Jean Monnet's, de Gaulle's strategy did not make things easier. He himself explains that Germany and Britain, in order to participate in the organization of Europe, would have to accept all sorts of impediments that he was not at all inclined to impose on France. A united Europe, field of action for the "primacy" of France, was supposed to function as a sort of fence around Bonn and London. De Gaulle's jealous concern for France's security, leadership, and freedom of action always prevailed over his thoughtful concern for France's association with others—which is why he viewed the Schuman Plan as nothing more than a liquidation of France's assets, thought Schuman and Monnet were only being donors of "gifts" to Germany, and regretted that the Treaty of Versailles had not been harsher.

A second tension, which had provided a main theme for *Salvation,* dominates *Renewal.* On one hand, de Gaulle wishes to gather the French together in *une grande querelle* directed by the government, which is answerable for France. (Economic *dirigisme* therefore seemed perfectly natural to him.) On the other hand, his obsession with unity and *grandeur* leads him constantly to excommunicate "intermediaries," i.e., the political parties, *notables,* the press, and "political, social, and economic interest groups." To him, their only function is to fragment opinion and foster recriminations. He considers them profoundly static, incapable of cooperating "with authority on anything constructive." *Renewal* bears the traces of his unending fight against a "hostile coalition of caucuses and scribblers."

Now, just as the limits on his grand policy of international balance of power and cooperation stemmed from de Gaulle's unbending conception of sovereignty, his hostility to the "ruling groups of yesterday" stemmed not only from their very nature, but also and perhaps primarily from his own conception of political power—a kind of monarchy tempered by plebiscite, which *a priori* renders all agents that intervene between the General Will and its "guide" as so many obstacles. (This includes the judiciary, which de Gaulle accused of meddling in politics as soon as it opposed him.) The Gaullist party is merely "the organization which had been formed to follow me above and beyond all the old parties." And, just as his ambitious foreign policy, which aims at nothing less than a transformation of the international system, would require support from and agreement with others, so his ambitious domestic policy of industrialization, competition, and scientific research requires in the long run the cooperation of intermediaries: leaders of economic and social organizations, local *notables,* bosses of political groups.

On these two points de Gaulle's intransigent Jacobinism has been modified by his successors. (Jean Lacouture called him "the great Jacobin cardinal," but should it not be "monarch"?) Abroad, their style is less belligerent, less sharp. Inside France, a transformation begun under de Gaulle has continued: the Gaullist "army of the faithful" has become a vast school of *notables* sensitive to the least movement of the nation; toward the *notables* of other parties, the policy that ranged from a cold war (described in *Renewal*) to an ill-fated attempt to capture them in a close mesh of social and regional participation has been abandoned, replaced by a major effort to seduce them into associating with the government; i.e., the new leadership has frankly acknowledged their permanence and given them back their prestige. All this has been done without abandoning either the guidelines of the General's foreign policy or the principles of the Constitution. This is a kind of accommodation—perhaps inevitable, since, in Péguy's words, "one cannot keep founding all the time," and since technicians must always come after the apostle.

We shall never know what de Gaulle thought of this.[3] He probably saw it as a dangerous return to the mistakes of the past, to laxity and mediocrity. His anguished call for eternal vigilance against the machinations of foreign states and of *notables* within the French state was not, in his view, merely a personal and therefore ephemeral quirk of character, but rather the expression of a national experience. He could also say to himself, not without pride, that, in any case, nobody could have inherited "what events established long ago as to the nature and extent of my task," and that it was preferable for the impossible legacy to fall to the faithful than to the foes. This overriding fear of a new fall, which led de Gaulle to act so rigorously on the international and domestic fronts, this obsession with decline, explain, to be sure, his suspiciousness of the outside world and his anger with the "country's ruling circles who had opted for decadence." But they explain far more: they are at the basis of the two Jacobin axioms of Gaullism as a method of adapting France "to the genius of modern times."

There is, first, the axiom of the centralized state. A people constantly exposed to the temptations of fragmentation, "contentious and at the same time conservative," can only be held together within the armor of a state which undertakes to carry out or orient all collective activities through the agency of *grands corps* of civil servants. At the end of his "reign"—and before the explosion of May 1968—de Gaulle had realized that it was necessary to call a halt to "the centuries-old drive toward centralization" and to launch various projects of "participation." However, his regional reform, the only actual fruit of this effort, in no way dispensed with the Jacobin corset but only loosened it a little. It offered Frenchmen, who refused, a larger part in the enterprises of the state, just as Kennedy—according to de Gaulle—offered France a larger part in the Atlantic Alliance, which de Gaulle refused.

To be sure, those who believe that the "de-Jacobinization" of the nation—or, in the phrase of the Club Jean Moulin, the "nationalization of the state"—is the condition *sine qua non* of transforming France into a modern society, played almost no part in the rejection of de Gaulle's regional reform, and there was no subsequent reform in the structure of French authority. But the question is: would France have this dual character, at once conservative and defiant, which perpetuates *immobilisme* and made the failure inevitable, if she did not live according to a system which slows down motion and can only change through crisis? De Gaulle, we know, remained respectful of basic French structures. Even if he saw that the intrigues and hostility of the *notables* were by-products of this system, he saw even more clearly that any drastic decentralization would initially deliver the nation to them, and he therefore feared that a deliberate overturning of structures would weaken France. He counted on the double pressure of big quantitative changes "conducted" by the state and of cautious adaptive reforms directed from above, for the eventual adjustment and correction of the traditional structures. But the fundamental question is whether these structures, these authority relations institutionalized in the administrative establishment and in business, are still susceptible of self-improvement, or whether their preservation (even if reformed) does not rather condemn France to the very mediocrity de Gaulle held in horror.

In foreign policy, the Jacobin axiom is that even in a century of superpowers, independence for a middle-size or small state still makes sense. Limited resources may prevent such a state from striking as hard or weighing as heavily as the superpowers, but they in no way keep it from being a modern industrial and military power. And only independence makes influence and ambition still possible. On this point de Gaulle never changed and never appears to have doubted—hence his policy toward atomic energy, computers, exploration of space, the Concorde, and the *force de frappe:* a less-than-great power is nothing but a smaller Great Power. But his partial failures—the penetration of France by so-called multinational companies, as well as the evident inadequacy of purely national enterprises—show rather that a middle-sized power that wants to keep its hands free runs the risk of being left with no hands. It is faced with a hard choice between continuing an independence which cannot achieve *grandeur,* and searching for *grandeur,* for "an undertaking as big as the earth," which requires a Europe infinitely more integrated, economically and politically, than de Gaulle would have tolerated. (This does not necessarily mean a technocratic Europe with a supranational bureaucracy, ambiguous goals of union, and no grand design, which he rightly denounced.) For de Gaulle, however, the choice between independence, as an end in itself and as an indispensable condition, and the great designs for which independence was supposed to be used, was inconceivable. Was the disagreement between him and the elites due only to their resignation to decadence, their old habit of submission, their rejection of "the very idea of national revival"—a sort of generalized Vichyism? Was it not also due to their conviction that the imperatives and ideals dear to the General, though impossible for France alone or even in association with other middle-sized powers, would be quite possible for a new supranational entity?

De Gaulle had made "being oneself" the guiding principle of his own life and that of France, and the harness of discipline was as necessary for mobilizing his own abundant faculties as the framework of the state was for France. There could be no question *either* of remodeling the structures from the ground up *or* of building a supranational Europe. A France with the state dismantled, a France dissolved into a federated Europe, would no longer be France. The same determination to exorcise the demons of doubt, dispersion, disorder, and decline, which made him say repeatedly that a great international enterprise was indispensable for "what the whole world expected of us" and for "the aspiration and self-respect of our own people," made him fear that a nation abandoned to its demons and weaknesses, lacking the strait jacket of the state, drowned in a federation where other, better disciplined or more powerful nations put their own mark on the design, would in fact sign its own death warrant.

De Gaulle's haughty will, which kept the leaders of France and foreign nations from his grave, and the fact that he did not revise it in eighteen years, say more than the *Memoirs* about his strength of faith in this Jacobinism stiffened against decadence. Only those who have not experienced and understood French history in the twentieth century can mock or be surprised by this attitude, which was the General's *raison d'être*. All the struggles of his life were based on a Pascalian gamble: if there was only a small chance for French *grandeur,* that chance must be taken and all actions predicated on its certainty. Because he could not resign himself to decline and because he saw history as a perpetual renewal, a constant redistribution of the cards, de Gaulle believed in teaching by example (in spite of everything) and "never tired of seeking in the shadows the glimmer of hope." And yet—because he had suffered from seeing elites "inclined toward [France's] subordination," because he knew his role was unique, and perhaps, who knows, because he guessed that he had not won his gamble—in his last volume, de Gaulle allows a tired melancholy to seep through his catalogue of the successes he achieved in forty months. The shadows are softened, the "brilliant sun" does not penetrate. Did he perhaps perceive that the gamble was lost because the old structures of France resisted change and because the world resisted French initiatives?

Let nobody, then, reproach the last Jacobin for not being what he could not be, for not having accomplished things that would have had to be based on an entirely different gamble (with equally uncertain chances of success), things that would, at the very least, have presupposed a nation confident, unified, and strong enough to leap into the adventure of internal self-government and European integration. Should this other gamble be attempted tomorrow, it will be because Charles de Gaulle accomplished so much.

II

Never has de Gaulle's style been more compelling, more effortless, and, on occasion, more pithy, than in the two completed chapters of *Endeavor.* The portrait of Pompidou is a masterpiece of deliberate ambiguity, which can be read in as many different ways as there are guesses about the true nature of the General's feelings toward his successor; his description of the transformation of France into an industrial nation pervaded by "the muted anguish of the uprooted" is another passage for the anthologies. And instead of the serene disenchantment of *Renewal,* the chapter in which de Gaulle describes—in full detail this time—his battle over the referendum of October 1962 is full of exhilaration, celebrating the victory of the hero against all parties (the Gaullists are again referred to not as a party or a "faction" but as a group "which had been created to support the policies of General de Gaulle"), and also, as at the time of Liberation, the way he rallied the French around him. Joy at obtaining the people's consent, joy at fulfilling at last the institutional reform that he had been unable to undertake in the days of the RPF and which he could begin only thanks to the Algerian war, illumines the whole chapter. It even succeeds in mellowing the next chapter, even though the second one deals with a series of economic and social troubles between 1962 and 1965.

And the substance is fascinating. As if he had vaguely felt that he would not reach the third volume, de Gaulle filled these chapters, especially the second, with anticipations. He is obviously eager to explain why reform had been so late in coming and had had to wait for "a thunderflash." Was it to himself or to his readers that he wanted to justify and legitimize his caution? He describes France in the process of thorough transformation but barely saved from a series of jolts and shocks, eager for tranquillity and racked by "routine selfishness and sectarianism," ready "to dissolve into innumerable individual anxieties and grievances" because the dangers and the anguish were over. On one hand, in such an "atmosphere of stagnation" the French inclination to divide and to suspect authority, their tendency "to clamor for progress while hoping that everything will remain the same," the way they target complaints on the civil service—all of this revealed the obvious weakness, "sickness, and instability" of France's social structure, especially in the areas of education and local administration. De Gaulle's analysis of its flaws and deficiencies is lucid and devoid of illusions. But, on the other hand, his favorite remedy, his own answer to the traditional defects of the French (to whom "everything, in the political, social, moral, religious, and national spheres, is always totally in dispute," so that no Presidential system imported from America could conceivably work), his way of overcoming the new tendency built up by "mechanized mass existence" (according to which "everyone resented what he lacked more than he appreciated what he had") —participation—was not yet applicable, according to de Gaulle. The climate was not right for it. After Algeria, what was needed, he says, was a period of peace and quiet, a grand effort at adaptation "in calmer seas." But given these obvious flaws of the social structure, given the many tensions created by rising expectations in a centralized and ossified system, how could France be made ready for reform? De Gaulle offers a double reply: first, by enforcing limited reforms that start the country in the right direction; second, by waiting for the event that would provoke consent—for "in politics as in strategy, business, and love, one must of course have the gift; one must also have the opportunity." "No institution can be reformed without its members' consent." The formula is basically true, even though it whitewashes public authority and dismisses all charges of state *immobilisme*. At any rate, this accounts for the differences between constitutional reform, which most French gladly accepted after the shocks of the postwar years, and partial reforms which met with all kinds of resistance. But it raises other important considerations.

The first concerns strategy. How does one wrest consent from the people? De Gaulle talks about thunder and says he was ready to take advantage of the storm "if one day it were to break." But he also says he did not wish it to come. Later, talking of participation, he explains: "Short of having to hammer out this reform in the fire of war or revolution, I would propose it to the people as soon as I had reason to believe that events had made them ready to accept it." But one sees the dilemma and the contradiction. As long as there is no storm, the weather does not favor large-scale reform, but if a storm breaks out, this must be proof of a failure of authority (in a country where everything depends on public initiative). To arrive as a savior after a storm (precipitated by the weakness of a "regime of parties" or by a plot of rebellious generals) is one thing; to use lightning after it has already struck decaying institutions which the "mood" of the public did not allow the government to rescue and renovate in time, is quite another. Implicitly, in the pages devoted to national education, de Gaulle recognizes that he did not sufficiently control opportunities there. But he throws the blame on the "stubborn, passive resistance" of the interests concerned: it would take "a tempestuous wind" to force the French university to reform. At least, in 1968, reform was adopted. But elsewhere, in local government and in business enterprises, the hurricane of 1968, far from bringing consent, only provoked a backlash of conservatism. Attempted acceleration, following slow driving and a nearly fatal crash, resulted in a change of driver, and in lots of brake action.

In 1969, if lightning, far from clearing the road for reform, struck the reformer, it was not simply because de Gaulle's strategy had gone wrong. There was also a substantive problem. The notion of "participation" was as fuzzy as de Gaulle's ideas on constitutional matters were clear-cut. What he had in mind, he writes, was "a change in the moral climate which would make man a responsible being instead of a mere tool." But morality is one thing and politics another. Politically, this "change in the moral climate" ran into enormous obstacles. First, organizing the economy "in such a way that each man would be a partner as well as an employee," turning "those who by their toil produce the wealth of the nation" into "responsible" human beings, supposes not only a total change in the behavior of French businessmen but also and above all a willingness of the workers to recognize the legitimacy of an economy based on profit. Second, how can one reconcile participation with *dirigisme,* an increase in the powers of cities and regions with the reinforcement of state authority, the autonomy of universities with the leading role of the state that "rightly has taken on the responsibility of teaching the young"? Either "the peaceful revolution of participation" was a true revolution—but then, what would be left of the economy of the bosses (businessmen in private enterprises, state managers in public enterprises), and what would be left of the Jacobin strait jacket? Or else, what would be left of participation; how would it differ from the traditional behavior of the French whenever they are allowed to express themselves but not take on responsibilities—i.e., protest? De Gaulle writes that the labor unions devoted themselves entirely to grievances "because they took no part in the studies and debates from which decisions stemmed." But, as French parliamentary institutions have shown at every level, mere participation in discussions is an incentive to demagogic escalation so long as final decisions are someone else's monopoly.

Endeavor does not give answers to these questions, but the elements of an answer are provided in some pages in the book and in de Gaulle's conversations with Malraux. To begin with, there is de Gaulle's nostalgia and search for consensus. What participation meant to him above all was the recovery of harmony, a return to the precious and privileged condition in which, above and beyond all conflicts of interests or clans, citizens agree on the fundamental principles of the body politic. It is not by chance that de Gaulle praises the *Social Contract* to Malraux. In *Endeavor,* his tribute to the public service of national education brings us back to the great epoch of Republican proselytism. When Malraux reminds him of how often he had been in the minority, de Gaulle replies, "I knew that sooner or later I would no longer be." In this mighty but clouded myth of participation, the desire to extend to all the French the family harmony in which he had been raised merges with a wish to recapture those great moments of fervor—the summer of 1914 and the summer of 1944. Participation is one of those chimeras without which, he says to Malraux, nothing great can be undertaken.

Let us assume that consensus was re-created, that divisive or "separatist" ideologies were blown away, that the concern for the national interest prevailed, that modernization for power was accepted as the great national design. In such an idyllic state, it would be easy to reconcile autonomy of the parts with direction by the state, participation of workers in management with the authority of the business heads. Alas, this presupposes that the problem has been solved. The real tragedy of the General, about which he laments discreetly in *Memoirs of Hope* (discreetly, because in the mind of this democratic monarch, even though France transcends the French, she does not exist without them, and there is therefore no question of indicting them) and against which he rails much more bitterly in front of Malraux (as he had many years before in front of Claude Mauriac), is the burden of having to carry the destiny of France during an eclipse of consensus, when even a great statesman can only administer and orate. Participation was the contemporary form of the social contract—what the Republic had been for France in the 1880s, *revanche* in 1914, the Liberation in 1944. The failure of the 1969 referendum thus broke this "contract with France" de Gaulle had mentioned to Malraux, not only because it proved that the French were no longer with him but above all because in his mind their "no" meant that they no longer believed in France and preferred their own divisive and destructive chimeras to her. As Malraux puts it, for de Gaulle the agony of France came from her "incapacity to believe."

If the concrete substance of participation remains vague, it is also because, like *grandeur,* it is a moral attitude rather than a code, a will to master France's destiny in the world. No form of government can cure the "spiritual sickness" of industrial civilization, but the reform of participation would at least mean a return to enthusiasm, hope, and exaltation; it would prove France's vitality. How familiar is this appeal for unity and *grandeur:* "What else have I myself ever been but someone endeavoring to teach?" If participation means not merely a plan for social justice but also the rally of the French for France, de Gaulle's final failure is even more tragic. But it was clear that in his view it was only the fault of the French; as for him, he told Malraux, "I gave back to France what she had given me." And the very importance he gave to his grand design shows his belief that the future might vindicate him—even if for the time being the French, as he told Malraux, "chose cancer."

III

Was de Gaulle's disappointment with his own time, a period in which "the immediate issue was not victory or annihilation but living standards," even deeper than he lets on in his own books? Malraux, in his so-called *reportage,* describes a gloomy hero who believes that the French had no more "national ambition," that he had only "amused them with flags," that Europe was dead and France threatened with death as a result, that he had "tried to raise France against the death of a world," that Christian civilization was now replaced by a dubious "faithless civilization." Some who worked closely with de Gaulle tend to think that Malraux, in his attempt to turn de Gaulle into a legend and stress the mythic aspects of his personage, made him sound too much like King Lear—or like a character in a Malraux novel. While de Gaulle had his moments of doubt and his premonitions of doom, he also was convinced that France would resume her march sooner or later, and that "real democracy is in front of us, not behind us: it has to be invented." Even Malraux does not leave out references to hope. But he does more than amplify the gusts of Gaullist pessimism on the desolate landscape of Colombey. He presents a man haunted by the thought of death, a man who seems rather different from the real de Gaulle. De Gaulle worried, of course, that death would interrupt his task, but he seems to have accepted it as a natural final point at the end of a well-filled life. Metaphysical anguish was not de Gaulle's style. Malraux the agnostic is bothered by de Gaulle's Christian faith, while remaining lucid and truthful enough to admit that the General's faith, like his France, was "a given, not a question." But de Gaulle, who discussed France, never talked about his religion. (He remarked to Malraux that nothing Caesar wrote tells us anything about *his* beliefs.) Malraux suggests that the General's faith "was so deep as to ignore any realm that would challenge it." How de Gaulle reconciled it in his own mind with his statecraft, we shall probably never know.

What, indeed, do we know about the most intimate de Gaulle—not the public personage, but the man who invented and became him? "It was part of my nature and a precept of my office invariably to keep my distance" (*"de ne me point livrer,"* reads the French text). Therefore, it is not surprising if those close to him tended either to project their own personality onto his, or to feel that they never acceded to his deepest self. Malraux, thirty years after the first appearance of this theme in *The Edge of the Sword,* comments that one tries in vain to "describe de Gaulle through psychology." Yet, whatever the digressions and distortions, Malraux gives us some of the best keys to understanding Charles de Gaulle. To be sure, there is a whole classical (or Roman) side of de Gaulle that came out of the education he received and out of the discipline of the army: personal austerity as well as the practice of *raison d'État,* a profound awareness of people's limits as well as a solemn, Latinate style, a total immersion in French history as well as a determination to play whatever card the French may have left somewhere in their past—be it in Louisiana! But it is the other side of de Gaulle that Malraux best reveals, not only because of his own romanticism but because it was the most enticing—it was the side that attracted Malraux and kept him fascinated for over a quarter of a century. Maybe the best way to describe it is as de Gaulle's will to (not just yearning for) transcendence. If, as Malraux suggests, there is in de Gaulle a "secret domain" which is neither that of Cincinnatus nor Washington's nor that of the great solitary religious figures, a domain whose supreme value is *refusal,* then, above all, what de Gaulle said "no" to all his life—like Malraux's heroes, or Nietzsche—is mediocrity, anonymity, and *le quotidien.* Life, he tells Malraux, does not mean "carrying one's suitcases" until death comes—it consists of freeing oneself from them. De Gaulle's horror of the fleeting and of the banal, which seems to echo Rimbaud, is not Malraux's invention. After all, de Gaulle described Malraux as "this inspired friend, this devotee of lofty destinies," who, by being "at my side . . . gave me a sense of being insured against the commonplace." His ambition was to escape from the ordinary, from the bureaucratic and mechanical routines of humdrum modern life, to stay alive in the memory of men, to be "a ferment, a seed," a carrier of hope (for "in the individual the end of hope is the beginning of death"). It was less a matter of defying death than of rising above it: by being an inspiration for action now and later and also by being—like those writers whose books he kept in his library—the author of deeds (political as well as literary) that "prevail over death." As a *mystique,* he had a thirst for eternity; he wanted to be a myth, because "nothing great is done without one." But as a *politique* he wanted the myth to take roots, like the trees of Colombey. For himself and for France—did he ever distinguish between the two?—the highest goal was to endure. To such a man, by contrast with Camus, transcendence meant the will to greatness, not the quest of "that relative degree of well-being and security which passes for happiness in this world of ours." Happiness was an illusion—or an-

other name for the commonplace. This intuition was already expressed in *The Edge of the Sword,* even before the birth of de Gaulle's
retarded child, on whom he lavished such deep and fiercely guarded
affection.

De Gaulle's cult of ambition and energy could have led him into
personal adventurism, like that of Malraux's early characters or like
Napoleon, whose hunger for *grandeur* de Gaulle admired but who, he
thought, had conceived his destiny as merely "that of an extraordinary
individual." What saved de Gaulle from this temptation was his "vocation of France." Was this vocation itself, perhaps, a transposition, a
way of both transcending and remaining loyal to his very close and
tight-knit family? It was not glory, it was a *cause* he sought. Individual
adventure would be a mere escape from mediocrity. De Gaulle's ambition was higher: he had to move and mold others on behalf of an
ideal that transcended him too. True *grandeur* was determined by
"the level of confrontation"; real transcendence meant "historical action," which entails "taking on, and sharing, the deepest passions or
the distress of many men." He carved, says Malraux with lapidary bril-
liance, "a solitude where he would not be alone"—isolation, which he
needed in order to think as well as to feel apart from "the commonplace," and community, especially in sorrow and anguish. Again, Malraux stresses the tragic side of de Gaulle's love for France. But there is
no doubt that it was in moments of national disaster—the war years,
May 1958, even the end of May 1968—that he achieved the communion he sought, and there is no doubt that those tragic colors were
worn by a man who had been brought up waiting for *revanche* in a
conflict-ridden nation, who spent half of World War I raging and
wasting in German prison camps, and who later witnessed his country
sinking into decline and sterility. By putting on the armor of knight-
errant for France, de Gaulle fulfilled himself. He also protected her,
for he had dedicated himself not only to rescuing her from distress,
but also to dispelling those clouds and mists—ideologies and other
"isms"—which, he thought, "destroyed her reality," and, above all, to
rallying the French.

Perhaps what attracted so many Frenchmen so often or so long to
this strange, impenetrable man, whose style of action and policies
could not fail to divide those whom he passionately wanted to unite,
and whose private shyness was matched by his public showmanship,
was something they vaguely sensed behind all these defenses and contradictions: a soul. According to Malraux, de Gaulle wondered
whether Saint Bernard—a neighbor across the ages, since Clairvaux is
close to Colombey—had had a heart, and de Gaulle said that Napoleon "had not had the time" to have a soul. The General had had
ample time, and a long record of encounters with private and public

grief. They had taught him that "sin is not interesting. The only ethic is that which drives man toward what is greatest in him. . . . Man is not made to be guilty." How far from Sartre's universe! There have undoubtedly been greater statesmen who have accomplished more, or whose visions and dreams far exceeded the confines of their nation. But has there ever been one who combined his culture's tensions more richly, or brought to a higher point its dominant features: passionate affirmation of the nation, seen and loved as a person, and an equally fervent rejection of humiliation, guilt, decline, drabness, indeed all forms of servitude; constant craving for action and responsibility, but also need for contemplation, isolation, and retreat; robust optimism, bursts of pessimism, and Christian faith. De Gaulle inscribed a French ambassador's copy of Volume III of the *War Memoirs,* on June 18, 1969, in Ireland: "Nothing is worth anything, nothing happens, and yet everything comes, but it does not matter" (Nietzsche). Beneath that quotation he added another one from Saint Augustine: "You who shall have known me in this book, pray for me!"

Will this reader of Chateaubriand—last of the classicists or first of the romantics—still make sense for the twenty-first-century man? From one point of view, classicists and romantics have so much in common, and it is so little like what the future may be: respect for traditions (even if they are not the same ones), a zest for spiritual concerns, an appreciation of history, the ability to be moved by great causes, the predominance of passion over calculation, a certain lofty cult of prowess, a sense of honor and glory. But, when de Gaulle, who presents and resents the agglomerate, mechanical, uniform, bureaucratic society from which stems that "voiceless anguish of the uprooted," invokes participation as the remedy and liberty as the ideal, or when he in fact offers his own epic story in order to show that fate can be mastered, he certainly believes it, but is he right? Tomorrow, in societies liberated from the scourge of large-scale wars and poverty, but driven by the pursuit of profit (individual or collective), by the troubles of growth, or by the ever more demanding imperatives of science and technology, will the values and the history of centuries marked by war and scarcity signify anything at all? Will anyone understand why men spilled so much blood?

A certain technocratic materialism, at best capable of organizing or rationalizing modern society, assumes that the prescientific era, in which rival nations and classes tore each other apart, in which *grandeur* was defined in terms of heroism—in other words, combat—was radically bad and must be superseded. And if de Gaulle rejected with so much fury the anonymous blend which supranationality seemed to entail for Europe, was it not partly because he held in horror that universe without borders, with uniform patterns of behavior, with forgotten traditions, which is already anticipated by the huge multinational enterprises, by calculations on return profit, by advertising companies and mass culture, and by the bargaining politicians whose horizons do not extend beyond the interests of their clients, or by the expertise of high civil servants whose supreme ambition is good management? Auguste Comte had opposed the industrial era and the military era. Will the culture of the first, based on applied science and computers, have anything in common with the culture of the second, common to Plutarch and to Michelet, to Plato and to Malraux? Or else, if de Gaulle was right, if the dream of technocracy were nothing but another illusion, and if the history of humanity were to remain that of conflict and antagonistic passions, will humanity disappear, victimized by a science and an industry placed at the service of old idols? Between spiritual poverty and enslavement to the challenged imperatives of the modern economy, and nuclear destruction, the future looks unreceptive to the lessons of Charles de Gaulle—unless statesmen will understand them, and find a way of avoiding both fates.

Whatever the future of his lessons, de Gaulle's prestige at present is intact. Since his death, his only implacable foes remain the ex-Vichyites or collaborationists who never forgave him for June 1940. The feelings of the others—even on the Left—range from grudging nostalgia to belated gratitude to continuing fervor. To him belongs credit for having given a solid foundation to the "European Europe" in the West, in place of a crucible of confusions; for having defined the only workable policy for eventual reunification of the continent; for having transformed the disaster of decolonization into a process which has made France stronger and better able to maintain ties with her former colonies; for having labored to replace domination by association everywhere; for having tried to reconcile respect for national integrity with the maintenance of the balance of power; for having re-established French unity without giving in to demands for vengeance; for having given France a modern, disciplined army; for having grasped the importance of economic transformation; and for having—at last— provided France with political institutions which are stable, legitimate, and capable of action. His is the glory of having fought not for glory but for *grandeur*. His is the greatness of having left France greater than he found her, and of all his life having produced extraordinary results from mediocre resources. He saved his country's honor and restored its self-respect, nourished the pride of Frenchmen with his achievements, acted in the interest of other nations' liberty as for his own, and fought for peace. Of what other statesman in the history of France can one say as much? He had time only to recount the heroic and tragic phases of his career: World War II, the Algerian war. After the departure of the statesman—dignified but disconcerting—the historic personage, anxious like Augustus "to depart life in style," succeeded beyond all expectation. He gave the French the chance to discover and display all they owed to him. He may have often manipulated and sometimes disappointed them, but he never deceived them, humiliated them, or inflicted unnecessary suffering on them. He left to the French of tomorrow a final testimony of his greatness as a writer and of his idea of France. Surrounded though he was at death by the gratitude of his people, the admiration of the world, and the "family harmony" he held so dear, one still cannot help thinking of him as a great Solitary, as in the poem "Le Jeu du Seul" by La Tour du Pin:

> Comprends-moi: j'ai soif de la gloire
> Avec la gorge amère des adolescents
> Quand ils prennent leur grand vol doré sur l'histoire
>
> D'un seul claquement de cœur!
> Car c'est la gloire en moi qui tressaille et qui vibre,
> Elle que je maintiens pour en jouir plus longtemps,
>
> Et moi qui suis patient, comme elle sera libre,
> Quand nous aurons notre hauteur. . . .
>
> Tu frémis de la folie d'un tel vol. . . .
> Regarde-moi . . . ai-je l'air de mentir?
> Car nous manquons de sang, je hais ce qui s'étiole
> De grandeur, je hais aussi ce qui s'enflamme
> Et renonce, n'ayant pas d'altitude au cœur. . . .*

---

* Understand me: I thirst for glory
With the bitter throat of adolescents
When they take their bold golden flight over history

With a single flapping of their hearts!
For it is glory in me which quivers and vibrates,
Glory which I preserve in order to enjoy it longer

And I who am patient, how free it shall be
Once we reach our full height. . . .

You shudder at the madness of such a flight. . . .
Look at me . . . do I look like a liar?
For we are poor in blood, I hate the wilting
Of grandeur, I also hate whatever catches fire
And gives up, for lack of altitude in its heart. . . .

IV
The Nation in the World

10

De Gaulle's Foreign Policy: The Stage and the Play, the Power and the Glory

The sound and the fury that raged around de Gaulle's foreign policy after his return to power in 1958 often made his action seem like a wild tale signifying nothing. And yet the purpose of his statecraft was never in doubt. He had an unalterable set of imperatives and a clear design. The imperative was to renew France's substance and power, to restore her influence abroad, and to have her play as independent and active a role on the world stage as the world and French resources allowed. This Gaullist vision in 1958 was no longer what it had been in 1945, or in the days of the RPF. The world had changed, and so had France.

I

Before discussing de Gaulle's own vision of France, and as a way of clarifying it, it is useful to discard many of the misinterpretations that have flourished in France and elsewhere about it.

De Gaulle was never foolish enough to confuse national independence with self-sufficiency or with a total absence of commitments or ties to other nations. His argument was, rather: never to accept bonds that cannot be removed and that might submit your nation's fate to the decisions of others long after the ties are no longer in your interest. What Arnold Wolfers has called self-abnegation [1] was to be ruled out, but certainly not intense cooperation and exchanges with others. A number of analysts have commented on the Napoleonic overtones of de Gaulle's foreign policy—sometimes it was even compared to that of Louis XIV—but in its inspiration the General's thought was at least equally derived from the Jacobin tradition.

This essay includes fragments from "De Gaulle, Europe and the Atlantic Alliance," *International Organization*, Winter 1964.

To any Frenchman who had lived through the humiliating years of the 1930s and 1940s—years of decline, then of occupation, followed by dependence and colonial disasters—this jealous concern for national sovereignty was understandable. It indicated de Gaulle's desire, in a nation which had been for a very long time a great power, to revive the sense of being master of its own destiny as far as was still possible. It reflected de Gaulle's sense of the need to restore self-respect, which France had lost during her long ordeal. In proportion as a nation's freedom of action is reduced, national pride, the vital spring of action, can be sustained only if the rulers make up in intensity what has had to be abandoned in scope. Also, the habit of dependence grows bit by bit: if a nation first becomes accustomed to relying on another nation for some of its essential needs, it risks becoming incapable of freeing itself, especially since dependence on allied and friendly powers is rarely irksome enough to precipitate firm resistance.

The same dislike of alienating one's fate explains de Gaulle's hostility to supranational integration, in Western Europe or within the Atlantic Alliance. In his view, either the supranational process concealed the final authority of one specific foreign power (the United States in NATO) or (in the hands of civil servants without political sense or responsibility) it risked creating a vacuum of will and a confusion of purposes that would benefit the most powerful manipulator or, at best, deprive the nation of control over policies and resources. On the other hand, de Gaulle, despite multiple threats and one boycott, never tried to disrupt the functioning of the Common Market, insofar as its joint policies had been decided by the member governments and thus embodied joint interests. In 1965–66, a common agricultural policy continued with French cooperation; in 1968, after the May crisis, France's resort to the safeguards provided by the Treaty of Rome for members in trouble was limited in scope and time.[2] Indeed, many of the common policies that do inextricably entangle the various West European economies were negotiated under French pressure.

To be sure, one can argue that de Gaulle was merely bowing to necessity—economic interdependence among industrial nations—and was actually trying to limit its effect,[3] but this is too sweeping an assertion. De Gaulle may have been suspicious of "transnational structures" that escape the control of national governments (or at least the French one) or express, in fact, the dominance of a foreign economic power; but he did favor various kinds of transnational exchanges (for instance in Franco-German relations), and he did not curtail cooperative policies among partners in the realm of economic and monetary affairs—again, so long as there was no risk of one nation being dominated by a bigger one. Recognizing a necessity and manipulating it so as to promote one's national interests is very different from denying it. De

Gaulle did not belong to the camp that believes that the economic concerns of modern citizens gradually replace and erode the old concerns of states—security, prestige, control, etc. But he was shrewd enough to realize that when economic issues are essential, the decisions to be made about them are *ipso facto* political, i.e., of vital concern to states.[4] Far from being unaware of the new forms of power, of being tied to the old chessboard of diplomacy and strategy, that lifelong worrier about the machine age realized that technology, the currency, the strength of the economy were essential arenas for the competition of states. What he denied was the equation of interdependence with harmony.

A second charge—of anachronism—focuses not on de Gaulle's constant stress on independence but on his vision of the ideal world order. This was not simply a return to the European order and the balance-of-power system of the eighteenth and nineteenth centuries. Here, as elsewhere, de Gaulle wanted to renovate, not resuscitate, old forms and notions that had proven beneficial both to France and to moderation. He believed that a multipolar world would be less unstable and less onerous for smaller powers—more respectful of their freedom of maneuver—than a bipolar one. He believed in moderation, maintained through balance-of-power policies and through maneuvers forcing the overly powerful to curb expansion or to give up his power, rather than through trans- or international agencies, which he considered to be mere festive forums in which the old game was pursued in decorous disguise, or traps for the unwary, or excuses for the meek and cowardly. To him as to Frederick the Great or Richelieu, Pitt or Bismarck, the way to get someone to do what one wanted was either to make a deal, if there existed the makings of a balanced bargain, or to put the other in so uncomfortable a position that he would have to give in. He did not have expectations of a world of pure democracy, with small powers counting as much as the big ones, or a world government of any sort. He did not believe in permanent alignments, or in the suppression of cabinet diplomacy by collective security or parliamentary diplomacy. Wilson's dream was a delusion in his eyes, and Roosevelt's rhetoric a disguise for hegemony. In these respects, he was indeed a classical European.

On the other hand, he seemed well enough aware of the differences between balance-of-power politics in the nuclear age and in pre-Hiroshima days. First, the use of force as a means of preventing or curbing hegemonial ambitions—the traditional device of balance-of-power systems—was now too risky: equivalents had to be found in the form of threats and crises. Second, the nuclear stalemate between the superpowers actually reduced their maneuverability and gave increased chances to middle powers. Third, the gap in actual might between middle powers and superpowers—or, to be precise, the gap in the *in-gredients* of power and in *usable* might—remained enormous, how-ever much the superpowers' achievements might be reduced or twisted in the direction of mutual denials rather than gains; [5] therefore, there was no chance for a state like France by herself to become a "third Great Power": only a European entity could. Fourth, France's own balancing policy had for centuries been aimed at keeping Germany di-vided and weak; France's alliances since 1871 had been designed pri-marily to provide security from Germany. De Gaulle, after 1944, had pursued the same policy out of fear of a German *revanche*. But after 1958, seeing Germany divided into two states and Europe as a whole dominated by Russia and the United States, he endorsed his Fourth Republic predecessors' post-1950 policy of reconciliation and even as-sociation with Bonn. Fifth, the restoration of French power after disas-ters in Europe had, in the past, taken the form of colonization outside Europe; de Gaulle himself, throughout the 1940s and 1950s, had deemed the supplement of power supposedly provided by the colonies and protectorates essential to France. But when he returned to power in 1958, he understood that the old benefits of colonization had turned into burdens. International politics still represented a competition in which power was the means to conflicting ends. But the nature of nec-essary power had been transformed. Militarily, there now was nuclear might, i.e., a capacity of unprecedented destruction, a way of knocking out a foe without first having to disarm him. Otherwise, industrial power was continuing its rise in importance. De Gaulle decided to concentrate on these kinds of power, and to cut off all the traditional devices that had stunted them. These old devices included industrial protectionism and the administration of colonies.[6]

A third charge was heard more and more often in the last years of de Gaulle's rule.[7] He was accused of not having any real design—except perhaps spoiling those of others—of caring not about the script, only the spectacle. There had never been a real play, only a de-termination to hold the center of the stage. Attempts to find a thread through the maze of Gaullist action ran into innumerable inconsist-encies and contradictions: he had coaxed and flattered the West Ger-mans at first, and later threatened them and staged a *rapprochement* with the Soviets. He had been the most intractable cold warrior over Berlin, against Nikita Khrushchev, and had later ceremoniously cele-brated Franco-Soviet friendship. He had called Israel an ally, only later to excommunicate Israel and the Jews. He could have obtained American aid for France's nuclear program, equality with England in this respect, a veto on U.S. nuclear weapons in Europe, a European political confederation, had he not "ignored the substance of power to keep faith with its shadow." [8] It was all maneuvers and scene-stealing, the argument went, and having upstaged so many other actors, he left France without any solid achievements (beyond decolonization) once he was gone from the stage.

He liked the stage, of course. But it is also true that he had a script —or rather a few clear principles and a vision—and he was perfectly inflexible as far as these were concerned. The things he could have obtained had he acted differently were either things he was not interested in, or things for which he would have to pay a price tantamount to giving up his *raison d'être*. The stupefying fact was not that he failed to give them up; it was that so many of his critics failed to understand that, wanting what he wanted, he could not behave in the "reasonable" way they would have preferred for him. However, when it came to tactics and timing and tone, these were dictated by *les circonstances*. Not only his own will condemned him to "eternal movement," [9] but also the rule of the game of world politics: whoever slows down or stays put falls behind. Coherence was provided by the design—and, to be sure, by de Gaulle's determination to keep the spotlight on himself (and France) each minute that the play lasted. It was neither a well-prefabricated classical drama nor pure improvisation; it was *commedia dell'arte*, in the sense that there was improvisation within the outlines of a script and with well-defined characters. The style was the policy; the style could hardly be imagined on behalf of a less ambitious policy, and it would have been difficult to wage his policy in a self-effacing style (nobody in France and abroad would have noticed it, whereas one of his main goals was to make everyone notice). Yet the policy was more than the style.

De Gaulle's design was a global revisionism of a special kind. A "revisionist" player means to distribute the roles in the play so as to increase his own part. A *status quo* player tries to preserve the existing distribution; a revolutionary player tries to change not only the roles but the play itself, usually on behalf of a grand ideology. What was special about de Gaulle's revisionism can best be understood by following Arnold Wolfers' distinction between possession goals and milieu goals. Ordinarily, a revisionist power aims above all at increasing its possessions—for instance, at recovering territories lost in a war, or gaining areas that can supply it with raw materials and markets, or annexing populations of the same ethnic origin. The French Fourth Republic, insofar as its policy-making process allowed it to have any clear design at all, was partly a *status quo* power (overseas, especially), partly revisionist (in its attempt to promote West European integration and in its flickering discontent with the structure of NATO). But its primary objectives were possession goals—security, a measure of control over German riches, the preservation of colonial territories and resources. When de Gaulle came to power, a radical redefinition occurred. Possession goals were not discarded but were, so to speak, moved from outside France to inside France.[10] Security was now sought through purely French efforts (cf. the nuclear deterrent) rather than through NATO. West German resources, having proven uncontrollable from the outside, would now be matched by the development of French industry. A growing economy and the end of financial dependence on allies would give France another prize possession—a strong currency and a vast stock of foreign reserves. The attempt to hold onto colonies would be abandoned. Possession goals were important as bulwarks of independence, secondarily as means with which to weigh on the international milieu. But the originality of de Gaulle's revisionism was his emphasis on milieu goals: his ambition was to transform the milieu. France was greedy for a role; the reshuffling he sought, ironically enough, was one that would have increased France's role by depriving others of *their* possessions.

De Gaulle's vision was that of a world in which there would be at least two layers of activity and power. There would be a layer of moderate international activity, not involving the use of force capable of upsetting the global balance of power or any important regional balance. In this layer, all states would be equally entitled to act and to be free from outside interference. Then, there would be another layer of activities capable of upsetting the balance—interstate or major civil conflicts into which big powers might be dragged. Here, it was up to the major states to exercise a kind of joint power of policing and settlement, comparable to that of the defunct European concert. But the major states were not merely the United States and the Soviet Union. A world dominated by them could only be unhappy, for lesser powers would have no real freedom of maneuver and the middle powers no real authority, while the domestic politics of such states could never be free of direct or indirect superpower penetration. A collision between superpowers would leave them all with no choice but precarious, passive neutrality or subordinate alignment. A collusion between super powers would turn them into stakes and subjects of a condominium. There had to be a concert in which the superpowers would be joined by others: China, a "European Europe," perhaps Japan. In such a scheme of world order, there would be a reasonable amount of autonomy for nation-states: they could move and compete without the fear of being caught into the superpowers' maelstrom, and without the temptation to exploit the superpowers' antagonisms. The superpowers would shift from their present dilemma—universal hostility or temporary complicity—to the more relaxed condition of partial adversary relations. The most interesting dimension of international politics would be the horizontal one—relations among the main powers—rather than the vertical one—relations between hegemonial states and their satellites or clients.

In order to achieve such a drastic change in the international milieu, two kinds of transformations were indispensable all over the world. First, the recovery of powers that, after World War II, had been reduced to being protégés of the Big Two was essential, as were other forms of weakening the superpowers. Either they had to lose their monopoly on certain kinds of power (for instance, their shared monopoly of nuclear weaponry or America's *de facto* control of the international monetary system) or they had to lose their grip on their temporarily enslaved or docile clients. De Gaulle's call was a call for emancipation. Second, in the specific case of France, it was necessary to turn the politically ambiguous policy of West European integration (conceived by Monnet as a counterweight to American influence,[11] but implemented without a clear design) into an instrument of emancipation, to reshape what had become a subdivision of the Atlantic Community dominated by the United States into *l'Europe européenne*. Both kinds of transformations were essential to de Gaulle. Europe was at times the *pièce maîtresse* of his policy, but West European cooperation was never an end in itself: it was good if it served the over-all strategy, bad (and therefore to be interrupted or redrafted) if the ultimate goal was forgotten. And it was never an exclusive concern: more interested in milieu than in possession goals, de Gaulle did not limit his revisionism to one continent. He knew that it was a time of "universal history," the first era for the first world-wide international system. Even after the end of decolonization, he continued to be absorbed by those French overseas interests which he had mentioned to Adenauer in their first meeting as being one of the great differences between Paris and Bonn.[12] (It is worth noting that among those interests he listed some on the American continent. It is hard to believe he meant the French West Indies only, and not also the emancipation of French Canada.[13])

De Gaulle was encouraged to pursue so sweeping a design by three factors that had already begun to mute the bipolar contest and to make room for lesser powers: new conditions on the use of force, which weighed particularly on the superpowers in the days of nuclear peril parity; the revival of nationalism; and the heterogeneity of the international system.[14] The first of these reduced American and Russian capacity to use massive force outside their zones of quasi-imperial domination, and reduced the likelihood of a general war between them. The second factor led de Gaulle to hope for an erosion of ideologies and a wave of rebellion against the superpowers' hegemonies, and the third prevented the superpowers from absorbing into their contest local conflicts whose roots and manifestations had little to do with the cold war. The second and third factors could also be counted on to offset any superpower attempt at condominium.

De Gaulle had to exploit these circumstances. He disposed of only two broad methods for getting others to play the roles he wanted them to play. One was to re-create France's own "substance and power." He would try to provide her with means of affecting the international milieu directly, of intervening in affairs and conflicts previously dealt with by the superpowers only, of acting in a way that would emancipate her from the one hegemony she had had to accept, of helping others to emancipate themselves from both, of making trouble for the hegemonists and their supporters. The other method was indirect: skillful maneuver to minimize contrary trends, to weave together and magnify the favorable strands, to convince hesitant potential partners, to impress the unconvinced with the prophetic soundness of his anticipations, to seize the right moment for a new move. Let me use shorthand and call the first method might (military, economic, financial, cultural) and the second one skill. It is obvious that both have limits. The might of a middle power like France, even when it is redesigned and built up imaginatively, remains modest. And even the most pyrotechnical skill cannot invent trends that do not exist or coerce nations that have the might to resist and react. It has been said that throughout his career as a statesman de Gaulle's fate was to try to do the utmost with limited resources. His method, untiringly, was to stretch scarcity, marshal mediocre means, transfigure poverty. He was aware of it—he told Adenauer on several occasions that France would collapse if she did not become a power again, but on the other hand that she could not achieve all he wanted by herself alone.[15] He had to get the support of others, yet he would not pay for it with the abandonment of his vision or his imperatives.

II

De Gaulle's pursuit of his design can be divided into three phases of unequal length. The first one lasted from May 1958 until the fall of 1962; the second, until the fatal spring of 1968; the third, until de Gaulle's resignation in April 1969. In the first, de Gaulle undertook two *grandes affaires:* the restoration of French power, and the attempt to turn the Community of the Six into his kind of Europe. The dominant perspective—which he wanted to alter, but from which he had to work—was still the cold war. In the second period, the perspective changed: after the Cuban missile crisis, an East-West détente gradually developed. De Gaulle went about exploiting this change globally—partly because it helped his emancipation from the Atlantic "cage," partly to compensate for the failure of his West European undertaking. This was the phase of thunderbolts, threats, boycotts, and vetoes. After the spring and summer of 1968, there were signs of a partial return to the policy of the first phase. Priority was again given to the restoration of French power, although there was a drastic shift in emphasis in what was implied, and while the perspective was still the détente (despite Czechoslovakia) there was a new interest in Western Europe.

In the first phase, the reconstruction of French power was the most urgent task. It had been the ambition of Mendès-France as well, several years earlier. But, to Mendès-France, modernization, productivity, and efficiency were partly their own rewards, partly means to the goal of *domestic* prosperity, reduction of social tensions, and greater justice. In de Gaulle's case, the new priorities of power were clearly geared to playing a stellar role on the world stage. This required, naturally, domestic appeasement. But in de Gaulle's book, domestic harmony depended on having a grand external design.[16] The kinds of power on which de Gaulle concentrated were all, primarily, instruments for action in the world.

The "priority of priorities" was the establishment of a strong state. Without it, there would be no peace in Algeria, no return to domestic concord, no possibility of having a consistent foreign policy. This had been de Gaulle's theme for almost fifteen years, and it had been vindicated by the shipwreck of the Fourth Republic. The adoption of the new Constitution by a huge majority of the French in September 1958 was a victory he could use on a number of fronts. To the Algerian rebels and to foreign powers, it said: I am not the Fourth Republic, *I* am credible, either in peace or in war. To the French Army, to Frenchmen in Algeria and in Metropolitan France, it meant a reassertion of authority and a promise of protection.

The next priority was freeing France from the Algerian burden. Nowhere was de Gaulle's mix of strategic determination and tactical flexibility more fascinating. The only thing clear about de Gaulle's conception in 1958 was that he believed France's empire was no longer essential to her modern power. And he had only two permanent imperatives (which he never abandoned). The first was to have a self-governing Algeria linked to France (self-governing because the *status quo* was untenable and integration would be a colossal, unbearably expensive, and politically doomed undertaking; linked to France because of the wealth of French interests in Algeria and because of France's self-image). The second was to achieve a settlement of the war that would enhance rather than wound French self-respect. But he had no dogma about the forms Algeria's "personality" and "solidarity" with France would take; as to the settlement, he had to revise constantly and, so to speak, descendingly his assessments of what was possible.

On the domestic front, de Gaulle showed little regard for the French in Algeria, whose clinging to past privileges he must have deemed utterly self-defeating. But he showed extraordinary prudence in dealing with the army, which represented dangerous power and had a deep and sensitive connection with French national pride. He took it out of politics and administration, tried to assure its docility by shifts of command, avoided direct confrontations, ordered it to pursue military victory in Algeria (which could only help a political settlement), but he was ambiguous about what it would do in Algeria after a cease-fire, remained extremely reluctant to negotiate on substance with the insurgents until the end of 1960 so as not to provoke it, and took various measures of repression against antiwar dissidents and protesters in order to protect its honor. Yet he did not let himself be stopped. His tactic was to advance toward a resolution of the Algerian war by stages and by leaning on the French public. (He promised self-determination in September 1959, and made a more specific announcement of an "Algerian Algeria" in November 1960. This led to the referendum of January 1961, which made substantive negotiations with the FLN possible.)

On the external front, de Gaulle's policy was one of constant but concealed retreat. His objective was to convince the FLN to accept his terms—he had to appear the master of his course—and so he changed them until they became negotiable. When the FLN resisted, he tried threats: the threat of building up a third force of moderate Muslims, of establishing temporary institutions, of partitioning the country. But the threats turned out to be empty, and potentially even more troublesome for the French than for the FLN. Anyhow, threats are better deterrents than "compellents"; while they may persuade a foe *not* to do something, they are bad at persuading him to negotiate. The one act that may have helped convince the FLN to settle rapidly was not of de Gaulle's making: it was the massive OAS terrorism of 1962. And so, de Gaulle had to make his offers more and more precise, and his concessions larger and larger. First, he offered no more than to negotiate a cease-fire with the FLN, with the idea that there would then be elections in Algeria and he would do *le reste* with the authorized, elected Algerian representatives. The FLN rejected this, as they had when Guy Mollet proposed it. Then, he suggested what *le reste* would be: three different options of self-determination—integration with France, total secession from her, or limited self-government and close association with her—and he revised the procedure a bit. Negotiations with the FLN would still aim only at a cease-fire, and would be followed by negotiations with all Algerian forces on the organization of a referendum. When this got nowhere, he again changed the substance and the procedure. The third, preferred, option became an Algerian Republic with its own diplomacy, and instead of two sets of negotiations there was to be only one—bargaining with all Algerian forces over a cease-fire, over the conditions of a referendum, and also over the terms of

Algeria's association with France. In fact, what prevailed was still a fourth formula, which in the beginning he had said he would never accept: negotiating with the FLN alone and agreeing on all substantive terms before a cease-fire. He had gradually given in, both on the outcome (independence for all of Algeria, the Sahara included) and on the procedure. But he had saved what mattered most to him: the Évian agreements incorporated *his* notion of a referendum in Algeria (the rule of the FLN would be chosen by the Algerians, not "imposed" by him) and of an interim regime between cease-fire and referendum. Independence was obviously more than what he had hoped to have to grant, but the agreements did arrange for preferential economic and cultural cooperation. If the agreements rapidly lost much of their value, most of the fault lay with the OAS, whose destructive rage led to the exodus of the Europeans from Algeria.

The main price de Gaulle had to pay in order to reach his objectives, the one great liability of his pragmatism and ambiguity, was that of time.[17] Time allowed him to carry public opinion and to disarm the army politically. (A faster settlement on approximately the same terms would probably have resulted either in major *secousses* or in a bleeding wound for French self-respect.) But the time it did take, that prevented dramatic shocks and deep wounds, bred other problems—two quite considerable upheavals in Algeria in January 1960 and April 1961, a multitude of acts of terrorism, and, in the intelligentsia, another great debate (argued in often purely moral terms, with little regard for the practical implications of ethical stances).

And yet the story of de Gaulle's extrication from Algeria is a success story. It was a grim tale of terror and debacle, but de Gaulle's temporizing taught the French that any protracted clinging to the old notion of power meant an Algerian France, not a French Algeria; his skill presented the ordeal as a victory for France's national interest, as a fulfillment of France's own liberal ideals, as a precondition for modern action on the world stage, and he succeeded thereby in orienting opinion toward new, less painful, more rewarding areas of concern. As a result, shortly after Évian, the turbulence gave place to startling silence. The old colonial army was liquidated, the *pieds-noirs* were absorbed, and public opinion—exhausted, or ashamed by OAS excesses, or shattered by the FLN's disintegration—was only too willing to turn the page.

Algeria, although it provided France with oil, had drained French resources and kept a huge part of her army unfit for modern warfare. But de Gaulle's removal of burdens aimed at freeing power, not at giving it up. France's influence in her former colonies was not abandoned. De Gaulle, here, converted French power: instead of direct or indirect administration, it now was to take the form of "cooperation," i.e., cultural, military, and technical assistance on a very large scale. This preserved France's hold on education and the economy in these areas, and thereby often political control or support for her foreign policy. France thus had the triple advantage of appearing as a champion of decolonization, being the leading provider of aid to the Third World, and keeping a political clientele.

The restoration of French power, even while the Algerian war was being fought, took the form of a series of measures designed to make the French economy more competitive, and to overcome the balance-of-payments crisis of the Fourth Republic. The devaluation of the franc in 1958 helped to boost French exports; de Gaulle used the Common Market as a means of forcing French industry out of its shell and as an opportunity to sell French industrial and agricultural exports. The restoration of power also meant accelerated development of France's nuclear program, without external aid. At this point, we have to turn to Gaullist strategy on the world stage.

When the General returned to power, the division of Europe into blocs was still the dominant reality. Khrushchev, elated by Sputnik, was forecasting the victory of East over West, and John Foster Dulles's anticommunism was as strong as ever. As in the days of the RPF, de Gaulle, while looking forward to a very different future, understood that in order to reach it one first had to survive in the present. With a Berlin crisis that started in November 1958 and lasted for more than three years, and with Soviet forces still uncomfortably close to France, de Gaulle adopted what might be called a temporarily anti-Soviet stance. His position was that for France to regain her great-power status, for Western Europe to coalesce, France and Western Europe first had to be secure. On this basis, de Gaulle justified a French nuclear force, made approaches to Adenauer, and proclaimed the "present necessity" of the Atlantic Alliance. But he was an "Atlanticist" with a difference. Whereas the American authors of the "situations of strength" policy had been vague about a future settlement with the Soviet Union, de Gaulle, as he told Adenauer at their first meeting, had not "given up" on the Russians, and wanted to "expand peace toward the East," including European Russia.[18] He deemed it essential to do nothing in the present that would *insulter l'avenir* (offend the future), hence his statement in 1959 recognizing the Oder-Neisse line as final. Indeed, convinced that the Soviets wanted to avoid war, and predicting their future search for a détente, he told his allies that to stand firm now, so as to prove to Moscow that pressure was unrewarding,[19] was the best way of insuring such a turn. Then too, ever since the early 1950s, de Gaulle had been dissatisfied with France's position within NATO, unhappy with the integration of military forces, complaining of the Americans' monopoly on decision-making in strategy and diplomacy, lamenting the Alliance's limited geographic scope.[20]

He thus opened two fronts in his battle. For the time being he would exploit all signs of American faltering in the protection of Western Europe's security, although he would do this circumspectly, given France's position and Soviet pressure.[21] For the future, he would try to prevent the kind of East-West accommodation that only consolidated the blocs, and try to promote a "thaw" that would lead to their dissolution. This meant that he would oppose bilateral U.S.-Soviet discussions on Europe, either as possibly detrimental to West European security at that time or as perpetuating the division for the future. And he would oppose the existing structure of NATO as dangerous, at that time, for Western Europe (deprived of a voice and utterly dependent on American nuclear protection) and incapable of leading to the right kind of thaw in the future. For the Russians could not be expected to make concessions so long as they were faced with a monolithic bloc under American command, whereas they *could* be expected, some day, to accept the restoration of a European order liberated from both hegemonies so long as their loosened grip on their satellites was shown to be compatible with security from Germany and was compensated by a parallel loosening of America's grip. The United States thought that the "thaw" would be hastened and broadened if the Soviet Union had a united Atlantic Community to deal with. De Gaulle, on the contrary, believed that in the long run the Soviets would prefer to deal with a Europe that was not simply an appendage of their principal rival—and that only such a Europe had a chance of emerging undamaged from an East-West deal. The Americans, curiously fatalistic in their opposition to de Gaulle, found it hard to believe that the "sense of history" could be other than a vast Atlantic Community, which would certainly include a unified and restored Europe but a Europe tied forever to the New World. The General had more ambition and pride for Europe.

Such was the Gaullist strategy. But it left one point unclear: what might be called the framework of action, or the costume the actor would wear in playing his role. De Gaulle had two alternatives. The first was the one he tried in a famous memorandum of September 1958: France could be one of three members in a Western directorate in charge of world-wide policy and strategy. It is clear that he expected a negative or elusive reply to this proposal from Eisenhower and Macmillan, but one should remember that this had also been his line in the days of the RPF, and that if it had by miracle been accepted, it would have allowed him to pursue his design—by blocking American inclinations toward a direct dialogue with Moscow, and by acting, in this triumvirate, as the only genuine voice of Europe. It would not have prevented, as a sideline, a policy of economic cooperation in the EEC, or a partnership with West Germany (aimed at preparing the future European entity larger than the Six, at boosting France as the European spokesman in the triumvirate, and at making a reform of NATO's structure possible). Despite being rejected in 1958, de Gaulle returned to the triumvirate idea in the specific instance of the Congo—when he feared that leaving the mess to the U.N. would only benefit one of the superpowers. It was not a way for de Gaulle to share *America's* responsibilities in leading the Atlantic Alliance, it was a way to try to make the Alliance do what *he* envisaged for it. In any case, a rather unsurprising refusal by London and Washington (coupled, to be sure, with suggestions for mere consultation among the NATO powers) left him free and determined to pursue the other alternative.

This meant putting on European garb. France would attempt to turn the Community of the Six into a model for a future pan-European entity, i.e., into a scheme of organized intergovernmental cooperation not only on economic matters but also on defense, foreign policy, and cultural affairs. The EEC would prepare for an enlarged Europe expanded toward the East and less dependent on the United States. For several years, multiple tugs of war went on. A bitter battle raged between de Gaulle and those West Europeans who were more concerned with procedures of unification—supranationality—than with the substance of policies to be adopted. They challenged his "European" credentials; he suspected their Europeanism, fearing that supranational institutions would encourage dependence, if not in the realm of means (economics), at least with respect to those traditional ends of statecraft: diplomacy and strategy. There was also a struggle between de Gaulle and the United States, unhappy with some EEC economic policies (especially in agriculture), and reluctant to get a European "partner" whose voice would be, in vital issues, so different from its own. There was a battle between de Gaulle and those West Europeans who considered their interests in trade or defense as identical with those of the United States, or closer to the United States than to de Gaulle. When Britain's application to join the Common Market was warmly endorsed by the United States and by several West European governments, all of which had previously championed supranationality, de Gaulle's conviction was confirmed that substance, direction, and goals, not procedures, were really at stake. But he could not overcome the resistance of his opponents, especially the Dutch, when the issue of Britain's entry complicated the already difficult negotiations on the Fouchet Plan for political cooperation.[22] Interestingly, this came at a time when American behavior—over Berlin, and over nuclear strategy, revamped from "massive retaliation" to "flexible response"—had created serious misgivings among West Europeans. But there were two ways of dealing with the Americans; de Gaulle's was a clarion call for emancipation; the other was the old strategy of the weak—cling to the stronger partner, convince and constrain him to support you. Adenauer oscillated between the two; the other powers opted for the second.

Both the Western triumvirate and the West European entente were tailored to serve two of de Gaulle's purposes. One was the pursuit with West Germans of a policy of reconciliation without equality. De Gaulle never ceased pleading for common Franco-German policies at the official level, and for vast exchanges and cooperation between young people, universities, etc., thus giving substance to an aim that had remained rather abstract under the Fourth Republic. In addition, however, the idea of France as part of an Anglo-French-American directorate would have consecrated the difference in status between France and West Germany. The second alternative, of a West European entente, seemed to erase this distinction. Were not the Six all equals, especially in an intergovernmental scheme? But in fact it preserved the difference. In the general orientation toward joint policies that would some day make pan-European reconciliation possible, West Germany would have to accept all kinds of restrictions—in its territorial claims, in the military realm. Also, the European defense entity de Gaulle had in mind did not include a "European" nuclear arsenal, i.e., he did not intend it to inhibit the construction of a French nuclear force or to annul the ban on German nuclear arms.

De Gaulle's nuclear policy would have been compatible with, indeed most necessary to, the tri-directorate: without nuclear weapons, France, next to the United States and Britain, would have been disadvantaged. It was also compatible with the Fouchet Plan: a European entity would have been crowned with, or supplemented by, a French nuclear force, just as NATO was capped by America's. So the building of the French arsenal was a vital part of de Gaulle's over-all policy. It allowed him to divert the army from its colonial nostalgia, and to rebuild it on lines closer to his early preference for an army of technicians, trained for mobility and surprise. It aimed at giving him a lever against American hegemony in NATO, at exploiting West European fears about the ultimate reliability of the American guarantee, and at encouraging them to accept as feasible, not just imaginary, the "European Europe" of his design.

De Gaulle placed himself in the cold-war perspective of the present. A French striking force, he argued, would certainly not be capable of devastating the entire Soviet Union, or of preventing the Russians—injured but not destroyed—from wholly devastating France. But it would nonetheless have a triple military function.

The first function has often been described in terms of the "triggering value" of a small striking force: it could serve to push into action the American thermonuclear arsenal. In case of extreme provocation of Western Europe by the Soviet Union, France's mere recourse to the *threat* to use atomic force (a threat which the Americans thought themselves less capable of issuing credibly except in the most serious circumstances), and the subsequent threat to annihilate France which the Russians would not fail to make, could *force* the United States to demonstrate its solidarity with France, i.e., to spread over France the umbrella of its nuclear protection, even if it had decided to avoid such a commitment. For France's "disobedience toward the United States" would never be reprehensible enough to justify abandoning her to Russian bombs. What was in question here, clearly, was a *preventive* triggering, destined to *deter* the Russians from attack or provocation rather than to serve *after* an attack. (And should the United States try to dissociate itself in advance, what better proof could it give of its willingness to ignore Europe's vital interests, as de Gaulle was charging?)

In the second place, the existence of an independent striking force and the threat it creates for the enemy could obstruct certain strategic conceptions which the Americans wanted to impose on NATO. These conceptions could not be implemented if any of the Allies possessed the means to undermine such a strategy. Under Robert McNamara's doctrine, American strategy in the event of limited Soviet military action in Europe was to use at first conventional weapons alone, and to resort to atomic weapons later, only if the Soviets persisted and only in "controlled" ways—against military objectives but not against cities.* This strategy could succeed only if: 1) the Soviet Union played the same game, an assumption which requires a frightening number of hypotheses and a considerable dose of optimism; and 2) if the allies of the United States were entirely under American control. If any ally had an autonomous nuclear striking force—necessarily directed, given its small size, *not* against military objectives but against Soviet cities, and destined to be brandished immediately in cases of extreme provocation—recourse to the strategy of options was made much more difficult. Insofar as the adoption of such a strategy might have encouraged the Russians to attempt certain moves (by making them believe that the risks would be small and controllable), one understood that the United States might prefer an increased risk of limited crises to the risk of an unlikely but final holocaust. One could also, however, understand why such a strategy was disquieting to many Europeans.

---

* This strategy, incidentally, presupposed a vast American superiority in thermonuclear weapons; if such were the case, however, how did one explain the American hesitation to brandish the atomic threat to deter the Soviet Union in Europe if not by the predominant desire to spare American territory?

Third, should the United States nevertheless weaken its nuclear protection of Europe, reserve it for extreme cases, and refuse absolutely to use the threat of atomic destruction to prevent limited Soviet moves against Europe, a French nuclear striking force would still have had the virtue of making the Russians pause. It would at least be able to inflict losses on the Soviet Union that the Soviet domination of France or even Western Europe would not outweigh. According to the reasoning of General Pierre Gallois, the prolific advocate of nuclear proliferation and graduated deterrence, the Soviet Union might *possibly* prefer to suffer enormous losses if the mastery of the world were at stake, i.e., in a direct conflict with the United States; but if the stakes were lower, less imposing forces would *certainly* suffice to make it hesitate. De Gaulle himself thought that the mere possession of nuclear weapons, even in small amounts, would influence the Russians.[23]

None of these arguments was unanswerable. How deeply de Gaulle himself believed in them—rather than in the much more general idea that renouncing an independent nuclear force meant resignation to permanent, barely influenceable dependence on other nations, and submission to small-power status in a world where the negative productivity of nuclear power was enormous—is unclear. He probably thought that, in case of war, nothing—conventional might or *force de frappe*—could save France from annihilation (hence his recurrent anguish of general war); but he also believed in the political benefits of a *force de frappe* in peacetime, and in its superior deterrent value, and in its over-all value as an insurance policy for the future.[24] It is likely that he deemed America's guarantee still probably sufficient to deter the Russians despite his well-publicized doubts. (He acted on that assumption in the Berlin crisis.) But it does not follow that he was insincere in wondering whether, if the improbable occurred, and the Russians ran risks they had so far avoided, the guarantee that had failed to deter would actually be carried out; and in wondering whether the Americans' new announced strategy might not encourage Moscow to run higher risks. What is clear is that he thought these arguments most useful in dealing with a military alliance he wanted to shake up, with West European partners who clung to the United States for security reasons, with a Soviet opponent who liked to rattle might and whose *interlocuteur* he wanted to become. Still, the results were paradoxical. The United States, having been tempted at times to help de Gaulle with nuclear aid—in exchange for some softening of his attitude toward NATO or toward "multilateral" NATO nuclear forces, i.e., in exchange for his giving up his designs—ended up, under Kennedy, more determined than ever to tighten its strategic control over NATO. As for the other West Europeans, they did not find here any added incentive to accept de Gaulle's design for Western Europe. For there was indeed an inevitable contradiction. He was blasting NATO as a mere appendage of America, since Washington's nuclear monopoly reduced its strategic and diplomatic functions to trifles. But could not the same be said of a West European entity led by France? If de Gaulle had been right in saying to Adenauer and Eisenhower: what matters for deterrence is the foe's certainty that nuclear weapons will be used against him if he moves, and this is only possible for the defense of one's own country, why should Bonn or Rome have thought they would be *more* protected by a handful of bombs available to Paris than by a huge arsenal in Washington? France's intentions might be more "European," but the credibility of her risking suicide for others was no greater than America's; and if there was doubt in both cases, then prudence made the American force more plausible, given its size and its capacity to be used in a first strike. France's nuclear program helped French emancipation, but it was not a tool for the reform of NATO or a goad to West European unity. Once again, a deterrent was neither a compeller nor a convincer.

The passage from the first to the second phase of de Gaulle's foreign-policy designs somehow got lost in the noise and smoke of the Skybolt affair, followed by his momentous press conference on January 14, 1963, when he barred Great Britain from the Common Market. Also, there was no abrupt discarding of old doctrines. In the years that followed, the EEC continued to be a focus of French policy—although exclusively as an aid to French power and as a hold on Bonn in the present, as well as a kind of useful beachhead toward that future de Gaulle still had in mind. But while occasionally calling again for political cooperation among the Six, he had no great desire to try the Fouchet Plan again, and he could have no illusion about the effect of his veto against Britain on the development of the EEC into a political-military entity. As for the Franco-German treaty of 1962, coming at the very end of the Adenauer era, far from being "the centerpiece of [de Gaulle's] European policy," [25] it was little more than a relic of his first phase—when he had hoped that entente with Adenauer would bring the other Four along—another beachhead for resuming the march toward European "organized cooperation" some day, and an instrument of reassurance designed to prevent Germany from straying too far: a deterrent, not a lever; a raincheck, not a deal.

De Gaulle had not succeeded in turning the EEC—or West Germany—into a partner for reform of NATO, and he knew from his experience in 1958 that to propose a reform by oneself was pointless. He had also noted that the Russians, while interested in making contacts with France, had never talked to him about Europe in general; and he knew that America's success in the Cuban missile crisis of 1962 would lead to direct deals between the superpowers—always dangerous, in his view. He now had to rely more on the negative uses of might (rather than bringing French power to bear on joint enterprises, he would have to make it difficult or painful for others to ignore it or contradict its aspirations) and on skill. Without Western or European stilts on which to advance, he had to maximize his nuisance power, to spend his energy on preventing others from consolidating what he wanted to destroy or from delaying what he wanted to hasten. That he was a master at using nuisance value in the service of an inflexible design, he had shown often during the war years. He now proved it again. Obstruction and nuisance, even magnified by style and elevated by a grand vision, are largely negative exercises. But given de Gaulle's analysis of the world, he must have thought that his power to deny and to hurt, if well used, would be sufficient to allow the favorable trends to unfold; and he would assist them by some positive moves as well.

There was still the problem of the framework. A Western tri-directorate was obviously ruled out. Partly this was because the United States, even at Nassau, offered no real sharing of diplomatic and strategic decision-making. At most (and even this was not too clear) it offered nuclear aid to France in exchange for the assignment of France's nuclear force to NATO, except when the French national interest would be at stake. This offer may have "meant recognition of France as the West's third and last nuclear power," [26] but it in no way included a sharing of what mattered most to de Gaulle—not the technology, but the command and the setting of goals; it also seemed tied to the establishment of a multilateral force controlled by the United States. And partly, the tri-directorate was out because, after the Cuban missile crisis, there was little point in placing oneself in a cold-war perspective. De Gaulle expected the Russians to seek a détente—and he wanted Western Europe, or at least France, to become a separate *interlocuteur*. The West European costume could be worn in matters under EEC jurisdiction, but not in strategic and diplomatic issues. Rather than choosing a single main framework, de Gaulle was therefore going to play with three different ones. Often, he would—as Pompidou put it—"play the role of Europe," i.e., act as the only European concerned with Europe's true long-term interests (even if this was true, it was an unauthorized act). Often, he would wear the hat of spokesman of the small, unaligned states, seeking freedom of maneuver and the right to noninterference from the power-greedy superstates (again, unauthorized). Often, he would wear a purely French hat: that of a middle power determined to be heard and to break into the charmed, or vicious, circle of the Big Two.

De Gaulle's strategy in the years 1963–68 can (of course) be divided into three parts. The first consisted of a long battle to prevent the reinforcement of the "hegemony" in whose orbit France had had to seek protection, a hegemony which had launched into a kind of global missionary course under Kennedy and Johnson (Frenchmen started talking about the danger of a unipolar world). This battle contained negative moves (essentially obstructions) and positive ones.

The main battlefield was Europe. De Gaulle had not turned Western Europe into *l'Europe européenne*. He now had to prevent it from becoming the "Atlantic" Europe, which the vague American notion of Atlantic partnership barely concealed. There were three fronts. One was France herself. De Gaulle saw the offer of nuclear aid that Kennedy made to France after the Nassau meeting of late 1962 as a gilded trap, an attempt to get her fully back into the Atlantic Alliance under U.S. control, and so he rejected it with noisy gusto.

Another front was West Germany. After Nassau, the United States engaged in a spectacular courtship of Bonn, in order to prevent any further seduction of Bonn by Paris (i.e., to kill what chances remained of a Franco-German entente becoming the embryo of a Gaullist independent Western Europe) and to prevent any imitation of Paris by Bonn in the nuclear realm. De Gaulle reacted vigorously. A Bonn-Washington axis meant not only the end of the hope of joint Franco-German action but—much more dangerously—the end of the dream of a reunited Europe and the permanent consolidation of the iron curtain. A West German defense establishment entirely tied to Washington meant that the United States would strengthen its grip on "its" half of Europe, and also contained a potential (if limited) danger of West German access to, and influence on, Washington's strategic and diplomatic decision-making. Gaullist obstruction of this axis took the form of ominous warnings and of a French rapprochement with the East European states and Russia, which suggested to Bonn that its liaison with Washington could lead not only to the end of all hopes of détente between Bonn and the East, but to French enmity.[27] The battle lasted throughout the years of Ludwig Erhard's chancellorship. His replacement by Kurt Kiesinger represented a partial victory for de Gaulle, insofar as the *Ostpolitik* of the new West German cabinet followed de Gaulle's lead, even though Bonn's defense policy remained "Atlantic."

The third front was the EEC. De Gaulle's two resounding "noes" to England, in January 1963 and November 1967, sprang only in part from his (quite genuine) fear that with British membership the Community would be transformed into a kind of loose free-trade area, harmful to existing French interests and to French efforts on behalf of a broad range of economic policies sharply different from those the United States might have wished. His vetoes came mainly from his conviction that Britain's entry would forever doom the hope of joint strategic and diplomatic policies different from America's. This conviction was particularly reinforced by the Nassau conference imbroglio. In the summer of 1962, Macmillan had hinted of a possible West European defense policy after Britain's entry into Europe, but he made no proposals, and de Gaulle was not a man to open a door on a mere vague promise. At Nassau, Macmillan accepted Polaris missiles on America's terms, and thus made a separate West European defense establishment (if Britain entered the EEC) impossible. De Gaulle's hostility to the Multilateral Nuclear Force (MLF) advocated by the United States at that time was due not only to its potential effect on West Germany, but also to the fact that it would tie the defense of the other Five more tightly to the United States, thus ruining prospects for any future *relance* of the Fouchet concept. And his boycott of EEC institutions in 1965 was due to a determination to prevent, even in an area in which essential French interests were at stake (agriculture), a leap into that supranational nirvana where his chances of directly influencing shared European policies might vanish. On the other hand, the EEC's own momentum offered him a chance to shape some joint *positive* moves against the United States: in the monetary realm, he tried for several years to get the Six to adopt a common policy limiting the scope of America's favored Special Drawing Rights. But these successes were small (there was never any common policy on U.S. investments).[28]

Europe was the main battlefield, but it was not the only one. De Gaulle's war against the supremacy of the dollar aimed at nothing less than a drastic reform of the Bretton Woods system and a rejection of the gold exchange standard, which had developed into a dollar standard, and which he accused of helping the United States keep running a deficit of its balance of payments, fostering inflation in the United States and abroad, and buying off other nations' resources. Here, he used France's growing strength, her reserves in dollars, to pressure the United States and the gold exchange standard—by converting them into gold. Negative measures were used on two other fronts. In Southeast Asia, the French virtually boycotted SEATO because of their disagreement with the United States over Vietnam. And in the Middle East, having interpreted Israel's victory in June 1967 as a gravely unbalancing act that marked a triumph of the pro-American over the pro-Soviet side, de Gaulle embargoed arms shipments to Israel.

For de Gaulle, a reinforcement of American might and influence meant perpetuation of the cold war. The second part of his strategy consisted in preventing a direct Soviet-American accommodation, which he considered equally bad for France and for Western Europe. Here, his means were meager. The danger of nuclear holocaust, highlighted by the Cuban crisis, and the pressure of China on Russia,

which de Gaulle had hoped would make the Soviet Union more ame-
nable to settlements, worked in favor of a Soviet-American dialogue.
Many West Europeans and most lesser nations saw in such a dialogue,
and in a relaxation of Soviet-American tensions, a precondition for a
world-wide détente, rather than an immediate threat to their interests.
During the Six Day War in the Middle East, the U.S.-Soviet conversation, first on the "hot line," later in Glassboro, New Jersey, was widely
greeted with relief. But de Gaulle was helped, paradoxically, by the
very trend he was so constantly battling: America's preponderance and
hubris. After the beginning of the bombing of North Vietnam (during
a visit by Aleksei Kosygin to Hanoi), the scope of a U.S.-Soviet rapprochement narrowed, and Johnson's policy of "peaceful engagement"
in Eastern Europe—a rival of de Gaulle's approach to Russia and its
satellites—never managed to get off the ground. After Glassboro, Russia's need to restore its credit with the Arab countries, Israel's intransigence and America's tacit support of it, made a Soviet-American *Dik-
tat* in the Middle East unlikely: it was a part of the world de Gaulle
wanted, perhaps more than any other besides Europe, to remove from
the superpowers' clutches. In the nuclear realm, the Big Two's incentive to a rapprochement was overwhelming. Here, de Gaulle once
more resorted to obstruction. He refused to sign the nuclear test ban
treaty, boycotted the Geneva talks on "complete and general disarmament," opposed the nuclear nonproliferation treaty.[29] He could not
prevent the superpowers from agreeing on the defense of their nuclear
preponderance, but he could keep them from turning it into a real
duopoly.

But the best way of preventing superpower *Diktats,* of avoiding a
re-enactment of Yalta, was to prepare for the advent of a new, post-
cold war, multipolar era. This was the third part of de Gaulle's strategy, the most ambitious and controversial: acting alone, he was trying
to realize a prophecy. Here also, there were three fronts: European,
global, and French. Again, Europe was the most important. Although
he could not make the EEC over, he still worked on behalf of his general European design. There was some progress toward joint policies
among the Common Market countries, if not in the realm of defense
and diplomacy, at least in the realm of foreign trade. The alliance of
France with the EEC Commission allowed the Six to present a common front in the "Kennedy round" of tariff negotiations. In agriculture, France remained the prime mover of the common policy. (Even
these successes, however, were gained only by means of threats and ultimatums, as in the case of the grain price agreement late in 1964.)

As for Western Europe's relations with Eastern Europe, de Gaulle
exploited what he thought was the right moment for his "opening to
the East" after the ouster of Khrushchev. This move served a number

of purposes. It seized the initiative for a détente away from the United States; offered the West and East Europeans the prospect of autonomous reunification and warned the United States that the Europeans themselves would try to determine their own future; convinced the Russians that they could afford some disengagement in exchange for a similar move by the United States and for a European settlement in which France and the Soviet Union would guarantee that there be no new German threat; told the West Germans that only in moving in such a direction, oriented by France and under France's guidance, was there any hope for an end of the "German anomalies." This was the gist of de Gaulle's press conference on the twentieth anniversary of Yalta. He pursued his policy in the East with a kind of "détente" offensive that took him to Russia, Poland, and Rumania, made him the self-appointed spokesman for West Germany's desire for reconciliation, and opened the way for economic and technological cooperation between France and the Eastern states. In the West, he announced in March 1966 his decision to withdraw France from the military institutions of NATO (a decision preceded, over the years, by several partial moves and by the failure to reassign French divisions to them after Algeria). This move was a signal to Moscow that France, unlike Britain or West Germany, was not tied to the United States and could be dealt with as a "nation with free hands," and a signal to the East Europeans that although the German "anomalies" had not been resolved, and there was still a need for NATO and the Warsaw Pact, there was no longer any justification for organized hegemony.[30]

On the second, global front, de Gaulle tried to bring to the surface the two latent, hidden layers of international activity mentioned earlier in this chapter. First, he called on the smaller nations to assert themselves, to refuse to be stakes or battlefields for the great powers. Hence his long journey to Latin America, his support of Biafra, and, above all, his startling appeal for a free Québec. (In that appeal, he was once more seized by his desire for renovation, for turning old obligations into new duties: de Gaulle's France had to use her influence for Québec's rehabilitation as a new nation, two centuries after the abandonment of Québec as a colony. In the cases of Québec and Biafra, his apparent violation of his own policy of nonintervention stemmed from a conviction that one was dealing here with nations struggling for self-determination.) In world trade conferences or in economic discussions at the U.N., the French often sided with the poorer nations' demands for price supports and market stabilization. Yet de Gaulle, unlike many of the small or new nations, was not interested in subverting the international hierarchy. For, second, de Gaulle wanted explosive situations handled by the major powers—not by the superpowers or the whole U.N. His recognition of China in January 1964

—after Mao's final break with Moscow, and at a time when the United States was in grave trouble in Indochina—was a way of exerting nuisance power at the expense of the two superstates, and a way of pointing to the convergence of interests between French revisionism and Chinese revolutionary policy. For Southeast Asia, de Gaulle's solution was predictable—a neutralization of the area, to remove it from the superpowers' contests—and his proposed method of achieving this aim was a settlement by the Big Five. For the Middle East, in 1967, he offered the same solution, and the method was a settlement by the Big Four and perhaps a Big Four police force. As for disarmament, he declared that only the nuclear powers could effectively negotiate it.

The last front was France herself. De Gaulle's decision to accumulate huge monetary reserves was intended to help force a reform of the world's monetary system in which gold (hoarded by France) would be the standard and the franc a world currency. French foreign aid was extended to countries other than her former colonies. French arms sales competed, often successfully, with America's. Above all, there was the nuclear *force de frappe,* now made operational. As France's strategy—if not de Gaulle's vision—changed, so did its rationale. It was no longer presented as principally a way of influencing American strategy,[31] but justified on the more general grounds that multilateral deterrence was superior to bipolar deterrence: that multilateral deterrence made calculations more uncertain, therefore risks higher, nuclear war more improbable, and large-scale conventional conflicts less likely. With the resulting neutralization of nuclear weaponry as a tool of diplomacy, middle powers would have a greater range for maneuvers; but in order to benefit from this, one would first have to have nuclear arms, because otherwise one might be victimized by the nuclear states' blackmail and be excluded from diplomatic settlements. Nor was the *force de frappe* any longer presented as primarily a way of deterring the Soviet Union from endangering French or West European security. Again in an attempt to realize a prophecy, de Gaulle in 1968 endorsed the so-called all-horizons (*tous azimuts*) strategy,[32] which underlined the gap between his and NATO's or America's policy.

To be sure, de Gaulle made full use of France's financial, economic, and military resources on behalf of his strategy—to the point of straining public support for the costs of his policy, as the May 1968 crisis demonstrated. The fear his West European partners had of affronting French might, the skill with which he exploited France's geographic and historical assets, his formidable obstinacy were all factors in his broad measure of success in blocking designs contrary to his own, and his partial success with economic cooperation and diplomatic détente between Eastern and Western Europe. In early 1968, everyone had endorsed the policy of "détente, entente, and cooperation" which he had been the first to define; but Washington was stuck in the Vietnam quagmire, and Bonn's initiatives had been rejected by Moscow as evil-minded and subversive. Only de Gaulle was *persona grata* in the East.

However, in his attempt to bring forth his envisioned world order, de Gaulle had resorted predominantly to exhortation and evocation. He could beacon and beckon; he could not build. No nation in Eastern Europe, not even Rumania, had followed his example in leaving NATO by leaving the military organization of the Warsaw Pact. West Germany's half-hearted and merely partial adoption of the policy he had advocated toward Eastern Europe had made the Russians even more insistent on everyone recognizing the *status quo* as the only basis of a European settlement. The détente was ambiguous, even if it had been initiated by West Europeans rather than Americans: it might lead either to a consolidation of the division of Europe, or to its erosion. De Gaulle had wagered on and pleaded for the latter. But Moscow and Warsaw pushed for the former, and refused the pan-European reconciliation proposed by him. The walls of Jericho had not collapsed. The Warsaw Pact and NATO were still formidable. In the Middle East, the influence of the superpowers remained decisive; in Southeast Asia, the United States was moving toward extrication from Vietnam; but Latin America had not emancipated itself from Washington any more than Eastern Europe from Moscow. China had turned inward during the convulsions of the cultural revolution. De Gaulle's European partners, during the pound sterling crisis and at the Stockholm meeting of March 1968, had refused to challenge the predominance of the dollar and actually given a new lease on life to the existing monetary system. So the outlines of de Gaulle's preferred future remained shadowy. On one level, the small powers' freedom of maneuver was being restricted by their internal weaknesses and by a factor otherwise in de Gaulle's interest: the East-West contest was cooling off, and this made it less important for the superpowers to court the small powers, and it encouraged the fragmentation among nonaligned nations. On another level, the weakening of bipolarity did not yet mean the emergence of multipolarity. The Big Two had their troubles, but neither in the Middle East nor in Southeast Asia were the Big Four or Five at work. For de Gaulle, nothing had been lost, and some things had been gained. But many more remained to be achieved.

At this point, the May explosion took place at home in France, followed by the invasion of Czechoslovakia. De Gaulle's first duty after the elections in June which marked the end of the domestic crisis was —once more—the restoration of French might. France's economy and finances appeared badly hurt by the long paralysis during the spring and by the subsequent flight of capital that resulted. But whereas in 1958 restoration had been directly and immediately geared to foreign affairs, this time the priorities shifted. *Grandeur* still meant "a grand undertaking," but that undertaking was domestic reform. The domestic reforms planned in 1968 were aimed primarily at removing those factors of discontent which had led to the explosion and crippled France in international affairs. That the ultimate goal was to resume playing a grand role on the world stage was clear enough: nothing was given up, not even the franc's exchange rate, despite formidable pressures to do so. But if there was no general retreat, there were at least detours or delays. To be sure, the austerity measures enacted in the fall of 1968 concerned domestic as well as foreign-policy expenditures. But the most urgent order of business was restoring the economy, threatened first with inflation, later with a recession, so as to keep it competitive within the Common Market; and the next order of business was to find the "third way" between pure capitalism and communism. Inevitably, there was some retrenchment. The foreign reserves had melted. (They would continue to do so. The French held onto the franc's rate with the help of the United States and of the monetary institutions it dominated.) Foreign aid was reduced. Development of the *force de frappe* was slowed down—which meant silencing, if not yet dropping, the claims to a *tous azimuts* strategy, which would have required a more grandiose scheme for land missiles and nuclear submarines. One major aspect of French strategy on the world front—a drastic reform of the international monetary system—had to be suspended, even though de Gaulle's New Year speech in 1968 defiantly mentioned most of the other aspects.

Necessarily, Europe once more became the dominant concern. As long as the trend of history seemed to be détente overcoming division, de Gaulle had been in the lead, but the Soviet Union's action in Czechoslovakia was a major blow to de Gaulle's design.[33] First, it meant that the Soviet Union was determined to defend the European *status quo* by force, rather than letting it be eroded away by even such mild currents as Alexander Dubček's brand of communism. The dream of "détente, entente, and cooperation" was obviously premature. But resignation to the *status quo,* for de Gaulle, meant perpetuating the "hegemonies," and that was unacceptable. Moreover, if West Germany concluded that "bridge-building" had been premature, this might lead (at a time when Bonn had grown more self-confident, and America less so, than in the days of Erhard and Kennedy or Johnson) to a new Washington-Bonn axis, leaving France in an essentially defensive position. Or if West Germany concluded that her only method of achieving reconciliation with Moscow and Warsaw and improving contacts with East Germany was the one demanded by Russia—accepting the *status quo,* and in effect recognizing the Soviet Union's supremacy over Eastern Europe—instead of the "revisionist" way promoted by de Gaulle, he would no longer be the only West European *interlocuteur* of the Russians. Indeed, for the conservative Russians, a *status quo* Bonn would be a better partner than a revisionist Paris, especially at a time when West Germany was enjoying an economic boom and a strong currency. Having made what to de Gaulle was the error of trying to achieve détente without engaging Moscow (and Warsaw), Bonn might now rush too fast and unreservedly toward Moscow. West Germany would thus become a purely national state in Europe, no longer restricted by its hope of gaining reunification through low postures and self-restraint, still encased in NATO, but under less exacting U.S. control than in the early 1960s. If de Gaulle chastised Kiesinger for the speed and showiness of Bonn's overtures to Prague in the spring of 1968, it could be less because he was accusing Bonn of being responsible for the Soviet Union's reaction in Czechoslovakia than because he sensed that after Prague, his own policy of détente would now put Bonn at the front of the stage and benefit the Russians. In either case, his policy of keeping a difference between France and West Germany was threatened.

The prospects for de Gaulle's design had become ever more distant, but his art had always been that of maneuvering in order to remove obstacles and rediscover usable paths. In the few months between the fall of 1968 and his own fall, he developed a new triple strategy.

The first part was a guarded attempt at a *relance* of his pre-1962 notion of a West European grouping, with its own policies, that could serve as a magnet to attract Eastern Europe. More than ever he wanted to preserve the chances of a West European entity capable of pursuing its own diplomacy and strategy. This implied, sooner or later —as he told Britain's Ambassador to France, Christopher Soames— both a complete overhaul of NATO (to be replaced ultimately by an alliance between the United States and the West European entity) and an *adieu* to the notion of a supranational government of Western Europe. But there was now a great tactical difference. Before 1962, he had been trying to evangelize the Five, and relied primarily on Adenauer's West German government in this effort. Now, he realized that any *relance* depended on removal of the irritant that had slowed down and poisoned the atmosphere in the EEC for six years: Britain's application for membership. Also, after the monetary crisis in November 1968, he must have reflected that the re-emergence of an economically very powerful and diplomatically more emancipated West Germany might lead Britain to a better appreciation of its common interests with France. (Had not the pound and the franc suddenly found themselves in the same leaking boat, and experienced a firm German refusal to change the mark?) And he must have thought that a weaker France could use Britain as a partner in an attempt to *encadrer* Bonn —now that the dream of a kind of pan-European *encadrement* under the guidance of Paris and Moscow was out of season. Finally, after Richard Nixon's election, he probably expected the "special relationship" between Washington and London to fade away, and Washington to be less discouraging, if London wanted to remember and pursue Macmillan's hints favoring military cooperation with France. In February 1969, de Gaulle's famous lunch with Soames (which the Wilson government chose to interpret as a possible trap) was an attempt at opening conversations in order to test the British conception of Europe. As in the days of the Fouchet Plan, de Gaulle gave "politics" precedence over economics; a political association was the precondition for an enlargement of the Common Market.[34] But the British were still unwilling to join on de Gaulle's terms; they expected these to change when he disappeared (they did); meanwhile, they tried to isolate him. The *relance* got nowhere, and served only to exacerbate relations between de Gaulle and the other Five, misinformed by Harold Wilson of an alleged attempt by de Gaulle to negotiate the transformation of the EEC and NATO behind their backs.[35]

And so the second and most urgent task—again—was the Sisyphean one of preventing Western Europe from becoming what he had opposed. The "threat" was no longer really that it would become an American appendage, given the shift in America's own priorities, but that it would become a kind of closed community, resigned to the *status quo* in the East and to dependence on the United States for defense. Thus, even after Prague, de Gaulle continued to resist Britain's entry *unless* Britain accepted not merely the economic provisions of the Common Market (which, as he also indicated to Soames, he knew would be *de facto* transformed by its enlargement) but also his politico-military conception of Europe. As long as Britain refused to discuss this with him, he would continue to veto her entry into the EEC and to try to thwart her attempt to outflank him in the West European Union (WEU). There, the British, acting somewhat like the Americans after January 1963, and cleverly exploiting a post-Czechoslovakia trauma in West Germany, were trying to beat him on his own procedural and substantive terrain: that of a common strategic and foreign policy for Western Europe, defined in a classic, intergovernmental way. In the WEU (whose purpose is to examine those very issues that are beyond the EEC's jurisdiction and that de Gaulle wanted settled as a *préalable* to Britain's entry into the EEC), the British rallied the other Five to *their* conception, or rather to their more evasive approach, thus isolating France. The Bonn government, eager to hold on more than ever to NATO for its security, and somewhat tempted to try the Soviet-preferred road of détente through acceptance of the *status quo,* now had two different reasons for closer relations with Britain. But the British tactic, and their exploitation of de Gaulle's offer of direct Franco-British talks (an offer partly aimed at averting such encirclement) could only confirm his conviction that Britain's entry into the EEC now would destroy whatever chances might still exist for his design of a "European Europe." Once more, to indicate his displeasure—and to show the West Germans that they could not have it both ways—he resorted to a boycott, this time of the WEU.

The EEC thus remained a beachhead toward his preferred future, but its present chances of expanding in scope or membership were nil. De Gaulle was back at the post-Fouchet, post-January 1963 situation, and would have to wait for a different British government. What could France by herself now do, in East-West relations?

Here we come to the third and last part of his strategy. After the failed *relance* and the familiar *blocage,* there was what could be called a holding operation. De Gaulle was protecting his options, not yet choosing a new path, waiting to see what the other actors would do, keeping his eyes on Moscow and Bonn. On one hand, he wanted to avert a return to the cold-war days and the blocs. His method consisted, paradoxically, of staging a rapprochement with the United States, manifested in effusive ceremonies when Nixon visited France in February–March 1969, and—just at the time of the fatal referendum—in a new strategic doctrine [36] that returned to the arguments of the Fifth Republic's first phase and placed France in the Western perspective. This rapprochement had a double purpose. One was to warn the Soviets that any further acts of force on their part could provoke France to return to the Atlantic orbit. The other purpose was to interpose France, so to speak, between Washington and Bonn. On the other hand, despite Czechoslovakia, de Gaulle repeated his faith in the policy of "détente, entente, and cooperation," both in a September press conference and during his October visit to Turkey, and renewed his appeal for improved relations with Eastern Europe and Russia. For to give this up would have meant, implicitly, vindicating the West German (or French) Atlanticists, and perhaps encouraging those West Germans who believed that the "bridge-building" tried in different ways by de Gaulle, Johnson, and Willy Brandt should be replaced by a new policy accepting Moscow's terms. As long as the doors between the two halves of Europe were still shut to Bonn but not to Paris, de Gaulle could hope to keep Bonn from abandoning the Kiesinger-Brandt policy in favor of a more Atlantic one, or in favor of resignation to the *status quo.* He continued to hope that France would be Moscow's *interlocuteur* for a European settlement. He thus had to act as if the Soviet action in Prague had been, in Debré's clumsy words, a mere *accident de parcours*. Hence de Gaulle's prompt resumption of close economic relations with Russia.

De Gaulle resigned several months before the West German elections that brought in a Brandt-Scheel cabinet and its dynamic new *Ostpolitik*. It is hard to guess how he would have reacted to these developments, or how he would have dealt with the new Conservative government in England. But some things are certain. He would not have given up his design. (And he would have pointed out, as he told Adenauer at their last meeting, that an arrangement on the basis of the *status quo* could only be temporary, and was not the equivalent of real peace.[37]) Also, he would have tried to be at least as active as Bonn. Maybe he would have attempted a *relance* of what had failed in early 1969—the Fouchet notion enlarged to Britain, a new spurt of West European cooperation to offset Moscow's attraction on Bonn and to replace Washington's fading control over Bonn. However, the immediate circumstances at the time of his departure were bleaker than at any moment since his return to power; his freedom of maneuver in achieving his design was small. This may have contributed to his gambling on a referendum: if a referendum could prove that he was still widely supported, his authority and durability on the world stage would be reasserted; without such evidence, there was little point in going on.

III

It may be worth while listing some of the precepts of de Gaulle's "operational code." We are dealing here with his tactics on the world stage. Let us take his operational code point by point.

1. International politics is a battle. Interests often converge, and possibilities for common action result from them, but nothing assures that this convergence will last. Indeed, it may have to be provoked, so to speak. As a result, friendships or enmities are never permanent, and one must always be on one's guard. The international milieu is a kind of jungle, moderated only by the beasts' self-restraint and by the combinations of power that force or encourage self-restraint, and the statesman must act accordingly.[38] There is no point in expecting even partners to show "mutual trust" (a phrase he removed from Fouchet's draft treaty when he personally revised it); there is no moral opprobrium attached to the use of threats or the resort to force in order to protect one's interests (Bizerte in 1961). And there is a permanent danger that one may be ensnared and trapped. (This explains de Gaulle's dislike for diplomatic niceties and distaste for protracted negotiations in which essentials risk slipping away under a mass of details. This was clear in his criticism of the negotiating procedure between the EEC

and Britain in 1962,[39] or his refusals to negotiate with the United States on any major issue.) "Pleading one's case" was not de Gaulle's way. His was the opposite of Britain's practice of trying to influence the United States by always being at its side, or of Bonn's many attempts to affect the United States by being docile: no one can coax anyone else away from his vital concerns—as shown by the United States in the Suez and Skybolt issues, or in its financial dealings with Bonn. De Gaulle's way of affecting and influencing was through unilateral decisions—through what he did and what he refused. He avoided negotiations whenever possible: they are usually too costly when one was weak, and often unnecessary when one was strong. They made sense only if they specified and refined an agreement already reached at the highest level. Nor was there any point operating in areas where one had no chance to make one's mark: getting out is often a better way of making a mark, for one's absence might be a nuisance to others, or at least a way of dissociating oneself from the *status quo*. Consequently, apparent isolation, although he may not deliberately have courted it, certainly did not scare him: it was both a (preferably passing) necessity of his kind of game and a *risque du métier*.

2. No nation should expect to receive something for nothing. There are few real gifts; he who expects charity ends up as a dependent. One of de Gaulle's key words was cooperation, one of his key concepts was reciprocity. To receive assistance without giving anything in return is bad not only for one's pride but also for one's status. To give assistance without expecting anything in return but gratitude is doubly foolish, for one will not get the gratitude and will probably incur resentment. But balanced arrangements have a chance to endure since each side can threaten the other with reprisals if it initiates a unilateral change. Nor should a nation expect to get what it wants in exchange for a mere promise: it must deliver something in return. De Gaulle applied this precept in negotiating with the Algerian FLN, and in twice vetoing Britain's entry into the Common Market. If you are in need of, or interested in, aid, do not ask for it; put yourself in the position of having your potential partner suggest it and ask for a favor or service from you in exchange. If you are alone in wanting a given policy change from a more powerful partner uninterested in it, do not ask for it (unless his refusal has the advantage of freeing your hands—this was the case with the American refusal of de Gaulle's plan for a tri-directorate of NATO); bide your time, and act by yourself (this is what de Gaulle did when he pulled France out of NATO when there was no chance of a joint Franco-German reform plan). The backlash from bold, unilateral action is less risky than a collective morass. And when a nation is forced by events to retreat or concede, and does not want to appear to be begging favors from an opponent

in return, it should make the concession unilaterally, as if it were a freely chosen act aimed at forcing the opponent to change his mind. (De Gaulle used this tactic in Algeria; it corresponded not only to his own style but also to the peculiar requirements of revolutionary wars.)

3. What matters is substance, not form. The desirable goal is equilibrium—not agreement or consensus. Even in the New World, U.S. power should be balanced.[40] Balance means moderation. But the balance of power is always shifting; the tapestry of international affairs is never finished. De Gaulle told Adenauer that as long as there was a threat of German *revanche,* he had to throw his weight on the Soviet side, but, as the threat now came from the East, he wanted to side with Bonn. Later, he said that if Bonn was won over to the Soviet side, he would have to cling to the United States.[41] When Bonn clung to the United States, he moved again toward the Russians. When, as he saw it, the balance of power was broken in the Middle East after the Six Day War, he swung to the Soviet side. In no case did his choice of partner mean an identification with him: it only meant a balancing act. For him, treaties and international agencies were no substitute for balancing policies: at best treaties could embody these; at worst they detracted from them. Under de Gaulle, only two major treaties were negotiated by France—the Évian agreements on Algeria, and a Franco-German treaty initiated by Adenauer.

4. If a nation's strength is deficient, it should use the method of the "elevator." When a nation has little power and wants more, it should try to rise to the desired level by using other nations. One hopes to continue until the day when, having arrived at the top level of power, one can send the elevator down. Or, to change the metaphor, one draws a check on other people's bank accounts: it is a loan, but there is no intention to repay. This is a method of some ruthlessness and complete cynicism used on behalf of power politics—*raison d' État*— according to the rules of traditional diplomacy.

For instance, with regard to Berlin in 1961, de Gaulle assumed a most intransigent position, which outraged the United States all the more in that France did not possess the military means to defend Berlin if intransigence led to war. To this charge French diplomacy could reply in two ways. First, the purpose of its hard line was not to provoke war but to deter the Russians from it by intimidating them. (This is what American strategic jargon calls "the rationality of irrationality.") Second, this intransigence had some diplomatic value to the extent that the Russians could not count on a Western disincli-means to deter the Russians and *had not decided not* to use it, i.e., to the extent that the Russians could not count on the Western disinclination to "play the game of chicken." Gaullist strategy was that of "irrevocable commitment"; American strategy was that of "the threat which leaves something to chance," to use the categories of Thomas Schelling.[42] Given American nuclear weapons, American strategy was sufficient to deter the Soviet Union, but not without disturbing the Germans a little. Thus, de Gaulle, in order to promote his rapprochement with Germany, could give himself the luxury of appearing to be suspicious of American intentions in the proportion that he knew their good intentions still existed.

De Gaulle's effort to create a French nuclear force was another instance of the use of America as an elevator. Without the nuclear umbrella of the United States, he would have had no chance of launching a policy opposed to that of Washington and aimed at making the umbrella less necessary. In 1966, his conviction that the United States would not abandon Western Europe allowed him to decide to withdraw France from NATO *and* to stay in the Atlantic Alliance, hoping to gain both from his challenge and from his last signs of loyalty.

Likewise, in his European policy, the General used Germany (or, rather, Chancellor Adenauer) as an elevator. Blocked in his plan for European political cooperation by Benelux, rebuffed by Italy, he could at least sketch out his kind of political organization of Europe by signing the Franco-German treaty of 1963 with the Chancellor. Bonn's need for French friendship also allowed de Gaulle repeatedly in the EEC to shape the common policies he wanted.

Finally, Europe itself served the General as an elevator. He spoke in the name of a Europe which did not exist, exploiting latent aspirations and repressed reservations about the United States that were widespread. In all these instances, he was exploiting to his advantage the facts of military and economic interdependence—facts that limit a statesman's freedom, and give him opportunities for maneuver, since they do not by themselves determine the shape of power relations. De Gaulle would, for the last time, exploit these facts during the monetary crisis in November 1968, receiving financial aid from the very nations whose currencies he had fought but who would have been in trouble had the franc collapsed.

5. The essence of the international game is to get others to do what you want. How to achieve this depends on your relations to them.

If a nation is in a position of strength—in the sense that it has assets which it can use against other nations, or represents a force they need or do not want to lose, or constitutes an obstacle which they must lift to realize their designs or pursue their vital interests—it may maneuver to the hilt. The advantage belongs to the offensive or the inflexible. To be sure, there is a theoretical risk of reprisals, especially when the opponent is militarily and economically more powerful. But, here again, military and economic interdependence will put a sharp limit on how far he can hurt you without hurting himself, whereas if one uses one's own advantages skillfully—military, financial, diplomatic, geographic, etc.—one can hurt him without harming oneself. For what matters is not comparative power but comparative vulnerability. An inferiority in power does not mean greater weakness if the stronger opponent is inhibited from retaliating. Boldness gives advantage: if a nation shows another nation that it can twist interdependence at the latter's expense, it can get away with it.[43] Thus, de Gaulle's way of forcing others to heed him often consisted of practicing a kind of *politique du pire*. If they insisted on following a course he deemed wrong, he would try to force them to keep to it until they realized how uncomfortable it really was, and rallied to his views; indeed, he would help make it uncomfortable. Guinea wanted full independence? She could get it, but at the cost of a complete removal of French participation in her affairs; the Guineans could find out about the flaws in Soviet aid by bitter experience, and alone. Erhard's West Germany wanted to cling to the United States? She would find, in such a case, that Paris was on the road to Moscow, reunification or détente between Bonn and Eastern Europe ever more distant, and Washington's demands becoming unbearable (they ended by toppling Erhard). The United States wanted to consolidate its control on West European defenses by launching the MLF? France would oppose the plan, refuse to join, increase thereby West Germany's hesitations, and let the conflicting expectations and reservations in Bonn, Rome, London, and the United States Senate and other branches of the American government kill the project. Britain wanted to keep its "special relations" with Washington *and* get into EEC? De Gaulle would veto the latter, and let the British suffer the loss of the former. Britain and the United States wanted to preserve the international monetary system? De Gaulle would show them how untenable the *status quo* could become, by withdrawing from the gold pool and refusing to help to ease the pressure on the pound and the dollar. Israel insisted on following a policy disapproved by de Gaulle? He would embargo French planes, force Israel to rely instead on the United States and discover that—as he had warned—the more the conflict became elevated into a superpower confrontation, the less Israel could either get peace on its terms or get it at all. Israel, Guinea, Britain were in no condition to retaliate. Bonn needed France too much, militarily and diplomatically, to retaliate on economic grounds. The United States could not attack the franc without endangering the dollar, and could not remove its military protection from France either.

If a nation is in a position of weakness, it is of course more difficult to get others where you want them. But it need not give up.

In Algeria, de Gaulle showed tactical flexibility, because disentanglement was absolutely necessary—an absolute that weakened the

French position. He got the FLN where he wanted it—at the peace table—only by making major concessions; and yet the final agreements were not merely a face-saving *abandon*. He gave in on independence, but obtained various guarantees and privileges because, even in his fundamental weakness, he still had cards to play. The FLN could not get to Algiers without his consent, even if he could not get out of Algiers without theirs; and once in Algiers, they needed what the French could bring them to build a viable state and economy. Thus, the provision of the operational code could be: when a nation has no alternative but to settle but has counters that will help make the settlement palatable, then bargain.[44] *

The other—and purest—case of weakness could be seen in his relationship with the Soviet Union. Ultimately, the achievement of the Europe he wanted depended on Russia's will. And he never expected mere good will from anyone, especially not the Russians. Of course, he wanted both "hegemonies" out of Europe or turned into nonhegemonic associations; and yet, while he handled the American antagonist by maneuver, denial, refusal, and blunt attack, after 1962 he handled the Soviet antagonist as a prospective partner, by seduction. The reasons for the difference are not hard to find. For one thing, the Soviet Union was the greater obstacle. If the Russians consented to German reunification and gave up control of the satellites, it is hard to imagine the United States hanging on in Western Europe. There was no point in getting the United States out of Europe by promising, in exchange, a *Europe de l'Atlantique à l'Oural,* but there was a point in trying to get the Russians out by assuring them that, in exchange, there would be no German nuclear threat and no American presence. Second, whereas de Gaulle had multiple leverage on the United States, he had none on the Soviet Union. He could make himself attractive to Russia by dissenting from Atlantic orthodoxy and showing himself eager for a détente. But there was no need for the Russians to give anything specific in return for these policies: to get him out of NATO all they had to do was to stop a bankrupt policy of bluster and threats over Berlin. Nor could he push his dissidence so far as to unbalance Europe—i.e., to weaken the West so much as to justify Moscow's hopes of perhaps extending Soviet hegemony westward. Nor could he actually weaken the Soviet hold on Eastern Europe: he knew that the Russians were still the key to what happened in those nations (whereas what happened in Western Europe could—with some will and vision—again be determined in Paris, Bonn, Rome, not Washington). All he had

---

* Contrast with de Gaulle's behavior over the Fouchet Plan discussions: in the absence of a genuine agreement on the functions of the proposed bodies and on their evolution, he did not care to make the concessions that would have allowed the Six to sign a *pro forma* agreement setting up these institutions.

was his own arguments, plus limited economic know-how: this was not enough to convince Moscow that his design for Europe could assure Russia's security and status better than or even as well as the *status quo,* that a "single" Europe, with a reunited Germany and without outside forces would better contain Germany than two Europes, with two Germanys and American and Soviet troops.

6. Present weakness, whether due to a lack of direct means of influencing the course of events or to unfavorable developments, is no reason for giving up if the course one is advocating happens to be the "right" one. "Right" is a complex notion: it does not mean a course that will necessarily prevail in the future, nor does it mean morally pure (de Gaulle had once written that Christian morality does not lead to empire). We have to go back to his vision. "Right" means: in accordance with the imperatives of active independence and great-power status for France, independence from outside domination for Europe, self-determination for genuine nations, and a balanced international system for all. One of de Gaulle's peculiarities as a statesman was his indifference to immediate success. Perhaps this was because his design was such a long-range one. But it was also because of his conviction that, even if this vision was never realized at all, he would still be vindicated by the ugliness of what would happen, or persist, instead. We are close to the universe of William of Orange: it is not necessary to hope in order to undertake, or to succeed in order to continue.

This trait sometimes came out in the form of an ambition to provide a last resort. In his West European policy, de Gaulle used the methods which had succeeded so well in France during the years of his exile in England, the RPF, and his first retirement at Colombey-les-Deux-Églises. He wanted to offer himself to the West Europeans as the supreme alternative, as the man to whom they could turn if American protection lapsed or if it jeopardized Europe's interests. He already had presented himself as the salutary recourse to Frenchmen, first against the Germans and their collaborators, and later when the Fourth Republic was crumbling. In those cases, in order to succeed, he had had to brush aside his rivals, to make the chasm that separated him from Vichy unbridgeable, and to contribute to the weakening of the Fourth Republic. It was a policy of poking a fire in order to demonstrate the helplessness of the firemen. Similarly, within the limits imposed by the need to preserve the security of NATO, he had to put his finger on its weaknesses and on American mistakes—for only thus could he play the role of the last alternative, the sole promoter of Europe's pride. In the days of the Resistance and of the RPF, he had told the French to remember France; in the 1960s, he told the West Europeans to remember Europe.[45]

At other times, de Gaulle seemed to want not so much to appear as a last resort in his own lifetime, but rather to be remembered after it as the man who had discerned clearly what others had failed to see. Here, we are indeed in the misty realm of prophecy more than in the muddy domain of politics. When, first in the summer of 1963 and three years later in Phnom Penh, he outlined the terms of a possible settlement for Vietnam; when he denounced the consequences of the gold exchange standard or the Six Day War; when he outlined the failings of Canadian or Nigerian federalism and called for Québec's or Biafra's freedom; when he discussed the rise of China or the reasons why the Soviet Union might want a settlement in Europe; when he called for a "European Europe"—it was as if de Gaulle was taking a raincheck on the future. Either he would be proven right as a prophet of progress or he would be proven right as a Cassandra.

7. Policy always runs on several tracks. If there are dead ends, there must also be exits from them. There must always be workable alternatives. De Gaulle was always careful not to compromise the present in his attempt not to insult the future. While pursuing a given policy, he kept several options *de rechange* open without losing sight of his goals, by contrast with statesmen for whom the preservation of options means the avoidance of choices. He never pushed his own feud with Washington to the breaking point: so long as Moscow was still on the Elbe, this would have been too dangerous. He never allowed his own rapprochement with Moscow to endanger his relations with Bonn, whose good faith he defended. His two rejections of Britain allowed for a change later, and indeed goaded London into becoming more "European." Also, any one move served several purposes, so that, if France were frustrated by events in one direction, he could still reach at least a subsidiary objective or retreat without any loss of face. This was clear enough in his Algerian tactics, even though the alternatives to a negotiated settlement were grim. His intransigence toward the Soviet Union, in his first phase, served three goals: to force the Russians off a dangerous course, to block direct Soviet-American agreements about Europe, and, should they be reached anyway, to be a catalyst for European resentments and European self-consciousness. Intransigence was thus both a virtue in itself—for it protected Europe—and a means toward Europe's return to the stage. Similarly, the French *force de frappe* was the leavening that would hasten the rise of the slow-baking European cake, and the vitamin that de Gaulle would give France to make her strong amidst a hostile world and a sickly Europe. And in his second phase, de Gaulle's decision to leave NATO was simultaneously: a way of further emancipating France from the "policy of blocs"; a signal to East European nations that might wish to follow France's example; a way of showing Moscow that there was an

alternative to an exclusive Moscow-Washington dialogue on Europe; a surgical cut that made it harder for Britain to join Europe on any terms other than de Gaulle's; and a means of putting pressure on Bonn.[46]

And yet could one not argue that, at the end, he had never gone beyond "square one," that none of the tracks led anywhere, and that the very complexity of his strategy had been self-defeating? [47]

IV

At the time of de Gaulle's resignation, and in the months that followed, his prophecy concerning the international system in general and Europe in particular seemed mistier than ever. His successors did not abandon the effort to build a West European entity through intergovernmental cooperation, nor did they give up the hope of overcoming the division of Europe. But revisionism has been toned down, and the change of methods reveals a change in the degree to which policy in the present is to be determined, dictated, driven by the vision of a distant future. And indeed, the vision itself is not quite the same. Pompidou's statement in early 1972 that West European unification was the precondition of France's keeping and enlarging her role in the world, the only alternative to mediocrity, and a requirement of her independence went far beyond anything de Gaulle had ever said in public: a conditionally useful tool had become a necessity.[48] The recognized lack of a West European consensus on defense and diplomacy was no longer an obstacle either to negotiations with England or to institutional attempts at harmonizing foreign policies among the Six. A lower priority for the realm of "high politics"—strategy and foreign affairs—dear to de Gaulle, and a higher priority to building Europe through economics meant a somewhat less dogmatically hostile attitude to supranationality in the EEC. And West Germany's spectacular initiatives toward the East and resignation to accepting the *status quo* as a precondition to détente were endorsed by de Gaulle's successors; they could not object to what seemed like a logical deduction from Gaullist advice and post-Czechoslovakia necessities, but they took a back seat in this new diplomacy. Except for the unchanged (but inactive) Mediterranean policy, and for a restatement of de Gaulle's program for Indochina, his global claims have been muted. Friendship with the Soviet Union prevails over the old dream of eventual European reunification. The "hegemonies" are tacitly accepted in the realms of diplomacy and security; the conflict with the United States is now limited to trade, agriculture, and (less and less) the international monetary system. The principle of independence remains a dogma; the principle of *active* independence, i.e., the search for major-power status, continues to inspire the construction of a *force de frappe* and the search for a European *relance*. But even these marching orders have been revised in the direction of greater modesty. Independence in industrial policy no longer means a costly effort at self-sufficiency, and major-power status is no longer sought all over the world, or in a daily and permanent challenge of the present international system. Die-hard Gaullists could argue that the essence of Gaullism has been abandoned, that *grandeur* is no longer an end in itself, merely a by-product of industrialization (Pompidou's priority), and therefore in danger of being ascribed to Europe rather than to France. "Pragmatic" Gaullists would have to reply that nothing has really been scrapped, that Europe was not "the beginning of French abdication" but the "national ambition" of a "strong and prosperous nation," [49] and that some things had to be suspended—that this was in the logic of the domestic priority de Gaulle proclaimed at the end, and of the temporarily unfavorable circumstances of the international system. There was enough in de Gaulle of both strategic inflexibility and tactical submission to *les circonstances* to feed the claims of each group.

Their quarrel, an anti-Gaullist could say, bears witness to de Gaulle's own failures. As of now, the Soviet Union's hold over Eastern Europe is undiminished. Bonn's reconciliation with Moscow and Warsaw has not resulted from increasing West European self-confidence (as de Gaulle had hoped) but from the effect of Russia's show of force and from the fear of a continuing decline in America's interest. Yet, again despite de Gaulle's expectations, the United States has not militarily "disengaged" itself from Western Europe, and no West European nation, not even France, is eager for large-scale U.S. withdrawals. West Germany has regained diplomatic autonomy as a normal nation— through the process of launching its own *Ostpolitik* and as a result of its agreements with the East European states. This coincides with pressures in the United States for the departure of American troops from Europe, yet it makes America's presence on the continent—i.e., a perpetuation of the "hegemonies"—*more* necessary to *encadrer* Bonn and to prevent either Soviet preponderance or a future Soviet-West German deal. As a result of all these facts, the next step in East-West relations in Europe is not merely a conference, largely European, on security and cooperation that will consecrate the détente and the political *status quo*, but also a primarily American-Soviet conference on arms-control measures—which might lead to balanced reduction of superpower forces, but would actually legitimize their European presence and their blocs. Britain has entered the West European Community at last, but as the outcome of bargaining on bread-and-butter issues, not as part of a grand balancing exercise dealing with defense, diplomacy, and world currencies. At present, France's departure from NATO serves more as an obstacle than as an incentive to a "Europeanization" of Britain's defense policy and nuclear force; and the only occasional suggestion for a European voice in defense comes from Britain—for a voice to be heard within NATO. (The notion is resisted by Paris and by Bonn.) Within the EEC, as in the past, different attitudes toward the United States lead to difficulties in diplomatic coordination, to divergences over monetary cooperation and to important nuances on the only real common policies in agricultural and external trade. Paradoxically but calculatedly, Bonn is somewhat more acquiescent of the Soviet-imposed *status quo* outside the EEC's boundaries, and, within the EEC, more Atlantic than Paris. This undermines France's challenge of Soviet military "hegemony" in Eastern Europe and France's attempts to exploit the crisis of America's world monetary hegemony.

American predominance in the world's monetary system, while badly shaken, has not been superseded: with an inconvertible dollar, the world is more than ever on a dollar standard, and the changes in parities decided in December 1971 and February 1973 have actually improved America's trading position, and forced its competitors to choose between having to float their currencies and absorbing unlimited amounts of dollars. In space, even on the American continent, U.S. predominance remains unchallenged. The Middle East conflict, engulfed in the dangerous logic of bipolarity, has stumbled into a new war marked once more by signs of confrontation, symptoms of condominium, and prospects of a decisive role for the United States. In the arms race, the distance between the Big Two and the challengers has grown, and even though the Strategic Arms Limitation Talks (SALT) have partly curtailed the future development of the superpowers' arsenal, the gap is now so huge that strategic arguments about multilateral deterrence are more than dubious.

What, then, happened to the Gaullist vision? Why did de Gaulle fail to realize his design? Why did he only partially achieve independence as a big power for France? We must go back to the earlier distinction I made between might and skill. We noted that de Gaulle had repatriated, so to speak, many of France's possession goals. His emphasis on economic growth and modernization, building a nuclear force, strengthening the franc—i.e., on the various facets of France's might—were aimed first of all at protecting France *from* the international milieu. They would of course be used, strategically, for offensive purposes, but their main function was defensive, or for reassurance. Moreover, actual French strength remained meager, partly because of specific weaknesses in the French economy, partly because the priority given to the world stage may not have been the wisest strategy for overcoming them, partly because the opportunities for a middle-size nation today are drastically reduced.[50] Last, but not least, the assignment of so many of France's resources to international efforts exacerbated the problem of getting and keeping public support. There was always (contrary to frequent assumptions, or hopes, abroad) general support for de Gaulle's policies. The vision, insofar as it was understood, was flattering to the French.[51] But it was difficult for *all* citizens to follow him in *all* of his acrobatics; he would raise hopes whose fulfillment was delayed for reasons that were hard to understand, and costly disappointment would follow. This was the story of peasant discontent in 1965. The big farmers' organizations had come to believe that the EEC would solve France's agricultural problems. When de Gaulle boycotted the EEC, in order to obtain a common agricultural policy on his terms, the peasants saw their dream of foreign markets for French milk and honey recede. The result was a loss of votes for de Gaulle on the first ballot of the Presidential Election in December 1965: the farmers were more concerned with specific goods than with French independence. De Gaulle wanted both, and had seemed ready to sacrifice the former to the latter. Then too, his establishment of priorities presupposed or required a willingness on the part of the citizens to accept certain sacrifices in their standard of living. Even more than the allocation of money (it would be hard to argue that French education, or the welfare system, or the production of consumer goods, or needy farmers were starved for public funds), it was a matter of the allocation of attention. Adenauer had once warned de Gaulle about young people's indifference to tradition, and citizens' desire for welfare above nuclear independence.[52] Whether the citizens increasingly came to think that independence was out of reach, or that the quest, even if successful, would be too costly, does not really matter. The confused unwillingness to accept the costs of *grandeur,* a preference for *grandeur* at low cost rather than no *grandeur* at all, or, rather, a desire to have both a prestigious foreign policy *and* more attention given to domestic problems led to the explosion of May 1968. De Gaulle wanted prosperity for *grandeur,* the French wanted *grandeur* as a by-product of propserity.

The heart of the Gaullist design had been to change the international milieu, primarily through the skillful exploitation of favorable trends and French assets. Here, de Gaulle operated under two very different handicaps: those beyond his reach, and those resulting from his style.

Since 1945, the international milieu has witnessed gigantic changes that have come about primarily as a result of revolutions and crises. De Gaulle could try to take advantage of favorable changes that revolutions and crises provoked (we have seen how he exploited the China-Russia break), and he could try to limit the harmful effect of other revolutions and crises on his design (as in the case of the Algerian revolution, or in Czechoslovakia). He could also try to help prevent damaging crises (over Berlin, successfully; in the Middle East in 1967, in vain). But his reach, here, was minimal. Almost by definition, revolutions are hard to manipulate from the outside. Biafra died, Québec delayed a showdown. As for the great crises, being in essence a peacetime substitute for general war, these "moments of truth" tend to reassert the latent bipolarity of the system, i.e., the fact that only two states have the ultimate power to plunge the world into war.

In addition to these two forces of change, there is a remarkable, novel inertia in an international system where states live with the safety net provided by the fear of general war, by economic and financial interdependence, and by the acute pressure of domestic concerns. When the international bonds woven by technology and a truly global economy were less compelling; when "social mobilization" had not yet led to multiple demands for welfare, education, prosperity; when force was not merely the *ultima ratio* but the normal test—the international system was less viscous, the milieu less resilient. The fact is, the bipolar distribution of power that resulted from World War II has evolved slowly; the American and Soviet blocs have disintegrated only insofar as determined statesmen have chosen emancipation and escaped retribution. (At least the superpowers have one option not available to lesser powers: that of reversing by force unfavorable trends in their sphere of domination.)

This inertia of the milieu has been a curse not only for Gaullist designs, but for the superpowers' own, more expansive plans. The grand American vision of an open world living according to the dream of universal free enterprise and constitutional democracy is a utopia; there has been no rollback of communism. The Communist vision has also been contained and cracked. The order of Versailles was fragile and brief. What might unfairly be called the order of Yalta has proved more durable. But a world order where no design prevails is also one where no design needs die: hope springs eternal, in a condition of mutual deadlock and lasting stalemate.

De Gaulle's action on the international milieu consisted mostly in carefully steering and stirring among conflicting currents, so as to keep away the bad ones and make room for others. De Gaulle helped, through his intransigence, to thwart Soviet designs on Berlin in the early 1960s. Later, he sunk the vessel of "Atlantic partnership." Similarly, he killed the British design for joining Europe without renouncing special relations with the United States and the Commonwealth. But Washington and Moscow, separately and together, blocked de Gaulle's "European Europe." The absolute necessity for all Western Europe to depend militarily on the United States; the Soviet Union's determination to preserve control in Eastern Europe; the hold, on many West Europeans, of Monnet's vision of a supranational process leading to integration with no tough questions asked *en route;* the tendency of many European statesmen to leave these questions (beyond their control) to the United States and concentrate instead on economic progress and social change; the continuing divergences among Europeans on those issues—all of this was beyond de Gaulle's reach.

Also, there were flaws in his vision and design. He seems to have overestimated the forces that would make his kind of Europe more attractive to the Soviet Union than the *status quo,* and he underestimated the resilience of Russia's ideology. Neither the economic difficulties of the Soviet Union, nor the rise of nationalism in Eastern Europe, nor the pressure from China were strong enough to make Russia's position in Europe unbearably uncomfortable. The rivalry with China, while increasing Russia's eagerness for accommodation and détente in the West, probably reinforced the determination to consolidate the Western front first, rather than exposing it to the unknown and incalculable, entailed by de Gaulle's scheme. The Soviet regime was such as to provoke a conservative and repressive reaction to forces of change, rather than a revisionist and adaptive one. De Gaulle was right in considering that ideology was a convenient disguise of national interests. But in this instance, the disguise had become the national interest, the *raison d'être:* Communist ideology and control by the Soviet elite were so thoroughly intertwined that lifting Soviet domination in Eastern Europe could lead to a fall of the regimes, and inversely the *dénaturation* of a Communist regime risked a loss of Russian control. For Russia, either would be fatal, in competition with the United States and with China, and at home. The Russian Communist global design may have become frayed, and her ideology as faith eroded, but ideology was still the cornerstone of control at home and abroad, the legitimizer of acts and costs. De Gaulle may have been too unideological to grasp this: the man who had reconverted an empire must have found it hard to conceive that other empire-holders would attach their entire fate to preservation of the *status quo.* In the circumstances of 1965–68, de Gaulle, out of wishful thinking and premature anticipation, imagined in Russia a far greater move away from totalitarianism at home, a greater willingness to let a "hundred flowers" bloom in Eastern Europe, a greater readiness to dissociate influence from domination, and a greater eagerness to get American troops out of Western Europe even at the cost of a parallel retreat of Soviet ones in the East, than existed. Worried about keeping what they had, the Soviet leaders preferred Americans on the Elbe, as long as there were Russians there too. The risks of explosion in one's own zone can be handled—as the Russians showed in Prague; what happens once one is out is less manageable. Between the bureaucrats in Moscow, wanting to hold on, and the strategist of mobility and blitz in Paris a dialogue of the deaf ensued. Imagination was on de Gaulle's side; power on theirs. In the very long run his analysis may still be vindicated. But the time scale was mistaken.

As for his designs, they also suffered from contradiction. De Gaulle wanted West Germany as a partner; he also wanted it under surveillance, restrained on the world stage while he pursued great-power status more than ever. He thought the two were compatible, because he expected that the West Germans would never give up the hope of German reunification, would need his support for it, and could not succeed in it or achieve the prerequisite détente unless they were willing to be modest and accept restrictions. As long as the chances for détente were slim (given Soviet hostility), why should the West Germans push Franco-German partnership so far as to exchange American protection (adequate and geographically remote, if often heavy) for French protection (rough, uncomfortably close, and infinitely weaker)? And, on the other hand, once Bonn were resigned to partition—if not forever or in its heart of hearts, at least for a long time and in all practical matters—why should the West Germans continue to walk with stooped shoulders, speak with low voices, and accept either French or even American chaperons on the world stage? Here again, in his eagerness for change de Gaulle underestimated the resilience of the *status quo*, its way of eroding even the proudest dreams of change. Again, his long-term analysis may be correct—but accurate timing was essential.

This brings us to the flaws in de Gaulle's style. His operational code had rather bizarre aspects. There was what one might call a streak of self-defeatism and a streak of defeatism. Both added to the difficulty of convincing others of the rightness of French policy: they provided counterincentives, in a world already poor in inducements. Realization of de Gaulle's vision required an extraordinary concordance of trends, events, and calculations: a great number of states coming to interpret their interests in *his* way, at approximately the same time. (To give an example from the past, in May 1967 he would have wanted Israel to trust the Big Powers with a settlement of the Gulf of Tiran issue; Egypt to stop bluffing, and to accept a compromise that would satisfy Israel; and both nations to use the opportunity to solve all their other differences too.) Yet his code of behavior was based on conflict (even as a way of producing compromise) more than on conciliation; and it made for contagion, more than for convergence. *I* may succeed, by being suitably obnoxious (or, when I am too weak for that, by being suitably prophetic) in persuading you that *you* are wrong in doing what you are doing. But is this enough to convince you that *you* ought to do what *I* say? Would you not rather learn from me that you ought to do something that would be truly *yours*, yet in *my* way, to use my book for *your* ends? I may force you to budge from your position; but, having been rudely dislodged, is it likely that you would come to mine?

There was an inherent contradiction here between a vision that required others to see their things in de Gaulle's way, and a method by which he refused to put himself in other people's shoes. Consequently, Erhard's failure did not make Kiesinger return to Adenauer's policy; after reliance on the United States and France, then symbiosis with the United States, West Germany began to emancipate herself from both. Britain may have moved closer to Europe after the lesson de Gaulle inflicted in 1963, but not enough to make Wilson any less suspicious of de Gaulle. Israel has indeed found reliance on the United States uncomfortable and Soviet involvement in Egypt calamitous, but not so much as to follow de Gaulle's free advice of November 1967. If he treated West European unity not as an unconditional goal but as a vehicle for French interests and ambitions, why shouldn't others do the same, and, like West Germany today, refuse to let themselves be burdened or diverted by it when and where it is of little use to them? To be sure, de Gaulle's great strength was to exploit opportunities of maneuver that others did not have, however much they might have wanted to imitate him. But after some years of maneuver, the willingness of anyone to serve the interests of other nations disappears; in the beginning they had let themselves be so used because they needed France. (The United States needed French lines of communication for NATO, Bonn needed reconciliation with France, the Soviet Union needed de Gaulle as an *interlocuteur de rechange,* etc.) But NATO learned to survive France's pullout; Bonn and London and Tel Aviv waited for *l'après-de Gaulle.* De Gaulle was probably not surprised by this. No method was perfect, but he considered the backlash from his own less dangerous than the by-products of meekness in the jungle.* Moreover, in a world of constantly shifting power and changing circumstances, there were no permanent conglomerations. The design was more a compass or a magnet than a final *terminus:* "In such matters nothing turns out exactly as one had hoped." [53] Things will never be, or never be for long, what they ought to be.

---

* Critics have often replied that much of contemporary international politics deals with economic issues that are most susceptible to a very different operational code: that of technocratic politics and interest-group bargaining; de Gaulle's style was often counterproductive, they say, because it was obsolete. This argument will be more fully discussed in Chapter 12. It exaggerates the degree to which "old" international politics is being *superseded* by the politics of economic interdependence; and even within the latter sphere, it underestimates the degree to which states continue in fact to manipulate interdependence and to shape it according to their power and will.

This brings us to de Gaulle's streak of defeatism. Things being what they are and states following only their interests as they see them, he seemed to say, one has to act on the pessimistic assumption that they will *not* see reality your way. This is the prophet's fondness for the self-fulfilling prophecy, characteristic of his internal as well as foreign policy, the other aspect of his frequent resort to *la politique du pire*. It is a technique that can be practiced as a way of teaching others the logical consequences of what is wrong with them, and also because *le pire* is an ever-present possibility for which one must be ready. Thus, in 1965, he exclaimed that no one knew where West Germany would be going, and staged a rapprochement with Moscow which made the prophesied detachment of Bonn more possible. Convinced that Britain as well as West Germany would tend to cling to NATO, he left NATO, thus leaving London and Bonn in a *tête-à-tête*. Having said that a vicious Middle Eastern circle of repression, revolt, guerrilla warfare, and Israeli expansionism was inevitable, he took measures that could not fail to result in encouraging Arab as well as Israeli intransigence. Again, de Gaulle could not be surprised: if things are what they are—unpleasant—one cannot change them to one's advantage by closing one's eyes to them, or act as if they would not turn out badly if one denied that they ever could, like those pacifists who believe that facing the possibility of war makes it likely. Rather, since the "evil"— each actor's tendency to see things his own way, whatever the results —is inherent in the game, the statesman must look for a way of either making these results so bad as to force the other actor to see things differently or else surviving the results. This assumes, of course, that the ultimate vision may not be realized at all or, if it is, only through long detours and bitter battles.

And yet, *le pire* is not *certain* to happen, and even though things will not be perfect, they can be made to be better, or to come about sooner. Here we come to another aspect of de Gaulle's operating style that upset statesmen and observers. His vision was extraordinarily long range: nobody, including de Gaulle, could put a date on its fulfillment—too much depended on *les circonstances*. And yet he was in a hurry to get things moving—a hurry that seemed to increase during his last years in office, and that made setbacks look worse, or more damaging, than they would have seemed if the General's predictions about the inevitable collapse of the walls of Jericho in the future had not been accomplished by so many insistent knocks. There may have been no inherent contradiction between the loftiness of his concepts and the frenzy of his tactics, but the contrast contributed to public discouragement among the French (whom de Gaulle himself had described as fickle) and to sarcasm among commentators (to whom the long range is what happens next year).

I must end on a note of caution, which invites us to take a different look at de Gaulle's achievements. He never expected the realization of his prophecies during his lifetime. Had they ever been more than a grand myth to make action and life worth while, to inspire the French out of the terrible shocks they had suffered? Should one measure him against his failure to do the impossible, or against his achievements?

In de Gaulle's personality, there was at one extreme a dreamer of grand enterprises, who set as a distant goal the kind of world that was indeed a transposition into modern terms of the historical periods most favorable to France's influence and power. Here, what was "right" was not necessarily what was reachable: *it was enough to move in that direction.* Even in this large perspective, his achievements were not minor. De Gaulle's attempt to overcome the "German anomalies" and to give greater play to forces of national emancipation in Eastern Europe remains the only valid European policy, i.e., the only one capable of succeeding at all in the long run, the only one worthy of Europe's pride even if it should fail. France's reconciliation with West Germany was managed in such a way that even today's "semidetached" West Germany is still loyal to the West, tied to France in the EEC. Under changed circumstances, Bonn is following today the policy of reconciliation with the East advocated by de Gaulle many years earlier; it is infinitely more eager for "détente, entente, and cooperation" with all its neighbors than for *revanche* against any, or new domination; it is increasingly aware that as its freedom to move alone theoretically grows, the directions into which it actually can move profitably are few: the Soviet sirens offer no condominium, and NATO and the EEC still offer a mast of security. The Common Market's horse, through the use of sticks more than carrots, is drinking where de Gaulle wanted it: his beatings neither killed it nor exhausted it. Britain has come closer to accepting the terms explicitly laid down by de Gaulle for its recognition as a worthy member of a Europe *"affranchie";* even if Pompidou was easier to satisfy with vague answers than the General, all the questions asked at Edward Heath's exam were some of de Gaulle's. And France has established herself as a worthwhile (or unavoidable) *interlocuteur* for both superpowers and as a still prestigious power among the nations of the Third World. The United States increasingly acknowledges the waning of the bipolar era and is striving to establish a new balance of power in a multipolar world: this is a belated tribute to de Gaulle's correct anticipation of major trends. The spectacular crises of the world monetary system in 1971 and 1973 vindicated the General's denunciations.

Nor should the more brutal aspects of de Gaulle's operational code and the more pessimistic Hobbesian or Brechtian aspects of his conception of world affairs blind one to the nature of his goals and his efforts. He tried to create a world in which total enmity would be replaced with only partly adversary relations, making room for détente without illusion and cooperation without servitude. This is the best détente one can strive for in a world of competing and unequal states. Intransigence was used on behalf of a design in which domination and hegemony would be replaced by association, in which iron or bamboo curtains would be lifted, and in which even the marks of French "superiority" (over, say, Germany) would be in the realms of available weaponry and diplomatic maneuver, not in the annihilating realm of actual control. The ideal was consistent. My role is to try to influence and weigh on *your* course, it is not to guide your hand and make the move *for* you. The nature and purpose of the constraints themselves would have been a moderate world order. Tactics derived from the battlefield and applied to the world stage aimed at dampening violent conflicts, and specifically at bringing peace back to France —embattled from 1939 to 1962—and at keeping her out of wars. In this de Gaulle succeeded, as he did in using favorable trends in order to end France's relation of psychological dependence on the United States, to separate France's necessary dependence on the United States for its security from any unnecessary abdication of strategic and diplomatic decision-making power, to penetrate the iron and bamboo curtains as far as possible, and to reconvert France's collapsing empire into a flexible, if flawed, association.[54] Whether another statesman could have attained the same results by "softer means" remains a matter of opinion. To my mind, the tougher methods rarely did lasting harm, often helped to clarify matters, and frequently got results.

At the other extreme, there was what could be called de Gaulle's minimum, but also unshakable, objective: to keep a base clear, from which France—when she was stronger and the winds more favorable —could again start to climb. The function of toughness here was to remove the obstacles and dodge the traps. Protecting France's chances, renewing her strength in order to protect them more easily and allow her to resume the march at every opportunity—this was his mission. Any diversions would only perpetuate the self-doubts, humiliations, and domestic torments that had resulted from the fall of France in 1940.[55] If the present was bleak and the future blocked, the alternative was a small but independent France, acting temporarily like the Swiss or Swedish hedgehogs, but—by contrast with them—tailoring her strength to the demands of future enterprises, actively making herself ready to turn independence into *grandeur* whenever possible. For his famous insistence on "free hands" for France meant not merely a command to others to keep their hands off, but a command to France to use hers for *une grande querelle* as soon as circumstances would allow. Meanwhile, his proclamations would show the way even when it could not yet be traveled.

In this task, de Gaulle's success was limited by the inexorable constraints that weigh on middle-size nations and transform the meaning or possibilities of "independence." Today, in order to have hands at all, such nations may have to join forces and accept some ties. These limits create a dilemma for his successors for which orthodox Gaullism provides no precise answer since it did not really pose the question. Is it better to opt for more "integrity," at the cost of making France more like Switzerland, i.e., of abandoning ambition? Is it better to preserve the ambition of the great role and the long march, at the cost of having entangling relationships with others with whom the role will have to be shared and whose direction may not be the same? Achieving his design for the world required a vast ambition, and appropriately huge means. Yet his imperatives for France stressed integrity above all. Ironically, many parts of de Gaulle's design seem closer to realization today than some of his imperatives: our multipolar world is not one in which France is a major, active member, even though she is an independent one. And as long as France or any other West European power insists on its independence, the West European entity remains in limbo and *grandeur* eludes both it and its members.

In the absence of a firm solution, de Gaulle at least provided a clear position. As long as France is mistress of herself, accepts the necessary entanglements lucidly, decides them herself, is vigilant about unwelcome effects, and can regain full freedom if these last come to prevail —in other words, as long as decisions are made in Paris, even if they are decisions for joint action—nothing is lost. The imperative of independence and the need for *grandeur* are both vital: there may be tension between them, but neither should be sacrificed to the other. And here, perhaps, lie de Gaulle's two greatest achievements. By his determination to protect and to renovate, by his ambition even to undertake what may often have been excessive, he has, as one critic put it, *"dé-ridiculisé"* France in the eyes of others, after many years of ridicule.[56] Respect or consideration was an integral part of his minimum goal. In the same way, he restored French self-respect. He was deeply convinced that, in the world of nations, he who does not keep running falls behind. Having restored French chances and maintained France in the race must have been a source of ultimate satisfaction to him.

11
Perceptions and Policies:
France and the
United States

Franco-American relations in the years of the Fifth Republic are a fascinating example of the importance of perceptions in foreign policy. The distinction between perception and reality in world politics is always arbitrary. For here as elsewhere perceptions are part of reality. The student of politics who looks only at patterns of behavior and leaves out the meanings that the actors give to their own and each other's conduct will become a specialist of shadows. Perceptions are more than a part of political reality: they mold it, they are the springs and fuel of action. And, of course, they are themselves shaped by reality.

The problem of perception-vs.-reality arises nevertheless for various important reasons. The perceptions of each government are shaped by its own and its nation's experience, a segment of reality that is not the same as any other actor's; the various attempts to shape reality project these different experiences onto the world stage. Distortion and conflict are thus insured by the selectiveness and parochialism of perceptions. Also the international system, although it imposes certain limits and imperatives of its own on the policies of all nations, is largely the outcome of their decisions and operations. The basic trends are often malleable enough to be twisted or even reversed by the main actors' moves. Thus, reality is in considerable part the product of a conflict of wills, of a contest of active perceptions competing for the privilege of defining reality. So long as the test is unresolved, each contender has, so to speak, his own reality; "real" reality is still in the making.

This chapter includes "Perceptions, Reality, and the Franco-American Conflict," published in *The Journal of International Affairs*, V. XXI, No. 1 (1967); parts of "Minimum Feasible Misunderstanding," published in the *New Republic*, April 5 and 12, 1969; and parts of "Franco-American Differences over the Arab-Israeli Conflict, 1967–71," *Public Policy*, Fall 1971.

Once the test is over, reality marks either the point of equilibrium reached by deadlocked wills or the scope of the triumph of the prevailing will; retrospectively, the perceptions that lost will now appear to the observer as having deviated from reality.

Thus uncertainty, complexity, and openness in the international system account for the creative role of perceptions, and for the difficulty in determining which perceptions have more weight and efficiency. All this in turn contributes to the fundamental uncertainty of world politics.

The present international system undermines and transforms many of the generally accepted components of "reality" in world affairs. Whereas it had been widely recognized that a high correlation existed between a state's material ingredients of power and its capacity to reach its goals, new conditions of the use of force and the spread of what one might call the legitimacy of the nation-state have lowered that correlation, reduced the inequality of the actors, and made the evaluation of power infinitely more complex. The purely objective ingredients are more difficult to translate into effective results, and the more subjective ones have gained more weight. A correct perception of the other actors' goals and handicaps, and of the limits within which maneuver is possible, can become a partial substitute for material power. When the physics of power declines, the psychology of power rises. Also, reality was usually defined in terms of who controlled what and who possessed what. The same new factors have led states to transfer their greed and expectations from physical mastery to the shaping of the international milieu—from tangibles to intangibles. What constitutes success and failure, what is "real" gain or merely "symbolic" or "illusory" achievement, is hard to say. Perhaps international politics today should be defined less as a struggle for power than as a contest for the shaping of perceptions. When force loses some of its prominence, power becomes the art of making you see the world the way I see it, and of making you behave in accordance with my vision. Past international politics were often played out in an arena of coercion-without-persuasion; now it tends to be an arena of more or less coercive persuasion.

The importance of perceptions in a system where the less powerful actors have acquired new leverage is further boosted by the increase in the number of nation-states. When the skills of persuasion have to be spread over so many players, the uncertainty of the game—to use a most fashionable term—escalates. Reality is the game, but the outcome is clouded. Each actor's perception of himself, of others, and of the game is shaped by his national situation, and the more nation-states there are, the more the divergences and the conflicts multiply. Any one power's ability to affect the milieu consequently decreases.

I. Battle: Perceptions and Issues

The history of Franco-American relations in the de Gaulle era can be divided into three parts. The first covered the time when de Gaulle was engaged on the domestic front, trying to extricate France from Algeria and to destroy the hopes of his internal adversaries who expected him to fade away immediately after the Algerian war. His relations with the United States were friendly. Despite clashes that revealed underlying conflicts of vision and policies, the General chose not to maximize the divergences.

A second phase began at the time of the settlement of the Algerian war in the spring of 1962, developed fully after de Gaulle's smashing victory at the elections of November 1962, and lasted until the spring of 1968. This was the phase in which the conflict was most acute. Both countries—or, to be more precise, the statesmen in charge of foreign affairs—started, to be sure, with a similar notion of reality; but the agreement was so narrow as to be almost meaningless, for what was obvious to them was far less significant than what was at issue. What was obvious to both was: 1) the existence of a struggle between two superpowers, the United States and Soviet Russia, one of whose main stakes was control of Western Europe; 2) the decline of Western Europe's influence because of the events of the 1930s and World War II; 3) the present necessity for Western Europe to seek military security in an alliance with the United States; 4) the imperative of managing the struggle in such a way as to avoid a nuclear war; and 5) the existence of an irresistible tide of decolonization (a fact the French were slow to recognize). This constituted reality for both, and yet there were conflicting visions of international affairs and conflicting diplomatic styles.

From 1947 to the end of the 1960s there was one dominant American image of international affairs and of America's role in them. World politics was seen as a contest, pitting the forces of order, stability, and evolutionary change against the forces of aggression and subversion. The former were supposed to contain the latter in such a way that statesmen with an evil intent would not only be thwarted, but also conclude that it was in their own best interest to mend their ways and play a responsible, "pragmatic," i.e., nonviolent, part in the global symphony. The forces of order were also supposed to encourage everywhere those political leaders and groups that stood for moderation. Shapers of American policy perceived the United States as being, by necessity and by vocation, the one nation that carried world responsibilities in this battle for order. Only the United States had the combination of power, values, institutions, and interests that made for leadership all over the globe. This is not to say that they considered the

United States to be a "global policeman" protecting its own narrow interests. American leaders, while obviously looking after national interests, nevertheless believed that the interest of mankind was identical to the higher interest of the United States; they saw the United States as the secular arm of an ideal of universal value, and they considered America's involvement in world affairs to be a necessary and proper substitute for the frequent failure of other nations to share the burden.

This view of international affairs encompassed the notion of a duel between two groups—one might call it a contest between black and white—and the idea of ultimate, if hard-won harmony. It provided the United States with an apparently simple criterion for evaluating other nations' behavior: they would be in or out of favor depending on whether their performance contributed to or detracted from the efforts to build an effective common barrier against the forces of disorder, on whether their acts advanced or retarded the attainment of ultimate harmony. And in the American approach one could discern what might be called an attitude of selfless superiority: superiority because of a deep conviction that the American sense of purpose and responsibility gave U.S. foreign policy a yardstick by which one could calculate everyone's best interest; selfless because the yardstick was used for a conception of the common rather than the purely American good.

French perceptions of international affairs clashed with America's at every point. French leaders—and especially de Gaulle—saw world politics as a *multiple* contest in which efforts to divide the contenders into two camps were both dangerous and futile: dangerous because it threatened peace as well as the independence of the weaker nations; futile because it was of the essence of the international milieu that ideological camps and military coalitions disintegrated under the strains of rival national interests. They considered any expectation of final harmony naïve: the range of choices ran instead to the gamut of grays, extending from bellicose instability to fragile moderation. In such a world, the French expected the dominant powers to seek to preserve and extend their sway, and to rationalize or disguise it under a cloak of ideological Messianism or altruistic universality. As for the smaller powers, though they may have no choice but to seek the protection of a giant, their interest and therefore their duty was thought to be in maintaining a margin of autonomy to preserve their own integrity and self-respect, and in safeguarding all chances to restore a system of world order that would moderate the clashes and balance the claims of the great powers.

Hence, there was a wide gap between the perceptions of the two nations. American leaders (and many scholars as well) believed that international politics in the nuclear age would be unstable if the number of major powers pursuing their national interests in traditional

ways increased too much, and more stable if the two superpowers over-
came their antagonisms and pooled their responsibilities *qua* great
powers, so to speak: such a duopoly would be tantamount to a conversion of the Soviet Union to America's notion of order. To the French,
this Soviet-American cooperation might perhaps insure peace and stability at the strategic level, but it would also impose intolerable restraints on smaller powers; in particular, it would probably consolidate the partition of Europe and preserve the *de facto* hegemony of
each superpower in its half of Europe.

There was also an interesting contrast in the two nations' perceptions of each other. The United States judged French actions during
the Fifth Republic as wicked, measured against the kind of world
order it deemed in the interests of humanity. The French attacks on
and secession from NATO were considered dangerous for Western security, as giving aid and comfort to the forces of chaos. The idea of a
French nuclear arsenal was considered wasteful and an encouragement
to irresponsibility. French nationalism was resented for being anachronistic, nefarious, and destructive. French attacks on the dollar and
demands for a return to the gold standard, French criticisms of the
Special Drawing Rights as inflationary and misgivings about American
investments in Europe were dismissed as absurd and mischievous.

In other words, the United States perceived French foreign policy as
a capricious if systematic demolition of everything that seemed promising in postwar Western policy. Disbelieving that a reasonable statesman could dismiss a world view as sensible as their own, or proposals
as generous or practical, Americans saw behind every Gaullist move a
calculation far more sinister, devious, or mean than it ever was. When
Robert Bowie or John Newhouse calls de Gaulle a tragic figure, he
expresses this perception aptly.[1] Although the perception of the immediate effect of de Gaulle's acts might be correct, there was a misperception of his purposes. American officials and commentators tended to
see an "atavistic" nationalism in his moves, to use Dean Acheson's
words, a desire to bring back the world of 1913. They failed to understand that his vision of a French return to *grandeur* was inseparable
from his vision of a new international system which differed profoundly from the world of the nineteenth century precisely because of
the restraints imposed by nuclear weapons, the emergence of many
new independent states, and the cooperative functional ties among nations. Convinced that American policy alone aimed at stability and
equilibrium, they could not comprehend that de Gaulle too desired
balance, albeit of a very different sort. American leadership was natural and benevolent. French attempt to exert leadership in Europe was
a megalomaniac's drive for impotent domination. De Gaulle's insistence on a European (i.e., French) presence in Soviet-American discus-

sions was dismissed as an arrogant nuisance. American experts, blinded by what de Gaulle's acts had done to Monnet's dream, did not perceive the European patriotism of de Gaulle.

American misperceptions of France resulted largely from an implicit conviction that the best a smaller Western power can hope to do is play the rather modest role assigned to it in the "grand design." French misperceptions of American policy were of a slightly different nature. Their preconceived notions did not concern what an orderly world *ought* to be but, rather, how a major power *tends* to behave. Americans criticized France for departing from a yardstick France did not *want* to observe; the French criticized the United States for behaving in a way that Americans quite indignantly deny *is* their mode of behavior. Americans resented the impact of French actions on the American design—de Gaulle's vision was half-misunderstood, half-rejected. This partial misperception of de Gaulle's intentions did not matter too much to the French, partly because the style of Gaullist (and indeed classical European) diplomacy is indifferent to intentions, partly because much American criticism dealt with the "consequences of General de Gaulle." On the contrary, France's quarrel with the United States was a quarrel about motives. The French were convinced that the United States acted as a hegemonial nation, slightly drunk with power, and resorted, like all empires, to moralistic window dressing of the naked *animus dominandi*. As a result, the French tended to misperceive the consequences of American acts—for instance by expecting, all too logically, American interventionism to be universal. But the main emphasis was on motivations. This was actually ironic, for the French were not denying America's good intentions: they were saying, in effect, that America's deepest drives were contradicting those intentions, that Americans were unaware of it—"we know you better than you know yourselves"—and that what mattered was not the pure heart (occasionally betrayed by impure execution) but the behavior dictated by the drive.

Americans, faced with French acts, bemoaned their effect. The French, faced with American acts, wasted little time deploring their effect, for they expected great powers to act that way—expected them to try to preserve their privileged position by rewarding the most docile and opposing the most rebellious of their allies, to reach agreements behind the backs of weaker partners, to use force in the defense of threatened positions, etc. Nothing could be more resented in the United States. For what was attacked, it was felt here, was the very integrity of America's policy, not merely its results; Americans denounced French moves, the French attacked America's self-image. As a result, the debate became acrimonious and fuzzy. It was acrimonious because the Americans felt unfairly blamed and insulted, even though the French attitude was far more cynical than sanctimonious. In effect, the French were saying: "Now it's your turn to behave that way, and our role to block you: thus turn the wheels of history." They were not saying: "You're behaving disgustingly." But when Americans are accused of playing power politics and of being as preoccupied with the promotion of their national interest as everybody else, they often react with the anger of hurt pride, for even though they may indeed *act* that way, they only rarely *think* in those tough terms—or at least they are not aware of it. And the debate was fuzzily elusive because most American leaders on the whole radically and indignantly rejected the analysis the French presented of U.S. actions. The French told the Americans: "We don't want to do or become what you prescribe for us." And the Americans told the French: "We are not at all what you say we are." France's interpretation of American policy battered America's values—it denied the existence of a special, selfless American conscience distinguishing America from all other previous leading nations, and it disappointed American expectations of harmony and friendship, especially between traditional allies.

It is easy to see in these two patterns of perceptions, or misperceptions, the effect of each nation's past. In the case of France, there is a long tradition of cabinet diplomacy, a long history during which France was often an imperial colossus, a long practice of world affairs in which the balance of power was equated with moderation and bipolar alignments were equated with war, a protracted distrust of Anglo-Saxon "sincerity" (exemplified in popular clichés as well as, say, in Michelet), a still considerable pride in having been the first modern state and modern nation, and the more recent experiences of World War II. All of these factors made for an understandable desire to play a tune of French making, rather than one which someone else had selected, and it helped the French to view the United States as just another dominant power, differing from its predecessors only in its relative greenness and in its capacity for self-delusion. In the case of the United States, at least until recently, history did not confer an understanding of or a sympathy for various aspects and practices of European diplomacy, such as the balance of power or self-assertive nationalism. Rather, it conferred a set of values that might be called missionary: a belief that involvement in world affairs in general, and resort to force or to the various wiles and black arts of world politics in particular, can only be justified—indeed, are made imperative—by the need to save the world from chaos and evil, and to establish a pluralistic and progressive order that corresponds to the highest interests of all. Moreover, the American history of long periods of isolation broken by briefer periods of involvement in international affairs did not prepare the missionary for the frustrating task of cooperating with others as equals. In a nation that Ralf Dahrendorf has called "the applied Enlightenment," the expectation of harmony, the faith in consensus among friends, encourages an anticipation of compliant collaboration by weaker partners, harnessed to their major ally by a common ideal. America's past leads to diplomatic shortcuts, ellipses, and illusions.

The two nations' positions on the chessboard of world politics was also important. The United States perceived international affairs and the behavior of France from the viewpoint of a superpower that sees itself as fighting an essentially defensive battle in a revolutionary international system. It tended almost of necessity to appreciate the moves of other nations in the light of the global strategy that it alone had the responsibility and means to define and apply. Consequently the United States reacted less impatiently to limited disagreements within its "camp" and to local challenges from restive associates than to a *défi* as broad and fundamental as de Gaulle's. Narrow dissents affect only the execution of a strategy whose over-all design is not challenged; they are minor disturbances in a centrally controlled system. Characteristically, the American replies to de Gaulle's memorandum of September 1958, asking for a Western three-power directorate of world-wide scope, consisted of suggestions for geographically limited and lower-level cooperation, as if the disagreements were narrow. British attempts to institute a dialogue with the Soviet Union were tolerated in Washington as a necessity of British domestic politics. But de Gaulle's overtures to the Soviet Union were greeted with dismay, for, unlike Britain, he had an over-all strategy different from Washington's. De Gaulle's policy seemed to question the very legitimacy of America's postulates, pretenses, and uses of power. American reactions reminded one at times of the shocked and angry responses of a colonial power when rebels ask for independence (ranging from "Aren't they ungrateful after all we've done for them?" to "We must reassert our leadership and teach them a lesson in power," to "They don't realize that by themselves they couldn't do a thing"). At times, American responses were like the reactions of people established in power and faced with a revolutionary opposition that wilfully defies the smooth, orderly procedures of channeled disagreement and denounces the invocation of legality and higher interest as hypocritical.

France's perceptions also were largely dictated by her position in the postwar world, the position of a Western power that needed and accepted America's military protection and at the same time had problems that were bound to create tensions with the United States. France was a power especially concerned with Germany and inevitably worried about any policy that would tend to produce complete equality between her and Germany. France also had suffered enormous losses from the "political collapse" of Europe and empire; she was inevitably worried about any policy that would tend to perpetuate the partition and divided dependence of Europe, or any policy that might dismiss her residual pretensions as a world power as anachronistic. If Americans saw their position as one of being on a global defensive, the French were global revisionists. The United States could not sympathize with a revisionism that appeared to Americans as obsolete and parochial. The French could not fail to resent an American strategy that left no room for their revisionism. Having to decide whether this strategy was deliberate or accidental, they chose the first interpretation because they could not believe that a power in America's position would *not* have a deliberate and consistent policy. Each nation, given its position, was led to a different interpretation of the uses and prospects of power in the nuclear age. The United States, with the biggest stock of military and economic power in the world, tended to minimize or ignore the very special difficulties that nations face today in translating such a supply into efficient uses, and to dismiss as illusory the claims of weaker nations, with comparatively tiny supplies of such power, to an active role. Americans considered these claims puffs, and the nations which made them capable of only "verbal" policies or gestures. France had tiny nuclear and mediocre industrial supplies, and for complex reasons little present desire, hope, or possibility of adding the supply of her West European partners to her own within an integrated community. She was therefore encouraged to exploit to the hilt the opportunities that the international system afforded to weaker states well endowed with all the intangible elements of power; these are much more evenly distributed than the material assets and much more exploitable when material assets are paralyzed or unusable. A vicious circle set in: Americans chalked up the "failures" of de Gaulle, failing to perceive that the game he played, with the means he had, was one whose results could not be assessed in the short run. And the French chalked up American failures and attributed them to *hubris,* without taking into account either the way Americans tried to justify their uses of power, or the way they tried to restrain those uses, or the fact that the international system impartially frustrated the designs of the mighty and the not-so-mighty alike.

Finally, the procedures the two nations follow in the making of foreign policy have accounted for a considerable misperception of each other. American decision-making, which combines a national bent toward *ad hoc* pragmatism and a terrifically complex process of intra-agency bargaining and bureaucratic consensus-formation, often makes for a series of short-term decisions.[2] The long range is dimly seen, perceived more in the form of general principles of a moral nature, ideal norms, than as a set of possible and desirable power relations and political connections. The magnitude of the tasks undertaken by American foreign-policy-makers and the nature of the machinery tend to produce crisis diplomacy—to yield decisions in and for emergencies, and to leave them intact (or to let their effects run their course) until the next emergency. For American decision-makers, France's diplomatic practices were doubly obnoxious. First, the intellectual *démarche* of a man like de Gaulle, moved by a long-range vision of a fundamentally political (rather than moral) nature, struck them, engaged as they were in the harrowing task of holding the line and coping with trouble all over the globe, as presumptuous and irrelevant. Second, the flexibility of his tactics—simultaneously pursuing courses that converged in the long run yet conflicted in the short run, leaving options open without avoiding essential choices or losing sight of final goals, and seizing the best moment for exploiting ambiguous trends—clashed with their habits and expectations.

For French decision-makers, the custom of starting with a long-range vision or at least with political guidelines was so strong that other nations were always judged as if they too acted in the same way. American moves were therefore seen not as improvisations but as an unfolding design, as elaborate and profound calculations. The French conduct of foreign affairs was diplomacy in the traditional style, heir to the policy of cabinets, calculations, and concealment, to balance-of-power politics and practical and limited alliances. The entire American tradition—that of Washington, Wilson, and Roosevelt—regarded this policy with distrust, as a permanent manifestation of cynicism, immorality, and Machiavellianism.

Neither American nor Gaullist diplomacy would get very high marks for the ability to cooperate with other nations as equals, to negotiate and to consult with skill and tact. But this common failing had different results on each side. On the American side, there was almost a mythology about negotiation, consultation, and cooperation: the methods used for domestic consensus-building were projected outside, disregarding the fact that techniques which work well among domestic partners united on fundamentals may be quite useless, in and of themselves, in producing agreement with foreign partners. What an American ally will experience as a merely routine system of supplying interallied information which does not in the least affect the American monopoly on ultimate decisions, Americans will celebrate as a genuine effort at sharing responsibilities. Consequently, they dismissed French charges about American domination in the diplomacy and strategy of NATO and considered French unilateral moves made without consultation with them as scandalous. They experienced French *faits accomplis* as acts of nihilistic defiance, not as reactions to a *status quo* disadvantageous to France. As for the French, they interpreted the contrast between American words (the ritual of harmony) and deeds (refusal to share supreme power) as evidence that the United States was determined to preserve its hegemony and as a license for them to retaliate in kind.

The three areas in which Gaullist and American perceptions clashed most vividly were Europe, Vietnam, and the Middle East.

In Europe, there was a clash over two related issues. Washington considered de Gaulle's rejection of the "Monnet method" of West European unification an exercise in retrograde nationalism; de Gaulle thought that America's support for this method was a clever attempt to control a rootless (*apatride*) conglomerate from the outside.[3] Concerning East-West relations in Europe, American policy-makers appeared to vacillate between two approaches. One was that of the old "situations of strength" policy: the first duty of the West was to organize its own camp. The later idea of an Atlantic partnership between Western Europe and the United States was a variation on this old design. The other approach, advocated by Zbigniew Brzezinski[4] and partly endorsed by President Johnson in 1966, was that of a deliberate and coordinated "opening to the East" designed to take advantage of changes in Soviet policy and of the growing desire in both parts of Europe for closer ties across the iron curtain. Both approaches shared one dogma: that the world needed American leadership and Western cohesion. In one version, only these two factors could provide Western Europe with military security and could exorcise "atavistic" intra-European rivalries; in the other version, only these two factors could, in the long run, succeed in shaking off Soviet hegemony in Eastern Europe. From both perspectives, French actions such as the blocking of supranational institutions in the EEC, the two vetoes of Britain's entry into the Common Market, the rejection of Kennedy's Nassau formula, and the final exit from NATO were perceived as foolish: they left the West fragmented, and they jeopardized European security by giving comfort to the Russians, by complicating allied communications, and by obliging the allies to rely more heavily on a nuclear deterrent whose plausibility had decreased; and France by herself could not promote an "opening to the East" that would be favorable to all Western interests. In both cases, French moves were seen as giving West Germany a bad example—that of a *Realpolitik* which deliberately discarded alliance mechanisms and tried to enhance national prestige by direct dealings with Moscow. Thus American officials disliked French moves partly because they were "unreal," and partly because they were only too real, i.e., capable of imitation.

However, the French considered that Atlantic "monolithism" was the main cause of division and immobility in Europe. They believed that West European security was sufficiently assured by the nuclear stalemate, and not significantly enhanced by a vast number of conventional forces arrayed against the Soviet Union. They denied that a Western bloc led by the United States could ever convince the Russians to consent to German reunification, especially since West Germany would have no incentive to accept the military and border concessions that would have to be the prerequisites to any reunification. In any event, they feared that America's drive for an entente with Russia would take precedence over any concerted Western effort to change the *status quo* in Europe. And the French did not believe that West Germany could follow their example and, say, repeat Rapallo: a West Germany detached from and angry at the West would still be potentially dangerous to the Soviet Union. Thus, to the French, their own design was the only sensible one. They believed that in the long run it would appeal to East Europeans tired of Soviet domination and get the Soviets to consent to German reunification in a framework in which Germany would be contained, so to speak, by European partners East and West. American hostility or skepticism toward this design was dismissed as the natural reaction of a monopolist who, deep down, wants to preserve the *status quo,* and whose obstinacy feeds the symmetrical obstinacy of the Russians. And yet, given the evolution in Western and Eastern Europe and the centrifugal pull of extra-European problems on the United States, the French felt that they were on the side of "reality." They believed that American policy-makers were fighting a losing rearguard battle against the new realities—indeed, against some of their own new inclinations.

Americans were prompt to point out the contradictions of Gaullism in Europe. Gaullism, they said, was using the European idea and West European institutions as a kind of smoke screen to flush out American predominance, but behind this screen purely French interests were being pursued without external interference—"Europe" meant a bar to the United States, but no leash on France. Also, Gaullism denounced the unreliability of America's nuclear guarantee of Western Europe, arguing that no nation can be expected to risk suicide for others, while it built a nuclear mini-force which it presented as more reliable to its European partners. But the French were equally good at perceiving the contradictions in U.S. policies in Europe. On one hand, the United States appealed to Atlantic solidarity in order to prevent the emergence of a West European viewpoint distinct from its own, but it also tried to safeguard from "Atlantic" constraints its own freedom of action in the Third World, at the U.N. and in its dealings with Moscow on arms issues. On the other hand, the United States asked for a "single partner" in Western Europe, shied away from any plan to let that partner have a separate military establishment, and used the absence of a "single partner" as a pretext for holding onto its monopoly of strategic and diplomatic decisions in NATO. Even when, after President Johnson's speech on October 7, 1966, American and French policies moved along comparable lines—in their approach to Germany and in their search for a détente in Europe—convergence meant competition rather than cooperation.

In Europe, the Franco-American conflict was one of "grand designs," of conceptions about the future, with each antagonist accusing the other of representing the past. But the conflict over Vietnam was more pathetic, because it was so retrospective on both sides. Each interpreted the Vietnamese situation in the light of its own recent past, projecting on a complex local reality the oversimplifying lessons it felt it had recently learned. The United States became engaged, step by step, in a series of *ad hoc*, incremental decisions whose tactical nature conflicted with, was transfigured into, and to some extent was compensated for by the sweeping general principles that served to rationalize American intervention: resistance to aggression, protection of national independence and of the right to self-determination, containment of communism, avoidance of new Munichs. Thus, the United States said it was exercising in Vietnam the sad prerogative of leadership and world responsibility; it was repeating the achievements of containment in Europe and Korea in more tragic and confusing circumstances; it was applying to China the lessons of twenty years of anti-Communist warfare—limited in means and objectives yet uncompromising in principles and scope. And the procedures used—overwhelming military might and calls for unconditional negotiations—were those that Americans habitually applied and that most of them consider fair.

The French read the story quite differently. Twenty years before, they had seen themselves as fighting for the West against Asian communism and as deserving full support from the United States; but the United States had argued that their stand was corrupted by colonialism, and charged them with throwing local nationalists into the arms of the Communists. Now the shoe was on the other foot. American officials sounded like French premiers of the early 1950s; French officials, journalists, and intellectuals described American policy as if Vietnam were Algeria all over again, only worse. At least the French were not aliens in Algeria, they pointed out, whereas the Americans were a foreign interventionist power in Southeast Asia. In a speech of September 1966 in Phnom Penh, de Gaulle analyzed America's predicament in "Algerian" terms: 1) It was an internal war (between natives and a Western power), not a case of aggression; 2) force alone offers no way out, because of the Western power's incapacity to find an organized native political force able to deprive the rebellion of its cause, cadres, and control; 3) the myth and mystique of "unconditional negotiations" are of little avail in such a war, for the rebel force will not engage in formal talks until the Western power has outlined its proposals about the political future of the disputed land in acceptable detail; 4) the prelude to a political settlement thus becomes the Western power's solemn commitment to total withdrawal; 5) no real prestige is lost by an honest confession of error and an intelligent effort at disengagement.

Two completely conflicting analyses led to a mountain of misunderstandings and a morass of mutual recriminations. American defenders of official policy were deeply hurt by this French analysis. They found traces of *Schadenfreude* in it, and a kind of delayed wish for revenge. (They did not notice that many of their bitterest French critics had also been in the vanguard of opposition to French colonialism.) Any comparison between a colonial situation and their own in Vietnam— between a Communist-led national revolution against imperialism and what they saw as Communist imperialism attacking a free nation —was an insult. The French position encouraged the enemy, and anyway France's advice came cheap, her present responsibilities being as small as her past responsibility loomed large. The French, for their part, considered the differences between Vietnam and colonial wars insignificant or illusory. The only reality they could see was the use of force by the most powerful white nation on earth against a small yellow people, for the preservation of a power position threatened by local revolutionary discontent. American denials were denounced as hypocritical or obtuse; once more they pointed to the contradiction between professions of intent and daily acts. The very fact that in Vietnam (by contrast with Europe) French views were deprived of immediate potency deepened the rift: while they increased American resentment, they gave good conscience to the French, who were moved to heights of self-righteous and indignant lucidity, now that their own record had been swept clean by decolonization.

The same conflict in the analysis of a complex reality led in 1967 to a dramatic Franco-American clash over the Middle East. No part of the world—not even Europe—offered such a clear demonstration of how two different visions of world politics can lead to discord. France and the United States had both supported Israel ever since 1948, and France, in the days of the Algerian war, had become Israel's main weapons provider. Franco-Israeli collusion during the Suez crisis had led to the muddled Middle Eastern war of October–November 1956. De Gaulle had celebrated Israel as an ally and treated Ben Gurion as a respected friend. But after 1962, French perspectives subtly shifted— and the Israelis either ignored or misperceived this. De Gaulle and the French Foreign Ministry were eager for a reconciliation with the Arab world, where France had important economic and cultural interests; de Gaulle was making his policy of cooperation with Algeria a kind of model of relations between an advanced nation and a poor one. This new approach ruled out unconditional support to Israel. Also, aware of the Soviet Union's increasing military aid to Egypt and of American military aid to and diplomatic support of Israel, de Gaulle saw with dismay one crucial part of the world being dragged into the East-West conflict, just as he was promoting a world-wide policy of disengagement from this conflict. The crisis of May 1967 was sudden, and its tangled and tempestuous development prior to the Israeli blitz testified once more to the potential for implacable escalation in any unresolved dispute. In de Gaulle's view, as long as no shots had been fired, there was still a chance for a peaceful settlement—one that might perhaps deal with all the issues, reduce superpower influence in the area, and thus allow for a resurgence of French influence. But as he saw it, a war (no matter which side started it) could only lead to one of his two nightmares, or perhaps to both: a confrontation between Russia and America, each supporting its clients, or a new Yalta, in which the two powers would settle the fate of the Middle East by themselves and perpetuate their predominance.

Hence de Gaulle advised Israel not to start a war and to trust *all* the great powers. Hence also he decided to blame whoever would shoot first, proclaimed neutrality when the war came, and adopted a punitive attitude toward Israel after the war was over. As he saw it, Israel's smashing victory had led to a rehearsal for superpower collusion, demonstrated by the Johnson-Kosygin meeting at Glassboro, and to an ominous perpetuation of the superpower confrontation in the Middle East. So long as the balance which Israel had broken in its favor was not restored, the Soviet Union could not afford to loosen her grip on, indeed had to escalate her help to, Egypt. This, in turn, consolidated the *de facto* alliance of Israel and the United States. French policy therefore aimed not at all to support Russia, but took the form of voting along with her in the U.N.; it aimed not to encourage Arab dreams of total revenge, but took the form of angry criticism of Israel; finally, it overtly blamed American interventionism, especially in Vietnam, for the Middle Eastern crisis. (The thought behind this startling shorthand was, presumably, as follows: America ever since the Cuban missile crisis had been moving almost unchallenged toward world preponderance. Its presence all over the world and its militant anticommunism had encouraged Israel to expect American backing in case of a clash with the Soviet Union. American *hubris,* manifested in a series of direct victories over the Russians in Berlin and in Cuba, in attacks on North Vietnam, in triumphs by proxy over Egypt, and in overwhelming advances in the arms race, would oblige the Russians to redress the balance, particularly in the Mediterranean. French freedom of maneuver had been dangerously impaired.)

De Gaulle acted as if the United States had always backed and encouraged Israel; and yet an analysis of U.S. policy since 1948 shows considerable hesitation and confusion between two courses of action vis-à-vis Israel. One of these could be termed a "great-power approach." It went back to the first Arab-Israeli conflict in 1948, and consisted essentially in treating this conflict as a local dispute. It stressed the responsibility of the U.N. in general and the permanent members of the Security Council in particular for maintaining peace in the area and settling the basic disputes. It thus postulated that the United States, as a great power with interests in both Israel and the Arab world, and with a responsibility for world peace, could, on behalf of the "international community," actively try to mediate. The other line of U.S. policy was what might be called "the strategy of commitment"; it developed in response to the Russians' own shift of policy against Israel and in favor of a strategy of military support to Egypt. It consisted in applying in the Middle East what had worked in other parts of the world: the drawing of clear lines to deter aggression, the adoption of military and diplomatic measures that would make it clear to Russia that its own designs and its allies' would not be unopposed, and in particular that the survival and security of Israel would be protected by the United States. Both strands of American policy were concerned with "containing" the Soviet Union, but in very different ways—the first, by depriving the Russians of the opportunities and leverage offered by Arab hostility to and humiliation by Israel; the second, by increasing the risks and costs of exploiting such opportunities. Neither course of action was ever pursued to the exclusion of the other.

Historically, French and American policies were, so to speak, moving in opposite directions: each nation had learned a different lesson from the Suez crisis. De Gaulle had concluded that France had to move away from Israel. The United States had concluded that it would not again force Israel to give up the fruits of victory without adequate compensation. Analytically, there clearly was a complete opposition between the American commitment to Israel and France's approach. But the U.S. "great power" line also differed markedly from Gaullist strategy. To be sure, the assumption that the Soviet presence in the Middle East could only benefit from the absence of a settlement and from perpetual high tension, the emphasis on the responsibility of the Security Council's permanent members, on the need to downplay the cold war, and on the role of the U.N. were all close to French postulates and interests. But the French always feared that the first course of U.S. action would ultimately lead to a direct U.S.-Soviet dialogue.

Insofar as both lines of U.S. policy had a strong anti-Soviet component, and the second line had a passionate pro-Israeli ingredient, French moves in 1967 were totally unacceptable to Washington. Since during the crisis the United States had not really chosen between or synthesized the two lines, the French analysis of U.S. policy was considered insulting: the most visible French action was official support of the Soviet Union, a "neutrality" that leaned heavily toward the Arabs, and an embargo that hurt the Israelis. The United States had been caught off guard by the Middle Eastern crisis, and only the speed of Israel's victory had saved American officials from having to agonize over whether to intervene actively or not. (In the days before the war, Israel had found American advice so tepid [5] that the Israeli cabinet's decision to strike had been largely inspired by the fear of leaving the nation's vital interests to a Big Four forum where only Russia showed any determination.) As Washington saw it, de Gaulle was blaming America for events entirely out of her control; he was bringing comfort to America's chief adversary, and encouraging among Russia's Arab protégés the illusion that peace should not be sought directly; he was conducting a vendetta born of personal pique against Israel, and shamefully sacrificing a former ally. Once more, the very notion of balance was proving completely contentious: for the Americans, de Gaulle, by punishing Israel, was trying to destroy the new, post-Six Day War balance in the Middle East; for de Gaulle, the French embargo against Israel was an attempt to redress the imbalance created by Israeli superiority before the Russians tried to do it themselves.

II. Rapprochement? Circumstances and Issues

During the crisis that rocked France in May 1968, American officials discovered that much as they disliked de Gaulle, they disliked the prospect of chaos in France even more. De Gaulle's ability to pursue his grand, long-term design had been impaired, not just by striking external setbacks such as the Czech invasion, but by the coincidence of this setback with his domestic troubles. At the same time, signs of a revision of American foreign policy appeared. Vietnam peace talks started. An exchange of warm cable messages between de Gaulle and Johnson, shortly after the monetary crisis of November 1968, signaled the beginning of a rapprochement. President Nixon's visit to Paris in March 1969 indicated that this rapprochement had become one of the new Administration's main objectives, and de Gaulle's almost effusive response showed that he sought it also. The rapprochement continued after de Gaulle's resignation. Pompidou reasserted France's friendship with the United States, and returned Nixon's visit a year later. But we must ask how far this reconciliation could go; one should avoid illusions about renewed friendships.

Franco-American difficulties of recent years had been both procedural (these could now be attenuated), conceptual (these can be partly alleviated), and over specific policies (more difficult to resolve).

The procedural problem was simple: neither the Democratic administrations nor de Gaulle showed much talent for, or willingness to, consult others before announcing decisions. American officials were always caught by surprise by de Gaulle's Olympian pronouncements— his recognition of Red China, his various condemnations of the Vietnam war, his two vetoes of Britain's application to the Common Market, his withdrawal from NATO, or his embargoes against Israel. The United States' failure to consult the European allies infuriated not only the French but also the West Germans, for instance throughout the early, decisive period of the nonproliferation treaty. President Nixon, whose National Security adviser, Henry Kissinger, had incisively criticized the highhandedness and arrogance of past administrations, promised during his European visit to be permanently more concerned with the susceptibilities of America's allies. Before August 1971, he kept his promise.

But insofar as Franco-American relations are concerned, would consultation on matters of common interest be feasible? Among America's allies, France under de Gaulle was the only one that claimed to be a world power *and also* insisted on taking positions independent of the United States. According to de Gaulle, great powers decide rather than bargain, inform rather than consult. *Ergo,* France did not consult the United States. And for the Americans to consult France on everything could easily have been a major burden for the American side, and an embarrassment for both. When the French recognized Red China without consulting West Germany, they explained that they knew that Bonn could not approve or follow suit, and preferred not to embarrass the Germans by asking for advice that would be disregarded. Under Pompidou, French claims to universal concerns have not been trumpeted, but the lesson of de Gaulle's style has not been lost. The so-called Mediterranean policy of post-de Gaulle France, marked by the agreement to sell jets to Libya, was launched without consultation. As for the United States, as they were before, the arms talks with Russia are closed to outsiders; policy in Asia, including Indochina, is an American monopoly; and the new international economic and monetary policy initiated in August 1971 has been almost belligerently unilateral (if only as a method to force allies to negotiate concessions). On the other hand, the disappearance of de Gaulle and the advent of Kissinger in Washington has removed much of the drama from the Franco-American stage.

Consultation is in any case no panacea; while it is infinitely better for friends or adversaries to be in touch and to enlighten each other about their goals, that by itself does not make them friends if the messages they exchange are divergent or hostile. Even if the Nixon Administration had shown itself determined to seek French opinions on every major subject, and vice-versa, a genuine rapprochement would follow only if the over-all conceptions and specific policies of the two governments came closer.

There is no doubt that this has to some extent occurred. The first turning point came in the spring and summer of 1968. Both governments found that their ability to give priority to foreign affairs was challenged by domestic turbulence. It was a time of internal fence-mending in both countries. De Gaulle, obliged to slow down his nuclear program and to wage battle with almost every important social group in order to save the franc, may not have abandoned his world vision, but neither he nor his successors could do much about it. When French capital fled France as a result of the May crisis, and also in reaction against the policies de Gaulle was pursuing in the aftermath of the crisis, the embattled franc and the troubled dollar were made to fight together for a revaluation of the Deutschmark—in vain. The "Group of Ten" extended large credits to France, and France in its predicament found the franc supported by the dollar it had battled, for Washington feared heavy pressure on its currency if the franc and the pound collapsed. This was no longer the time for France to wage war on the dollar. The devaluation of the franc in August 1969 marked the official ending of France's open, all-out campaign for a drastic reform of the world's monetary system, although the system's crises in 1971 and 1973 vindicated and revived French criticisms of it. Priority now went to strengthening the French economy (and the new approach to that goal is far less hostile to U.S. investments). De Gaulle's last referendum campaign was fought—for the first time—exlusively on domestic grounds, without any reference to foreign affairs. As for the United States, internal divisions over Vietnam, the campus crisis that sprang from the Vietnam war but really exceeded it, the concern for law and order led to a desire for a policy of restraint and to a kind of battle fatigue with the whole outside world.

External failures also contributed to this change of stance. The Vietnam disaster, the prolonged disarray of the Atlantic Alliance, the staggering costs of the arms race and "world responsibility" led to an agonizing reappraisal in Washington. The Soviet invasion of Czechoslovakia had an enormous impact in France, and an embarrassing one in the United States. The heart of de Gaulle's "revisionism" had been the notion of a gradual reunification of Europe, and this required: 1) a reassertion of national autonomy in Eastern as well as Western Europe; 2) a Soviet willingness to let this occur; 3) an American willingness to withdraw American forces from Europe, so as to allow for a parallel withdrawal of Soviet forces and the ultimate dissolution of the two rival military blocs; 4) a cooperating group of states in West Europe agreed on this direction and policy. Czechoslovakia showed that—to put it mildly—the moment was not ripe. The Gaullist notion, which had so deeply annoyed American policy-makers, of a vast European settlement negotiated primarily among Europeans obviously had no meaning at present. (A Conference on European Security and Cooperation would be a consecration of the *status quo*—not the kind of settlement the General had wanted.) De Gaulle's new warmth toward America was his way of marking his displeasure with Soviet behavior—an indirect way, since, for lack of any better alternative, he, like Willy Brandt, refused to give up his Eastern policy. His successors' support for West Germany's accelerated *Ostpolitik* could be interpreted as preserving his ultimate vision, insofar as Bonn's reconciliation with Moscow and Warsaw and Bonn's acceptance of the Oder-Neisse line are the prerequisites to that "détente, entente, and cooperation" de Gaulle had called for. But French support for an *Ostpolitik* that recognizes East Germany and the "realities" of the post-Yalta order shows that the road to a reunited Europe freed of the "hegemonies" will be longer, more arduous, and less rewarding for France than de Gaulle had hoped. Whether France's new, relatively "low posture" drastically changes the long-range Gaullist vision of international affairs or not, it revises the time perspective enough to make a partial rapprochement with the United States possible.

On the American side, indeed, the revision appeared to go further. Here, a new approach toward France came from a new conception. The Nixon Administration moved toward a view of American interests closer to de Gaulle's. It desires a world in which the preservation of a camp is less important than the pursuit of the national interest, in which the superpowers' special responsibilities do not obliterate the concerns of other parties, in which it is neither possible nor wise for a Great Power to expect conformity and docility from its friends, in which a system of order capable of moderating conflicts will be possible only if Great Power interventions are curtailed, regional balances of power are established, and middle powers given greater responsibilities, in which stability will result from a balance-of-power diplomacy pursued among several major actors. Insofar as de Gaulle's great objective was a world in which lesser states would not be trampled by the superpowers' duel or duopoly, and where middle powers like France could again play a global role, rapprochement became natural. The tactical self-restraint on behalf of the old Gaullist vision was new on the French side, and what was new in the United States was a vision of self-restraint and equilibrium as being in the interests of America.

It is undeniable that the "old Gaullist vision" cannot be the same without de Gaulle. De Gaulle had a fierce determination with which he held and pursued it when the moment was ripe, or held it in reserve when circumstances were hostile. Nobody else can be expected to pick up this fierceness: here, indeed, the General's vision *was* his character. And there was the simple fact of a single inspiration. There may be a greater similarity between two differing policies carried out pluralistically, than between two like policies one of which is waged by a single mind, and the other by several men and bureaucracies. In the latter case, almost inevitably, the long-term goal becomes less compelling, the short-term concerns more imperative. Procedure shapes perception: on both sides of the Atlantic, now, under presidents interested in but not driven by foreign affairs, policy is at least as much a bargaining process as a chain of command.

Even in its new approach, however, what the United States looks for (instead of dependents or clients) is partners, states that will be free to pursue their own policies, yet cooperate with the United States so as to keep divergences minimal or edgeless. Indeed, Kissinger's request in April 1973 that the West Europeans subordinate their economic integration to a common Atlantic design reads like a return to the old concept of Atlantic partnership with, if anything, a less benevolent United States at the head of it. De Gaulle, because of his personality as well as his conception of France, had stressed French independence. And one of his legacies is the preservation of a distinct French personality and policy. This prevents rapprochement from ever veering into alignment. Also, Nixon's diplomacy has been marked by tactics very similar to de Gaulle's, especially in the year of shocks, 1971 — politically at Japan's expense, economically with both Japan and Western Europe as targets.

For the United States, consulting middle powers is one thing; building them up is another. Encouraging them to take a share of the burden previously carried alone is one thing; encouraging them to pursue policies that may be quite different from America's all over the world is another. Kissinger's balance-of-power world is one in which the United States, Russia, and China are "more equal" than the other states. And even if it takes a more modest view of its world-wide responsibilities, the Administration nevertheless still sees Western Europe as having merely regional concerns, and the United States as a superpower. France is not in that league; the difference in rank and power cannot fail to create apprehensions and suspicions in the weaker partner, especially as France is formally or *de facto* excluded from superpower negotiations or confrontations whose outcome will affect her fate, her status, or her opportunities.[6]

Only as the lessening of differences in vision brings about specific policy changes will the Franco-American rapprochement be serious. Let us examine again the areas of discord.

The United States' willingness to negotiate in Paris its extrication from Vietnam created one opportunity for rapprochement. But its slowness at making concessions which the French deemed necessary, and its belief that renewed military action, in Cambodia or in the air war, could improve its bargaining position, strained relations despite the spectacular quasi-reconciliation with China. There was no longer any debate about the need for American extrication from Vietnam, but a tactical disagreement about the speed, terms, and acceptable costs. French policy remained that outlined in de Gaulle's speech in Phnom Penh. It encompassed different assessments about the need for, and prospects of, pro-Western regimes in Vietnam and in other Southeast Asian states.

In the Middle East, France's recognition of the limits to her industrial independence in Europe and her dependence on Arab oil supplies has meant that her "Mediterranean policy" continues to show Gaullist continuity. The breakdown of the special relationship between France and Algeria in 1971 only increased the determination of French officials to pursue their course of action in the eastern Mediterranean, as if to show that Algeria's "defection" did not affect their ties with Egypt. To give up this policy would mean recognizing the superpower predominance or aligning France with the United States.

Since 1969, however, the Big Four talks over the Middle East have been no panacea for France. At first, as de Gaulle had surmised, Arab inferiority and Russia's determination to hang on in Egypt made for intransigence; the process of big-power escalation continued in the form of growing Soviet support for Egypt. In this state of tension, the French government arranged to sell arms to Libya—again for the same reasons she had been anti-Israel in 1967, and again to a huge outcry in the United States and France. Throughout 1970 and 1971, the greater the superpowers' involvement, the higher the peril of direct collision, and the stronger was the temptation of avoiding it by collusion: the Four Power talks became a screen behind which Big Two bargaining went on actively. The decisive forces, either for war or for peace, were the superpowers alone—so long as there was no formal settlement. France's vision still led her to want a settlement in which the superpowers would not be the only guarantors. (Nor do the French want the Americans to be the only ones to pressure Israel for concessions. If each superpower "delivers" its client, even a settlement would not reduce their "hegemony.") But insofar as de Gaulle was right in believing that in the absence of a settlement there was no room left for France, his successors, in order to find room, have had to behave as if the Soviet-American hold on the Middle East had not increased—i.e., as if de Gaulle's gloomy view had not been correct. President Anwar el-Sadat's expulsion of Soviet military forces from Egypt could not fail to please them, for it showed the plight of a superpower that provides a client state with neither victory nor settlement, and it made Egypt's need for settlement more acute. Yet France's strategy suffered from wishful thinking about her capacity to reverse the trend. This is the paradoxical corollary of her correctly gloomy analysis of the likely effects of superpower involvement.

The American predicament was more complex. Washington itself remained institutionally divided and the policy-makers hesitated between the contradictory implications of the two strands of American policy in the Middle East, discussed earlier in this chapter. And, of course, success for either course of action also depended on factors beyond America's command.

The relation between French and American policy in the Middle East was bound to remain touchy. The French have kept asking the Americans: "Do you see what you are doing?" and the Americans have brushed aside French warnings with the question: "What use are you?" There had been some rapprochement because Paris and Washington preferred peace to war, and feared that war might result from diplomatic laxity and military escalation. But for Paris almost any settlement was deemed a diplomatic and military improvement, whereas Washington could either, within certain limits, play a game of chicken in order to obtain a settlement favorable to "its" side, or else continue to stay in a state of neither war nor peace. A partial settlement—such as the reopening of the Suez Canal—might have represented the best short-term compromise between the two elements in U.S. policy, but also one of the most embarrassing conclusions for France. It would have consecrated the military commitments of the superpowers and demonstrated that any political solution depended on the superpowers alone.

Had a general settlement been (miraculously) reached, would it have reinforced or impaired the Soviet and American positions? Both cases can be argued, but whatever the outcome, it is certain that France's role in bringing it about would have been small. The French undoubtedly would have discovered that both the Soviet and the American influence would persist. Still, it would at least have had a chance of gradually disconnecting the Middle East dispute from the cold war—one of France's major goals. The Americans might, over time, have found advantages in sharing with France and Britain responsibilities that they once faced alone. Prospects for joint participation in multilateral arrangements would have improved.

However, no settlement obtained, and (as was likely) hostilities resumed. They badly hurt prospects for Franco-American cooperation. Washington has been dragged again into the very cycle of collision and collusion which the French had so desperately wanted to avert. Paris again dissociated itself from Washington's commitment to Israel during the war, and found itself shut out of Washington's "great power" attempt to move toward a settlement. France reaffirmed its 1967 stand, but it now amounted to a policy of mere deploration and to a recognition of impotence (West European as well as French). The only alternatives are a bipolar agreement imposed on the parties, or a resumption of war fed by the rival superpowers. Neither is attractive to, nor leaves much room for the French.[7]

The most important area of Franco-American relations remains, of course, Europe. For here is the core of French policy—after de Gaulle even more than under him.

The first range of issues are military ones. Gaullist military policy aimed at reversing the postwar trend which made France an "integrated" member of the Atlantic Alliance, while the "Anglo-Saxon" powers held onto their strategic nuclear forces, in effect, under national command. De Gaulle, having focused on the creation of a French national deterrent, then having taken France out of NATO, turned the treaty into a classical alliance between France and the fifteen other NATO nations. One thing is clear: de Gaulle's successors, while more eager than he to proclaim the "fundamental" nature of the American alliance,[8] are no more willing than he either to bring France back into NATO or to abandon the *force de frappe*. A complete Franco-American rapprochement here requires: 1) military cooperation on eventual joint action between French forces in West Germany and France, and NATO forces in Western Europe, and also between France's and America's strategic nuclear forces; 2) American willingness to provide military assistance to France's nuclear program within the limits of the MacMahon Act. (Such assistance has, of course, been given to Britain for many years.)

It is obvious that these issues soon turn out to be more than bilateral. Cooperation at the operational level between the French Army and the NATO armies in Europe has much improved. But it meets only part of the old French grievances. One of de Gaulle's reasons for leaving NATO was that he was annoyed at being merely associated with the execution of a strategy decided in Washington, despite the façade of NATO councils. (NATO officially endorsed the strategy of "flexible response" only after France's exit, but many years after it had become operative American doctrine.) What his successors presumably want—and what many French officers are known to want—is top-level cooperation between French and American military leaders *and* defense ministers. This is the kind of cooperation de Gaulle had hinted at in his memorandum of September 1958. But can Washington meet these wants without *ipso facto* exposing NATO as a fraud, or rewarding the French exit from it? The present institutional setup provides no solution. Consequently, both sides are satisfied with letting the matter rest.

As for American aid to France's program, it would again appear to many as rewarding the proliferation of nuclear weapons and indeed as a bonus to a nuclear force that (by contrast with Britain's) is not "assigned" to NATO. With the West Germans already less than enthusiastic about the nonproliferation treaty, which consecrates their non-nuclear position, any obvious American aid to a French nuclear force might add insult to injury. Again, the present institutional framework makes Franco-American cooperation difficult. The United States has created a certain Alliance machinery and France has bolted out of it; cooperation really requires the drastic abandonment of its past policy by one or the other party. The French are not the ones likely to give in; and Washington is not likely to change its stand *unless* a new perspective transcending Franco-American relations is introduced.

In the realm of issues which involve France, the United States, and the rest of Europe, a number of developments since the invasion of Czechoslovakia have transformed reality enough to allow the two governments to deal with each other in new ways.

Insofar as East-West relations are concerned, there has been a dramatic switch since 1969. Until Czechoslovakia, de Gaulle had grandly wooed Russia and Eastern Europe. The Russians were on the defensive, resisting with smiles those aspects of de Gaulle's offensive that would have hurt their interests, and resisting with fury the West German opening to the East pursued by Kiesinger's coalition cabinet. The Americans encouraged the West Germans (thus deepening Soviet misgivings) and resented de Gaulle. After Czechoslovakia, de Gaulle's departure, and with the new West German cabinet of Willy Brandt, the roles changed. A determined "offensive" was waged by Bonn; Russia proved receptive and relaunched its own old offensive for a European security conference with renewed vigor. Once more, the United States was in the wings—but so, now, was France, which had become less important to the Soviet Union. Washington and Paris endorsed Bonn's policy, but out of necessity more than enthusiasm. Both had indeed hoped for a reconciliation between West Germany and the East European states, yet neither had thought that things would move quite so far or quite so bilaterally.

As a result, a Franco-American rapprochement has come about on two points. One is Berlin—the scene of earlier discord between de Gaulle and the United States, in the days when de Gaulle was the toughest European foe of the Soviet Union. Paris and Washington have been eager to consolidate West Berlin's security, and to consider Berlin the last remaining symbol of the four-power stewardship of the German problem. The settlement of 1971, which entailed Soviet concessions, satisfied all parties. The other point concerns the Soviet call for a European security conference. Both governments were at first reluctant: the United States did not want to have a one-sided mechanism in which the Russians could play on the rivalries and mutual fears of the Atlantic allies, and discourage the eventual reinforcement of the Common Market (for instance by trying to prevent any future "spillover" from economic to military organization). The French feared that a conference might actually consolidate and perpetuate both "hegemonies," albeit, perhaps, at a lower military level. But both sides have overcome their objections: the United States, in order not to appear to resist the desires of most West Europeans, and as a way of giving momentum to their own policy of détente with Russia; the French, because military matters have been largely removed from the agenda, and a conference that dealt mainly with cooperation would give momentum to the old Gaullist notion of spreading "détente, entente, and cooperation." The United States would not object to the conference if it led to some East European emancipation (as the Rumanians and Finns hope) without weakening the cohesion of the West; the French would not mind if it led to East *and* West European emancipation.

But there is one subject of persistent disagreement: what is called in the jargon "Mutual Balanced Force Reductions (MBFR)." The Americans, despite the formidable technical complexities of this issue, have accepted the Soviet proposal to negotiate on it, in order to appease two restless constituencies. Americans at home have demanded unilateral U.S. reductions, out of conviction that the European balance of power rests essentially on the American nuclear guarantee, or because they believe there is no real danger of war now that all parties are eager for détente, or because they resent Western Europe's failure to raise more forces of its own, or because of the simple-minded fear (derived from Vietnam) that a military presence abroad leads to military involvements. And in Europe, there are allies that press for MBFR for reasons of their own. But the French oppose MBFR. Officially, the main reason is the old Gaullist hostility to blocs: MBFR would have to be negotiated between the Warsaw Pact and NATO, and would restore or prolong the military predominance of Washington and Moscow. But there is another reason. Both a European security conference leading to a broad diplomatic détente and various pan-European cooperative schemes, *and* the simple maintenance of the present military *status quo* would save France from having to face the issue of a future West European defense entity. This issue is doubly unpleasant for the French, first because West Germany might dominate such an entity, and secondly because such an entity could seriously jeopardize good relations with the Soviet Union. Paradoxically, France's policy of military independence-with-security, and diplomatic friendship with the Soviet Union and East Europe requires a security conference but no MBFR. France fears that MBFR might mean American withdrawal, and in effect favor the Soviet Union, especially if the superpowers agree on an overt or disguised neutralization of Germany. Bonn thinks MBFR would be a barrier to American unilateral reductions, and fears that without it the rising costs of defense would in effect make the European part of NATO fall behind the Soviet Union.

Along with the desire to prevent a Washington-Bonn axis that would consolidate Europe's division and limit French freedom of maneuver, France has always been guided by fear of a Bonn-Moscow intimacy. The Soames-de Gaulle conversation in February 1969 suggests that de Gaulle was worried by the economic strength West Germany displayed in the monetary crisis of November 1968, and perhaps anticipated the diplomatic consequences of the May crisis and the Czech invasion; he was moving toward an overture to Britain. In a very different way (through the EEC, not through direct talks on issues outside the EEC's domain; by lifting the veto ahead of EEC negotiations, not as the outcome of successful extra-EEC talks) de Gaulle's successors have also turned to London. The Common Market has been extended to new members, a monetary union has been started (albeit shakily), and some foreign-policy harmonization has been attempted. This is happening at a time when the United States formally proclaims its continuing interest in West European unity, and acknowledges its lack of concern for any specific form of it. Moreover, Pompidou's new approach, which aims at a West European entity defined primarily by its financial, industrial, agricultural, and monetary joint policies, avoids the head-on collision with the United States which de Gaulle's emphasis on joint strategic and foreign policies had provoked. Thus, there has been a rapprochement on what used to be the most divisive of all the issues.

But a new source of tension has appeared as a direct consequence of the very factors that make rapprochement easier in the realm of diplomacy and strategy: this is the new American conception of balance of power and *Realpolitik,* and the reassertion of the priority of domestic interests in the United States. As long as the cold war prevailed, the political advantages that Americans expected from West European unity were such that they willingly paid an economic "price" in exchange: they accepted a rather protectionist EEC agricultural policy and EEC trade advantages for Western Europe's former colonies—two French demands. (It should be added that the Common Market had huge economic advantages for U.S. investments.) Today, with the "old" cold war against Russia less compelling, American commercial interests which feel threatened by the EEC's (and Japan's) economic policies speak out more vigorously, and find strong support in Congress and in the Treasury and Commerce Departments. Also, the remedies for the United States' balance-of-payments deficit are more likely to be found at the expense of America's major competitors—now considered strong enough to look after their own interests—than at the expense of the American economy: unemployment at home is a greater concern than the possibility of a recession abroad. Yesterday, the EEC achieved its greatest progress in such areas as a common external tariff, preferential association agreements, and a common agricultural policy; and Washington welcomed EEC decisions even if they irritated specific interests within the United States. Today, the United States declares war on EEC policies that, as Nixon said in early 1972, "encourage the development of a world divided into discriminatory trading blocs," and EEC countries run into serious difficulties in trying to cope with the repercussions of the international monetary crisis. Parity fluctuations have jeopardized the EEC's agricultural policy and its attempt at a monetary union of the Nine. America's attack on the EEC's agricultural and external economic policies, Kissinger's decision to link military and economic issues in U.S.-West European discussions, and American monetary moves and suggestions on world monetary reform, are putting maximum pressure on points that are always potentially explosive for the members of the EEC.

Ultimately, Franco-American relations depend largely on America's choices. In the Nixon-Kissinger policy, tension exists between the wish for self-restraint and an aggressive pursuit of the national interest, between the wish to let the West Europeans build their own entity and the inclination to keep Europe (and Japan) closely tied to the U.S. as permanent allies in a basically tripolar contest, between the objective of preserving NATO and the tendency to consider the emergent European community as an economic rival. Sooner or later, these ambiguities will have to be resolved. A Franco-American rapprochement, today as always, requires that the United States accept a "European Europe." This does not mean that the United States should not try to get the best possible deal from it, on matters of trade for instance, but it should abandon its attempts to play on intra-European divisions, or its effort to dissolve the EEC's common-trade and agricultural policies, or its claim to a permanent *droit de regard* on policies affecting U.S. interests. Even less does it mean hoping for a resurrection of Monnet's Europe. The enthusiasm that propelled it is gone. De Gaulle or no de Gaulle, the supranational process does not work well when the geographic and functional scope of the enterprise expands: there must be either a leap into real federalism or continued tough interstate bargaining.

The choice for the American Administration, therefore, would consist in recognizing: 1) that any new steps toward West European cooperation depend not on a resurrection of the old "Atlantic priority," which the inclusion of Japan, the thaw in the cold war, and Western Europe's own quest of a détente with Moscow have made implausible, but on a minimum acceptance of the old, if now mellowed Gaullist vision; 2) that the long-term interests of the United States and of Western Europe can be reconciled on this basis unless the United States resorts to a trade war through competitive devaluations and subordinates the restoration of an effective global monetary system to the establishment and guarantee of a trade surplus; 3) that the United States cannot and should not force the Gaullist vision on reluctant Europeans, but can facilitate in various ways the gradual development of a West European entity, based on the cooperation of Paris, London, and Bonn, and endowed with a strategic and foreign policy of its own.

The following changes would be required on America's part, in the strategic-diplomatic realm. First, since it is in America's long-run interest that Western Europe not rely forever on Washington for every aspect of its defense, the United States should avoid pressuring West Germany, and to some extent Britain, to rely on American armaments, or to make their own weapons manufacturers form a frequently exclusive partnership with their American counterparts. There will be no West European defense system unless there is more cooperation among West European weapons producers. Ultimately such a defense system will require specialization and standardization of West European armaments. America should do nothing to prevent this, even if it must sacrifice arms sales for it.

Second, Washington cannot insist that the present military structure of NATO is sacred. While the Nixon Doctrine encourages America's allies to "do more" for their conventional defense, the United States has so far preferred it when this increase takes the form of European financial contributions to keep American forces at their present levels, rather than that of a separate West European defense organization (which would entail a reorganization of NATO on a less unequal basis). The divisions and inhibitions of West Europeans continue; many of them cling to the present organization of NATO as if they wanted to be forever liberated from greater responsibilities. But the prospect of a decline of NATO, as a result of either unilateral American troop cuts or an MBFR agreement, and also the need to minimize, in U.S.-West European relations, that dependence on American forces and weapons which is like a faucet which Washington can always turn on for blackmail, should make the gradual emergence of a West European defense entity imperative.

It is up to Washington to initiate the gradual transformation of

NATO's military structure, for otherwise one may have to wait a very long and wasted time for West European initiatives. The present military integration, i.e., the actual subordination of European armed forces to largely American commands, should be loosened up. This would make a gradual rapprochement between the European members of NATO and France possible. If not the enlarged EEC (one of whose members is a neutral), the WEU could serve as the framework for this transformation, if it is made clear that the immediate purpose is a rapprochement with France, and the ultimate goal is a separate West European organization allied to the United States.[9]

The emergence of a West European military and political entity is tied up with the problem of nuclear weapons. In the past Britain dismissed the notion of a European nuclear force, but the French continue to believe that there is no point building a united Europe if it has no deterrent of its own. And it is impossible to see how a national nuclear deterrent could be meaningfully "integrated" or supranationalized. In these circumstances, the only logical solution to the puzzle lies in Anglo-French nuclear cooperation within the framework and at the service of a West European political entity. Prime Minister Heath, for several years when he was out of power, called for such cooperation. Here again, American initiatives are required. Washington should encourage Britain to engage in serious talks with France over nuclear cooperation. A French government convinced of America's willingness to accept the notion of an Anglo-French nuclear deterrent cooperating with its own, and a British government convinced that Washington would prefer this to the politically onerous and militarily indifferent "special nuclear relationship" between Washington and London, could then discuss joint targeting and joint production.[10] This is hardly possible so long as Britain's nuclear forces are assigned to NATO, i.e., under U.S. command and strategy. Here also, NATO must be changed to allow for joint strategic decision-making by its nuclear powers. One could make a case against it, if the alternative were the gradual extinction of the British and French deterrents; but the real alternative seems to be a costly duplication of efforts by London and Paris, and a delaying of the moment when West European cooperation spills over into defense.

All these measures would represent drastic changes of American policy. When President Nixon went to Europe early in 1969, nobody could have expected him to have made such decisions. But the pace of diplomacy since 1969, especially in Soviet-American affairs, makes them more necessary. The gradual emergence of a West European defense entity would enable the Americans and West Europeans to engage the Russians in serious, protracted negotiations on arms control in Europe, without provoking the usual anguish among West Europeans. It would put the main responsibility for a long-term effort for European and German reunification where it belongs: on neither American nor German shoulders, but in the hands of all West Europeans. Since a military organization must be at the service of a political one, the development of a West European entity is a prerequisite. This in turn requires, in trade and monetary matters, enlightened American proposals and tactics that would help unite rather than divide the Nine. Whether a West European organization does or does not lead to continental reunification, it would relieve the United States of many of the psychological and military burdens it has carried in recent years.

What is required, beyond the change in America's image of itself, is a clearer long-term vision of world order—one in which American privileges in the world monetary system and predominance in strategic decision-making would be curtailed. Is this conceivable in Washington? If the answer is yes, a fundamental rapprochement between the French and the Americans, and also between the various West Europeans would be possible. If the answer is no, relations among West Europeans will remain volatile, and relations between the United States and France will, at best, be those of a "minimum feasible misunderstanding."

The future of Franco-American relations depends essentially on Washington's European policy. Pompidou's France has, more than de Gaulle's, made Western Europe the primary field and supreme ambition of her foreign policy. De Gaulle's global and direct challenge to the United States has been replaced by a more limited, defensive, and indirect effort to convince other West Europeans to preserve their joint enterprise from American demands. Between the superpower, which tends to put on its allies the responsibility for its handicaps in the world economic contest, and the ally, which tends to blame America's own moves but cannot by itself make the Americans change their perceptions and policies—a subtle test of will goes on.

12

Obstinate or Obsolete?
France, European
Integration, and the Fate
of the Nation-State

I

The critical issue for every student of world order is the fate of the nation-state. In the nuclear age, the fragmentation of the world into
countless units, each of which has a claim to independence, is obviously dangerous for peace and illogical for welfare. The dynamism
that animates these units—when they are not merely city-states of limited expanse or dynastic states manipulated by the Prince's calculations, but nation-states that pour into their foreign policy the collective pride, ambitions, fears, prejudices, and images of large masses of
people—is particularly formidable.[1] An abstract theorist could argue
that any system of autonomous units follows the same basic rules,
whatever the nature of the units. But in practice, i.e., in history, their
substance matters as much as their form; the story of world affairs
since the French Revolution is not simply one more sequence in the
ballet of sovereign states; it is a story of fires and upheavals propagated
by nationalism. A claim to sovereignty based on historical tradition
and dynastic legitimacy alone has never had the fervor, the self-righteous assertiveness which a similar claim based on the idea and feelings of nationhood presents: in world politics, the dynamic function of
nationalism is to constitute nation-states by amalgamation or by splintering, and its emotional function is to supply a good conscience to
leaders who see their task as the achievement of nationhood, the defense of the nation, or the expansion of a national mission.[2]

This is where the drama lies. The nation-state is at the same time a
form of social organization and—in practice if not in every theory—a

First published as "Obstinate or Obsolete: the Fate of the Nation-State and the
Case of Western Europe," in *Daedalus*, Summer 1966.

factor of international nonintegration. But those who argue in favor of a world under more centralized power or integrated in networks of regional or functional agencies, tend to forget Comte's old maxim that *on ne détruit que ce qu'on remplace.* Any new "formula" would have to provide world order, of course, but also the kind of social organization in which leaders, elites, and citizens feel at home. There is currently no agreement on what such a formula is; [3] as a result, nation-states—often inchoate, economically absurd, administratively ramshackle, and impotent yet dangerous in international politics— remain the basic units despite the remonstrations and exhortations. They go on *faute de mieux* despite their alleged obsolescence. Indeed, they profit from man's incapacity to bring about a better world order, and their very existence stands as an obstacle to their replacement.

If there was one part of the world in which men of good will thought that nation-states could be superseded, it was Western Europe. Pierre Hassner, one of France's most subtle commentators on international politics, has reminded us of E. H. Carr's bold prediction of 1945: "We shall not see again a Europe of twenty, and a world of more than sixty independent states." [4] Statesmen have invented original schemes for moving Western Europe "beyond the nation-state," [5] and political scientists have studied their efforts with a care from which emotional involvement was not absent. The conditions seemed ideal. After World War II, nationalism seemed at a low ebb, and an adequate formula and method for building a substitute had apparently been devised. Thirty years after the end of the war—a period longer than the interwar era—observers have had to revise their judgments. The most optimistic put their hope in the chances which the future may still harbor, rather than in the propelling power of the present. Less optimistic ones, like myself, try simply to understand what went wrong.

My own conclusion is sad and simple. The nations in Western Europe have not been able to stop time and fragment space. The political unification of Europe might have succeeded if, on one hand, its nations had not been caught in the whirlpool of different concerns, arising from profoundly different internal circumstances and outside legacies, and if, on the other hand, they had been able or obliged to concentrate on "community-building" to the exclusion of other external and domestic problems. The involvement of policy-makers in issues among which community-building is merely one has meant that the divergences among foreign policies have increased, not decreased.

Every international system owes its inner logic and its unfolding to a diversity of domestic determinants, geohistorical situations, and outside aims among its units. Every international system based on fragmentation tends to reproduce diversity through the dynamics of unevenness (so well understood by Lenin, albeit applied only in the economic realm by him). But there is no inherent reason why a fragmented international system need rule out certain developments in which critics of the nation-state have put their bets or their hopes. Why must the system be built of a diversity of *nations?* Could it not be a diversity of regions, of "federating" blocs superseding the nation-state, just as the dynastic state replaced the feudal puzzle? Or else, could not the logic of conflagration-fed-by-hostility lead to unification, the kind of catastrophic unification among exhausted yet interdependent nations which Kant sketched? Let us remember that the unity movement in Europe was an attempt to create a regional entity, and that its origins and dynamics resembled, on the reduced scale of a half-continent, the process Kant dreamed up in his *Idea of Universal History.*[6]

The answers are not entirely provided either by the legitimacy of national self-determination, the only principle which transcends all blocs and ideologies, since everyone pays lip service to it, or by the newness of many nation-states, which wrested their independence from another power in a nationalist upsurge and are unlikely to give up what they obtained so recently. But conversely, the legitimacy of the nation-state does not by itself guarantee the nation-state's survival in the international state of nature, and the appeal of nationalism as an emancipating passion does not assure that the nation-state must everywhere remain the basic form of social organization in a world where many nations are old and settled and where the shortcomings of the nation-state are obvious.

No, the real answers are provided by two unique features in the present international system. First of all, it is the first truly *global* international system. Regional subsystems have only a reduced autonomy; the "relationships of major tension" blanket the whole planet; interdependencies in the world economy affect all the non-Communist nations and begin to affect the Soviet group of nations. Domestic polities are dominated not so much by a region's problems as by purely local or purely global ones; these join to divert a region's members from the affairs of their area, and indeed make isolated treatment of those affairs impossible. As a result, each nation, new or old, is placed in an orbit of its own from which it is quite difficult to move away: the attraction of regional forces is offset by the pull of all the other forces. Or, to change the metaphor, the nations that coexist in the same apparently separate "home" of a geographical region cannot escape the smells and noises that come from outside through all the windows and doors, or the view of outlying houses from which the interference issues. With diverse pasts, moved by diverse tempers, living in different parts of the house, inescapably yet differently subjected and attracted to the outside world, the residents react unevenly to their exposure and calculate conflictingly how they could either reduce the disturbance or affect in turn the people in the other houses. Adjusting their own relations within the house is subordinated to their divergences about the outside world; the "regional subsystem" becomes a stake in the rivalry of its members about the system as a whole.

The common home could still prevail if the residents were forced to come to terms, either by one of them, or by the fear of a threatening neighbor. This is where the second unique feature of the present situation intervenes. What tends to perpetuate the nation-states decisively in the present system is the new set of conditions that govern and restrict the rule of force: Damocles' sword has become a boomerang, and the ideological legitimacy of the nation-state is protected by the tameness of the world jungle. Force in the nuclear age is still the "midwife of societies," insofar as revolutionary war begets new nations or new regimes in existing nations; but the use of force along traditional lines for conquest and expansion—a use that made "permeable" feudal units obsolete and replaced them with modern states built on "blood and iron"—has become too dangerous. The legitimacy of the feudal unit could be undermined by the rule of force—the big fish swallowing small fish by national might; or subtly and legitimately, so to speak, through dynastic weddings or acquisitions that consolidated larger units. But a system based on national self-determination rules out the latter, and a system in which force is a blunted weapon rules out the former. The new restrictions on violence even tend to pay to national borders the tribute of vice to virtue: violence that dons the cloak of revolution, or that persists in the form of interstate wars only when these accompany revolutions and conflicts in divided countries, perversely respects borders—it infiltrates them rather than crossing them overtly. Thus, all that is left for unification is what one might call "national self-abdication" or self-abnegation, the eventual willingness of nations to try something else. But global involvement hinders rather than helps here, and the atrophy of war removes the most pressing incentive. What a nation-state cannot provide alone—in economics or defense—it can still provide through means far less drastic than hara-kiri. For while it is true that economic interdependence in all its forms—trade, investments, travel, the management of monetary institutions—has weakened the autonomy of the nation-state, eroded its monetary, business, or tax policies, submitted its government to a host of transnational pressures,[7] it is not clear that a merger of nations would plug the sieve's holes rather than make the sieve bigger.

These two features bestow solidity to the principle of national self-determination, and resilience to the U.N. They also give shape to the "relationship of major tension": the conflict between the United States and the Soviet Union. As the superpowers find that what makes their power overwhelming also makes it less usable (or usable only to deter one another and to deny each other gains), lesser states discover that under the umbrella of the nuclear stalemate they are not condemned to death, and that they indeed have an impressive nuisance power. Thus, as the superpowers compete in a muted form all over the globe, the nation-state becomes the universal point of salience, to use the language of strategy—the lowest common denominator in the competition.

Other international systems merely conserved diversity; the present system profoundly conserves the diversity of nation-states despite all its revolutionary features. Rousseau's dream, concerned both with the prevalence of the general will (i.e., the nation-state) and with peace, was to create communities insulated from one another. In history, where "the essence and drama of nationalism is not to be alone in the world," [8] the clash of noninsulated states has tended to create more nation-states and more wars. Today, Rousseau's ideals come closer to reality, but in a most un-Rousseauian way. The nation-states prevail in peace, they are not superseded because a fragile peace keeps the Kantian doctor away, they are not replaced because their very involvement in the world preserves their separateness. The "new Europe" dreamed of by the Europeans could not be established by force. Left to the wills and calculations of its members, the new formula did not jell because Europeans could not agree on their role in the world. The failure of an experiment made under apparently ideal conditions tells us a great deal, for it shows that a unification movement can fail not only when a surge of nationalism occurs in one important part but also when differences in how the national interest is assessed rule out agreement on the shape and purpose of the new, supranational whole.

The word nationalism is notoriously slippery. What I suggest is the following threefold distinction, which may be helpful in analyzing the interaction between the nation-state and the international system:

1. There is *national consciousness* (what the French call *sentiment national*)—a sense of "cohesion and distinctiveness," [9] which sets one group off from other groups. My point is that this sense, which has important effects on international relations when it is shared by people who have not achieved statehood, is rather "neutral" once the nation and the state coincide. That is, the existence of national consciousness does not dictate foreign policy, does not indicate whether a people's "image" of foreigners is friendly or unfriendly, and does not indicate whether or not the nation's leaders will be willing to accept sacrifices of sovereignty. One cannot even posit that a strong national consciousness will be an obstacle to supranational unification, for it is perfectly conceivable that a nation might convince itself that its "cohesion and distinctiveness" will be best preserved in a larger entity.

2. For lack of a better phrase, I shall call it the *national situation*. Any nation-state—indeed, any state—is, to borrow Sartre's language, thrown into the world. Its situation is made up of internal features (these, in an individual, would be called heredity and character) and its position in the world. The state of national consciousness in the nation is only one element in the situation. It is a composite of objective data (social structure and political system, geography, formal commitments to other nations) and subjective factors (values, prejudices, opinions, reflexes, traditions toward and assessments of others, and others' attitudes and approaches). Some of its components are intractable, others flexible and changeable. Any statesman, whether a fervent patriot or not, must define the nation's foreign policy by taking this situation into account; even if he is convinced of the obsolescence of the nation-state (or of *his* nation-state), the steps he can and will take to overcome it will be affected by the fact that he speaks—to borrow de Gaulle's language this time—for the nation as it is in the world as it is. He cannot act as if his nation-state did not exist, or as if the world were other than it is. The national situation may facilitate unification moves, even when national consciousness is strong. It may be an obstacle, even when national consciousness is weak. The point is that even when the policy-maker tries to move "beyond the nation-state" he can do so only by taking the nation along, with its baggage of memories and problems—with its situation. I do not want to suggest that the situation is a "given" that dictates policy; but it sets up complicated limits that affect freedom of choice.[10]

3. I will reserve the term *"nationalism"* for a specific meaning: it is one of the numerous ways in which political leaders and elites may interpret the dictates, or suggestions, of the national situation. It is one of the ways of using the margin the national situation leaves. Whereas national consciousness is a feeling, and the national situation a condition, nationalism is a doctrine or an ideology—the doctrine or ideology that gives absolute value and top priority to the nation in world affairs. The consequences of this may vary immensely. Nationalism may imply expansion (i.e., the attempt to establish the supremacy of one's nation over others) or merely defense; it may entail the notion of a universal mission or, on the contrary, insulation. It may be peaceful or pugnacious.[11] It is less a determinant than a criterion of choice, an attitude that shapes the choices made. But whatever its manifestations or content, it always follows the rule common to all manifestations of nationalism: it always pours the content into one mold, the preservation of the nation as the highest good. Nationalism thus affects, *at least* negatively, the way in which the freedom of choice left by the national situation will be used; indeed, it may collide with, and try to disregard or overcome, the limits which the situation sets.

The relation between these three factors is complicated. Nationalism (in the sense of the will to establish a nation-state) can be triggered by, and in turn activate, national consciousness in oppressed nationalities; but in colonial areas as well as in mature nation-states, nationalism can also be a substitute for a weak or fading national consciousness. In nation-states that are going concerns, national consciousness encourages nationalism only in certain kinds of national situations. A nationalist leader may assess the national situation in exactly the same way a nonnationalist one does, but the former may promote policies the latter would have rejected and oppose moves the latter would have undertaken. That bane of international relations theory, the national interest, could be defined as follows: N.I. = National situation x outlook of the foreign-policy-makers.

It is obvious that a similar national situation can result in differing foreign policies, depending in particular on whether or not there is a nationalist policy-maker. It is obvious also that the national interests in different nations cannot be defined in easily compatible terms if the respective outlooks are nationalist, even when the situations are not so different. But the same incompatibility may obtain, even if the outlooks are not nationalistic, when the situations are indeed very different.

II

Let us now look at the fate of the six nation-states in continental Western Europe, first by examining the basic features of their national situations, then by commenting upon the process of European unification, later by discussing its results, and finally by drawing some lessons.

Western Europe in the postwar years has been characterized by features that have affected all of its nations. But each of these features has affected each of the six nations in a different way.

The first feature—the most hopeful one from the viewpoint of the unifiers—was a temporary demise of nationalism. In the defeated countries—Germany and Italy—nationalism was associated with the regimes that had led the nations into war, defeat, and destruction. The collapse of two national ideologies that had been bellicose, aggressive, and imperialistic brought about an almost total discredit for nationalism in every guise. Among the nations of Western Europe on the Allied side, the most remarkable thing was that the terrible years of occupation and Resistance did not result in a resurgence of chauvinism. Amusingly enough, it was the French Communist Party that displayed the most nationalistic tone; on the whole, the Resistance movements showed an acute awareness of the dangers of nationalist celebrations and national fragmentation in Western Europe. The Resistance itself had a kind of supranational dimension; none of the national Resistance movements could have survived without outside support, and the nations whose honor they saved were liberated rather than victorious. All this militated against any upsurge of the kind of cramped chauvinism that had followed the victory of World War I, just as in Germany the completeness of the disaster and the impossibility of blaming traitors crushed any potential revival of the smoldering nationalism-of-resentment that had undermined the Weimar Republic. There was, in other words, above and beyond the differences in national situations between indubitable losers and dubious winners, the general feeling of a common defeat and the hope of a common future: Resistance platforms often emphasized the need for a union, or federation, of Western Europe.

The demise of nationalism affected the various nations of the half-continent differently. There were significant differences in national consciousness, for one thing. In liberated France, nationalism was low, but patriotic sentiment was extremely high. The circumstances in which the hated Nazis were expelled and the domestic collaborators purged amounted to a rediscovery by the French of their own political community: the nation seemed to have redeemed its "cohesion and distinctiveness." On the contrary, in Germany especially, the destruction of nationalism seemed to have been accompanied by a lowered national consciousness as well: what was distinctive was guilt and shame, and the all too cohesive nation-state was torn apart by partition, occupation zones, regional parochialisms blessed by the victors. Italy was in slightly better shape than Germany, in part because of its Resistance movements.

The defeated nations—Germany in particular—were in the position of patients on whom drastic surgery has been performed and who lie prostrate, dependent for their every movement on surgeons and nurses. Even if one had wanted to restore the nation to the pinnacle of values and objectives, one could not have done so except with the help and consent of one's guardians—and they were unlikely to support such a drive. In other words, the situation set strict limits on the possibility of any kind of nationalism, expansive or insulating. The lost territories were beyond recuperation; a healing period of *repli,* comparable to that which had marked the early foreign policy of the Third Republic, was not conceivable either.

On the other hand, France and, to a lesser extent Belgium and Holland, were not so well protected. For, although the prevalence of the nation meant little in the immediate European context, it meant a great deal in the imperial one: if the circumstances of the Liberation kept national consciousness from veering into nationalism in one realm, the same circumstances tended to encourage such a turn with respect to the colonies. Cut down to size in Europe, these nations were bound to act as if they could call upon their overseas possessions to redress the balance; accustomed, through their association of nationalism with Nazi and Fascist imperialism, to equate chauvinism only with expansion, they would not be so easily discouraged from a nationalism of defense, aimed at preserving the "national mission" overseas. The Dutch lost most of their empire early, and found themselves in not so different a situation from the German and Italian amputees. The Belgians remained serene long enough not to have nationalistic fevers about the huge colony that seemed to give them no trouble until the day when it broke off—brutally, painfully, but irremediably. The French, however, suffered almost at once from dis-imperial dyspepsia, and the long, losing battle they fought gave continual rise to nationalist tantrums. The French inclination to nationalism was higher anyway, because there was one political force that was clearly nationalist. It had presided over the Liberation, given what unity it had to the Resistance, and achieved a highly original convergence of Jacobin universalism and "traditionalist," right-wing, defensive nationalism. This was the force of General de Gaulle. His resignation in 1946 meant, as Alfred Grosser suggests,[12] the defeat of a doctrine that put priority not only on foreign affairs but also on *Notre Dame la France*. The incident that led to his departure—a conflict over the military budget— was symbolic enough of the demise of nationalism. But his durability, first as a political leader, later as a "capital that belongs to all and to none," reflected a lasting French nostalgia for nationalism; and it was equally symbolic that the crisis which returned him to power was a crisis over Algeria.

The second feature common to all the West European national situations, yet affecting them differently, was the "political collapse of Europe." Europe did not merely lose power and wealth: such losses can be repaired, as the aftermath of World War I had shown. Europe, previously the heart of the international system, the locus of the world organization, the fount of international law, fell under what de Gaulle has called "the two hegemonies." The phrase is, obviously, inaccurate and insulting. One of those hegemonies took a highly imperial form, and thus discouraged and prevented the creation in Eastern Europe of any regional entity capable of overcoming the prewar national rivalries. But the American hegemony in Western Europe, different as it is, has been a basic fact of life, even though it was more "situational" than deliberate. Its effects were better than usual, insofar as the hegemony was restricted to areas where the European nations had become either impotent or incapable of recovery on their own. The dominated had considerable freedom of maneuver, and indeed the American presence prodded them into recovery, power recuperation, and regional unity; it favored both individual and collective emancipation. But the effects were in a way worse, because the laxity meant that each party could react to this feature of all the national situations—i.e., American hegemony—according to the distinctive *other* features of the national situation. American domination was only one part of the picture. Hence the following paradox: American prodding and the individual and collective impotence of West European nations ought logically to have pushed the latter toward unity-for-emancipation. But the autonomy that each West European nation retained gave it an array of choices: between accepting and rejecting dependence on the United States, between unity as a weapon for emancipation and unity as a way to make dependence more comfortable. It would have been a miracle if all the nations had made the same choice. To define one's position toward the United States was the common imperative, but each one has defined it in his own way.

At first, this diversity did not appear to be an obstacle to the unification movement. As Ernst Haas has shown,[13] the movement grew on ambiguity. Those who accepted American hegemony as a lasting fact of European life as well as those who did not could submerge their disagreement while building a regional entity: for the former, it was the most effective way to continue to receive American protection and contribute to America's mission and, for the latter, it was the most effective way to challenge American predominance. But there are limits to the credit of ambiguity. The split could not be concealed once the new Europe was asked to tackle matters of "high politics"—i.e., go beyond the purely internal economic problems of little impact or dependence on relations with America.[14] It is therefore no surprise that this split should have disrupted unification in 1953–54, when the problem of German rearmament was raised, and in 1962–68, when de Gaulle challenged the United States across the globe.[15]

This is how the diversity of national situations operated. First, it produced (and produces) a basic division between nations I would call resigned, and nations I would call resisters. The resigned ones included the smaller countries, aware of their weakness, realizing that the Soviet threat could not be met by Europeans alone, accustomed to dependence on external protectors, grateful to America for the unique features of its protection, and looking forward to an important role for Europe but not in the realm of high politics. In the past, Italy had tried to act as a great power without protectors, but those days were over, and acceptance of American hegemony gave the creaky Italian political system a kind of double cushion—against the threat of communism, and also against the need to spend too much energy and money on rearmament. For the smaller states as well as for Italy, acceptance of U.S. hegemony was like an insurance policy which protected them against having to give priority to foreign affairs. Germany, on the other hand, accepted dependence on the United States not merely as a comfort, but as a necessity as vital as breathing. West Germany's geographical position put it on the front line, its partition contributed to making security a supreme goal, the stanch anticommunism of its leadership ruled out any search for security along the lines of neutrality. There followed not only acceptance of American leadership but also a wish to do everything possible to tie the United States to Western Europe. Gaining equality with other nations was another vital goal for Germany, and it could be reached only through cooperation with the most powerful of the occupying forces. Defeat, division, and danger conspired to make West Germany switch from its imperialistic nationalism of the Nazi era to a dependence which was apparently submissive, yet also productive (of security and status gains) under Adenauer.

As for the resisters, they, like the West Germans, gave priority to foreign affairs—but not in the same perspective. The French reading of geography and history was different.[16] To be sure, the French saw the need for security against the Soviet Union, but the "tyranny of the cold war" operated differently in France. French feelings of hostility toward Russia were much more moderate than in Germany, and, although it may be too strong to speak of a nostalgia for the wartime Grand Alliance, it is not false to say that hope of an ultimate détente allowing for European reunification, a return of the Russians to moderation, and an emancipation of the continent from its "two hegemonies" never died. The French time perspective has consistently differed from, say, the German: the urgency of the Soviet threat never overshadowed the desire for, and belief in, a less tense international system. Whereas West Germany's continuity with its past was wrecked and repudiated, France (like Britain) looked back to the days when Europe held the center of the stage and forward to a time when Europe might again be an actor, not a stake: the anomaly was the present, not the past. Also, on colonial matters, France (more than Britain) often found little to distinguish America's reprobation from Soviet hostility. And France worried not only about possible Soviet thrusts but also about Germany's potential threats: the fearful anticipation of a reborn German national consciousness and nationalism has marked all French leaders. An additional reason for dreading the perpetuation of American hegemony and the freezing of the cold war was the fear that such a course would make Germany the main beneficiary of America's favors. Germany looked East with some terror, but there was only one foe there; when the French looked East, they saw two nations to fear; each could be used as an ally against the other—but for the time being the

Soviet danger was the greater, and if Germany was built up too much against Russia, the security gained in one respect would be compromised in another.[17]

The diversity of national situations also operated in another way. As I have suggested, situations limit and affect but do not command choices. A general desire for overcoming the cold war and American hegemony did not make for a general agreement on how to do so. What I have called the resisters were divided, and this division became decisive. If all the resisters had calculated that the best way to reach France's objectives was the construction of a powerful West European entity which could rival U.S. might, turn the bipolar contest into a triangle, and wrest advantages from both Russia and America, the "ambiguity" of the movement (between resigned *and* resisting forces) might not have damaged the enterprise until much later. But those who reasoned along the lines just described—like Jean Monnet —were sharply divided from those who feared that a sacrifice of national sovereignty to supranational institutions might entail loss of control over the direction of the European undertaking. Two kinds of people took this second line: the nationalists who were still eager to preserve all the resources of French diplomacy and strategy, in order, in the present, to concentrate on overseas fronts and, later, to promote whatever policies would be required, rather than let a foreign body decide; and, on the other hand, men like Mendès-France, who were not nationalists in the sense I use the term in this chapter, but who thought that the continental European construction was not France's best way of coping with her situation, who thought priority should be given to the search for a détente, the liberalization of the empire, the reform of the economy.[18]

The success of the European movement required, first, that those suspicious of European integration remain a minority—not only throughout the six nations but in their leadership, not only in the parliaments but above all in the executive branches. This requirement was met in 1950–53 and in 1955–58, but not in the crucial months for EDC in 1953–54, and no longer after 1958. The movement proceeded after 1958 in a dialectic of ambiguity. However, there was a second requirement for success: that the "minute of truth"—when the European elites would have to ask about the ultimate political direction of their community—be postponed as long as possible; i.e., that the cold war remain sufficiently intense to impose even on the "resisters" priority for the kind of security that presupposed U.S. protection—priority for the *urgent* over the *long-term important*. But this requirement was shaken during the brief period of nervous demobilization that followed Stalin's death in 1953–54, and then was gradually undermined by a third basic feature in Europe's postwar situation. Before we turn to it, one remark must be made: in French foreign policy, "resistance by European integration" prevailed over "resistance by self-reliance" only so long as France was bogged down in colonial wars; it was this important and purely French element in France's national situation whose ups and downs affected quite decisively the method of "resistance." [19]

The divisions and contradictions described above were sharpened by a third common feature which emerged in the mid-1950s and whose effects developed progressively: the nuclear stalemate between the United States and the Soviet Union. The effect of the "balance of terror" on the Western Alliance has been analyzed so often and well [20] that nothing needs to be added here; still, we might usefully inquire how Europe's gradual discovery of the uncertainties of America's nuclear protection affected the other factors we have discussed above.

The first thing we can say is that the nuclear balance of terror worsened the split between French "resistance" and West German "resignation." The dominant political elites in West Germany thought it merely added urgency to their previous calculation of interest. From the West German position, the nuclear stalemate was thought to increase the danger for the West: the United States was relatively weaker, the Soviet Union stronger and more of a threat. Indeed, the Social Democrats switched from their increasingly furtive thoughts of neutrality to outright endorsement of the Christian Democratic support of NATO. If America's nuclear monopoly was broken, if America's guarantee was weakened, West Germany needed a policy that was respectful enough of the United States' main concerns, so that the United States would feel obligated to keep its mantle of protection over West Germany and not be tempted into negotiating a détente at its expense. West German docility would be the condition for, and counterpart of, American entanglement in Europe. The West German reaction to a development that (if General Gallois' logic were followed) might lead to the prevalence of "polycentrism" over bipolarity was to search for ways of exorcising the former and preserving the latter. On the whole, the smaller nations and Italy, while not at all fearful about the consequences of polycentrism (quite the contrary), were nevertheless not shaken out of their "resignation." The mere appearance of parity of nuclear peril was not enough to make them eager or able to give priority to an activist foreign policy.

In France, the balance of terror reinforced the attitude of resistance. The goal of emancipation now became a real possibility. A superpower stalemate meant increased security for the lesser powers: however much they might complain about the decrease of American protection, there was a heightened feeling of protection against war in general. What the West Germans saw as a liability, the French considered an opportunity. West Germany's situation, and its low national consciousness, induced most German leaders to choose what might be called a "minimizing" interpretation of the new situation. France's situation—its high national consciousness and, after 1958, Gaullist doctrine—induced French political elites to choose a "maximizing" interpretation. They believed that the increasing costs of the use of nuclear force made actual use less likely, U.S. protection less certain but also less essential, Europe's recovery of not merely wealth but power more desirable and possible. This recovery of power would help bring about the much desired prevalence of polycentrism over bipolarity.[21]

As this feud shows, the balance of terror heightened the division over method among the "resisters." On one hand, it provided new arguments for those who thought that emancipation could be achieved only by uniting Western Europe; that individual national efforts would be too ridiculously weak to amount to anything but a waste in resources; but that a collective effort could exploit the new situation and make Western Europe a true partner of the United States. On the other hand, those who feared that the "united way" could become a frustrating deviation reasoned that the theory of graduated deterrence justified the acquisition of nuclear weapons by a middle-size power with limited resources and that this acquisition would considerably increase the political influence and prestige of the nation. The increased costs of force ruled out, in any case, what in the past had been the most disastrous effect of the mushrooming of sovereign states—a warlike, expansionist nationalism—but they simultaneously made the value of small- or middle-size nations good again. According to this argument, the "united way" would be a dead end, since some, and not exactly the least significant, of the associates had no desire for collective European power at the possible expense of American protection.

Until the nuclear stalemate became a fact of European life, opposition to a supranational West European entity had come only from a fraction of the "resisters." In the early 1950s the United States had strongly—too strongly—urged the establishment of a European defense system, for it had not been considered likely to challenge America's own military predominance. In the 1960s the United States no longer urged the West Europeans to build such a system. American leadership developed a deep concern for maintaining centralized control over NATO forces, i.e., for preserving bipolarity, and a growing realization that Europe's appetite would not stop short of nuclear weapons. As a result, some of the "resigned ones," instead of endorsing European integration unreservedly, for the first time now showed themselves of two minds: they were willing to pursue integration in economic and social fields, but less so in matters of defense, lest

NATO be weakened. It is significant that the Dutch resisted de Gaulle's efforts in 1960–62 to include defense in a confederal scheme, and that West German leaders put some hopes in the MLF—a scheme that would have tied European nations one by one to the United States—rather than in a revised and revived EDC. Inevitably, such mental reservations of those who had been among the champions of supranationality could only confirm the suspicions of "resisters" who had distrusted the "Monnet method" from the beginning. Thus, the national situation of West Germany in particular—a situation in which the U.S. policy of reliance on West Germany as an anchor for U.S. influence on the continent played an important part—damaged the European movement: West German leaders were largely successful in their drive to entangle the United States but found that the price they had to pay was a decreasing ability to push for European integration. European integration and dependence on the United States were no longer automatically compatible.

This long discussion of the different responses to common situations has been necessary as an antidote to the usual way of discussing European integration, which has focused on process. The self-propelling power of the unifying process is severely constrained by the associates' views on ends and means. In order to go "beyond the nation-state," one must do more than set up procedures in adequate "background" and "process conditions." A procedure is not a purpose, a process is not a policy.

III

Still, since the process of European integration is its most original feature, we must examine it, too.[22] We have been witnessing a kind of race between the logic of integration set up by Monnet (analyzed by Haas) and the logic of diversity (analyzed above). According to the former, the double pressure of necessity (the interdependence of the European social fabric, which will oblige statesmen to integrate even sectors originally left uncoordinated) and of men (the action of the supranational agents) will gradually restrict the national governments' freedom of movement. In such a milieu, nationalism will become a futile and anachronistic exercise, and the national consciousness itself will, so to speak, be impregnated with an awareness of the higher interest in union. The logic of diversity, by contrast, sets limits on the degree to which the "spill-over" process can curtail the governments' freedom of action; it restricts to the area of welfare the domain in which the logic of functional integration can operate; indeed, insofar as discrepancies in other areas prevail, even issues belonging in the area of welfare may become infected by the disharmony, because of the links that exist among all areas. The logic of integration is that of a blender which crunches up the most diverse products, replacing their different tastes and perfumes with one, presumably delicious juice. One expects a finer synthesis: ambiguity helps because each "ingredient" can hope that its taste will predominate at the end. The logic of diversity is the opposite: it suggests that, in areas of key importance to the national interest, nations prefer the self-controlled uncertainty of national self-reliance, to the uncontrolled uncertainty of the blending process; ambiguity carries one only part of the way. The logic of integration assumes that it is possible to fool each one of the associates some of the time because his over-all gain will still exceed his occasional losses, even if his calculations turn out wrong here or there. The logic of diversity implies that losses on one vital issue are not compensated for by gains on other issues (especially not on other less vital issues): nobody wants to be fooled. The logic of integration regards the uncertainties of the supranational function process as creative; the logic of diversity sees them as destructive past a certain threshold. Ambiguity lures and lulls the national consciousness into integration as long as the benefits are high, the costs low, the expectations considerable. Ambiguity may arouse and stiffen national consciousness into nationalism if the benefits are low, the losses high, the hopes dashed or deferred. Functional integration's gamble could be won only if the method had sufficient potency to promise a permanent excess of gains over losses, and of hopes over frustrations. Theoretically, this may be true of economic integration. It is not true of political integration (in the sense of "high politics").

The success of the approach symbolized by Monnet depended, and depends still, on his winning a triple gamble: on goals, on methods, on results. As for goals, it is a gamble on the possibility of substituting motion as an end in itself, for agreement on ends. It is a fact that Europe's transnational integrationist elites did not agree on whether the object of the community-building enterprise ought to be a new superstate—i.e., a federal potential nation, à la U.S.A.—or whether the object was to demonstrate that power politics could be overcome in cooperation and compromise, that one could build a radically new kind of unit, change the nature and not merely the scale of the game. Monnet himself was ambiguous on this score; Walter Hallstein leaned in the first direction, many of Monnet's public relations men in the second.[23] Nor did the integrationists agree on whether the main goal was to create a regional "security-community," [24] i.e., to pacify a former hotbed of wars, or to create an entity whose position and strength could decisively affect the cold war in particular and international relations in general. Now, it is perfectly possible for a movement to use its continental nationalists as well as its antipower idealists, its inward-looking and outward-looking politicians—but only as long as there is no need to make a choice. Decisions on tariffs do not require such choices. Decisions on agriculture begin to raise basic problems of orientation. Decisions on foreign policy and membership and defense cannot be reached unless the goals are clarified, nor can decisions on monetary union (past the first stage of narrowing fluctuations between currencies). One cannot be all things to all people all of the time.

As for methods, there was a gamble that supranational functionalism would irresistibly rise. Monnet assumed, first, that national sovereignty, already devalued by events, could be chewed up leaf by leaf like an artichoke. He assumed, second, that the dilemma of the West European governments—having to choose between an integration that tied their hands and stopping a movement that benefited their people —could be exploited in favor of integration by men representing the common good, endowed with superior expertise, initiative, deadlines, and package deals. Finally, he assumed that this approach would take into account the interests of the greater powers and prevent the crushing of the smaller ones. The troubles with this gamble have been numerous. Even an artichoke has a heart, and it remains intact after the leaves have been eaten. It is of course true that successful economic and social integration in Western Europe would considerably limit the freedom governments continued to enjoy (in theory) in diplomacy and strategy, but why should one assume that they would not be aware of it? As the artichoke is slowly eaten, the governments become ever more vigilant. To be sure, their dilemma suggests that they might not do anything about it: they would be powerless to save the heart. But this would be true only if governments never put what they consider essential interests of the nation above the particular interest of certain categories of nationals, if superior expertise were always either a supranational monopoly or the solution of an issue at hand, if package deals were effective in every argument, and, above all, if the governments' representatives were always determined to behave in an EEC way, rather than as agents of states that are unwilling to accept a supranational community whatever the conditions. Functional integration may indeed give lasting satisfaction to the smaller powers precisely because it is for them that the ratio of "welfare politics" to high politics is highest, and that the chance of gaining benefits through intergovernmental methods that reflect rather than correct the power differential between the big and the small is poorest. But this is also why the method is not likely *à la longue* to satisfy the bigger powers as much: facing them, the supranational civil servants, for all their skill and legal powers, are a bit like Jonahs trying to turn whales into jellyfish. Of course, the idea is ultimately to move from an administrative procedure, in which supranational civil servants enter a dialogue with national ministers, to a truly federal procedure in which a federal cabinet is responsible to a federal parliament; but what is thus presented as linear progress may turn out to be a vicious circle, since the ministers hold the key to the transformation, and may refuse it unless the goals are defined and the results already achieved are satisfactory.

There was a gamble about results as well. The experience of European integration would mean net benefits for all and bring about progress toward community formation. Progress could be measured by the following yardsticks: in the realm of interstate relations, an increasing transfer of power to new common agencies, and the prevalence of solutions "upgrading the common interest" over other kinds of compromises; in the realm of transnational society, an increasing flow of communications; in the area of national consciousness (which is important both for interstate relations, since it may limit the statesmen's discretion, and for transnational society, because it affects the scope and meaning of the communications), an increasing compatibility of views about external issues. The results achieved in Western Europe so far are mixed: dubious on the last count, positive (but not unlimited) on the second, and marked on the first by unexpected features. There was some strengthening of the authority of the EEC Commission until 1965, and in various areas there was some "upgrading of common interests." On the other hand, the Commission's unfortunate attempt to consolidate those gains at de Gaulle's expense in the spring of 1965 brought about a startling setback for the whole enterprise; in their negotiations, the members have conspicuously failed to find a common interest in some vital areas (energy, transport, industrial and investment policies), and sometimes reached apparently "integrating" decisions only after the most ungainly, traditional kind of bargaining, in which such uncommunity-like methods as threats, ultimatums, and retaliatory moves were used. In other words, either the ideal was not reached, or it was reached in a way that was its opposite and its destroyer. If we look at the institutions of the Common Market as an incipient political system for Europe, we find that their authority is limited, their structure weak, their popular base restricted and distant.[25]

It is therefore not surprising if the uncertainty about results already achieved contributes to uncertainty about future prospects. The divisions among partisans of integration make it hard to predict where the "Monnet method" will lead if the process were to continue along the lines so fondly planned by the French *inspirateur.* Will the enterprise become an effective federation, or will it become a mere façade behind which all the divergences and rivalries continue to be played out? It was nonetheless remarkable that Gaullist and American fears should converge in one respect: de Gaulle consistently warned that applying the supranational method to the area of high politics would dilute national responsibility in a way that would benefit only the United States; incapable of defining a coherent policy, the "technocrats" would leave vital decisions to the United States, at least by default. On the contrary, many Americans have come to believe on the basis of some of the EEC's actions in agriculture and trade that a united Europe would be able to challenge U.S. leadership much more effectively than the separate European states ever could. The truth of the matter is that nobody knows: a method is not a policy, a process is not a direction; the results achieved so far are too specialized and the way in which they have been reached is too bumpy to allow one to extrapolate and project safely. The face of a united Europe has not begun to emerge; there are just a few lines, but one does not know whether the supranational technique would finally give Western Europe the features of a going concern or those of a Fourth Republic writ large—the ambitions of a world power or the complacency of parochialism. The range of possibilities is so broad, the alternatives are so extreme, that the more the Six, and now the Nine, move into the stormy waters of high politics, the less they, and outside powers such as the United States that may be affected by their acts, are willing to extend the credit of hope and to make new wagers: neither Gaullist France nor America has been willing to risk a major loss of control. Contrary to the French proverb, in the process of functional integration, only the first steps do not cost much.

Two important general lessons can be drawn from a study of the process of integration. The first concerns the limits of the functional method: its relative success in the relatively painless area where it works relatively well lifts the participants of EEC to a new level of issues where the method does not work well any more—like swimmers whose skill at moving quickly away from the shore brings them to a point where the waters are stormy and deep, at a time when fatigue is setting in, and none of the questions about ultimate goal, direction, or endurance has been answered. The functional process was used in order to "make Europe"; once Europe began being made, the question had to be asked: "Making Europe, what for?" The process is like a grinder, a machine that works only when someone keeps giving it something to grind. When the members of EEC start quarreling and stop providing, the machine stops. For a while, the machine worked because the European governments poured into it a common determination to integrate their economies in order to maximize wealth. But with their wealth increasing, the question of what to do with it was bound to arise: a capability of supplying means does not *ipso facto* provide the ends, and it is about the ends that quarrels broke out.

Each member state is willing to live with the others, but not on terms too different from his own; and the Nine are not in the position of the three miserable prisoners of *No Exit*. Transforming a dependent "subsystem" proved to be one thing; defining its relations to all other subsystems and to the international system in general has turned out to be quite another.

The model of functional integration—a substitute for the kind of instant federation that governments had not been prepared to accept —shows its origins in important respects. It is essentially an administrative model, which relies on bureaucratic expertise to promote a policy that political decision-makers are technically incapable of shaping (something like French planning under the Fourth Republic). The hope was that in the interstices of political bickering the administrators could build up a consensus, but it was a mistake to believe that a formula that works well within certain limits is a panacea—and that even within the limits of "welfare politics" administrative skill can always overcome the disastrous effects of political paralysis or mismanagement. Moreover, the model assumes that the basic political decisions, to be prepared and pursued by EEC civil servants but formally made by the governments, would be reached through a process of short-term bargaining, by politicians whose mode of operation is empirical muddling through of the kind that puts immediate advantages above long-term pursuits. This model corresponds well to the reality of parliamentary politics with a weak executive branch—for example, the politics of the Fourth Republic—but it was a mistake to believe that all political regimes would conform to this rather sorry image, and to ignore the disastrous results that the original example produced whenever conflicts over values and fundamental choices made mere empirical groping useless or worse than useless.[26]

The second lesson we should draw from the origin of the integration model is even more discouraging for advocates of functionalism. To revert to the analogy of the grinder, what happened in 1965 was that the machine, piqued by the slowing down of supply, suddenly suggested to its users that in the future the supplying of material to be ground be left to the machine. Bureaucratic institutions tend to become actors with a stake in their own survival and expansion. The same thing happens often enough within a state whose political system is ineffective. But here we are dealing not with one but with several political systems, and the reason for the relative ineffectiveness of the EEC's Council of Ministers may be the excessive toughness, not weakness, of the national political systems involved. In other words, by trying to be a force, the bureaucracy here, inevitably, turns into a factor that the nations try to control or at least affect. A new complication is thus added to all the substantive issues that divide the participants. Thus, the agricultural problem could have been solved "technically," since the governments had previously reached basic compromises, and had more or less agreed on the relations between Common Market and outside agriculture. But the way these accords were reached left scars, and the nature of the agreement meant a victory for one state (France) over another (West Germany). The whole issue was reopened, due not to the states' but to the Commission's initiative. In the crisis of 1965, the Commission's overly bold proposal for a common agricultural policy (along pro-French lines) *cum* supranationality (against French determination) did allow some of the Six, hostile in fact to the substantive proposals, to endorse the Commission's plan and stand up as champions of supranationality, while knowing that the French would block the scheme; the French, eager to get their partners committed to a protected agricultural market, preferred to postpone the realization of this goal rather than let the Commission's autonomy grow, and used the Commission's rashness as a pretext for trying to kill supranationality altogether; and the West German government, not too kindly disposed toward the Commission whose initiatives and economic inspiration were hardly in line with Erhard's views, found itself defending it (its head, now under French attack, was a German). To be sure, the Commission's dilemma had become acute: either its members resigned themselves to being merely patient brokers to their quarreling clients, and letting them set the pace; or else they tried to behave according to the ideal type of the Monnet method *and* as if a genuine community had already been established. But if prudence meant sluggishness, anticipation meant delay. Since 1965, all the important issues—including Britain's entry—have been hammered out between governments. The Commission has been discreet. This has not ended the arguments about the need for "stronger" institutions. Haggling about the kind of machinery one wants is a polite method for appearing to want to keep working together, while disagreeing completely on what one wants the machinery for.

IV

We must come now to the balance sheet of the "European experiment." The most visible result is the survival of Europe's nations. To be sure, they survive transformed: swept by the "age of mass consumption," caught in an apparently inexorable process of industrialization, urbanization, and democratization, they become more alike in social structure, in economic and social policies, even in physical appearance; there is a spectacular break between the past, which so many monuments bring to constant memory, and a rationalized future that puts them closer to American industrial society than to the issues of their own history. These similarities are promoted by the Common Market itself. It is of no mean consequence that the prospect of a collapse of the EEC should bring anguish to various interest groups, some of which fought its establishment: the transnational linkages of businessmen and farmers are part of the transformation. And no West European nation is a world power any longer in the traditional sense—i.e., in the sense either of having physical establishments backed by military might in various parts of the globe, or of possessing in Europe armed forces superior to those of any non-European power.

And yet they survive as nations. In foreign affairs and defense, not only has power not been transferred to European organs but France has actually taken power away from NATO. Differences in the calculations of national interest broadened with the advent of the balance of terror, as I have already argued. Even when, after 1968, these calculations came closer, they converged on avoiding rather than promoting foreign and defense policies: Brandt's Bonn has wanted to avoid upsetting Washington or Moscow; Pompidou had decided to lift the European car out of the bog by no longer raising the issues that had, with de Gaulle at the wheel, stuck it there. Paradoxically, the post-Czechoslovakia rapprochement in the *Ostpolitiken* of Paris, London, and Bonn has not brought about much of a "spill-over" into European political cooperation. Policies toward the United States have remained different, and even the *Ostpolitiken* are not identical. A common inability to affect the superpowers' détente or their rivalry in the Middle East has not been translated into a common stand either on force reductions (or build-up) or on oil-sharing. As for intra-European communications, the indubitably solid economic network of the EEC has not been complemented by a network of social and cultural communications; the links between some European societies and the United States are stronger than the links among them. Even in the realm of economic relations, the Common Market for goods has not been complemented by a system of pan-West European enterprises: firms that are unable to compete with rivals in the EEC often associate with American firms rather than merge with their European rivals; or else the mergers are between national firms and help to build up national monopolies. Finally, European statesmen express views about external issues that often appear to reflect and support their divergent definitions of the national interest; or, while superficially favorable to "Europe," they fail to show any active enthusiasm or great passion.[27] There is no common European outlook. Nor is there a common *projet,* a common conception of Europe's role in world affairs or Europe's possible contribution to the solution of problems characteristic of all industrial societies.

To some extent, the obstacles lie in the present condition of national consciousness. In two respects, similarities have emerged in recent years. There has been a rebirth of German national consciousness, largely because the bold attempt at fastening Germany's shattered consciousness directly to a new European one did not succeed: the existence of a West German national situation gradually reawakened a German national awareness, and reduced the gap between West Germany and France in this area. Moreover, the national consciences in Western Europe are alike in one sense: they are not like Rousseau's general will, a combination of mores and moves that define the purposes of the national community with intellectual clarity and emotional involvement. Today's national consciousness in Europe is negative rather than positive. There is still, in each nation, a *"vouloir-vivre collectif."* But it is not a "daily plebiscite" *for* something. It is, in some parts, a daily routine, a community based on habit rather than on common tasks, an identity that is received rather than shaped. Thus West Germany's sense of "cohesion and distinctiveness" is the result of the survival and recovery of a West German state in a world of nations rather than a specific willed set of imperatives. In other parts, national consciousness is a daily refusal rather than a daily creation, a desire to preserve a certain heritage (however waning, and less because it is meaningful today than because it is one's own) rather than a determination to define a common destiny, an identity that is hollow rather than full, and marked more by bad humor toward foreign influences than by any positive contribution.

To be sure, negative or hollow national consciousness need not be a liability for the champions of integration: general wills à la Rousseau could function as obstacles to any fusion of sovereignty. But a patriotic consciousness that survives in a kind of nonpurposive complacency can be a drag on any policy: it does not carry statesmen forward in the way an intense and positive "general will" prods leaders who act on behalf of national goals, or in the way in which European federalists have sometimes hoped that enlightened national patriotisms would encourage Europe's leaders to build a new European community. The French may not have a sense of national purpose, but, precisely because their patriotism has been tested so often and so long, because pressures from the outside world have continued throughout the postwar era to batter their concerns and their conceits, and because modernization, now accepted and even desired, also undermines their cherished traditional values and their still enforced traditional authority patterns, French national consciousness resists any suggestion of abdication, resignation, *repli*. (So much so that the "Europeans" themselves have presented European integration as an opportunity for getting French views shared by others instead of stressing the "community" side of the enterprise.[28]) West Germany's national consciousness, on the other hand, is marked by a genuine distaste for or timidity toward what might be called the power activities of a national community on the world stage; hence the West Germans tend to shy away from the problems of "high politics" which a united Europe would have to face and avoidance of which only delays unity; a tendency, at first, to refuse to make policy choices and, later, to pretend (to oneself and to others) that no such choices are required, that there is no incompatibility between a "European Europe" and an Atlantic partnership and a reconciliation with the East. In one case, a defensive excess of self-confidence makes unity on terms other than one's own difficult; in the other case, an equally defensive lack of self-confidence projects into the foreign undertakings of the nation and weakens the foundations of the common European enterprise.

And yet, if the "national consciousness" of each European nation could be isolated from all other elements of the national situation, one would, I think, conclude that the main reasons for the endurance of the nation-state lie elsewhere.

They lie, first of all, in the differences in national situations, exacerbated by the interaction between each of the West European member states and the present international system. Earlier, we looked at specific instances of such differences; let us return to them in a more analytic way. One part of each national situation is the purely *domestic* component. In a modern nation-state, the importance of the political system—in the triple sense of functional scope, authority, and popular basis—is a formidable obstacle to integration. It is easier to overcome the parochialism of a political system with only a slender administrative structure, than it is to dismantle a political system which rests on "socially mobilized" and mobilizing parties and pressure groups, and which handles an enormous variety of social and economic services with a huge bureaucracy. To be sure, it was Monnet's hope and tactic to dismantle the fortress by redirecting the allegiance of parties and pressure groups toward the new central institutions of Europe, by endowing the latter with the ability to compete with the national governments in setting up social services. In other words, the authority of the new European political system would deepen as its scope broadened and its popular basis expanded. The success of this attempt to dry up the national ponds by diverting their waters into a new, supranational pool depended on three prerequisites which have not been met: with respect to popular basis, the prevalence of parties and pressure groups over executive branches; with respect to scope, the self-sustaining and expanding capacity of the new central bureaucracy; with respect to both scope and popular basis, the development of transnational political issues of interest to all political forces and peoples across boundary lines.

The executive establishment of the modern political state has one remarkable feature: it owes much of its legitimacy and power to the support of popularly based parties and pressure groups, but it also enjoys a degree of autonomy that allows it to resist pressures, manipulate opposition, manufacture support. Even the weak Fourth Republic evaded pressure toward "transnationalism" and diluted the dose of "bargaining politics" along supranational lines. Even the EEC civil servants' careers are made and unmade in national capitals. Above all, each nation's political life continues to be dominated by "parochial" issues: each political system is like a thermos bottle that keeps the liquid inside warm, or lukewarm. It is as if, for the mythical common man, the nation-state were still the most satisfying—indeed, the most rewarding—form of social organization in existence.[29] If we look at the states' behavior, we find that each reacted to the transnational forces that vitiated its autonomy by trying to tighten control on what was left. Multinational enterprises erase borders, but research, development, and technology, far from being "Europeanized," have been nationalized. The growing similarity and interdependence of West European industrial societies have not led to political integration. Indeed, insofar as all of them have become the scene of constant, often unruly group bargaining—what Raymond Aron has termed the politics of querulous satisfaction—their ability to divert attention to integration has been small. And, within the EEC's institutions, empirical muddling through—the political mode of operation of such societies—has been powerless to overcome paralysis whenever the members were divided (industrial and energy policy, social and regional policy, space, control of foreign investments) or to allow for the drastic revision of policies which incremental adjustments cannot save (agriculture).

The European political process has never come close to resembling that of any West European democracy because it has been starved of common and distinctive European issues. If we look at the issues that have dominated European politics, we find two distinct categories. One is that of problems peculiar to each nation—Italy's battle of Reds vs. Blacks, or its concern for the Mezzogiorno; Belgium's linguistic clashes; West Germany's "social economy" and liquidation of the past; France's postwar constitutional troubles and party splintering, later the nature and future of Gaullist presidentialism and the fall-out from May 1968. Here, whatever the transnational party and interest-group alignments in the EEC, the dominant motifs have been purely national. The other category of issues are international ones (including European unity). But here, the *external* components of each national situation have thwarted the emergence of a common European political system comparable to that of each nation. Here, the weight of geography and history—a history of nations—has kept the nation-states in their watertight compartments.

It is no accident if France, the initiator of the European-unity process, has also been its chief troublemaker; for by reason of history and geography France's position differed from everyone else's in the Community (and was actually closer to Britain's). For West Germany, integration meant a leap from opprobrium and impotence to respectability and equal rights; for the smaller powers, it meant exchanging a very modest dose of autonomy for participation in a potentially strong and rich grouping. France could not help being much more ambivalent, for integration meant on one hand an avenue for leadership and the shaping of a powerful bloc, but, on the other, the acceptance of permanent restrictions on French autonomy. A once-great power inherits from its past a whole set of habits and reflexes that make it conduct policy as if it were still or could become again a great power (unless those habits and reflexes have been smashed, as Germany's were). In other words, integration meant an almost certain improvement in the national situation of the other five nations; but for France it could be a deterioration or an adventure.[30] There is no better example here than the issue of nuclear weapons. Integration in nuclear matters meant, for France, giving up the possibility of having a nuclear force of her own, perhaps never being certain that a united Europe would create a common nuclear deterrent, at best contributing to a European nuclear force that would put West Germany in the same position as France. But the French decision to pursue the logic of diversity, while giving her her own nuclear force, also made a European nuclear solution more difficult and increased France's distance from West Germany. Moreover, a geographical difference corroborated the historical one: France had lasting colonial involvements. Not only did they intensify national consciousness; they also contributed to France's ambivalence toward European integration. The worse France's overseas plight became, the more European integration was preached as a kind of compensatory mechanism. But this meant that European integration had to be given a "national" rather than a "supranational" color; it meant that the French tried to tie their European partners to France's overseas concerns, much against these partners' better judgment; above all, it meant that there was a competition for public attention and for official energies between the European and overseas components of French foreign affairs. The great-power reflex and the colonial legacy combined in a policy of cooperation with France's former imperial possessions despite the cost; overseas cooperation is presented as a policy that has transfigured the colonial legacy and that manifests the great-power reflex.[31]

Thus, national situations multiplied the effects of differences among the various national consciences. But the endurance of the nation-state in France is due also to a revival of nationalism. Even without de Gaulle, the differences analyzed above would have slowed down European integration; but his personal contribution to the crisis of integration was enormous. Not only did he raise questions that were inescapable in the long run but he tried to impose his own answers. De Gaulle changed French policy from ambivalence toward supranational integration to outright hostility; from a reluctance to force the European states to dispel the ambiguities of "united Europe" to an almost gleeful determination to bring out differences into the open. De Gaulle also changed the national situations of the others, which sharpened antagonisms and led to a kind of cumulative retreat from integration.

It is true that the General was an empiricist, and that his analysis of the European situation was to a large extent irrefutable. What could be more sensible than starting from what exists (the nation-states), refusing to act as if what does not yet exist (a united Europe) were already established? But pragmatism is always at the service of ends, explicit or not. (The definition of a bad foreign policy could be: a foreign policy that uses rigid means at the service of explicit ends, or whose flexible means do not serve clearly-thought-out ends.) De Gaulle's empiricism was a superb display of skill, but on behalf of a thoroughly nonempirical doctrine. It is obvious that his distrust of supranational integration, perfectly comprehensible as a starting point, nevertheless resulted in a kind of freezing of integration and perpetuation of the nation-state. If his chief foreign-policy objective had been the creation of a European entity acting as a world power, his "empirical" *starting point* would have been a most unrealistic *method*. But it was not his supreme objective, and Europe not his supreme value.

De Gaulle's doctrine was a "universalist nationalism." That is, he saw France's mission as world-wide, not local and defensive; but this meant that Europe was just one corner of the tapestry; a means, not an end. "Things being what they are," it is better to have separate nation-states than it is to have a larger entity; while the latter could undoubtedly act better as a forceful competitor in the world's contests, it would have to be coherent to do so, and it was more likely to be incoherent, given the divisions of its members and the leverage interested outsiders possess over some of the insiders. The size of the unit was less important than its "cohesion and distinctiveness," for effectiveness is not merely a function of material resources: if the unit has no capacity to turn resources to action, the only beneficiaries are its rivals. In a contest with giants, a confident David is better than a disturbed Goliath. This is a choice that reflects a doctrine; de Gaulle's refusal to gamble on European unity went along with a willingness to gamble on the continuing potency of the French nation-state. Joseph Schumpeter defined imperialism as an objectless quest; de Gaulle's nationalism was a kind of permanent quest with varying content but never any other cause than itself.

Every great leader has his built-in flaw, since this is a world where

roses have thorns. De Gaulle's was the self-fulfilling prophecy. Distrustful of any Europe but his own, his acts made Europe anything but his.
Here we must turn to the effect of his policy on France's partners.
First of all, there was a matter of style. Wanting European cooperation, not integration, de Gaulle refused to treat the Community organs
as Community organs; but, wanting to force his views about cooperation on nations still attached to the goal of integration, he paradoxically had to try to achieve cooperation for a common policy in a way
that smacked of conflict, not cooperation, of unilateralism, not compromise. Thus we witnessed not just a retreat from the Monnet
method to, say, the kind of intergovernmental cooperation that marks
the Organization for Economic Cooperation and Development (OECD),
but to a kind of grand strategy of nonmilitary conflict, a kind of political cold war of maneuver and "chicken." With compromises wrested
by ultimatums, concessions obtained not through package deals but
under the threat of boycotts, it is not surprising if even the Commission ended by playing the General's game instead of turning whatever
cheek was left. Its spring 1965 agricultural plan was as outright a challenge to de Gaulle as his veto of January 1963 had been an affront to
the Community spirit. Just as de Gaulle had tried to force West Germany to sacrifice her farmers to the idea of a European entity, the
Commission tried to call his bluff by forcing him to choose between
French farmers' interests and the French national interest in a "European Europe" for agriculture, on one hand, and his own hostility to
supranationality and the French national interest in the free use of
French resources, on the other. Playing his game, the Commission also
played into his hands, allowing him to apply the Schelling tactic of "if
you do not do what I ask, I will blow my brains out on your new
suit," and in the end buying his return at the price of a sacrifice of integration.[32] In other words, he forced each member state to treat the
EEC no longer as an end in itself; and he drove even its constituted
bodies to bringing grist to his mill.

But de Gaulle's effect on his partners was a matter of policy as well.
Here we must examine Franco-German relations. Had West Germany
been willing to follow France, he would have given priority to the
construction of a "half-Europe" that would thereafter have been a
magnet (as well as a guarantee of German harmlessness) to the East.
West Germany's refusal led him to put a "Europe from the Atlantic to
the Urals" on the same plane as a "European Europe" in the West; for
the containment of West Germany, no longer assured in a disunited
Western Europe of the Six, could still be gotten in a larger framework.
The implications were important. First, there was a considerable
change in West Germany's national situation. Whereas for more than
fifteen years the United States and France tacitly carried out Robert

Schuman's recommendation—"never leave Germany to herself"—the Franco-American competition for German support, the Gaullist refusal to tie West Germany to France in a federal Europe (so to speak, for the knot's sake), and America's disastrous emulation of the sorcerer's apprentice in titillating German interest in nuclear strategy or weapons-sharing, had all been factors that loosened the bonds between Germany and the West. Consequently, the domestic component of West Germany's national situation was also affected. Still concerned with security as well as with German reunification, but less and less able to believe that loyalty to their allies would deliver all the goods, the West German leaders and elites felt less dependent and constrained. Of course, objectively, the external constraints remain compelling. But de Gaulle's effect on Germany was, if not a rebirth of German nationalism, at least a change in the situation that gives national German action some chances. The temptation to use economic power to reach one's goals and the example of one's allies competing for accommodation with one's foe could not be resisted forever, especially when the past was full of precedents. To be sure, a nationalist Germany may well find itself as unable to shake the walls or to escape through the bars as Gaullist France was unable to forge the "European Europe." But the paradox of a revisionist France, trying to change the international system to her advantage despite her complete lack of "traditional" grievances (lost territories, military discrimination, and so forth), and a Germany with many grievances behaving in fact like a *status quo* power, could not last forever. The result, after 1969, was a West German *Ostpolitik* that followed France's example and solemnly acknowledged the inviolability of the *status quo,* yet in so doing asserted Bonn's right to an independent foreign policy. Of course, a less aggressively ambitious France might not have prevented West Germany from trying to follow its own path one day: the possibility of someone else's imitative *hubris* is no reason for *effacement;* but because the "essence and drama" of nationalism lie in the meeting with others, the risk of contagion—a risk that was part of de Gaulle's larger gamble—could not be disregarded.

Thus the nation-state survives, preserved by the resilience of national political systems, by the interaction between separate nations and a single international system, and by leaders who believe in the primacy of "high politics" over managerial politics and in the primacy of the nation.

V

This long balance sheet leaves us with many questions. What are the prospects in Western Europe? What generalizations can we draw from the whole experience? Is there no chance for the European Community? Is it condemned to be, at best, a success in economics and a fiasco in "high politics?" [33]

While nothing (not even the Common Market) is irreversible, no important event leaves the world unmarked, and after the event one can never pick up the pieces as if nothing had happened. This is true of the Common Market, and it is true also of General de Gaulle. It is not easy to sweep under the rug the curls of dust he willfully placed in the sunlight; it is not easy to ignore the questions he asked, even if his answers were rejected, since they are the questions any European enterprise would face sooner or later. Even the passing of his kind of nationalism has not transformed the national situations of the European states so deeply that all the cleavages discussed here have suddenly disappeared. To be sure, the failure of Britain's policy of maintaining close ties with the United States led to an "agonizing reappraisal" in London that in turn led to Britain's third, and successful, application to the EEC. In this respect, as well as in the rest of the Common Market, de Gaulle's disappearance eased the strains. France stopped trying to promote cooperation through cold war and lifted the veto on Britain. Yet Pompidou has combined a more conciliatory style with the Gaullist habit of raising questions about ends, at least in the economic part of the enterprise to which he has decided to devote his efforts. Even in this more moderate realm, the results have been mixed and do not disprove the previous analysis.

The diversity of national situations has been manifest again. The only part of Pompidou's grand design that his EEC partners have endorsed, a monetary union, has been badly battered. The common float of West European currencies, decided in March 1973, is limited (excluding the pound sterling and the lira) and fragile. West Germany's preference for economically liberal solutions, and the priority she gives to the fight against inflation, have made her suspicious of too strictly monetary a scheme, for she fears that would allow other nations to pursue both more statist and more lax economic policies while counting on help from the strong German mark to save them from trouble. But France's priorities—on full employment and peace and quiet on the labor front, even at the price of inflation, on modernizing without provoking widespread discontent, and on preserving the common agricultural policy (essential to protect her peasants from currency fluctuations)—and the French civil service's fondness for controls have led her to put monetary union ahead of economic harmonization. Moreover, the French have another target beyond EEC—the position of the dollar as a world currency—and they want to use monetary union as a lever to limit the influx of short-term capital from outside Europe. The West Germans (and, in all likelihood, the British) are opposed to controls on capital, out of a deeper attachment to and need for free trade, and out of a continuing desire not to antagonize the United States. But the economic union many Germans would prefer is considered by the French as something in which European distinctiveness would be diluted to America's advantage, and as a potential Deutschmark zone.[34] In order to prevent a new slowdown following the Community's enlargement, Pompidou tried to go beyond the economic realm by proposing a political secretariat, à la Fouchet, and to give his European policy the momentum of popular support, through a referendum. But the former proposal only underlined the old battle about institutions—which conceals, as before, a contest between French designs for Europe (hence her refusal to have that secretariat located in Brussels, along with NATO) and the others' desire to postpone the question of ends by escaping into supranationality. And the fiasco of the French referendum (which confirmed the relative indifference of French public opinion and proved that Pompidou's temporary return to the politics of ambiguity had not paid off[35]) forced him to dig in his heels in more orthodox Gaullist fashion. The road is rocky, and the car sputters, even after the smooth but modest European summit conference of October 1972. America's demands for EEC "concessions" on agriculture and external trade policy, and America's overt linkage of economics and security have once again divided the EEC between those who, for domestic or foreign-policy reasons, are eager to accommodate Washington, and France's desire to build a "European Europe"—at least in the economic realm, where Western Europe's collective power is greatest, and whose importance in world politics has grown apace with détente and the nuclear stalemate.

These setbacks do not mean that the European enterprise is doomed. One can conceive of a set of circumstances in which a speedy forward march could succeed: Western Europe could become West Germany's least frustrating framework at a moment when MBFR or U.S. unilateral cuts might oblige Bonn's leaders to envisage a spill-over of EEC into defense and diplomacy, Western Europe could be seen as Britain's best avenue of leadership in such circumstances, Western Europe could serve as the best compensation for a French political system that would again be beset by domestic troubles and in which "Europe" would be once more an alibi. Western Europe could become a full-fledged economic, military, and diplomatic entity through a major external shock inflicted by either superpower or by both, or through a deliberate, gradual transformation planned in concert with Washington and acceptable to Moscow. But such progress depends on the timely convergence of too many variables to be counted on—and now, in the external component of each West European state's national situation, not only American but Soviet moves and positions have a decisive (if divisive) effect. Within the Community's institutions, daily reality brings a permanent confrontation of national interests that may erode the nation-state's edges but perpetuates their will to exist.[36]

The European experience is of general significance. It tells us about the conditions which the national situations of the units engaged in an attempt to integrate must meet, lest the attempt be unsuccessful. Those situations ought to be similar, of course; but what matters is the nature of the similarity. Insofar as domestic circumstances are concerned, two conditions are essential. The units must be political communities, not in a substantive sense (common values, à la Rousseau) but in a formal one (many links of communications, and common habits and rules, across regional differences and across the borders of ethnic groups, tribes, or classes).[37] In other words, transnational integration presupposes integration within each unit.* These units need not be nation-states, in the sense of communities endowed

---

* The distinctions I suggest are like marks on a continuum.

1. At one end, there are *cooperative arrangements* whose institutions have no autonomy from the various governments (OECD, the U.N. in most respects). These arrangements range from truly cooperative to hegemonial, i.e., from representing all the members to asserting the domination and extending the will of one of them.

2. Then there are *entities* with *central institutions* that have some authority, in the sense of legal autonomy from the components and legal power all over the territory. But these are *not* political communities in the formal sense, because there may be discontinuities in communications or transactions among the components, or because the cleavages within the entity deprive the central institutions of autonomy or effective power. (States such as the Congo or certain Latin American republics fall in this category, supranational entities like the EEC, and, within the limits of effective military integration, NATO.) These entities may be very resilient if they are states, endowed with international personality and institutions that have a formal monopoly or at least superiority of force over internal challenges; but if they are supranational (and especially if they are not simply an arrangement disguising the hegemony of one of the members), they are likely to be unstable, since the "central" institutions will be challenged by the central institutions of the component states. In other words, supranational entities will tend either to retrogress toward stage 1 or to progress toward stage 3.

3. Next come entities that are *political communities* in the *formal* but not the substantive sense. That is, their central institutions have autonomy and power, there are common habits, and the community's rules are enforced across internal barriers, but the central institutions do not have legitimacy all over the territory, and the habits and rules are not based on common values concerning the polity. This is the case with many nation-states which have "national consciousness" but are not political communities in the last sense.

4. Here I refer to nation-states whose central institutions are wholly autonomous, effectively powerful and legitimate, and whose society has shared values concerning the polity. These are political communities in the *substantive* sense. Needless to say, there are not many of them. The difference between stage 3 and 4 is largely a difference in the level and scope of consensus. I would reserve the term national to states in those two stages.

with external sovereignty under international law; but if a newly independent state is a mere shell with no true community yet, the divisions within the population will badly hinder any trans-state integration: domestic integration is a prerequisite for it and will be a primary goal of any leader who tries to be more than the representative of a sect, class, tribe, or ethnic group. This explains why Latin American integration remains a chimera, and also why it has been so difficult in Africa and Asia to move beyond the nation-state. In many cases, the state is there, but not yet the nation.

Students of supranational integration have rightly stressed the importance of pluralistic social structures and elite groups in the units that try to integrate. But success here also requires that in each unit there be executive leaders who represent those sections of the elites which advocate union and whose power depends on the support of the integrationist elites and groups. Since many of the new states are single-party states with so-called charismatic (or should one say authoritarian?) leaders, this internal condition for unification is often missing.

As far as external conditions are concerned, what matters is not that the units be in "objectively" similar situations but that there be "subjective" similarity—a conviction on the part of the policy-makers that the similarity exists. The implication—and this is crucial—is that one must examine more than the relation of each unit to the international system at the moment. The similarity that matters is a similarity in the way different statesmen interpret historical and geographical experience and outline the future in the light of this experience. Integration means a common choice of a common future, but that requires certain attitudes about the past and the present.

As for the past, supranational integration is likely to be more successful when the voyager's baggage is light. If the state's past international experiences have been long or complex, if the state has enjoyed an autonomous existence on the world scene for a long time, integration will not be easy. Is it an accident that the only successful example of voluntary unification in the modern world is that of the United States (a fusion of units that had been colonies, not states, where neither the machinery of the state nor foreign-policy traditions had had time to develop)? In one sense, ridding a nation of overseas commitments (such as France and Britain have done) should make their luggage lighter. But, as we have seen in the case of France, old burdens tend to be replaced by new ties, the old *imperium* leaves lasting concerns, and the old responsibilities leave a continuing sense of responsibility.

The kind of similarity required in the present concerns the relation of the units to the international system. When a similarity in national situations is one of distance or insulation from the system, as was the case of the American states and to a large extent the case of Switzerland after the Reformation, concentration on the difficult job of unification becomes possible. A capital obstacle to integration anywhere in the world today is the loss of such distance, the impossibility of such insulation in the echo chamber of the present international system. But this obstacle can sometimes be removed.

For there is a second question: the degree of compulsion in the international system. When the national situations are similar because of an overwhelming external threat (as was originally the case with the Swiss cantons and the American ex-colonies), unification for survival or security may be imperative. A compelling threat can make up for different pasts and impose a common destination. One can argue that this was Western Europe's condition in the first ten years after the end of World War II, but a countervailing force could be seen in the different pulls of different pasts, with different kinds of involvements in the international system. The nations of Western Europe assessed differently the degree to which the threat from the East superseded other aspects of international politics. It was not an accident that the nation which considered the menace entirely compelling was Germany, divided and literally confronted with the threat, to the exclusion of almost everything else. It was not an accident that France and Britain never let the threat from the East dominate their entire foreign policy. In any case, Western Europe today is no longer dominated by the Soviet threat. Today's international system inflates each national situation, while it removes some of sovereignty's sting. In a way, the relative impotence of force, the postponement of the minute of truth, should reduce the significance of all differences in national situations. But since this is still a competitive system of fragmented states, Rousseau's iron logic applies: each state tries to exploit whatever margin of difference it has; and, since it ultimately matters much less than before, the incentive to unification in order to "pull more weight" is slim. The breakdown of the Soviet and American camps and the kind of weightlessness that nations have in the new international system because of the restrictions on force encourage different visions of the future, or a tendency to take the hazards and chances of a diverse present as they come, rather than planning too much for an inscrutable future. A rational observer, outside the contest, can argue that— precisely because the stakes in the international contest are more symbolic than real—nation-states ought to be willing to unite, for the outcome would be a new actor whose power could really be great enough to make a difference. But the logic of competition operates the other way. It conforms to the French proverb: one thing possessed is worth more than two things promised. In the immediate postwar system, it seemed that European nations were obliged to choose between insecurity apart or an Atlantic shelter together. The "halfway house" of Western Europe got started but did not progress far before the advent of an era in which separateness became attractive again.

The dialectic of fragmentation and unity gives the drama of Europe much of its pathos. In a "finished world," dominated by two giant powers, in a crowded world that resists the sweep of any one power's universal mission, there is something absurd and pathetic in the tenacious persistence of separate European national wills. Yet precisely because so many of the differences among them are expressed in the realm of foreign affairs, integration becomes difficult.

It has become possible for scholars to argue that integration is proceeding *and* that the nation-state is more than ever the basic unit without being contradictory, for recent definitions of integration "beyond the nation-state" point not toward a new kind of political community, but merely toward an "obscur [ing of] the boundaries between the system of international organizations and the environment provided by member states." [38]

There are important implications here. One is, not so paradoxically, that the nation-state is vindicated as the basic unit. So far, anything that is "beyond" is "less": cooperative arrangements with a varying degree of autonomy, power, and legitimacy exist, but there has been no transfer of allegiance to their institutions, and their authority is limited, conditional, dependent, and reversible. There is more than a kernel of truth in the federalist critique of functional integration. So far, the "transferring [of] exclusive expectations of benefits from the nation-state to some larger entity" [39] leaves the nation-state as the main focus of expectations, and as the initiator, pace-setter, supervisor, and often destroyer of the larger entity. In the international arena the state is still the highest possessor of power, and while not every state is a political community, there is as yet no political community more inclusive than the state. To be sure, the military function of the nation-state is in crisis, but since the whole world is "permeable" to nuclear weapons, any new type of unit would face the same horror, and since the prospect of that horror makes conquest less likely, the decline of the state's capacity to defend its citizens is not total, nor even so great as to force the nation-state itself into decline.

The endurance of the nation-state is demonstrated not only by the frustrations of functionalism but also by both the promise and the failure of federalism. On one hand, federalism offers a way of going "beyond the nation-state," but it consists in building a new and larger nation-state. The scale is new, not the story, the gauge, not the game. The federalist model applies the Rousseauistic scheme for the creation of a nation to the "making of Europe"; it aims at establishing a unit marked by central power and based on the general will of a European people. The federalists are right in insisting that Western Europe's best chance of being an effective entity would be not to go "beyond the nation-state," but to become a larger nation-state in the process of formation and in the business of world politics: i.e., to become a sovereign political community in at least the formal sense. The success of federalism would be a tribute to the durability of the nation-state; its failure so far is due to the irrelevance of the model. Not only is there no general will of a European people because there is as of now no European people, but the institutions that could gradually (and theoretically) shape the separate nations into one people are not the ones that are most likely to do so. The internal problems of Europe involve matters that can be resolved by technical decisions by civil servants and ministers, rather than general wills and assemblies. (A general will to prosperity is not very operational.) The external problems of Europe are matters for executives and diplomats. And when the common organs set up by the national governments try to act as a European executive and parliament, they have to do so in a fog maintained around them by the governments, and are slapped down if they try to dispel the fog and reach the people themselves. In other words, Europe cannot be what some nations have been, a people that creates its state. Nor can it be what some of the oldest states are and many of the new ones aspire to be: a people created by the state. It has to wait until the separate states decide that their peoples are close enough to justify setting up a European state that will weld the many into the one; and we have just examined why such a joint decision has been missing. The factors that make the federalist model irrelevant to diverse and divided nations also make all forms of union short of federalism precarious. Functionalism is too unstable for complete political unification. It may integrate economies, but then either the nations will proceed to a full political merger (which economic integration does not guarantee), in which case the federal model will be vindicated, or else the national situations will continue to diverge, and functionalism will be merely a way of tying together the pre-existing nations in areas deemed of common interest. Between the cooperation of existing nations and the breaking in of a new one there is no stable middle ground. A federation that succeeds becomes a nation; one that fails leads to secession; half-way attempts like supranational functionalism must either snowball or roll back.

But the nation-state survives transformed. Among the men who see "national sovereignty" as the nemesis of mankind, those who put their hopes in regional superstates are illogical, those who put their hopes in a world state are utopian, those who put their hopes in functional political communities more inclusive than the nation-state are too optimistic. What has to be understood and studied now is, rather than the creation of rival communities, the transformation of "national sovereignty." The model of the nation-state derives from the international law and relations of the past, when there were only a few players on the stage and violence was less risky; it applies only fitfully to the situation today. The basic unit has become more heterogeneous as it has proliferated; the stage is occupied by players whose very numbers force each one to strut, but its combustibility nevertheless keeps them from pushing their luck. The nation-state today may be a new wine in old bottles, or in bottles that are sometimes only a mediocre imitation of the old; it is not the same old wine.[40] What must be examined is not just the legal capacity of the sovereign state but the *de facto* capacity at its disposal. Granted the scope of its authority, how much of it can be used and with what results? There are many ways of going "beyond the nation-state," and some modify the substance without altering the form or creating new forms. To be sure, as long as the old form is there, as long as the nation-state is the supreme authority, there is a danger for peace and for welfare. Gullivers tied by Lilliputians rather than crushed by Titans can wake up and break their ties. Men who slug it out with fists and knives, prisoners in a chain gang, are all men, yet their freedom of action is not the same. An examination of the international implications of "nation-statehood" today and yesterday is at least as important as the ritual attack on the nation-state.

Prospects of genuine European unification would improve if the international system created conditions and incentives for moving "beyond the nation-state." In a world where many more units succeeded in becoming genuine nations with pluralistic structures, and where, on the other hand, multipolarity led to greater autonomy for the subsystems and to new interstate wars, the conditions of unification would be met at least in some parts of the world: a less universal and intense involvement in global affairs, a more compelling threat of violence, greater internal harmony might allow the nation-state to supersede itself. But even so, the result might simply be an agglomeration of smaller nation-states into fewer, bigger ones. There are more things in the heaven and earth of the future than in any philosophy of international relations.

Conclusion:
Decline or Renewal?

13

The Nation: What For?
Vicissitudes of
French Nationalism,
1871-1973

In several of his books Raymond Aron has examined the role of the nation-state in international relations, often speculating on the fate and weakness of the French nation in the age of empires, industrial civilization, and nuclear weapons. My aim here is to pursue this question at a time when Frenchmen are again seeking to determine their collective destiny.

The France of the great Revolution was the first modern nation-state. Not only did it combine on one territory "community of culture, military order and political unity," [1] like England and Spain in the seventeenth and eighteenth centuries, but in addition it brought about an intense "social mobilization" that gave rise to national feeling. Its leaders showed the will to preserve freedom of action for the nation-state in the world and considered it the supreme form of social organization, which is the essence of nationalism. France therefore provides an excellent specimen for the elucidation of the uses of nationalism, and the study of its sources. With regard to its uses, questions arise as to what extent French nationalism has unified the political "community," deeply divided first by the French Revolution and then by the industrial revolution, and to what extent it has allowed French leaders to define a coherent strategy that maintains French integrity and freedom of action in the world. As for the sources, we must try to settle the dispute between those political scientists who cling to the old model in which foreign policy is paramount and nationalism is a "response" to the "challenge" of the international state of war or nature, and others who believe, on the contrary, that the choice of any foreign

This essay was originally written for a *Festschrift* honoring Raymond Aron, *Science et conscience de la societé* (Paris, 1971). It has been translated by Nancy Roelker and the author.

policy, "nationalist" included, is largely determined by internal factors, i.e., by interests, factions, and beliefs, social, economic, and political. Is it *raison d'État* or class (or party) interest? Which of the two ingredients, the nation's position in the world or its internal character, lies at the core of the nationalist attitude?

Beyond these questions lies a further one. What is the pragmatic justification of nationalism, an ideology which sanctions the division of the human race into pseudospecies (to borrow a phrase from Erik Erikson)? In the realm of values, nationalism poses problems of differing magnitudes. The "absolute" justification, often expressed in the nineteenth century and revived by the Gaullists, is that nationalism makes an essential contribution to humanity; if not a guarantee of international harmony, it is at least a necessary condition for it. Despite Woodrow Wilson or de Gaulle, the twentieth century has made us skeptical of this claim. The only "absolute" justification of nationalism lies in the absence of any legitimate supranational authority, in the equivocal nature of units larger than the nation, to which one later regrets that "men have not given their faith and their devotion." [2] But the question of pragmatic or relative justification remains. Has nationalism served its national community (whatever the effects on others)? Has it synthesized the potentials and mobilized the means of the nation, within the limits imposed by internal social and political factors on one hand, and the imperatives of the international situation on the other? In other words, has nationalism been able to transform the national feeling on which it rests into policies that promote the nation's unity and interests? [3]

To answer these questions thoroughly would require a big book, especially since a historical sociology of French nationalism that examines them systematically has not yet been attempted.[4] I shall limit myself here to a very brief outline of the main features in order to place the dilemmas of the present in some perspective. A thorough study would begin with the messianic fervor of the Revolution, and it would include Napoleonic imperialism and the nationalist enthusiasm of the liberals in the Jacobin tradition, which was revived among some pre-Marxist French socialists and reached its height in the Commune. But in this chapter, I shall confine myself to the period that begins with the establishment of the Third Republic.

I

The founders of the Third Republic held to a doctrine: they wanted to build a Republican political regime and a complex social system around the idea of the nation.[5] There is no doubt that the springs of their nationalism were internal. As representatives of a liberal bourgeoisie and lower middle class which had not had their fair share of political power since the beginning of the nineteenth century, they desired to construct at last a group of stable institutions that would protect them against both reaction and revolution. Unlike the conservative liberals (mostly aristocrats and upper-class bourgeois), they understood that a regime too narrowly controlled by the traditional elites would not offer stability—hence their acceptance of universal suffrage, their appeal to new social strata, and the recourse to parliamentary government. But how were the Jacobin overtones in the concept of national sovereignty to be reconciled with the goal of social stability and with the distrust both of the executive and of any assembly too open to popular pressures? Here valuable assistance came from Rousseau, Michelet, Edgard Quinet, and Charles Renouvier. The new state would be at the same time the guardian of the general interest—from the very fact of its identification with the whole citizenry—and limited in extent, dealing only with matters that all citizens had in common. The new state owed the people justice, not happiness; equality before the law, not equality in material terms. Thus the problem of class differences would not be included in the purview of the state. The notion of a general will limited to the general welfare served as a principle of exclusion, just as in the constitutional sphere the difference between "national" sovereignty and "popular" sovereignty served as a principle of discrimination.

But the idea of the nation fulfilled a third function: that of a principle of standardization. The poor and the rich, the clergy and the working class, the army and the small farmers, those to whom the Revolution was the great disaster of the history of France and those to whom it was the great hope—all would be taught a certain conception of France. (It is well known from the books of Ernest Lavisse, the educational program of Jules Ferry and his aides, and the speeches of Third Republic politicians.[6]) What Émile Durkheim in *L'Éducation morale* called the French characteristic of confusing national temperament with the conscience of mankind is at work here. By glorifying a personified France, the contribution of her rationalizing genius to humanity, and the duties of each Frenchman toward France, it was hoped that the nation would become "a single army, in divisions composed of thousands of men, marching in a single step, moved by the same thought, seeming to form one being." [7] By associating France with the Republic, one would attract Frenchmen intellectually and sentimentally to a moderately Republican regime from which they were actually and constitutionally quite far removed. By extolling the values of moderation, sobriety, individual labor, respect for family and property; by preaching a savings-bank morality; by sanctioning discipline as the foundation of moral upbringing as well as of public order;

by promoting the ideal of a general culture based on history and the abstract sciences, and by concocting a mixture of the Ten Command-ments and bourgeois values—by these means all ranks of society would be consolidated. A synthesis would emerge in which respect for authority as well as criticism of it, revolutionary currents (in a bour-geoisie that had emancipated the individual) as well as traditionalism (in a society where barriers between classes were as important as the demand for equality within each class itself) would all take their place.

Philosophically, this desire for synthesis reflected the tradition of Rousseau and Kant, carried on subsequently by those positivists who—unlike Comte—continued in the tradition of the *philosophes* rather than turning conservative. Historically, it reflected a long and bitter experience of drastic alterations in domestic political regimes, and es-pecially the lessons of the Revolution of 1848, the Second Empire, and the Commune. But this synthesis-and-stability-oriented nationalism re-flected also another factor in the national situation—the external com-ponent.

In an international system like the one established by the Congress of Vienna—pluralistic but composed of states constituted quite differ-ently from one another—nationalism could not clearly guide French statesmen to any one foreign policy. It was unclear whether France's leading position and freedom of action would be better protected by a policy like Richelieu's—divide and conquer, above all maintain the balance of power—which Proudhon among others advocated, or, on the contrary, by what Hans Morgenthau has called a policy of "univer-sal nationalism," which at that time would have meant exploiting the French revolutionary heritage by encouraging the formation of na-tion-states in Europe so as to achieve a greater similarity between the several states, and at the same time weaken some of France's rivals. The debate continued ever more hotly under the Second Empire. Just as the expansion of the First Empire had awakened outside France a national spirit fatal to Napoleon's ambition and to French conquest, the encouragement Napoléon III gave to nationalist groups ended by stimulating the unification of Germany at the expense of the previous balance of power, including France's position and even French terri-tory.

The result was the demand for *revanche;* more precisely, Republi-can nationalism performed a two-pronged and overriding external func-tion. On one hand, it was felt that the national community must be strengthened so that a humiliation like that of 1871 could never hap-pen again. This implied an intellectual and moral reform—not so much on Renan's terms as in the Republican schoolbooks'.[8] On the other hand, it was necessary to exploit the then-present international situation and outwit the Germans. The defeat of 1871, with the loss of Strasbourg and Metz, had given French nationalism an anti-German direction which slanted French policy in the balance of power, and at the same time weakened the balance's flexibility—one of the conditions required for its stability—by changing what had been a fluid balance of changing alliances into a rigid and dangerous equilibrium of blocs.

Thus the internal and external sources of French nationalism coincided, and so did the function of internal unification and that of diplomatic and strategic mobilization. But this was not sufficient to bring Frenchmen together as nationalists. In the first place, there were deep differences of opinion about the ultimate objectives in foreign policy. Despite the desire for *revanche* and the patriotic zeal it aroused, the international system always leaves a margin of choice to statesmen (even when they are moved only by so-called realistic considerations of national interest), and there are always different ways of defining that interest as soon as one goes beyond the mere survival of the nation or its security in the narrowest sense. The desire for *revanche* offered no solution to such problems. As early as the 1880s it was evident that different avenues were open to patriotic Frenchmen who wished to restore French *grandeur*. Should one seize the first opportunity to fight and win the second round of the duel with Germany, or would it be better to wait and count on the slow weaving of alliances or on the external advantages that time, patience, and Republican diplomacy would bring to bear? Should French eyes be fixed on the "blue line of the Vosges," or should France grasp the occasion for colonial conquests? From the beginning, Republicans—opportunists, Radicals, Boulangists—were divided on these two sets of questions.

Later, a third source of division appeared, more serious in that it involved not a conflict over tactics but between degrees of nationalism. Did *revanche* justify a domestic and foreign policy of active preparation for war and an aggressive policy of colonial conquest? Were peace and the renunciation of might-makes-right really less important than *revanche?* Were respect for world law and concern for world peace too low in the hierarchy of national interests? Should the drive for power and for the reconquest of the lost provinces be kept within the limits imposed by the ideals in whose very name France understood her role as a great power? Should purely national values and universal values be reconciled, so that *revanche* would result only from a legitimate, defensive war? [9] In the broadest definition of nationalism both sets of arguments are included, because the proponents of both are concerned with the independence and rank of the nation. But in the eyes of those to whom *only* narrowly national values are important, the others, who would limit the nation to the realization of certain ideals, are at best half-hearted patriots. This was the tenor of the debate in the years before World War I.

It was soon apparent that the ideal of the model citizen on whom both the political regime and the educational system were predicated would not be enough to unify Frenchmen within their own borders. A synthesis built on an ideal is always fragile and incomplete; it will only take hold if accompanied by precise measures of social integration. But, by its very premises, the Republican formula could not do this and go beyond the primary school, the army, and minimal social legislation. There was no question of extensive fiscal or social reforms that would appease the urban workers. Moreover, any synthesis based on an ideal *ipso facto* cuts off from the community those who cannot accept its fundamental principles. The Republican formula could not satisfy those who rejected bourgeois values, the ideal of the individual rising through work and savings, and still less could it satisfy those who would not accept the legitimacy of a government founded on popular consent, the lay state, the celebration of the principles of 1789.

The Boulangist movement revealed for the first time the numbers and ardor of those who were excluded. In a country like the United States, where a majority of citizens share the same beliefs, the ideological character of the national synthesis is disguised; but in a country divided into sharply distinct schools of thought, a synthesis that claims to rally the people around important ideals and beliefs that stem from only one of the constituent rival groups can succeed only if those who begin by standing aside eventually join the majority. This was the case of certain groups in France in the 1890s.

But Boulangism is of major importance from another point of view. It showed how those who were excluded could themselves join under a nationalist banner. Confronting an unsuccessful nationalism of synthesis, there appeared a nationalism that claimed to be concerned only with the unity and *grandeur* of France but that was nevertheless divisive. It is true that the official nationalism was also in some respects exclusive; for example, the Republicans cast doubt on the patriotism of clericals. But one could say that they were really only excommunicating those who excluded themselves by refusing to enter the Temple, while the nationalism of the excluded was above all a repudiation of the high priests themselves. Even when both shared a conception of the national interest in foreign policy and the same dependence on a certain social order in France, the nationalist "outs" refused to believe that anything could be done until the high priests were driven from the Temple. They either denied the legitimacy of the democratic principle or accused the Republicans of having usurped it for their own advantage. In the Republican case, exclusion of their foes was the unfortunate result of the partial failure of their synthesis; in the case of the opposition it was the necessary preliminary to any synthesis.

Since its problem was to unite highly diverse groups against the official would-be unifiers, nationalism itself provided the necessary cement—a counternationalism, outbidding that of the Republicans and attempting to destroy them with their own weapons. This shows the extent to which even those who oppose democracy must come to terms with universal suffrage in a democratic system: for counterrevolutionaries to draw on nationalism as a unifying element—what a tribute from virtue to vice! But what better way was there to reconcile the proto-*poujadisme* of the lower classes, the proto-*maurrasisme* of the old conservative elites (who had supported Boulanger), and later, the plebiscitary Jacobinism of the discontented *petite bourgeoisie* which wished France to assume an aggressive stance, the nostalgia for the old days of the provincial gentry, the romanticism of the army, the protectionism of *rentiers* and skilled workers, and the aristocratic pretensions of the intelligentsia (to whom Maurras appealed)? The sources of this mélange included jingoist impatience (Paul Déroulède), morose contemplation of France's declining position in the world (Maurras) or of the weakening of the values of *vieille France* (Édouard Drumont or Paul Bourget), a mixture of all these (Barrès), or resistance to social "uprooting" and fear of being pushed down into the proletariat (most of the recruits in the movement). What mattered was not the causes but the target—the Republican regime.

The springs and functions of opposition nationalism were identical to those of official nationalism. Both sought to raise conflicting interests to a level where they would merge with the general welfare; both were designed to serve at the same time as cement and as a sponge to wipe out differences. The counternationalism was primarily a reactionary response, planned to take the place of the official nationalism by making it appear that the legally constituted regime was itself the only obstacle to France's great internal reconciliation and salvation. Because Maurras believed that France was in the hands of a faction, supported by four "estates" oriented to their own selfish interests, he convinced himself that he alone represented unfragmented nationalism, and he created a political myth, principally defensive, which was nothing but a mirror image of the Republican myth. And because Barrès, himself a member of Parliament, was not really convinced that the official line represented only a faction, his expression of nationalism was more ambivalent.

At all events, the crisis of French nationalism in the late nineteenth century resulted from the clash of an inadequate official doctrine with an all-out counterdoctrine. The Dreyfus Affair was the result of this confrontation. A half-hearted and tardy desire to correct a judicial error inevitably took the form of reminding the army that it existed to serve the nation and was therefore subject to the civilian authority which was the nation's voice; opponents of the regime denounced even the correction of the error as inimical to the nation, as an act which weakened France in relation to her enemies. In one camp, an attempt was made to rally the nation through Republican principles, which many people deplored because they believed it was a deliberate suspension of the ongoing process of internal reconciliation and a dangerous subordination of the national interest to the interests of one party. In the other camp, an outraged defense of the motherland identified primarily with the army and the Church, took priority, and it saw the government as the main enemy. Each accused the other of wasting or usurping the national patrimony and aiding France's enemies by creating divisions among Frenchmen.

Analysis of nationalism as a divisive factor before 1914 leads one nevertheless to more subtle considerations. Frenchmen were tearing each other apart largely in the name of the same deity—the nation. The fight was over which form of government, which social system, which foreign policy would best defend it. In the background of the disagreements there was a common point of reference, and since the field on which the rivalry between the two camps was being played out was nationalism, it tended to be strengthened by the contest, as each tried to prove itself more worthy of France than the other and more eager to serve her.

Of course, in a country less torn by ideological struggle, those excluded from the official doctrine would not have tried to join under another, but still single, doctrine; and in a less intensely patriotic country, even if they had, it would not have been under the banner of nationalism. Boulangism made its attack on the parliamentary Republic in the name of the very social values and international ambitions held by the Republic itself. To be sure, Maurras wished above all to save "his" France from social disintegration, but that France, hierarchical and monarchical as it was, was at least as good a bourgeois and peasant refuge as the Republican and egalitarian France of Alain; Maurras's anti-Germanism was no different from that of Clemenceau or Poincaré. There was, of course, a noisy debate from 1900 to 1914 between nationalists and internationalists led by Jaurès, but one must not overlook Jaurès's precept about domestic policy to his followers—the real outcasts in a society where fear of the workers and resistance to industrialization remained strong. He told them that social progress would follow upon the acceptance, the exploitation, and the glorification of a Republican form of government. In foreign policy, Jaurès had a deep commitment to national defense and countered the pessimism of the nationalists about the existing situation, not in the name of some vague supranational ideal, but with generous, although myopic, optimism about a kind of Internationale of moderate nations. For Jaurès, in other words, thanks to the Republic, the French proletariat had a motherland and felt that they should defend her if she were attacked. Thus, even the great split between Left and Right preserved a consensus around the nation. Each ideological camp was both a divisive *and* an integrative force.

What held this limited consensus together, despite the breaches mentioned above? On the home front, the Republic, despite the crises, had succeeded in providing a framework. In terms of citizenship, the public school had inculcated in the young patriotism and a conception of society; in 1914 these had not yet been eroded either by the defeatism of some Syndicalists and Socialists or by the damaging contrast between the actual conditions of the workers and the *petit-bourgeois* ideal taught in the schools. And in terms of the class struggle, the Republic had kept the allegiance of the workers; their disappointment in the regime's social policies had not shaken their conviction that universal suffrage and civil liberties represented enormous progress. The position of the upper classes was strong enough to neutralize their natural hostility to the Republic and their bitterness at being excluded from or kept a minority in the new political class.

In foreign policy the escalation of dangers had brought about a sudden change. Pacifist defeatism was out of fashion, and the prudence represented by Caillaux came up against a hardened intransigence. Colonial expansion and the maintenance of France's position in Europe were complementary. The conscripted army thus had to play the same role in promoting a national consensus that the school did—despite the Dreyfus Affair. Although the international situation had become explosive to a point which considerably limited the options of a nation determined to engage in the power game, the logic of the balance of power still prevailed, and domestic and foreign policy were kept in fairly watertight compartments. The Internationale existed, to be sure, but it was neither an instrument for any one of the European powers (none of which had a Socialist government) nor a supranational movement with a single, clear ideology. It was, rather, a coalition of minority movements, each one prey to the dramatic tug of war between the shared ideology of class struggle on one hand, and the reality of conflict between nations and its own loyalty to its nation on the other.

The coat of arms of the pre-1914 Republic was division on a ground of national unity. But this unity, which permitted France to survive the ordeal of the war, concealed elements of danger whose dimensions were not to be measured until much later. One weakness of the regime (heir to all its predecessors in this respect) was its failure to develop *corps intermédiaires* between the people and the state. The Republic remained the form in which Frenchmen could love France without intermediaries. The French were thus unable "to deal with a society organized according to functional interests, in which coordination and compromise predominate," and, by the same token, they tended to bestow on the political parties, groups, and associations to which they belonged the emotional intensity of their attachments to the motherland. For the old-time French militant "the organization [whether party or union] was in the last analysis only the national community transposed." [10] But to transfer one's attitude toward the whole community to one part of it is to risk magnifying the differences between groups almost to the point of civil war (or at least ideological conflict) in the name of peace and national *grandeur*.

External circumstances had also facilitated the development of French national unity in support of the Republic's foreign policy. Germany since the fall of Bismarck had contributed greatly to the rapprochement of her adversaries by her power politics and her abandonment of the Iron Chancellor's network of alliances. As a result, French revisionism could find support in British and Russian concerns for the balance of power, and France's weaknesses—limited resources, unprogressive economy, and demographic stagnation—could be offset by powerful allies. If the alliance failed, it would be the end of the dream of *revanche* and perhaps even of the balance of power.

At any rate, between the 1870s and 1914 an important change occurred, reflecting at the same time the internal exhaustion of a society disinclined to change and a deterioration of France's position vis-à-vis Germany—in spite of her colonial empire. The nationalists of the early days of the Republic and even the Boulangist counternationalists had been militant; they had blown trumpets, they had addressed themselves to the future, they had called for a modernized and greater France. Gradually, the emphasis shifted, as much for those who followed Jules Méline as for those who followed Maurras,[11] from confidence to caution, from the conquest of the future to the preservation of the past, from ambition for great undertakings to the defense of the patrimony and an attempt to arrest the decline. Gambetta's optimism was replaced with Barrès's "regressive" fascination with death, or Maurras's "aggressive" hatred of death-dealing foes. Even the about-face shortly before the war was primarily a patriotic reflex in the presence of a revived menace. But a purely defensive unity was doubly dangerous: if the main object in joining together for the salvation of the motherland was to conserve those benefits one owed to her, was there not a risk of encouraging each group in its selfish calculations, with the likelihood that some day only a policy quite the opposite of national unity against outside dangers would arise for the protection of those gains? Was there not a risk of some day sacrificing, for the sake of her survival, the rank and relative power of the motherland?

II

The 1914 war plunged the world from a multipolar balance-of-power system into a revolutionary situation. In time of war, the function of nationalism is simple: to unify the people for victory. Initially, the *union sacrée*—the patriotic cooperation of all parties—came about in a way that surpassed all hopes. But later disappointment crept in, and the Russian Revolution introduced an ideological element into the world scene for the first time since Napoleon had perverted the messianic ideology of the French Revolution into a mere drive for hegemony. A state emerged whose goal was neither to dominate others nor to establish a balance of states, but, rather, to transform the social order everywhere. At that moment the international system became more complex and heterogeneous: to the uncontrolled competition between states was added the rivalry of alternate models of society.[12] In such an international system a state which preserves its domestic consensus subordinates the fluctuations of domestic policy to the necessities of the world contest; the external springs of nationalism are the dominant ones. But in a state divided internally along ideological lines, there is, strictly speaking, no subordination of domestic to foreign concerns but, instead, an inextricable interlocking between them. Every choice of foreign policy produces a break in the domestic order; every position taken on the domestic front has repercussions on foreign policy. Every attempt to act as if foreign policy should be dictated only by questions of power and balance is at odds with the rules of a new game in which the old ideological conflicts within nations are linked up with the conflicts among nations.

In fact, at first sight the choices of foreign policy seem to be dictated by internal considerations, but the internal confrontations are really only the transposition of international confrontations, and the opposing forces within a nation begin to represent ideological forces that are at war outside its borders. Foreign policy *is* dominated by internal forces, but domestic policy is a reflection of important foreign conflicts. Wars between states become civil wars and vice-versa.[13] This development radically challenges nationalism.

World War I destroyed what had allowed French nationalism to play a unifying and guiding role. A small but growing fraction of the Syndicalist and Socialist left moved outside the Republican framework. The longer the war went on, the more these groups rebelled, both against the prospect of a victory that would once again sanction the rights of the strong, on the international plane, and against the deceptions of the *union sacrée,* which would not benefit Frenchmen oppressed at home. Jaurès had warned that "from a European war . . .

there could arise . . . over a long period, crises of counterrevolution, furious reaction, exacerbated nationalism, stifling dictatorship, monstrous militarism, a long series of reactionary violence and deep hates, reprisals and enslavements." [14] French Socialists and Syndicalists, won over to a patriotism of national defense, had played this barbarous game of chance. Although initially convinced that priority should be given to the protection of rights already gained by the working class in France, they were upset by the injustices and sacrifices of war, and they became much more concerned with strengthening the supranational community of hope than in defending the national community of burdens. When the war spawned the Russian Revolution, the mirage of working-class emancipation gave birth to the French Communist Party, and this war-born rupture of the internal consensus brought the foreign ideological conflict into the heart of the nation; the new party passed under the control, not of the heirs of syndicalism or French revolutionary socialism, but of Moscow's men. This was a serious blow to the claim of synthesis and to the unifying function of the Republican regime, and it encouraged the counternationalism of the opposition, which badly needed new sources of support against the Republic after the latter had succeeded in winning the war.

The war had also completely changed France's position in Europe. Victory was followed by the United States' withdrawal into isolationism, Britain's resumption of its balance-of-power policy, and the exclusion of the Soviet Union from the international community. France was the leader of a Pyrrhic victory. She was still the neighbor of a weakened but resourceful Germany which would in turn seek *revanche,* so she had to be guided by the need for security. But in a revolutionary situation, this need forces even a state dedicated to preserving the *status quo* to develop means of intervening everywhere against any attempt to subvert or overthrow it. How could this duty of general vigilance, this necessity of a widespread deterring presence be embodied in France? She was too exhausted to play the role, imposed by the new situation, of the beast in the burrow. She was deprived of even the traditional possibilities in a balance of power by the drastic changes on the map and in politics. Conflicts of opinion over the national interest went much deeper than they had before the war, even among those for whom French integrity and freedom of action was still the essential concern. To maintain her position France needed ampler means, a more determined will, a more mobile army, and a wider strategy than before the war, but in fact victory had made her means weaker, her vision more narrowly European, and her army less flexible.

This transformation in the international sphere and domestic change reinforced each other: the emergence of a French Communist Party directed from Moscow made an alliance with Russia against Germany difficult for France. The Soviet policy of fanning the conflicts among capitalist states by openly supporting German resistance to the victorious Allies widened the breach between the French Communist Party and the "national" political parties. Among these, those who cared the most about limiting or reducing Communist dissent naturally showed a certain sympathy for the aggressive regimes that had arisen in neighboring states, even when they were pursuing policies hardly compatible with the interests of France as defined in traditional terms. Thus, even the aim of returning to the *status quo ante* in which foreign and domestic policy were clearly separated risked distorting the former. It was easy to deny the contradiction as it applied to Fascist Italy, for had not the old Italy been France's ally? But the problem was much harder to resolve in relation to Hitler's Germany, because there was a conflict between the traditional anti-German line and the new anti-Communist line, between two expressions of the will for national cohesion, one on the foreign scene and one on the domestic. And internal economic and political crises made France's European position still more difficult. For many Frenchmen, domestic recovery was becoming a prerequisite for any active foreign policy, but since economic recovery involved a choice between social systems, each one of which had the name of a foreign power, the impossible dream of separation between the domestic and foreign spheres became a nightmare.

It becomes almost futile to investigate the functions and sources of French nationalism in the years between the wars. Domestic crises and international affairs combined to bring about a kind of eclipse of nationalism. National feeling persisted as a wish to live together apart from others, for neither the Communists nor the Fascists (except for a handful) wished France to disappear; but insofar as the well-known "plebiscite of every day" also implies a wish to live together with one another, national sentiment was seriously weakened by the quarrels of the 1930s, with the result that it was virtually impossible to define coherent nationalist attitudes. The forces that had made for integration now contributed to the breakdown. The old tune of Republican nationalism—unify France in support of the government and against Germany—rang false. The Republican synthesis had been destroyed and the pre-1914 framework was in ruins. The nationalism of the public schools was replaced by an increasingly passionate pacifism among schoolteachers. Domestic crises deepened the gulf between Left and Right; even the followers of the regime, eager for unity and reconciliation, sought synthesis by exclusion: the Left hating all those who smelled of fascism to whatever degree, and the Right hating Communists and fellow travelers. When the Popular Front took in the Communists, a large part of the Right abandoned the regime.

The relative degree of domestic unity that France achieved in 1938–39 by expelling the Communists from the majority was certainly not an expression of resistance to Germany but, rather, an expression of the policy symbolized by Munich. The same Republican defensiveness that had aroused French pride on the eve of World War I now led to withdrawal and apathy. The situation was abominable. The government was weakened by repeated economic setbacks, and it needed time to restore national unity, but the passage of time only worsened France's situation in Europe, easy prey to Hitler's rapacity given the exhaustion of France and Britain. The international situation was giving out contradictory signals about the course to take. There could be no question of allowing Germany to attack French territory, but the desire to resist from now on had to be accommodated, for better or for worse, to the desire for peace, since another war— even victorious—would only bring further exhaustion, perhaps fatal this time, and more difficulties on the home front. The Left feared a consolidation of the Right; they either wished to exorcise the painful memory of the summer of 1914 (because of their disillusion in the *union sacrée* and the postwar conservative Bloc National), or else they dreaded the contagion of authoritarianism. The Right wanted to exorcise the memory of 1917, for they feared the triumph of communism.

The policy of France, the leading conservative power in a revolutionary international system, resulted in two quite different kinds of mistakes. Not only was she acting as if it was still the era of powers with limited interests (a mistake Britain also made), as if Hitler were only a Bismarck with bad manners, a leader one could coax into compromise, but she was also unable to play the classic game that any conservative state can play with revisionist ones in a balance-of-power system. The return of the United States to isolationism and Britain's hesitations certainly made the game more difficult, but the general reluctance to make an alliance with the Soviet Union after 1934 cannot be accounted for exclusively by the effects of such an alliance on domestic politics or by the unfavorable reaction in France to the Great Purges. France's obstinate continuation of a purely defensive policy— lethal for her alliances to the East and calamitous in March 1936— showed the extent to which the remains of the old nationalism, the cult of the army and the will to *grandeur,* had been stunted and dwarfed. For a state on the defensive in a revolutionary situation, the search for security generally knows no limits, but France took the opposite path and withdrew to the Rhine.

Domestic divisions and apathy in foreign affairs continued to reinforce each other. Within France, the quarreling factions were convinced that no satisfactory foreign policy was possible so long as domestic accounts were not settled—in more elegant terms, until there was a "reordering of domestic priorities." Conversely, the desire for peace at almost any price aggravated the tendency toward civil war: the advocates of peace attacked the "warmongers" ever more violently, convinced that peace depended on eliminating them. Whether their purpose was a more effective onslaught on their domestic enemies or whether they were motivated by sincere pacifism, the *Munichisme* which resulted was an anticipation of Vichy.

There were still some Republicans of the traditional sort but, even in the 1920s, before the great internal turmoil, France's weakness on the world scene had caused Poincaré's German policy to fail. In the 1930s, the crisis worsened; Paul Reynaud's foreign policy would have required alliances, mobilizations, and a revolution in strategic doctrine that neither the French economy nor domestic politics nor the climate of opinion would have tolerated. The traditional Republicans were few and divided; when, like Henri de Kérillis or Louis Marin, they sought domestic allies to enlarge their political base they could find them only in circles of doubtful republicanism, whose will to oppose Germany was weakening. If, like Reynaud, they wanted to remain loyal to the regime as well as to the traditional anti-German reflex, they were isolated. Republicans of the Left, Radicals or Socialists, paid lip service to a nationalism even more qualified than that of Caillaux and Jaurès. Overconfident in the Wilsonian ideal of moderate international relations through cooperation and arbitration, seduced by the idea of collective security (but preferably without recourse to force), they criticized, at least at first, the Treaty of Versailles as being too harsh. For a long time they tended to apply to Hitler's revolutionary Germany the defensive and conciliatory precepts preached by Jaurès toward the Germany of Wilhelm II. Before 1914, to stand for peace and negotiation, to want to keep the dynamics of alliances from escalating into bloodshed, was not necessarily to weaken France's international position; but in the era of Hitler the same ideas had entirely different consequences. The ways of defending peace cannot be the same in different international systems. To qualify or moderate nationalism in the 1930s was to compromise it.

The Republicans on the Right, like Flandin and the leaders of the PSF, were doing much the same, but in a somewhat different way. They also put the maintenance of peace first (except in case of direct attack), but less out of idealism than out of concern to spare France's weakened national resources.[15] Moreover, they gave priority to internal reorganization over foreign policy, because their chief aim was to return to *domestic* "equilibrium," which meant, above all, to get rid of the Communists and Socialists. For them, domestic considerations not only overruled foreign ones, but tended in fact to make internal unity as impossible for France as international leadership. On this ground, where the desire to keep things unchanged meant conservatism at home and defensiveness abroad, the right-wing Republicans, with their devalued nationalism, met the counternationalists, with their perverted nationalism.

The history of this perversion is no less fascinating or depressing for having been so often analyzed.[16] In the 1930s, the counterdogmas of Maurras spread beyond the confines of the old narrow circles of the Action Française. His criticism of the regime finally seemed justified, as much by corruption and ineptitude in financial affairs, inability to overcome the depression, and the threat of the Popular Front to social order at home, as by the weakening of France's position abroad. In one sense, Maurras and his followers were clinging to their 1900 belief that the Republican regime was incapable of defending France's domestic or foreign interests, and therefore that it must be changed. But whereas the old nationalism of the excluded had at least been one expression of nationalism, in the 1930s it was merely nationalist jargon concealing a profound transformation in substance.

Even if the ideological priorities were the same—in that, according to Maurras, only the restoration or rather the establishment of a monarchy would arrest decline—a reversal had taken place in regard to practical priorities. Faced with the German menace of 1914, Maurras, whose nationalism sprang primarily from external considerations, had advocated war, even one conducted by the Republic. "Salvation first" was the tactical form of his imperative, *politique d'abord!* But in the 1930s, given the domination of domestic factors (immortalized by Thierry-Maulnier in 1938), salvation itself required first a change in the regime. A German victory over France and a victory of Republican France over Germany seemed likely to be equally fatal for Maurras's France. The most urgent need was to avoid an alliance with the Soviet Union and prevent war, and then to reform the government, so as to be better prepared to confront foreign perils later on. In the Europe of the 1930s, this conditional nationalism subordinated French power and positions to a defensiveness that in this case smacked of civil war.

The impeccable nationalist credentials of Maurras's "return to order," inspired by a collection of French theorists (La Tour du Pin, Frédéric Le Play, Comte, Hippolyte Taine among them), were suddenly called into question, now that this "order" was no longer Maurras's abstract system (more baroque than classical) but the reality of foreign regimes dedicated to "law and order" as perceived through the blinkers or rose-colored glasses of envious Frenchmen. They had to convince themselves that Mussolini's Italy and Franco's Spain were *ipso facto* in accord with France's national interest. This shows that the old ideal, which gave priority to the national interest defined in terms of foreign policy (and which Maurras accused the Republican "ideologues" of betraying in their foreign alliances) was really dead. Henceforth, the national interest would be defined in domestic terms, even when France's position in the world was at stake. All that remained of the old nationalism was an anti-German feeling, simultaneously sincere and ineffectual, and a glorification of the colonial empire. But the empire was really used as an alibi for withdrawal, to disguise as high policy what was essentially nothing but the abandonment of Europe. (This was also true among conservative Republicans.)

There is no doubt that the inspiration for this transformed policy was still "national," since the two objects of "invincible nostalgia," [17] unity and *grandeur,* still had an appeal. Once again, only the "national" label could hold together and justify such heterogeneous groups: old elites in decline, businessmen frightened by the increased power of the Left, *petits-bourgeois,* artisans, and peasants hurt by the crises, all of whom had to be mobilized against the "grave diggers." Since the legal government had revealed itself as fragile, one could more easily rationalize calling the growing opposition the "real nation," and justify denouncing official France as anti-France. But in politics results count more than intentions, and in reality this contorted nationalist position gave priority to a domestic upheaval that was clearly counter to the desires of most Frenchmen, and entailed the overthrow of the legally constituted government while giving Germany a free hand. This is why I call it perverted nationalism.

Still further to the Right was a small group of real dissidents who were a-national or antinational. The admiration which Maurras and his diffuse following showed for "regimes of order" stopped at the German frontier. They were not in favor of National Socialism. But the Fascist groups and intellectuals went further. Some, like Drieu la Rochelle, Brasillach, and Doriot before 1939, went only a little beyond Maurras, although enough to alienate them from him markedly after June 1940. Their orientation remained "national" in theory, in that they certainly did not favor German victory; but their desire to protect France extended to advocacy of reconciliation with Hitler, and, at home, to an imitation of the National Socialist "regenerative" measures that had so "benefited" Germany. Whereas Maurras's "integral nationalists" explained that only an original, reborn France (or a France returned to her own origins) could face up to the eternal enemy, the Fascists said that only a Fascist France could make deals with him without harm to herself. Some French Fascists, like Rebatet, went even further, to the point of out-and-out defeatism, so disgusted were they with their own country. Significantly and paradoxically, the only prewar "warmongers" who called for national solidarity, resistance to Germany, and strengthened alliances, were the Communists. After qualified nationalism and perverted nationalism, we now have to include off-and-on nationalism, which went off again with the pact between Hitler and Stalin.

In this period French nationalism both exploded and faded. Often, the immediate cause of the agony was the domestic crisis, which pushed some to favor withdrawing from the world until the house was in order, and prevented others from finding even the beginnings of a way to bring about order that did not entail a drastic showdown with their domestic opponents. But, in the last analysis, France was the victim of what I shall call the tyranny of outside forces. The main factors of internal division—communism, Depression—were themselves a sign of this. The French inability to master events had assumed frightening proportions. Every choice of policy involved risks. The most advantageous choices in foreign policy, such as intervention in March 1936, were ruled out by the lack of military and diplomatic preparedness, itself a result of World War I and the Depression. All the other choices —appeasement or resistance after 1937—were terrible.

To the extent that nationalism is a call for action, the principle of the "hiding hand" applies: the less people understand the consequences of an undertaking, the more anxious they are to start it.[18] In 1914, except for Jaurès, who anticipated that the war would last so long and cost so many men? The Syndicalists, firmly opposed to all foreign wars, had done so not in the name of peace, but for a different sort of war aim: social revolution. In 1939, there was no longer the ideal of *revanche* to overcome the memories of the previous nightmare, nor a "hiding hand" to encourage illusions about how short or easy the new war might be; but there was a hiding hand encouraging illusions about the advantages of appeasement. For France to succeed in playing a more effective role on the world scene, in the international system of the 1930s, a different nation was needed: less divided, less on edge, less tired. For France, as she was, to retain rank and power, another international system was needed. Neither the nation nor the system had recovered from the last war ordeal.

The depth of the abyss was reached during the crisis of the German occupation, collaboration, and resistance. The Vichy of Pétain and Darlan serenely carried on the pre-1939 perverted nationalism, all the while believing that they were resuming the great game of the years after the Franco-Prussian War. To be sure, a similar problem existed: to rebuild national unity around certain beliefs, so that France might re-establish herself in the world after a defeat. But Vichy was doomed to fail in its attempt at internal unification: counterrevolutionary theories did not have the historical relevance that had characterized the Republican synthesis, and consequently they served at best as good words, at worst as a license for purges; in addition, reconciliation in a humiliated and occupied country could only come from a foreign policy acceptable to the majority, so that the ideological and practical priority given to the "national revolution" became clearly absurd.

The Vichy regime could hardly act as if foreign policy was a matter that could be attended to later, à la Maurras, nor could it openly rally Frenchmen to the ideal of *revanche,* as the Republican leaders had after the Treaty of Frankfurt. Once more, foreign and domestic factors interlocked to produce tragedy. A rigorous wait-and-see foreign policy (not to be confused with the postponement of formulating one), intended to rebuild France's strength before war resumed, would have required a different domestic policy, a less suspicious and domineering Germany without the weapon of blackmail provided by French war prisoners and ideological collaborationists. The infernal machine of collaboration, even if it had been limited to what I have called "involuntary state collaboration," would have gradually destroyed a policy of wait-and-see. As it moved, it pushed Vichy down the slope of submission, at the foot of which, in November 1942, there was no other choice but to give in or give up.

Of course, there is no doubt that Pétain and Laval sincerely wished to protect France and the empire, nor that they had ambitions to save France's chances in case of a German victory. But "political decisions are not taken in the future perfect." [19] From the moment official Vichy collaboration anticipated and drew checks on the account of German victory, thus encouraging other, more eager collaborationists to outbid the government, there was, if not a betrayal of, at least a desertion of the national interest, because "there were national reasons for preferring the allied camp to the German camp" [20]—unless, like the unfortunate Laval, one believed that an Allied victory would mean the Bolshevization of France. In Laval's case, the abandonment of the national interest stemmed as much from miscalculation, largely due to the obsessive fear of internal revolution, as from a preference for a Nazi Europe.

The threat of death that hung over France's national community during the war had at least two major consequences: one was to bring to an end the perverted nationalism that had become the final expression of the anti-Republican counterdoctrine and the Maurrasian theory in which these dogmas had become frozen. The other was the nationalist upsurge of the Resistance. Of course, there were many nuances in it, but all were included in a great consensus, oriented simultaneously toward domestic reform and toward regaining French rank, power, and prestige.

III

This unity was not destined to last much beyond the Liberation. Although the widespread devaluation of nationalism of the 1930s had disappeared and the Resistance's intentions were good, the postwar at-

mosphere resembled that of the years between the wars more than that
of the great days of the Third Republic. Once again a revolutionary
international situation made it impossible to separate domestic and
foreign policy. France's presence in the camp of the victors in no way
ended the tyranny of outside factors on her internal situation, and she
was in an even weaker position to master the storms. To be sure (although it took some time for the French to realize this), these storms
did not threaten her very existence, as the Nazi hurricane had, and the
will to master them had been revived by the bitter experience of
dependence—first on Britain before the war, and then on the Allies
(for de Gaulle) or the Germans (for Pétain) during the war. These
were favorable changes, but others were unfavorable. Europe was
downgraded by comparison to the two superpowers, which had at
their disposal unrivaled space, resources, and new weapons. For the
lesser "Great Powers," like France, the nightmare was no longer that
one could not hold a place in the first rank against a fanatical enemy,
but rather that one might become a victim of superpower collision, or
collusion, be a mere object rather than a subject, however deficient.
To the old question, "What *should* the nation do in a world it can
neither dominate nor balance?" was added a brand new question,
"What *can* the nation still do?" But this was hardly perceived as yet.
Was the erstwhile *raison d'être* of the nation on the world scene—the
search for a certain degree of power, for a role to play, even the protection of one's own integrity—still possible? Was it not, rather, necessary
to choose between the ultimate objectives of national action, which remained valid, and independence itself, in case the latter had become
untenable and maybe an obstacle to reaching these goals?

The answer to this new question depended to a large degree on the
internal aspects of France's national situation. A nation capable of mobilizing its forces can do more than a disorganized one, but the Republican framework had not been revived. The old integrative forces
—school, army, ideological blocs—were in eclipse. The ideological
blocs were being eroded—except for the Communists; the school and
the army, while less destructive of nationalism than they had been between the wars, simply were not very effective. The large and powerful
Communist party—well entrenched in the industrial centers, threatening the parliamentary game, and practicing a kind of lopsided nationalism by opposing American influence and the revival of West
Germany, but not the Soviet Union—underlined the continuity of the
French crisis, by which I mean the considerable alienation of many
Frenchmen seeking a different social order, represented by a great foreign power. The new Constitution for the Fourth Republic was a
scarcely disguised return to a pluralistic democracy, but it lacked common beliefs or intellectual synthesis. Once again, the capacity of the

government to unify a majority of Frenchmen depended on its ability to develop a coherent foreign policy. Otherwise, external affairs were likely to tyrannize domestic policies, which would make Frenchmen more likely to tear each other apart. The heterogeneity of the international system would exacerbate the divisions of the body politic, and these, in turn, would weaken France in world competition, just as in the period between the wars. Unfortunately, the postwar international system again gave off quite contradictory signals to France, and her leaders did not succeed in working out a coherent strategy. If they focused on security, there were two threats—from the Soviet Union and from Germany. To protect France from both by a policy of neutrality was to disregard the lesson of the prewar years and to lose whatever influence France might still have on Germany. But to favor one or the other power would aggravate internal dissension, increase French dependence on the United States, and sooner or later contribute to the revival of Germany. And if they relied upon maintenance of the empire (rebaptized the French Union) as a preliminary condition for France's return to a respectable rank and for an increase in her power, this might deplete the nation's resources.

The initial foreign policy of the Fourth Republic was remarkably orthodox in a nationalist sense. It comprised repressive measures against Germany; participation in a West European alliance against a possible German threat in the future, and in an Atlantic Alliance against the Soviet threat; defense of the French Union against indigenous nationalist movements. Only the Council of Europe—faint echo of the supranationalist visions of the Resistance—seemed to offer something new. This strategy, though logically coherent, was not sound, because once again the international system was unfavorable and French resources were sufficient. Lacking adequate national means and foreign support, it was impossible for France to maintain a "hard line" simultaneously in Europe and overseas. Each in itself required resources and assistance that were not forthcoming, as was evident already in 1948 in Germany, and again in the Suez crisis of 1956. It was therefore necessary to change course—hence the slow and painful decolonization, begun in 1954, and the move toward the political integration of Europe as early as 1949.

It proved impossible, however, to find a new equilibrium between the imperatives and restrictions imposed from without and nationalist concerns. European integration, although intended to protect the nation's security and increase the resources of the members in an enlarged framework, seemed likely instead to limit French freedom of action while restoring the resources and rank of Germany. To preserve some degree of military freedom, France's Parliament, in 1954, killed the EDC. But by reluctantly allowing West Germany to rearm within the framework of NATO, so as to keep the French Army intact, France was in fact locking herself in the Atlantic cage, becoming ever more dependent on the United States, from which predicament the political and military integration of Western Europe might have freed her. In other words, the French government was merely condemning France to a choice between different forms of dependency, without thereby guaranteeing that her power, her rank, her security, or her prestige would be improved. Far from overcoming the tyranny of outside forces, the bind in which France found herself increased it. Within France, this tyranny was represented by the "Europeans," the *Atlantistes* (often the same as the "Europeans"), and, of course, the Communists. The program of atomic armaments, drawn up to re-establish a margin of superiority over Germany and some degree of freedom of action vis-à-vis the United States, was not really compatible with either European integration, *or* the Atlantic Alliance, *or* France's current resources. Moreover, the slow pace of decolonization, and especially the refusal to extend it to Algeria, could lead paradoxically to the exhaustion of French resources and to greater dependence on allies, called in to help in the name of anti-Communist solidarity.

The balance-of payments crisis which occurred at the end of the Fourth Republic demonstrated the imbalance between ends and means. The crisis over EDC and the Algerian tragedy which caused the regime to collapse showed that France's obvious inability to reach her goals alone did not prevent many Frenchmen from accusing the government of betraying the interests of the nation, as France retreated in Europe (where Germany moved ahead) and overseas (where the rebels pushed ahead), in both cases at the expense of the French Army. There was an imbalance between ends and means, contradictions among the ends, and a considerable margin of uncertainty about the purpose of each of these undertakings. Traditional desires for protection (of the army and of the empire) were mixed with daring initiatives such as European integration, but protection seemed only to increase dependence, and audacity involved risks. What strikes the observer with the benefit of hindsight is not so much the presence and crisscrossing of the two great international divisions—the cold war and decolonization—within France's Parliament.[21] It is the spectacle of men seeking the traditional *raison d'État* and trying almost desperately to adjust a certain conception of national wealth, power, and influence (as de Gaulle would say)—a conception learned in school, strengthened in the war, intimately bound up with France's "civilizing mission," the Roman heritage of Imperial France, and a degree of leadership in Europe—to a world where the inflated nationalism of the superpowers and of colonial rebels challenged the very essence of a European-type nation-state. Since neither the international situation nor the resources favored such an adjustment, internal dissension and resentment toward the rest of the world were inevitable. This was true whether failure stemmed from divisions in the leadership, as with the EDC, or from the brutal contrast between hostile realities and the united—even obstinate—determination of the leaders to defend positions they thought essential to the rank, power, and prestige of the nation, as in the case of Indochina or Algeria.

In its weak executive and multiplicity of factions, the Fourth Republic resembled the Third in the 1880s. A specific parallel can be drawn between the Boulangist movement and the rise of the RPF. In each case, ultranationalist impatience on the part of those who were disappointed by a timid foreign policy led to antiparliamentary sentiments in which constitutional reform came to be the *sine qua non* of the fight against decline. The adherents of both movements claimed to be motivated exclusively by the national interest, in contrast to the party interests represented by the government. Both claimed to unify Frenchmen under the banner of intransigent nationalism abroad and a strong government at home.

There was another marked resemblance between the RPF and the Maurrasism of the period between the wars. In addition to excommunicating the government, the RPF accused the Communists of seceding from France and denounced them as the Trojan horse of a foreign state whose doctrine and policy threatened France's independence as a nation—once again *raison d'État* and domestic political concerns were linked. But there was no similarity between the content of the perverted nationalism of the extreme right in the 1930s and the exacerbated nationalism of the RPF, or between their respective results. In the 1930s, widespread Maurrasism has pushed a tired regime further toward "appeasement" of Germany, and into a myopic withdrawal, while Gaullism in the Fourth Republic usually reinforced the opponents of any abandonment of sovereignty and sounded the call for presence in the world.

There were both similarities and differences between the Gaullist "ultras" and the "integral nationalists" of the period before 1914. Whereas the latter had developed a counterrevolutionary doctrine to oppose to the Republicans, the Gaullist ultras, facing a Republic equipped with a Constitution but no faith, could only offer another Constitution. The Gaullists were animated chiefly by a feeling of national humiliation, and they tirelessly attacked the government's "policy of abandonment," whereas the ultranationalists before 1914, less discontent with the Republic's foreign policy, had attacked primarily its domestic policy and the Republican elites. However, in the fight over the EDC, when the French Army was at stake, the struggle took on some of the characteristics of the Dreyfus Affair.

Neither the RPF nor its predecessors before and after 1914 went so far as to break the law, despite the General's castigations and Maurras's call for the kitchen knife. Still, de Gaulle in 1940 had given priority to the latent national will for rehabilitation and *grandeur* over respect for Pétain's legality. Legitimacy, for de Gaulle, lay not in mere legality but, rather, in the combination of national independence and consent of the people—both in jeopardy in 1940, both regained in 1944. It was a unique situation. There was indeed "an asymmetry in regard to the criterion of the nation," [22] between Gaullists and collaborationists (and even between Gaullists and followers of Pétain). But a precedent had been set, and it was followed by the "ultras" in Algiers in May 1958. Motivated by an explosive combination—by the defense of specific interests but also by an ideal which transfigured and transcended them—these fanatical military men and colonists with their backs to the wall arrogated to themselves the right to cut "the silken thread of legality," again in the name of the superior interest and integrity of the motherland. Their own conception of the national interest required sacrifices in terms of both resources and values, much greater than were required by decolonization. The "asymmetry" (between "ultras" and officials) was less striking than in 1940–44, but it went in the opposite direction. In 1940, de Gaulle well understood the international system, and the probable evolution of the French people, as well as the enormous cost of the different kinds of collaboration. In 1958, the ultras were mistaken about everything. The case of the 1958 ultras was made worse by the fact that the Fourth Republic was a freely elected representative government, whereas the regime de Gaulle had defied, although it had popular consent at the outset, was nevertheless founded in the trauma of defeat and had rapidly become a dictatorship. The perverted nationalism of the 1930s had contributed to undermining the regime, the blind nationalism of the ultras went so far as to overthrow it—with the help of available Gaullists, moreover. After nearly three quarters of a century the lesson was clear. Any nationalism that gives ideological or practical priority to the destruction of a pluralistic representative government and makes this a prerequisite for defense of the national interest in fact works against that defense, by dividing the people and thus making the national situation worse. Such a nationalism is bound also to give the world an image of France's interest that is distorted by the diversion from external to domestic objectives and by the oversimplification which attributes all troubles to the regime alone.

IV

De Gaulle's second "reign" presents the most fascinating attempt to develop the "great enterprise" of the Third Republic in a new perspective: to rebuild national unity and to outline a foreign policy based on a nationalist ideal. We have seen that the springs of Republican nationalism were internal; the problem was to give to a new leadership and to the people that supported it the backing, the weight, and the prestige of a certain conception of the nation. But the Republicans also had the obligation and the ambition to respond to the challenge of the defeat of 1870. In de Gaulle's case, the chief motivation was the desire for *grandeur* on the world scene—and how longstanding it was! This encompassed his rage against dependence, against the tyranny of external factors, against the bad card (or inept playing of the cards) France had been dealt in the game of international relations. But there was also a motive in terms of domestic policy: not only to unify Frenchmen in "great undertakings" without which civil strife would fester but also to establish a strong government. What was needed was to break the vicious circle which, for forty years, had tied the heterogeneity of the international system to that of the nation, and to mobilize the French around a policy whose main object was nothing less than to diminish the former.

The Republicans had tried to unify Frenchmen through particular philosophical and political ideas at home and the goal of *revanche* abroad. One might call this a doctrinaire nationalism. Since any doctrine induces qualifications, reservations, and differences of interpretation, the unity desired was never completely achieved. General de Gaulle's aim was quite different: he sought to unify France by means of an attitude, a state of mind, rather than precise dogmas and policies. To him, the nation was both a fact, a product of history, and a value, derived from and embodied in her culture. Nationalism was a duty, in the sense in which a code of behavior is a set of norms.[23] Specifically, the aim was to rally Frenchmen around a man, *l'homme de la nation,* who would translate and interpret the *élan vital* of the nation according to the necessities and possibilities of the moment. This is an "existential" construct, instead of the "essential" construct of the Third Republic. Barrès, Péguy, and others had attacked the static features of the Third Republic; de Gaulle's construct was so dynamic and fluid that it could lean sometimes to the Left and sometimes to the Right without being identified with any one group and never definitively alienating any.

Naturally, de Gaulle's nationalism, like that of the Republicans, could not avoid producing some divisions. In domestic affairs, all those who did not accept the concentration of power in a single man were hostile. In foreign policy, the opposition included those who thought that the mystique of independence threatened the gains made by the Fourth Republic when it interlocked France with the European and Atlantic communities; those who conceived of the nation as a collection of lands, none of which should ever be alienated; and those who gave priority to domestic needs. In other words, all those who defined the national interest primarily in terms of defense and the acquisition of possessions—markets, colonies, means of production or consumer goods—looked on independence as a means only. (For them, security was something to be obtained either by the maintenance of national forces or by membership in an alliance whose forces were equal or superior to those of the presumed enemy.) They considered themselves good patriots, and resented de Gaulle's sarcasm, aspersion, and curses.

For de Gaulle, these benefits, possessions, and goods were certainly not negligible, but he thought them inherently fluctuating. To identify the survival and *grandeur* of the nation with any particular configuration of them, therefore, would be to lose flexibility. And to him none of them had value unless the nation was independent. In the final Gaullist analysis, freedom of action was the necessary condition of salvation. It is less serious to lose territory or to be without this or that resource, because these disadvantages can be remedied, whereas dependence on others in exchange for territory or resources may be fatal. De Gaulle and his critics both realized that the middle-size nation-state cannot do everything, but they drew different conclusions. His conclusion was an absolute imperative: what France could still do was to "remain herself" and use what she had as well as possible to obtain the rest—in other words, to act like the General himself.

Everyone knows that the effect was a continuing and ardent struggle between the old parties—heirs of the Republicans—and de Gaulle at home, and that a long and bloody battle over decolonization in Algeria was fought between him and the French nationalists who were wedded to the idea of France inseparable from a French Algeria, a colonial army, and the *mission civilisatrice*. But it would be a mistake to conclude that the policy of unifying Frenchmen at home was therefore a failure. In fact, the political parties and the ultras were both fighting rearguard actions, and they were gradually used up, worn out, and left behind by the General's dynamic strategy. By offering France a government that was strong but not dictatorial (thus rallying the heirs of the Jacobins as well as those of Maurras, lay Republicans as well as clericals) and an active foreign policy that abandoned yesterday's positions to run faster toward those of the future, that destroyed only to replace, that rejected narrow protectionism in favor of a dynamic opening up, de Gaulle made his opponents appear either as advocates of dependence or as old-fashioned, divisive fanatics. And he succeeded, over a period of ten years, in persuading Frenchmen to turn away from those who resisted him.

Even so, one arrives at May 1968. The weaknesses of de Gaulle's domestic policy and the mistakes derived from centralization undoubtedly were important in that crisis. But one must distinguish between the two: centralization was an essential element of the regime created by the General, and a vital ingredient in his nationalism, whereas domestic policy was generally subordinated to foreign affairs. De Gaulle had gambled on gathering Frenchmen around him as the country raced to make itself a modern nation capable of playing a major world role. He had gambled on the possibility of greatly improving the national situation by exploiting more effectively the international opportunities of a middle-size state while transforming French society at the same time. The problem, then, was to develop a "coherent [strategy] seeking to maintain [French] integrity and freedom of action on the world scene." This strategy may be described as the answers to a series of questions. First question: what *should* France do? Answer: preserve her independence so as to increase her influence. Second question: what *can* France do toward this end? Answer: make herself more dynamic, modernize her power, transform herself as a nation just as de Gaulle had advocated that the French Army transform itself in the 1930s. This implied a redistribution of the nation's responsibilities, in order to get rid of those which increased her dependence on others (hence disengagement from the "servitude" of NATO and the campaign against supranational institutions in Europe), or limited her means (tariffs), or exhausted her resources while lowering her prestige (decolonization). As a corollary, it implied accepting, even seeking, new responsibilities which would enlarge France's role while leaving her free (hence the policy of aid to the Third World, and especially the *force de frappe*). It also implied a policy of increasing the nation's resources and using them according to a new order of priorities, such as making the economy competitive, encouraging science and technology (especially in advanced sectors like atomic energy, aeronautics, and electronics) while making sure that the essential sectors remained in French hands. It meant obtaining a large balance-of-payment surplus to be used to advantage in world politics, giving priority to a strengthened franc over the satisfaction of domestic needs not essential to foreign policy. Third question: *how* should France use her resources and enlarge role? Answer: in the service of world-wide revisionism, by contributing to changing the international system in a way that would raise France's prestige and rank. One way was to hasten the shift from a bipolar world to a multipolar world (hence de Gaulle's many efforts to obstruct anything that might consolidate the two "hegemonies," his support of independence movements in the Third World and the emancipation of satellite states). Another way was to subordinate West European cooperation to French independence and the prior satisfaction of French economic interests, and to a design for the gradual unification of the entire continent.

This extraordinarily bold gamble sought to eliminate the tyranny of outside factors in various ways. Having united Frenchmen as much as possible around the necessity to act on the world scene, de Gaulle sought to hasten the return of a moderate and balanced international system and thus to break the linkage between foreign policy and domestic unrest, to rid the latter of the poison injected by revolutionary world politics, even if internal dissension could not be wholly eliminated. This plan was based on a reading of the international system which made sense at a time when the balance of terror was restraining the superpowers and when France was experiencing rapid industrialization and an increase in the birthrate. A more logical plan than observers of day-to-day Gaullist policy (often wildly fluctuating) have recognized, it was designed to provide France with the tangible and intangible benefits that a middle-size nation can anticipate: security and markets, but also influence and presence on the world scene without sacrificing freedom of action. Yet he did not win his gamble, despite the success of French decolonization, the acquisition of prestige, and the lessening of some elements of dependence. Why?

Assuming that the golden rule of independence is sound, de Gaulle's interpretation of the possibilities offered by France's situation was too optimistic, although it was not utopian. The present international scene is most resistant to the efforts of any power to transform it quickly. Even the superpowers have a hard time. In Europe, French global revisionism clashed with the conceptions of her neighbors, and de Gaulle was not able to impose his own "European Europe." The superpowers can at least use all sorts of incentives to bring about change when they cannot force it. But a middle power like France usually has to settle for exploiting tendencies of which she controls neither the origins nor the outcome. Some tendencies are easily *reversible,* as the Soviet Union proved by crushing budding East European nationalism in Prague; others depend on the internal developments in other countries, the superpowers included, which France cannot influence. Still others can only be exploited if one has powerful levers; thus, the weakness of the "dollar-exchange standard," which de Gaulle understood well, could not, while he was in power, be corrected in the way he wished because he found no allies, and the franc was found to be even more vulnerable.

Also, France's own internal characteristics did not lend themselves to fulfillment of the General's ambitions. This time the domestic consequences of foreign policy unbalanced the scale. At bottom, the trouble lay in the traditional fragility of the French economy (in spite of the progress made). Industry was unable to expand without inflation and often incapable of producing goods required by the "great ambition" at competitive prices. This was due partly to its structures and partly to French attitudes. The partial sacrifice (or rather insufficient expansion) of certain essentials (housing, hospitals, telephones, highways), the use of resources to accumulate reserves or for cultural and social investments (schools, social security) rather than for higher wages (which would possibly have hindered the competitiveness of business) were indeed the expression of a choice, but they resulted, paradoxically, in depriving the government "of all flexibility and freedom to maneuver," [24] in direct contradiction to the principal goal sought. With a more productive industry and less hostile relations between management and labor, the gamble would have been less risky. But with things as they were, it meant heading for an explosion, especially as there was a contradiction between the strong government essential to the great ambition and the means needed to make it work. The centralized state exacerbated social tensions in the public sector, and in the attempt to ease them in the private sector it held back modernization by subsidizing marginal producers and shopkeepers.

One may grant that de Gaulle had defined in an inspired way what a nation like France should do in a world like that of the 1960s. One may argue that the external obstacles might have been merely delaying, not insurmountable factors. One can maintain that domestic obstacles could have been overcome by a policy in less of a hurry about an immediate world role (although with that still as the main priority), more concerned with an early reform of structures. It would have stressed qualitative changes that would have brought about, later, decisive and lasting quantitative changes, rather than quantitative progress and innovations which the rigidity of French structures, the persistence of antieconomic attitudes, and the narrowness of French castes doomed to fragility. Even so, one is still obliged to recognize that a prior question had not yet been answered: *could* France, a middle-size state, still do what as a nation she *ought* to do? Was it not the very notion of "active independence" itself that doomed the great Gaullist design to failure?

The design was reasonable for a world in which diplomacy is a billiard game, in which each state can be conceived as a self-contained entity—large, medium or small, independent or dependent, but solid and impenetrable (unless it is a conquered or satellite nation, in which case it is not a real state). In such a world, a frontier is a real barrier, not a mere checkpoint or an absurd symbol easily overrun or undermined. In such a world, each self-respecting nation-state produces the goods it needs or buys them abroad. In either case it controls them. The real tragedy for de Gaulle and for France was that at the moment when the balance of terror made it possible for a middle-size state to regain some freedom of action on the traditional international diplomatic-strategic chessboard, the evolution of industrial society and the balance of terror itself gave international relations a new chessboard

—technological, economic, and monetary—and here the independence of a small or middle-size nation-state was gravely compromised.[25] At the very time when the old dialectic of interstate affairs—the logic of diversity, the weakening of bipolarity, and a drastic change in the function of military power—removed the desire or the necessity for the nation-state to disappear into larger entities, the new dialectic, dominated by the logic of solidarity and by economic imperatives, suddenly robbed the middle-size nation-state of a considerable part of its substance. The form remained, but the matter was drained away.

What does "independence" mean in these circumstances? If it is the nation's abstract freedom to define strategic and diplomatic options, and if the state has none of the necessary means (weapons, modern technology, capital) either because they do not exist or because they are controlled by other states or foreign companies, the freedom means nothing. If independence means national control of all the means of action on the world scene, no European state is independent. If there is national control of the available means but these are largely specialized (as with Sweden) or dependent on the availability of foreign markets (as with Japan), i.e., if the control is only partial, reduced impenetrability combines with a *de facto* dependence or deprives the nation of any active, ambitious world role. The Gaullist dream was to provide national control over the entire range of means essential to an ambitious role, even if France were destined to remain inferior to the two superpowers in quantitative terms—as in a metaphor used by de Gaulle in 1965, "no matter how large the glass we are offered by others, we prefer to drink from our own when toasting them." But at present a middle-size state is not a great power on a smaller scale: there is a difference in kind. Behind the gigantic effort to modernize, the Gaullist concept had a traditional base, an atavism for Colbert and mercantilism. It is the image, so familiar to schoolchildren in the Third Republic, of a country which has all necessary resources and activities: France, or the-world-on-a-human-scale, *not* merely a particular fraction of the world. The attempt either to accomplish alone, in a small way, that which only the great powers can undertake (be it nuclear power, a space program, computers or supersonic planes), or to close the gap by a combination of national efforts, and the attempt to open France's borders so selectively that the only flows allowed inside would be those which would strengthen France's independent economy, led to disappointing results.

The purely national enterprises of the Fifth Republic—such as color television, a purely French nuclear power program, the *Plan Calcul* for computers—have gone badly. Resources have been too widely dispersed, or the relative weakness in resources and haste to achieve independence have concentrated the available means on a technique that has not turned out to be profitable, or innovations have been exploited prematurely, or the rigidity of structures thwarted the intelligent exploitation of the innovations. Cooperative enterprises with other European states in armaments, space, and for the development of the Concorde have suffered from the absence of shared priorities, from national selfishness, and from the added weaknesses of the separate states.[26] So one returns to the fundamental dilemma. The middle-size nation-state cannot by itself rise to the level of modern power; the simultaneous satisfaction of rising needs at home and the acquisition of tangible and intangible goods abroad seems to require the end of independence. Does it then boil down to a choice between pure and simple dependence of the nation-state on (and penetration by) another, i.e., the tyranny of outside forces, and the repudiation of the nation-state, or, rather more accurately, the dissociation of the nation from the state?

V

Despite his setbacks in foreign policy, de Gaulle's nationalist strategy achieved some extraordinary results at home. The man who said, fifty years after the Battle of the Marne, that there was only one history of France, left, when he abdicated, a country closer to domestic appeasement than the one he had found. He had continued the liquidation of ideological divisions begun during the dreadful war years. Even the French Communists are now less clearly agents of the tyranny of outside forces than they used to be (due partly to a rather chauvinist reaction, anti-Arab during the Algerian war and anti-American later; partly to a greater separation from the Soviet Union, reflecting internal changes in Russia as well as tensions between Russia and China and the Czech affair; partly to reaction against the New Left since 1968). Like other countries moving, not without difficulty, into the postindustrial era, France proves to be a society resistant to great undertakings, syntheses and over-all world visions, which are both divisive (since there are conflicting visions) and integrative (for the believers). This does not mean, naturally, that there is perfect harmony on the home front, nor that ideological arguments, attitudes, and styles left over from the past are not still to be found. But France is less deeply and permanently divided. National feeling is very strong,[27] but it does not need to be made into a doctrine or counterdoctrine. For the first time in modern French history, the transition from the rule of a charismatic personality to ordinary successors has taken place without a constitutional crisis. The very conditions of his departure from power have consolidated and legitimized de Gaulle's regime.

But if the national consciousness is stronger and less fragmented than in the past, the scope for French nationalism is not more promising, for reasons that are less dramatic and more basic than in the period between the wars. On the domestic front, a distinction must be drawn between the willingness to live together (which seems to me greater, despite 1968 and some regional "nationalisms"), the will to maintain one's own separate way (still an indisputable French characteristic), and the determination to maintain independence for the nation-state. This latter, while still powerful, is weaker than in the past. Modernization and the increased internal harmony have inevitably been achieved at the cost of a certain devaluation of the past, especially insofar as it had become a source of division and, most recently, of humiliation. But the past was also one of the springs of nationalism. (One might say, of this turn of events, that nothing fails like success!) In addition, a technological society, with its outlook turned to the future, with the constant need to update its scientific information, with a burgeoning youth who care more about the civilization of the future than about the old quarrels recounted in history books, is less burdened with traditions and rituals. As Girardet points out, security itself, at least from neighbors, encourages relaxation of the once tense national stance. In his pessimistic moments, de Gaulle saw in himself, rightly or wrongly, the last champion of the history of France as a nation-state playing a great role in the world. In trying to counteract the antiheroic nature of this society, its hostility toward any integration other than functional, de Gaulle attempted to infuse Frenchmen with his own brand of nationalism, since a new Christianity or a religion of humanity would not do. He called on France "to be herself," i.e., different from others, in order to console her for the fate of becoming like others. The assumption was that foreign policy could still be the great stage on which national personalities confront each other, as in the time of Hegel. But the greater the General's success in modernizing France, the less this remedy took hold. The gap increased between his active nationalism and the passive patriotism of the French. As time passed, their admiration for his acts turned to skepticism about his goals.

Does this mean that an industrial society concerned with the future and reconciled to (or detached from) its past is immune to nationalism? One only has to consider the United States to realize that the contrary is true. But, for France, there were two problems—domestic and international. The domestic difficulty had for ten years been concealed by de Gaulle's postulate that the primacy of foreign affairs would bring about domestic reform and smother domestic divisions and doubts. Instead, discontent about social policies, rigid structures, provincial dissent in a country no longer threatened from the outside and no longer *encadré* in forces of national integration or along nationwide class lines, technocratic centralization, and uneven growth resulted in the May 1968 delirium. It taught de Gaulle that the domestic function of nationalism—unity—could not be performed if nationalism did not have a domestic component, as it had had under the Third Republic, or if that component was limited to popular support for strong central political institutions. The demand for "participation" meant that the French saw domestic, social, and regional reform no longer as an eventual by-product of the modernizing changes dictated by their country's world role, but as a necessary *préalable* to the national consensus. De Gaulle's failure in 1969, to give clear substance to and to gain approval for "participation," showed that in the absence of this consensus, and despite the disappearance of old ideological issues and cleavages, the very notion of "participation" would be resisted by conservatives, revolutionaries, and more drastic reformists alike. His successors have not solved this problem. They have, on the whole, dodged it. France today is too solid for dissolution, too complex—both too relaxed and too bickering—for the older kind of nationalism that de Gaulle's nostalgia still desired.

The second difficulty applies to the other middle-size European powers as well as to France: of what *use* is the nation now? There is no doubt that de Gaulle realized that withdrawal and acceptance of dependence on others might revive French internecine quarrels, accelerate French decline by pettiness and protectionism, sour the French in general (marinating in resentful chauvinism) and the intellectuals in particular. He believed that the only way to avoid this was to appeal to France's presence and action on the world scene. It is high time to give him credit for this, even if one disagrees with his remedy. For that remedy to succeed, he would have had to win his own personal gamble—that it was still possible for France to have a history as a nation-state in the old sense.

Does this mean that after de Gaulle had tried to speed up French internal modernization and to adapt the French nation-state as much as possible to the new international system, one suddenly discovers that this "renewed" France has no role to play? Let us examine this question more closely. For some Frenchmen, submission to a postindustrial order and to the consumer society in its liberal-capitalist form is itself an abdication; an "Americanized" France is no longer France. The problem here is how any nation can preserve its character and retain individuality while the social order is standardized across all frontiers. To ask for the preservation of all traditional characteristics would be to refuse modernization, necessary both for social progress and for the exercise of influence abroad; but to demand the preservation of uniqueness is certainly not unreasonable. This is partly the business of cultural nationalism, where the nation-state still has a role to play and where it has the necessary means (through the schools, universities, social policy, urbanism, and its influence over the mass media). And there must also be a vision, a plan. But does it make sense to ask for a plan at the level of the nation-state when it cannot even afford to pay for its own industrial society?

This brings me to economic and financial considerations. In these domains, sovereignty is leaking away on all sides. "Americanization" as I have described it above results from a lack of imagination, from an inability to discriminate between the good and bad aspects of a certain experience, to draw lessons from its failings. But there is another kind of "Americanization," which reflects the decline of the French state's capacity to control financial transactions and monetary fluctuations (except at costs damaging to the nation's competitiveness). It shows too the limits of France's national resources—a limited market, too little capital, overrigid structures, companies that are too small, closed management circles, high prices, ingrained habits. *This* Americanization results from American preponderance in certain spheres (like computers and spatial telecommunications) and is also expressed by the presence on French soil of multinational business firms directed by Americans. This kind of Americanization can be partially reduced through basic changes in French industrial structures and attitudes toward industry, which would improve management and increase available capital and manpower. And yet, the examples of West Germany and even Japan (despite Tokyo's resistance to U.S. investments) show that this is not enough. There seems to me no doubt that this is a "menace" to the nation-state. Even though it offers some benefits for the citizens from the strictly economic point of view (maximum production of goods at lowest prices), serious limitations are imposed on national freedom of action by the diversion of capital, labor, know-how, and brains; the loss of control over the monetary market and the goods' destination; the subordination of some sectors of the economy or some regions of the country to imperatives that do not correspond to national interests or development needs and are dictated by extranational considerations. These amount to dependency by penetration.[28]

Of course, the question needs to be asked, who profits? In some respects, these American businesses abroad can serve as more or less voluntary agents of U.S. foreign policy, either because they are subject to American law, or because they are tightly tied into the "military-industrial complex," or because their establishment abroad achieves an objective of Washington's foreign policy. In such cases, their presence makes the host country dependent in the traditional sense upon another state. In other respects, however, this phenomenon merely reflects the lessening control of states on, or the transnationalization of, the economy. The power of the state is reduced as these businesses escape national legislation or slip between laws of different nations; transnationalization occurs because criteria of production and management are based on world-wide or regional, rather than national, considerations. This is a unique kind of dependence. To say that it is only a more indirect and better disguised form of dependence on the United States disposes of the question too easily. Large multinational corporations are not mere instruments of American power. But it is true that the headquarters of most of these firms are located in the United States, that there is a profound imbalance in this respect, that American foreign policy can make good use of them (in a world eager for technology and products) to exploit its advantages or to compensate for its weaknesses on the chessboards of interstate relations, and that American foreign economic policy aims at a trade surplus that would finance investments abroad. Is the loss of economic sovereignty for a middle-size state like France really the same when the "multinational" business that controls a given sector of the economy is a private French firm with foreign subsidiaries as when it is a French subsidiary of a foreign firm?

Thus, the medium-size nation-state loses whether it is dependent on a foreign state or on a foreign business group. The lack of national control over certain important resources can weigh heavily on a state's foreign policy, deflect its direction, limit its ambitions, and inhibit changes. We also know that such a nation cannot really assure its own security against a superpower. Conventional weapons are of little avail against nuclear weapons, and small nuclear forces that can contribute to deterrence when coordinated with the strategic forces of a superpower are likely to be of little use by themselves.[29] For France, one alternative, whose case has been argued too often to repeat it here, is to "build Europe," i.e., to create a multinational state whose resources would be comparable to those of the superpowers. There is no question that a Western Europe equipped with common institutions and decision-making powers could do more—and more effectively—than poor old *"Europe à la carte,"* tied down to its national constituent parts, in military and industrial matters. But even a federal Western Europe would have difficulty in developing a substantial nuclear deterrent force. The British and French forces are too different to be merged easily, West Germany has taken a vow of nuclear virginity, and the lag by comparison to the superpowers is tremendous in the era of MIRV and even limited ABM.

Western Europe has already been and will continue to be penetrated, if only by the preference European businessmen have shown for affiliation with American firms as opposed to European ones. Regaining economic independence, or rather acquiring an economic position comparable to that of the United States, is therefore most uncertain.

One problem at the outset would be the necessity of combining some of the quasi-monopolies which each European government has encouraged as a means of resisting American domination. Not all the rigidities and lags can be blamed on the limited national market. They are the products of centuries of history, residues whose crust hardens even as societies become more standardized and open. An enlarged European market would not abolish them overnight, and a centralized supranational power could only succeed if the nations themselves cooperated.

A third reason for skepticism is the eternal problem of a common plan. If it is hard to answer the question, "What use is the nation?" it is even less easy to answer another, "Of what use would Europe be?" If the answer is, "To obtain power," one must know what type of power and for what ends. Is it diplomatic and military power in the classical sense of foreign policy? This brings me to the crucial problem against which de Gaulle bruised himself: is the world scene still the field for great performances by Europe's peoples? Is the search for influence in the world a sufficient incentive to accomplish the transition from the nation-state to a federated Europe? Could a united Europe really have played a decisive role in Vietnam or the Middle East, as we are so often told? Could it have prevented the occupation of Czechoslovakia? I have said that a Europe with nuclear weapons comparable to those of the superpowers is inconceivable, and the known interest of the United States in preserving Western Europe from invasion remains a sufficient deterrent. Europe equipped with conventional armies and weapons—no European nation alone can produce the entire range of those needed—could replace the American troop presently based there, but their mission would be essentially one of defense and a contribution to deterrence. Now, this is a mission that Europeans—if they wanted it, which is not obvious today—could just as well accomplish in the framework of a West European alliance, with a division of labor with regard to the production of arms. Federation is not necessary in military terms—not so much because any federation presupposes a unified policy (which is always true) or because Europeans are deeply divided (which is less true today), as because the common policy they might agree on does not require such an upheaval. On the traditional chessboard, one does not become a great power by putting together small or medium states: the realization of what is possible for Europe can be accomplished by a mix of national actions and coordinated actions. If the object is the long-range unification of the continent with peaceful penetration of Eastern Europe and the gradual breakup of the blocs, federation is either unnecessary or insufficient. West Germany (resigned to a long partition but anxious for bonds with her half sister) does not need, and Eastern Europe (resigned to a long domination by the Soviet Union, but anxious for inconspicuous bonds with Western Europe) has little to gain from a federation that sought to contain Bonn and to emancipate Prague and Warsaw.[30]

The old diplomatic-military chessboard offers no decisive incentive to abandon the national framework. If we turn to the new chessboard, it is indeed the desire for common economic power (including an arms industry on a European scale) and the fear of being victimized by the winds of economic interdependence buffeting Europe's states which justify the idea of a federation. But we are faced again with ambiguity in the ultimate goals. At a time when military conquest no longer pays off, it is a complex matter for the state to translate economic power into foreign influence. The returns on traditional military and colonial power are very low, but the returns on modern economic power are uncertain and often indirect, in that the state itself is not always the beneficiary. Economic power is an important element in the rank of a state, but at present the productivity of even high rank is in question: it may entail some capacity to resist penetration (though not decisively in Western Europe), but not the capacity to dominate outside one's borders. Indeed, not even the dominant economic and financial world power, the United States, is any longer capable of imposing its preponderance and escaping the costs of interdependence, despite its enormous assets on all chessboards. Today, at least in Europe, the idea of economic power means more for the welfare of the people of a nation than for the political *grandeur* of the political community on the world scene.

Perhaps we have entered a new era, not that of the traditional balance of power or that of the revolutionary system, but rather one of a world political society in which internal and foreign policy, interstate and transnational phenomena are linked, as in revolutionary systems. But instead of insoluble conflicts and life-and-death confrontations between states, there may henceforth be a certain degree of calm. Conflicts will continue and take place on a tightrope, but over a triple net provided by the balance of terror, international solidarity in the domestic and monetary spheres, and the priority of domestic needs. Does this mean that there is no more interest in foreign affairs when they begin to look like the dubious rivalries and complicated manipulations in domestic politics? This is not true everywhere. Many states, like Israel and Egypt, India and Pakistan, South Africa, and North Vietnam, still have "great quarrels" with immense stakes, in which nationalism is a guide and a cement. But (happily for them) this is no longer true of the states of Western Europe—including Germany, given the military and psychological obstacles to reunification. Today, there may be only three powers that can dream of a foreign policy on a grand scale. The United States and the Soviet Union have arsenals to maintain, empires to preserve, clients to protect, and a serious clash to avoid. China opposes them both in the name of anti-imperialism, and tries to force open the vise in which they caught her. For these three the traditional game of foreign influence still makes sense, though even for them frustrations outweigh the gains. And American and West European policies may push Japan into trying once again to compete on all chessboards all over the world. But the nation-state of Western Europe, conscious of being outside the race, is not sure that by joining a federation it would be able to re-enter the racetrack or that it would acquire any real advantages: hence its reluctance to sacrifice itself.

This may not be true forever. If some quarrel between small states escalates into violence between the superpowers, or if two of the three powers mentioned above come to blows, the West European oasis could come to an end. In that case, the states of Western Europe would rediscover foreign policy—as victims of the others' races. But as long as the oasis lasts, their own desire to leave it for the race is feeble, as is the possibility that they could influence the racers. By the same token, the probability is great that if the policy of others ends by destroying the European oasis, it will also end badly for the non-European racers themselves.

There remains today the goal of collective welfare, which is a reasonable incentive. But is reasonableness enough, insofar as, like a convalescent still haunted by illness, the European state only really responds to atavistic incentives—fear of sudden annihilation and the search for glory? Perhaps the final incarnation of the ambition to be different from others, at the moment when one feels that one becomes banal, is to stay at home alone. In the case of France, a certain basic conservatism which has survived all the changes, and a continuing desire to emulate others resist the temptation of European federalism.

On the other hand, the twin desires to escape dependence and increase prosperity incontestably offer a motive to "go beyond the nation-state" in some degree. The French nation-state might abandon the age-old ideal of total self-sufficiency and accept cooperation with its neighbors to the point of genuine functional federalism in particular sectors—for instance, in such matters as currency exchange rates and some advanced industries. But, at the same time, for purposes of domestic policy and cultural autonomy, it would retain *formal* sovereignty in other sectors, such as budget, agriculture, wages, housing, education, and military uses of nuclear power, while making sure to harmonize its policies with other states, so that much of the *content* of that formal freedom would in fact be given up. This would entail a degree of specialization in the French economy, and the acceptance of penetration by multinational enterprises in several sectors otherwise condemned to be perpetually outclassed and out of date. The French nation-state would thus tolerate some dismantling of its traditional powers, in favor either of foreign enterprises, or supranational institutions, or a pooled sovereignty with other states. But the internal legitimacy of the nation-state would stand firm, and it would continue to be the highest object of allegiance, the everyday horizon of French citizens, the privileged distributor of goods, even if it had not itself produced them all.

It is easier to predict the survival (by default) of the European nation-state than to describe the ultimate ends of its action, when the threat of brutal domination is fading and a zone of peace obtains between peoples in Europe, and when the world-society offers only a choice between the gray prose of everyday transactions and the sinister poetry of battle. Acceptance of this situation need be interpreted as "resignation to decline" only if one conceives of the nation as a personage seeking glory. It is perhaps time, for the salvation of the human race, to restrict glory as a goal to individuals, and, for the sake of the nation itself, to conceive of it as a community—different from others, to be sure, but not an object of worship.

And yet in the case of France, such a way of looking at the nation raises serious problems. French nationalism today does not experience the same anguish and perversions as in the 1930s. But the difficulty of finding a role for the nation-state, the fact that the tyranny of external forces now takes the insidious form of economic penetration (rather than that of military threats or the blatant allegiance of domestic groups to foreign ideologies, against which patriotism can be mobilized)—these are additional factors depriving nationalism of its old integrative power. Today, nationalism neither unites nor provides clear guidance. But there is enough residual nationalism in the Gaullist legacy, enough strength in the will to separateness, enough uncertainty and discord about the role of a European entity, to weaken any impetus to supersede the nation, any drive toward a European nationalism.

Another problem is posed by the French state itself. From its origins to de Gaulle, whether dominating over or dominated by French society, it has had one overriding mission: defense and expansion in the world. This vocation has allowed it to be a catalyst for French nationalism even when its specific institutions and philosophic basis were not acceptable to all Frenchmen; a right-wing nationalism could thus compete and converge with a Jacobin one. Today, however, the state is shaken by a profound change in its relations to society and in its external mission. This explains why orthodox Gaullists are uncomfortably caught between their paean to détente and their constant stress on the naturally dangerous state of international politics; why those other believers in the state, the Communists, continue to pose as champions of a threatened independence. Today, the state must justify itself in purely utilitarian and defensive terms: as provider of services and as the only center of cohesion. (Even universal military service is defended on these grounds.) But these are dangerous arguments, for it is only too easy to show that the state, as traditionally constituted, performs those roles badly.

Thus, today, for domestic and external reasons, the French state no longer defines or crystallizes French nationalism, and nationalism in French society no longer serves as a forceful inspiration for the state. Given the human costs imposed in the past by the state and by what Erikson calls "pseudo-speciation," this might be a reason to rejoice. But as long as nationalism and the state flourish elsewhere, one may well ask whether the condition in France (or in other European states) represents progress or peril, evidence of wisdom or of decline.

14

The State:
For What Society?

I

For centuries, the drama of France as a political community has been a drama about the relations between French society and the state. The story of the successive balances and imbalances between these two is far more interesting than the story of the often accidental succession of regimes and revolutions. A history of the French polity since the end of the wars of religion could begin by showing how Richelieu's theory and practice, and Louis XIV's embellishments (and excesses) established a certain kind of equilibrium between France's feudal society and the *ancien régime*. It was an equilibrium established around the state, which dampened all potential conflicts not only by eliminating independent sources of power but also by domesticating the nobility, assuring a minimum of social mobility, and exerting various material and spiritual controls over the mass of the people. Moreover, the state encouraged new productive activities. To perform its functions, it developed a bureaucracy the size and might of which have often been exaggerated, but which was far more potent than in any other country. France's characteristic style of authority, and the citizens' dependence on and resentment of the state resulted from this system of relations.

In the eighteenth century, the dream of a static equilibrium became a nightmare of disintegration. Tocqueville has given us the best description of the process. The state of Louis XIV was tied to the feudal order but supposed to be above it. The state of his unfortunate successors proved incapable of preventing a gradual emancipation of the Third Estate from the corset of the bureaucracy and its own capture by the privileged groups that Richelieu and Louis XIV had wanted to dominate. Thus, the state became the stake in a battle for the control of France's economic, social, and political future. By the eve of the

443

Revolution, the state had become incapable of reforming either itself or French society and was irrelevant to many of the economic, social, and intellectual changes that were sweeping France. It was also the major obstacle in the way of translating these changes into a reform of social rights and duties and a reform of political power, demanded by a majority of the people.

Napoleon's regime can be seen as an ambitious attempt to provide the new society which had emerged from the Revolution with the same kind of state-society equilibrium that had prevailed in the seventeenth century. But even before the empire's destruction on the battlefields of Europe it became clear that the old formula could not work any more. A turbulent society rent by profound ideological and class cleavages required a far more powerful machinery for state control. The bureaucracy's corset became a strait jacket. But the bourgeois who had emancipated themselves from the *ancien régime* were not going to accept a role of mere service and submission to Napoleon forever— certainly not once the regime had accomplished its mission of restoring order and stability and "the tranquillity of possessions." The half-century that followed saw a series of experiments aimed at finding a new kind of equilibrium between French society, increasingly determined to participate in and control its state, and the French state, which remained the prize of all the contests between ideologies and classes.

A new equilibrium was achieved under the Third Republic. To be sure, the so-called Napoleonic machinery of the state was not dismantled. It remained *formally* centralized: the formal powers of local government were minimal, and the political and administrative system was dominated by a hierarchical distinction between the law, expression of national sovereignty, and administrative decrees and regulations made by state agents or local authorities within the framework of and in conformity with the laws. But behind this permanent façade, a radically new relation between state and society developed. The substantive meaning of centralization varies completely, depending on that relation. It means one thing when the state dominates and controls society; it means quite another when the state merely expresses, protects, and guarantees social order.

The paradox of the "Republican synthesis" [1] lay in the fact that the state was sufficiently the heir to the *ancient régime* and the Napoleonic system to remain a common frame of reference, a stake, and often a scapegoat for all groups. The well-established French style of authority and the values it embodied made each social class, or stratum, determined to get its rights enshrined in, and its interests protected by, the law of the state. Each ideological bloc, or school of thought, dreamed of central institutions that would make its own clientele the basis of support and the chief beneficiary of the state. But, at the same time, the function of the state was reduced, by broad consensus, to that of a watchdog for the stalemate society, a pragmatic fixer of its minor flaws, and a perpetuator of its structures and values. To be sure, the Republican state took over one function that its ideological opponents denounced as quasi-totalitarian: public education—and this could not fail to make it appear even more essential, and centralizing, than before. It is interesting to note that the *ancien régime* had neglected this, and Napoléon I had been interested only in higher and secondary education for an elite: dominant states eager to control society have, in the French experience, been skeptical about the virtues of primary mass education. The primary-school system of the Third Republic was really a service undertaken by the state for society. Of course, the Republicans hoped—publicly—that the citizens who would come out of the schools would "vote well." But the purposes of the school system were to inculcate the values of the stalemate society; to provide channels of individual ascent in society, which would guard against social upheavals; and to promote sufficient ideological faith, thanks to which the effects of social differences and antagonistic beliefs would be cushioned, and the consensus of society around its limited, representative state confirmed. The strait jacket was becoming merely a warm set of clothes. Society, supposed to be able to take care of itself as long as its practices and structures were legitimized by the state, in return legitimized a state which had been organized to perform no more than the limited functions society entrusted to it, and to shackle or blunt those of its inherited instruments that might exceed those limits.

In order to define the real weight and role of the state, it is therefore not enough to talk about centralization. One has to ask and answer a series of questions:

1. What are the state's functions? In the case of the Third Republic, they were public order and justice, national defense and education, and piecemeal economic protectionism. The weakness of the executive branch, the peculiarities of what can only improperly be called a party system, the habit of government by center coalitions—all these contributed to keeping these functions from expanding.

2. Where and by whom were the rules made? Laws were made at the center, by Parliament—but this implies that they were drawn up and elaborated by the nation's representatives, a political class which reflected quite faithfully the aspirations of the groups whose social consensus preserved the stalemate society: bourgeois, *petits-bourgeois,* and peasants.

3. How were the rules applied? At the national level, by the civil service's central bureaucracy, but the bureaucracy operated under three kinds of checks, which amounted to a process of bargaining with

the participation of the public's representatives. There was the check exerted by cabinet ministers and their own *cabinets ministériels* (staffs), who had to please both the parliamentarians and the voters. There were the deputies and senators, intervening on behalf of their constituents, in the often picturesque manner immortalized by Robert de Jouvenel.[2] Also, in the case of the school system, the unions representing *lycée* and public-school teachers and even university professors had a considerable effect on the activities of the Ministry of National Education—indeed, one might almost say that they captured it. At the local level, one finds a similar picture. The local agents of the state, i.e., the *préfets* and their subordinates, had to engage in a double process of negotiation: with the territorial representatives of the electorate as well as with the functional representatives of interests—these were the *notables,* spokesmen for a predominately rural and small-town society. Moreover, the deputies and senators had a role here too: as national representatives of their constituents, they could put pressure on the local bureaucrats.

Thus, one sees that centralization meant little more than "uniform rules decided at the center"; that the Third Republic's centralization differed considerably from the *ancien régime*'s. The functions of the state were not the same, and they no longer had to be shared with the possessors of offices bought from the state and transmissible to heirs; the making of uniform rules by the state was no longer limited by the survival of various territorial and social forms of feudalism; there was greater institutionalized participation of the public in making and enforcing rules. Instead of authoritarian but spotty centralization, the centralized system was democratic in its foundations, and tempered by a network of "parallel relations" between bureaucrats and representatives of districts or interests at every level. Behind the classical façade of the administrative state, the reality was the adoption and protection of the corporate interests of the groups under administrative supervision (*tutelle*) by the administration exerting it: in other words, a beleaguered state. But, at the same time, the interests' representatives derived their influence less from formal grants of independent authority based on universal suffrage, than from bargaining power in the enforcement of *tutelle* from above. Thus, as Pierre Grémion has pointed out, they, in turn, "internalized the logic of the civil service."[3]

In this symbiosis between a limited state and a stable society, the carriers of Republican legitimacy—i.e., the elected representatives, from the local mayor to the national deputy—played a key part. Obviously, the system presupposed a profound congruence between the values of French society and those embodied by the political system, a broad consensus on what both should be. Congruence was not perfect, nor consensus total. Society was divided into a huge number of mainly small *communes* and districted to the disadvantage of the cities, so the network of local *notables* did not leave much room for representatives of the urban proletariat—which the rest of French society wanted to keep from growing. But what could have become a serious source of disturbance for the social order was partly minimized by the central political system. Until the appearance of the Communist party, the workers' representatives elected to Parliament shared the ideology of Republican government, and indeed harangued their supporters about its virtues; their deputies and senators thus participated in the elaboration and enforcement of the rules, even if they very rarely sat in the cabinets. While the political institutions in Paris minimized the major cleavage in French society, French society minimized the major cleavage in the French political system: that between the extreme right and the majority of Frenchmen who believed in government by consent and in parliamentary institutions. Those who remained ideologically hostile to the Republican lay state and to public education often had strong local positions in the rural and small-town elites. They could take part in the subtle modification of the rules at the local level; moreover, they were part of the social consensus on a limited, protective state.

The intricate balance of the Republican synthesis was thus made up of a series of compensatory mechanisms. The relatively depoliticized network of relations between *préfets* and *notables* provided for a delicate integration around the rules, and compensated for the potentially divisive effects of class antagonisms and ideological camps. Class solidarity and ideological affinities provided a kind of nationwide integration above and beyond the society's fragmentation into almost 40,000 *communes* and into the many categories of peasantry, commerce, *artisanat,* small business, and professions; they compensated for the "individualism" of a country where voluntary associations were often weak, brittle, and negative. The "commanding heights of society" were occupied by a formidably self-confident and domineering bourgeoisie, and the cream of the civil service: the *grands corps* were reserved to the bourgeois elite of graduates from the *grandes écoles*. But the political system saw to it that the power of domination culturally, economically, and administratively enjoyed by the *haute bourgeoisie* would be compensated by the political domination of representatives of the lower middle classes and peasants, by their parliamentary control over the bureaucracy, and by a public-school system aimed at refreshing the "inheritors" with regular additions of *boursiers*.

The 1930s subjected this fine Swiss, or rather French watch to pressures that broke it. A society tied so closely to its state, even when it is a limited state, tends to blame it for everything that goes wrong. The predicament of those who wanted to preserve the stalemate society was worsened by the very fact that a *limited* state was of its essence. They sought a solution by further limiting state functions (through devolution to corporate groups) while they made state rule-making more authoritarian and rule-enforcing more elitist. When this collapsed in 1944 into a horrid mélange of fascism and impotence, nothing less than a total reconstruction of the relations between the state and society became necessary.

The postwar Fourth Republic was a transitional period. Earlier balances were replaced with contradictions. The vastly expanded functions of the state gradually transformed the social and economic bases of French society. Yet the state's organization remained uncomfortably like that of the Third Republic—hence the conflict was exacerbated between an expanding "technocratic" bureaucracy and the traditional system of weak cabinets and splintered legislatures, and between society itself and a class of politicians and *notables* that seemed increasingly irrelevant to its concerns. Querulous dissatisfaction replaced the old consensus. Well-organized interest groups put more and more pressure on the rule-makers at the center—where it mattered. The rule-makers, craving for constituent support, were caught between the old logic of representing interests and the new ambition of modernization. It is not surprising that the two most important expressions of modernization—planning and the opening of borders to European economic integration—were undertaken by the executive: "While the legislature had to decide the number of donkeys in the national stud . . . the national economic Plan [could be] adopted without reference to Parliament." [4] Both the Schuman Plan and the Common Market had to be sold to the French deputies as ways of regaining initiative in *foreign* policy. The modernizing administration symbolized by Jean Monnet worked behind a parliamentary scene where, as Herbert Luethy's famous book suggested,[5] the clock still marked the time for all those who demanded special favors and shelters. The logic of the system of representation and the logic of state action, once combined or fused, were now at odds. The parliamentarians and local *notables* gave the impression of being stifled by the new bureau-technocracy, and submerged by the waves that a changing society kept hurling at the shores of the traditional political system. State legitimacy was being eroded.

It is a recurrent, bizarre feature of modern French history that growing contradictions between state and society end in a breakdown due not to them, but to external reasons: the European coalition against Napoleon in 1814–15, the Prussians in 1870, the Nazis in 1940, the Algerian settlers in 1958. The Fifth Republic is now more than fifteen years old. It has made drastic social and economic modernization a "national ambition," in sharp contrast to the ambivalence of the

Fourth Republic on this score. It has also reorganized completely the central institutions of the state. And there is no new balance, no new synthesis. But there are major problems that the rest of this chapter will try to explore.

II

I have no intention of either analyzing at length the transformation of French society or describing in depth the overhaul of the state. On the first point, anyone curious about the figures and facts of French economic growth since the end of World War II now disposes of an almost definitive French study which combines a wealth of statistical information with commendable caution in its attempted explanations.[6] On the second point, several fine texts abound.[7] It is the relation between state and society that I want to discuss.

The stalemate society—this halfway house between France's feudal and rural past and the dreaded industrial future, this haven for an undynamic bourgeoisie driven by acquisitiveness rather than profitability, *patrimoine* and property rather than market expansion, security rather than risk-taking—was a unique construction. It removed France from most of the schemes devised by sociologists, whether Comtian, Marxist, or Weberian. Today, the residues of the past are visible and important, but they are far more salient in the realm of state-society relations than in society itself (except for business-worker relations). Today, France is a special instance of the general case: modern industrial society. France is becoming at the same time a "classical" and an "advanced" industrial society.[8] (Whether there is as sharp a break between the two types, as some theorists have suggested, will not be discussed here. It is enough to say that in the advanced, ownership matters less than managerial skills and economic less than intellectual capital, the tertiary sectors expand, and previously sharp separations between functions, activities, and roles fade away.)

This does not mean that what makes France distinctive—the weight of her preindustrial past and of traditional patterns of behavior toward authority and conflicts—must fade away. But it means that many of the problems France faces, which some of the French tend to blame on the idiosyncrasies of French traditions, habits, and style, are problems that plague other societies as well. At a time when the French are protesting strongly about inequality, American writers, disillusioned by the failure of the promise of liberalism, explain that a good measure of inequality is inevitable and fine (at least as long as it can be justified by the requirements of meritocracy), while others try to find new ways to decapitate the ever-growing hydra of injustice.[9] Nor is the problem of participation unknown in the United States, a country where the electorate stays at home on Election Day in amazing numbers, whose faith in Federalism—old or new, sincere or tactical—cannot substitute for the states' and cities' inadequate resources, and whose rock-bottom minorities (the very poor, the migrants, blacks or Indians or Mexicans: they overlap) do not feel fully included in the political system, nor provided with effective power or rights just because they have the vote. Nor is the classical mode of representation anywhere able to insure either an adequate participation of the representatives in a process of decision dominated by the executive and its experts, or a sufficient supervision by the representatives of the way in which decisions are enforced.

But it is the French case that concerns us here. The study of French growth mentioned above confirms the analysis which my Harvard colleagues and I presented in *In Search of France* about a dozen years ago. "New men and new attitudes" account for the changes in society. They released a pent-up potential for growth which had been thwarted in the 1930s and in the war years. From below, the pent-up demand for more goods and better housing and services served as one motor of expansion. From the top, a few groups of men in the bureaucracy and in the nationalized enterprises provided guidance, institutions, information, and public financing. In between, organized interests served as relays for modernization, higher productivity, new methods of production and distribution. The study points out that the emancipation of France from the stalemate society was made easier by some of that society's own chief assets, once they were turned in a new direction. The high value it placed on hard work resulted in an impressive number of work-hours per week; the thirst for instruction meant the labor force was well educated. Another asset was the centralized state bureaucracy. But here we come back to our theme: the different meanings of centralization. What changed French society most was a completely new recourse to, and considerable extension of, a pre-existing machinery, as well as the society's old habit of dependence on the state. When the watchdog became a greyhound, those who had been holding the leash had to learn to run.

Let us review our earlier questions. What are the functions of the state? Today, to the earlier ones, we must add: nothing less than the transformation of society. Industrialization, the reconversion of a dwindling agricultural sector, the social-security system and policy of "social transfers," a policy of regional balance (*aménagement du territoire*), urbanization, the development of a modern network of communications and telecommunications—these are all undertaken either under state guidance or by state agencies. There is, to be sure, a link between the old *colbertisme* and the modern French state. But what a difference there is between state participation in developing commercial and manufacturing activities when economic development was a side issue, and a state where economic growth is *the* collective goal!

What are the instruments of the state for these new functions? What are their effects on the state itself? These questions were of no great importance earlier. In the Third Republic, the machinery of the state, whose features have been analyzed in depth by Michel Crozier and synthesized at length in this volume, had instruments adequate to its limited tasks. (In public education, centralization, stratification, and the independence of each stratum insured technical excellence, the diffusion of Republican ideology, and the security of the teachers—as long as the whole system fitted a society that was geared to individual mobility, respectful of class distinctions, and neither deeply divided nor confused about the social functions of education.) But today these questions are essential, and Crozier and his collaborators have examined them in detail.

What are the instruments of state used to fulfill the state's new functions? Beyond the bewildering variety of institutions, agencies, public enterprises, and acronyms, the answer is simple: on the whole, they are patterned after the old ones, and very often they are the old ones. A splendid case study [10] shows how one of the *grands corps*—the engineers of the Ponts et Chaussées—established by the *ancien régime* and, for a century and a half, organized as little more than a federation of local services living in "tight complicity" with the local (mainly rural) communities they served, has in a few years been completely reorganized according to all the canons of the "Crozier model," in order to take over urban development. We need more such case studies—for instance, of the nationalized enterprises. But what we know, say, of the French telephone system, or of public television and radio, or of the social-security system allows for this generalization: the new functions are mainly being performed according to an old model that tends to "reproduce" itself automatically.

What is the effect of the new and old functions and tools on the state itself? There is a sharp contradiction between the logic of the French bureaucracy, and the nature of many of the new functions or the new conditions in which social change forces older functions to be performed. The old logic was to proceed by uniform, impersonal rules in areas where the state had a monopoly of means, or at least privileged advantages. Administrations had clearly delimited jurisdictions, a high degree of vertical integration, and walls separating one from another; the rights and obligations of personnel were rigidly defined and stratified along "caste" lines. This was the logic which Saint-Simon denounced as wasteful; as he saw it, it was appropriate for a society of landed property-owners and *hommes de loi;* as many of his disciples discovered, it also worked for a society of engineers proud of technical prowess. But it does not fit a state in search of profitable industrial development, whose mode must be selective objectives, diversified programs, and comprehensive plans; not minimal regulations or technical achievements, but collective mobilization and harmonization. This kind of state needs managerial talents. It requires the capacity to combine activities in different milieux and to make fundamental reorganizations. For instance, the state must not only introduce new methods and disciplines in public instruction, but also adapt education to the needs and demands of the economy, and to a society that offers students other means of information and sources of knowledge.[11]

How the French state has reacted to this contradiction is far from simple. One response might be called adaptive reinforcement. If urban planning, for instance, or industrial policy is hampered by the tendency of each ministry or service to prepare its own projections and pursue its own concerns, a solution is found in increasing the powers of "horizontal" administrations that play the role of mediators and arbiters at the top of the bureaucratic pyramid. This is the role of the Ministry of Finance and of the top *grands corps*. While this solution reduces the disadvantages of vertical splintering, it increases the horizontal stratification and, as regards the *grands corps,* increases the weight of centralization.[12]

A second reaction might be called adaptive change. When the new state functions are in areas where the civil service enjoys no monopoly of expertise and must either enlist the cooperation of private entrepreneurs or compete with them, the state has sometimes modified the old model, so as to approach the logic of economic rationality more closely. Often this only occurred after a long process of trial and error, a *dirigiste* phase leading to intolerable snags or expenses (such as the dead end of the purely French program of nuclear energy and the hapless Concorde). But these changes *have* affected the nationalized enterprises in recent years, once the recommendations of the Nora report of 1967 were put into partial effect by the Chaban-Delmas cabinet. It has meant greater autonomy, as well as risk, for these enterprises.

The third response is the worst one. When the bureaucracy has a monopoly, and conditions are such that horizontal action on top cannot remedy the situation, internal *blocage* may reach disastrous proportions. One example is that of telecommunications—with fragmentation into disparate networks, and a glaring incompatibility between what ought to be industrial management and what remains the bureaucrats' code (*statut*) concerning the rights and duties of the white-collar personnel. Another example, both sad and comic, is that of the ORTF, with its factions, fads, apparently unshakable routine, and inert opposition to reform. Here, any autonomy would be resisted by both the personnel and the government. A third (and worst) example is that of secondary and university education. Centralization, in the sense of reinforcing the services of the Ministry of Education as against the teachers, would of course be the opposite of a solution, even if it were politically conceivable, for what the *lycées* and universities need is freedom to experiment. Instead of this, a recent commission has found a pattern as depressing as it is familiar: the attempt to give "unchanged schooling to a radically different public" has made "the institution unable to take charge . . . through a real strategy of innovation, of the changes forced upon its members." The institution has responded to the new challenge in the old way: multiplying new categories of personnel, new curricular labyrinths and barriers, which thwart innovation and perpetuate "the separation of disciplines, the limited initiative of schools, the absence of cooperation among teachers, their predominant individualism and resulting isolation." And, the report goes on, while all of this may have fitted the old, obsolete conception—"the transmission, by a prestigious master, of an unchallenged culture to students who recognize the culture as valid and the master as its distributor"—social changes have turned the old "cultural priesthood" into "a more humble and operational task: a response to the students' needs." [13]

The French state was able to adapt or modify the old model when it had a relatively clear yardstick—economic development, the basis of what I have called, in an earlier chapter, France's consensus by default —and when change was not opposed by its personnel, as has been the case in education, where no consensus on new ends and means exists. But all three of these responses have one result in common: a malaise within the civil service between the upper echelons and the middle and lower ones. If centralization means (among other things) the dissociation of decision from execution, then the personnel that merely executes is squeezed between superiors whose role is no longer merely to lay down impersonal rules (which the lower strata can interpret in order to apply them) but to plan the future, and a public that is in far greater contact with the bureaucracy and expects not distance but service, not routine but efficiency. Urbanization and the extension of the state's activities have tarnished the old prestige of the *fonctionnaire,* once a minor king in the village or the small town. He still has the security provided by the code—a frequent cause of *blocage.* But, in a society that has begun to value the roads to wealth, the old careers, in which prestige, security, and some functional leeway compensated for mediocrity of earnings and slow promotions, no longer seem so attractive.

The answer to the question of the effect of the new functions on the state is somewhat more complex than that which critics of the French bureaucratic model often give. But, on the whole, it is fair to suggest that while the state has incited French society to change, French society has only rarely forced the state to change, and pressures for change internal to the state have been almost nonexistent.

I must now return to some of the questions I asked earlier: how are decisions made? How are they applied? It has become difficult to separate these two questions precisely because of the change in state functions—i.e., because of the preponderance of programs over rules —and also because of the constitutional innovations of 1958, which restrict the traditional domain of the law and the role of Parliament. The executive has the power to make regulations outside the domain reserved to the law and, with Parliament's consent, ordinances *within*. Even when the rule-making power is in the hands of the legislators (as in the case of education), they often can do no more and no better than enact a *loi-cadre,* which leaves all detailed measures to the executive. The bills voted by Parliament are themselves almost always of executive origin. Even in the Fourth Republic, when the state had already begun to expand, the sovereignty of the legislature, buttressed by its committees' actual control of the legislative process and by the National Assembly's mastery of the agenda, preserved the formal separation between rule-making and rule-enforcement. There is now a continuum of administrative decisions, and the greatest difference between it and the processes of the "Republican synthesis" lies in the crisis of representative legitimacy. Yesterday, rule-making was democratic and rule-enforcement was shared with the nation's representatives at various levels. Today, only the façade of the old processes remains, and a new reality of quite a different sort emerges; it is here that we find the biggest leap in centralization.

Take the case of the ministers, who used to be, in rule-enforcement, watchdogs for the public. Today, they serve in cabinets whose composition and life depend primarily on the President of the Republic, and whose relation to Parliament is exactly the opposite of what it used to be—in the sense that the executive is able to force the Assembly to vote for budgets and bills prepared in the ministries, instead of the Assembly being able to harass and coerce the cabinet. The ministers— many of whom were trained as civil servants—tend to see themselves more as technicians doing a job than as politicians supervising an essentially static bureaucracy. It is striking that the wave of scandals in 1972, which threw the bodies of various deputies ashore, did not reveal any minister drowned in corruption. Indeed, it showed the ministers fending off demands from parliamentarians. In past regimes, ministers saw to it that Parliament's laws were carried out by the civil service; the bureaucrats' weapon against them was obstruction.[14] In the Fifth Republic, functional and constitutional factors give the bureaucracy the power of initiative, and tend to make the minister the man who chooses among, and legitimizes, the bureaucracy's schemes, and who sometimes reconciles them with political necessities (or realities). When the ministers are themselves elected representatives— which has not always been the case, especially in the early years of the regime—and when they have the confidence of Parliament, their role is one of democratic participation, but it is more tenuous than in the parliamentary regimes.

Take the case of the deputies—who used to play a national role in rule-making, as well as a national and local role in rule-enforcement. I have already mentioned the decline of their rule-making power for technical and constitutional reasons. But there is another reason for this decline: the existence of a reasonably coherent majority coalition which, even though it has the constitutional power to overthrow the cabinet, actually has an interest in supporting it and in avoiding a dissolution of the Assembly. To be sure, the importance of the deputies in law-making increases when the majority is narrow, and when the Gaullist party alone does not have an absolute majority. But in 1967, when the Gaullists and their allies obtained a majority of only a handful of votes, the regime resorted to ordinances instead of laws, and so long as the allies of the Gaullists have no alternative other than a coalition with them, their own contribution cannot amount to much. The smaller the law-making role of the deputies, the greater their inclination to intervene in enforcement on behalf of their constituents. But when intervention is no longer closely tied to the very persuasive power of ultimate rule-making, and to the power of making and unmaking cabinets, it is far less effective.

The top civil servants regard the deputies as spokesmen for fractional interests only. The remarkably high proportion of former bureaucrats in the new National Assembly of 1973—almost one third—indicates that the change in the political regime of the Fifth Republic has affected not only the power but the composition of the old political class. The agents of the state at the regional or departmental level can fend off the deputies' interventions far more than they could before. Indeed, the transfer of state power from the central services to the ones at the level of the *départements* (deconcentration) allows the ministers to deflect the pressures from their parliamentary colleagues to levels where career civil servants can politely resist. Yesterday, as agents of the executive, these were essentially servants of a general interest defined by Parliament and in a subtle way they depended on the legislators, who were often powerful enough not merely to bring down cabinets, but to bring rewards to friendly bureaucrats. Today, the hierarchy of command has been reversed.

Of course, legislators everywhere are affected by changes in the functions of the state, and in parliamentary systems with stable majorities the dominance of the executive is a general phenomenon. But the Fifth Republic combines features of both cabinet and Presidential systems, and it does so at the representatives' expense. In a parliamentary regime, the dominating executive is an emanation from the majority's parliamentary group. In the French case, it emanates from the President: its power comes from above, confidence only from below.

Take, finally, the traditional local *notables:* the political ones, elected by the citizenry directly or indirectly, and the functional figures, who, while beyond the pale of *formal* legitimacy conferred by political election, belong to publicly recognized institutions such as chambers of commerce or agriculture. The network of *notables* still exists—only its meaning is gone. What gave them their bargaining power was their representativity: this was real, not formal, and they did indeed express the concerns of a largely rural or small-town society. The balance of complicity and mutual dependence between the *préfets* and the *notables*—the old game in which a *préfet* vindicated the *notables* in the eyes of their public by "interpreting" the rule, and the *notables* strengthened the *préfet* vis-à-vis his superiors by applying it—has been destroyed. To obtain from the *préfet* adaptive changes in national plans decided by complex bureaucracies in Paris would in any case be more difficult than to negotiate derogations from or adjustments of impersonal rules. But insofar as decisions and programs continue to be made at the local level of the bureaucracy, the activities carried out locally demand other *interlocuteurs* than a self-perpetuating caste of local elites whose districts were drawn ages ago, who do not represent the new urban and industrial occupations, and who do not properly reflect the alignments of local political forces in nationwide elections. Yesterday, in various parts of France, the political *notables* were strongholds of the opposition to the regime, and gained a certain influence through the local bargaining processes. Today, these shelters have become ghettos. There is, to be sure, a residual use for the old game in the remaining rural parts of France, and if a deputy also happens to be a local *notable,* the combination restores some of his power. Yesterday, each one sufficed, since a kind of sovereignty was conferred by election; today, each one is insufficient in itself, but their addition gives its beneficiary some influence over the real exerter of sovereignty—the minister in Paris or his local agent. But this too is a small residue. The change from the past is symbolized by the reversal of old career patterns: yesterday, the local *notable* used his position to become a deputy, then a minister; today, among the Gaullists, civil servants become parliamentarians or ministers, then seek local office.[15] The efficiency of the old *notables* is further limited by the ways local budgets are drawn up: many expenditures are compulsory, and others are at the charge of the national government—which also provides a growing amount of the local districts' resources.[16]

In one case, the local *notables'* representativity has not declined—indeed, perhaps the reverse. I am speaking of the mayors of large or growing cities. But there are two enormous differences now. The mayors' *interlocuteurs* tend to be, not the *préfets*, but the administration in Paris—sometimes the ministers or the President himself: partly because of the nature of the problems, which are nationwide (industrial or housing policy), partly because the technical administrations functioning at the local level have preferred to reinforce the authority of the distant central services to that of the *préfet*, partly because of the development of horizontal coordination at the center. Urban issues tend to become national problems. Moreover, yesterday's delicate game was not only about equilibrium, it was also about legitimacy: the administrative and the *notable* systems confirmed each other. Today, should the mayors demand adjustments of decisions or changes of plans deemed unreasonable by the administration, its monopoly of technical expertise, control of funds, power of rewarding cooperation are such that the mayors' choice is quite often—for instance in the matter of creating new towns—between grudging acquiescence, and being pushed aside. (In the case of the new towns, there is another imbalance: the complex new legal units established under recent laws, while endowed with most of the powers of the component *communes*, end up being run at least temporarily by the *notables* who represent the components, and who therefore speak for the old rather than the new social order.)

Thus, the decline of the old network of representation and *notabilité* results partly from institutional and economic changes, partly from institutional obsolescence. And yet it is clear that the administration does not make and apply its decisions without some outside participation. Here we find, at last, some counterweights. In times past, they could all be called legitimate, either because they were part of the representative system or, in the case of the economic *notables*, because they expressed the interests of a society with a broad consensus on the defense of these interests and on the local institutions set up for their protection. Today's counterweights have no comparable legitimacy, because they all are the expressions of private interests. Now, a nation that has traditionally accepted the idea that only the state represents the general interest continues to look with suspicion on private groups. The "Republican synthesis" had organized checks and balances *within* the state. (Even the local economic interests were expressed in *Chambres* that had a partly public status.) Counterweights outside the state are seen as leading to either the "dismemberment" or the "colonization" of the state, i.e., they destroy the general interest.

What are these counterweights? First, they are far more central than they used to be: group consultation and bargaining take place mainly in Paris. Second, we should note that this centralized bargaining tends to erase the old sacrosanct barrier between public and private, which speeds the erosion of the old legitimate network: the mayors and other local *notables* have to bargain not only with agents of the state but also with the state's huge economic partners—industries, promoters—sometimes even with multinational firms, which they are simply not equipped to counterbalance. And the process now takes different forms, each one of which lacks legitimacy. The most visible is acknowledged bargaining, with labor unions or business associations or farmers' or shopkeepers' representatives. "Acknowledged" does not necessarily mean "open": while the convention signed in 1966 between the government and the steel industry indicated in general terms the commitments of the industry and those of the state, we know little about how the negotiations were handled and about the amount of state aid.[17] As in the old system, the partners are mutually dependent and, sometimes, complicitous. But while state planning, in its earlier phases, tried to put a cloak of legitimacy over the whole system of *concertation,* the gradual shrinking of the Plan has removed that cloak.[18] This process of bargaining is an inevitable, and often beneficial, part of France's political life, and the Chaban-Delmas and Pierre Messmer cabinets tried to give it a new brand of legitimacy in the guise of generalized "contracts" for everything from wages to urban development. But it is clear that the Left distrusts what it sees as a new symbiosis between business and government; the bargaining between state and labor, and usually between state and shopkeepers, remains antagonistic; and many of the representatives resent the extraparliamentary *concertation.*[19]

Far less visible is what might be called informal interpenetration. There is a quasi-symbiosis between, say, some of the "weaker" bureaus in the Ministry of Industry, and the branches or professional organizations with which they are in contact. Of course, this reminds one of the old local symbiosis between the civil servants and the activities under their supervision; here again, the state "internalizes" the interests it ought to control or guide, in exchange for which the interests accept state directives. But there are differences. The implications are not the same at the central level of a dynamic society as they are at the local level of a static one. Yesterday's interests were defended by acknowledged *notables,* today's *notables* do not have such public recognition and are often unknown. Another form of interpenetration—the messiest—consists in the complex bargaining that occurs between the multitude of services in charge of urban and regional development, and the army of eager, competitive, and greedy contractors and speculators. (Many of these last have obviously tried to use Gaullist parliamentarians as intermediaries, and have successfully exploited the loopholes, contradictions, and errors in the jungle of French rules and plans.) Another form is sometimes referred to as the "technostructure" —a Galbraithian term applied to a fluid group composed largely of members and ex-members of the *grands corps:* those who play some of the key coordinating, supervisory, and managerial roles in the state, and those who, having left the service of the state but not their school or rather caste ties, play comparable roles in private industry or banking: an elite within the interest groups, and a natural counterpart of the state elite. Because these kinds of interpenetration are secretive, we have no adequate case studies on the adoption and enforcement of most of the programs that are shaping France and that require cooperation between the state and private interests.

Finally, at the local level, particularly in cities, where the national services need local support to carry out development plans, the obsolescence or technical incompetence of the old functional *notables* often allows the administration to select its own correspondents, i.e., to choose among possible counterplayers. Since the natural tendency is to lean on supporters and to avoid politics—according to the conviction or myth that the state transcends political divisions and aims at the common good through "the best" technical means—this obviously becomes more a way of circumventing than of solving the problem of participation.[20]

France today is a society in flux, then, and it has not yet found a way of institutionalizing the extension of its state. One must distinguish between the general *political orientation* of the state and its *policy process,* what has been called, above, rule-making and rule enforcement. One can argue that the political orientation is more democratic in the Fifth Republic than in the two previous Republics. The election of the President by the people, his power to dissolve the Assembly and to resort to referendums, even the fact that the cabinet emanates from him rather than from the mysterious deals negotiated among the deputies—all this implies a clearer, more direct, perhaps also more continually used link between the electorate and the general direction of the state. But this does not tell us what the state plans and decisions will be; it tells us something about the scope of the state's functions— whether they will be extended or abridged or confirmed—and something about the spirit in which they will be carried out, but very little about the actual content of the measures that will be taken in the discharge of these functions. It is in this latter respect that relations between state and society have become unbalanced, less "participatory," less legitimate. In earlier periods, the representative regime—national as well as local—legitimized not only the bureaucracy (whose authority derived from the rules voted by Parliament and was confirmed by its subtle game with the local *notables*) but also the checks and balances exerted by the elected parliamentarians and *notables*. Today, the political system legitimizes mainly the bureaucracy, whose authority derives from the program established by an executive based on universal suffrage in both of its components (Presidency and cabinet). The legitimate representative network has only insufficient countervailing powers, and both formally constituted and informal interest groups, not to mention the hidden forces, are outside the political system. To paraphrase Pierre Grémion, the representative does not decide, the decision-maker is not representative. This is true in other democracies also, but it is a source of special malaise in the French polity, where the countervailing powers within the political system are weaker than elsewhere and where public recognition, i.e., the granting of formal rights and duties by the state, is a precondition for legitimacy.

The unfortunate reform bill of April 1969 was a flawed attempt to come to grips with the problem. It tried to write a new, regional role for elected political representatives, who would take part in the process of policy decision and enforcement, and to legitimize functional representation by giving delegates from interest groups seats both in regional assemblies and in the Senate. In one respect, this construction was worthless: the regional assemblies would have consisted of delegations from those very territorial and economic *notables* whose relevance to the problems of the present had vanished—although the bill tried to give to the political regional councillors a more urban basis than that of the present departmental ones. In another respect, the project was double-edged. Making a region's national deputies members of the regional assembly seemed like giving them a new and more effective local role, but it was also a way of insuring Gaullist control; what was a counterweight to the state from one angle appeared as a reinforcement from another. But the plan also proposed including in the Senate delegates selected by the national economic and social interest groups, and this was a daring attempt at dealing with the whole problem. The fact that this part of the plan became the focus of maximum opposition showed that the guardians of the old legitimacy were not prepared to accept a new one, and revealed a lack of consensus not so much about the political institutions of the regime, but about the new society itself. In the bill, the new Senate had only advisory powers; this suggested the drafters' own ambivalence about legitimizing new checks on the bureaucracy at the central level.

In France's limited state of yesteryear, representation provided both for government and for participation; it insured the right balance between state and society. Today, representation provides personnel and support for the government but does not insure proper participation;

the latter would require a new and different scheme of representation, which has not yet emerged—precisely because the right balance has not been agreed upon. The old state, because its functions were limited, exercised a control over French society exactly adjusted to its functions. A quiet town can be "covered" by a handful of *gendarmes,* well informed by influential citizens, whereas even an army of policemen cannot control a turbulent city in which the old influentials have lost their authority and the new ones, being controversial, may be ill-informed or contribute to the disruptions. In present-day France, the old stable relationship between the bureaucracy's limited capacity for collective action and the equally limited one of the *notables* is broken, and a state with a hugely increased capacity is confronted with organized interests whose own capacities have multiplied; the meetings between them range from open collisions to obscure collusions. It is not surprising if the public feels, at times, that the state has become an unstoppable monster and, at times, that the state has lost grip over society and over interests that impose their will by force or funds or favors.[21]

III

What is the effect of the new state on France's changing society? Top civil servants and Jacobin politicians argue that the cacophony of private interests in a country which has no consensus on its social future or recognition for their legitimacy, means that the state continues to be the only agent of progress. Traditional dependence on the state and the "Malthusian" social attitudes prevalent for so long also make state initiative indispensable. (Michel Debré's memoirs are a kind of apotheosis of this view.[22]) Defenders of this attitude can point to the spectacular urbanization of France, with its proliferation of plans and *schémas;* to the expansion and rising productivity of French agriculture; to the modernization of much of French industry; to grand public and private undertakings, such as the building of the industrial complex of Fos and the transformation of the coast of Languedoc; to the collective agreements signed with unions in recent years, etc.—in general, to the state's proven capacity to mobilize resources and talents, to serve as a magnet and instigator. They show how the characteristics of the French civil service have been used to society's advantage. The habit of proceeding by universal rules has made a nationwide approach to growth possible, and the state's control of credit and taxation has allowed it to orient private activities; its symbiosis with local clienteles gave it a leverage on them; its monopoly of the general interest helped it pressure labor and business unions into negotiating and following public guidelines. But the critics of the Jacobin tradition, when they do not indulge in the demagogy that has become characteristic of Servan-Schreiber, point to a whole series of drawbacks.

The first has to do with the way in which the state twists, prevents, or delays change by the very style of its action and by the reproduction of its own patterns. The vertical integration of services that barely communicate with one another has resulted, for example, in an industrial policy of *ad hoc* interventions that were completely contradictory—support to laggards as well as to new technologies, to small as well as to big firms.[23] A concern for national prowess regardless of cost has led to the creation of monopolistic industrial "giants" whose internal cohesion is artificial and weak. The tendency of each government service to use expertise and information as a source of control has encouraged firms and interest groups to act in the same way. The goal of economic efficiency has been slowed down by the top bureaucrats' habit of relying on business leaders whom they know instead of gambling on newcomers. In return, even in a modern industry like electronics, entrepreneurs may choose a strategy of relying on state support, cartelization, and insulation from the market, instead of a strategy of internal reorganization and open competition.[24] The old "corporatist" solidarity of services with the groups under their *tutelle* has protected backward sectors—inefficient farmers or shopkeepers or artisans—that weigh on the budget and delay modernization. (There are, of course, also strictly political causes for these practices.) Fos, a source of pride to the Jacobins, is a prize example for their critics, who point out the bad coordination and forecasting by squabbling services, reluctant industrialists, and hostile *notables*.

More important perhaps is a second effect: the contribution of state action to insecurity and inequality. Our earlier analysis of homeorhesis has emphasized French sensitivity to both these matters. The traditional style of authority was a guarantee of security and a way of cushioning inequality. The endurance of this style is one of the proofs of a continuing and widespread desire to combine growth with, and achieve welfare through, the defense of *droits acquis,* the avoidance of competition, and the limitation of risks.[25] In the days of the Republican synthesis, social groups on the whole had limited expectations—except the workers, whose dream of collective ascent was millennial. Security and the hope of individual ascent in society made inequality bearable. Today, social groups expect collective ascent. But insecurity and the frustrations that such expectations meet make inequality far less tolerable. The insecurity that inevitably accompanies rapid economic and social change breeds a fear of being shut out of the collective elevator. Hence the *lycéens'* and university students' phobia about restricted admissions and about anything else—from the abolition of military deferments to the creation of new curricular labyrinths—that might be interpreted as an oblique way of making opportunities more unequal. Hence also the unskilled workers' determination to destroy their status label, which exposes them to precarious conditions of employment and living and makes them pariahs. A rising tide makes some sailors fearful of being submerged.

Moreover, even though the tide lifts all the ships, the bigger ones still tower over the small ones. Individual ascent from a stable basis meant there was always a possibility of rare but spectacular breakthroughs into the top castes, through hard work plus savings or intellectual capital. Many Frenchmen believed that if not they, at least their sons, could make it into the elite. Castes were acceptable, indeed desirable, as expressions of vested, or wrested, rights. Today, the hope for collective ascent encourages an expectation of a collective breakthrough to the top, yet the only results are an improvement in the lot of all strata of society, rather than greater mobility. And so, the elite, once an object of admiration and hope, is now an object of envy and frustration.

This resentment is made worse by France's new mass education. Its competitiveness and uncertainties breed insecurity, rewarded by access not to the top, but to levels of employment (and security) that had required no such hardships in the past. As in inflation, it costs more to get the same. At the same time, the supply of coveted goods is small, since the elite castes have barely been enlarged while the demand has increased—both because of the aspirations fed by mass education, and because the enlarged role of the state makes its top functions more magnetic.[26] Even though, in recent years, equality of opportunity has actually increased in the school system, this "democratization" does not lead to equality of results. Ascent to the top remains exceptional and is more of an ordeal than it was. Moreover, the devaluation of school degrees—which mass education produces just as inflation devalues the currency—gives better chances for access to the elite to the already privileged sons of *grands bourgeois,* who have inherited assets that offset the devaluation; and this offsets the gain in equality of opportunity. At a time when the transformation of society in advanced industrial countries tends to erode old class barriers and replace them with status differences and symbolic discriminations, the stratification characteristic of the French style of authority perpetuates class barriers. Here, as in other aspects of French society, institutions that in a different context played a positive role now tend to have a negative influence. Yesterday's advance is today's privilege. In the earlier class society, for instance, the rigid "strata" of the civil service offered a double escape from class: each level contained persons from different class origins; and even insofar as class differences persisted between strata, the "bureaucratic phenomenon" (prevalent in industry as well) tended to transform a hierarchy of social classes into a functional hierarchy. Moreover, each stratum used to be highly valued for the security it provided. This is still the case—but the double price that has to be paid, in the miseries of mass education that must first be endured, and the likelihood that promotions will never take one beyond the caste, creates resentment. Until now, the craving for security—perhaps even heightened by the insecurity and anguish experienced in school and at the university—is still the stronger. Will this be the case forever?

Finally, the tide does not raise equally all those ships that do not sink. We do not know much about the full scope of inequality in France, but we know that wage differentials are enormous. French top executives are among the best paid, French workers at the bottom—not to mention immigrants—are assuredly not. More than one third of them earn less than 1200 francs per month, more than one third of the top executives earn more than 6000; average hourly wages are below those in Germany and Italy. France is, among the original six nations of the Common Market, the country which assigns the smallest share of its national income to remuneration of wage earners, and where the undistributed income of corporations is highest.[27] We know that the spectacular contraction of the population active in agriculture has left 400,000 holdings of less than 5 hectares at one end, 25,000 of more than 100 at the other, with 15 per cent of the farmers receiving more than half of the agricultural income.[28] We know that the contrast between traditional shops and modern supermarkets is growing, and that while the number of workers and employees has risen in most industries, there has been very little concentration among the smaller ones; in 1966, those which employed fewer than a hundred wage earners still accounted for 37 per cent of the active population in industry, versus 37 per cent in 1926. We know about growing regional disparities. While some of these inequalities are old, many are due to the unevenness of postwar expansion and not just to old historical cataclysms or the slow sedimentation of a stable society.

It would be, of course, unfair to blame the bureaucracy for all the insecurity and inequality that accompany accelerated economic change in France. But the state not only controls the levers of change but also proclaims modernization as its goal; the citizens of a country that used to seek security in economic stability tend therefore to say the state is at fault when the escalation of change leads to insecurity, and when, far from preserving the existing hierarchy of ranks and statuses while lowering the barriers between them, change results in massive upheavals and in higher barriers (as at the end of the eighteenth century). It cannot be denied that the Fifth Republic has tried valiantly to combine expansion with security for as many groups as possible, and has done so with measures to improve equality of opportunities. But these measures suffer from a double handicap against them: a highly unequal base at the start, and the almost insoluble nature of the problem in the first place. The statutes protecting civil servants, the efforts made on behalf of professional retraining, a sprinkling of measures to help reconversion or ease the departure of peasants and shopkeepers from their jobs, a rain of subsidies to farmers or industrialists, the encouragement to monopolistic "national champions," the constant tinkering with the social insurance systems—all of this shows the regime's care not merely for its electoral base but also for a basic demand from the whole public. But by definition total security is unachievable in a dynamic society, and the losers who compare their fate with the winners blame the state for not helping them enough, instead of praising it for having tried. Moreover, in attempting to provide French students with security by giving them free access to secondary and higher education and national diplomas endowed with equal value, the state has in fact contributed to their insecurity, since the lack of equality in results is far more glaring in a uniform system than in a diversified one, while nonrestricted admissions are offset by the terror of exams and the fear of compulsory assignment to a discipline or school.

The state has also failed to take measures that would have decreased inequality in results, and taken others that have actually made it worse. Here, we find a mélange of economic choice and political calculation. For fifteen years, the development of France as an industrial society has been in the hands of technicians supported by a modern yet conservative coalition. If the majority had been "progressive," would there have been the same accord, or symbiosis, between technocrats and politicians? Would the politicians have thwarted effective growth? We do not know. But we know that the Fifth Republic chose to give priority to collective power (in de Gaulle's version) and aggregate growth (in Pompidou's, which overlapped with de Gaulle for six years), over any set of measures that might have produced more equality but slowed down growth, or might have diverted public funds from power- and production-oriented activities. Lower taxes have always been preferred to higher social investment; private investments and savings have been encouraged; even when taxes had to be raised, as in the fall of 1968, the burden was carried by the consumers but lightened on business. Now, while increasing prosperity has allowed ever more consumers to buy more goods—and thus achieve collective improvement—state policy has resulted in a scarcity of public goods. This is particularly burdensome for those who need them most: the poor, the old, the very young, the handicapped. Public housing is insufficient, urban public transportation is deficient, and while schools have been built in huge quantities, the same cannot be said of hospitals or old-age homes.

The regime has refrained, on the whole, from "structural reforms" that might allow conditions and incomes to become more equal. The formula (in the political sense) of Pompidou's rule has been to modernize France while respecting not only traditional values—order, work, authority, respect for the family, "moderation"—but also what François Bourricaud calls the primary institutions of France: private property, the *grands corps,* the *lycées* and universities, the territorial districts dating from Napoleon.[29] With only slow and limited procedures for communal *regroupements,* France is still dotted with *communes* that are too small to join in the race for expansion or to resist the onslaught of promoters and state experts. A number of state agencies are supposed to help the *regroupement* of small-farm land, but they lack legal and financial means to buy enough land at a time of rising prices and intense speculation. French agriculture is still organized with excessively small average lots, overproduces some goods and underproduces others, and has low productivity at the bottom. The failure to tax adequately profits on real-estate booms also contributes to a glaring contrast between often shabby public housing and luxury residential districts.

The state has also worsened inequality by deliberate strategies aimed either at accelerating growth or at appeasing the regime's supporters. A policy of subsidies to farmers and businesses that has often helped the fat get fatter is pursued on technical and political grounds. The tax and social-security systems do little to offset inequality in incomes. More than 60 per cent of the state's revenue comes from indirect taxes, which hit the poor hardest; the income tax is riddled with exceptions, deductions, and reductions that leave 45 per cent of the French untaxed (and 77 per cent of agricultural income). Recent legislation aims at applying the same rates and regulations to those whose income is withheld and to non-wage earners (who still manage to conceal from three fifths to three fourths of their real income). Inheritance taxes are insufficiently progressive; shareholders are excessively favored. Taxation is heavier on those low-income families that family allowances try to help, than on others. The financing of the social-security system is actually regressive, and the ratio of expenditures for social security to GNP is below that of the other five original Common Market countries.[30] A prehistoric system of local taxation results in a terrible inequality in fiscal pressure: it is highest in the poorest communes. Even the measures taken by the state to remedy this situation have tended to perpetuate it, given the absence of structural reform. More doles to small shopkeepers, at the taxpayers' or supermarkets' expense (under the pretext that competition has to be made "fair"); more tax advantages for artisans and small enterprises; more piecemeal aid to backward or declining areas, too unsystematic to allow for a take-off or to reverse a fall; even the overdue measures to raise bottom wages, or the choice of a rate of industrial growth that will not accelerate the flight from the countryside: all these measures divert resources from structural reform and serve to humanize poverty rather than attack the roots of inequality. Also, given the tax system, they weigh more heavily on the poor than the rich—although, in this instance, it means that the poorer farmers, shopkeepers, etc., are largely subsidized by the workers.

The last form of inequality which the state has promoted is inequality in participation. In the present vacuum of legitimacy that mars the relations between the bureaucracy and the *administrés*, they cannot help but feel that only *les gros* have access to power. *Les gros* are the ones who benefit from what I have called secretive interpenetration. In the case of visible bargaining with the state, leaders of business, farm, or shopkeepers' associations tend to represent the prosperous and established. Labor-union leaders tend to emphasize the problems of the industrial sector rather than those of the plant or workshop, where the issues concern basic dignities, better working conditions, *and* participation—characteristics of a society pressing for a share in decisions that actually shape daily lives.[31] Of course, there have always been unorganized citizens, particularly among the young and underprivileged, or the immigrants and nonunionized *petits*. But their numbers have grown, and their plight has worsened in a society where collective actions and demands prevail, where urban sprawl breeds both deviant behavior and social segregation by districts, and where the natural protector of those whom Alain called *les négligents*, the deputy or the *notable*, has lost influence. These unorganized forces—*isolés* or, in the case of the students or immigrant workers, masses—are much more dependent on public goods than in the past, when these were rare and less controlled by the state. Such dependence ought to incite these forces to organize. But the fact that they benefit from public goods whether they organize or not is not conducive to action.[32] And yet the less they do, the more unequal is the various social groups' participation, and also their share of the goods.

It is not surprising that French society's reaction to the titanic activities of the state are highly ambivalent. Wastes, delays, and *blocages*, inequality and insecurity on one hand, considerable economic growth, a rise in living standards, and residual pride in being among the most advanced (or at least a sense of security from external threats) on the other hand—these are the considerations that influence the citizens' behavior. It is exemplary in its very ambivalence. In two Presidential Elections, all but one referendum, and five legislative elections, the French have supported the regime and legitimized its activities. Never was that support higher than . . . in June 1968! Yet there is no legitimate countervailing system; hence group-bargaining is frequently chaotic, and tidal waves of protests occur. The causes for this have been discussed too often in this book to be described again. But the manifestations deserve some comment.

One reason why collective bargaining with the state must so often be clandestine, or why it becomes confrontation, is that the gap is so large between base and top, between small members and big organizers. The top does not want to wholly alienate the former, so they must either act behind the scene when they can, or—when they cannot, or refuse to, act as "accomplices" of the state—they must drive a hard bargain, protect their autonomy, and reject anything that smacks of "integration." While theoretically a functional integration of interest groups of the kind de Gaulle had conceived of might help to legitimize the system as a whole, it would de-legitimize its functional components in the eyes of their members. Moreover, the more clandestine or friendly bargaining there is between the *patronat* and the state, the more intransigent the unions.

The explosions of protest are usually either deliberate manipulations of crisis by organized interests, or anomic manifestations of impotent discontent by the unorganized. Often, they occur when the former make hurried and harried decisions aimed at avoiding their being left behind and outbid by the latter. Alain called French protests of his time a manifestation of *le citoyen contre les pouvoirs,* and this description referred to a then prevalent attitude of individual distrust of the elites, whose mischief each citizen hoped Parliament could mitigate; this suspiciousness did not paralyze the limited French state or the dispersed French economy. The same formula today describes actual breakdowns, recurrent acts of violence, and massive disobedience by collective forces who consider Parliament hopeless and who aim to challenge a powerful state. While such bizarre offspring of Sorel's general strike may be analyzed as inherent to the French style of authority —as I have done in other chapters—there is a difference in degree and in meaning. Take the case of the university students in 1968 and 1973, of the *lycée* students in 1973. The *proximate* mechanism can be described as a protest against police repression or against specific laws, a kind of *chahut*. But one is dealing here with a *mass* phenomenon. The old *chahut* was a protest inspired by a widely accepted view of how superior authority should behave—indeed, it amounted to a demand that the challenged superior conform to the view. The new *chahut* is a declaration of total nonconfidence in the challenged institution itself, rather than in any individual teacher. As the commission on secondary schools put it: yesterday there was a model, today there is none. The same is true of the *lycéens'* protest against the *Loi Debré:* beyond their attack on the end of military deferments, the *lycéens* were denying the value of universal military service—one of the key institutions of Old France. Shopkeepers' revolts like those of Poujade or Nicoud appear different, for their enraged followers seem to have had in mind the archetype of Old France; the *lycéens* and university students denounce the irrelevance of the old model in a realm where it has been most faithfully and impractically preserved. Yet even the *petits* who block roads or besiege tax collectors know that *papa*'s France, like *papa*'s Algeria, is dead. It is the absence of any other workable model that makes *chahut* not only universal but permanent.

In the days of the Third Republic, the consensus on the stalemate society and the limited state made a single question—how should this society be governed?—the focus of all ideological differences and class fears; for the organization of political institutions, the way in which leaders would be selected, would determine the balance of benefits within French society. Today, there is an apparent consensus on how the nation should be governed and its national political personnel selected, but the issue is of far smaller significance, and amounts to little more than a legitimization of democratically based efficiency. The important question—for what goals should this institutional system work? —remains unanswered. To be sure, the French agree on one point: economic growth is a necessary purpose. Almost nobody, except a minority of intellectuals and *gauchiste* students, challenges this goal. But the expansion of goods and services and better living conditions are intermediate goals, or rather means to ends, and there is no common vision of these. One might argue that modern industrial society by the very nature of its dynamism is not susceptible to the same degree of conceptualization as the more stable societies of the past—hence the decline or irrelevance of old ideologies. But this is only partially true, for the indefiniteness of modern society can be reduced and shaped.

When we come to the point of defining a coherent set of ends, we find contradiction, ambivalence, and division. To each group, the way in which modernization is achieved matters as much as the objective itself, and yet the ways desired are neither compatible with one another nor compatible with the objective. It is not so much, as a recent study gloomily suggests, "that the themes which are at the origin of France's economic modernization are those of a small part of the population, the *patronat* and the high civil service." [33] It is rather that each group wants modernization: 1) in the "homeorhetic" way, 2) with better living conditions and more public goods, and 3) with easier access to positions of responsibility and a greater sense of participation. These are irreconcilable, if sometimes "nonnegotiable," demands. The same study is therefore right in indicating that much of business insists on keeping its protected markets, that the minor civil servants are disoriented by the evolution toward a system that requires initiative (concentrated on top) rather than regulation and *tutelle,* that the *cadres* feel left out of decisions, the *petits* threatened with extinction, the workers comparatively victimized, and the professions and intellectuals in danger of losing their monopoly of prestige in favor of production and commerce—activities they neither understand nor respect.[34]

A profound ambivalence marks the attitude of those who accept the material benefits of modernization but condemn the general "quality of life" in an advanced society. This ambivalence is particularly evident among French students. Their protest against a life of *métro, boulot, dodo* is not simply Rimbaud's complaint about the dailiness of life. Nor is it only an expression of frustration on the part of those who, having at last acceded to the temples of culture (in a society that values culture so highly that not even the Communists endorse the critique of the school system as "reproducing" a bourgeois model), discover that it affords them neither an escape from mediocrity nor the respect of others. Their ambivalence expresses a basic truth about French society, and the *ressentiment* of intellectuals who detest the displacement of prestige brings it out into the open (many insights owe their existence to resentment): the type of society that lives for growth alone leaves much to be desired.

The division that the French reveal on ends has to do with the subject of this chapter: the ideal articulation between state and society. The political organization of France's central institutions—the system of national representation and the relations between branches of government—no longer determines who benefits. This depends rather on the existence, nature, and location of all the counterweights to the modern state machine, and on the social ends to which its vast functions are put. As elections show, one half of the French seem satisfied with the present scope and uses of state functions, and are not deeply displeased *qua* citizens with the current system of counterweights (even if, *qua* members of specific groups, they often behave quite differently). But the other half appears unhappy about the kind of economic growth that celebrates the profit motive as its best fuel. They would like to expand the state's functions still more and use them to redistribute incomes and power more drastically, to control better and sharply restrict *les gros*. Some of them hope that the resulting increase in the weight of the state will somehow be counterbalanced either by a restoration of the representatives' role at different levels or by a measure of *autogestion* in state enterprises. Others—the Communists—are untroubled by the problem of counterweights, as befits those who want the state to master society. In neither camp is there a clear view of how the proper balance between state and society should be created.

To sum up: a consensus on economic progress is neither an agreement on common values nor an agreement on the structures and institutions of a new society. This may help to explain the new quantitative and qualitative dimension of protest. In the stalemate society, the proletarian minority that was out of the consensus was torn between two attitudes. One, inspired by the dream of a new, just society where productive work would be the supreme value and the workers the ruling class, was a total rejection of bourgeois values, of structures that left the proletariat out as a class and allowed in only individuals resigned to abandoning their class for individual ascent into the bourgeois order. The other attitude was resignation to a compromise with that society—just enough for gains in material conditions and dignity, even though the workers remained at the bottom of the ladder. This double bookkeeping was expressed in revolutionary ideology and reformist practices, in parties and unions sucked into the daily politics of French society, and in grand prefigurations of the vanishing Apocalypse, such as the strikes of the spring of 1936. Today, all groups of French society except those on the very top indulge at times in similarly schizophrenic behavior. Yet none has a vision comparable to the old working-class dream, fed by currents as different yet converging as Proudhon, Marx, or Jaurès. Nineteenth-century ideologies of the future look obsolete, while contemporary "applied Enlightenments" or "applied Socialisms" seem uninspiring or downright repugnant. So the moments of grand protest are marked less by ideological Messianism than by "grand refusals" and confusion. The absence of a consensus on the new, emerging France explains the same mix of pragmatic exploration of all available means of collective ascent within the existing, controversial social order, and moments of total *contestation,* the same oscillation between negotiating collective demands for improvements *in* society and delivering ultimata for a change *of* society. In an advanced nation where the old "independent" bourgeoisie is being replaced by salaried middle classes, where the peasants themselves are caught in the market relations of capitalism,[35] it is no surprise if the behavior of the workers should become a model for everyone. This may in turn explain why the old barrier between the "consensus groups" and the workers is eroding, and the fence between the Communists and other citizens is coming down.

But are we not, after many detours, back at the familiar model of French behavior? Yet it is now in such worsened condition that Crozier's thesis that it is "exhausted" seems wholly convincing. On top, rigid castes "reproduce" themselves in techniques for action and matrices of security; at the bottom, mass protest recurs and group-bargaining is made difficult by the groups' basic dissatisfaction, by the need not to alienate their own suspicious members, and by rigidities that centralization and stratification produce. Thus the state is often faced with forces than can cooperate neither with it nor with one another. Yet we have to remember that if this picture were the whole truth, the changes in French society could be explained only by assuming that the state is neither so indispensable nor so much a cause of paralysis as Crozier's analysis suggests.

IV

For many years, reformist sociologists (not to be confused with *réformateur* politicians) have advocated a *déblocage* of French society. This, they argue, should come through a deliberate bending of the rigidities of the administrative style: by opening and diluting the *grand corps,* experimenting (in education, urban development, new forms of agriculture), generalizing the contract method, giving increased autonomy for and diversifying the universities, promoting decentralization. Or it should come from the skillful use of breakdowns, the deliberate creation of crises of uncertainty that would oblige partners to establish new face-to-face relations. This is what Crozier refers to as institutional investment and institutional learning.[36]

These suggestions raise two different kinds of problems. The first has to do with society: is not the customary behavior of the French the major obstacle to any attempt at changing their behavior? The second has to do with the political system: what support does it provide for such reforms? Unfortunately, the advocates of reform are so convinced of its salutary effects that they tend to minimize one and to avoid the other.

I have discussed the vicious circles in customary French behavior elsewhere (see Chapter 6) and will not develop my arguments here again. In the absence of a social consensus, it may be easier to provoke crises than to exploit or end them; as Bourricaud remarks, there is only a delicate margin between Crozier's invitation "to break the traditional mechanisms" and *casser la barraque* (blowing up the joint). [37] Moreover if, as Jean-Claude Thoenig points out, the rigidities of castes and strata correspond to a widespread desire to avoid face-to-face conflicts, and to reduce political and social disputes to administrative ones, if the strata amount to "circuits of mutual avoidance," [38] their destruction or collapse would result in a rise in tensions within each and well-routinized conflicts between them. The absence of agreement on means of resolving these conflicts or on goals could easily lead either to the kind of chaos that only the state—once again—could clean up or lead to an actual increase in centralization. This latter eventuality had already occurred in the universities. The academic authorities have demanded that the Ministry of Education resolve the uncertainty and discord about the scope and substance of new zones of autonomy. It is all very well to advocate responsibility, but if one has correctly analyzed the old style of French authority relations as a deliberate flight from it, can one expect those on whom initiative is suddenly thrust to be overjoyed? It is all very well to advocate "participation" —for instance, that of all the factions, union representatives, and strata delegates in secondary education, in planning for its overhaul —but if their confusion and contradictory interests lead to complete deadlock or oblige the state to impose its own scheme after all, would not more harm than good have been done?

For France to draw the vaunted benefits from the "learning process" of the new institutions, they would have to be established first. But there is no sign of great enthusiasm on the part of those who would have to run them and devise their rules. Studies of the regional reform of 1964 [39] show how the attempt to establish, rather experimentally, new regional institutions strengthened the pre-existing departmental administrations, which felt threatened, and reinforced the center. The new bodies also made no dent on industrial and urban policies, which continued to be handled outside and above them. The growing role of the *grands corps* and of horizontal central administrations is an obstacle to decentralization, for they see in it—conveniently—both a loss of influence and a loss of effectiveness.[40] As for the citizens, they still seem to prefer to be "powerless rather than impotent." One notices this particularly in the behavior of municipal governments. They would rather have their accustomed if financially and geographically unmanageable domain than mergers that would involve a painful redistribution of roles. In the case of middle-size or large cities, their leaders often prefer the newer version of the old game—the prestige that comes from direct deals with the state, now the government itself—to the acquisition of greater powers that would expose them if they failed in their task, and whose enforcement might be too absorbing to allow the simultaneous pursuit of a career in Parliament or government.

The reformists reply that no real institutional devolution—i.e., one that would make it hard for those in charge to push decisions back to the center, and give them adequate resources in exchange—has really been tried. This is a good point, but it is only one more argument in an endless dialogue of the deaf. It is more important to examine new forms of behavior, or signs that show that the old ones are perhaps untenable, in areas we can already observe. In other words, where are the French getting ready for "institutional learning"?

There *are* new patterns of conduct. While the caste phenomenon is as tight as ever at the top of the bureaucracy and, as we have seen, reproduces itself all along the line, there is a contradiction between the rigidities of access and *statut*, the habits derived from the "circuits of avoidance" (such as the tendency to treat urban issues as purely technical ones, or the way information is retained by the lower strata), and the new role of initiation, promotion, negotiation, and orientation played by the *grands corps*. To be sure, they are not eager to share or lose their monopoly of expertise and coordination. But a less rigidly hierarchical *statut*, and less restrictions on entry, might actually help them do their new work more efficiently.

Outside the civil service, one finds profound—if not complete— changes of behavior. In institutions thoroughly independent of the state and untouched by the "bureaucratic phenomenon"—the family, the Church, which may serve, over time, as, respectively, a school and an agent for more responsible or "participatory" behavior—changes have occurred for a wealth of economic and intellectual reasons, in response to social transformations and transnational currents. As for institutions that rely in part on the state, but realize that it cannot provide them with an alibi for immobility, and that too much dependence could mean a loss of their traditional autonomy, the only alternative to extinction is self-help and adaptation. This has been characteristic of the *patronat* (despite its continuing reluctance toward competition), once it understood that the alternative in matters of modernization, management, and even labor relations was not merely mediocrity but decline, and now that borders were open in Europe. And it has also been characteristic of the major peasants' unions (despite serious tensions between them and spokesmen for the poorer farmers), once they understood that trying to keep a large fraction of France's active population on the farms would be detrimental to their own welfare, that the irreversible rural exodus and its endorsement by the government made the old policy of sole reliance on price supports alone untenable, and that the Common Market was a major opportunity. It has been less characteristic of the labor unions, whose conflicted relations with the state are still closer to the old authority patterns.

In other instances, the old pattern persists—but this is rapidly becoming suicidal. The best example can be found in secondary and higher education. Some protection against insecurity and conflicts may once have been afforded by the ridiculously complex stratification of personnel, the rigidity of their *statuts*, their attachment to a pedagogic concept that is obviously obsolete, the fragmentation of responsibility, their isolation from the outside world, their division into noncommunicating disciplines, their dependence on uniform directives. But the protection has collapsed: the teachers' and administrators' own sense of irrelevance is the worst of insecurities, and while they can all still unite against attempts at authoritarian change, the piecemeal way that adaptation to mass education has occurred and the automatic reproduction of unequal castes have provoked severe tensions among categories, whose juridical distance is made less tolerable by the similarity of the services they render.[41] In the case of the middle and lower ranking personnel in the ministries, a modicum of security and autonomy is still enjoyed, but the price they pay for their power to "muddle through alone" is a sense of being left out. (This is true, increasingly, of the cadres of private enterprise and bureaus.)

Few people are as badly equipped for "participation" as a nation whose traditional style is deliberately nonparticipatory. That style was tied to a specific economic and social order—preindustrial, later "French bourgeois"—and to a limited state, and both are dead. The new demand for participation, incoherent and inchoate as it may be, shows that the French feel the increasing irrelevance of their old style. The preceding shifts and strains indicate that certain kinds of "institutional investments" could exploit these changes and tensions (while carefully avoiding the creation of new, additional insecurity, insofar as it is possible). One would consist of pursuing the partly covert, partly acknowledged cooperation between the state and the farm and business unions. In the case of business, this could be done to encourage a greater acceptance of competition, a greater willingness to experiment with management reform and with more humane and decentralized methods of production—at a time when the revolt against the assembly line and the demand for some *autogestion* are growing. In the case of the farmers, cooperation ought to encourage new forms of collective production—cooperatives or shareholding companies, and the development of agricultural and food industries in the countryside; here, state guidance could overcome the residues of the old "corporatist" mentality.[42] In both instances, cooperation should also make a more coherent policy of regional balance possible, provoking a take-off in backward areas and a reconversion of the declining ones. With the labor unions a continuation of the contractual policy might begin to induce some changes in their behavior (although substantive policy changes would also be required on both sides).

Another type of institutional investment would be educational reform, along the lines recommended, for secondary schools, by the recent commission, whose suggestions could well be extended to a new, less misguided, gradual reform of higher education. These ought to be complemented by two imperatives: a clear limitation on the number of cases in which final decision is rolled upward from the teaching establishments to the Ministry of Education, and the abandonment of "national diplomas." The latter move would, in effect, create competition among various universities, and while this is anathema to most of the teachers and students, it would reduce psychological insecurity by introducing variety into the rat race, and legitimize the inevitable inequality of results.

A third kind of institutional change, connected to the last, would affect other parts of the state. The limited autonomy given to public enterprises could be expanded. In new areas of social and economic policy, autonomous offices or agencies in charge of urban or regional development, public housing, and telecommunications could exploit the new managerial roles played by top services. Broadening the *grands corps,* emphasizing training in management, and changing conditions of entry—which might mean an end of the monopoly of the *grandes écoles,* or at least an end to the rigid separation between them and the universities—could make the elite more flexible and adequate. If the elite becomes less of a closed *caste,* its customary "reproduction effect" might be beneficial throughout the civil service.

But there are caveats which must be observed. There would of course be resistance to change among those concerned—for the same reason which, in international relations, explains the unlikeliness of disarmament or world federation: the well-known hardships of the present, even when they are increasingly less under control (as is the case of French schoolteachers, or of states caught in "mad momentums" of arms races or overwhelmed by private capital onslaughts on their currencies), tend to seem less risky than the unknown problems a mutation would bring with it. In addition, those on top might fear that a change in conduct might mean a loss in power, and those below sometimes seem keener about acceding to the privileges monopolized on top than about abolishing them once and for all. Were these resistances overcome, the measures I have listed would still leave major issues unsettled. Among them, there is the problem of inequality and the issue of the unorganized. There is the problem of making the cadres participate formally in the management of enterprises and services; there is the dissatisfaction of the workers with conditions and authority relations in the plants, and with public housing and transportation. And there is the whole formidable issue of decentralization. This involves not only the grant of more powers to existing local governments but a drastic redesign of their limits, a reduction in the number of levels, a change in a system that gives to rural areas far greater representation than to the growing urban ones, and a willingness to pour some content into the empty new regions established in 1972.* Moreover, there is resistance both from the top bureaucracy and from

---

* A serious study of decentralization would have to ask about each unit of local government:

    1. What are its powers, functional and financial?

    2. What are its relations to the central government? In particular, does it have its own executive and technical staffs? Or is the executive appointed by the central government (the *préfets*) or submitted to a *tutelle* by the agents of the central government (which is the case of the mayors), and must it resort to the central government's experts (as is the case for urban development)?

    3. Are its agents elected? How? And on what basis?

the existing networks of *notables,* and there is no widespread popular demand from below. Tocqueville remains the best interpreter: in the absence of a tradition of local government, those who do not like the way the state deals with their areas prefer to change the policy of the state, i.e., the government, rather than the territorial distribution of powers.[43] Urban civic associations, the Groupes d'Action Municipale (GAM), have tried to transcend the traditional class and party divisions in their cities in order to short-circuit traditional *notables* and use whatever autonomy French law gives the *commune* (so as to prove, for instance, that urban planning need not be a state privilege). But their relative failure shows that in the absence of sufficient financial power and expertise, and as long as most mayors cling to the game of dependence on the state, the attempt to play a *new* game in the *old* structure is doomed. The fact that several GAM leaders—including the best known one, the mayor of Grenoble—have sought national political office, is an admission of defeat, or a recognition that the road to local reform runs through national politics.

A third caveat is that all these reforms—expanding new patterns of behavior or making changes or creating conditions for further changes of behavior in the areas that are still "blocked"—depend on a political will. It is not enough to demonstrate that a *déblocage* is possible, that a reduction of inequality and centralization is essential. One must also have a political force for carrying them out and making a better alternative available. Who will come out for institutional investment?

I must, here, return to the French political system, and evaluate its performance. In earlier chapters I have tried to show its own responsibility in the perpetuation of protest and in the events of 1968. The decline of Parliament has increased the distance between political leaders and the public. Presidential control of the cabinet has tightened under Pompidou, whose training into politics was as Premier, under a President who had "reserved domains" but left considerable freedom in other areas to those in charge. This has made the regime, paradoxically enough, even more "personal" than in the early days of the Fifth Republic. Yet in other respects some of its initial handicaps have been overcome. A decade ago, there was still enormous confusion in the party system. The logic of the Presidential election and the need for the President to have a majority in Parliament have simplified, although not eliminated, the confusion. "Bipolarization," an ugly word, describes the trend quite well. The existence of a majority around the President's program has led to an alliance between its adversaries on the Left—the Socialist-Communist front of 1967, the "common program" of the Left of 1973; it has also taught the Left that disunity does not pay: hence the fall in its support in June 1968, when the Communists and Socialists faced their voters in disarray, and the futil-

ity of the PSU, which represents interesting ideas and a genuine programmatic alternative to the Communists and Socialists, but must, on
the second ballot, deliver its small electorate to the big Leftist parties
it criticizes. In turn, the two coalitions have condemned the poor
"Centrists" to a rather comic fate. They argue that they are a safeguard against the terrible peril of "polarization," that they preserve a
chance for the old tradition of government by the center or a Third
Force. In order to survive, they concentrate their attacks on those in
power. And yet, on the second ballot, their supporters predominantly
vote for the candidates of the coalition that the Centrist leaders so vir-
tuously denounce.[44] Even in the tough conditions of 1973, the majority returned to power thanks to the Centrist electorate but without
any need for Centrist votes in Parliament. It seems clear that their inclusion in the majority is now just a matter of finding the right moment.[45] To be sure, each of the two great coalitions is heterogeneous,
and herein lies some uncertainty for the future. But the trend is likely
to continue.

Ten years ago, the French party system suffered from atavistic divisions and intractable new problems. But since the end of the Algerian
war, the only unmanageable issue was May 1968, and it was overcome, if not resolved. As for the more traditional divisions, two have
eroded. One is the religious issue. Even as late as 1968, religious
practice was a better indicator of a Frenchman's voting behavior than
his class or occupation.[46] But in March 1973, for the first time, many
practicing Catholics appear to have voted for the new Socialist party
—led by a man, François Mitterrand, who was born a Catholic and
casually told a journalist he would probably die a Catholic too.[47] The
other could be called a division-over-de Gaulle issue—the split between
a Gaullist party that was little more than an "army of faithful," led
from above, without any program of its own, and all the other parties,
whose origins were in the parliamentary regimes of the past. The General is gone and the Gaullist party, while it remains in many respects
different from the others [48] (in particular because of its relative lack
of roots at the local level), has nevertheless evolved into a more autonomous, national, and durable force.

All these improvements make it likely that the institutions will last,
that a kind of synthesis between heroic leadership and routine political authority has been found, flexible enough to offer leeway between
the extremes. But stable and accepted institutions are not a guarantee
of reform in state and society, and those very same improvements also
explain why there is no majority to carry out a "reformist" program.

In the past twenty years, two men (both, incidentally and paradoxically, former Radicals) have tried to move in that direction. Mendès-
France was less concerned with "institutional investment" than with

economic efficiency, the precondition of effective modernization in 1954. Chaban-Delmas, in his appeal for a new society in 1969, came out for a series of *déblocages*—through decentralization and regional reform, systematic *"concertation"* with the unions as well as business and farmers, greater emphasis on structural problems, public investments, autonomy for public enterprises and the ORTF. On balance, he promised more aid to the poor than reduction of the causes of poverty. It was by no means a very daring effort at reform, for even at the outset he had to take into account Pompidou's views on education (as an ex-*boursier* he finds nothing wrong with the system that made him what he is) and his party's fears of "disorder" and its highly ambivalent views on the subject of inequality. His program gradually shriveled up, due to the combined reticences of Pompidou and the Gaullist coalition, just as Mendès-France had been defeated by Parliament. Regional reform was emasculated, decentralization was replaced by *déconcentration,* structural measures—for instance those tending to give the state better control over real estate for public housing, urban planning, and the concentration of farmland—were abandoned, and there was no progressive tax or social security reform. Only *concertation* and some grants of autonomy to public enterprises and (temporarily) to the ORTF were left—not without parliamentary grumbling.[49] As the nation approached election time, pressures for a shift developed both in the Élysée and in Parliament. Chaban-Delmas was dismissed by Pompidou. While the new Premier, Messmer, pursued his predecessor's contractual policy with the unions, it was clear that the spirit was no longer quite the same. Chaban-Delmas and his advisers thought that the majority should not only keep but try to increase its supply of voters among the workers; Messmer seemed more concerned with preserving social peace for expansion. Moreover, a more spectacular effort was made to shower subsidies, tax relief, and price supports on the coalition's faithful: shopkeepers, artisans, farmers. The result of this shift and of the orientation imposed earlier on Chaban-Delmas was a policy that did a great deal for economic expansion, but did not resolve the problems with which this chapter—and Chaban-Delmas's advisers—have been concerned.

"Bipolarization," in the French political context, implies features that militate against the adoption of the reformist program. The first is the appearance of so-called "catch-all parties." In the Fourth Republic, with proportional representation, each party was more afraid of losing some fraction of its narrow base than hopeful of making any gains by wresting voters away from its rivals: hence, a defensiveness of programs, a desperate emphasis on ideological purity—to compensate for the daily dirtying of hands in coalition governments. The logic of the new system is the opposite. When each coalition tries to expand

and gain control of voters in the middle, *le marais*,[50] the result inevitably is a program that tries to promise something to everyone, is vague enough to bring hopes to all, and antagonizes only those who would in no case vote for it anyhow. Both the Gaullists and the new Socialist party have succeeded as catch-all parties of this kind. In both instances, we are regaled with plans for modernization—both sides proclaim their devotion to a high rate of growth—for higher living standards for every group, and for a motley array of structural reforms. In both instances, we find a mixture of conservatism and promises of innovation. What is striking in the Gaullist case is the absence or poverty of everything that touches on the issues which the reformists deem essential (for instance in the Premier's program of Provins, in January 1973). The axes remain expansion plus "humanization." What is striking in the Socialist case is not so much the expected attempt to deal seriously with the problems of inequality, but the prudence of proposals on decentralization,[51] on educational reform, on the civil service itself. Louis Blanc is more of an influence than Proudhon. The fact is that *le marais* and the discontented to whom both sides appeal are profoundly ambivalent about reforms. They include people who genuinely aspire to greater equality and participation—among the new middle classes of cadres, for instance, or among the professions—and people with deeply conservative reflexes who desire law, order, and more help from the state. The logic of catch-all parties is incrementalism.

Another feature militating against reform has to do with the peculiarities of each "pole." The present dominant coalition in Parliament is a mix. Valéry Giscard-d'Estaing's Independents are men with deep roots in the old soil of the *notables*. They accept the necessity of modernization but are anything but champions of reform. The vast Gaullist party is itself composite. Many of its deputies are ex-civil servants, businessmen, cadres, representatives of the new industrial France, eager for economic expansion, but not keenly concerned about territorial, structural, or educational reform. Others are old Jacobins, aware of *blocages* and inequities, yet convinced that reducing the power of the state would be fatal, and that generalized participation would be chaos. The handful of left-wing and reformist Gaullists exerts little influence. The Centrists who rallied to Pompidou in 1969 have little originality.

What has given the Gaullist party its general cast has been Pompidou's own strategy and it is as unreformist as can be in a number of ways. His policy seems based on one idea: there are already so many changes taking place because of industrialization that adding more would be too much; the role of the state should consist therefore in allowing modernization to proceed while minimizing its social costs. He seems convinced that French behavior patterns are fixed and that the dream of changing them is utopian. His *politique* aims at building a broad alliance between the Gaullist party and the *notables:* hence his regional "reform" carefully preserves their powers and prerogatives, and he has tried to expand the grass-roots influence of Gaullism directly (although Gaullist showing in municipal and departmental elections has been mediocre) and indirectly, by alliances and patronage.[52] Both the policy and the politics aim at proving that France can, in de Gaulle's words, "marry her time" without leaving the old ancestral home. The results have been a double-edged success. On one hand, the Gaullist majority's influence has increased among the aged, in the countryside, in the old Radical and conservative strongholds in central France and the Southwest; and the support of *notables* probably protects it from the danger of sudden extinction which hit the RPF. On the other hand, what appears as a guarantee of long life from one angle looks like a choice for a shrinking base from another. Not only have these *politics* reinforced the conservatism of the *policy* but they have resulted in a serious loss of support among workers, members of the professions, and city-dwellers, categories in which the Socialists have made considerable gains; the majority coalition is a modern conservative party whose strength is greatest in declining social groups, and it has failed to rally together all categories of Frenchmen, as de Gaulle had wanted and partly obtained.

The other political pole is an uneasy alliance. If the new Socialists are a "catch-all party," the Communists are a countersociety and a centralized organization of militants.[53] In the French polity, they perform one major service, and a number of disservices. They contribute to the integration—into a "separatist" society, perhaps, but one which industrialization and détente have made much less of a ghetto than in the late 1940s—of a huge mass of workers, employees, civil servants, professionals, farmers (in dwindling numbers) who might otherwise join the ranks of the turbulent unorganized. A coalition of alienated citizens and well-integrated ones whose political views happen to be on the far left, it is a bulwark against anomie. But the first disservice comes precisely from the social heterogeneity of the party's electorate; the predominance of workers in the membership and direction cannot obliterate it, nor can it be concealed by the continuing reference to the working class as the single engine of history, or the continuing refusal to accept analyses of social change such as Garaudy's. The Communists too must have a catch-all program—and the fact that they need allies if they are to come to power often tempts them into outbidding Socialists in "openness." Here again, we find political leaders making promises for all (except the monopolists, who will pay for change). Their old attachment to Jacobin ideology (not to mention the party's own organization) and their respect for traditional French education, due both to the ideology of the Republican school and to the importance of school and *lycée* teachers in the party, seriously limit the Communists' reformism.

A second disservice resides in the cast which Communist participation gives to the "common program" of the Left. The stress is not on the timid decentralizing residues or vague *autogestion* references of the Socialist program, but on vast nationalizations, and indeed on the control of an expanding state by the parties and unions that speak for "the masses." The problem of participation is not so much solved as dodged by the assumption that a state ruled by the organized instruments of the masses would *ipso facto* be representative—Jacobin Leninism or Leninist Jacobinism. Added to the Louis Blanc version of socialism, it certainly helps weed out not only Proudhon but Sorel. The fierce *étatisme* of the Communist program, the relentless insistence on the primacy of the Communist party in the coalition, the rather obvious contradiction between the promise of economic growth and financial solvency, and the cost of the social measures promised, continuing fears about the fate of freedom—all of this has for fifteen years kept the Left from crossing the threshold of 46 per cent of the vote; it scares not only those whom any radical attempt at dealing with inequality would offend but also those who are sympathetic yet do not believe that participation or better representation is achieved by increasing the weight of the state and by relying on central politics alone. Consequently, there has been no alternation between the two coalitions: the Gaullist, or Pompidou, coalition remains in control.

Are there factors that could unfreeze the situation? Yes, but they do not necessarily serve the reformist cause. In the next Presidential Election of 1976, each side will try once again to court *le marais*. The Right will want to regain lost ground among those who deserted it, and will want to make sure that Centrist voters, on the second ballot, will again surrender to the logic of "bipolarization" and support it. The Left has to get more Centrist voters, and also knows that a Presidential battle (in which, on the second ballot, no Communist is likely to be in the race) has a better chance of attracting them than a legislative election. The trouble is that the Centrists are not a homogeneous force either.[54] Their electorate is clearly more conservative, closer to Pompidou's strategy, than their leaders, who are divided (between Servan-Schreiber's shrill reformism and Jean Lecanuet's nuances) and ambiguous (they talk about participation and decentralization, but represent a notoriously unreformist tradition of mainly Christian-Democratic *notables* and parliamentarians). It is likely that both coalitions will try to cut through the ambiguities by focusing on the problem of inequality: the Left will promise more extensive measures (but not other kinds of reforms), and the Right will promise to "humanize" (rather than dealing with causes). Clearly, the Left cannot afford to be very daring in the search for more votes. As for the Right, its attempt at regaining lost ground cannot take precedence over the need to hold onto its present constituency. The problem of the socio-economically shrinking base can be solved only by slowing down expansion, which is the last thing the regime wants, or by shaping it in such a way as to rescue Pompidou's politics. Not only has he been courting the network of *notables* but he is trying to arrest their decline, and thereby to pump some new life into the old symbiotic relation between the *notables* and the state, by stressing that the time has come to save family farms, to build "middle size towns" rather than *métropoles d'équilibre,* to support middle-size businesses rather than national champions, to develop individual housing rather than *grands ensembles,*[55] to grant small shopkeepers the right to veto supermarkets.[56] Whether the new France can be fitted into the mold of the old one, whether the old scheme of representation can be sufficiently revived to solve the problem of participation—at least at the local level—by restoring balance between a less "colossal" (yet untransformed) state and the *notables* (for instance in the new regions) remains to be seen, but it seems Pompidou's gamble. It is obviously a strategy of adaptive restoration, not reform. The capture of the indispensable Centrist electorate is sought less through programmatic appeals than through the politics of alliance with *notables* at the local level, where the roots of Centrist influence are, and through the politics of parliamentary *ouverture. Ouverture,* or liberalization, the dream of Giscardians and Centrists, means a dilution of the Gaullist party's predominance, greater leeway for the deputies in legislation, a lessening of the imbalance between executive and Parliament. Here again, we find not reform but adaptive and very partial restoration, for the problem of participation at the national level is even less likely to be solved by a slight rise in the deputies' stocks than, at the local level, by a resurrection of the *notables* of yesteryear. In both instances, the problem of functional, as opposed to political, representation is still unsettled.

The election of another President from the right-wing coalition in 1976 would probably clinch the *ralliement* of the Centrists. Despite their leaders' brave proclamations, the "sociological weight" (Lecanuet's own term) of their electorate would mean a consecration of the Pompidou strategy. The election of a Socialist President would create quite another problem. He would need a new Parliament. If the new Assembly had a "united Left" majority, the main problem would be that of the relations between Communists and Socialists. Any vigorous promotion of the reformist measures advocated by many of the younger Socialists around Mitterrand would only strain the alliance to the breaking point, and a kind of prudent minimalism might be the only salvation—an agreement on various measures to fight inequality, a minimum of nationalizations, but not the whole "common program" (particularly not that part of it which was designed to weaken the Presidency, and which a left-wing President would have no incentive to carry out)—and certainly not the reformist program. If there is no clear left-wing majority in Parliament, or if the Socialist President should have to break the alliance with the Communists, there would be a return to that "Third Force" strategy that the Centrists dream of, the Gaullists' allies secretly hope for. But it is hard to see how any coherent reformist program would emerge: one would be back at *immobiliste* government, this time under Presidential leadership, with some better chance of stability, yet with obviously greater room for parliamentary maneuvers. This would hardly be a cure for the over-all problem of counterweights to the state.

V

France is becoming more "like the others." In foreign affairs, the post-de Gaulle Republic has abandoned the General's global reformism. It has accepted in fact the permanence (or should one say the provisional permanence) of the division of Europe. It has consequently avoided any further showdowns between Western Europe and the United States on military issues. While it has continued its atomic armament, it has shown no enthusiasm for a West European defense entity or program. While France has tried to bring out a "European personality" in the monetary realm, she has had to compromise both with West Germany's repugnance for any economic confrontation with the United States and with Britain's demand for a special treatment of the pound. France clearly lacks the power to impose her own views on international monetary reform, and her desire for a European point of view here has led her to retreat even further from the earlier Gaullist stand on gold and fixed parities. Foreign affairs, as in other West European countries, is hardly a vital priority, and what is original in France's positions (thanks to de Gaulle) is no longer disturbing, or is being blunted for the sake of West European unification, or trans-Atlantic harmony, or pan-European détente.

In domestic affairs, many features of the French landscape resemble those of her neighbors: an erosion of old ideological camps; a predominance of the executive over Parliament; a reasonably stable and coherent majority; a Constitution that is openly challenged by few, deeply resented only by the Communists, and could be made even more of a common charter by the reduction of the President's term to five years, proposed by Pompidou; large-scale bargaining with corporate interests; domination of industry and the tertiary services by big bureaucratic organizations and the rule of experts. And yet, many special characteristics remain. France's modern economy is marked by a degree of inequality that was tolerated and somewhat mitigated in the old society but causes increasing tensions now. The centralized state suffers from its enormous weight. Local government exhibits its peculiar weaknesses, acceptable only as long as the centralized state was limited and the old game in which local authorities gained in "captive power" what they lacked in autonomous power made sense. France's top elites are still closed, authoritarian, basically conservative in their approach to institutional problems—even when they are innovative and pragmatic in solving functional ones. The Communist party neither grows nor shrinks, is neither a revolutionary force nor a new social democracy, and clouds the chances of the French Left of either reaching or staying in power. There is a proclivity to mass protest among the unorganized and the young. The acute crisis of mass education exceeds, for institutional reasons, comparable crises in other sectors. These are the "purely French" features of today.

Many of these are aspects of the problem with which this essay has been concerned: the quest for a new balance between state and society. In the 1870s, a consensus for a certain kind of society and for a limited state finally made possible a consensus on political institutions and on their proper insertion into society. A century later, the fragile but resilient consensus favoring a state with extended functions and supporting the political institutions of the Fifth Republic has not yet brought about an operational consensus on society. Nor has it allowed for a legitimate set of checks and balances that would insure the participation of the citizenry not only in the election of the President and the representatives but in new forms of representation, in the creation of a legitimate elite of *notables* characteristic of the new society. At present, the citizenry has a kind of legitimizing role at the point where state action is initiated, but none at the points where state action is applied. This is why new forms of decentralized representation are needed, functional as well as political, and why the weight of the state itself must be reduced. Otherwise, the state will be permanently overloaded by the burden of bargaining with organized interests on all issues, major and minor, and periodically overwhelmed by the demands of the unorganized who find no place within existing institutions and associations.

De Gaulle, always on bad terms with France's old *notables*, had looked for ways to eliminate them, and had groped toward the creation of a new elite: first at the center, through weakening the old parties and recruiting a new Gaullist political class; finally all over France, through the establishment of regional institutions and a new

Senate in which new territorial delegates and the representatives of modern economic activities would have their say. But his attempt was bound to be insufficient, partly because his Jacobin fear for the unity of state and nation led him to keep the new regional assemblies limited in power and to resist having their members voted in by direct universal suffrage, partly because his tactical pragmatism led him to carve out a considerable role for the old *notables* (at least for a while) rather than eliminating them at once. And the attempt failed because they opposed it anyhow. Pompidou's own efforts to lean on them, to insert Gaullists among them, and to mold France's development into their antiquated ways, are no solution at all. Indeed, so long as a new legitimate elite of notables has not been created, there will be a serious problem of political leadership at the center: at present, the government must be selected either from among parliamentarians (many of whom are far more representative of the old than of the new France, on the Left as well as on the Right) or from among civil servants (whether they have gotten themselves elected or not). It is not surprising if the lack of daring and imagination, as Messmer himself has suggested, are "the worst enemies" on top.

And yet the very absence of a social consensus results in political coalitions that either avoid or distort these issues. A final paradox lies in this fact: there was more of a consensus on the social order in an age of deep ideological abysses than there is today. A widely shared set of beliefs about the good society allowed for disagreements about how man should be governed. A pragmatic agreement on how he should be governed does not resolve the problem of the nature of the society he should live in. To be sure, as long as everyone recognizes that it will be an advanced industrial society, and as long as most Frenchmen want it to be a liberal polity, the scope of divergence is relatively narrow. But it remains broad enough to preserve the familiar special features, to perpetuate the dialogue between Jacobin doctrinaires or conservative pragmatists and Tocquevillean reformists, to prolong the ambiguities of political programs, and to allow one to predict new turbulence and tribulations in the drama of the relations of the French with their state.

Notes

1. The Vichy Circle of French Conservatives

1. See Henry W. Ehrmann, *Organized Business in France* (Princeton, N.J., 1957).
2. See David B. Truman, *The Governmental Process* (New York, 1951).
3. A fine account of these events is to be found in William L. Shirer, *The Collapse of the Third Republic* (New York, 1969).
4. René Rémond, *The Right Wing in France* (Philadelphia, 1967).
5. Alexis de Tocqueville, *The European Revolution and Correspondence with Gobineau* (New York, 1959), p. 155.
6. Charles Maurras, *De la Colère à la justice* (Geneva, 1942).
7. See, for the case of Brittany, Suzanne Berger, *Peasants against Politics* (Cambridge, Mass., 1972).
8. Maurras, *La Seule France* (Lyons, 1941).
9. Henry Bordeaux, *Les murs sont bons* (Paris, 1941), a dreadful popular novel.
10. See, for instance, Pierre Nicolle, *Cinquante Mois d'armistice* (Paris, 1947); also Richard Kuisel, "The Legend of Vichy Synarchy," *French Historical Studies,* Spring 1970.
11. See Volume II of Albert Mallet, *Pierre Laval* (Paris, 1955).
12. Raymond Aron, in *L'Âge des empires et l'avenir de la France* (Paris, 1945).
13. I have explored this development in further detail in *Le Mouvement Poujade* (Paris, 1956).

2. Self-Ensnared: Collaboration with Nazi Germany

1. Saint-Paulien (M.-Y. Sicard), *Histoire de la collaboration* (Paris, 1964).
2. Michèle Cotta, *La Collaboration, 1940–44* (Paris, 1964).
3. See S. Hoffmann, C. P. Kindleberger, L. Wylie, J. R. Pitts, J.-B. Duroselle, and F. Goguel, *In Search of France* (Cambridge, Mass., 1963), pp. 21–60.

4. On *collaboration d'état,* see the important contributions of: Eberhard Jäckel, *Frankreich in Hitlers Europa* (Stuttgart, 1966), and Robert O. Paxton, *Vichy France: Old Guard and New Order, 1940–1944* (New York, 1972). Paxton documents impressively the scope and continuity of voluntary *collaboration d'état.*

5. See in particular Raoul Girardet, "Note sur l'esprit d'un fascisme français, 1934–39," *Revue française de science politique,* V, No. 3 (July–September, 1955), 524–46; Paul Sérant, *Romantisme fasciste* (Paris, 1959); Robert J. Soucy, "The Nature of Fascism in France," *Journal of Contemporary History,* I, No. 1 (1966), 27–55, and *Fascism in France: the Case of Maurice Barrès* (Berkeley, Cal., 1972), pp. 283*ff.*

6. Soucy, "The Nature of Fascism in France," p. 41.

7. See Soucy, "Le Fascisme de Drieu la Rochelle," *Revue d'histoire de la 2ⁱᵐᵉ guerre mondiale,* April 1967, pp. 61–84.

8. Soucy, "The Nature of Fascism in France," pp. 44*ff.*

9. On Joseph Darnand, see Jacques Delperrié de Bayac, *Histoire de la milice, 1918–45* (Paris, 1969).

10. Compare with England making the same discovery—much faster, but equally reluctantly—after World War II.

3. In the Looking Glass: Sorrow and Pity?

1. Robert Aron, *The Vichy Regime* (New York, 1958).

2. André Malraux, *Felled Oaks* (New York, 1972).

4. The Rulers: Heroic Leadership in Modern France

1. This is not true of Erik Erikson's work.

2. For a recent effort, see James D. Barber, *The Presidential Character* (New York, 1972).

3. Compare Harry Eckstein's notion of congruence, in "Theory of Stable Democracy" (mimeo., Princeton, N.J., 1961).

4. I hesitate to call them "illegitimate leaders," since they may possess or develop a legitimacy of their own, or "revolutionary leaders," since the word "revolution" carries an implication of social purpose that might be misleading.

5. See Nathan Leites, *On the Political Game in France* (Stanford, Cal., 1959).

6. See Michel Crozier, *The Bureaucratic Phenomenon* (Chicago, 1964). See also William R. Schonfeld, "Authority in France" (Ph.D. dissertation, Princeton, 1970), in which he brilliantly shows how this style emerges from the French school system. A part of this thesis is in Schonfeld's *Youth and Authority in France* (Sage professional paper, Beverly Hills, Cal., 1971).

7. See S. Hoffmann, *et al., In Search of France* (Cambridge, Mass., 1963). See also Laurence Wylie, *Village in the Vaucluse* (Cambridge, Mass., 1957); and Jesse R. Pitts's review of Crozier in *Analyse et prévision,* SEDEIS, I (1966), 51*ff.*

8. Philip Williams, *Crisis and Compromise* (Hamden, Conn., 1964).

9. On homeorhesis, see C. H. Waddington, "The Desire for Material Progress as a World Ordering System," *Daedalus*, Spring 1966, p. 667. The dread of insecurity is displayed in essays written by French *lycée* students about their future; see Gérard Vincent, *Les Lycéens* (Paris, 1971).

10. See Crozier, p. 262 of English edition; and Gabriel A. Almond and Sidney Verba, *The Civic Culture* (Princeton, N.J., 1963).

11. *In Search of France,* p. 18.

12. Pitts, *ibid.,* p. 243.

13. See Nicholas Wahl, in Samuel Beer and Adam B. Ulam, eds., *Patterns of Government* (New York, 1958 edition).

14. Williams, *op. cit.,* p. 443.

15. Raymond Aron, *Démocratie et totalitarisme* (Paris, 1965).

16. Consider Pétain's slow promotion before 1914, Mendès-France's withdrawal in 1945, and de Gaulle's withdrawal in 1946 and again in 1955.

17. See Jean-Raymond Tournoux, *Pétain and de Gaulle* (New York, 1966), p. 381.

18. See de Gaulle's speech in Paris, August 20, 1964, in André Passeron. *De Gaulle parle, 1962–66* (Paris, 1966), p. 234.

19. Secrecy—a way of preserving oneself from others' encroachments—is characteristic both of French people and of each "stratum." See Henry W. Ehrmann, *Organized Business in France* (Princeton, N.J., 1957). The much greater unavailability of archives to researchers in France than in other open societies is another example of the same phenomenon.

20. Alexander Werth, *Lost Statesman* (New York, 1958), p. 120.

21. Pitts, *In Search of France, loc. cit.*

22. On *le peuple* vs. *la population,* see Emmanuel d'Astier de la Vigerie, *Sept fois sept jours* (Paris, 1961).

23. See Jean-Marie Cotteret and René Moreau, *Le Vocabulaire politique du Général de Gaulle* (Paris, 1969), pp. 42*ff.*

24. Jean Plumyène, *Pétain* (Paris, 1964).

25. See A. W. De Porte, *De Gaulle's Foreign Policy, 1964–66* (Cambridge, Mass., 1968). De Gaulle himself confirmed this in *Memoirs of Hope* (New York, 1971).

26. See André Siegfried, *De la 3ᵉ à la 4ᵉ République* (Paris, 1956), p. 171.

27. See Lewis Edinger, *Kurt Schumacher* (Stanford, Cal., 1965), p. 272.

28. See Tournoux, *op. cit.,* p. 390.

29. One recalls his remark, in *Felled Oaks* (New York, 1972), to André Malraux, comparing himself to the comic strip hero Tintin. Even in foreign affairs, the impudent challenger also behaved as one of a handful—indeed a fully legitimate—*Grand;* whereas in domestic affairs, the imperious quasi monarch waged a permanent *Fronde* against the entrenched elites.

30. This point is incisively made by Peter Gourevitch in "Political Skill: a Case Study," *Public Policy,* XIV, 239–76 (1965).

31. See *In Search of France,* pp. 34*ff.*

32. This principle, stated in de Gaulle's *Le Fil de l'epée* (Paris, 1932), explains much of his post-1958 colonial policy, his exit from NATO, and

his recurrent "empty-chair policy" (at the Geneva Disarmament Conference, the WEU boycott in 1969, etc.).

33. See "Les Élections legislative de Mars 1967," *Cahiers de la Fondation nationale des sciences politiques,* No. 170 (Paris, 1971), especially François Goguel's analysis of the results, pp. 315*ff.*

34. This case is brilliantly argued by Peter Larmour, in "De Gaulle and the New France," *Yale Review,* Spring 1966.

35. Press conference, February 4, 1965. Quoted in Roy Macridis, ed., *De Gaulle: Implacable Ally* (New York, 1966), p. 83.

36. De Gaulle's handling of the Algerian crisis was a case in point. In order to convince a stuck and sizzling army to sacrifice the old vested interests of the nation overseas, of the settlers in Algeria, of the colonial army itself, he showed that an obstinate and futile pursuit of victory would actually wreck the new "equilibrium" of France; he showed that the army could find in conversion to atomic defense a far more prestigious equivalent of its imperial glories. Once again, total change—but in orderly harmony—was presented as the answer to both the irresistible pressure for change and the fear of changes in the hierarchy of statuses.

37. For a thoughtful discussion of the problem of change in French bureaucracy, see the July–September, 1966 issue of *Sociologie du travail,* Michel Crozier, ed., as well as his book *The Stalled Society* (New York, 1973).

38. There was a first serious warning: the sudden drop (more drastic than after May 1968) in de Gaulle's popularity at the time of the miners' strike in the spring of 1963: the strike was the result of a social change (the decline of the coal industry) and of the state's haughty handling of discontent. De Gaulle deals with it, rather defensively, in the last chapter of *Memoirs of Hope.* A good analysis of public opinion in 1963 and in 1968–69 is to be found in Jean Charlot, ed., *Les Français et de Gaulle* (Paris, 1971). Most remarkable is the finding that, except in 1959, a majority of the French never believed that France's economic situation would improve, and that they never judged that their standard of living had improved. Equally remarkable is the widespread hostility to changing jobs or residence.

39. See de Gaulle's own remarks in the second and last finished chapter of *L'Effort* (the second volume of *Memoirs of Hope*); also, Bernard Tricot, *Les Sentiers de la paix* (Paris, 1972), p. 349. At the end of the Algerian war, Tricot told de Gaulle: "Algeria was our last adventure. . . . Now it seems we're going to become a sort of big enterprise, we'll only be concerned with problems of management." De Gaulle answered, "Don't worry, we'll put passion into it!"

40. See Charlot, *op. cit.,* pp. 75*ff.* The French consistently approved de Gaulle's foreign-policy goals but, after the middle of 1967, began to doubt that they could be achieved.

41. See Ronald Inglehart, "The Silent Revolution in Europe," *American Political Science Review,* December 1971, pp. 991–1017; and Inglehart and Leon Lindberg, "Political Cleavages in Post-Industrial Society: the May Revolt in France," forthcoming; also, Charlot, *op. cit.*

42. Charles Morazé, in *Le Général de Gaulle et la République* (Paris, 1972), pp. 154*ff.,* comments on the French attachment to gold, the view of eco-

nomics as the accumulation of wealth rather than the exchange of goods, and other aspects of the old mercantilism.

43. The conception of Premier Jacques Chaban-Delmas and his advisers may have actually been closer to Crozier's. For reasons discussed on pp. 478–79, their three-year practice fell short of his ideas and their hopes.

44. Compare Pétain's references to the permanence of the soil, the tree, etc., with the last two pages of de Gaulle's *War Memoirs* (New York, 1960), a prose poem to both the permanence and constant renewal of nature.

5. *The Ruled: Protest as a National Way of Life*

1. The classification used here was proposed by Raymond Aron in his lectures *La Lutte des classes* (Paris, 1964).

2. Gabriel A. Almond, in his introduction to Almond and James S. Coleman, eds., *The Politics of Developing Areas* (Princeton, N.J., 1960), pp. 37–38.

3. See Raymond Aron, *Opium of the Intellectuals* (New York, 1958).

4. The best study remains Val Lorwin, *The French Labor Movement* (Cambridge, Mass., 1954). See also Jean-Daniel Reynaud, *Les Syndicats en France* (Paris, 1967).

5. See my *Le Mouvement Poujade* (Paris, 1956).

6. Jean-Paul Sartre, preface to Paul Nizan, *Aden Arabie* (Paris, 1960).

7. See Alain Touraine, *Le Communisme utopique* (Paris, 1968), p. 45. (English translation: *The May Movement* [New York, 1971]).

8. For instance: from extreme Left to Right in cases such as Alexandre Millerand, Aristide Briand, Pierre Laval; from extreme Right to Center, in the case of many Poujadist deputies or Gaullist leaders under the Fourth Republic; under the Fifth Republic, from extreme Right to Center in the case of Poujade himself, and from Left to Center in the case of Michel Debatisse, the militant leader of the young peasants' movement, the Centre National des Jeunes Agriculteurs (CNJA), who became a mainstay of the moderate rural organization the Fédération Nationale des Syndicats d'Exploitants Agricoles. Albert Camus's bitter play *L'État de Siège* is a lively allegorical treatment of the whole theme of protest and failure, with the return, at the end, of the politicians who fled when the plague struck.

9. See Hadley Cantril, *The Politics of Despair* (New York, 1958).

10. See, in addition to *The Bureaucratic Phenomenon* (Chicago, 1964), Michel Crozier's book *The Stalled Society* (New York, 1973).

11. The gradual absorption of the prewar PSF and postwar RPF into the parliamentary system could be analyzed as the result of such a process. The Daladier cabinet, to a large extent, followed a policy of "La Rocque-ism without la Rocque," just as many of the cabinets of the Fourth Republic, in their anticommunism and economic program, followed a line of "Gaullism (RPF-style) without de Gaulle," and the nationalist Mollet government of 1956 can be said to be Poujadism without Poujade.

12. See Laurence Wylie's admirable studies, *Village in the Vaucluse* (Cambridge, Mass., 1957), and *Les Français* (Englewood Cliffs, N.J., 1970). See

also Jesse R. Pitts's provocative unpublished Harvard dissertation, "The Bourgeois Family and French Economic Retardation" (1958), and William R. Schonfeld, "Authority in France" (Ph.D. dissertation, Princeton, N.J., 1970).

13. Crozier, "Le Citoyen," *Esprit,* February 1961, p. 210.

14. For a fine illustration and defense, see Émile Durkheim's *Education morale* (Paris, 1934). For a recent keen and detailed critique, see OECD, *Review of National Policies for Education: France,* April 1970.

15. See also Crozier, "The Cultural Revolution," in Stephen R. Graubard, ed., *A New Europe?* (Boston, 1964), pp. 602–30.

16. Maurice Merleau-Ponty, quoted by René Rémond, "Les Intellectuels et la politique," *Revue française de science politique,* IX, No. 4, 867.

17. Concern for underdeveloped peoples has become one of the principal subjects of French left-wing intellectuals: a fascinating mixture of generosity, a quest for a new universalism despite France's decline as a world power, and an expression of *mauvaise conscience.*

18. For instance, the slogan, long repeated by Sartre, that since the Communist party represents the proletariat, and the proletariat is the "universal class" or the carrier of *le sens de l'histoire,* the intellectual should support the Communists.

19. However, even the withdrawal from *engagement* does not necessarily mean giving up the search for universal laws: in the mid-1960s, "structuralism" (including Althusser's "structuralist" Marxism) went looking for "structural" laws of society but turned its back on history and on the meanings of human action. It thus was both a new form of scientism, and a repudiation of two centuries of prophetic but persistently disappointing philosophies of history.

20. See the "great debate" between Sartre and Camus after the publication of *The Rebel* in *Les Temps modernes,* Summer 1952. The hero of Sartre's last play, *Les Séquestrés d'Altona,* is a typical rebel; in *La Critique de la raison dialectique,* the "group" is a band of rebels. The fascination exerted by China's cultural revolution is that for a "rebellion" ordered from the top to revive fervor.

21. Raymond Aron, *D'une sainte famille à l'autre* (Paris, 1969), p. 59.

22. J.-M. Domenach, "Le Modèle américain," *Esprit,* October 1960, p. 1525.

23. Crozier, "The Cultural Revolution," p. 606.

24. From an unpublished prospectus by Crozier and Joseph Bower.

25. See, for instance, Colette Audry's subtle hatchet job on Léon Blum, *Léon Blum ou la politique du juste* (Paris, 1955). Maurras was not any kinder to right-wing politicians. Mendès-France has been treated much more respectfully, as a kind of tragic hero, because he refused the usual deals and half-measures. (Indeed, *Le Canard enchaîné* once called his cabinet, which it supported, not really a government but the opposition in power!) But the most fascinating example remains that of the character assassination of Jaurès by intellectuals as diverse as Péguy, Sorel, and Maurras. There is still no first-rate French assessment of Jaurès.

26. Crozier, "The Cultural Revolution," p. 627.

27. The search for universality has been another major reason for the appeal of communism. But it has also been another source of tension, for com-

munism meant accepting the Soviet Union as a model and leader. Consequently, whenever the Soviet Union behaved as a great power rather than as the carrier of an Idea, fellow travelers fell out and intellectual party members deserted (cf. Merleau-Ponty at the time of the Korean war, or Garaudy after the occupation of Czechoslovakia).

28. See Edgar Morin, *Commune en France* (Paris, 1967). (English translation, *The Red and the White* [New York, 1970].)

29. Pitts, "Adieu à la France de papa," *La Caravelle,* Cambridge, Mass., Autumn 1959.

30. See S. Berger, P. Gourevitch, P. Higonnet, and K. Kaiser, "The Problem of Reform in France: the Ideas of Local Elites," *Political Science Quarterly,* September 1969.

31. Morin, "Intellectuals: critique du mythe et mythe de la critique," *Arguments,* IV, No. 20 (1960), 38. See also the change of *Espirt*'s line under Domenach after 1957.

32. See the remarks of Jean Duvignaud, "L'Intervention des intellectuels dans la vie publique," *Arguments,* pp. 45–46.

33. On this last point, see the remarks by Serge Moscovici in his monograph *Reconversion industrielle et changements sociaux* (Paris, 1961), pp. 311–12.

34. See Suzanne Berger's perceptive analysis, "Bretons, Basques, Scots and other European Nations," *Journal of Inter-Disciplinary History,* III, No. 1 (Summer 1972), 167–76.

35. For a brilliant study of how the regional reform of 1964 amounted in fact to an increase of authority for the state (embodied by the regional *préfet*), and has therefore been resisted by departmental civil servants and local political *notables,* resented by economic interests in areas where local society was well organized, and approved by them in areas dependent on support from Paris, see Pierre Grémion and Jean-Pierre Worms, *Les Institutions régionales et la société locale* (Paris, 1968).

36. This is one of the themes of H. Stuart Hughes's *The Obstructed Path* (New York, 1968).

37. Even a book that was an attack on the elitism of French education—its admission procedures into secondary and higher education, and its cultural model—was written in a style "for initiates." See Pierre Bourdieu and J.-Cl. Passeron, *Les Héritiers* (Paris, 1964).

38. Nothing is more revealing than a public-opinion survey on *Les Français et l'État,* undertaken in March–April 1970 and published by the Societé Française d'Enguêtes par Sondages (SOFRES). Sixty-four per cent saw the protection against social risks as the primary function of the state; 63 per cent saw civil servants as being "apart"; 59 per cent wanted as much or more state intervention in the economy as at present; civic virtue was defined as obedience or good private behavior, not participation; 73 per cent considered themselves deprived of influence on the state. For an analysis, see *Projet* (June 1971). The hold of the traditional style is also confirmed by Annick Percheron. "La Conception de l'autorité chez les enfants," *Revue française de science politique,* February 1971, pp. 103–128.

6. Confrontation in May 1968

1. See the bibliography prepared by Laurence Wylie, Franklin Chu, and Mary Terrall and published by the Council for European Studies (1973); for a review, see Philippe Bénéton and Jean Touchard, "Les Interprétations de la crise de mai–juin 1968," *Revue française de science politique,* June 1970.

2. See Annie Kriegel, "Dans le brouillard de l'université française," *Figaro littéraire,* May 25, 1970, as well as the OECD report, *Review of National Policies for Education: France,* April 1970, p. 9. In 1962–63, the less vocational faculties, Letters and Sciences, had 65 per cent of the students, compared with 32.8 per cent in 1945. In the days when they were small, they "formed" the top secondary school and university professors. There were now more students than even a growing secondary education and university system could absorb, and many of the teaching outlets available would, at least for the bourgeois students, have amounted to a *déclassement.*

3. In a public-opinion poll held in September 1968, 56 per cent of the students questioned listed anxiety about future jobs as the primary reason for the explosion.

4. Daniel Singer, *Prelude to Revolution* (New York, 1970)—a stimulating study; Singer's careful analyses are wrapped in a kind of apolitical, utopian, socialist-revolutionary wishful thinking, which confuses industrialism and capitalism and indulges in often fanciful class reductionism. The conclusions to which his excellent observations led this reader were very different from his own.

5. See pp. 138–39.

6. I am relying here on the analysis in George Ross's unpublished Ph.D. dissertation on the CGT, Harvard University, 1972.

7. The best account is by Jean-Daniel Reynaud *et al.,* "Les événements de mai et juin 1968 et le système français de relations professionnelles," *Sociologie du Travail,* January–March and April–June 1971.

8. On January 1, 1968, de Gaulle told Pompidou, who, at a traditinal New Year's ceremony, had expressed considerable pride in his government's achievements, that there were three dark points: demography, job opportunities for the young coming out of school, and worker-management relations. He does not seem to have endorsed the temporizing tactics of the Minister of Education, Alain Peyrefitte.

9. See Stanley Hoffmann, *et al., In Search of France* (Cambridge, 1963).

10. See Albert Hirschman, "The Principle of the Hiding Hand," *The Public Interest,* Winter 1967.

11. See the brilliant analysis by Raymond Boudon, "La Crise universitaire française," *Annales,* May–June 1969, and also his "Analyse secondaire et sondage sociologique," *Cahiers internationaux de sociologie,* July–December 1969. I have relied heavily on his highly convincing and exhaustive demonstration.

12. For a critical study, see OECD study by C. Grignon and J.-Cl. Passeron,

Innovation dans l'enseignement supérieur: expériences françaises avant 1968 (Paris, 1970).

13. Ironically enough, Peyrefitte was in the midst of bringing out some reforms when the explosion came, but it was too little, too late, and too secret.

14. Michel de Certeau and Dominique Julia, "La Misère de l'université," *Études,* April 1970, pp. 522–44.

15. Michel Crozier, "French students: a letter from Nanterre-la Folie," *The Public Interest,* No. 13, Fall 1968, pp. 151–59. See also A. and V. Zolberg, "The Meanings of May," *Midway,* Winter 1969, pp. 91–109, and François Bourricaud, *Universités à la dérive* (Paris, 1971).

16. In an unpublished paper on "Basic Cleavages of French Politics and the Disorders of May–June 1968," Philip Converse and Roy Pierce show the high correlation between advanced education and participation in demonstrations, especially among professionals and *cadres moyens.*

17. There now was a marked discrepancy between greater laxity at home and continuing "discipline" in school. Gerard Vincent, in *Les Lycéens* (Paris, 1971), showed that the students hugely resented the *lycée,* but not their parents.

18. See Bourricaud, "Alain Touraine à la recherche du sujet historique," *Preuves,* July–September, 1969, pp. 118–25. Also, R. Dulong, "Les Cadres en mai–juin 1968," *Sociologie du travail,* July–September 1970.

19. In addition to Reynaud *et al., op. cit.,* see Gérard Adam, F. Bon, *et al., L'Ouvrier français en 1970* (Paris, 1971).

20. In western France, some peasant organizations joined the demonstrations in May 1968.

21. See Alain Schnapp and Pierre Vidal-Naquet, eds., *Journal de la commune étudiante* (Paris, 1969).

22. George Ross, *op. cit.,* shows that if the CP had wanted the Grenelle settlements approved by the workers, it would not have submitted them to the Renault workers, who benefited least from them.

23. Annie Kriegel points out, however, and quite rightly, that the party has been good at "recuperating" leftist themes and slogans: see "Le parti communiste et la 5ème République" in Club Nouvelle Frontière, *Radioscopie des Oppositions* (Paris, 1973), pp. 115–38.

24. See the restrained but suggestive remarks by Christian Fouchet in *Au Service du Général de Gaulle* (Paris, 1971).

25. One could of course argue from the case of Italy in 1970 that in a weak parliamentary regime with a less heavily centralized bureaucracy, no "concentrated May" would occur in the first place; none did under the Fourth Republic. But given the volatility of the situation, which in a few days turned a small incident at the Sorbonne into a nationwide revolt, it would be hard to assert that no parliamentary system could have been submitted to a similar shock—at least in France.

26. In July 1972, Pompidou dismissed Premier Jacques Chaban-Delmas shortly after he asked the National Assembly for a vote of confidence, a gesture Pompidou did not approve. The lesson de Gaulle had taught Pompidou has been well learned.

27. This is further developed in "Participation in Perspective," *The Embattled University, Daedalus,* Winter 1970, pp. 177–221.
28. See Raymond Aron, *The Elusive Revolution* (New York, 1970), pp. 66–7: "If the University is not a preparation for anything, it must be reserved for a minority; if it is to be open to a larger number, it must prepare them for more than reading Virgil with the aid of a dictionary."
29. In April 1970, a survey of workers undertaken by the Fondation Nationale des Sciences Politiques showed that 46 per cent of them were satisfied with the present statute of the enterprise. Quantitative demands came far ahead of the demand for participation, nationalization, or *autogestion*. In line with the argument about authoritarianism presented above, the lowest percentage of workers satisfied with the statute of the enterprise (38 per cent) was among the workers in the larger firms (those employing more than 2000 workers), the highest (59 per cent) in enterprises employing fewer than 10 workers. It was the workers in the large factories who took the biggest part in the May 1968 strikes. (Cf. Converse and Pierce, *op. cit.*)
30. Compare Michel Crozier, *The Stalled Society* (New York, 1973), Chapter 9.
31. Bourricaud, "Alain Touraine," p. 24.
32. Jean-Jacques Servan-Schreiber and Michel Albert, *Ciel et terre* (Paris, 1970).
33. This was acknowledged by Edgar Faure: see *Ce que je crois* (Paris, 1971). His successor, Olivier Guichard, temporized. He appointed an independent commission, whose eminently sensible report, released in June 1972, was immediately denounced in classic terms by all the teachers' unions. It proposed a change in the training and pedagogic function of the teachers, a gradual unification of their castes, and autonomy for the secondary schools. The unions attacked with particular vehemence the idea that promotions should depend on decisions made by the schools' heads—*proximate* superiors—rather than on inspection and decision by the distant ministry. Whatever student and parent "participation" has been introduced in *lycées* since 1968 has contributed to its discredit, for the absence of autonomy on curriculum, management, etc., has reduced it to an empty symbol. Moreover, in conformity with the classical style, students, while resenting authoritarianism, also expect the teachers to have authority, and despise those who play at being the students' equals. See Vincent, *op. cit.*
34. One of Edgar Faure's top aides, Jacques de Chalendar, significantly describes the "representative system" of the new university as close to that of French *communes: Une loi pour l'université* (Paris, 1970).
35. The study by Pierre Grémion and Jean-Pierre Worms, *Les Institutions régionales et la société locale* (Paris, 1968), should have led one to expect this reaction. See also Grémion and Worms, "L'État et les collectivités locales," *Esprit,* January 1970, pp. 20*ff.*
36. Bourricaud, "Une Reprise en main difficile." *Preuves,* No. 218 (May–June 1969), p. 47.
37. So far, the best study of the project's origins and substance is: *La*

Réforme régionale et le référendum du 27 avril 1969, Cahier de l'Institut d'Études Politiques de Grenoble, Paris 1970. The consultation which preceded the draft revealed the *notables'* ambivalence toward financial autonomy for the regions: they both desired it as a victory over the state, and feared the responsibilities it would have entailed.

38. Maurice Faure, *Journal officiel,* Assemblée Nationale, April 26, 1972, p. 999.

7. The Hero as History: de Gaulle's War Memoirs

1. Charles de Gaulle, *War Memoirs,* I: *The Call to Honour* (New York, 1955); II: *Unity* (New York, 1959); III: *Salvation* (New York, 1960). Only Volume I of the American translation was published in an edition that includes (under separate cover), along with the narrative text, the documents that figure at the end of each of the French volumes. My references to the documents are taken from the French edition: Charles de Gaulle, *Mémoires de guerre,* I: *L'Appel* (Paris, 1954); II: *L'Unité* (Paris, 1956); III: *Le Salut* (Paris, 1959).

2. Charles de Gaulle, *The Edge of the Sword* (New York, 1960), p. 58.

3. In a long and moving letter sent to Roosevelt in October 1942, de Gaulle tried to explain the difference between personal or partisan politics and the politics of Free France. This forceful document was unanswered. The reader may find it in Volume II, *L'Unité,* pp. 382–85.

4. *Edge of the Sword,* p. 80.

5. De Gaulle condemns Hitler not only because Hitler attacked France, but also because "he based his colossal plan on the strength he attributed to man's baseness. Yet men are made of souls as much as of clay" (III, 198). Similarly, Laval's sin was "to approach matters by their underside" (II, 335).

6. De Gaulle once defined France as both *"integrée à l'Europe"* and *"étendue sur le monde entier"* (II, 516, French ed.).

7. Translated as "the higher rationality of Europe" (III, 179)!

8. For instance: in 1940–42, in order to get the French to resist Vichy, de Gaulle repeatedly stressed that they all were resisting—and since they were, why should France's allies still deal with Vichy instead of with Free France alone? In 1958, in order to get French settlers in Algeria to change their traditional attitudes, he "understood them" on May 13, 1958, to have expressed their desire to give equal rights to the Muslims.

9. *"Se rétablir . . . sous des formes nouvelles"* (I, 342, French ed.).

10. Thus *grandeur* does not depend on a colonial empire: what should be avoided is having the colonies "cut themselves off" from France *and* the French forces getting bogged down in them (III, 253—the translation is bad). This is a crucial clue to de Gaulle's policies after 1958.

11. De Gaulle had committed himself not to fight "against France"; but Vichy, in his eyes, was not France: Vichy was the gravedigger of France's independence, status, and self-respect (I, 95; III, 282–86).

12. The Fourth Republic merely fumbled with *grandeur,* and it had popular support. Vichy, he thought, betrayed France's interests—hence his revolt.

13. This whole passage is inadequately translated.

14. However, de Gaulle confesses to being fascinated by Assemblies, as was Barrès (III, 117).

15. See III, 185. Premiers Michel Debré and Maurice Couve de Murville fitted de Gaulle's description perfectly. So, initially, did Premier Georges Pompidou, but when he became a political leader in his own right, with his own constituency, de Gaulle began to cool toward him and to question Pompidou's *sens de l'État.*

16. Raymond Aron, *France: the New Republic* (New York, 1960), pp. 44–45.

17. See on one hand, Volume II of de Gaulle's *Discours et messages* (Paris, 1970) and *Dans l'attente, 1946–1953* (Paris, 1970); on the other hand, Vincent Auriol's *Journal du septennat, 1947–1954,* Vol. I: *1947* (Paris, 1970) and *Mon Septennat, 1947–1954* (Paris, 1970).

18. Philip Williams, *De Gaulle's Republic* (London, 1960).

19. *Ibid.,* p. 215.

8. De Gaulle as Political Artist: the Will to Grandeur

1. De Gaulle's biographers do not give much detail, they do not indicate their sources, they copy one another often without acknowledging it, and sometimes they contradict each other. The most interesting indications are in Georges Cattaui, *Charles de Gaulle: l'homme et son destin* (Paris, 1960), and Jean-Raymond Tournoux, *Pétain and de Gaulle* (New York, 1966). (Further citations from Tournoux's work refer to the French edition, Paris, 1964). A factually much richer biography by André Frossard has been published serially in a Paris weekly, *En ce temps là: de Gaulle* (1972–73).

2. Cattaui, *op. cit.,* p. 20.

3. De Gaulle, *Mémoires de guerre* (Paris, 1954, 56, 59) I, 1. All references in this chapter to the *Mémoires* are to the original French editions; the translations are ours.

4. Cattaui, *loc. cit.*

5. Compare André Malraux, *Antimémoires* (Paris, 1967), p. 157: "I think that, ever since his decision of June 18 [1940] hope had a tragic character for him." We think this tragic vision developed much earlier.

6. Tournoux, *op. cit.,* pp. 24–25; Philippe Barrès, *Charles de Gaulle* (Montréal, 1941), p. 30.

7. Compare Roger Wild, "De Vaugirard au Quartier Latin," *Revue des deux mondes,* March 15, 1962, pp. 275*ff.*

8. *Le Fil de l'épée* (Paris, 1932), p. 87.

9. The impact of *Cinna* on de Gaulle deserves a long (if hypothetical) discussion. In Act II, when Augustus appears, his first statement refers to *"cette grandeur sans borne et cet illustre rang"* that he has acquired. Then there is his discourse on the melancholy of domination, the *"destin*

des grandeurs souveraines" that deprives them of friends they can trust, his call for lucidity, and his final mastery—*je suis maître de moi comme de l'univers."* All this is reflected in *Le Fil de l'épée.* In the first volume of *Mémoires d'espoir,* De Gaulle actually quoted Augustus: when recriminations against him became excessive, he quieted himself, he says, by repeating the verse: *"Quoi, tu veux qu'on t'épargne, et n'as rien épargné."* *Le Renouveau* (Paris, 1970), p. 312.

10. There is an extraordinary passage in *Vers l'armée de métier* (Paris, 1933, p. 217), where de Gaulle explains that whoever possesses the potential for leadership qualities cannot develop them by exerting them only in "military categories": *"La puissance de l'esprit implique une diversité qu'on ne trouve point dans la pratique exclusive du métier, pour la même raison qu'on ne s'amuse guère en famille."*

11. Emmanuel d'Astier de la Vigerie, *Les Grands* (Paris, 1961), p. 90.

12. *Mémoires de guerre,* I, 2.

13. Speech at Saint-Cyr in 1957. Quoted in Tournoux, *La Tragédie du Général* (Paris, 1967), p. 227.

14. Tournoux, in *Pétain et de Gaulle,* p. 39, correctly suggests that Charles was younger than his classmates in his studies; this would have accentuated his sense of being different and superior.

15. *Mémoires de guerre,* I, 2.

16. The text may be found in Tournoux, *Pétain et de Gaulle,* pp. 29–36.

17. Gustave Nadaud, *Chansons à dire* (Paris, 1887), pp. 303–6.

18. Compare his press conference of November 27, 1967: apropos of *"l'après gaullisme,"* he said: *"Tout a toujours une fin. Chacun se termine."* *Le Monde,* November 29, 1967, p. 4.

19. That feather seems to owe a great deal to Rostand's *Cyrano de Bergerac* and Cyrano's *panache.*

20. *Le Fil de l'épée,* p. 87. In *Mémoires de guerre,* de Gaulle talks of several leaders (Churchill, FDR, Hitler) as "seducers."

21. *Ibid.,* pp. 86, 87.

22. Cattaui, *op. cit.,* p. 23.

23. Jean Lacouture, in *De Gaulle* (Paris, 1964, p. 15) notes that de Gaulle in his *Mémoires de guerre* (I, 2) describes his ambition to *"rendre à la France quelque service signalé"* as *"l'interêt de la vie,"* not as duty. In 1958 in Dakar, when faced with picketers asking for independence, he exclaimed that when de Gaulle is there, *"on ne s'ennuie pas."* André Passeron, *De Gaulle parle, 1958–62* (Paris, 1962), p. 462.

24. *Le Fil de l'épée.*

25. See Cattaui, *op. cit.,* p. 23, and Tournoux, *Pétain et de Gaulle,* p. 25.

26. Compare *Vers l'armée de métier,* p. 197. *"Le rôle du chef est toujours de concevoir d'après les circonstances, de décider et de prescrire en forçant sa nature et celle des autres."*

27. See Eugen Weber, *The Nationalist Revival in France: 1905–1914* (Berkeley, Cal., 1959).

28. De Gaulle, *La Discorde chez l'ennemi* (Paris, 1944; first published in 1924).

29. *Ibid.,* p. viii. On p. x, he celebrates the *"jardin à la française"* with its

"magnificent harmony," despite the "noble melancholy" that sometimes pervades it because "each element, by itself, could have shone out more" but only "at the expense of the whole."

30. See, on his experiences at the École de Guerre, Tournoux, *Pétain et de Gaulle*, Part I, chaps. 5–6, and pp. 380*ff*; also Jacques Minart, *Charles de Gaulle tel que je l'ai connu* (Paris, 1945).

31. Cattaui, *op. cit.*, p. 29; Gaston Bonheur, *Charles de Gaulle* (Paris, 1958), p. 32.

32. *La Discorde chez l'ennemi*, p. ix.

33. On Péguy's influence, see Édmond Michelet, *Le gaullisme—passionnante aventure* (Paris, 1962). The prose poem that ends the third volume of de Gaulle's *Mémoires de guerre* closes with the image of the Old Man who "never tires of watching, in the shade, for the glimmer of Hope."

34. *La France et son armée* (Paris, 1938), p. 228.

35. Alexander Werth, *De Gaulle* (New York, 1965), p. 60.

36. H. Stuart Hughes, *Consciousness and Society* (New York, 1958), pp. 117–18.

37. Quoted by Lucien Nachin in his preface to de Gaulle's *Trois études* (Paris, 1945), p. xlvi.

38. *Mémoires de guerre*, I, 2.

39. *La France et son armée*, p. 274.

40. *Mémoires de guerre*, I, 60.

41. See Tournoux, *Pétain et de Gaulle*, p. 41.

42. Compare, in *La France et son armée*, p. 191: "*grandir sa force à la mesure de ses desseins, ne pas attendre du hasard, ni des formules, ce qu'on néglige de préparer, proportionner l'enjeu et les moyens: l'action des peuples, comme celle des individus, est soumise à ces froides règles.*"

43. See above, Chapter 7, pp. 227–29.

44. Malraux, op. cit., p. 152. *Le Fil de l'épée* was based on lectures and articles written between 1927 and 1932.

45. *Les Jeunes Gens d'aujourd'hui* (Paris, 1913).

46. Compare, *Vers l'armée de métier*, p. 221: "*les puissants se forment eux-mêmes. Faits pour imprimer leur marque, plutôt que d'en-subir une, ils bâtissent dans le secret de leur vie intérieure l'édifice de leurs sentiments, de leurs concepts, de leur volonté.*" This is a constant theme both in this book and in *Le Fil de l'épée*.

47. *Le Fil de l'épée*, p. 83.

48. *Vers l'armée de métier*, pp. 217–18.

49. Ibid., pp. 224*ff*; *Le Fil de l'épée*, pp. 96–97; Nachin, *Charles de Gaulle* (Paris, 1944), pp. 88–89.

50. *Le Fil de l'épée*, p. 88.

51. François Mauriac, *De Gaulle* (Paris, 1964), p. 24.

52. *Le Fil de l'épée*, p. 77*ff*.

53. See also *Vers l'armée de métier*, p. 154, about the "perpetual return" of human affairs.

54. *Mémoires de guerre*, II, 67.

55. Malraux, *op. cit.*, p. 155.

56. *Mémoires de guerre*, II, 312.

57. *Ibid.*, III, 287.

58. Passeron, *De Gaulle parle, 1962–66* (Paris, 1966), p. 132. (TV interview, December 13, 1965).

59. Compare de Gaulle's lectures at Saint-Cyr in 1921, in Tournoux, *La Tragédie du Général*, pp. 513*ff.*

60. Compare de Gaulle's balanced judgment on Napoleon in *La France et son armée*, pp. 149–50.

61. Compare d'Astier, *Sept fois sept jours* (Paris, 1961): *"comme un grand prélat glacé dont la France est le royaume qu'il ne veut pas partager et qui n'est peut-être pas de ce monde"* (p. 102). See also Malraux, *op. cit.*, p. 135; Pierre Bourdan, *Carnets des jours d'attente* (Paris, 1945).

62. *Mémoires de guerre*, I, Chapter 2.

63. Compare *"le caractère esthétique des choses militaires,"* in *Vers l'armée de métier*, p. 142.

64. *". . . César, qui ne procède que des exigences profondes de son temps, est un homme sur la scène,* c'est-à-dire forcément un artiste" (emphasis added). Letter to M. de Bourbon-Busset, quoted by Tournoux, *La Tragédie du Général*, p. 486. In *Mémoires de guerre*, I, 47, he called Churchill *"le grand artiste d'une grande Histoire."* See also the reasons he stated for admiring François Mauriac: one was Mauriac's appreciation of the aesthetic dimension of de Gaulle's enterprise (in Jean Mauriac, *Mort du Général de Gaulle*, Paris, 1972).

65. *"De même que le talent marque l'œuvre d'art d'un cachet particulier de compréhension et d'expression, ainsi le* Caractère *imprime son dynamisme propre aux éléments de l'action. . . . Moralement, il l'anime, il lui donne la vie, comme le talent fait de la matiére dans le domaine de l'art."* *Le Fil de l'épée*, pp. 54–55.

66. Compare the quotations in note 9. The final call for a master, in *Le Fil de l'épée*, is a call for a *"ministre, soldat ou politique."*

67. When General Georges Catroux, a much higher-ranking general, joined de Gaulle in October 1940, there was no doubt any more about de Gaulle's leadership.

68. *"Il faut qu'un maître apparaisse, indépendant en ses jugements, irrécusable dans ses ordres, crédité par l'opinion. Serviteur du seul État, dépouillé de préjugés, dédaigneux de clientèles; commis enfermé dans sa tâche, pénétré de longs desseins, au fait des gens et des choses du ressort . . . assez fort pour s'imposer, assez habile pour séduire, assez grand pour une grande œuvre. . . ."* (*Vers l'armée de métier*, p. 227); Robert Aron, in *An Explanation of de Gaulle* (New York, 1966, p. 70), quotes this revealing sentence from de Gaulle's *Mémoires de guerre:* "In human endeavors, due to a long and slow effort, a sudden, unique spurt may be achieved in different and disparate spheres." A good account of de Gaulle's own course.

69. *Le Fil de l'épée*, p. 15.

70. *Le Renouveau*, p. 311.

71. See, for instance, Colonel Passy, *Souvenirs* (Monte Carlo, 1947), I, 122; André Gide, *Journal 1942–49* (Paris, 1950), p. 185.

72. D'Astier, *Les Grands*, p. 124.

73. Malraux, *op. cit.*, p. 150.
74. Compare Henri Amouroux, *Pétain avant Vichy* (Paris, 1967).
75. *Ibid.*, p. 151. The General's gift for sarcasm was often displayed to his aides and visitors. See Claude Mauriac, *Un autre de Gaulle* (Paris, 1971). (English translation: *The Other de Gaulle* [New York, 1973]).
76. Passy, *op. cit.*, I, 123.
77. D'Astier, *Les Grands*, p. 137.
78. Compare *Mémoires de guerre*, III, 288–89. He spent very little time as a "private" person after his resignation in January 1946. He made his first public statement in June, and after the failure of the RPF, he wrote *Mémoires de guerre*, still unfinished in 1958 when the Fourth Republic collapsed.
79. In *Mémoires de guerre*, II, 287, de Gaulle says that he decided, after his resignation in 1945, to stay in metropolitan France so as to show that the flood of insults *"contre moi"* could not touch him. A few lines farther, he speaks of "de Gaulle."
80. Malraux, *op. cit.*, p. 134. Gide, *Journal 1942–49* (Paris, 1950), p. 185.
81. Bourdan, *op. cit.*, p. 35.
82. Passy, *op. cit., passim;* compare also Major-General Sir Edward Spears, *Two Men Who Saved France* (London, 1966), pp. 148*ff.*
83. D'Astier, *Sept fois sept jours*, pp. 60–61, writes: *"Il n'aime pas les hommes. Il aime leur histoire, surtout celle de la France, dont il agit un chapitre qu'il semble écrire au fur et à mesure dans sa tête."*
84. *"C'est pourquoi, dans les heures tragiques où la rafale balaie conventions et habitudes, ils [les chefs] se trouvent seuls debout et, par là, nécessaires." (Vers l'armée de métier*, p. 221.)
85. Pierre Viansson-Ponté, *Les gaullistes* (Paris, 1963), p. 49: insults leave de Gaulle cold, but he is concerned about how the press treats "his historical figure."
86. *Le Fil de l'épée*, p. 89; *Mémoires de guerre*, II, 322.
87. *Le Fil de l'épée*, p. 70; *Mémoires de guerre*, III, 243.
88. Malraux, *op. cit.*, p. 135.
89. See Jean-Marie Domenach, "Un nihilisme surmonté," *Esprit*, December 1970.
90. See Jerome Bruner, *On Knowing* (Cambridge, Mass., 1962), p. 29; the characteristics listed in this paragraph are borrowed from this stimulating essay.
91. Tournoux, *Pétain et de Gaulle*, p. 389. The phrase came from an evaluation by one of de Gaulle's superiors in 1942.
92. *"Le dialogue traditionnel, dans les affaires de l'État, lui était étranger."* Malraux, *op. cit.*, p. 156.
93. D'Astier, *Les Grands*, p. 108.
94. Compare François Mauriac, *op. cit.*, pp. 22–23.
95. Albert Hall speech, June 18, 1942, in *Mémoires de guerre*, I, 672*ff;* see also I, 1.
96. Compare Lacouture, *op. cit.*, p. 164*ff.*
97. Malraux, *loc. cit.*
98. Tournoux, *Secrets d'État* (Paris, 1960), p. 351.

99. Portrait of Mussolini, *Mémoires de guerre*, III, 172.

100. Malraux, *op. cit.*, p. 156: *"nous et le destin du monde."*

101. *Vers l'armée de métier*, p. 197.

102. *Mémoires de guerre*, III, 232.

103. See Tournoux, *Pétain et de Gaulle*, pp. 383*ff*, and d'Astier, *Les Grands*, pp. 119*ff*.

104. Compare the portrait of Stalin in *Mémoires de guerre*, III, 78. He quotes Stalin as saying "after all, only death wins." In *Felled Oaks* (New York, 1972) Malraux mentions de Gaulle quoting this quip of Stalin again.

105. *Mémoires de guerre*, I, 111.

106. Compare *Mémoires de guerre*, II, 294.

107. Compare his refusal to participate in any public ceremony or go to any public edifice used by the Fourth Republic. On his failures, see his press conference of November 1953, in Alexander Werth, *op. cit.*, pp. 227–28.

108. *Mémoires de guerre*, II, 240–41.

109. A good example is provided by Maurice Schumann, his wartime spokesman on the BBC. The day after de Gaulle's return to liberated Paris, Schumann met him at his office in the War Ministry, and was greeted with these words: *"On ne m'y reprendra plus."* (Never again!): Frossard, *op. cit.* No. 54, p. 27.

110. Compare Erik Erikson's concept of virtue, in "Human Strength and the Cycle of Generations," *Insight and Responsibility* (New York, 1964).

111. *Mémoires de guerre*, I, 1; see also III, 21, and Passeron, *De Gaulle parle, 1962–66*, pp. 134–37.

112. The epigraph to *Le Fil de l'épée* is a quotation from Hamlet, *"être grand, c'est soutenir une grande querelle."* ("Rightly to be great/Is not to stir without great argument.") See also *Mémoires de guerre*, I, 1.

113. *Mémoires de guerre*, III, 290.

114. *La France et son armée* (Paris, 1938), p. 277.

115. *Mémoires de guerre*, I, 1.

116. See Konrad Adenauer, *Erinnerungen*, II (Stuttgart, 1966), 428–29; III (Stuttgart, 1971), 102–3, 140–41, 228–29.

117. Oxford speech, November 25, 1941: *Mémoires de guerre*, I, 565*ff*; also *Mémoires d'espoir*, pp. 189–90.

118. Compare de Gaulle's remarks on Syria and Lebanon, while serving there in 1930: "People here are as foreign to us (and vice versa) as ever." Only two possibilities existed, according to him: coercion or departure (Nachin, *Trois études*, pp. 56–57). He later applied both. At least one possibility was thus ruled out—that which had served as the myth of the French empire under the name of assimilation and was to serve as the myth of French Algeria under the name of integration.

119. See the comparison of the French and the Germans in *Vers l'armée de métier*, pp. 22–23.

120. See the press conference of May 19, 1958, in Passeron, *De Gaulle parle 1958–62*, p. 5.

121. *Mémoires de guerre*, II, 321.

122. Malraux, *Antimémoires*, p. 130.

123. See the portraits of Hitler and of Laval in *Mémoires de guerre*, III, 173–75.

124. Compare Tournoux, *La Tragédie du Général*, p. 278.

125. In *La France et son armée*, writing about the 1890s—the years of his childhood—de Gaulle said: France "cultivates melancholy, while enjoying her wealth." His task in the 1960s seemed to be to increase her wealth without melancholy—by means of an active foreign policy.

126. See Lloyd and Suzanne Rudolph, *The Modernity of Tradition* (Chicago, 1968), pp. 199–200.

127. Compare Louis Terrenoire, *De Gaulle et l'Algérie* (Paris, 1964), p. 58, reporting that de Gaulle in March 1958 told him: "People are worried about France, but this feeling of national concern has not yet become a personal anxiety."

128. Passeron, *De Gaulle parle 1958–62*, p. 7.

129. *Mémoires de guerre*, III, 238, 650 (Bayeux speech of June 16, 1946).

130. Compare Eugène Mannoni, *Moi Général de Gaulle* (Paris, 1964), p. 106: "The R.P.F. merely taught de Gaulle what he had already known: in History's absence, solitude is preferable to promiscuity."

131. See above, Chapter 4, pp. 90–91.

132. *Mémoires de guerre*, II, 311.

133. Malraux, *Antimémoires*, p. 140.

134. Emmanuel d'Astier de la Vigerie is the best example.

135. Jacques Soustelle is the best example.

136. *Mémoires de guerre*, III, 271.

137. Photos taken on de Gaulle's return from Montréal to Orly Airport in the middle of the night show de Gaulle elated and combative, surrounded by sleepy and sullen cabinet ministers.

138. Malraux, *Antimémoires*, p. 156.

139. *Le Fil de l'epée*, p. 79.

140. See Stanley Hoffmann, "Paradoxes of the French Political Community," in S. Hoffmann, *et al.*, *In Search of France* (Cambridge, Mass., 1963).

141. Compare d'Astier, *Les Grands*, p. 99; Tournoux, *La Tragédie du Général*, p. 194; Léon Noël, *Comprendre de Gaulle* (Paris, 1972), pp. 140*ff*.

142. Compare d'Astier: "I am a French ant, that brings . . . a bit of material for his history. . . . I have been in a theater of history, I want to go back to life, to my life." *Sept fois sept jours*, pp. 60–61. See also Malraux, *Antimémoires*, p. 131.

143. Compare Paul de la Gorce, *De Gaulle entre deux mondes* (Paris, 1964), Chapter 10, on de Gaulle's hesitations over economy and financial policy in 1944–45.

144. *Mémoires de guerre*, III, 289.

145. *Vers l'armée de métier*, p. 154.

146. Compare Tournoux, *La Tragédie du Général*, pp. 502–03.

147. *Cinna*, Act IV, Scene 2.

148. Tournoux, *La Tragédie du Général*, *loc. cit.*

149. See Raymond Aron, *La Révolution introuvable* (Paris, 1968), pp. 38*ff*, 95*ff*. See also François Bourricaud, "Une Reprise difficile en Mains," *Preuves*, No. 218 (May–June, 1969), pp. 38–48.

150. Compare de Gaulle's television interview, June 7, 1968: "Until now, our structures and our groups . . . have resisted this kind of change."

151. Malraux, *Les Chênes qu'on abat,* (Paris, 1971), p. 164.

152. See above, Chapter 6, pp. 166–67.

153. Raymond Aron, *op. cit.,* p. 43.

154. See Stanley Hoffmann, "De Gaulle's Legacy to Pompidou," *The New Republic,* July 12, 1969, pp. 19–21.

155. Television interview, April 10, 1969.

156. His timidity as a domestic reformer had already shown, in comparable circumstances, when he refused to follow Mendès-France's austerity plan in 1945.

157. Television interview, June 7, 1968: "Such a reform, nobody, including me, can undertake alone. It has to be sufficiently accepted and the circumstances must be right. . . . Now, there has been a shock, a terrible shock, which must have opened the eyes of many."

158. De Gaulle, speech of March 11, 1969.

159. In the television interview of June 7, 1968, he compared himself to the angel in a "primitive painting," who tried to keep a crowd from letting itself be driven to hell by devils, and pointed in the opposite direction —only to become the target of the crowd's anger.

160. It is not at all clear that, had de Gaulle remained in power until 1972, his successor (after fourteen years of Gaullist rule) would have been a Gaullist.

161. These quotations are from our earlier conclusion. For another assessment, see Emmanuel Berl, "Le crépuscule du magicien," *Preuves,* Nos. 219–220 (July–September, 1969), pp. 82–85. For an evaluation close to ours, see Charles Morazé, *Le Général de Gaulle et la République* (Paris, 1972), *passim.*

9. Last Strains and Last Will: de Gaulle's Memoirs of Hope

1. The quotations in this essay come from Terence Kilmartin's uninspired translation of the *Les Mémoires d'espoir* (Paris, 1970 and 1971), published in the United States as a single volume. Memoirs of Hope (New York, 1971). The translations from André Malraux are my own, made before the appearance of the American version of *Les Chênes qu'on abat* (Paris, 1971), *Felled Oaks* (New York, 1972).

2. See Claude Mauriac, *Un autre de Gaulle* (Paris, 1971).

3. But we can guess. In addition to Malraux's tantalizing report, we have a scrupulous account by Jean Mauriac (the other son of François) of de Gaulle's last year and a half: *Mort du Général de Gaulle* (Paris, 1972). See also Jean d'Escrienne, *Le Général m'a dit* (Paris, 1973), pp. 42*ff.*

10. De Gaulle's Foreign Policy: the Stage and the Play, the Power and the Glory

1. Arnold Wolfers, *Discord and Collaboration* (Baltimore, 1965), pp. 67*ff.*

2. See Leon N. Lindberg and Stuart A. Scheingold, *Europe's Would-Be Polity* (Englewood Cliffs, N.J., 1970), pp. 141*ff.*

3. See the writings of Edward L. Morse, in particular: "The transformation

of foreign policies: modernization, interdependence, and externalization," *World Politics,* April 1970; "Defense Autonomy in Gaullist France" (Morristown, N.J., 1972); and *Foreign Policy and Interdependence in Gaullist France* (Princeton, N.J., 1973).

4. See Konrad Adenauer's *Erinnerungen,* III (Stuttgart, 1967), 167.

5. On this distinction, see my *Gulliver's Troubles* (New York, 1968), Chapters 2 and 3.

6. De Gaulle is trenchantly clear on this point in the *Memoirs of Hope* (New York, 1971), pp. 37*ff.* and 143*ff.*

7. See, for instance, Pierre Hassner, "From Napoleon III to de Gaulle," *Interplay,* February 1968.

8. John Newhouse, *De Gaulle and the Anglo-Saxons* (New York, 1970), p. 343.

9. *Ibid.,* p. 48.

10. Not entirely (cf. the importance of the agricultural Common Market, i.e., of access for French produce in the Community's other eight countries' markets, or the continuing reliance on overseas resources such as Sahara's oil, although largely through private companies), but to a spectacular extent. Compare *Memoirs of Hope,* p. 165.

11. See Jean Monnet's memorandum of May 3, 1950, reproduced in *Le Monde,* May 9, 1970.

12. *Erinnerungen,* II (Stuttgart, 1966), 430. De Gaulle (*Memoirs of Hope,* p. 177) says he told Adenauer that "from a strictly national point of view, France, unlike Germany, had no real need of an organization of Western Europe."

13. See *Memoirs of Hope,* pp. 238*ff.*

14. See Stanley Hoffmann, "International Organization and the International System," in *International Organization,* Summer 1970.

15. *Erinnerungen,* II, 429, and III, 138, 203.

16. This is uncompromisingly reasserted in *Memoirs of Hope:* world responsibility is the condition of internal transformation, stability, and progress without which France would be doomed to decline (p. 166).

17. See Bernard Tricot—one of the chief negotiators on the French side—defending de Gaulle on this point in his excellent memoirs *Les Sentiers de la paix* (Paris, 1972), pp. 377*ff.*

18. *Erinnerungen,* II, 429.

19. *Memoirs of Hope,* pp. 201, 214, 228–29.

20. See the volume of de Gaulle's speeches of that period, *Dans l'attente, 1946–1953* (Paris, 1970), especially pp. 510*ff.*

21. *Memoirs of Hope,* p. 203.

22. See Alessandro Silj, "Europe's Political Puzzle" (Harvard University, Center for International Affairs, 1967); Robert Bloes, *Le Plan Fouchet et le problème de l'Europe politique* (Bruges, 1970). Christian Fouchet, in *Au Service du Général de Gaulle* (Paris, 1971), is unenlightening, but Maurice Couve de Murville, in *Une Politique etrangère* (Paris, 1971), throws light on the mysterious episode of the new, tougher draft presented by France in January 1962.

23. *Erinnerungen,* III, 170–71. *Memoirs of Hope,* pp. 213–15. For a rebuttal

of all these arguments, see Raymond Aron, *The Great Debate* (New York, 1964).

24. See Wilfred L. Kohl, *French Nuclear Diplomacy* (Princeton, N.J., 1971); also, Michael J. Brenner, "Strategic Interdependence and the Politics of Inertia," *World Politics,* July 1971.

25. Newhouse, *op. cit.,* p. 227. Couve de Murville, *op. cit.,* pp. 253*ff,* makes clear that the initiative for the treaty came from Adenauer, in an anti-Soviet perspective.

26. Newhouse, *op. cit.,* p. 226. The details he gives are usually right, the interpretation is wrong.

27. "From time to time de Gaulle indicated a willingness to trade German interests for some recognition from Moscow," Newhouse, *ibid.,* p. 33. Aside from de Gaulle's far-sighted stand on the Oder-Neisse line, it is impossible to find any evidence to buttress this charge. Indeed, in Moscow and Warsaw, de Gaulle stressed the non-*revanchiste* nature of Bonn, and he never took on East Germany any line softer than Bonn's.

28. On de Gaulle's monetary policy, see Morse, *Foreign Policy and Interdependence in Gaullist France.*

29. Couve de Murville, in his inimitable cool way, dismisses it as a Soviet-American deal about Germany, *op. cit.,* pp. 209–10.

30. Couve de Murville discusses both Bonn's dismay and Czech and Polish fears that France's exit from NATO would boost Bonn's influence there, *op. cit.,* pp. 207*ff,* 269*ff.*

31. Except in the writings of General André Beaufre; certainly not in the *Revue de défense nationale.*

32. See General Pierre Ailleret's article, "Défense dirigée ou défense tous azimuts," *Revue de défense nationale,* March 1968.

33. Although it seems that he had foreseen both Soviet intervention and Czechoslovakia's forced submission.

34. Couve de Murville, *op. cit.,* pp. 427–28.

35. De Gaulle had actually suggested to Christopher Soames that if a further exploration showed that there were reasons to begin serious discussions, the other Five should then be informed. This was not reported by Harold Wilson. Wilson's account, in his memoirs, is not entirely candid.

36. See General Michel Fourquet, "Emploi des différents systèmes de forces dans le cadre de la stratégie de dissuasion," *Revue de défense nationale,* May 1969. For an analysis, see Edward A. Kolodziej, "France Ensnared: French Strategic Policy and Bloc Politics after 1968," *Orbis,* Winter 1972.

37. *Erinnerungen,* III, 225.

38. André Frossard, *En ce temps là: de Gaulle,* No. 34 (1972), has a remarkable letter of de Gaulle to his mother, dated December 20, 1936, in which he commended the Franco-Russian pact of 1935 "whatever our horror of Russia's regime," because the only imperative was stopping or defeating Hitler. He also predicted that Italy would give France *le coup de pied de l'âne* (hit her when she was down).

39. *Erinnerungen,* III, 166, 181.

40. *Memoirs of Hope,* p. 240.

41. *Erinnerungen,* II, 429; III, 45.

42. Thomas Schelling, *The Strategy of Conflict* (Cambridge, Mass., 1960).
43. West Germany played the same game at the tense monetary conference in Bonn in November 1968.
44. This does not necessarily mean negotiate formally. De Gaulle's way of bargaining was to grant unilateral concessions, followed by negotiation on details. However, as Tricot (*op. cit., passim*) shows, these were far from trivial.
45. *Erinnerungen,* III, 210.
46. He succeeded in getting Bonn to agree to the continued stationing of French troops in West Germany.
47. See Newhouse, *op. cit.,* p. 65. See also my *Gulliver's Troubles,* p. 420.
48. Pompidou speech of April 11, 1972. In *Felled Oaks* (New York, 1972), André Malraux reports that de Gaulle actually interpreted "Europe's death" as a tragedy for France.
49. Pompidou speech, April 13, 1972.
50. See Chapter 13, pp. 430–33. For instance, state encouragement to "national champions" in industry, or the emphasis on a purely French but not always profitable technology may have perpetuated old flaws in the French approach to economic affairs.
51. Compare Jean Charlot, ed., *Les Français et de Gaulle* (Paris, 1971), pp. 45*ff* and 75*ff.*
52. *Erinnerungen,* III, 102–3.
53. *War Memoirs,* III, 721 (New York, 1968). See also *Memoirs of Hope,* p. 166.
54. For an interesting and critical review of the policy of cooperation with France's former colonial territories, see *Esprit,* July–August 1970.
55. *Erinnerungen,* III, 228; *Memoirs of Hope,* pp. 299–301.
56. See Emmanuel Berl, "Le Crépuscule du magicien," *Preuves,* July–September 1969, pp. 82–85.

11. Perceptions and Policies: France and the United States

1. See John Newhouse, *De Gaulle and the Anglo-Saxons* (New York, 1970), p. 352.
2. For a more detailed analysis, see my *Gulliver's Troubles* (New York, 1968), Part III.
3. See *Gulliver's Troubles,* Chapter 11.
4. See Zbigniew Brzezinski, *Alternative to Partition* (New York, 1965).
5. This is confirmed by Lyndon B. Johnson's own account in *The Vantage Point* (New York, 1971), p. 293.
6. For a critique of the new American foreign policy, see Stanley Hoffmann, "Will the Balance Balance at Home?" *Foreign Policy,* Summer 1972; "Weighing the Balance of Power," *Foreign Affairs,* July 1972; and "Choices," *Foreign Policy,* Fall 1973.
7. For an equally gloomy view of French prospects, see Edward A. Kolodziej, "The Mediterranean Policy: the Politics of Weakness," *International Affairs,* July 1971.
8. See the *Livre Blanc sur la Défense Nationale* (Paris, 1972), p. 2.

9. See the concrete proposals by François Duchêne, "A New European Defense Community," *Foreign Affairs,* October 1971.
10. For concrete suggestions, see Michael J. Brenner, "Strategic Interdependence and the Politics of Inertia," *World Politics,* July 1971; Ian Smart, "The Prospect for Anglo-French Nuclear Cooperation," Adelphi Paper No. 78 (London, 1971); and Andrew Pierre, *Nuclear Politics* (New York, 1972).

12. Obstinate or Obsolete? France, European Integration, and the Fate of the Nation-State

1. See Pierre Renouvin and Jean-Baptiste Duroselle, *Introduction to the History of International Relations* (New York, 1966).
2. In a way, the weaker the foundations on which the nation rests, the shriller the assertions become.
3. On this point, see Rupert Emerson, *From Empire to Nation* (Cambridge, Mass., 1962), Chapter 9; and Raymond Aron, *Peace and War Among Nations* (New York, 1964), Chapter 11.
4. E. H. Carr, *Nationalism and After* (London, 1965), p. 51, quoted in Pierre Hassner, "Nationalisme et relations internationales," *Revue française de science politique,* XV, No. 3 (June 1965), 499–528.
5. See Ernst B. Haas, *Beyond the Nation-State* (Stanford, Cal., 1964).
6. On this point, see my essay "Rousseau on War and Peace," in *The State of War* (New York, 1965).
7. See for instance Richard Cooper, "Economic Interdependence and Foreign Policy in the 70's," *World Politics,* January 1972; and Robert O. Keohane and Joseph S. Nye, Jr., eds., *Transnational Relations and World Politics* (Cambridge, Mass., 1972).
8. Hassner, *op. cit.,* p. 523.
9. Karl W. Deutsch, *Nationalism and Social Communication* (Cambridge, Mass., 1953), p. 147.
10. A more systematic and exhaustive analysis would have to discriminate rigorously among the various components of the national situation. If the purpose of the analysis is to help one understand the relations between the nation-state and the international system, it would be especially necessary to assess: 1) the degree to which each of these components is an unchangeable given (or a given unchangeable over a long period of time) or, on the contrary, an element that can be transformed by will and action; 2) the hierarchy of importance and the order of urgency that political elites and decision-makers establish among the components.
11. See Raoul Girardet, "Autour de l'idéologie nationaliste," *Revue française de science politique,* XV, No. 3 (June, 1965), 423–45; and Hassner, *op. cit.,* pp. 516–19.
12. Alfred Grosser, *French Foreign Policy under de Gaulle* (Boston, 1965).
13. Haas, *The Uniting of Europe* (Stanford, Cal., 1958).
14. See my discussion in "The European Process of Atlantic Cross-Purposes," *Journal of Common Market Studies,* February 1965, pp. 85–101. The

success of internal economic integration raised these external issues far earlier than many expected.

15. The latter case is self-evident; the first, less so, since the crisis over EDC was primarily an "intra-European" split between the French and the Germans. But there was more to it than this. EDC was accepted mostly by nations who thought that Europe could not and should not refuse to do what the United States had demanded—i.e., rearm in order to share the defense of the half-continent with the United States and incite the United States to remain its primary defender; EDC was rejected by nations who feared that it would freeze existing power relationships.

16. Although there was a minority of "resigned ones" in France, like Paul Reynaud.

17. An impressive continuity marks French efforts to preserve the difference between France's position and West Germany's: from the *préalables* and protocols to EDC, to Mendès-France's Brussels proposals, to de Gaulle's opposition to any nuclear role for Germany.

18. France's "integrationist resisters," like Monnet himself, often chose not to stress the "resistance" aspect of their long-term vision, but nevertheless aimed ultimately at establishing in Western Europe not a junior partner of the United States but a "second force" in the West. Mendès-France's political vision never put the nation at the top of the hierarchy of values, but in 1954 (especially in his ill-fated demands for a revision of EDC at the Brussels meeting in August) and in 1957 (when he voted against the Common Market), his actual policies did put priority on national reform over external entanglements.

19. It is no coincidence that EDC was rejected six weeks after the end of the war in Indochina, that the Common Market treaty was signed by France while war raged in Algeria, that de Gaulle's sharpest attack on the "Monnet method" followed the Évian agreements that ended the Algerian war. The weight of the French national situation affected and inflected the course of even so nationalist a leader as de Gaulle. Even he went along with the "Monnet method" (however grudgingly) until the end of the Algerian war. It is not a coincidence either that the French leaders most suspicious of the imprisioning effects of the EEC were those who labored hardest at improving the national situation by removing colonial burdens (Mendès-France, de Gaulle), and that the French rulers who followed Monnet and tried to orient the pride of France toward leadership of a united Europe were those who failed to improve the national situation overseas (the MRP, Mollet). The one French politician who sought both European integration *and* imperial "disengagement" was Antoine Pinay.

20. Especially by Henry Kissinger in *The Troubled Partnership* (New York, 1965) and Raymond Aron in *The Great Debate* (New York, 1964).

21. One should not forget that the original decisions that led to the French nuclear *force de frappe* were made before de Gaulle, and oppositin to the national deterrent came from men who did not at all object to de Gaulle's argument that Europe as a whole should stop being a client of the United States.

22. See my previous discussion in "Discord in Community," in F. Wilcox

and H. F. Haviland, Jr., eds., *The Atlantic Community* (New York, 1963), pp. 3–31; and "Europe's Identity Crisis," *Daedalus*, Fall 1964, pp. 1244–97.

23. See, for instance, Max Kohnstamm, "The European Tide," in Stephen R. Graubard, ed., *A New Europe?* (Boston, 1964), pp. 140–73.

24. See Karl W. Deutsch, *et al., Political Community and the North Atlantic Area* (Princeton, N.J., 1957).

25. Under authority, I include three distinct notions: autonomy (the capacity to act independently of the governments, particularly financially), power (control over acts of others), and legitimacy (being accepted as the "rightful" center of action).

26. Compare decolonization. Along similar lines, see Francis Rosenstiel, *Le principe de "Supranationalité"* (Paris, 1962).

27. See the analysis of a recent French public-opinion poll by Raoul Girardet, "Du fair national aux necessités européenes," *Contrepoint,* Spring 1971.

28. On this point, see Raymond Aron and Daniel Lerner, eds., *France Defeats EDC* (New York, 1957).

29. See Emerson, *loc. cit.*

30. Britain's refusal to join EEC, before 1961, could not fail to increase French hesitations, for integration without Britain meant equality with Germany, and a clear-cut difference between France's position and Britain's, i.e., a reversal of French aspirations and traditions. Britain has on the whole rejected the "resignation-resistance" dilemma—and as a result, both the aspects of its foreign policy that appeared like resignation to U.S. predominance and the aspects that implied resistance to decline have contributed to the crisis of European integration: for France's vetoes in January 1963 and November 1967 meant a French refusal to let into Europe a power that had just confirmed its military ties to the United States, but Britain's previous desire to play a world role and aversion to "fading into Europe" encouraged France's own misgivings about integration.

31. See Grosser, *op. cit.,* Chapter 4.

32. See Thomas Schelling, *Strategy of Conflict* (Cambridge, Mass., 1960).

33. The best balance sheet (despite its jargon) is in Leon N. Lindberg and Stuart A. Scheingold, *Europe's Would-Be Polity* (Englewood Cliffs, N.J., 1970). For a more detailed assessment of current developments, see my contribution to Wolfram Hanrieder (ed.), *The United States and Europe in the 70s* (forthcoming).

34. For a good discussion of the 1971 crisis, see Guy Berger, Edward L. Morse, and Michel Albert's articles in *Revue française de science politique,* April 1972.

35. The question asked of the voters—whether to approve Britain's entry into EEC, given "the new perspectives open to Europe" (undefined) —was too clever by half. Pompidou's speeches veered from "Europeanism" to "Gaullism," and a sizable part of the Gaullist electorate abstained or deserted.

36. See Maurice Couve de Murville, *Une Politique étrangère* (Paris, 1971), p. 382.

37. Haas's definition of a political community in his *The Uniting of Europe,*

p. 5 ("a condition in which specific groups and individuals show more loyalty to their central political institutions than to any other political authority") is not very helpful in the case of states marked by severe domestic cleavages. There might be more loyalty to the center than to any other political authority merely because there is no other *political* authority, and yet one would still not be in the presence of anything like an integrated society.

38. Haas, *Beyond the Nation-State,* p. 29.
39. Haas and Philippe C. Schmitter, "Economics and Differential Patterns of Political Integration," *International Organization,* XVIII, No. 4 (Autumn 1964), 705–37, 710.
40. Some assert that it is not even the old bottle, so great are the effects of transnational forces on the nation-states. See Keohane and Nye, *op. cit.*

13. The Nation: What for? Vicissitudes of French Nationalism, 1871–1972

1. Raymond Aron, *Peace and War Among Nations* (New York, 1966), p. 294.
2. *Ibid.,* p. 296.
3. On the distinction between "national situation," "national consciousness," and "nationalism" see above, Chapter 12.
4. Which of course does not mean that solid historical studies or indispensable analyses do not exist. See in particular the writings of Raoul Girardet, "Introduction à l'histoire du nationalisme français," in *Revue française de science politique,* VIII, No. 3 (September 1958), and *Le Nationalisme français, 1871–1914* (Paris, 1966).
5. I have described this in "Paradoxes of the French Political Community," *In Search of France* (Cambridge, Mass., 1963).
6. See especially Pierre Nora, "Ernest Lavisse: son rôle dans la formation. du sentiment national," in *Revue historique,* July–September, 1962.
7. Léon Bourgeois, cited by Georges Burdeau, in *Traité de science politique,* V (Paris, 1953), 378.
8. In particular, the famous *Tour de la France par deux enfants,* that bible of patriotism for children, by "Bruno" (Mme. Alfred Fouillée) (Paris, 1884).
9. Compare Jean Jaurès, *L'Armée nouvelle.*
10. Charles Roig and F. Billon-Grand, *La Socialisation politique des enfants* (Paris, 1968), p. 164.
11. And of course for the followers of Barrès, who moved from concern for the working class in the Boulangist period to romanticizing a province of Lorraine lacking all industry, in his nationalist myth. See the remarks by Jean Plumyène, "Nationalisme et instinct de mort," *Contrepoint,* Spring 1971.
12. See Aron, *op. cit.,* Chapter 5.
13. For a different view, see Arno J. Mayer, *Dynamics of Counter-Revolution in Europe* (New York, 1971).
14. Cited in Jaurès *Textes choisis* (Paris, 1959), p. 131.

15. This concern was also very strong on the Left, as for Daladier.
16. See especially Charles Micaud, *The French Right and Nazi Germany* (Durham, N.C., 1943) and Eugen Weber, *Action française* (Stanford, Cal., 1963).
17. Girardet's "Introduction," *Revue française de science politique,* September 1958, p. 525.
18. Albert Hirschman, "The Principle of the Hiding Hand," *The Public Interest,* No. 6, Winter 1967.
19. Aron, "De la trahison," *Preuves,* No. 116 (October 1960), 7.
20. *Ibid.,* p. 6.
21. This is the theme of Alfred Grosser, *La IVe République et sa politique exterieure* (Paris, 1961).
22. Aron, "De le trahison," p. 6.
23. See P. G. Cerny's suggestive "De Gaulle, the Nation-State and Foreign Policy," *Review of Politics,* April 1971.
24. François Bourricaud, "Une Reprise en main difficile," *Preuves,* No. 218 (May–June 1969).
25. See Raymond Vernon, *Sovereignty at Bay: the Multinational Spread of U.S. Enterprises* (New York, 1971).
26. See the excellent study by Robert Gilpin, *France in the Age of the Scientific State* (Princeton, N.J., 1968). See also Vernon, "Rogue Elephant in the Forest," *Foreign Affairs,* April 1973, pp. 582*ff.*
27. See the figures of a poll quoted by Girardet, "Du Fait national aux nécessités Européenes," *Contrepoint,* Spring 1971, pp. 11–12. They show that this feeling is far stronger than class or generational consciousness, especially strong among workers and *petits-bourgeois,* and that a majority think that a loss of independence would be bad for France's future, their standard of living, and their freedom.
28. A fine set of papers and arguments on this subject is to be found in *Analyse et prévision* (SEDEIS), June, November, December 1970.
29. See Aron, *République impériale* (Paris, 1973), pp. 217–27.
30. For a contrary opinion, see Pierre Hassner, "Change and Security in Europe," Part II, Adelphi Paper No. 49 (London, July 1968).

14. The State: For What Society?

1. See Stanley Hoffmann, *et al., In Search of France* (Cambridge, Mass., 1963), pp. 3*ff.*
2. Robert de Jouvenel, *La République des camarades* (Paris, 1914).
3. From an unpublished paper by Pierre Grémion, "La Fonction latente de la tutelle dans l'expérience de planification," November 1972.
4. Philip Williams, *Crisis and Compromise* (Hamden, Conn., 1964), p. 221.
5. Herbert Luethy. The German and French titles were respectively *Frankreichs Uhren gehen anders* and *La France à l'heure de son clocher* (in the United States: *France against Herself,* New York, 1955). See also Warren C. Baum, *The French Economy and the State* (Princeton, 1958).
6. Jean-Jacques Carré, Paul Dubois, and Edmond Malinvaud, *La Croissance française* (Paris, 1972).

7. See for instance Williams and Martin Harrison, *Politics and Society in de Gaulle's Republic* (London, 1971); and Suzanne Berger on the French political system, in S. H. Beer and Adam B. Ulam, eds., *Patterns of Government* (3rd ed., New York, 1973).

8. See *Plan et prospectives, 1985: la France face au choc du futur* (Paris, 1972).

9. See for instance Daniel Bell, "Meritocracy and Equality" in *The Public Interest,* No. 29 (Fall 1972), 29–68; he discusses, among many others, John Rawls's *A Theory of Justice* (Cambridge, Mass., 1971) and Christopher Jencks's *Inequality* (New York, 1972).

10. Jean-Claude Thoenig, *L'Ère des technocrates* (Paris, 1973).

11. See the perceptive analysis by Jean-Pierre Worms and Pierre Grémion in a round table on "Administration et Pouvoir économique," *Esprit,* January 1973, pp. 51–70.

12. I have used an unpublished report by the Centre de Sociologie des Organisations on the Ministry of Industry and its environment, January 1970. Among the new horizontal services, one of the most interesting is the Délégation à l'Aménagement du Territoire et à l'Action Régionale (DATAR): a small staff attached to the Premier's office. For a description, see *Actualités-Documents,* a publication of the Comité Interministeriel pour l'Information, No. 101 (Feburary 1973).

13. "Rapport de la Commission d'études sur la fonction enseignante dans le second degré" (mimeo, June 15, 1972).

14. Compare Ezra N. Suleiman, *Politics, Power, and Bureaucracy in France* (Princeton, N.J., 1974), on the top French civil service.

15. Compare "Prospective du système politique," (mimeo, Centre d'étude et de recherche sur l'Administration économique et l'Aménagement du Territoire, Institut d'Étùdes Politiques de Grenoble, 1972).

16. See Jean de Savigny, *L'État contre les communes?* (Paris, 1971); also Michel Longepierre, *Les Conseillers généraux dans le système administratif français* (Paris, 1971).

17. See Jack Hayward, "Steel Masters and Public Servants," an unpublished study prepared for a conference on Enterprise and Government in Western Europe (Harvard University, Center for International Affairs, January 1973).

18. On the evolution of the plan, see the various writings of Lucien Nizard, in particular: "De la planification française," *Revue française de science politique,* XXII, No. 5 (October 1972), 1111–1132, and "Administration et Société," *ibdem,* XXIII, No. 2 (April 1973), 199–229.

19. Five heads of parliamentary committees, members of the Gaullist party, in July 1971 denounced the "politique de concertation" which makes "pressure groups the favored *interlocuteurs* of the government."

20. See François d'Arcy and Bruno Jobert, "La Planification urbaine," (mimeo, Centre d'étude et de recherche sur l'Administration économique et l'Aménagement du Territoire, Institut d'Études Politiques de Grenoble, July 1972).

21. Carré, Dubois, and Malinvaud, the authors of *La Croissance française,* with a fine art of understatement note that in markets dominated by a

monopoly or oligopolies, the statement of industrial objectives is more "an ingredient of the enterprises 'strategy' than an effort of objective evaluation" (pp. 582*ff*).

22. Michel Debré's *Une Certaine Idée de la France* (Paris, 1972) can be read as the testament of a certain kind of Gaullist who is at the same time Rousseauistic, Jacobin, intensely patriotic (in the Third Republic school sense), reformist in a strictly administrative rather than participatory sense, and very distant from the conservative Pompidou strategy described below.

23. See Lionel Stoléru, *L'Impératif industriel* (Paris, 1969), Chapter 3.

24. I have used the findings of John Zysman, who is working on a study of France's electronics industry ("French Industry between the Market and the State," MIT Ph.D., 1973).

25. *Plan et prospectives, 1985,* pp. 136*ff.*

26. I have used here the ideas of Pierre Bourdieu, expressed in his many writings on French education and on the "strategies of reproduction" of social groups.

27. See Georges Spénale, "Expansion et équité," *Le Monde,* March 17, 1973, p. 38, using various French and OECD statistics; also, Gilbert Mathieu in *Le Monde,* March 14, 1973, p. 19.

28. See Pierre Le Roy, *L'Avenir de l'agriculture française* (Paris, 1972).

29. See François Bourricaud, "Les 'Réformateurs' introuvables" in Club Nouvelle Frontière, *Radioscopie des oppositions* (Paris, 1973), pp. 80–114.

30. See Maurice Parodi, *L'Économie et la société française de 1945 à 1970* (Paris, 1971), Chap. 11.

31. See Gérard Adam, Jean-Daniel Reynaud, and Jean-Maurice Verdier, *La Négociation collective en France* (Paris, 1972), pp. 67*ff.*

32. See Bourricaud, "Le Modèle polyarchique et les conditions de sa survie," *Revue française de science politique,* XX, No. 5 (October 1970), 893–925.

33. *Plan et prospectives, 1985,* pp. 163*ff.*

34. *Ibid.,* p. 166. The authors point out that at the present time the function that public-school teachers used to play as the countryside's ferment is being performed by farmer's organizations.

35. For a rather laborious attempt at squeezing France's peasantry into Marxist schemes, see the essays by Gervais, Servolin, and Jollivet in Cahiers de la Fondation Nationale des Science Politiques, *L'Univers politique des paysans* (Paris, 1972).

36. Michel Crozier, *The Stalled Society* (New York, 1973). See also *Plan et prospectives, 1985* (which reflects his influence profoundly), pp. 151*ff.*

37. In Bourricaud, "Les 'Réformateurs' introuvables," p. 109.

38. Thoenig, *op. cit.,* p. 152.

39. See Grémion and Worms, "L'Expérience française de régionalisation au cours des aneés 60," unpublished paper for the Seminar in Rome, September 1972; also Grémion's earlier study, "Réforme régionale et democratie locale," *Projet,* April 1970, and his article, "La Théorie de l'apprentissage institutionnel et la régionalisation du 5ème plan," *Revue française de science politique,* XXIII, No. 2 (April 1973), 305–320.

40. On these points, see Suleiman, *op. cit.,* and Thoenig, *op. cit.,* Chapter 9.
41. The same analysis could be applied to scientific research. It owes its security to its bureaucratic status and management, but the price paid—isolation from universities and industry—is, in the long run, sterilizing.
42. Le Roy, *op. cit.,* p. 45*ff.*
43. The election of Servan-Schreiber in Nancy in 1970 appears to have been more a protest against government policy than a demand for "regional power."
44. This was the case not only in the legislative elections of March 1973 but also in the referendum election of April 1972: see the analysis by Alain Lancelot, *Projet,* July–August 1972.
45. For a detailed analysis of the elections of March 1973, see Jean Charlot, ed., *Quand la gauche peut gagner* (Paris, 1973).
46. See "Basic Cleavages of French Politics and the Disorders of May–June 1968," unpublished paper by Philip Converse and Roy Pierce.
47. *Le Point,* January 15, 1973, p. 76.
48. Compare Mark J. Kesselman, "Systèmes de pouvoir et cultures politiques," *Revue française de sociologie,* October–December 1972, pp. 485–515, and "Changes in the French Party System," *Comparative Politics,* January 1972, pp. 281–301.
49. See Jean Bunel and Paul Meunier, *Chaban-Delmas* . . . (Paris, 1972), a sympathetic yet critical account of his three years in office.
50. Compare Emeric Deutsch, Denis Lindon, and Pierre Weill, *Les Familles politiques aujourd'hui en France* (Paris, 1966), and the study by Converse and Pierce mentioned in note 46.
51. While there was mention of the need for a popularly elected regional body, little was said about the crucial point: the powers of the local governments.
52. Another interpretation is offered by Gilles Martinet in *Le Système Pompidou,* a suggestive study that, however, gradually substitutes muckraking for analysis (Paris, 1973).
53. Compare Annie Kriegel, *The French Communists* (Chicago, 1972); also, a paper written by Georges Lavau for an MIT conference on communism in France and Italy, October 1972.
54. Cf. Alain Duhamel, "Le Paradoxe centriste," *Projet,* February 1973, pp. 128*ff.*
55. See Pompidou's message to Parliament, *Le Monde,* April 5, 1973.
56. The *loi Royer* voted by Parliament in the fall of 1973 establishes departmental committees composed of equal numbers of local representatives and shopkeepers' delegates, with the power to authorize or veto the creation or extension of large stores and markets.

Index

Abetz, Otto, 32, 33, 37, 38
Acheson, Dean, 336
Action Française, 33, 34, 36, 115, 418
Adenauer, Konrad, 51, 245, 323; de
    Gaulle policy toward, 289, 294,
    314; European integration and,
    297, 300; policy toward United
    States, 300, 327, 373
Africa, 190, 395
Alain (Émile Auguste Chartier),
    122, 130, 153, 410, 467
Algerian war, 24, 51, 132, 424; de
    Gaulle tactics during, 79, 85, 102,
    115, 193, 233, 238, 263, 271-72,
    316-17; Franco-American relations
    after, 334, 344; party system and,
    478; protests over, 112, 126, 149,
    247; the Right and, 135; role of
    FLN in, 242, 257-58, 292-93, 313-
    314; settlement of, 169, 291-94
Almond, Gabriel, 112-13
Althusser, Louis, 115
Ambler, John, 69n
Americanization, 435-36
Anglophobia, 31, 116
Anti-Americanism, 126-27, 129, 433
Anticommunism, 6, 31, 32-33, 37-38,
    294, 344, 373
Antimemoirs, 255-56

Anti-Semitism, 34, 36-37, 47, 54, 57,
    97, 205
Arabs, 142; Algerian war and, 433;
    de Gaulle policy toward, 328, 345-
    346; Franco-American relations
    and, 346-48, 353-55
Aragon, Louis, 129n
Arms talks, 322, 349, 357-58, 360,
    393. *See also* Nuclear weapons
Army, French, 24, 166, 291, 410;
    changes in, 424-25; de Gaulle view
    of, 228-29, 260-61; protest move-
    ments within, 112, 115; *Putsch* of
    1961, 261
Aron, Raymond, 114, 132, 149, 151,
    197, 240, 386, 403
Artisans, 111, 118, 122, 158-60
Asia, 190, 395
Auriol, Vincent, 199
Authoritarianism, 153-54
Authority, 65-184; centralization of,
    140, 153, 160, 246, 446, 453; con-
    frontation in May 1968 and, 145-
    184; crisis, 71-76, 237-38; fragmen-
    tation of, 120-21, 160; legitimacy
    of, 79-80, 88-90; in modern French
    leadership, 68-110; nature of po-
    litical system and, 66, 74-76, 119-
    123, 130-32, 170; revolt against,

517